George Skoch

EYEWITNESSES TO THE INDIAN WARS, 1865–1890

Also by Peter Cozzens

No Better Place to Die: The Battle of Stones River

This Terrible Sound: The Battle of Chickamauga

The Shipwreck of Their Hopes: The Battles for Chattanooga

The Darkest Days of the War: The Battles of Iuka and Corinth

The Military Memoirs of General John Pope

General John Pope: A Life for the Nation

Battles and Leaders of the Civil War, Vol. 5

The New Annals of the Civil War (with Robert I. Girardi)

Eyewitnesses to the Indian Wars, 1865–1890:
  Vol. 1, *The Struggle for Apacheria*

Eyewitnesses to the Indian Wars, 1865–1890:
  Vol. 2, *The Wars for the Pacific Northwest*

Eyewitnesses to the Indian Wars, 1865–1890:
  Vol. 3, *Conquering the Southern Plains*

EYEWITNESSES TO THE INDIAN WARS, 1865–1890

The Long War for the Northern Plains

EDITED BY PETER COZZENS

STACKPOLE
BOOKS

Copyright © 2004 by Stackpole Books

Published by
STACKPOLE BOOKS
5067 Ritter Road
Mechanicsburg, PA 17055
ISBN: 0-8117-0080-1

All rights reserved, including the right to reproduce this book or portions thereof in any form or by any means, electronic or mechanical, including photocopying, recording, or by any information storage and retrieval system, without permission in writing from the publisher. All inquiries should be addressed to Stackpole Books, 5067 Ritter Road, Mechanicsburg, Pennsylvania 17055.

Printed in the United States of America

*For my colleagues in the United States Foreign Service,
whose integrity, dedication to duty, and heroism
too often go unrecognized*

CONTENTS

List of Illustrations and Maps xi
Preface xiii
Introduction xv

PART ONE:
Platte River Bridge and the Powder River Expedition, 1865

S. H. Fairfield	The 11th Kansas Regiment at Platte Bridge 2
Henry E. Palmer	The Powder River Indian Campaign of 1865 ... 13
Charles W. Adams	Raiding a Hostile Village 43
Ovando J. Hollister	An Interview with General Connor 45
Albert M. Holman	A Fifteen Day Fight on Tongue River 49

PART TWO:
Red Cloud's War, 1866–68

"W"	A Bloody Prospecting Trip in the Bighorn Mountains 58
William Murphy	The Forgotten Battalion 64
George Weber	Cold Cheer at Fort Kearny 79
John Guthrie	A Detail of the Fetterman Massacre 81
Anonymous	Letters from Fort Phil Kearny 84
Thomas W. Cover	The Murder of John Bozeman 88
James Bridger	Indian Affairs in the Powder River Country 90
E. A. Brininstool and Samuel S. Gibson	The Wagon Box Fight 93
George B. Grinnell	An Indian Perspective on the Wagon Box Fight 101

PART THREE:
The Yellowstone Expedition, 1873

George A. Custer	Battling with the Sioux on the Yellowstone ... 104
Louis E. Hills	With General George A. Custer on the Northern Pacific Surveying Expedition in 1873 120
Charles Braden	The Yellowstone Expedition of 1873 128
Samuel J. Barrows	Crossing the Big Muddy [Creek] 150

PART FOUR:
The Black Hills and Beyond, 1874–76

George A. Custer	The Black Hills Expedition: Dispatches and Letters 156
William Ludlow	The Black Hills Expedition................ 172
William H. Wood	Reminiscences of the Black Hills Expedition.. 176
Alfred Bear	Story Told by Strikes Two and Bear's Belly of an Expedition under Custer to the Black Hills in 1874.................. 179
Guy V. Henry	A Winter March to the Black Hills 183
Philip H. Sheridan	The Black Hills 188
Frederick Schwatka	The Sun Dance of the Sioux 192
Robert E. Strahorn	"Alter Ego" on the Powder River Expedition .. 200
Thaddeus H. Stanton	A Review of the Reynolds Campaign 227

PART FIVE:
The Summer Campaign of 1876

Daniel C. Pearson	Military Notes, 1876..................... 236
Henry W. Daly	The War Path.......................... 250
Anonymous	Brave Boys Are They: The Newspaper Correspondents with Crook's Army..................... 261
James E. H. Foster	From Fort Fetterman to the Rosebud 265
Charles King	Custer's Last Battle 282
Charles A. Eastman	The Indian Version of Custer's Last Battle 299
Theodore W. Goldin	On the Little Bighorn with General Custer.... 310
John Silversten	Reminiscences of the Reno Fight 338

Edward S. Godfrey	Captain Benteen's Command	341
William D. Nugent	Thrilling Experience Near the Custer Battlefield	343
Theodore W. Goldin	Terry and Crook	345
Frederick Schwatka	With Crook's Expedition	350
Andrew S. Burt	Dispatches from Crook's Column	367
John G. Bourke	The Battle of Slim Buttes	378
John F. Finerty	The Fellows in Feathers: An Interview with General Crook	385
Charles S. Diehl	Terry's Tribulations	391

PART SIX:
The Winter Campaign of 1876–77

Jerry Roche	The Dull Knife Fight	414
Nelson A. Miles	Rounding Up the Red Men	431
Frank D. Baldwin	Winter Campaigning against Indians in Montana in 1876	442
Edwin M. Brown	Terror of the Badlands: The Sioux Expedition, Montana Territory, 1876 and 1877	451
David T. Mears	Campaigning against Crazy Horse	463

PART SEVEN:
The Odyssey of the Northern Cheyennes, 1871–90

George A. Woodward	Some Experiences with the Cheyennes	470
Edgar B. Bronson	A Finish Fight for a Birthright	482
Albert G. Forse	Across the Country with the Cheyennes	515

PART EIGHT:
The Death of Crazy Horse, 1877

Jesse M. Lee	The Capture and Death of an Indian Chieftain	528
Henry R. Lemly and E. A. Brininstool	The Murder of Chief Crazy Horse	542
Valentine T. McGillycuddy	The Death of Crazy Horse	549

PART NINE:
The Ghost Dance and Wounded Knee, 1890–91

George Sword	The Story of the Ghost Dance	554
Lloyd S. McCormick	The Wounded Knee and Drexel Mission Fights	559
William F. Kelley	The Indian Troubles and the Battle of Wounded Knee	578
Edmond G. Fechet	The True Story of the Death of Sitting Bull	597
Frederic Remington	The Sioux Outbreak in South Dakota	607
Charles W. Taylor	The Surrender of Red Cloud	611
Edward S. Godfrey	The Battle of Wounded Knee Creek	615
August Hettinger	Personal Recollections of the Messiah Craze Campaign	620
Courtney R. Cooper	Short Bull's Story of the Battle of Wounded Knee	630

Notes ... 637
Index ... 679

ILLUSTRATIONS AND MAPS

Maj. Gen. Grenville M. Dodge.... 4
An attack on the escort 5
Platte River Bridge, as sketched
  by a member of the 11th
  Kansas Volunteer Cavalry 10
Old Fort Kearny, Nebraska 14
An army wagon train en route
  to Fort Laramie 20
Pumpkin Buttes 23
Policing up stragglers 32
Hauling artillery on Connor's
  march along Tongue River.... 36
Chief Red Cloud 59
Brig. Gen. Philip St. George
  Cooke 74
The death of Lieutenant
  Grummond 82
The Fetterman Fight 85
Jim Bridger 91
The wagon-box corral on
  Piney Island 95
An Indian delegation in
  Washington 105
Construction crews and army
  guards on Northern Pacific
  Railroad 106
George A. Custer as a
  major general of volunteers .. 108
Rain-in-the-Face 135
"To Horse!" 157
Cavalry on the march 168
Scouts on the march 180
Maj. Guy V. Henry 184
Trespassing prospectors on
  the lookout for Indians 190
Spotted Tail 193
Selecting the sun pole 195

The charge on the sun pole 197
A Sun Dance devotee 198
General Crook's headquarters
  at Fort Fetterman 201
Maj. Thaddeus H. Stanton 228
An attack on a hostile village ... 230
Cheyenne warriors 237
Frank Grouard 252
Sitting Bull 259
Crook's command crossing
  Crazy Woman's Fork 267
Signaling for a talk 271
"A number of Indians were seen
  running about the crest" 272
In the camp of the Crow and
  Shoshone scouts 275
Dismounted—the fourth troopers
  moving the led horses 279
An artist's conception of the
  battle of the Rosebud 281
Charles King as a young
  lieutenant 283
Indian scouts watching
  Custer's advance 288
The end of Custer's command .. 295
Two Moon 302
"Crazy Horse with the Oglalas
  came forward with a
  tremendous yell" 307
The last of Custer 308
Romance on the Hudson;
  reality on the plains 311
Unhorsed 323
Chasing down a runaway
  pack mule 328
Editorializing the Little Bighorn. 336
On Reno Hill 339

Brig. Gen. Alfred H. Terry 346
William F. "Buffalo Bill" Cody . 354
Capt. Anson Mills............ 362
A conference with the
  Indian allies 369
Lieutenant Schwatka's charge
  through the village at
  Slim Buttes............... 380
Buying cavalry horses for
  the Indian War 398
Mackenzie's attack on
  Dull Knife's village 424
Nelson A. Miles as a
  major general............. 432
Colonel Miles meets Sitting Bull
  between the lines 435
The battle of Wolf Mountain ... 437
The surrender of Little Chief ... 439
The Lame Deer fight.......... 441
Crossing the ice-bound
  Missouri River 445
Sitting Bull attacking Miles's
  supply train 454
Little Wolf.................. 474
The murder of Sergeant
  Mularkey 476
"The head men of the tribe
  appealed to the government" . 486
Cavalry in a blizzard.......... 498
The defiance of Dull Knife..... 503
Dull Knife's Cheyennes
  struggling toward the divide. . 505
Captain Wessells sets out after
  Dull Knife's band.......... 508
Fighting the entrenched Cheyennes
  on Hat Creek Bluffs........ 512
"The little washout was
  a shambles" 513
Wovoka.................... 555
The Ghost Dance 556
An unconscious ghost dancer... 557

Another view of a Ghost Dance . 558
A parley with Big Foot........ 565
Yellow Bird throws dust
  in the air................. 569
The opening of the fight at
  Wounded Knee............ 570
Henry's squadron rescues the
  7th Cavalry near Pine Ridge . 573
Sioux dead at Wounded Knee... 577
Ghost dancers in prayer 579
The battle of Wounded Knee ... 588
The wounding of Lieutenant
  Hawthorne 589
Digging trenches at Pine Ridge . 591
Sioux of the Standing Rock
  Agency.................. 598
The death of Sitting Bull 604
A cavalryman in winter uniform. 608
Watching the Brule stronghold. . 610
Sioux dead at Wounded Knee... 617
An infantryman in winter
  uniform.................. 622
Corporal Weinert working his
  Hotchkiss gun 628
The last scene 635

Maps
Battlefield of Platte Bridge....... 7
Fort Philip Kearny 67
The Fetterman fight 70
The battle of the Rosebud...... 253
Custer's final approach to
  the Little Bighorn.......... 290
Custer's battleground 292
Plan of Reno's defense on
  the bluff 325
Fort Robinson and vicinity..... 495
The 1890–91 Sioux campaign .. 560
The Wounded Knee battlefield.. 563

PREFACE

Eyewitnesses to the Indian Wars, 1865–1890: The Long War for the Northern Plains is the fourth volume of a five-volume series that seeks to tell the saga of the military struggle for the American West in the words of the soldiers, noncombatants, and Native Americans who shaped it. Volume Five will feature accounts that transcend a particular region or conflict, including eyewitness biographical sketches of key military figures; narratives of army wives, junior officers, and enlisted men; accounts of garrison life; writings and speeches of army officers on Indian policy; narratives of army scouts; and discussions of Indian-fighting doctrine and tactics.

It is the purpose of the present volume to offer as representative a selection of original accounts pertaining to the campaigns on the Northern Plains as may be assembled under one cover. As in earlier volumes, most of the accounts presented here are taken from contemporaneous newspapers and magazines, or from unpublished manuscripts.

Several considerations guide the choice of material for inclusion in the *Eyewitnesses to the Indian Wars* series. The events described must have occurred between the end of the Civil War and the tragedy at Wounded Knee. With but few exceptions, the articles featured were published during the authors' lifetimes. Articles published within the last fifty years have been excluded, as they are for the most part readily available.

My goal in editing the selections in this volume has been to present accurate and annotated texts. I have added notes to correct errors of fact, clarify obscure references, provide historical context where needed, offer capsule biographies of contributors, and identify more fully persons mentioned in the text.

Editing of the text has been light. Many nineteenth-century writers had a penchant for commas, for commas and hyphens in combination, and for semicolons. I have eliminated them where their overuse clouds the meaning or impedes the rhythm of a sentence. I have regularized capitalization, punctuation, and the spelling of names and places. I have replaced references to an officer's brevet, or Civil War volunteer, rank with their regular rank at the time of the events described. Thus Bvt. Maj. Gen. George A. Custer becomes Lt. Col. George A. Custer, Bvt. Maj. Gen. John Gibbon becomes Col. John Gibbon, and so forth. Lieutenant colonels are referred to as colonel when only their last name is mentioned in the text, thus Colonel Custer; this courtesy follows normal military usage.

INTRODUCTION

The long war for the Northern Plains commenced well before the white man began carving up the Native American domain in the latter decades of the nineteenth century. The Teton Sioux, the principal victims of white acquisitiveness, had themselves seized much of the region from the Crow Indians earlier in the century, and they would continue to wage war for Crow lands even as the white noose around them tightened.

A hundred or more years earlier, the Chippewas had driven the Sioux from present-day Wisconsin, across the Mississippi River and into western Minnesota. Chippewa pressure in turn compelled the Sioux to displace the Cheyennes, whose villages ranged between the Mississippi and Upper Red Rivers. The Cheyennes withdrew to the Missouri River in 1676, according to their most reliable historian, where the Sutaios, a people who spoke a similar dialect, opposed their further advance. The two tribes fought for a time, then formed an alliance, and together they crossed the Missouri River below the Cannonball and took refuge in the Black Hills. There Lewis and Clark found them in 1804.

Several Sioux tribes followed, pushed by the Chippewas and drawn by the rich game of the plains in about equal measure. The Siouan family originally had consisted of seven autonomous but related groups or tribes. As they spread westward, the Sioux tribes coalesced into three divisions. The four tribes remaining along the Minnesota River became known collectively as the Santees, or Nakotas. They were a semi-sedentary people who harvested wild rice, moved on foot, hunted animals of the forest, and fished. Two tribes, the Yanktons and Yantonais, abandoned the Minnesota woodlands in favor of the prairies east of the Missouri River. They pursued the buffalo on horseback and had no fixed villages, but did retain some characteristics of the Santees. Together the two tribes were known as the Dakotas. Their combined population was estimated at seventy-five hundred in 1867.[1]

It is the westernmost group, known as the Lakotas, or Teton Sioux, that appear most prominently in *The Long War for the Northern Plains*. The Lakotas constituted nearly half the strength of the entire Sioux confederacy, numbering between fifteen and twenty thousand people divided into the following seven subtribes: the Blackfeet (a Siouan people not to be confused with the Blackfeet tribe farther to the northwest), Brules, Hunkpapas, Miniconjous, Oglalas, Sans Arcs, and Two Kettles.

The Lakotas were the true horse-and-buffalo Sioux of popular imagination.[2] Less well known was the fact that their culture was scarcely two generations old at the time of their first serious conflict with the whites in the 1850s. By then, each Lakota subtribe had laid claim to its own hunting grounds, which it defended vigorously against the Crows, Assiniboines, Crees, and other non-Lakota denizens of the Northern Plains.

The largest of the Lakota sub-tribes were the Oglalas and Brules. They wintered in villages congregated along the North Platte River and in the summer ranged northward to the upper Powder River and eastward through the Black Hills to the Missouri in pursuit of buffalo. North of the Big Cheyenne, or Belle Fourche, River lay the hunting grounds of the Miniconjous and Two Kettles; farther north, on the grassy plains between the Missouri River and the mouth of the Yellowstone River, lived the Hunkpapas, Blackfeet, and Sans Arcs, small subtribes that often camped and hunted together.

The horse and buffalo were crucial to the Lakota way of life. Buffalo meat was the dietary staple. The hide, fur, and bones provided clothing, shelter, and nearly every domestic article imaginable. A man measured his wealth in the number of horses he owned. He purchased his wife with horses, and he would risk his life to steal them from other tribes or to recover his own stolen horses or those of his band.

The political systems, spiritual beliefs, and ceremonies of the Lakotas derived from the habits and characteristics of the buffalo. Lakota legend traced the tribe's creation to the miraculous appearance of the White Buffalo Woman, who gave them the Sacred Calf Pipe, the smoking of which brought spiritual union with all things—animate and inanimate—and a channel to *Wakan Tanka,* the Great Mystery. "There was nothing sacred before the pipe came," the Lakota Left Heron explained. "There was no social organization, and the people ran around the prairie like so many wild animals."[3]

Kinship was all important to the Lakotas. The extended family, or band (*tiyospaye* in the Lakota tongue), was the cement of tribal society. Bands camped and hunted as a unit and normally came together as a tribe only once a year, in June for the annual Sun Dance.

The Sun Dance was central to the sacred life of the tribe. White Buffalo Woman had commanded the Lakotas to perform the rite in order to retain tribal vigor and the favor of *Wi,* the sun deity, who reigned over the natural and spiritual worlds and defended the cardinal virtues of the people. The Sun Dance ceremony lasted twelve days, culminating in the dance itself, a rapturous manifestation of self-sacrifice and piety in which participants lacerated their arms and moved about the sun pole, suspended by ropes attached to their bodies by means of skewers inserted beneath the chest or back muscles. "I must give something that I really value to show that my whole being goes with the lesser gifts [to Wi], explained a Lakota warrior. "Therefore I promise to give my body."[4] After the dance, the tribe broke up into bands for the buffalo hunt.

The cardinal virtues that the Lakota man assiduously cultivated in himself, and for which the tribe supplicated Wi in the sun dance, were bravery, fortitude, generosity, and wisdom. Foremost among these was bravery. War and the hunt were the two great endeavors of the Lakota male. Success in the former, through strictly prescribed war honors, determined a man's place in the tribe and was the path to prestige and leadership.

Individual valor meant more than group victory. Loosely adhering to a common objective, each warrior fought to further his own interest. War chiefs planned larger raids or battles, but they exercised little control once the fighting began. The greatest single Lakota war honor—that of first coup, striking a live enemy with a coup stick—required far more courage than a white soldier in ranks shooting a rifle was ever called upon to display.

Closely related to bravery was the virtue of fortitude, which the Lakotas defined as the capacity to endure pain and discomfort and the ability to maintain an aura of dignity and reserve under trying circumstances.

The first two virtues served the individual in his quest for social esteem and stature; the third, generosity, benefited the tribe. In the Lakota view, property existed to be given away to less fortunate members of the tribe. Prestige derived not from how much one had, but from how munificent one was in distributing it. "A man must take pity on orphans, the crippled, and the old. If you have more than one of anything, you should give it away to help those persons," said a Lakota.[5]

The final virtue, wisdom, was the most difficult to attain. In the Lakota world, wisdom meant superior judgment in matters of war and the hunt, tribal welfare, and the spirit world. Also of great value in Lakota culture was the gift of prophesy, as manifested in dreams and visions that came true. Those who possessed the gift were called *Wichasha Wakan,* or men of sacred power. Sitting Bull, the most influential of the Lakota chiefs, was also a renowned *Wichasha Wakan.*

A chief held far less power than the white man imagined. He led by example and governed with the advice and consent of a council of elders. Every decision represented consensus; without it, no decision was made. Families were bound to obey a chief only in matters of war and peace or the communal hunt. To compel obedience in such instances, the chiefs relied on the fraternal warrior societies that defined the life of the warrior. From these societies came the *akicita,* or policemen, who enforced the rules that the chiefs laid down. Working with the *akicita* were the four "shirt wearers," warriors of proven prowess whom the tribal council appointed to enforce council dictates.

Relationships with other peoples were fairly simple. To the Sioux, one was either an ally or an enemy (one might, however, stage truces with enemies for the purpose of trade, particularly in guns and ammunition). The names by which they were known reflect this dichotomy. *Sioux* was a French corruption of *Nadowe-is-iw,* the name the Chippewas gave them, which meant "snake" or "adder," and by metaphor, "enemy." *Nakota, Dakota,* and *Lakota* were the name they gave themselves in the Santee, Yankton, and Teton dialects, respectively. These terms signify "ally" and were extended to any people with whom peace had been formally concluded.

The principal non-Teton beneficiaries of the appellation Lakota were the Northern Cheyennes and the Northern Arapahos. Both tribes had split into a northern and southern branch in the 1830s, after George Bent established a fort and trading post on the Arkansas River. Those bands that gravitated to Bent's Fort became the southern branches of both tribes; those that roamed north of the North Platte River, the northern branches.

The Cheyennes and Arapahos shared many characteristics of the Lakota and themselves had been close allies since at least the mid-eighteenth century. Originally located northeast of the Red River Valley of Minnesota, the Arapahos crossed the Missouri River when the Cheyennes left Minnesota. The Arapahos were known as a kindly and accommodating people, while the Cheyennes were the most warlike tribe on the plains. Despite their very different temperaments, the Cheyennes and Arapahos faithfully shared in one another's struggles and, after making peace with the Lakotas in the 1840s, in the conflicts of that tribe as well, particularly against their common enemy, the Crows.

Not until the 1850s did the Lakotas perceive the *wasichus,* or white men, as a serious menace. Before the Mexican War, few whites had ventured onto the plains. Most Americans believed the "Great American Desert," as the region became known after the Louisiana Purchase made it part of the United States, would never be fit for anyone but wandering Indians. The government confidently erected a chain of forts to mark the eastern edge of the "Permanent Indian Frontier" and give little more thought to the plains.

All that changed in 1848. From Mexican defeat, the United States gained a huge domain in the Southwest; the subsequent resolution of the disputed Oregon border with Great Britain opened that territory also. Suddenly the United States stretched from coast to coast. Long trains of emigrant wagons wound their way along the Platte River road, through the heart of the Plains Indian lands, toward California goldfields and rich Oregon farmlands.

Nearly seven thousand increasingly restive Lakotas, as well as nearly all the Northern Cheyennes and Arapahos, lived along the Platte. Government officials hurried west to negotiate an Indian treaty that would allow whites unimpeded travel across the Great Plains. At Fort Laramie, representatives of the Plains tribes gathered to "touch the pen" to the first of many agreements that they would only vaguely understand. In exchange for protection from white aggression, the Native American signatories of the Fort Laramie Treaty agreed to permit the government to build roads and military posts on the plains. They also pledged to cease warring upon other tribes. To encourage compliance with the treaty, the government promised the signatory bands annuities in the form of clothing, blankets, weapons, and ammunition.

For a time an uneasy peace reigned. But the treaty bore the seeds of future discord. No chief could curb inter-tribal warfare, embedded as it was in the Plains Indian culture. Fissures opened among the Lakotas. Most were willing to accept annuities and stay clear of the emigrant roads, but the Hunkpapas and Blackfeet opposed the treaty categorically.

The arrogant stupidity of a green lieutenant temporarily united the factious Lakotas against the whites. On August 19, 1854, Lt. John L. Grattan marched thirty soldiers into the camp of the friendly Brule chief, Conquering Bear, to demand the surrender of a Minneconjou visitor who had killed a stray ox from an emigrant train. Conquering Bear hesitated, and Grattan opened fire. When the smoke cleared, Conquering Bear lay mortally wounded, and Grattan and his men were dead.

The so-called "Grattan massacre" brought the Lakotas into armed conflict with the army. The War Department called upon Col. William S. Harney, a hulking, intimidating man, to bring the Lakotas to terms. Harney accepted the challenge. "By God, I'm for battle—no peace," he bellowed as he set out up the Platte with six hundred soldiers.[6] On September 3, 1855, Harney attacked the village of Little Thunder, the successor to Conquering Bear as head chief of the Southern Brules, on Blue Water Creek, north of the Platte. Little Thunder escaped, but more than half of the village's 250 occupants were killed or captured.

Stunned by the defeat, the Lakotas answered Harney's summons to a treaty council at Fort Pierre on March 1, 1856. They agreed to cease hostilities and to accept the authority of head chiefs (an office that had never before existed in Lakota society) whom Harney appointed and whom the U.S. government would hold accountable for the behavior of their people. The Indian Bureau objected to Harney's negotiating in its stead, and the Senate rejected the treaty, but "The Butcher," as the Lakotas called Harney, had so overawed the tribes that they forswore war against the *wasichus* for nearly a decade.

The Cheyennes too felt the force of the *wasichu* soldiers. In response to army road surveys through the heart of their homeland, restive young warriors had lashed out against travelers along the Platte route. Small clashes between war parties and army detachments during 1856, for which both sides bore blame, led the War Department to outfit a spring 1857 offensive under Col. Edwin V. Sumner to "severely punish" the Cheyennes. Sumner killed few Indians in the campaign that followed, but he destroyed many lodges and food stores before the onset of winter. The Cheyennes and their Arapaho allies relented, and for the next seven years, gold-seekers and settlers made their way unmolested through the Cheyenne and Arapaho country to new diggings in the foothills of the Rocky Mountains.

Gold precipitated the next major clash between the Lakotas and the army. Its discovery in Montana and Idaho in the early 1860s generated heavy traffic along the Upper Missouri River and the established emigrant roads, and also led to the opening of new routes. Lakota war parties struck back, but their raids drew little notice from a U.S. government preoccupied with civil war. Not until the summer of 1862, when years of festering grievances caused the Santees of Minnesota to rise up, did the Northern Plains again command national attention. Hundreds of white settlers died before Minnesota volunteers defeated the rebellious bands, sending the surviving Indians reeling onto the plains and into the arms of their Dakota kinsmen. Frightened whites in turn fled the Dakota Territory. By the spring of 1863, nearly a quarter of the homesteads along the Upper Missouri River lay abandoned.

Responding to rumors that a large force of hostile Santees and Dakotas had gathered near Devil's Lake under the leadership of Little Crow, chief of the Minnesota hostiles, to strike at the frontier settlements, Maj. Gen. John Pope, commander of the Department of the Northwest, mounted an offensive to crush Sioux resistance in the Dakota Territory. Two expeditions set out in July: The first, under Brig. Gen. Henry H. Sibley, was to march up the Minnesota River toward Devil's Lake; the second, under Brig. Gen. Alfred Sully, was to move up the Missouri from Iowa to cooperate with Sibley.

Although they had not intended to join Little Crow, the Lakotas became embroiled in the struggle nonetheless. Hunkpapa and Blackfeet hunting parties inadvertently mingled with Little Crow's fleeing warriors and in July, were drawn into battle against Sibley. Bested in engagements at Dead Buffalo Lake on July 26 and Stony Lake on July 28, the Dakotas, Santees, and their reluctant Lakota allies retired across the Missouri River. When Sibley turned back toward Minnesota, the Dakotas and Santees recrossed the Missouri to follow the buffalo and restock meat stores lost in the July battles. Sully's column struck their camp at Whitestone Hill on September 3, killing one hundred Indians and destroying huge quantities of food and equipment. Before returning to Sioux City, Sully built and garrisoned a post downriver from Fort Pierre, evidence that the *wasichus* intended to maintain their grip on the Upper Missouri. The Dakotas slipped back east of the Missouri for the winter, and the Lakotas withdrew deep into their own country.

Sully was back the following summer. Pope had received intelligence reports from Upper Missouri trading posts and the British Red River settlements indicating that larger numbers of Lakotas and Yanktonais Sioux planned to join with Little Crow's Santees to close navigation on the Missouri, dispute the overland passage of Montana-bound gold-seekers, and fight any soldiers sent out to stop them.

By mid-July 1864, nearly fourteen hundred Sioux lodges had assembled in the Badlands of western Dakota. Marching toward them along the Cannonball River was Sully, with twenty-two hundred troops. On July 28, five miles south of the Sioux village at the base of the Killdeer Mountains, the two forces clashed. Confident warriors left their village standing and assembled their families on the hills to watch the fight. But Sully's artillery swept the Sioux from the field, and in their haste to escape, the Indians left behind valuable supplies and some one hundred dead.

Low on rations, Sully felt obliged to forgo pursuit and instead cross the Badlands in order to meet transports on the Yellowstone River with much-needed supplies. Although the Sioux had escaped, Sully could rightly boast of having "met the combined forces of the Sioux nation at points they chose to give us battle, and in these engagements completely scattered them in all directions."[7] More importantly, his expedition had pushed the military frontier nearly to the Montana Territory.

Once again, the badly outgunned Sioux had suffered a stunning defeat at the hands of the "Long Knives," as they called the Federal soldiers. The legacy of Killdeer Mountains was profound. Sully had planted garrisons in the heart of the Hunkpapa and Blackfeet homeland, leaving units at the trading posts of Forts Union and Berthold and building a permanent post, Fort Rice, on the Missouri River ten miles above the mouth of the Cannonball. Killdeer Mountains also renewed factionalism among the Upper Missouri Lakota. Several hundred sought peace, but most rallied around the Hunkpapa war chief Sitting Bull, who vowed to drive the *wasichus* from Sioux country at any cost. From a tactical standpoint, the battle of Killdeer Mountains taught the Lakotas to avoid pitched battle with the Long Knives, and it convinced them of the need for better firearms and more reliable sources of ammunition.

On the Great Plains, the year 1865 opened to unprecedented bloodshed, thanks in large measure to a ruthless volunteer colonel named John M. Chivington, who, intent on getting up an Indian war, had massacred Black Kettle's band of Southern Cheyenne at Sand Creek in eastern Colorado.

Retribution was swift. In January, the Cheyennes and their Arapaho and Lakota allies struck hard along the Arkansas and Platte River emigrant routes, burning wagon trains, wrecking ranches, cutting a hundred miles of telegraph lines, and slaughtering indiscriminately. Old-timers would call 1865 "the bloody year on the plains." Every tribe from Texas to the Yellowstone River was at war with the whites, and friendly Indians were leaving reservations by the hundreds to join the hostiles.

In the Powder River country, the Oglalas took up the lance under the leadership of Old-Man-Afraid-of-His-Horses and Red Cloud. Along the Upper Missouri, the war fever that Sand Creek engendered added greatly to the prestige—and numbers—of Sitting Bull's Hunkpapa war faction. Lakota and Cheyenne war parties swept across the Northern Plains, not only attacking whites, but also striking westward to seize more Crow land in order to replace their supply of buffalo and other game animals, which had grown scarce before the tide of advancing *wasichu* emigration.

The army made ready to respond. General Pope, now commander of the sprawling Military Division of the Missouri, which extended from Texas to the

Canadian border, fashioned plans for a concerted offensive against all the warring tribes. His objectives were twofold: to put an end to depredations against the settlements, and to secure for emigrant travel the principal land and water routes across the plains. In the north, Pope faced the dual problem of clearing the Platte route of marauding bands and of helping secure a new trail that John M. Bozeman and John Jacobs had blazed through the Powder River country to the Montana goldfields two years earlier. With the coming of spring, emigrants in droves would gather at Fort Laramie, the trailhead. Because the Bozeman Trail passed through some of the best Lakota hunting grounds, along the eastern base of the Bighorn Mountains, conflict was inevitable.

In his planning, Pope was ably seconded by the commander of an expanded Department of the Missouri, Maj. Gen. Grenville Dodge. Together they evolved a strategy for smashing the Great Plains tribes in the early spring, before the grass returned to the plains and the Indians resumed their raids on the emigrant routes. Three expeditions were to strike simultaneously, one in the south and two in the north. The northern campaign would be a joint pincer movement, similar to that which Sully and Sibley had attempted in the Dakotas the year before. Marching north from Fort Laramie into the Powder River country, Brig. Gen. Patrick E. Connor was to first build a fort and supply station, then strike at Sioux and Cheyenne camps near the Bighorn Mountains. General Sully would approach the Powder River from Sioux City. He was to punish Lakotas who had attacked Forts Rice and Berthold during the winter, then turn west to fight several hundred lodges of hostile Sioux, Northern Cheyennes, and Arapahos, believed to be in the Black Hills. Driving this group before him, Sully was to press on to the Powder River country, establish a fort on the river, and trap any remaining Indians between him and Connor.

Pope had predicated his strategy on two premises: that Civil War veterans in large numbers would be available for duty in the West, and that Pope and Dodge would be left to treat with hostile tribes as they saw fit. There would be no weak-kneed treaties, no annuities that rewarded depredations, and no civilian traders to corrupt the Indians with alcohol and arm them with new rifles.

It was a fine plan Pope and Dodge had devised, but circumstances disrupted their spring offensive. With the end of the Civil War, the Union volunteers wanted nothing more than to go home. No sooner did troops arrive in the West than they deserted by the hundreds. Entire regiments threatened mutiny. Other factors also conspired against the generals. Heavy rains, overflowing rivers, tardy supplies, inadequate transportation, and a lack of cavalry mounts prevented Connor and Sully from starting on schedule.

Presaging three decades of War Department, Indian Bureau, and congressional wrangling over Indian policy, the second pillar of Pope's planning for the Northern Plains also fell before the campaign had begun. Public revulsion over the Sand Creek massacre caused Congress to add $20,000 to the Indian Appropriations Act to finance a new treaty with the Lakotas of the Upper Missouri, which Gov. Newton Edmunds of the Dakota Territory would negotiate. Pope objected. He denied Edmunds military protection for his peace commission and curtly informed the governor that "there are no Sioux Indians in Dakota Territory with whom it is judicious to make such treaties of peace as you propose."[8] Pope also appealed to Washington to restrain Edmunds, but as the summer wore on, rising costs and congressional opposition caused the War Department to waiver in its support of Pope's aggressive designs.

While Pope and Dodge planned and fretted, the Indians struck. In late July, the chiefs decided the time had come for the massive war expedition that they had been plotting since May in retaliation for Killdeer Mountains and Sand Creek. Between one and three thousand Lakota, Cheyenne, and Arapaho warriors assembled to attack Platte Bridge Station, a critical post located at the North Platte River crossing of the Oregon Trail, some 130 miles west of Fort Laramie. A company of the 11th Kansas Cavalry and detachments of the 11th Ohio Volunteer Cavalry and the 3rd U.S. Volunteers, former Confederate prisoners known as "Galvanized Yankees," garrisoned the stockade. The principal leaders of the war party were Dull Knife, White Bull, and Roman Nose of the Cheyennes, and Old-Man-Afraid-of-His-Horses and Red Cloud of the Oglalas.

Having observed small parties of hostile Indians nearby, the commander at Platte Bridge, Maj. Martin Anderson, decided to send a detachment under the popular and capable Lt. Caspar W. Collins to reinforce the twenty-five-man escort of a train of empty wagons approaching the river from the west. Concealed in the hills north of the Platte, the main Indian war party watched Collins's twenty-man party leave the stockade. A half mile beyond Platte Bridge, the Indians attacked, killing Collins and four of his men. They also ambushed the wagon train, killing and mutilating all but three members of the escort and burning the wagons. With that, the allied tribes considered the war over, and the great war party broke up to hunt buffalo.

For the army, the war had scarcely begun. Interceding in Pope's spat with Governor Edmunds and the Indian Bureau, Ulysses S. Grant, the commanding general of the army, gave Pope's planned offensive his ringing endorsement. Although welcome, Grant's approval did not end Pope's woes. Nervous Minnesotans and the timid commander of the Department of the Northwest, Maj. Gen. Samuel R. Curtis, conjured up an imaginary hostile force at Devil's Lake, and General Sully forwarded seemingly credible reports that three thousand Sioux lodges were coming to Fort Rice to make peace. They weren't; on June 2, Sitting Bull's Hunkpapas attacked Fort Rice. Other reports reached Pope that large numbers of hostiles had assembled at Bear Butte, on the northeastern edge of the Black Hills (these reports were correct at the time they were made, but before Pope could respond, the Indians in question had attacked Platte Bridge and then dispersed to hunt buffalo). The reports from the Black Hills were especially troubling because a government-sanctioned road-surveying expedition under James A. Sawyers of Sioux City was about to push up the Niobrara River, intending to pass through the Black Hills country en route to Virginia City, Montana.

Pope had deflected Curtis's nervous appeal for help, and Sitting Bull had foiled the intentions of the Lakota peace faction, but the Black Hills threat compelled Pope to alter his plans. Pope called off Sully's expedition, detailing part of his command as an escort to Sawyer's surveying party, and gave his former mission to Connor. "You must deal with these Indians in the Black Hills and establish the post at Powder River," Pope told Dodge on June 3.

Dodge and Connor moved to comply. They organized a three-pronged expedition into the Powder River country. The columns were to rendezvous on Rosebud Creek, a tributary of the Yellowstone, on or about September 1. Col. Nelson Cole led the Right Column, composed of eight batteries of the 2nd Missouri Volunteer Light Artillery, mounted as cavalry; eight companies of the 12th Missouri Volunteer Cavalry; and a train of 140 wagons—fourteen hundred men in all. Cole's command was to march up the Loup Fork of the North Platte River, attack any hostiles that might be lingering at Bear Butte, and then march around the northern edge of the Black Hills to the rendezvous.

Lt. Col. Samuel Walker commanded the Center Column, composed of six hundred men of his own 16th Kansas Volunteer Cavalry. He was to march from Fort Laramie to the Black Hills, and then continue on to the Powder River and the Rosebud rendezvous.

General Connor marched up the Bozeman Trail with the Left Column, which he in turn divided into two sections. The main body, which he accompanied, totaled 475 men, including the famed Pawnee scouts of Frank North. A second section, detached at Horseshoe Creek, was commanded by Capt. Albert Brown of the 2nd California Volunteer Cavalry and consisted of 116 men and 84 Omaha scouts. Brown was to continue up the North Platte to Platte Bridge, then head northwestward to Wind River, and finally eastward to a union with Connor at his new post on Powder River.

Nothing went as planned. The late start, poor guides, bad leadership, early storms, and clever harassing tactics by the Indians all contributed to the complete failure of the expedition. Cole eventually met up with Walker north of the Black Hills, and together the two commands limped across the sun-swept plains, while horses and mules gave out and rations dwindled. On September 5, near the mouth of the Little Powder River, the exhausted Bluecoats stumbled upon the same Lakota, Cheyenne, and Arapaho village that had staged the Platte Bridge raid. More than a thousand warriors sallied forth from the hills and bluffs protecting the village to give battle. A sharp fight raged for three hours before the Indians broke off the fight. The Cheyennes withdrew to the Black Hills in search of buffalo, but the Lakotas were compelled to fight again on September 8 when Cole and Walker blundered upon their village in the Powder River Valley. This time, the Bluecoats barely escaped annihilation. No sooner did they break free of the Indians than blustery winds and an early snowstorm lashed at the men and animals. Horses and mules died in droves; in one night alone, Cole lost 414 animals and Walker nearly 100.

Connor's Pawnee scouts found the battered commands of Cole and Walker on September 13 and guided them to Fort Connor, as Connor called the "rather rude affair" his men were constructing on the Powder River. Apart from routing an Arapaho village on August 29, Connor's men had seen relatively little action, and the general was anxious to assemble another expedition and take the field from Fort Connor. Before he could act, orders reached him from Pope, breaking up his sprawling District of the Plains into four small districts and directing Connor to return to his old command, the District of Utah, "at the earliest practical moment." Connor and the other district commanders were to "return to a purely defensive arrangement for the security of the overland routes" and "reduce troops and expenditures without delay."[9]

Pope's peremptory orders emanated from the government's desire to accelerate the mustering out of volunteer regiments and from War Department displeasure with Connor. The high cost of the campaign, along with Connor's pronouncement that he intended to kill every Indian male over the age of twelve, had caused a clamor for his recall. Connor left for Salt Lake City in late September, and the Powder River expedition came to a dismal close.

Seldom during the long war for the Northern Plains was government policy consistent, or even coherent. In the late summer of 1865, Indian Bureau peace commissioners sent runners with invitations to a conference at Fort Sully to the very Indians then battling Cole and Walker in the Powder River country. Few came, but that did not prevent the superintendent of Indian affairs, Edward B. Taylor, from assuring Washington that the treaties that emerged from the council would bring lasting peace to the Northern Plains.

On paper, it seemed so. Once again, the Indian signatories had agreed to withdraw from the emigrant routes in exchange for annuities. The problem was, the peace chiefs had no following of consequence. Red Cloud and the Oglalas remained aloof, and Sitting Bull and the powerful Hunkpapa war faction scoffed at the notion of dealing away land for rations and trinkets. Said Sitting Bull to a group of reservation Assiniboines: "The whites may get me at last, but I will have good times till then. You are fools to make yourselves slaves to a piece of fat bacon, some hardtack, and a little sugar and coffee."[10] True to his word, in the spring of 1866 Sitting Bull renewed his war against Fort Rice.

Maj. Gen. William T. Sherman, the new commander of the Division of the Missouri, needed peace badly, if only for a time. The volunteer regiments of the Civil War were mustering out far faster than the Regular army could be recruited and posted. Until he could bring the military establishment in the West up to strength, Sherman had to adopt a defensive strategy. "All I ask is comparative quiet this year [1866]," he wrote Grant's chief of staff, "for by next year we can have the new cavalry enlisted, equipped, and mounted, ready to go and visit these Indians where they live."

Perhaps conscious of the emptiness of the 1865 treaties, the peace commissioners tried to entice more chiefs to sign. For a moment, it appeared as if they might succeed in negotiating a meaningful agreement. Old-Man-Afraid-of-His-Horses, Red Cloud, and several other prominent war leaders came in to Fort Laramie to hear what the emissaries of the Great Father had to say. But Sherman and his subordinates proved the agents of their own discomfiture. Rather than trust to a treaty to secure the Bozeman Trail, Sherman ordered three military posts built along the eastern edge of the Bighorn Mountains. On May 13, 1866, the 2nd and 3rd Battalions of the 18th U.S. Infantry Regiment marched from Fort Kearny, the 3rd Battalion to garrison posts along the Platte Road, the 2nd to protect the Bozeman Trail. The regimental commander, Col. Henry B. Carrington, a career staff officer with no combat experience, traveled with the 2nd Battalion, expecting to win over the Sioux and Cheyennes with "patience, forbearance, and common sense."

But common sense was at a premium in the frontier army. Certain that the Indians would capitulate in council, Colonel Carrington marched his seven-hundred-man battalion into Fort Laramie at the very moment the peace commissioners were negotiating the terms of travel along the Bozeman Trail. Red Cloud expressed the outrage of the gathered chiefs at Superintendent Taylor's evident deceit. "The Great Father sends us presents and wants us to sell him the road," stormed the Oglala war leader, "but White Chief goes with soldiers to steal the road before Indians say Yes or No." With that, Red Cloud and the Powder River chiefs broke off talks, vowing to kill any white who dared enter their lands. Again Taylor prevaricated. Standing Elk and Spotted Tail, Lower Brule chiefs whose hunting lands lay far from the Bozeman Trail, were happy to give away what was not theirs, and they signed the treaty, as did the chiefs of the dissipated bands that lived about the fort, the so-called "Laramie Loafers." But young Brule warriors were for war, and they decamped for the Powder River country after Carrington's column passed by. Spotted Tail told Taylor of these defections and advised that *wasichus* venturing north had best "go prepared, and look out for their hair." His warning fell on deaf ears. "Satisfactory treaty concluded with the Sioux and Cheyennes," Taylor wired the Indian Bureau. "Most cordial feeling prevails."[11]

Carrington got a healthy dose of Lakota cordiality when he entered the Powder River country. On June 17, the 2nd Battalion, 18th U.S. Infantry, marched north from Fort Laramie. Carrington detached one company to garrison Fort Reno (formerly Fort Connor). The remainder of the battalion continued up the Bozeman Trail to Piney Creek, at the base of the Bighorn Mountains. There Carrington set his men to work building his headquarters post, which he named Fort Phil Kearny. On August 3, he detached two companies to plant a third post—Fort C. F. Smith—ninety-one miles faurther up the trail. Within a week of Carrington's arrival at Piney Creek, Red Cloud struck. With his Oglalas were several thousand Minneconjou, Sans Arc, Brule, Cheyenne, and Arapaho warriors. War parties stole stock, ambushed supply trains and details sent to gather logs from the nearby "pinery," and killed anyone foolish enough to stray from the fort alone.

Carrington fought off the attacks and kept up the construction. Fort Phil Kearny was completed in December, a testimony to Carrington's engineering prowess, but his command was ill prepared for battle. Although two-thirds of his men were raw recruits, Carrington set aside no time for drill or training before winter shut in the garrison. The battalion was armed with old muzzle-loading Springfield rifles, hardly an ideal weapon for engaging swift-moving mounted warriors. More troubling still, Carrington's subordinates were as overconfident as he was cautious, and they demanded he take the offensive. Word of unrest among the officers reached Carrington's superior, Brig. Gen. Philip St. George Cooke, the superannuated commander of the Department of the Platte. Not only did Cooke take no action to quell the disaffection, but he also gave but scant attention to Carrington's requests for cavalry, breech-loading rifles, and ammunition. A handful of reinforcements arrived in November, bringing the garrison of Fort Phil Kearny to a mere 402 officers and men. Camped in the hills and ravines around the fort were more than two thousand hostile warriors.

Those numbers would hardly have troubled Carrington's reckless young subordinates, had they been aware of them. Capt. William J. Fetterman, the most troublesome of the malcontents, boasted that he could ride through the Indian country with eighty men.

Fetterman had a chance to make good his boast on December 6, when the wood train was attacked two miles from the fort. Carrington ordered Fetterman to take thirty-five cavalry and a handful of mounted infantry, relieve the wood train, and follow the hostiles along their customary withdrawal route around the west end of the Sullivant Hills. Carrington, meanwhile, would lead twenty-five mounted infantry up the Bozeman Trail and swing behind the Indians. The plan went awry when the war party of about one hundred turned on their pursuers, stampeding the green cavalrymen. Lt. Horatio S. Bingham and a sergeant were killed, and five enlisted men wounded.

Red Cloud commanded in person. Since August, he and the other war chiefs had been planning "two big fights with the whites," similar to the Platte Bridge affair—one at Fort C. F. Smith, and the other at Kearny. Apparently the December 6 action was the first such attempt, the attack on the wood train having been made to decoy pursuing soldiers into an ambush.

Red Cloud tried the ploy again on December 19, but Capt. James Powell, commanding the relief detachment, did not take the bait. Captain Fetterman, however, was easily lured. On the morning of December 21, a war party under the daring young Oglala Crazy Horse attacked the wood train, forcing it to corral. Ensconced among the hills and ravines north of Lodge Trail Ridge were another two thousand warriors. Carrington ordered Powell out again, but Fetterman, claiming seniority, demanded the assignment. Carrington relented, and Fetterman set out for the pinery with three officers, seventy-six men, and two civilian volunteers. Ignoring Carrington's orders that he not pursue the Indians beyond

Lodge Trail Ridge, Fetterman charged pell-mell after Crazy Horse's decoy party, over the ridge and along the Bozeman Trail, straight into an ambush. Not a man survived. Carrington retrieved the mutilated corpses and retired into the stockade to accept a siege.

Five days after the Fetterman fight, Sitting Bull's Hunkpapas attacked Fort Buford, built at the mouth of the Yellowstone earlier that year. They besieged the fort so effectively that, until spring, the War Department believed the garrison had been slaughtered.

The Fetterman disaster and presumed destruction of Fort Buford stunned and outraged the army. Making perhaps the most infelicitous public utterance of his career, Sherman told Grant, "We must act with vindictive earnestness against the Sioux, even to their extermination, men, women, and children."[12] Colonel Carrington was also a recipient of Sherman's wrath. "I know enough of Carrington to believe that he is better qualified for a safe place than one of danger," he wrote a colleague in disgust. A three-hundred-man relief column arrived at Fort Phil Kearny in January 1867 to lift the siege. With it came an order replacing Carrington with Lt. Col. Henry W. Wessels. General Grant cast a wider net for a scapegoat and replaced Cooke as department commander with Bvt. Maj. Gen. Christopher C. Augur.

Wessels tried to launch a winter offensive, but the biting cold and deep snow drove him indoors. Red Cloud's people also withdrew, and the stillness of winter descended over the Bozeman Trail.

Spring brought badly needed supplies to Forts Smith and Kearny. Particularly welcome was a July 1867 shipment of seven hundred Springfield-Allin breech-loading rifles to replace the old muzzleloaders with which the garrisons, and Fetterman's command, had ineffectually battled the Indians.

That the soldiers would find ample employment for their new rifles was evident, as Red Cloud returned to the warpath with a vengeance. Harassing attacks closed the Bozeman Trail to all but heavily guarded trains, and the garrisons of Forts Smith and Kearny were forced to fight for wood and water. To protect wood-cutting parties and their military escorts against attack, in early July civilian contractors built a corral of fourteen wagon boxes on an open plain near the Fort Phil Kearny pineries.

Dropping their hit-and-run tactics, in August the Indians launched simultaneous assaults on Forts Smith and Kearny. On the first, some eight hundred Lakota, Cheyenne, and Arapaho warriors attacked a six-man hay-cutting party, armed with repeating rifles, and its twenty-man army escort, armed with the new breechloaders, in a large hayfield northeast of Fort C. F. Smith. Retiring to a brushwood corral, the soldiers held off their assailants for four hours at a loss of three killed.

The next day, a war party of one thousand Minneconjous under High Back-Bone and Oglalas under Crazy Horse attacked the Fort Kearny wagon-box corral. Fifty-one men of Company C, 27th U.S. Infantry, under the command of Captain Powell and Lt. John C. Jenness, had drawn escort duty a week earlier.

Armed with breech-loading rifles, they repelled the Indian assault at a loss of three killed and two wounded.

Red Cloud and his allies lost heavily in these assaults, but they retained their iron grip on the Bozeman Trail. To the north, Sitting Bull held sway in the country around Fort Buford. The tenacity of Indian resistance brought another call for peace in Washington. A commission had been sent out in June to treat with the Lakotas. Old-Man-Afraid-of-His-Horses greeted them with a cheeky demand for ammunition for hunting, and the discussions came to naught. But the commissioners were sympathetic to the Lakota and in their report concluded that the government had no right to put a road through the Powder River country.

Neither the army nor the administration seriously contested that view. The steady progress of the Northern Pacific Railroad, which was projected to connect St. Paul, Minnesota, with Seattle, Washington, had become more important to the future of the nation than was a shortcut to the Montana goldfields. Consequently, on April 29, 1868, the Indian Bureau concluded a treaty with Red Cloud and his allied chiefs, in which the Indians relinquished all claims to the country east of the Bighorn Mountains, in exchange for the abandonment of the Bozeman Trail and the three forts that guarded it. Red Cloud also agreed to remove his people to an agency in Nebraska.

In the summer of 1868, the army left the Powder River country, and the Lakotas burned down the forts. Red Cloud had won his war.

In the Yellowstone country, Sitting Bull continued to fight. With no faith in *wasichu* promises, he remained staunchly opposed to treaty making of any sort. His friend and fellow Hunkpapa war chief Gall and a few lesser chiefs signed a treaty at Fort Rice in July 1868 that addressed none of the fundamental Hunkpapa grievances—that is to say, the detested Upper Missouri forts, steamboat traffic on the river, and white encroachment on tribal hunting grounds. Instead, the government created for the Lakotas a "Great Sioux Reservation," encompassing all of present-day Sioux Dakota west of the Missouri River; the treaty vaguely defined the Powder River country west of the reservation as "unceded Indian territory." Referring to what would prove a problematic concession, Article 16 of the treaty read: "The United States hereby agrees and stipulates that the country north of the North Platte River and east of the summits of the Bighorn Mountains shall be held and considered to be unceded Indian territory, and also stipulates and agrees that no white person or persons shall be permitted to settle upon or occupy any portion of the same; or without the consent of the Indians, first had and obtained, to pass through the same." By inference, Lakotas who wished to live by the chase rather than on government rations might continue to roam this tract.[13]

Gall's treaty was of no interest to Sitting Bull, who attacked Fort Buford two months after its conclusion. Nor did it appease nonreservation Lakotas, among whom Sitting Bull continued to rise in influence. In 1869, tribal elders accorded him the unprecedented office of supreme chief of the Lakotas (principally the Minneconjou, Sans Arc, Blackfeet, northern Oglala, and his own Hunkpapa sub-tribes) and the Yanktonais. Crazy Horse of the Oglalas became his staunchest ally outside the Hunkpapa tribe.

Competing with Sitting Bull for the allegiance of the Lakotas was Red Cloud. As agency life took root, the two factions drifted apart culturally. The westward migration of the buffalo, which the nonreservation bands followed into the unceded territory, brought about a growing physical drift as well. Between the two factions were large numbers of Lakotas who gravitated to the agency for food in the winter months and to the unceded territory to join in the hunt in the spring and summer.

As the 1870s opened, Sitting Bull was principally concerned with conquering the Crow land upon which the buffalo now grazed. He wrested the upper Powder River country from them, pushing the western frontier of the Lakotas to the Bighorn River. Sitting Bull's attention was drawn sharply to its eastern limits in 1873. Between 1870 and 1872, the Northern Pacific Railroad had progressed from Minnesota to the bank of the Missouri River, frightening off the buffalo and bringing white settlers in droves. At its new western terminus, a town, Bismarck, and a large cavalry post, Fort Abraham Lincoln, sprang up. Ahead of the railroad, protected by large military escorts, surveyors worked up the Yellowstone River Valley toward the Rockies. An expedition in 1871 went unchallenged, and two the following year—one west from Fort Ellis, Montana, under Maj. Eugene M. Baker, a second east from Fort Rice, Dakota, under Col. David S. Stanley—met with only limited resistance. But once finished with the Crows, Sitting Bull turned his attention to the new *wasichu* threat.

On June 20, Colonel Stanley again set out from Fort Rice, this time with nineteen companies of infantry, ten companies of the 7th Cavalry under Lt. George A. Custer, 350 civilians, a detachment of white and Indian scouts, and a train of 725 wagons. Two steamboats were chartered to haul supplies along the Yellowstone River. A greater provocation could hardly be imagined, and on August 4, near the mouth of the Tongue River, the Lakotas struck. Three hundred warriors tried to draw Custer, who was reconnoitering forward of the main column with two troops of cavalry, into an ambush. Custer detected the ruse and fought off the attackers for three hours until reinforcements arrived, then chased the hostiles off. A week later, the 7th Cavalry encountered a large war party under Sitting Bull on the north bank of the Yellowstone, below the mouth of the Bighorn. Again Custer prevailed, pursuing the Lakotas ten miles to the tune of the regimental anthem, "Garry Owen."

After the fight, known as the battle of the Yellowstone, Sitting Bull drew his people away to the south. Stanley swung north to the Musselshell River and in late September returned to Fort Rice. Perhaps Sitting Bull thought he had succeeded in keeping the *wasichus* out of the unceded territory, but it was the Panic of 1873, and not Indian resistance, that brought construction on the Northern Pacific to an abrupt halt at Bismarck; not until 1879 would it be resumed.

A threat no less profound than the railroad confronted the Lakotas in 1874. There had long been rumors of gold to be found in the Black Hills, or *Paha Sapa*, as the Lakotas called the mountain range that towered over the western third of the Great Sioux Reservation, but the region had remained unknown and unexplored. The Panic of 1873 and the growth of Dakota stimulated the gold talk anew, and the territorial legislature petitioned the federal government for a geological survey to determine the mineral wealth of the region.

The commander of the Division of the Missouri, Maj. Gen. Philip H. Sheridan, also was interested in the Black Hills. He hoped to build a military post at its eastern base in order to deter Lakota war parties from raiding off the Great Sioux Reservation. Both the secretaries of war and the interior gave their support to Sheridan's plan, and in July 1874 Custer led the 7th Cavalry, a detail of army engineers, two "practical miners," and an entourage of newspaper reporters into the Black Hills.

Sitting Bull watched the expedition angrily. Apart from a vague mystical attachment to the Black Hills, the Lakota esteemed the game-rich region as an unfailing source of food, a sort of meat reserve on the hoof. "I heard Sitting Bull say that the Black Hills was just like a food pack and therefore the Indians should stick to it," said the Oglala Standing Elk.[14]

In his report of the expedition, Custer was circumspect regarding the gold potential of the Black Hills. But the press whipped up a gold frenzy nonetheless, and prospectors made ready to descend on the hills with the first thaw in 1875. President Grant's declaration that the army would expel all intruders deterred few; as the New York *Tribune* editorialized, "If there is gold in the Black Hills, no army on earth can keep the adventurous men of the west out of them."

Not that the army had any heart for the job. Brig. Gen. George Crook, the commander of the Department of the Platte, sympathized with the interlopers, as did most of the troops assigned to the task, and by the summer of 1875 some eight hundred miners had made their way into the Black Hills.

Hoping to avert war, the government offered Red Cloud and the reservation chiefs $6 million dollars for the Hills. A decade on the reservation had given the chiefs a shrewd appreciation for the value of a dollar—and of the value the *wasichus* attached to their land—and they scoffed at the paltry sum the Great Father offered them. "Our Great Father has a big safe, and so have we," declared Chief Spotted Bear. "The hill is our safe." The commission returned empty handed. Of their Native American interlocutors, the commissioners reported, "We do not believe their temper or spirit can or will be changed until they are made to feel the power as well as the magnanimity of the government."[15]

Having failed to purchase the Black Hills, the Grant administration decided to steal them. On November 3, 1875, President Grant, Secretary of War William W. Belknap, Secretary of the Interior Zachariah Chandler, Indian Commissioner

E. P. Smith, and Generals Crook and Sheridan huddled secretly in the White House to concoct a stratagem for securing the Black Hills. All agreed on war as the only solution. Grant gave two orders aimed at deflecting blame to the nonreservation Indians for what amounted to illegal and naked government aggression. First, the directive barring miners from the Black Hills would continue in effect, but the army would not enforce it. Second, the hunting bands would be directed to leave the unceded territory and settle on the reservation. Remove the Indians, fill up the Black Hills with white settlers, and the issue of title became moot.

Six days after the meeting, a pliant Indian Bureau inspector, E. C. Watkins, provided a veneer of legitimacy to the planned land grab. Returning from a tour of the friendly Crow and Ree reservations and of the white settlements bordering the unceded territory, in which he had heard lurid tales of Lakota depredations—many of which were true—Watkins concluded, "The true policy, in my judgment, is to send troops against them in the winter, the sooner the better, and whip them into subjection."[16] Secretary Chandler and Smith concurred. On December 6, Smith instructed the agents for the Red Cloud and Spotted Tail agencies to send out runners to notify all Indians in the unceded territory that they had until January 31, 1876, to report to an agency; otherwise they would be considered hostile and turned over to the War Department.

Not that there was any chance of runners reaching the winter camps in time for the nonreservation bands to comply, even if they had been of a mind to, which, as Sitting Bull had made clear to Frank Grouard, an adopted captive turned army scout, earlier that fall, they were not. At a council of chiefs to consider the government offer to buy the Black Hills, Sitting Bull had spoken emphatically against any sale. "He said he had never been to an agency and was not going in," remembered Grouard. "He was no agency Indian. He told me to go out and tell the white men at Red Cloud that he declared open war and would fight them wherever he met them from that time on." Grouard undoubtedly embellished; Sitting Bull—and Crazy Horse—intended to fight only a defensive war to protect Lakota hunting lands.

Unaware of the government ultimatum, or of the forces gathering to fight them, the nonreservation bands had scattered for the winter, and January 31 came and went without a response. On February 8, 1876, Sheridan directed his department commanders, Brigadier Generals Alfred H. Terry and George Crook, to begin their offensives into the unceded territory.

Terry's column never got started. He had planned to make a quick strike with the 7th Cavalry against Sitting Bull's village, which Terry believed to be located on the Little Missouri River, a relatively short march from Fort Lincoln. But scouts now reported the Hunkpapa camp to be two hundred miles farther west. Closer to home, heavy snows had shut down the Northern Pacific Railroad, upon which Terry depended for supplies, and prevented the concentration of the 7th Cavalry at Fort Lincoln. Sheridan reluctantly accepted the fact that nothing could be expected of Terry until the spring or summer.

Matters appeared more promising in Crook's Department of the Platte. By the end of February, Crook had gathered nearly one thousand men and a large store of supplies at Fort Fetterman, Wyoming. On March 1, he set out along the old Bozeman Trail with five troops of the 2nd Cavalry, five troops of the 3rd Cavalry, and two companies of the 4th Infantry. Crook assigned nominal command of the expedition to Col. Joseph J. Reynolds, the elderly commander of the 3rd Cavalry. A brutal "norther" pounded the command with snow and sent temperatures plummeting below zero. Crook persevered, and on the evening of March 16 his scouts discovered a Cheyenne village of 105 lodges nestled in a cottonwood grove along the Powder River and surrounded by high bluffs. Crook permitted Reynolds the honor of attacking the camp with three of the five cavalry squadrons that formed the expedition, while Crook stayed behind with the pack train and the remainder of the command.

Reynolds fumbled badly. He had hoped to attack the village at dawn from two directions, but Capt. Alexander Moore failed to get his supporting squadron into position on the bluffs east of the village as planned. The rough terrain slowed the attacking squadron, commanded by Capt. Henry E. Noyes. Not until 9 A.M. did the assault begin. Noyes sent Capt. James Egan with forty-seven pistol-wielding troopers, accompanied by Lt. John G. Bourke and newspaper correspondent Robert E. Strahorn, on a mad dash into the village, while he rode down the Cheyenne pony herd with the other troops. Most of the two hundred warriors of the village withdrew to the rocky bluffs that Moore's dismounted squadron was to have secured and opened fire on Egan's lone group. Colonel Reynolds belatedly committed Capt. Anson Mills's reserve squadron to the attack, which saved Egan from annihilation, and Moore eventually traipsed into the village, allowing the troops to secure the lodge area. But the half-naked warriors clung to the bluffs tenaciously, throwing the much larger force of well-clothed soldiers on the defensive. Reynolds panicked and at 1:30 P.M. burned the village and withdrew up the Powder River to rejoin Crook. In his haste, Reynolds forgot to assign anyone responsibility for the pony herd, and most of the animals ran off.

Crook was furious. Not only had Reynolds lost the pony herd and stupidly burned much-needed buffalo robes and provisions in the village, but in permitting the Indians to escape, he undoubtedly also had alerted every Indian camp within a day's march to the soldiers' presence. Reluctantly, Crook returned to Fort Fetterman. His aborted campaign had done little more than convince the roaming bands that the government had marked them for extermination. Alerted to the army's intentions and aroused to resist, the nonreservation chiefs decided to gather into one powerful camp for survival.

A disgusted Sheridan made plans for a summer campaign. Three columns would take to the plains to find and engage the Indians—in concert if possible, but independently as necessary. Crook was to refit and again march north from Fort Fetterman, this time at the head of fifteen troops of cavalry, four companies of infantry, civilian packers, and Indian scouts, for a total of nearly thirteen hundred officers and men. Col. John Gibbon was to march east from Fort Ellis, Montana, with four troops of cavalry and six companies of infantry totaling some four hundred officers and men. Custer was to march west from Fort Lincoln at the head of his own 7th Cavalry and six companies of infantry. If all went well, Custer would sweep the hostiles westward toward the Bighorn River, and Crook would shove them back on Custer. Gibbon, operating along the Yellowstone, would intercept any Indians seeking escape north.

Gibbon took the field first, leaving Fort Ellis on March 30. The Fort Lincoln column set off on May 17. General Terry, not Custer, was in overall command. Custer had fallen into disfavor with President Grant for his testimony before a congressional committee investigating allegations of corruption against Secretary of War Belknap. Grant initially prohibited Custer from taking any part in the campaign, but a tearful appeal from Custer and a strong endorsement from Terry caused Grant to relent to the point of permitting Custer to go with his regiment. The last in the field, Crook cut loose from Fort Fetterman on May 29 to retrace the steps of his March expedition.

While Terry and Crook groped for the enemy, the largest gathering of Indians the Great Plains had ever seen was coming together in the Powder River country. Reynolds's destruction of the Cheyenne village not only had united the nonreservation bands, but it also stimulated a spring exodus from the agencies of unprecedented size. Previously, young warriors had drifted to the unceded territory primarily to hunt buffalo; now they came out to hunt soldiers too. How many Sioux and Cheyennes assembled in the summer of 1876 is a matter of debate. The best estimate calculates the size of the village of nonreservation bands, or "winter roamers," at 105 lodges in mid-March, a figure that swelled to 461 lodges by June 7.[17] Two weeks later, the migration from the agencies brought the village to nearly 1,000 lodges, or just over seven thousand persons, of whom some eighteen hundred were adult males.

The village was organized into six tribal circles. The largest was that of the Hunkpapas of Sitting Bull and Gall at 260 lodges, to which some twenty-five lodges of Yanktonais and Santees had attached themselves. The Oglala circle of Crazy Horse constituted some 240 lodges. The Minneconjou circle counted 150 lodges; the Blackfeet circle, in which had gathered the Brules, Blackfeet, and Two Kettles, totaled 120 lodges; and the Sans Arcs circle, 110. The Cheyenne allies of the Lakotas contributed 120 lodges.

The size of their village and the inevitability of their fate, should the bluecoats find them, steeled the Indians to stand and fight rather than flee and scatter, as was their wont when pursued, and their resolve also benefited from a mystic vision of rare import. In mid-June, near the Rosebud encampment of the grand village, the Hunkpapas held a Sun Dance at Sitting Bull's behest. The ceremony afforded Sitting Bull the opportunity to fulfill a vow to Wakan Tanka that he would give of his flesh for the welfare of his people. His friend Jumping Bull cut fifty small pieces from each of the chief's arms, then Sitting Bull danced.

For several hours, he danced around the sun pole until, stopping suddenly, he fell into a faint. He swayed but did not drop, and onlookers eased him to the ground. When he awoke, Sitting Bull spoke of the vision he had had. From the sky, he had seen many horses and soldiers falling, feet upward, into the Lakota camp. "These soldiers do not possess ears," a voice proclaimed. They would die, a gift from Wakan Tanka, but the Lakotas were not to plunder their bodies. Word of Sitting Bull's vision spread quickly among the six tribal circles.

Eager to fulfill the prophecy, on the morning of June 17 a party of six hundred warriors under Sitting Bull and Crazy Horse rode forth from the village, now on Davis Creek, back up the Rosebud. Their objective was the Wyoming column of George Crook. The day before, Crook had cut loose from his wagon train and crossed from the Tongue to the Rosebud. As his column paused along the creek bed for coffee on the morning of the seventeenth, the Lakota attacked from high ground to the northwest. Only the stiff resistance of his Crow and Shoshone scouts prevented Crook from suffering a stunning defeat. As it was, he barely had time to deploy his units in a long skirmish line before the spreading Indian attack closed on his command from the west, north, and east. The battle raged back and forth over the hills and ravines north of Rosebud Creek, each side alternately gaining and losing ground. Believing that Crazy Horse's village lay just a short distance down the Rosebud, Crook dispatched two cavalry squadrons under Captain Mills through a long gorge to find and attack it. Crook was mistaken. A fierce assault on Maj. William B. Royall's squadron at noon caused him to realize that he could not support Mills in the event he found the village, and he issued orders for his recall. Fortunately for Crook, Mills left the Rosebud and returned to the battlefield cross-country, falling on the rear of the Lakotas and Cheyennes as they were massing for an attack. Mills's approach scattered them, and the fighting sputtered out before 2 P.M.

Thoroughly shaken, Crook skulked back to his supply base on Goose Creek and refused to move until reinforced. Because he had retained possession of the battlefield, however briefly, Crook claimed a victory. But General Sheridan knew better, and in a private letter to General Sherman, he blasted Crook for mismanaging the affair.

Sitting Bull and Crazy Horse had far better grounds for claiming victory. Soldiers had not fallen from the sky into their camp, but the Lakota had driven off a force nearly twice their number. They celebrated that night, then moved their village the next morning to the valley of the "Greasy Grass"—the Little Bighorn.

Neither Terry nor Gibbon knew of Crook's fight and subsequent retreat. The two had opened communications on June 1, and eight days later they met aboard the supply steamer *Far West*. Clashes between his scouts and Lakota war parties led Gibbon to conclude that the hostile village was on either the Tongue River or Rosebud Creek, but Terry wanted confirmation. On June 10, he sent Maj. Marcus A. Reno with six troops of the 7th Cavalry to scout the upper reaches of the Powder and Tongue Rivers. Reno exceeded his orders and continued on to the Rosebud, where he found a heavy Indian trail, perhaps nine days old, well north of the headwaters of the Rosebud and leading west.

Terry was unjustly angry with Reno, as the major's unauthorized detour had kept him from setting off in the wrong direction and provided at least some intelligence upon which to shape plans. On the evening of June 21, Terry, Custer, and Gibbon conferred in the cabin of the *Far West*. All assumed that the Indians would run if confronted; the object, recalled Gibbon, was "to prevent the escape of the Indians, which was the idea pervading the minds of all of us."[18] That the Indians might stand and fight seems to have occurred to no one.

To Custer and the 7th Cavalry would go the honor of fixing and, if possible, striking a decisive blow at the enemy, who were believed to be making for the Little Bighorn River. Terry, with Gibbon's command, would take up a blocking position at the mouth of the Bighorn River. "The march of the two columns [Terry's and Custer's] was planned," wrote Terry's adjutant on July 1, "as to bring Colonel Gibbon's force within cooperating distance of the anticipated scene of action by the evening of the twenty-sixth." But there was no expectation of simultaneous attacks by both columns, as partisans of Terry later insisted. Such a plan would have required exact knowledge of the location of the Indian village, which none present on the *Far West* possessed. As Maj. James Brisbin, the chief of Gibbon's cavalry, recalled in a letter written on June 28: "It was announced by General Terry that Colonel Custer's column would strike the blow, and Colonel Gibbon and his men received the decision without a murmur. The Montana column felt disappointed when they learned that they were not to be present at the final capture of the great village, but General Terry's reasons for affording the honor of the attack to Colonel Custer were good ones."[19] Those reasons were the greater mobility and strength of Custer's 7th relative to Gibbon's mixed command of infantry and cavalry.

On the morning of June 22, Custer received his orders, which were highly discretionary in nature, certainly for someone as independent minded as Custer. They read as follows:

> Camp at Mouth of Rosebud River
> Montana Territory
> June 22, 1876

Lt. Col. Custer, 7th Cavalry
Colonel:
  The brigadier general commanding directs that, as soon as your regiment can be made ready for the march, you will proceed up the Rosebud in pursuit of the Indians whose trail was discovered by Major Reno a few days since. It is, of course, impossible to give you any definite instructions in regard to this movement, and were it not impossible to do so the department commander places too much confidence in your zeal, energy, and ability to wish to impose upon you

precise orders which might hamper your action when nearly in contact with the enemy. He will, however, indicate to you his views of what your actions should be, and he desires that you should conform to them unless you shall see sufficient reasons for departing from them. He thinks that you should proceed up the Rosebud until you ascertain definitely the direction in which the trail above spoken of leads. Should it be found (as it appears almost certain that it will be found) to turn towards the Little Bighorn, he thinks that you should still proceed southward, perhaps as far as the headwaters of the Tongue, and then turn toward the Little Bighorn, feeling constantly, however, to your left, so as to preclude the possibility of the escape of the Indians to the south or southeast by passing around your left flank. The column of Colonel Gibbon is now in motion for the mouth of the Bighorn. As soon as it reaches that point it will cross the Yellowstone and move up at least as far as the forks of the Big and Little Horns [sic]. Future movements must be controlled by circumstances as they arise, but it is hoped that the Indians, if upon the Little Horn, may be so nearly enclosed by the two columns that their escape will be impossible.

The department commander desires that on your way up the Rosebud you should thoroughly examine the upper part of Tulloch's Creek, and that you should endeavor to send a scout through to Colonel Gibbon's column, with information of the result of your examination. The lower part of the creek will be examined by a detachment from Colonel Gibbon's command. The supply steamer will be pushed up the Bighorn as far as the forks if the river is found navigable for that distance, and the department commander, who will accompany the column of Colonel Gibbon, desires you to report to him not later than the expiration of time for which your troops are rationed, unless in the meantime you receive further orders.

                Very respectfully, your obedient servant,
                E. W. Smith, captain, 18th Infantry,
                Acting Assistant Adjutant General

At noon on the twenty-second, the 7th Cavalry rode out of camp near the mouth of the Rosebud, 31 officers, 566 enlisted men, and 31 Indian scouts strong. Six mule packers, five scouts, newspaper reporter Mark Kellogg, and Custer's vacationing nephew, Autie Reed, brought the total to 647.

At 7:45 P.M. on June 24, having covered seventy-three miles in two and a half days, Custer reached the Busby Bend of the Rosebud, the point where the Indian trail diverged to the west. There, according to Terry's instructions, he "*should* still proceed southward," presumably to give Gibbon time to get into place. But Terry had assumed the village to be near the *upper* Little Bighorn; the trail, however, suggested that it lay far closer to the Yellowstone River.

When his scouts brought word that the hostiles had crossed the Wolf Mountain divide to the Little Bighorn, Custer elected to keep on the trail. He told his officers they would make a night march to the divide, rest there during the twenty-fifth while the scouts reconnoitered the village, then attack on the morning of June 26.

At dawn on the twenty-fifth, Custer's tired troopers drew rein at the eastern base of the divide. From a mountaintop called the "Crow's Nest," his Ree scouts spotted smoke from the Lakota village, fifteen miles to the northwest. Custer followed them up the mountain. He saw nothing, but while scanning the horizon, he received reports that the hostiles were watching the regiment's movements. Convinced that he had been discovered, and fearful that the Indian village might flee before him, Custer elected to attack at once. Topping the divide at 12:07 P.M. on June 25, Custer halted briefly to split the regiment into four elements for the assault. To Capt. Frederick W. Benteen he assigned three troops with orders to scout to the left, or south, in case the Indian village, being warned of the approach of the 7th Cavalry as Custer presumed, withdrew upstream rather than downstream toward Gibbon's blocking force. Should Benteen find no sign of hostiles in that direction, he was to hurry back to the main command. Custer accorded Major Reno three troops and the lead in the advance to the Little Bighorn. He left one troop behind to guard the pack train, and with the five remaining troops—a total of 221 officers and men—followed on a parallel course on the north side of a stream, since named Reno Creek.

Six miles northwest of the divide stood a lone tepee; in it were the mortal remains of a warrior killed in the Rosebud fight. At the burial lodge, Custer called a halt and summoned Reno to the right bank. The time was 2 P.M. While they waited for Benteen to rejoin the column, interpreter Fred Gerard climbed a knoll near the tepee. Catching a glimpse of Indians and pony herds milling in the distance, he yelled to Custer, "Here are your Indians, running like devils!"

Custer remounted the command and, trusting Benteen to catch up, started off with Reno in advance. The two columns trotted on for three miles down Reno Creek to a spot since called "The Flat." A line of bluffs hid the Little Bighorn. Behind the bluffs rose a cloud of dust, which to Custer's excited mind could only mean that the Indians were running away. He told Reno to attack or, as Reno recalled it, "to move forward at as rapid a gait as prudent, and to charge afterward, and that the whole outfit would support me."

But the whole outfit did not support him, at least not in the manner Reno had expected. He thought Custer would support him from the rear. Instead, probably prompted by word from Reno that the Indians were not fleeing, Custer swung his column to the north and rode downstream, under cover of the bluffs, to attack the lower end of the village. Fording the Little Bighorn a few minutes before 3 P.M., Reno led his command of eleven officers, 129 men, and thirty-five scouts on an accelerating run down a flat valley toward the Indian village that to the startled major looked endless. As warriors poured forth to challenge—not run from—his advance, Reno grew cautious. Dismounting his men in the open, he formed a thin skirmish line facing the village, his right flank anchored on a belt of timber along the river.

Contrary to what Custer thought, the Lakotas and their Cheyenne allies had little notice of the approach of the 7th Cavalry. Not until Custer reached the lone burial lodge on Reno Creek did anyone see them. And Reno's cavalry was across the ford on the Little Bighorn before word of his approach passed through the village.

With the exception of the *akicita* on police duty, most of the men were asleep in their lodges or beneath the cottonwood trees shading the riverbank. They had danced and feasted late into the night, and the hot and cloudless day encouraged lethargy. Pandemonium now ensued, as the men scrambled for war paint, weapons, and their ponies. Women and children hurried to strike lodges and pack travois for flight. Among the gathering warriors was Sitting Bull, astride a black horse, shouting, "Brave up, boys, it will be a hard time. Brave up."

The first notice Reno had of Custer's change of plans came when he saw him atop one of the bluffs on the far side of the river, waving his hat encouragingly. The gesture did little to settle Reno's nerves. The hostile throng to his front was growing steadily, and a number of mounted Indians had turned his left flank. After just fifteen minutes in the open, Reno withdrew into the timber's edge, forming a new line fronting west. Among the attackers arose the cry, "Crazy Horse is coming!" Scores of mounted Oglalas pitched into the fray, lending weight to the attack Sitting Bull's Hunkpapas had begun. Again the soldiers fell back, this time to a clearing deep in the timber.

Here the battle lost coherence. Panic-stricken, Reno galloped out of the timber and into the open valley to the southeast, with little on his mind beyond reaching the bluffs across the Little Bighorn. Men mounted and followed as best they could; at least seventeen were left behind in the confusion. The retreat quickly deteriorated into a rout. "Indians covered the flat," remembered the Cheyenne chief Two Moons. "They began to drive the soldiers all mixed up—Sioux, then soldiers, then more Sioux, and all shooting. The air was full of smoke and dust. I saw soldiers fall back and drop into the riverbed like buffalo fleeing."[20]

The Lakota counted many coups during the stampede. Forty were killed, including two officers and a surgeon, thirteen wounded, and seventeen left in the timber on the left bank before the ninety-one tired and terrified survivors of Reno's column gathered at 4 P.M. on a flat hilltop, since named Reno Hill, overlooking the valley.

Reno's retreat freed up all the Indians to fight Custer, who at that moment was leading his column down a ravine that opened on the upper end of the Medicine Tail Coulee. Undoubtedly Custer was worried. The hostile village stretched for miles along the river bottom; far from fleeing, the Indians were massing to attack; and Benteen was nowhere in sight. Custer told Adj. William W. Cooke to send a courier on the back trail after the errant captain. Cooke scribbled a message—"Benteen. Come on. Big Village. Be quick, bring packs. W. W. Cooke. P.

S. Bring packs"—and handed it to a dull-witted trumpeter, Giovanni Martini, or John Martin, as his enlistment papers read, to carry.

Custer did what he could to salvage the situation. He posted three troops on the north slope of a ridge some three thousand feet east of the river, and toward which three ravines led from the Indian village. Perhaps to stall for time, Custer apparently sent two troops under Capt. George Yates down the Medicine Tail Coulee to threaten the village and hold the principal ford, but a volley from the riverbank drove them off. This is speculation; nothing of the ensuing fight is certain except that the Lakotas and Cheyennes attacked from every direction of the compass, and that Custer and all his men—save the Crow scout Curley, who made his escape sometime during the action—perished.

The fighting probably ended a few minutes before 5 P.M. Crazy Horse, White Bull, and Gall of the Lakotas and Two Moon and Lame White Man of the Cheyennes figured prominently in the fight. As befitted a head chief with responsibility for his people, Sitting Bull remained with the women and children to protect them in case other soldiers appeared. Gall summed up the final moments of the struggle, as Custer and a handful of officers and men clung to a hilltop and fought hand-to-hand with exultant warriors. "The men were loading and firing, but they could not hit the warriors in the gully and the ravine," said Gall. "The dust and smoke was black as evening. Once in a while we could see the soldiers through the dust, and finally we charged through them with our ponies. When we had done this, the fight was over."[21]

Not quite. Reno's shattered battalion still clung to its hill. Benteen rode up with his battalion at about 4:20 P.M., and the pack train reached Reno Hill perhaps an hour later. The sounds of firing from Custer's last stand downstream were clearly audible, but Reno was in no frame of mind to respond. Capt. Thomas B. Weir galloped off without orders at 5:05 P.M. with D Troop to join Custer. Benteen followed fifteen minutes later with three troops, and Reno waved along the remainder twenty minutes after that. But it was a case of far too little, too late. Pausing on a high point a mile and a half northwest of Reno Hill, Weir and Benteen saw only a huge cloud of smoke in the distance and a huge, angry horde of mounted Indians milling about and shooting at objects on the ground. That the warriors were pumping bullets into dead troopers, or that Custer's command had been annihilated, occurred to no one. When the Indians tired of the game, they swarmed toward Weir Point, and the troopers withdrew to Reno Hill, where Benteen set up an elliptical defense perimeter, open toward the river, with the pack train, picketed horses, and the wounded clustered in a shallow depression in the center.

At dawn on June 26, the battle resumed. Forming a cordon around Reno Hill, the Indians poured a heavy fire into the defenders, occasionally launching sorties. Water parties scurried to the river to fill canteens under covering fire. Men fell in considerable numbers along the firing line, but it held. At noon, the Indians began to leave, and by midafternoon, the firing had dwindled to an occasional ragged volley. With the setting sun, an enormous parade of Indian families with loaded travois filed up the west bank of the river, cheered on their way by Reno's troopers. Only two tepees, burial lodges for slain warriors, remained of the great village.

Sitting Bull had encouraged the warriors to break off the fight. "Let them go now," he said of the soldiers, "so some can go home and spread the news. I just saw more soldiers coming." He had not, but word had reached him of the approach of Gibbon from the north.

On the night of June 26, the Indian procession camped on the benchland southwest of the Little Bighorn Valley, sleeping in the open. The next night, they raised their village, again in the valley. On the fourth night, they staged a victory dance. Sitting Bull's Sun Dance vision had been fulfilled, but it left the chief joyless. "I feel sorry that too many were killed on each side," he later said, "but when Indians must fight, they must."[22]

More fighting was sure to come, but for the moment, feeding the large gathering was of greater concern to the chiefs. Game was scarce, and in early August the village broke up to hunt buffalo. In early August, Sitting Bull led his Hunkpapas, with some Minneconjous and Sans Arcs, down the Little Missouri to the Killdeer Mountains. A second contingent followed Crazy Horse up the Little Missouri toward the Black Hills. Warriors who had held back now left the agencies to join the hostiles.

During the month of July, neither Terry nor Crook disturbed the hostile camp in its peregrinations through the Powder River country. Both commands awaited reinforcements, Terry on the Yellowstone, and Crook at the base of the Bighorn Mountains. A stunned Congress voted funds to build the two forts on the Yellowstone that Sheridan wanted, and it lifted the ceiling on army strength to permit the enlistment of an additional twenty-five hundred cavalry privates, men who came to be known as the "Custer Avengers." The secretary of the interior also yielded to Sheridan's demand that the army be given control of the Lakota agencies.

Learning of the Custer disaster on July 10, Crook summoned the 5th Cavalry, which he had earlier moved to the upper Cheyenne River to disrupt traffic between the Red Cloud agency and the hostiles. A forced march brought Col. Wesley Merritt and the 5th to War Bonnet Creek, where on July 17 he turned back a large war party of agency Cheyennes making for the hostile camp. On August 3, Merritt joined Crook at Camp Cloud Peak. Crook sent his wagon train back to Fort Fetterman, and on August 5 he started for the headwaters of the Rosebud with a force of two thousand. Terry, meanwhile, had been reinforced by six companies of the 22nd Infantry under Lt. Col. Elwell S. Otis and six companies of the 5th Infantry under Col. Nelson A. Miles. On August 8, he started up the Rosebud from his supply depot at its mouth with a command of seventeen hundred officers and men.

Terry and Crook met unexpectedly on August 10. Through pounding rain and deep mud, they followed the Indian trail east to the Tongue and Powder. Morale sank, and Crook chafed under the command of Terry, whom he thought unduly cautious. For a week, the expedition bivouacked at the mouth of the Powder River, awaiting supplies. On August 26, Crook cut loose from Terry and headed for the Little Missouri. Terry shifted his army down the Yellowstone to the mouth of Glendive Creek and pondered his next move. The only orders he had received from Sheridan were that he establish a temporary cantonment at the mouth of Tongue River and leave Colonel Miles, with the entire 5th Infantry and Otis's six companies, to hold the Yellowstone River Valley during the winter. A note from Crook on September 3 advising that the trail had given out at Beaver Creek, a tributary of the Little Missouri, and that the tribes had scattered, convinced Terry that nothing more remained to be done, and he disbanded the expedition.

In his haste to break free of Terry, Crook had packed rations for only twelve days and stripped his command of baggage. Constant showers turned the plains to paste and slowed the march to a crawl; Lt. John G. Bourke likened the column to a "brigade of drowned rats." After losing the Indian trail, Crook dropped into the Little Missouri Valley and headed east toward the head of the Heart River. There he picked up a fresh trail leading south. On September 5, with only two days' rations remaining and Fort Lincoln four days' march to the east, Crook elected to follow the trail south. Scouts carried dispatches to Fort Lincoln asking Sheridan to have provisions rushed to meet the column at Custer City, in the Black Hills. With luck, Crook would reach the Black Hills in seven days.

Crook's decision troubled even his most devoted subordinates. Adjutant Bourke scribbled in his diary, "We have great confidence in Crook, but cannot shake off a presentiment of dread as to the possible consequences of our bold plunge, without rations, across an utterly unknown zone of such great width as that lying between us and the Black Hills."[23] As the rains continued, the rations gave out, and horses and mules dropped by the dozens, it seemed Bourke's presentiment would be realized. But luck was with Crook. On September 8, an advance party of 150 men under Captain Mills, which Crook had dispatched on the strongest of the remaining horses to the Black Hills to buy provisions, stumbled undetected upon a Minneconjou camp of thirty-seven lodges at the head of the Moreau River, near Slim Buttes. Nearby were the villages of Crazy Horse and Sitting Bull, who had come down from the Killdeer Mountains.

Mills attacked the next morning. He drove the occupants into the hills and held his ground until Crook came up with the main column at noon. Fifteen Minneconjous trapped in a gulch near the camp took a toll on Mills's troopers until persuaded to surrender; among them was Chief American Horse, mortally wounded. Late in the day, some two hundred warriors from Crazy Horse's camp attacked Crook but were driven off. The famished soldiers gulped down dried meat and pemmican, packed what they could for the march to Custer City, then destroyed the Indian village. By the time they reached the Black Hills four days later, Crook's troops were again hungry, their mounts nearly crippled.

So ended the summer campaign of 1876, with just the shabby victory at Slim Buttes (the Minneconjous whom Mills attacked had intended to surrender at an agency) to show for nearly five months in the field. Fearing public opprobrium himself, Sheridan dared not draw too much attention to the failings of his subordinates. Better to let matters rest. "The fact of the case is," Sheridan confided to General Sherman, "the operations of Generals Terry and Crook will not bear criticism, and my only thought has been to let them sleep. I approved what was done, for the sake of the troops, but in doing so, I was not approving much, as you know."

The campaign had wrecked Terry and so demoralized his officers and men that "they were afraid of the Indians," said a major who joined the command in October. "I was impressed with the opinion that both [Sheridan and Terry] felt that the campaign against the Sioux had been a failure, for which they would be held responsible by the people. Especially was this the case with General Terry, who was nervous, excited, and depressed in spirits; he had changed much since I had last seen him in 1869."[24] Morale was little better in Crook's command.

Lakota and Cheyenne morale, on the other hand, remained strong. A few hundred Indians returned to the agencies, but many more left to join the hostiles. To prevent a further exodus, General Crook ordered Col. Ranald S. Mackenzie and his crack 4th Cavalry regiment, recently arrived from the Indian Territory, to surround Red Cloud's camps near the Red Cloud agency and seize the arms and ponies of the occupants. Crook then deposed the venerable chief, replacing him with the more tractable Spotted Tail as chief of the agency Lakotas. General Terry, meanwhile, assigned the 7th Cavalry the same duty at the Missouri River agencies, a bit of cheap revenge for the Little Bighorn fiasco.

Close on the heels of the army came another commission, this one to coerce the agency chiefs into relinquishing all claim to the unceded territory and the Black Hills. The commission curtly informed them that no rations would be forthcoming until they did so (Congress had conditioned further appropriations for subsistence on such a settlement.) A handful of chiefs, including Red Cloud and Spotted Tail, placed their marks on the agreement. None of the war chiefs signed, if they were even aware of the agreement. Their subjugation—complete and final—became Sheridan's obsession. Disarming the agency Indians was the first step in his strategy of total war. Next, he would plant two forts in the heart of the Lakota hunting lands, from which mobile columns would campaign constantly against the hostiles until they surrendered unconditionally.

Undoubtedly anxious to redeem his reputation, General Crook moved swiftly. On November 14, he set out from Fort Fetterman with twenty-two hundred men to do battle with Crazy Horse, whose camp was thought to be located near the Rosebud battlefield. En route, scouts brought word of a large Cheyenne village in the Bighorn Mountains just west of Crook's line of march. Crook ordered Mackenzie to find and attack it with ten troops of cavalry. On the cold, misty morning of November 25, 1876, Mackenzie's troopers swept down upon two hundred lodges of the Cheyenne chiefs Dull Knife and Little Wolf in a canyon of the Red Fork of the Powder River. Mackenzie lost six killed and twenty-six wounded, but the Cheyenne lost everything they owned. Hungry and nearly naked, the survivors stumbled northward through subzero temperatures to join Crazy Horse's village. Crook did not pursue. And as December brought with it howling blizzards and continued arctic cold, he called off his campaign altogether.

Col. Nelson A. Miles displayed greater vigor. The object of his campaign was Sitting Bull, who had laid down the challenge when he attacked Miles's supply trains between the Tongue River cantonment and the Glendive Creek depot in mid-October. Miles tried to parley with Sitting Bull, but their respective demands—Sitting Bull that the whites leave his country, Miles that the Lakota surrender and repair to the agencies—admitted of no compromise. On October 21, Miles attacked Sitting Bull's village near the head of Cedar Creek. Although outnumbered, the "walk-a-heaps" of his 5th Infantry dealt the mounted Lakotas a decisive defeat in a two-day running battle that cost the Indians their winter food stocks and camp equipment and led the Miniconjous and Sans Arcs to defect from Sitting Bull. They offered to surrender to Miles, who, unable to feed two thousand Indians, retained five chiefs as a guarantee their people would go to the agencies. Only a handful did; the remainder trekked up the Powder in late November to join Crazy Horse's rapidly swelling camp.

Despite the harsh winds and bitter cold, Miles remained in the field to press the war against Sitting Bull, whose Hunkpapas had struggled north toward the Missouri, hoping to make good their material losses at the Fort Peck agency. Pausing just long enough to resupply and refit with winter clothing, much of which consisted of buffalo coats and leggings that the soldiers fashioned themselves, on November 5 Miles departed the Tongue River cantonment. "I shall endeavor to follow the Indians as long as possible," Miles assured his wife, "even to their retreats where they think we can not go."[25]

He made good his promise. Operating in three battalions, for six weeks the 5th Infantry chased Sitting Bull back and forth across half of Montana. Miles's favorite subordinate, Lt. Frank D. Baldwin, struck the decisive blows. With a hundred men, he gave battle to Sitting Bull on December 7 and drove his band across the Missouri River. Baldwin kept on the trail and on December 18 attacked the Hunkpapa camp of 122 lodges near the head of Redwater Creek. The Indians fled south into the hills, abandoning what little they had managed to set aside for the winter. Baldwin returned to the Tongue River cantonment in late December, having marched 716 miles in the dead of winter. Sitting Bull turned north with the fifteen lodges still loyal to him. Together with the camps of Gall, Iron Dog, and a few hundred defiant Minneconjous and Sans Arcs, he crossed the *chanku-waken*—the sacred road—into Canada in May 1877. "They told us this line was considered holy," remembered a young follower of Sitting Bull. "They called that a holy trail. They believe things are different when you cross from one side to another. You are altogether different. On one side you are perfectly free to do as you please. On the other you are in danger."[26]

Reinforced by the Cheyenne fugitives of the Mackenzie fight, Crazy Horse had plenty of fight left in him. During the last days of December 1876, he staged raids against Miles's cantonment in an effort to draw the "walk-a-heaps" up the Tongue River into an ambush. Miles took the bait. With five companies of the 5th and two of the 22nd Infantry, he marched up Tongue Valley toward the Oglalas and Cheyennes, who lay in wait on a spur of the Wolf Mountains. On the afternoon of January 7, 1877, Miles's scouts captured a party of Cheyenne women and children returning from a visit to a neighboring camp. A war party tried unsuccessfully to recover them and, in so doing, prematurely sprang Crazy Horse's trap. The next morning, when five hundred warriors assailed his command, Miles was ready for them. Both sides fired off a good deal of ammunition, without doing much damage, until a blizzard blanketed the field of battle at noon. The Indians withdrew, and Miles returned to the cantonment to trumpet his great victory to Sherman and Sheridan.

General Sheridan intended to renew the campaign in the spring, with Miles in command of five regiments of cavalry and infantry and the freedom to ignore department boundaries, but the Wolf Mountains debacle, along with the difficulty of feeding so many people, fragmented the Tongue River village and strengthened the peace faction to the extent that further fighting appeared unnecessary. General Crook availed himself of the changed mood and sent Spotted Tail among the hostiles on a peace mission. Surrenders followed apace. During the spring, nearly three thousand Indians turned themselves in at the Red Cloud, Spotted Tail, and Cheyenne River agencies. At Camp Robinson on May 6, Crazy Horse and his Oglalas capitulated, surrendering nearly twelve thousand ponies to the army.

After Sitting Bull and his confederates crossed in Canada, the only hostile camp of consequence remaining south of the international border was that of Lame Deer, a Minneconjou who vowed never to surrender. Miles set out after him with a squadron of the 2nd Cavalry. In a brief fight on May 7 on the bank of Muddy Creek, a tributary of the Rosebud, Lame Deer was killed and his band scattered. Miles spent the remainder of the summer hunting down the fugitives and building the two forts that Sheridan had long wanted in the heart of the hostile country: Fort Keogh, beside the Tongue River Cantonment, and Fort Custer, at the confluence of the Big Horn and Little Bighorn Rivers.

Scattered hostilities would continue until 1881, when Sitting Bull abandoned his Canadian sanctuary to surrender the paltry few who remained faithful to him, but the relentless campaign of Bear Coat Miles in the winter and spring of 1877 had broken the back of Lakota resistance.

Two tragic and sordid affairs stained the army's record in the waning years of the 1870s. In both, blood was shed unnecessarily.

The first incident claimed just one life, but it was that of Crazy Horse. His presence on the reservation troubled both the whites and agency Indians, who feared he might touch off an explosion. There was good reason to fear an outbreak, as conditions at the agencies were far from ideal. Crazy Horse was displeased that Lakota warriors had signed up to scout for the army against the Nez Perces, who were then making a bid for Canada, and he believed they might also be employed to chase down Sitting Bull. Crazy Horse also was angry that surrendering Cheyennes had been herded south to a reservation in the Indian Territory against their will. There was no real evidence that Crazy Horse intended to foment trouble—despite his legitimate grievances, he had resigned himself to agency life—but the army was taking no chances. General Crook used a failed conference between Lt. William Philo Clark and Crazy Horse over the recruitment of scouts for the Nez Perce War as the pretext for the chief's arrest. Ironically, Crazy Horse had conceded to serve with Clark, vowing to fight until there were no more Nez Perces left, but Frank Grouard bungled the translation, saying Crazy Horse would fight until there were no *white men* left. On September 5, the chief was taken into custody. In a scuffle to disarm him two days later, Crazy Horse was mortally wounded, whether by an army bayonet or a Lakotas knife remains uncertain. But the army was happy to see him dead, and though they mourned him, many skittish Lakotas were relieved at his passing. "It is good," said a Miniconjou chief; "he has looked for death, and it has come."[27]

Nothing could excuse the injustice done the Northern Cheyenne bands of Dull Knife and Little Wolf. Dragged to the Cheyenne and Arapaho agency in the Indian Territory in August 1877, the Northern Cheyennes died of disease by the score during the winter of 1877–78. With the prospect of another deadly winter before them, in September 1878 Dull Knife and Little Wolf led three hundred of the tribe on a desperate trek fifteen hundred miles northward, toward their old country. It was not a raid or a hostile action in any sense. The Cheyennes simply wanted to go home, and they tried to avoid contact with the soldiers sent after them. Both chiefs set down strict prohibitions against killing or molesting settlers, which a few warriors unfortunately violated.

In Nebraska, the bands separated. Little Wolf continued north in the hope of reaching the Yellowstone Valley. Dull Knife and his followers surrendered to a cavalry patrol near Camp Robinson on October 23 in the mistaken belief they would be granted a home in the north. Instead, they were imprisoned in army barracks at Camp Robinson and told they would remain in confinement until they agreed to return to the Indian Territory. His people would rather die than go south again, Dull Knife told the post commander, Capt. Henry W. Wessells. When persuasion failed to sway the Cheyennes, Wessells cut off their food, water, and fuel. Driven nearly mad by thirst and hunger, the Cheyennes shot their way out of the barracks on the night of January 9, 1879, with rifles the women had secreted at the time of surrender. Nearly half were shot or froze to death before the ordeal ended. Moved by their suffering, the Indian Bureau consented to resettle them at Pine Ridge.

Little Wolf and his band eluded capture. Fortunately, their odyssey ended peacefully. Cheyenne chief Two Moons, who had served under General Miles since April 1877, persuaded them to join his people at Fort Keogh, where Little Wolf's men signed on as scouts. At General Miles's insistence, Dull Knife and the surviving members of his band were permitted to move to Fort Keogh three years later, and in 1884 an executive order set aside the Tongue River reservation as the permanent agency of the Northern Cheyennes.

"I now regard the Indians as substantially eliminated from the problem of the army," said General Sherman in 1883. "There may be spasmodic and temporary alarms, but such Indian wars as have hitherto disturbed the public peace and tranquility are not probable."

In the main, Sherman was correct. With the exception of the Geronimo outbreak in 1885, no hostilities of consequence occurred for the next seven years. But tensions were mounting on the Lakota reservation. Indian agents, schoolteachers, and missionaries hammered away at the old ways in an effort to make over the Lakotas in white man's image. They compelled the children to attend schools, tried to make Christian farmers of the adults, and promoted factionalism to break up the tribal relationship; Indians were either "progressive" or "nonprogressive," and rewarded or punished accordingly, usually by a withholding of rations. Meanwhile, the fraud that had longed plagued agency management continued. Hunger and want were frequent, as unscrupulous contractors and agents diverted food and other supplies.

Nor were the reservation lands inviolate. The Dawes Act of 1887 called for the division of tribal lands into individual allotments. As the Great Sioux Reservation contained twice the land needed for allotments, the remainder was to be opened up to white settlement. Two years later, a commission, of which their old nemesis George Crook was a member, wrested from the Lakotas nearly half their reservation. Ration cuts followed. Crops failed, and disease swept the agencies. In their despair, many Lakotas found hope in the message of a messiah, who promised a millennium of Native American rebirth, preceded by a violent cleansing of the land of the *wasichus*.

Or so the Lakota believers interpreted the prophesy of Wovoka, a gentle Paiute shaman whose Ghost Dance religion foretold a new day in which all Native Americans, living and dead, would be united in a world free of whites. Through a rigid regimen of prayer, dance, and song, one might "die" and catch a glimpse of the world to come. Violence, however, would not speed its coming. Wovoka, who had been raised with a white family, preached a doctrine of tolerance. "Do no harm to anyone," he preached to the pilgrims who came from tribes throughout the West to hear his message. "You must not fight."

Those words were lost on the Lakota emissaries Short Bull and Kicking Bear, who brought back from their pilgrimage a call to arms and a promise that properly fashioned "ghost shirts" would stop *wasichu* bullets.

The perverted Ghost Dance of Short Bull and Kicking Bear won adherents by the hundreds and brought the Pine Ridge and Standing Rock agencies to the verge of anarchy. In November 1890, the army intervened at the direction of President Benjamin Harrison. Elements of the 2nd and 8th Infantry and 9th Cavalry occupied the agencies, and Brig. Gen. John R. Brooke, commander of the Department of the Platte, set up a temporary headquarters at Pine Ridge.

The presence of soldiers split the Lakotas into two factions—"friendlies" and "hostiles"—which in composition roughly paralleled the progressive and nonprogressive division that the agents had engendered. The hostiles were not truly hostile, at least not yet; they simply were unwilling to abandon the Ghost Dance. Withdrawing to remote corners of the reservation, they continued to dance. The Brule and Oglala "hostiles" took refuge on an elevated plateau between the White and Cheyenne Rivers called Cuny Table, praying and dancing under the tutelage of Short Bull and Kicking Bear.

At the Cheyenne River agency, the Ghost Dance craze had taken hold of the Minneconjou bands of Hump and Big Foot. At Standing Rock, home to the Hunkpapas, Sitting Bull had privately rejected the tenets of the religion, but he availed himself of the emotions it stirred among his people to try to win their allegiance back from the Indian agent, the domineering but capable James McLaughlin. Hump was quickly pacified, but not so Big Foot and Sitting Bull, and General Miles ordered their arrest.

Agent McLaughlin and Lt. Col. William F. Drum, commander at nearby Fort Yates, elected to effect the arrest of Sitting Bull with Indian police. A detachment of the 8th Cavalry under Capt. Edmond G. Fechet would stand by within supporting distance. The plan went tragically awry. At dawn on December 15, a platoon of Lakota police under Lt. Henry Bull Head surrounded Sitting Bull's cabin and seized the chief. Sitting Bull was resigned to his fate until his son began deriding him for cowardice. A humiliated Sitting Bull resisted arrest; followers swarmed to his rescue, and a fight broke out. By the time Fechet showed up, six policemen and as many ghost dancers lay dead or dying. Among them was Sitting Bull. The surviving Hunkpapa ghost dancers and their families fled the agency.

The army also bungled the arrest of Big Foot. The task fell to Lt. Col. Edwin V. Sumner, commander of a "camp of observation" at the forks of the Cheyenne River, near Big Foot's village. Learning that Big Foot's commitment to the Ghost Dance had wavered, and fearful of provoking a fight, Sumner elected not to arrest him. What Sumner did not know was that Big Foot had received an invitation from the Oglala chiefs to come to Pine Ridge and mediate their disputes. On the night of December 23, Big Foot and his people left their village and headed south.

An infuriated General Miles dispatched the 7th Cavalry to intercept the Minneconjous. On December 28, four troops under Maj. Samuel M. Whitside found them. Big Foot consented to a military escort, and the two parties camped for the night in the valley of Wounded Knee Creek, twenty miles from the agency. During the night, regimental commander Lt. Col. James W. Forsyth arrived with orders from General Brooke to disarm Big Foot's band and marched them to the railroad for transport to Omaha.

The Indians awoke December 29 to find their camp surrounded by five hundred soldiers and a battery of Hotchkiss guns. Forsyth assembled the men and demanded their guns. Soldiers fanned out to search the tepees. As tensions rose, a medicine man named Yellow Bird exhorted the warriors to resist. There was a scuffle; a gun went off; a group of young men threw off their blankets to reveal hidden rifles. Raising them, they let go a volley into the nearest soldiers. Hand-to-hand fighting followed. Hotchkiss guns raked fleeing Lakotas, turning a ravine in which many sought refuge into a mass grave. The troops tried to avoid shooting women and children, but the confusion was too great, and the warriors too thoroughly intermixed with noncombatants, to make for a clean fight. Sixty-two of the 150 or more dead Lakotas were women and children. Big Foot and Yellow Bird were among the dead. At least fifty more Indians were wounded. The 7th Cavalry suffered twenty-five killed and thirty-nine wounded, losses sufficiently heavy to refute the oft-leveled charge that Wounded Knee was a massacre. It was great tragedy, but no one had set out to kill Indians.

Fighting continued the next day when the 7th Cavalry stumbled into a trap set by hostile Brules and Oglalas near the Drexel Mission church. Only the timely arrival of Maj. Guy V. Henry's squadron of the 9th Cavalry prevented a possible repetition of the Little Bighorn. With this latest evidence of his subordinates' incompetence, General Miles took personal charge of the situation. In the greatest concentration of army forces during the Indian Wars, he ringed the hostile camp, which numbered four thousand people, of whom nearly a thousand were fighting men, with thirty-five hundred soldiers. Two thousand more were posted in supporting distance. The overawed Lakotas began drifting back to the agencies.

On January 15, 1891, Kicking Bear of the Minneconjous, who had been one of the eleven Lakota emissaries to Wovoka's Paiute village the previous autumn, handed his rifle to General Miles. With his surrender, the uprising ended and the Ghost Dance vanished. The four-decade war for the Northern Plains was over; the *wasichus* had proven invincible. As the historian Robert M. Utley observed: "The Ghost Dance was the Indian's last hope. Accommodation had failed. Retreat had failed. War had failed. And now Wounded Knee made it plain that religion had failed. No choice remained but to submit to the dictates of the government."[28]

Speaking in 1891 of the *wasichu* and his government, an old Sioux lamented, "They made us many promises, more than I can remember, but they never kept but one; they promised to take our land, and they took it."[29]

PART ONE

Platte River Bridge and the Powder River Expedition, 1865

The 11th Kansas Regiment at Platte Bridge

S. H. FAIRFIELD[1]

Kansas Historical Collections 8 (1904): 352–62

That mighty army of boys in blue that went forth at country's call to fight for freedom and native land is fast melting away. It is disappearing like the morning cloud and the early dew. In the passing away of Comrade Henry Grimm,[2] one of the victims of the Platte Bridge massacre, the campaign of the 11th Kansas Regiment against the Indians at the close of the Civil War is brought vividly to my mind.

Henry Grimm was wounded in a battle with hostile Indians at Platte Bridge, Wyoming Territory, 120 miles west of Fort Laramie.[3] The battle lasted during the three days of July 25, 26, and 27, 1865. It may be interesting to the present generation to learn something from those who were actual participants in those eventful, exciting times of forty years ago, the results of which meant so much for the future of Kansas and tolled the death knell for the "poor Indian."

Kansas was menaced on her eastern border by a large Confederate army and numerous bands of bushwhackers thirsting for Kansas blood, and on the south and west by nearly all the hostile tribes of Indians of the whole country, who had been driven westward and still westward for centuries, until at last, on the Western Plains, they came to a halt and said to the pale-faced brother, "Thus far we will go, and no further." They were willing, however, to make a treaty of peace, the terms of which were that the white man should not settle on any more of their lands; that their hunting grounds should not be invaded nor their game destroyed (thus taking away their only means of subsistence), and that no inroads should be made through their territory. But the white man had discovered gold and rich minerals in the mountains beyond the plains, and thousands of seekers for the yellow metal rushed through the Indian country, killing and destroying their game. Long trains of wagons were winding their way over the plains; the mysterious telegraph wires were stretching across their hunting grounds to the mountains; engineers were surveying a route for a track for the iron horse; and all without saying as much as "by your leave" to the Indians. Too plainly their game would soon be gone, their hunting grounds taken from them, and they themselves without a country.

The destruction, under Colonel Chivington, of a Cheyenne village,[4] where all of their old men, women, and children were massacred, terribly exasperated the tribes. In their desperation they started on the warpath, all the numerous tribes of Indians on the plains and in the mountains banding together in the death struggle for their homes and hunting grounds. One military commander declared that never in all the history of the tribes did they do such fighting. General Mitchell[5] said that the tribes engaged in the Northwest were the Cheyennes, Arapahos, Kiowas, Brule and Oglala Sioux, a portion of the Blackfeet, and a large part of what were known as the Missouri River Sioux. All were well supplied from some source, said to be the Mormons, with the best of modern firearms and ammunition.[6]

In 1865, after gold was discovered in Colorado, that territory had more than fifty thousand inhabitants, and all the supplies for this multitude, as well as for the numerous forts and posts on the plains and in the mountains, and in New Mexico, had to be hauled from the Missouri River in wagons, distances of five hundred to one thousand miles. There was no railroad nearer than St. Joseph, Missouri. All of the lines of communication from the Missouri River to the mountains had to be guarded by soldiers, and all the trains passing over these routes were obliged to have a heavy escort. Major General Dodge,[7] in his report to the secretary of war, said that the Indians held the entire overland route from Julesburg to Junction Station, near Denver; that they had destroyed the telegraph lines, captured trains, burned ranches, and murdered men, women, and children indiscriminately, and that on the southern route a similar state of affairs existed; that every Indian tribe capable of mischief, from the British possessions on the north to the Red River on the south, was at war with us, and that not a train or coach of any kind could cross the plains in safety without being guarded. As soon as troops could be spared from the eastern army, they were hurriedly transported to the Department of the West, some twenty-five thousand troops being sent to the western frontier.

Our regiment, the 11th Kansas Cavalry, under Col. P. B. Plumb,[8] on its return from the campaign against General Price,[9] October 21 to 26, 1864, was ordered to Fort Riley, to be put in readiness for the campaign on the frontier. February 20, 1865, we took up the line of march for Fort Kearny, although one-third of the regiment were still dismounted, and fully one-half not properly clothed, owing to the lack of supplies at Fort Riley. Four days out the mercury dropped to thirty degrees below zero, yet the march was continued for days and weeks without fuel, except such as was made from buffalo chips. At Fort Kearny,[10] the regiment was inspected, its unmounted men were supplied with horses, and it was again started on the march. We crossed the Platte River at Julesburg, where the river was half a mile wide, amidst floating ice, and camped on the north bank for several days, during a driving snowstorm. From this point we proceeded up the North Platte some two hundred miles to Fort Laramie. Here the regiment was distributed to various posts and stations throughout the northern subdistricts of the plains, commanded by Col. Thomas Moonlight.[11]

Maj. Gen. Grenville M. Dodge. GRENVILLE M. DODGE. *BATTLE OF ATLANTA.*

Most of the posts had stockades, built of logs twenty feet long, set in the ground close together and pinned, and portholes made through them. These stockades held a company or more of men, with their horses and transportation. A part of the regiment was stationed at the different posts for over one hundred miles up the North Platte—Horseshoe Creek, La Bonta, Deer Creek, and Platte Bridge. All these posts had stockades and were from thirty to thirty-five miles apart. Troops from these posts guarded the overland telegraph, furnished escorts, and scouted the country for marauding parties of Indians.

On May 20, two hundred Indians attacked the Deer Creek station, captured some thirty horses, and were repulsed by forces under Colonel Plumb. On the twenty-seventh, Colonel Moonlight captured Two Face and Black Foot, Sioux chiefs, with their bands. They had with them a Mrs. Eubank and her little daughter.[12] She had been captured by the Cheyennes on the Little Blue and was in a pitiable condition. Moonlight says that he "tied the two chiefs up by the neck with a trace-chain, suspended from a beam of wood, and left them there without any foothold." I remember seeing the cruel savages hanging by the neck on one of the hills north of the fort. Seven hundred Indians were fed for several weeks, but as it was costly to keep them there, they were ordered to be sent to Julesburg. Captain [W. D.] Fouts of the 7th Iowa, with three troops of cavalry, left Fort Laramie as escort to these seven hundred Indians. He also had in charge 185 lodges of Sioux Indians, numbering about two thousand.

On the second day out, near Fort Mitchell, on the North Platte, the Indians mutinied and made an attack on the escort, killing and mutilating Captain Fouts and several of the soldiers, and then the whole outfit fled across the river. A dispatch was sent to Colonel Moonlight at Fort Laramie, who immediately started in pursuit with a force of California, Ohio, and Kansas troops. When 120 miles out, in the early morning at the camp on Dead Man's Fork, he was attack by a large force of Indians. After a sharp engagement, they succeeded in stampeding his horses. This necessitated the abandonment of the pursuit. Moonlight burned his saddles and took up the weary march back to Fort Laramie on foot. On his

An attack on the escort. W. F. BEYER. *DEEDS OF VALOR.*

arrival there, he was relieved of his command by Brig. Gen. Patrick E. Connor,[13] commander of the District of the Plains, and ordered to Fort Leavenworth, to be mustered out of the service. It was a cruel order and a great injustice to a brave soldier. Colonel Moonlight was the peer of any officer that ever drew [a] sword west of the Missouri River.

The feeling among the soldiers was bitter against General Connor, and there were those among them who would have released him [Moonlight] from his command on short notice and without requiring him to report to Fort Leavenworth for muster out. He kept the 11th Kansas in the Indian country two months after they had been ordered home by the government to be mustered out, and then took their horses and transportation from them out on the desert, hundreds of miles away, letting them find their way to civilization.

General Connor gave the following order to the commanders of his expedition: "You will not receive overtures of peace or submission from Indians, but will attack and kill every male Indian over twelve years of age." How will this compare with General Weyler, the Spanish butcher, in Cuba? Someone has said that you only have to scratch the skin of a civilized man to find the savage.

On May 11, five companies of the 11th Kansas, under Colonel Plumb, were ordered to Fort Halleck, 120 miles from Fort Laramie, to reopen and protect the route of four hundred miles from Camp Collins, Colorado, to Green River. For two hundred miles of this distance, the Indians had full sway. They had captured all the horses and destroyed all the stage company's property. Colonel Plumb distributed his five companies at different points along the entire line and again opened the overland communication between the East and the West. The stages, loaded with United States mail, were drawn by cavalry horses. Soldiers were drivers. His troops were constantly on duty protecting the telegraph line, escorting trains, and repelling attacks of the Indians, who were always on hand, ready to strike at any unguarded point.

The wily foe well understood that if the soldiers' horses could be stampeded, they had them at a great disadvantage, and they hovered around the posts and lines of travel, watching for a chance to make a dash when the troops were off their guard or in small bodies. The headquarters of the troops on the North Platte were at Platte Bridge, under command of Maj. Martin Anderson[14] of the 11th Kansas Cavalry, Company I, of the same regiment, under Captain [James E.] Greer, being on duty there.

Platte Bridge was a strategic point. It was here that the savages from the Powder River country crossed to the lines of travel on the southern overland route, where they reaped a rich harvest, intercepting travel, plundering and robbing richly laden trains, United States mail, and valuable express. The military forces at the bridge were a hindrance to their predatory raids, and the redskins were determined to remove the soldiers out of their path. This made the post a dangerous one for a small body of troops to hold. The Indians were always bold and ugly at that point. June 26, Lt. W. Y. Drew of Company I, with twenty-five men, while repairing the telegraph line, had a hard scrimmage with some three hundred warriors that pounced down upon them. On July 2, the whole of Company I was attacked by several hundred Indians, some twelve miles from the bridge. Major Anderson then ordered a detachment of troops from D, H, and K Companies to report at headquarters at the bridge for duty, thus bringing up the number of enlisted men to 120, [with] two tepees of Snake Indians. This force was wholly inadequate to be stationed in the heart of the Indian country swarming with savages.

About the middle of July, I went with a mail detail of twelve men from Platte Bridge one hundred miles down the line toward Fort Laramie. We were gone ten days, having to travel mostly in the night, as it was unsafe to travel by daylight in small bodies. While at Horseshoe Station, we learned that the Indians had appeared again along the North Platte and in our rear, in large numbers, and

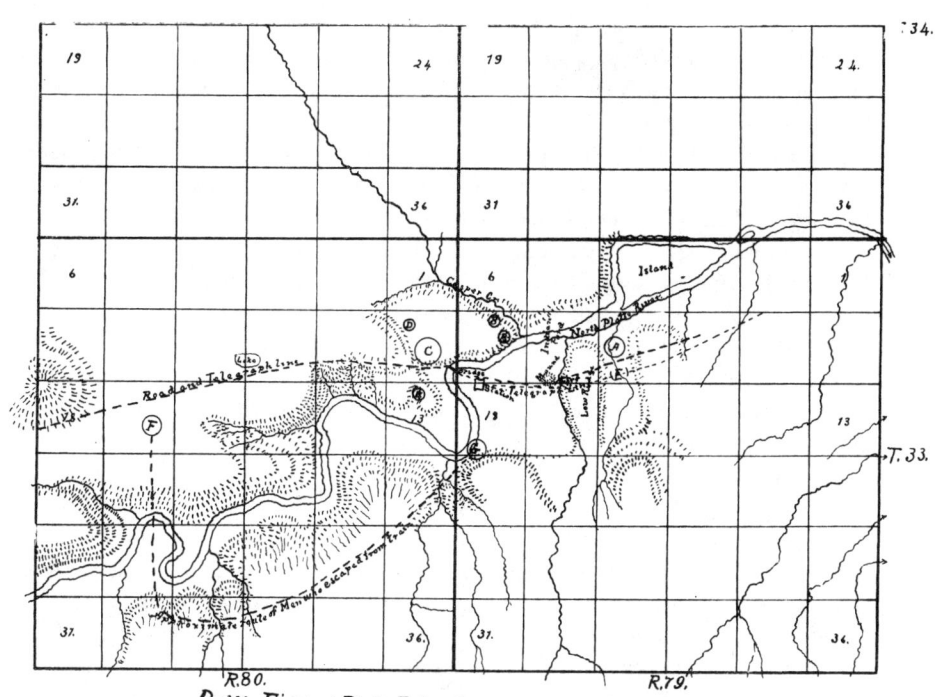

Battlefield of Platte Bridge. KANSAS HISTORICAL COLLECTIONS, 1904.

were liable to give us serious trouble on our return. We arrived at Deer Creek, where our company was stationed, on July 24. Another detail of twelve men under Cpl. Henry Grimm relieved us and proceeded to Platte Bridge with the mail. They arrived there on the twenty-fifth; also a small detachment of the 11th Ohio from Sweetwater Bridge. The Indians had been hanging around the bridge for several days and were bold and saucy, which indicated that they were there in force. In the early morning of July 25, a small band attempted to stampede the horses that were grazing just below the bridge on the south side of the river, where Company I, commanded by Captain Greer, was camped, but the soldiers finally succeeded in getting them into the stockade.

Reinforcements coming from the post, the Indians were driven back. The Indians rallied, and in their turn drove our boys back and recovered the body of their dead chief.

About 9 A.M. on the twenty-sixth, a train of wagons from Sweetwater, escorted by twenty-five men, under command of Sgt. Amos J. Custard,[15] Company H, 11th Kansas, was seen coming over the hills some two or three miles away. The howitzers were fired to warn them of danger.

A detail of twenty-five men, under Sergeant Hankammer, including the mail party under Corporal Grimm, was ordered to go to the relief of Sergeant Custard. Lt. Caspar Collins, 11th Ohio, who had just arrived with Grimm's mail party, volunteered to take command of the detachment.[16] They crossed the bridge to the north side of the river, and at full speed made their way toward the hills. They had proceeded about half a mile when, from behind the hills and out of the ravines, came swooping down upon them hundreds of Indians,[17] yelling, whooping, shooting arrows and rifles, and riding in circles about them like so many fiends, while a large body of them, coming down from the bluffs, attempted to get between them and the bridge. Captain Greer, Company I, seeing the peril threatening the brave boys under Collins, charged across the bridge with the balance of his company and poured a deadly fire into the howling savages, driving them back, and thus opening a way of retreat for Collins and his men, if they succeeded in making their way through the hundreds of savages that surrounded them. Collins, finding that more than half of his men were killed or wounded, gave [the] command for everyone to make for the bridge. It was a race for life. [Sebastian] Nehring, a private of Company K, 11th Kansas, not understanding the order, dismounted to fight from a deep washout in the road. Grimm, looking around, yelled to him in German, "To the bridge!" That was the last that was seen of poor Nehring. [Pvt. George] Camp, also of Company K, lost his horse and then ran for dear life, but when within a few rods of safety was overtaken and tomahawked.[18] Sergeant Hankammer's horse was wounded, but carried him safely to the bridge and there dropped.

A wounded soldier fell from his horse and called out to his comrades, "Don't leave me! Don't leave me!" Collins turned and rode back to the man, and thus lost all possibility of saving his own life. The brave lieutenant was mounted on a magnificent horse and might have escaped, had he not gone back on this errand of mercy. It was a miracle that any man escaped. Our friendly Snake Indians reported that they heard the order given by the chiefs of the wild Indians, "Stop firing! You are killing our own men." This, added to the fact that the Indians were so massed, was what probably saved our boys.

The bridge across the Platte was of one thousand feet span, and the stockade was on the south bank of the river, near the bridge. Our soldiers held the bridge and stockade, although the Indians crossed the river above and below the bridge and fought desperately, harassing our forces on every side throughout that day and a part of the next.

On the evening of July 26, two men came out of the chaparral in a bend of the river on the south side, about one-half a mile above the bridge. A party went out to rescue them. They proved to be boys from Sergeant Custard's command. They said that when they heard the howitzers in the morning, Custard ordered a corporal [James Shrader] to take five men[19] and go forward to see what the firing meant. They had proceeded but a short distance when they were cut off from Custard's escort. Pursued by the Indians, they struck for the river, but only three of them succeeded in crossing to the south bank, and one of these was killed before the friendly shelter of the chaparral was reached.

The nineteen men remaining with the train under Custard were also surrounded, but made a brave fight from 10:00 A.M. until 3:00 P.M. From that time there was an ominous silence, which, to the troops at the bridge, boded ill for Custard and his men.

Five squadrons of the 6th Michigan Cavalry at Laramie were ordered by forced marches to Platte Bridge to relieve the garrison. Major Anderson, on the evening of the twenty-sixth, sent a telegram to Lieutenant [Josiah M.] Hubbard, at Deer Creek, giving an account of the battle, but the Indians, during its transmission, cut the wires, so the message as received was only fragmentary.

Major Anderson issued an order to Lieutenant Hubbard, at Deer Creek, to reinforce him at once, as his troops were nearly out of ammunition, and he could hold out but a short time. Two friendly Snake Indians were paid $150 to take the order to Deer Creek, thirty-five miles distant. They started from the bridge after dark, took to the mountains and followed down the range, and delivered the order just at dawn the next morning. Lieutenant Hubbard put his company in readiness at once and made a forced march to the bridge.

Arriving there about 3:00 P.M. in the afternoon, we were cheered lustily as we came in. The main body of the Indians had apparently withdrawn. The next morning, we took an ambulance and went out to gather up our dead. We found Nehring with his arms bound to his body by telegraph wire, his hands and feet cut off, his tongue and heart cut out, and otherwise horribly mutilated. Nearly one hundred arrows were sticking in his body; a long spear pierced it through to the ground. Lieutenant Collins was found a half mile from the bridge, stripped and cut up in a fiendish manner.[20] The Company I soldier was also stripped and mutilated, but for some reason Camp's body had escaped such awful indignity. The arrow that pierced Grimm was pulled through after the feather end was cut off. The arrow in his spine remained there for over four hours during the battle. He begged the doctor to take it out and not let him die with it in his back.

On the afternoon of the twenty-seventh, twenty-five of us boys, under Lt. Phil Grimm, went out in search of Sergeant Custard and his men. We followed the telegraph road among the hills. Several miles from the bridge, we came to a washout where the boys had made a stand.

On three sides, the embankment was three or four feet high, but on the west there was only slight protection. Into this washout they had driven one of their wagons, and from behind such meager embankments the poor fellows fought for their lives for five long hours. Here we found the mangled and mutilated bodies of Sergeant Custard and his eighteen men. Seventeen of them had been left lying upon their faces, their bodies pinioned to the ground with long

Platte River Bridge, as sketched by a member to the 11th Kansas Cavalry.
KANSAS HISTORICAL COLLECTIONS, 1904.

spears. They had been stripped and cut up in a shocking manner. The wagoner was strapped to his feedbox, and hot irons from the hubs of the wagon wheels were placed along his back, apparently when he was alive. The charred remains of one man were among the coals where the wagon was burned.

The next day, another detail of twenty-five men, under command of Lieutenant Hubbard, went out and buried the poor fellows where they had sacrificed their lives so dearly. A long ditch was dug and lined with blankets. In it the dead were laid side by side, with rubber blankets spread over them, and then the bodies were covered with the sand of the desert. How many Indians were killed in the battle will never be known. In a communication from General Dodge, he says, "Information from our scouts shows that their loss of life must have been greater than at first supposed. The Indians threw away all the scalps they had taken from our men, a sure sign that they had lost more than they had killed."

It was estimated that over two thousand Indians were engaged in the fight, and that over one-third of Major Anderson's forces were killed or wounded.

A few days after the battle, our regiment was relieved by the 6th Michigan, and we were ordered to Fort Leavenworth to be mustered out; so we soon took up our line of march for the white man's country. Between Fort Laramie and Julesburg, all of our serviceable horses were taken from us, and we were left to plod our way several hundred miles on foot. At Fort Kearny, our transportation was also taken from us and all of our belongings dumped on the banks of the Platte River. After having served our country faithfully for three years, we felt that we were cruelly and unjustly treated. But the curses of the boys rested on General Connor, commander of the district, and not on our country.

There was possibly some excuse for the officers in command. They were at their wits' end as to how to furnish equipment for the contemplated campaign. Troubles arose which were unlooked for when they planned the expedition into the heart of the Indian country. Even before they were sent to the plains, most of the horses were worn out by the hard campaigns in the South. Transportation for the troops was insufficient. Added to these difficulties were the insubordination and desertion of the troops. The soldiers claimed that the term for which they enlisted had expired, and that they were entitled to be mustered out, but by some arbitrary power were held in service. Many of the officers were arbitrary and tyrannical, and the soldiers were wicked enough to believe that the general officers were not anxious for the strife to come to an end, but were fighting the Indians on the same principle that boys used to torment hornets, punching their nest just to see them fight. The War Department of the plains and the various Indian agents were at swords' point. One was for extermination; the other demanded a treaty of peace. General Dodge, in a communication to General Pope, says, "I desire that the government may understand that it has either got to abandon the country west entirely to the Indians or meet the war issue presented; that there are fifteen thousand warriors in open hostility against us in the north, and about ten thousand in the south, and never before have we had so extensive a war on the plains, so well armed and supplied as now."

Had the military arm of the government in the West been let loose, it would have wiped the redskins off the face of the earth. But a different spirit pervaded the country. It was tired of bloodshed, turmoil, and strife. As soon as the clouds of war had passed over in the South, the people began to breathe easier, but on looking westward, they beheld a dark, ominous cloud rolling up in the sky. They were alarmed and began asking what it meant. Commissioners were sent out by the president to see what was behind the cloud. The secretary of war wrote [Lt. Gen. Ulysses S.] Grant, "The president is much concerned about the Indian expedition. The secretary declares his inability to meet an expedition so large and unexpected, and not sanctioned by the government. Have you any information to relieve the president's anxiety or to satisfy him as to the object or design of the expedition? Who planned it?"

General Grant to Secretary [Edwin M.] Stanton: "They have been planned under General Pope's direction. I will go to St. Louis in a few days and look into this matter myself."

General Grant to General Pope, commanding the Department of Missouri: "The quartermaster and commissary generals report requisitions of such magnitude coming from Leavenworth as to alarm them. Look into this and stop all unnecessary expenditures."

General Pope's headquarters were at St. Louis, and he instructed his generals in the field to plan and manage the campaign against the Indians and make requisitions on the government. They, being on the ground, would know what was best. This proved to be erroneous, for reckless expenditures were made without the approval of the government. The United States quartermaster reported on August 6, 1865, to the secretary of war that $10 million of supplies had been sent to the army in the West, exclusive of the outfit of the troops, wagons, animals, clothing, and stores taken with the troops in their own trains. Had the expedition which had already started been allowed to go on as planned by General Pope and his generals, the Treasury of the United States would have been in a condition similar to that of England at the close of the Boer War.

The peace commissioners sent out by the president, with authority to make treaties with the warlike Indians, in conjunction with the United States Indian agents, succeeded in getting the chiefs of most of the tribes in council. A cessation of hostilities was agreed upon until October, when the chiefs of the tribes would meet in council, with the commissioners appointed by the president, to make treaties of perpetual peace, and thus the war was practically ended, and most of the troops in the Indian country were relieved from duty and ordered back to their various states to be mustered out of the service.

Our regiment having been furnished transportation from a train returning from the mountains, we again took up our weary tramp of three hundred miles for home. We did not have the appearance of returning heroes; neither did we look like a very formidable foe. We scattered along the road like so many schoolboys, but always brought up at night with the wagons that held our grub and blankets.

It cheered our hearts when we first saw our dear old Kansas, with her fields of waving corn and broad prairies covered with green, so unlike the desert we had left behind. Arriving at Fort Leavenworth, muster-out rolls were prepared and, just three years from the time we were enlisted into the service for three years or during the war, we were mustered out. As soon as the boys were free, they made for their homes, to enter again the peaceful walks of life. Friends of a large number of the soldiers came with wagons to take them home, but many had to go on foot, for railroads were an unknown quantity in Kansas in those days.

The Powder River Indian Campaign of 1865

HENRY E. PALMER[1]

In *Civil War Sketches and Incidents, Papers Read by Companions of the Commandery of the State of Nebraska, Military Order of the Loyal Legion of the United States* (Omaha: By the Commandery, 1902): 59–109[2]

In August 1864, I was ordered to report to General Curtis,[3] who commanded the Department of Kansas, at Fort Leavenworth, and was by him instructed to take command of a detachment of the 11th Ohio Cavalry, sixty men, everyone of them lately Confederate soldiers with John Morgan on his raid into Ohio, captured there and confined at Columbus. They had enlisted in the Federal service under the pledge that they were to fight Indians and not Rebels. I was to conduct these men to Fort Kearny and there turn them over to Captain Humphreyville of the 11th Ohio.

On my way out, near Big Sandy, now Alexandria, Thayer County, Nebraska, I met a party of freighters and stagecoach passengers on horseback, and some few ranchmen, fleeing from the Little Blue Valley. They told me a terrible story: that the Indians were just in their rear, and that they had massacred the people west of them—none knew how many. All knew that the Cheyennes had made a raid into the Little Blue Valley, striking down all before them. After camping for dinner at this place and seeing the last citizen disappear toward the states, I pushed on to the Little Blue and camped in the valley, where we saw two Indians about five miles away on a hill as we went into camp.

Next day I passed Eubank's ranch, where we found the bodies of three little children, from three to seven years old, who had been taken by the heels by the Indians and swung around against the log cabin, beating their heads to a jelly. Found the hired girl some fifteen rods from the ranch staked out on the prairie, tied by her hands and feet; naked, body full of arrows, and horribly mangled. Not far from this was the body of Eubank with whiskers cut off and body most fearfully mutilated. Mrs. Eubank was missing. The buildings had been fired and the ruins were yet smoking. Nearly the same scene of desolation and murder was witnessed at Spring Ranch. Camped that night at Liberty farm.

Next day we passed wagon trains, in one place seventy wagons loaded with merchandise, en route for Denver. The teamsters had mounted the mules and made their escape. The Indians had opened boxes containing dry goods, taking great bolts of calicos and cloth, carried off all they wanted, and had scattered the

13

Old Fort Kearny, Nebraska. GRENVILLE M. DODGE. *BATTLE OF ATLANTA.*

balance around over the prairie. Bolts of cloth had been seized by Indians on horseback, who had dropped the bolt, holding on to one end of the cloth, and galloped off over the prairie to stretch it out. Five wagons loaded with coal oil, in twenty-gallon cans, had been inspected by the Indians; some fifteen or twenty cans had been chopped open with hatchets to see what was inside. Non of them had sense enough to set the coal oil on fire, otherwise the entire train would have been destroyed, though several wagons had been fired and burned. These Indians had attacked the troops at Pawnee Ranch, August 9, 1864, under the command of Capt. E. B. Murphy of the 7th Iowa Cavalry, and had driven them into Fort Kearny. Murphy had only thirty men. Captain Murphy returned August 15 with 110 soldiers and plainsmen and a mountain howitzer and renewed the fight. By this time, about August 20, the main body of the Indians was far away in the Republican Valley, en route for Solomon River. I followed their rear guard to a point near where the town of Franklin, in Franklin County, Nebraska, on the Republican, now stands. Camped there one night, and then marched north to Fort Kearny. On that day's march, we saw millions of buffalo.

This raid on the Blue was made by the Cheyennes under the command of Black Kettle, George Bent, Two Face, and others. Mrs. Eubank and a Miss Laura Roper were carried away captives. We ransomed them from the Indians, who brought them into Fort Laramie in January 1865. Just prior to this outbreak on the Little Blue a number of the same Indians had attacked a train near Plum Creek, thirty-one miles west of Fort Kearny, on the south side of the Platte, and had killed several men.[4] From Plum Creek they moved on down the Little Blue, passing south of Fort Kearny.

Col. J. M. Chivington,[5] commanding the 1st Colorado, was in command of the District of Colorado, headquarters at Denver, and during October and November 1864, made several raids after these Indians. On November 29, 1864, Colonel Chivington, with three companies of the 1st Colorado and a detachment of the 3rd Colorado under command of Col. George L. Shoup, attacked Black Kettle, who with White Antelope, George Bent, and other bands were encamped on Sand Creek, 175 miles southeast of Denver. He attacked them just at daylight after a forty-mile ride in the dark by the troops. The Indians were surprised and 416 were killed—men, women and children. The fight was made in the village, and the troops had no time to pick for the men and save the squaws. This was the first great punishment the Indians of the plains had received since Harney's fight at Ash Hollow.[6]

On January 7, 1865, the military and stage station at Julesburg, at the old California crossing on the south bank of the Platte, was attacked by the Indians. Capt. Nicholas J. O'Brien, familiarly known among white men as "Nick O'Brien," and by the Indians as O-sak-e-tun-ka, was in command of the troops. The Indians (Sioux and Cheyennes), to the number of about one thousand, chased the stagecoach into the station, killing one man of the escort and one horse. Captain O'Brien left a sergeant and twelve men in the fort to handle the two pieces of artillery and, mounting the rest, thirty-seven men and one officer beside himself, went to met the savages. As the men neared the top of the hill, they saw the large force opposed to them, but never flinched. The Indians charged on them with great fury and killed fourteen of the soldiers. Captain O'Brien ordered his force to fall back, which they did in good order, leaving their dead comrades to fall into the hands of the Indians. The redskins endeavored to cut them off from the fort, and came very near doing it. The men finally gained the fort and held the enemy at bay with the artillery—two mountain howitzers. Night put an end to the conflict. The Indians withdrew during the night, and in the morning no one was in sight. The soldiers went out to find the bodies of their dead comrades; found them, but nearly all were beyond recognition—stripped of clothing, horribly mutilated, their fingers, ears, and toes cut off, their mouths filled with powder and ignited, and every conceivable indignity committed on their persons. The Indians, as they afterwards admitted, lost over sixty warriors.[7] None were found on the field, as they always carry away their dead with them.

These events emphasized the fact that there was an Indian war on the plains, extending from the settlements bordering on the Missouri River in Nebraska and Kansas from the Arkansas River to the Platte. There were at this time no settlements in Nebraska Territory north of and along the Platte River except the little hamlet of Fremont, a few buildings at Columbus, a ranch at Lone Tree (now Central City), and a ranch and blacksmith shop at Grand Island. Fort Kearny was located on the south bank of the Platte about six miles from the present city of Kearney, Nebraska. The Platte, Smokey Hill, and

Arkansas River routes were the three great highways from the Missouri River to the mountains and the Pacific coast beyond. More than five thousand teams loaded with freight and passengers passed a given point on the Platte in one month in 1864. Russell, Majors, and Waddell were transporting millions of pounds of freight for the government.

Colorado, with its population of sixty thousand people; Utah, with as many more; and Montana, Idaho, Oregon and California were depending largely on freighters and overland travel. Ben Holliday's overland coach, a daily stage with a capacity of from twelve to fifteen passengers—fourteen days from Atchison, Kansas, to Sacramento, California—and the Pony Express, ten days, were the fastest means for communication until Creighton's telegraph line was completed in 1864. This was the situation when the Indian war startled the frontier settlers. Only four years previous, April 1860, I had crossed the plains from Omaha to Denver all the way on foot, part of the time alone, never more than seven in the party; hundreds of thousands of people, men, women, and children, had crossed in straggling parties, armed and unarmed, and not one Indian outrage had been committed. From some cause unrecorded the storm had gathered, and without warning savage hosts were assailing citizens and soldiers along a thousand miles of unprotected frontier.

In the winter of 1864, some time in December, I think, Bvt. Brig. Gen. Tom Moonlight was placed in command of the District of Colorado and, until in May 1865, had his headquarters at Denver. Some time during this month he made his headquarters at Laramie. March 30, 1865, the District of the Plains was created and Brig. Gen. P. E. Connor was ordered from his command at Salt Lake to take command of the new district, with headquarters first at Fort Kearny, then at Denver, and in June at Julesburg. At Laramie, Colonel Moonlight organized an expedition to punish these marauding Indians. Before starting out on his expedition, he learned from some of the trappers that two white women were with Two Face's band near the south base of the Black Hills. Through interpreters, trappers, and Oglala Sioux, communication was opened up with these Indians, and for a large number of ponies, blankets and a quantity of sugar, etc., the two white women were purchased from the Indians and brought into Laramie. Two Face and two of his best warriors, Black Foot and Black Crow,[8] came in with the prisoners to surrender them. The armistice was violated. Two Face and his warriors were arrested and hanged in chains about two miles north of the fort on the bluffs, where their bodies were allowed to hang until the crows carried away all the flesh from their bones.

One of these women, Mrs. Eubank, was the wife and mother of the massacred party at Eubank's ranch, near Spring ranch, on the Little Blue in Nebraska, now one of the best settled portions of this state. I had known Mrs. Eubank before the Indian troubles—met her at her home in the spring of 1861, just after she had moved from Ohio to brave the dangers of a pioneer life and do the cooking for stagecoach passengers on the old Ben Holliday line. She was a fine looking woman, full of youth, beauty, and strength, but a short time married, with bright prospects for the future. I remember, too, that her log cabin was unlike anything else I had seen on the road west. The dirt roof, supported by heavy timbers, was hidden by cotton cloth, which gave to the interior of the cabin a clean, tidy look; the rough board floor was covered with a plain carpet; real china dishes, not greasy tin pans and cups, appeared upon the table. That, with a fine dinner, made an indelible impression upon my mind. As I stood at the smoking ruins of her home in August 1864, knowing that her body could not be found, and wondering if she were a captive among the Indians, I thought then, would I ever see her again alive? A few weeks after her rescue from the Indians, I met her again at Fort Laramie. The bright-eyed woman appeared to me to be twenty years older. Her hair was streaked with gray, her face gave evidence of suffering, and her back, as shown to General Connor and myself, was a mass of raw sores from her neck to her waist, where she had been whipped and beaten by Two Face's squaws. The sores had not been permitted to heal and were a sight most sickening to behold. The poor woman was crushed in spirit and almost a maniac. I sent an escort with her and her companion, Miss Laura Roper, with an ambulance to Julesburg, where they were placed upon a coach and returned to the East. Miss Roper lived and married in Beatrice, Nebraska. Mrs. Eubank went back to her friends in Ohio, and I have never heard from her since.

Moonlight's raid after the Indians was a failure. Through mismanagement he allowed his command to be ambushed [on] June 18, 1865, his horses captured, and several men killed, retreating to Fort Laramie in time to receive an order from General Connor to report to the commanding officer at Fort Kearny, Nebraska, for muster out of service.

My regiment, the 11th Kansas Cavalry, was ordered upon the plains in February 1865. We left Fort Riley, Kansas, on the sixteenth. After experiencing a most fearful snowstorm and blizzard, the command, about six hundred strong, reached Fort Kearny, Nebraska, on March 3, 1865, and in a few days pushed on to Lodge Pole Creek and camped near the present town of Sidney, where they went into winter quarters; remaining there, however, only a few weeks, when they were ordered to Mud Springs, where they again attempted to build winter quarters; from there to Laramie, Platte Ridge, and Fort Halleck; then they were strung out on the overland stage route with some 2,500 men in all, guarding the through-mail line. I had returned to Fort Leavenworth from Fort Kearny on detached service, and in June 1865, was ordered to report to General Connor, whom I found at the old California crossing on the Platte.

General Connor had with him two companies, L and M, of the 2nd California Cavalry, and a detachment of the 11th Ohio, under command of Captain Humphreyville,[9] and Captain O'Brien with his company of the 7th Iowa Cavalry, and two mountain howitzers, manned by Captain O'Brien's men and commanded by him. The command was delayed several hours trying to cross the Platte, June 24, 1865, which was then receiving snow water from the mountains, and was even with the bank. The crossing was made by swimming the stock and floating over the stores, wagons, etc., in wagon boxes covered with tarpaulins.

The men were also crossed on these rafts. We camped on the Lodge Pole. In the afternoon after the first day's march from the Platte, the men indulged in fishing in Lodge Pole Creek. Trout and pike were hauled out by the bushel with gunnysack seines. While we were cooking our fish, forty mules (that had made themselves useful drawing headquarters' wagons and ambulances, etc.) feeding on the opposite bank of the creek, about one hundred yards from headquarters, were frightened by a jackrabbit. One of the mules leading the band was feeding close to a large jackrabbit sitting behind a bunch of sagebrush. Lieutenant Jewett, aide-de-camp, and myself happened to discover the rabbit just before the mule saw it. Jewett remarked that he thought we would see some fun when the mule got a little closer to the rabbit. Sure enough, when the mule got within a few feet of the bunch of sagebrush, Mr. Jack gave a monstrous jump to change location. The mule gave a snort and started back among the herd on a gallop. All the rest of the mules joined the leader, becoming more frightened at every jump, and away they went for the hills about a mile away, no stop or halt until they disappeared. The general ordered a squad of cavalrymen to gather their hobbled animals and start in pursuit. This was done, but "nary" a mule was seen afterwards. When the cavalry reached the hills, they were met by a band of Indians, who beat them back. Before we could assist them, both Indians and mules were far away, and before we got near them, they were across the North Platte, near Ash Hollow, en route for the Black Hills. Next day, June 26, 1865, we were attacked by Indians near Mud Springs and gave them a lively chase, the fight not ending until about 10:00 P.M., when the men gathered in camp to prepare supper.

Soon after the return to camp, General Connor decided he must send Lieutenant Oscar Jewett, his aide-de-camp, who had had great experience in Indian warfare, to Chimney Rock, some thirty miles north, where a large supply train in charge of Leander Black was encamped. Overhearing the instructions to Lieutenant Jewett, that he must go alone and run the risk of riding among the Indians, I begged General Connor to allow me to accompany Jewett. At that time I had not been assigned to any particular duty—was simply a passenger in the general's ambulance, en route to join my company, which was supposed to be stationed at Platte Bridge, on the North Platte, west of Laramie. To impress the general with my claims, I gave him to understand that I had seen much of the Indians and was as capable of dodging their arrows as Lieutenant Jewett. After some hesitancy, the general consented that I might go, but instructed us to ride at least six hundred yards apart, one behind the other. We left at 11:00 P.M., and before daylight next morning were in the camp of the supply train and had the men aroused, ready to meet an attack expected at daylight. The ride was a very interesting one, the night being as dark as I ever experienced, and neither one of us heard or saw the other until we met in Black's camp.

Next day General Connor issued an order assigning me to duty as acting assistant adjutant general, District of the Plains. Our march from this point (Chimney Rock) to Fort Laramie was devoid of anything particularly exciting. We were detained at Fort Laramie until July 30 awaiting supply trains. During this time, expeditions were organized by General Connor, supplied with trains of provisions and munitions of war, and started for a general rendezvous at the mouth of the Rosebud, near the south bank of the Yellowstone River. One of these expeditions, composed of the 16th Kansas, under command of Lt. Col. Samuel Walker,[10] left us at Laramie, marching in a northeasterly direction up the Rawhide, across the Cheyenne to the Belle Fourche, along the west base of the Black Hills to the right of Devil's Tower, toward the Little Missouri until he intercepted Colonel Cole's[11] command. Walker's command, designated as the center column, was composed of six hundred men of the 16th Kansas cavalry.[12] He was ordered to march July 29, but his command mutinied and refused to go, claiming that they had enlisted to fight Rebels, not Indians; that the war for which they enlisted was over and they should be mustered out. Two mountain howitzers double-shotted with grape and canister were sent to Walker's camp to help him enforce his order; the ringleaders were arrested, and his command marched away July 30 and did valiant service before their return in October. He took forty days' supplies packed on mules.

The right column of the Powder River Indian expedition was commanded by Col. Nelson Cole of the 2nd Missouri Light Artillery, and was composed of 797 officers and men of the 2nd Missouri Light Artillery serving as cavalry and 311 officers and men of the 12th Missouri Cavalry—in all 1,108 men, not including guides. He marched from Omaha, Nebraska, to Columbus, thence up the Loup, north fork, to its head, thence north across the Niobrara, Cheyenne River, to the east base of the Black Hills, around the north side, through the present site of Fort Meade, near the present city of Spearfish, on to the Little Missouri and to Powder River, intercepting Walker's command on the Belle Fourche. He was ordered to meet Connor at the mouth of the Rosebud.

About July 9, I was relieved as acting assistant adjutant general by Capt. C. J. Laurant, a regular assistant adjutant general, who had been sent by General Dodge to report to General Connor. The general refused to let me join my company and issued an order announcing me as his acting assistant quartermaster, and instructed me to provide transportation, forage, etc., for the expedition.

I found that there were only about seventy government wagons at Fort Laramie; that the commissary stores and forage required for the expedition and required by the command under Colonels Cole and Walker would require in the neighborhood of two hundred wagons to transport the same. I was compelled to press citizens' outfits into service. I pressed into service forty wagons belonging to Ed Creighton, which was under the charge of Thomas Alsop; captured Tom Pollock's train of thirty wagons and other trains until I had a train of 185 wagons.

General Connor's command left Fort Laramie on July 30, 1865, en route for Powder River. Our column was known as the "Left Column of the Powder River Indian Expedition," and was composed of 68 men belonging to Company F, 7th Iowa Cavalry, under command of Capt. N. J. O'Brien, with 1st Lt. John S. Brewer, 2nd Lt. Eugene F. Ware; 60 men of Company E, 11th Ohio Cavalry,

An army wagon train en route to Fort Laramie.
GRENVILLE M. DODGE. *BATTLE OF ATLANTA*.

under Captain [Levi G.] Marshall; 70 men of Company K, 11th Ohio Cavalry, Capt. J. L. Humphreyville; 67 men of Company M, 2nd California Cavalry, commanded by Capt. Albert Brown; 49 men of Company L, 2nd California Cavalry, commanded by Capt. George Conrad; 14 men, a detachment of the 2nd Missouri Artillery; 15 men, a detachment of the Signal Corps of the United States Volunteers, under command of Lt. J. Willard Brown, assisted by 2nd Lt. A. V. Richards; 15 men on detached service from Company G, 11th Ohio Cavalry, commanded by Lt. John B. Furay, serving in the Quartermaster's Department; 95 Pawnee scouts under command of Capt. Frank North; and 84 Winnebago and Omaha Indians under command of Capt. E. W. Nash; together with six companies of the 6th Michigan Cavalry, numbering about two hundred men, under command of Col. J. H. Kidd. The Michigan troops were intended as a garrison for the first military post established, to be located on Powder River, and were not properly a part of the left column of the Powder River Indian expedition. Not including the Michigan troops, we had, all told, 358 soldiers and 179 Indians, together with about 195 teamsters and wagonmasters in the train, which was in the direct charge of Robert Wheeling, chief train master. The general's staff was limited to five officers: Capt. C. J. Laurant, A.A.G.; Capt. Sam Robbins, 1st Colorado Cavalry, chief engineer; myself as quartermaster; Capt. W. H. Tubbs, A.C.S.; and Lt. Oscar Jewett, A.D.C.

We arrived at the south bank of the Platte August 1, expecting to cross at the La Bonta crossing.[13] The general, with his guides and advance guards, had arrived the night before, expecting from information furnished by his guides that he would find a good crossing here. Our guides, ten in number, chief among whom were Maj. James Bridger, Nick Janisse, Jim Daugherty, Mick Boyer,[14]

John Resha, Antoine LeDue, and [James] Bordeau, were supposed to be thoroughly posted on this country, especially with the region so near Fort Laramie, where they had been hundreds of times. But the treacherous Platte was too much for them. The spring flood that had just passed had washed away the crossing, and after ten hours' diligent searching, not one of the cavalry escort could find a place to cross the river without swimming his horse and endangering his life. Coming up with the train, which did not reach camp until afternoon, I found the general thoroughly discouraged and more than disgusted with his guides. The river had been examined for four miles each way from La Bonta crossing, and not a place could be found where it would be possible to cross a train. The alternative was presented to march to Platte Bridge, 130 miles out of our regular course. Soon after parking the train, I rode off by myself on my government mule up the river, searching for an antelope. Without noticing the distance traveled, I was soon nearly five miles from camp and out of sight of the same over a sharp bluff near the river. Just beyond this bluff, I discovered a fresh buffalo trail leading down into the water, and across the river on the opposite side could distinguish tracks that the buffalo had made coming out of the stream. Curious to know how they could cross so straight without swimming in the rapid current, I rode my mule into the river and crossed on a good, solid bottom.

Returning by the same route, I marked the location in my mind and rode back to camp in time for supper. Soon after feasting on antelope steak that I had captured on my expedition, and having lit my pipe, I strolled up to General Connor and asked if he proposed crossing the Platte at this point, or if he intended to go around by the bridge. The general seemed put out by my question, which, under the circumstances, he considered aggravating, and answered me rather roughly that we would have to go round by the bridge. I told him that if it was the train that bothered him about crossing, I would guarantee to have it on the opposite bank of the river by daybreak the next morning. The general's reply was, "Very well, sir; have it there." After 9:00 P.M., when all was still in camp, I detailed a gang of teamsters, about forty men with picks and shovels, and marched them up the river to the buffalo trail and set them at work making a road. It being a moonlit night, the work was easily prosecuted, and by break of day on the morrow the lead team of the 185 wagons stood, leaders in the river, waiting the command to march. As soon as it was light enough to distinguish the opposite shore, I rode in ahead of the leaders and gave the command "Forward!" There was no break or halt until the train was parked opposite the general's camp, all before sunrise. In fact, the entire train was parked, the mules turned loose to graze and the men preparing their breakfast, when the sentinels on the opposite bank of the river discovered the train beyond the Platte and gave the alarm to the general, who rushed out of his tent undressed to see what he did not believe was true. He immediately ordered "Boots and Saddles" to be sounded, and in a short time the entire command was with us. After breakfast, our column moved on, passing over a country perfectly destitute of grass or timber, and scarcely any water.

August 2 and 3, we made thirty-three miles, following up the north bank of the Platte. August 4 opened with a cold, drizzling rain. Broke camp at 6:00 A.M. Weather soon cleared off. Found roads hilly; in fact, no roads at all. No wagon had even been near our line of march. Captain Brown, with two California companies, was ordered to push on, following up the Platte, while we struck off to the right. They were to march by way of the south slope of the Bighorn Mountains into the Wind River Valley and thoroughly reconnoiter that region of country, and to rejoin us within twenty or twenty-five days near the Crazy Woman's Fork of the Powder River, which stream they were to strike near its head and follow down until they intercepted our command. The Omaha or Winnebago scouts under command of Captain Nash, eighty-four men, accompanied them. Flanking parties were reinforced on our line of march today, the Pawnee scouts composing same; also a party of the same scouts two or three miles ahead of the command. Every precaution was taken to guard against surprises. Parties were sent ahead for Indian signs, the guides reporting several strong indications of war parties having traveled the country ahead of us. Our course after leaving the Platte was in a northwesterly direction. Camped in some hills, where we found stagnant pools, grass very poor, country very rough, almost impossible to get the train through. We marched only ten miles and reached camp at 1:30 P.M. Streams were "doubled up" nearly every hill; no wood at this camp.

August 5. Moved from camp at sunrise, traveled over several high ridges, and made camp at Brown's Springs at 10:00 A.M. Grass and water excellent. Stock looking well so far, no accidents of a serious nature having happened since we started. General Connor very vigilant and careful about being surprised; he superintends every movement himself and is very sanguine that our expedition will be successful. Distance traveled today, eight and one-half miles, as measured by the general's ambulance odometer.

August 6. Left Brown's Springs at 6:00 A.M., Sunday, everything moves off in the usual manner; course nearly north. Saw Pumpkin Buttes at 1:00 P.M., which the guides say is thirty miles from Powder River.[15] Some careless soldiers fired the grass near our camp last night. The fire, getting beyond control, serves as a beacon light to the hostiles and gives great uneasiness to our guides, who fear that the Indians will be signaled thereby and may congregate in large numbers too large for our little command. At the starting of this fire, the flames ran across the camp toward two powder wagons. Volunteers from the general's headquarters camp, together with some soldiers, rushed through the fire to the powder wagons and dragged them to a place of safety; in doing so had to pass over burning grass. Today our left flankers killed three buffalo. Made camp on the dry fork of the Cheyenne at 10:00 A.M. Grass and water plenty. No water visible, but any quantity of it within a few inches of the surface in the sandy bed of the river. Empty cracker boxes were sunk in the sand, sand scooped out, and soon water could be dipped up by the bucketful, enough to water all the stock and to supply the camp. The last of the train did not reach camp until dark; distance marched only twelve miles.

Pumpkin Buttes. GRENVILLE M. DODGE. *BATTLE OF ATLANTA.*

August 7. Broke camp at the usual hour; roads very heavy today; distance traveled eighteen miles. The train did not all arrive in camp until after midnight. Our camp was at some springs in a cozy little valley, where we found plenty of grass and enough wood to cook our buffalo meat. Five buffalo killed and brought in today; any quantity of buffalo and antelope in sight on both flanks. Teams gave out today, many of the mules refusing to pull.

August 8 was spent in recuperating the stock; not a wheel was turned today. (I refer to my dairy from this date on for only important events of the expedition; will not try to record the incidents of each day's march.)

August 9. We obtained our first view of the Bighorn Mountains at a distance of eighty-five miles northwest, and it was indeed magnificent. The sun so shone as to fall with full blaze upon the southern and southeastern sides as they rose toward Cloud's Peak, which is about thirteen thousand feet above sea level, and the whole snow-covered range so clearly blended with the sky as to leave it in doubt whether all was not a mass of bright cloud. Although the day was exceedingly warm, as soon as we struck this ridge we felt the cooling breezes from the snow-clad mountains that was most gratefully appreciated by both man and beast. In front and a little to the northeast could be seen the four columns of the Pumpkin Buttes, and fifty miles farther east Bear Butte, and beyond, a faint outline of the Black Hills. The atmosphere was so wonderfully clear and bright that one could imagine that he could see the eagles on the crags of Pumpkin Buttes, forty miles away.

August 11. Broke camp at the usual hour; traveled down Dry Creek; passed two or three mud holes, where the stock was watered. After eight miles marching, got to a spot where we could see the long-looked-for Powder River. Saw columns of smoke down the river, indicating an Indian village a few miles away. It proved to be a fire which the hostile Indians had made a day or two before. Powder River is, at this point, a very rapid stream, water muddy like the Missouri; timber very plenty, ranging back from the river from one-half to one mile; grass not very good. Train reached camp at 2:00 P.M. and camped in the timber on the riverbank. In the evening, the general, some members of his staff, and the guides, with an escort, went down the river to see if there were any signs of the Indians. Found a "good Indian" very lately sewed up in a buffalo skin and hung up in a tepee. Many such sights along Powder River. The country traversed by the general was similar to the campground.

August 12. Train remained in camp. An exploring expedition was sent up the river under the command of Lieutenant Jewett, with orders to proceed twenty miles, to look for a better location for a military post. Twenty-five of the 6th Michigan Cavalry went up the river with Lieutenant Jewett to the crossing of the old traders' trail from Platte Bridge to the Bighorn Mountains, and past the same to the Bozeman Trail. Lieutenant Jewett found bottoms on both sides of the river, banks heavily timbered, flanked by high, bold bluffs, with Indian signs all along the stream—scarcely a mile where there had not been Indian villages, some within a few weeks, some that were probably made years and years ago. Some camps gave evidence that the Indians had very large droves of horses, as the trees were badly girdled. Numerous Indian burial trees were found with lots of "good Indians" tied up in them. Several bands of buffalo were seen during the day. Lieutenant Jewett returned to camp the same day, having made a fifty-mile march.

August 14. The first timber was cut today for building a stockade, the general having decided to erect a fort[16] on the west bank of the river at this point on a large mesa rising about 100 feet above the level of the river and extending back, as level as a floor, about five miles to the bluffs. A very fine location for a fort, the only disadvantage being scarcity of hay land. Our stockade timber was cut twelve feet long and was from eight to ten inches in thickness. These posts were set four feet deep in the ground in a trench. Every soldier and all the teamsters who could be urged to work were supplied with axes, and the men seemed to enjoy the exercise, chopping trees and cutting stockade timber.

August 16. Command still in camp waiting for a train of supplies from Fort Laramie before we proceed. Indian scouts discovered a war party today, and the soldiers gave them a running fight, Captain North's Pawnees in the advance, with only a few staff officers, who were smart enough to get to the front with the Pawnees. Captain North[17] followed the Indians about twelve miles without their being aware of our pursuit; then the fun began in earnest. Our war party outnumbered the enemy, and the Pawnees, thirsty for blood and desirous of getting even with their old enemy, the Cheyennes, rode like mad devils, dropping their blankets behind them and all useless paraphernalia, rushed into the fight half naked, whooping and yelling, shooting, howling—such a sight I never saw before. Some twenty-four scalps were taken, twenty-nine horses captured, and quite an amount of other plunder, such as saddles, fancy horse trappings, and

Indian fixtures generally. The Pawnees were on horseback twenty-four hours and did not leave the trail until they overtook the enemy.[18] There was a squaw with the party; she was killed and scalped with the rest. On their return to camp, they exhibited the most savage signs of delight, and if they felt fatigued did not show it; rode into camp with the bloody scalps tied to the ends of sticks, whooping and yelling like so many devils. In the evening, they had a War Dance instead of retiring to rest, although they had been up more than thirty hours. The War Dance was the most savage scene I had ever witnessed. They formed a circle and danced around a fire, holding up the bloody scalps, brandishing their hatchets and exhibiting the spoils of the fight. They were perfectly frantic with this, their first grand victory over their hereditary foe. During the War Dance, they kept howling, "Hoo yah, hoo yah, hoo yah, hoo yah," accompanying their voices with music (if such it could be called) made by beating upon an instrument somewhat resembling a drum. No one who has ever witnessed a genuine Indian War Dance could form any conception as to its hideousness—the infernal "Hoo yahs" and din-din of the tom-tom. These howling devils kept up the dance, much to our amusement, until long after midnight, when finally the general, becoming thoroughly disgusted, insisted upon the officer of the day stopping the noise. After considerable talk, Captain North, their commander, succeeded in quieting them, and the camp laid down to rest; but this War Dance was kept up every night until the next fight, limited, however, to 10:00 P.M.

August 19. Several of the staff officers, myself included, went on a buffalo hunt in the afternoon. We killed several buffalo. One of the scouts reported having seen a large body of Sioux Indians. Captain North started with his company in pursuit; killed one Indian chief and captured six head of horses. Colonel Kidd went out in another direction with twenty-five men and reported from five hundred to one thousand Indians. Captain O'Brien and Lieutenant Jewett, with fifteen men, went ten or twelve miles down the river and camped until 3:00 A.M. of the twentieth, then struck across the country toward camp, but saw no Indians. Captain Marshall, with forty men of the 11th Ohio, went in pursuit of another band of Indians and captured eleven head of stock. All of these scouting parties returned to camp; some on the nineteenth, some not until the twentieth.

August 22. Broke camp at sunrise; started from Powder River going north, leaving part of the train at the fort, also all the 6th Michigan Cavalry. Traveled twenty-three and one-half miles and made camp on Crazy Woman's Fork of the Powder River, so named because of the fact that some fifteen years before, a poor, demented squaw lived near the bank of the river in a "wickiup"[19] and finally died there. The water of this stream is not as good as that of the Powder River, more strongly impregnated with alkali; grass not very good; sagebrush abundant, some timber on the stream. Saw some signs of Indians, but none very recent. About noon today, Capt. Albert Brown, with his Company L, 2nd California Cavalry, joined us. He had been on a three weeks' scouts—left us August 4 for the Wind River country—had followed the Wind River Valley to a point west of the south end of the Bighorn range, and then east to Crazy Woman's Fork; and down this valley to our command; had seen no Indians, game in abundance.

August 23. Left Crazy Woman's Fork at 6:00 A.M.; traveled north five miles; came to a dry creek; passed several of the same kind during the day; did not find any running water; stock suffered some from want of same. The country is rolling, still seems more compact and gives us a much better road than we had on the south side of the Powder River. The Bighorn Mountains, lying right to our front, seem to be within rifle range, so very near that we could see the buffalo feeding on the foothills; the pine trees, rocks, and crags appear very distinct, though several miles away. Fourteen miles from Crazy Woman's Fork, we struck the Bozeman wagon trail, made in 1864. Made camp at 3:00 P.M.; grass splendid; plenty of water, clear and pure as crystal and almost as cold as ice. The stream was full of trout, and the boys had a glorious time in the afternoon bathing in the ice water and fishing for trout with hooks made of willows. Several bands of buffalo had been feeding close to camp, and about 5:00 P.M. about twenty-five cavalrymen rode out and surrounded a band and drove them into a corral formed of our wagons, and there fifteen were slaughtered and turned over to the Commissary Department.

The general and a few of his staff officers, myself included, went up the stream to a high mesa some three miles above camp and got a beautiful view of the country and the surrounding hills; returning ran upon a monstrous grizzly, which took shelter in a little plum patch covering about an acre of ground. One of our party, train master Wheeling, with more daring than the rest of us cared to exhibit, rode up within a few rods of the patch; the bear would rush out after him, when he would turn with his mule so quickly that the bear could not catch him, the bear close to his heels, snapping and growling, at the same time receiving the fire of our Sharp's rifles. After receiving the same, Mr. Grizzly would retire, and again Wheeling would draw him out of the plum patch, and again we would pour cold lead into his carcass. The fight was intensely interesting. When we downed the grizzly, we found we had perforated his hide with twenty-three balls. The animal was one of the largest of its species; we agreed that it weighed about 1,800 pounds.

From this point on to Montana—in fact, along the whole base of the Rocky Mountains to the British possessions—the country is perfectly charming, the hills are covered with a fine growth of grass, and in every valley there is either a rushing stream or babbling brook of pure, clear snow water filled with trout, the banks lined with trees, wild cherries, quaking asps [sic], some birch, willow, and cottonwood. No country in America is more picturesque than the eastern slope of the Bighorn Mountains.

August 25. Broke camp at the usual hour; pushed on north, passing along the base of the Bighorn Mountains. Crossed several streams, one of which we named Coal Creek, because of the fact that near the center of the stream lay a block of coal about twenty-five feet long, eight feet thick, and about twelve feet wide, the water having washed through a vein of coal that cropped out at this point. We found coal here enough to supply our forges and to enable the blacksmith to do some needed repairs. Seven miles from Coal Creek, we came to a very pretty lake about two miles long and about three-fourths of a mile wide, which Major Bridger told us was De Smet Lake, named for Father De Smet.[20] The lake is strongly impregnated with alkali—in fact, so strong that an egg or potato will not sink if thrown into the water. Large, red bluffs are to be seen on both sides, and underneath the lake is an immense coal vein. Not many miles from this lake is a flowing oil well. A scheme might be inaugurated to tunnel under this lake, pump the oil into the lake, set the tunnel on fire, and boil the whole body of alkali water and oil into soap. Made our camp on the Piney Fork of the Powder River, about two or three miles below the present site of Fort Kearny, where now is a flourishing city known as Buffalo, county seat of Johnson County, Wyoming. Just after we had gone into camp, a large band of buffalo that had been aroused by our flankers came charging down the hill directly into camp. Many of them turned aside, but several passed through among the wagons, much to the dismay of our animals, most of which were tied, taking their meal of grain. One monstrous bull got tangled in the ropes of one of our tents and was killed while trampling it in the dust.

August 26. Left Piney Fork at 6:00 A.M. Traveled over a beautiful country until about 8:00 A.M., when our advance reached the top of the ridge dividing the waters of the Powder from that of the Tongue River. I was riding in the extreme advance in company with Major Bridger. We were two thousand yards at least ahead of the general and his staff; our Pawnee scouts were on each flank and a little in advance; at that time, there was no advance guard immediately in front. As the major and myself reached the top of the hill, we involuntarily halted our steeds. I raised my field glass to my eyes and took in the grandest view that I had ever seen. I could see the north end of the Bighorn range, and away beyond, the faint outline of the mountains beyond the Yellowstone. A way to the northeast, the Wolf Mountain range was distinctly visible. Immediately before us lay the valley of Peneau [or Peno] Creek, now called Prairie Dog Creek, and beyond, the Little Goose, Big Goose, and Tongue River Valleys and many other tributary streams. The morning was clear and bright, with not a breath of air stirring. The old major, sitting upon his horse with his eyes shaded with his hands, had been telling me for an hour or more about his Indian life— his forty years' experience on the plains; telling me how to trail Indians and distinguish the tracks of different tribes; how every spear of grass, every tree and shrub and stone was a compass to the experienced trapper and hunter—a subject that I had discussed with him nearly every day. In fact, the major and myself were close friends. His family lived at Westport, Missouri. His daughter, Miss Jennie, had married a personal friend of mine, Lieutenant Waschman, and during the winter of 1863, I had contributed to help Mrs. Bridger and the rest of the family, all of which facts the major had been acquainted with, which induced him to treat me as an old-time friend.

As I lowered my glass the major said, "Do you see those 'ere columns of smoke over yonder?" I replied, "Where, Major?" to which he answered, "Over there by that 'ere saddle," meaning a depression in the hills not unlike the shape of a saddle, pointing at the same time to a point fully fifty miles away. I again raised my glass to my eyes and took a long, earnest look, and for the life of me could not see any column of smoke, even with a strong field glass. The major was looking without any artificial help. The atmosphere appeared to be slightly hazy in the long distance, like smoke, but there were no distinct columns of smoke in sight. Yet knowing the peculiarities of my frontier friend, I agreed with him that there were columns of smoke, and suggested that we had better get off our animals and let them feed until the general came up. This we did, and as soon as the general with his staff arrived, I called his attention to Major Bridger's discovery. The general raised his field glass and scanned the horizon closely. After a long look, he remarked that there were no columns of smoke to be seen. The major quietly mounted his horse and rode on. I asked the general to look again; that the major was very confident that he could see columns of smoke, which, of course, indicated an Indian village. The general made another examination and again asserted that there were no columns of smoke. However, to satisfy curiosity and to give our guides no chance to claim that they had shown us an Indian village and we would not attack it, he suggested to Captain North, who was riding with his staff, that he go with seven of his Indians in the direction indicated to reconnoiter and to report to us on Peneau Creek or Tongue River, down which we were to march. I galloped on and overtook the major, and as I came up to him overheard him remark about "these damn paper-collar soldiers" telling him there were no columns of smoke. The old man was very indignant at our doubting his ability to outsee us, with the aid of field glasses even. The joke was too good to keep, and I had to report it to the general. In fact, I don't believe the major saw any columns of smoke, although it afterwards transpired that there was an Indian village in the immediate locality designated. Bridger understood well enough that that was a favorable locality for Indians to camp, and that at most any time there could be found a village there. Hence, his declaration that he saw columns of smoke.

Our march down Peneau Creek was uneventful, the road being very good, much better than we had before found. This stream takes its name from a French trapper by the name of Peneau, who had been trapping for beaver. A band of buffalo close by tempted him to take a shot, which he did, slightly wounding a large bull. The bull took after him, and Peneau fled for his life. Just as he reached the steep bank of the creek, some fifteen or twenty feet above the stream, Mr. Bull caromed on his rear and knocked Peneau clear over the bank head foremost into the creek, the bull tumbling in after him. Fortunately the fall was more disastrous to the bull than to the man, who was able to make his escape. Such is the story as told to me by Major Bridger. Our camp that night was in the valley of Peneau Creek, not far from Tongue River, sixteen miles from Big Piney.

August 27 and 28. Traveled down Peneau Creek and Tongue River; country near the river very barren; no grass. After camping, four of the Omaha scouts went a short distance from the camp and met a grizzly, which they imprudently fired upon. The grizzly closed upon them, killing one of the scouts and fearfully mangling two others before a relief party could drive away the bear. Just after sunset of this day, two of the Pawnees who went out with Captain North toward Bridger's columns of smoke two days previous came into camp with the information that Captain North had discovered an Indian village. The general immediately called me to his tent and instructed me to take command of the camp, keeping the wagons in corral, protect the stock, and hold the position until he should return; that he was going out to fight the Indians. I had never been baptized with Indian blood, had never taken a scalp, and now to see the glorious opportunity pass was too much. So I begged the general to order Lieutenant [John S.] Brewer of the 7th Iowa Cavalry, who had just reported to me as being ill, to remain with the train, and that I be allowed to accompany him in the glorious work of annihilating the savages. The general granted my request. The men were hurried to eat their supper, then being prepared, and at 8:00 P.M. we left camp with 250 white men and eighty Indian scouts as the full attacking force. From our calculation as to distance, we expected to strike the village at daylight on the morning of the twenty-ninth.

Our line of march lay up the valley of Tongue River, and after we had passed the point where our wagons had struck the stream, we found no road, but much underbrush and fallen timber; and as the night was quite dark, our march was very greatly impeded, so that at daylight we were not within many miles of the Indian village. The general was much disappointed at this delay, which compelled us to keep closely under cover, and in many instances to march along by the water's edge under the riverbank in single file, to keep out of the sight of the Indians. I had worked myself to the extreme advance and, like possibly many others in the command, had begun to think that there was no Indian village near us, and that we would have no Indians to fight. Arriving at this conclusion, I had become somewhat reckless and had determined that Captain North, who had joined our command soon after we left camp, should not reach the village in advance of myself. As we rode along close together conversing, I managed to forge in ahead of him just as we dropped down into a deep ravine; the bank on the side just beyond the stream was much higher than the bank from which we came, and the trail led up to this steep bank.

As I rode up the bank and came to the top, my eyes beheld a sight as unexpected to me as a peep into Sheol. Just before me lay a large mesa, or table, containing five or six hundred acres of land covered with Indian ponies, except a portion about one-half mile to the left, which was thickly dotted with Indian tepees full of Indians. Without a moment's hesitation, I grasped the bits of my horse with my right hand and his nostrils with my left to prevent him from whinnying, threw myself from the saddle, dragging the horse down the bank against Captain North's horse, and whispered to him that we had found the village. Captain North held my horse while I ran back, motioning the men to keep still. In fact, the general had issued orders when we left camp that no man should speak above a whisper, and that when the horses attempted to whinny, they should be jerked up with a tight rein. During the last half hour of our march, several men had become somewhat careless and were not as cautious as they had been during the night.

I soon met the general, who was close to the advance, and told him of my discovery. The word was passed back for the men to close up and to follow the general, and not to fire a shot until he fired in advance. General Connor then took the lead, rode his horse up the steep bank of the ravine, and dashed out across the mesa as if there were no Indians just to the left; every man followed as closely as possible. At the first sight of the general, the ponies covering the tableland in front of us set up a tremendous whinnying and galloped down toward the Indian village. More than a thousand dogs commenced barking, and more than seven hundred Indians made the hills ring with their fearful yelling. It appeared that the Indians were in the act of breaking camp. The most of their tepees were down and packed for the march. The ponies, more than three thousand, had been gathered in, and most of the warriors had secured their horses; probably half of the squaws and children were mounted, and some had taken up the line of march up the stream for a new camp. They were Arapahos under Black Bear and Old David, with several other chiefs not so prominent.[21]

The general watched the movements of his men until he saw the last man emerge from the ravine, when he wheeled on the left into line. The whole line then fired a volley from their carbines into the village without halting their horses, and the bugles sounded the charge. Without the sound of the bugle, there would have been no halt by the men in that column; not a man but what realized that to charge into the village without a moment's hesitancy was our only salvation. We already saw that we were greatly outnumbered, and that only desperate fighting would save our scalps. I felt for a moment that my place was with the train; that really I was a consummate fool for urging the general to allow me to accompany him. I was reminded that I had lost no Indians, and that scalping Indians was unmanly, besides being brutal, and for my part I did not want any dirty scalps; yet, I had no time to halt; I could not do it, for my horse carried me forward almost against my will, and in those few moments—less than it takes to tell the story—I was in the village in the midst of a hand-to-hand fight with warriors and their squaws, for many of the female portion of this band did as brave fighting as their savage lords. Unfortunately for the women and children, our men had no time to direct their aim; bullets from both sides and murderous arrows filled the air; squaws and children, as well as warriors, fell among the dead and wounded.

The scene was indescribable. There was not much of the military in our movements; each man seemed an army by himself. Standing near the "sweat-house," I emptied my revolver into the carcasses of three warriors. One of our men, a member of the 11th Ohio Cavalry, a fine looking soldier with as handsome a face as I ever saw on a man, grabbed me by the shoulder and turned me about that I might assist him in withdrawing an arrow from his mouth. The point of the arrow had passed through his open mouth and lodged in the root of his tongue. Having no surgeon with us of a higher grade than a hospital steward, it was afterwards, within a half hour, decided that to get the arrow out of his mouth, the tongue must be, and was, cut out. The poor fellow returned to camp with us, and at this date I am unable to say whether he lived or died. Another man, a sergeant in the Signal Corps by the name of Charles M. Latham, was shot in the heel. He had been through the entire war in the Army of the Potomac and wore a medal for his bravery; had passed through many battles and escaped unharmed. This shot in the heel caused his death; he died a few days afterward with lockjaw. The Indians made a brave stand trying to save their families and succeeded in getting away with a large majority of their women and children, leaving behind nearly all of their plunder. They fled up a stream now called Wolf Creek, General Connor in close pursuit. Soon after we left the village, General Connor advised me to instruct Captain North to take his Indians and get all the stock he could possibly gather. This was done, and with a few stragglers, I followed a small band of Indians up the main Tongue River about three miles, until they gathered recruits enough to turn upon us and force us back.

General Connor pursued the fleeing savages fully ten miles from camp, when he found himself accompanied by only fourteen men: Our horses had all become so fatigued and worn out that it was impossible to keep up. The general halted his small squad and attempted to take the names of his brave comrades, when the Indians, noticing the paucity of his numbers, immediately turned upon him and made a desperate effort to surround him and his small squad of soldiers. They fell back as rapidly as possible, contesting every inch, reinforced every few moments by some stragglers who had endeavored to keep up. With this help, they managed to return to camp, where Captain North and myself had succeeded in corralling about 1,100 head of ponies.[22] One piece of artillery had become disabled. The axletree of the gun carriage, a mountain howitzer, was broken. We left the wheels and broken axle near the river and saved the cannon. The command rendezvoused in the village, and the men were set to work destroying Indian property. Scores of buffalo robes, blankets, and furs were heaped up on lodge poles, with tepee covers and dried buffalo meat piled on top, and burned. On one of these piles we placed our dead and burned their bodies to keep the Indians from mutilating them. During our halt, the Indians pressed up close to the camp and made several desperate attempts to recover their stock, when the mountain howitzer, under the skillful management of Nick O'Brien, prevented them from completing their aims. Our attack upon the village commenced at 9:00 A.M. The rendezvous in the village was about 12:30 P.M. We remained there until 2:30 P.M., and in the time intervening, we destroyed an immense amount of Indian property—fully two hundred fifty Indian lodges and contents.

Policing up stragglers. W. F. BEYER. *DEEDS OF VALOR.*

At 2:30 P.M. we took up the line of march for the train. Captain North, with his eighty Indians, undertook to drive the stock; they were soon far ahead, while the rest of the force was employed in beating back Indians. The Indians pressed us on every side, sometimes charging up to within fifty feet of our rear guard. They seemed to have plenty of ammunition but did most of their fighting with arrows, although there were some of them armed with muskets, with which they could send lead in dangerous proximity to our men. Before dark, we were reduced to forty men who had any ammunition, and these only a few rounds apiece. The Indians showed no signs of stopping the fight, but kept on pressing us, charging upon us, dashing away at the stock, keeping us constantly on the move, until 11:45 P.M., when the last shot was fired by our pursuers.

At this time, I had gone ahead with an order from General Connor to Captain North relative to handling the stock. Having completed my work, I halted by the side of the trail and waited for the general, who was with the rear guard. I remember, as I was getting off my horse, I heard the last shot fired some two or three miles in the rear. After I had dismounted, I realized that I was fearfully tired, so tired that I could not stand up. I sat upon the ground and in a moment, in spite of myself, was in a sound sleep, and was only awakened by being dragged by my horse, which was an Indian pony that I had saddled from the captured stock. Nearly all our men had remounted themselves while we were rendezvousing in the Indian village, otherwise we would not have been able to keep out of the way of the pursuing Indians. My lariat was wrapped around my right hand, and with this the pony was dragging me across the prickly pears when I awakened. Realizing that I was on dangerous ground, I quickly mounted my pony and listened long for the least sound to indicate whether the general had come up or not. There was no noise—not a sound to be heard, the night intensely dark and myself so bewildered that I scarcely knew which way to go. Again jumping from my horse, I felt with my hands until I found the trail and discovered that the footprints of the horses went in a certain direction. Taking that as my course, I rode away as rapidly as possible, and after three miles hard riding overtook the general and his rear guard, who had passed me while I was asleep. All congratulated me on my narrow escape.

We arrived at camp at daylight, after marching fully 130 miles without any rest or refreshments, except the jerked buffalo with which the boys had filled their pockets in the Indian village.

The incidents of this fight would make interesting reading. Many acts of personal bravery cannot be recorded. Suffice it to say that every man was a general. Not a command was given by the general after the first order to charge— not a man in the command but that realized that his life was in the balance. We must either whip the Indians, and whip them badly, or be whipped ourselves. We could see that the Indians greatly outnumbered us; that our main dependence was upon our superior equipments—we were better armed than they. As for fighting qualities, the savages proved themselves as brave as any of our men. The fight commenced at 9:00 A.M. and was offensive until after 11:00 A.M., when the general was driven back into camp with his small squad of men; from that time until midnight, we fought on the defensive. Yet we had accomplished a grand victory. Two hundred and fifty lodges had been burned with the entire winter supply of the Arapaho band. The son of the principal chief (Black Bear) was killed, sixty-three Indians were slain, and about one thousand head of ponies captured. While we were in the village destroying the plunder, most of our men were busy remounting. Our own tired stock was turned into the herd, and the Indian ponies were lassoed and mounted. This maneuver afforded the boys no little fun, as in nearly every instance the rider was thrown or else badly shook up by the bucking ponies. The ponies appeared to be as afraid of the white men as our horses were afraid of the Indians. If it had not been for Captain North with his Indians, it would have been impossible for us to take away the captured stock, as they were constantly breaking away from us trying to return toward the Indians, who were as constantly dashing toward the herd in the vain hope of recapturing their stock.

Many exciting scenes were witnessed upon the field of battle. During the chase up Wolf Creek with the general, one of North's braves picked up a little Indian boy that had been dropped by the wayside. The little fellow was crying, but when picked up by the soldier-Indian fought like a wildcat. One of our men asked the Indian what he was going to do with the papoose. He said, "Don't know; kill him, mebby." He was told to put him down and not to injure the bright little fellow. The Indian obeyed, and at least one papoose owed his life to the kind-hearted soldier. Several of our men were wounded, some of them quite severely. Three or four afterwards died of their wounds. Two of our soldiers, white men, I forget their names, were found among the dead, and three or four of North's Indians were killed. Lieutenant Jewett, the general's aide-de-camp, the general's bugler, and orderly were among the wounded. Lieutenant Jewett was shot through the thigh and through the hand, and yet was compelled to ride over sixty-five miles after receiving his wounds.

We were absent from camp thirty-three hours, had marched 130 miles, and during that time had had nothing to eat except a few hardtack and some jerked buffalo meat. If there is a better record to the credit of the volunteer cavalry soldier, I am not aware of the fact. We brought back to camp with us eight squaws and thirteen Indian children, who were turned loose a day or two afterwards.

August 30 and 31, we marched twenty-two miles down Tongue River. September 1, early in the morning, a cannon shot was heard. No two persons could agree from what direction the sound came, but as this was the day fixed for the general rendezvous of Cole and Connor's commands near the mouth of the Rosebud, some eighty miles away, it was supposed that the sound came from that direction. General Connor directed Captain North, with about twenty of his Indians, and Captain Marshall, with thirty men of the 11th Ohio Cavalry, to push on rapidly to the rendezvous to communicate with Cole. Marched fifteen miles.

September 2. Did not leave camp until 1:00 P.M. Marched down the river eight miles. Valley has narrowed up very much, and the country appears rough and irregular. Last night several "medicine wolves" were heard prowling in the hills near camp. Ever since we left Fort Laramie, our camp has been surrounded with thousands of wolves, making the night hideous with their infernal howling; but not until tonight have we heard the medicine wolf, which old Bridger claims to be a supernatural sort of an animal whose howling is sure to bring trouble to the camp. Bridger, Nick Janisse, and Rulo, being very superstitious, were so frightened at this peculiar howling that they took up their blankets and struck out for a new camp, which, according to their theory, was the only way of escaping from the impending danger. They went down the river about half a mile and camped in the timber by themselves.

September 3. Has been a cold, dreary day, raining most of the time; some snow. Weather very disagreeable for a mounted man compelled to march sixteen miles in the snow and rain.

September 4. Weather not quite so cold as yesterday—not disagreeable; country very rough; scarcely any grass, not a bear was seen for miles on the march. Passed down Tongue River; was compelled to cross the stream dozens of times. A messenger from Colonel Sawyers' train of emigrants came into camp at night with the news that his train was attacked by the Indians, supposed to be the same ones that we had fought; that Captain Cole of the 6th Michigan and two of his men were killed; that the train was parked and the men doing their best to defend themselves. From him we learned that Colonel Sawyers,[23] with about twenty-five wagons and one hundred men, were en route from Sioux City to Bozeman by way of the Bighorn, or Bozeman route; that they had passed over the country by way of the Niobrara, North Fork of Cheyenne, between Pumpkin and Bear Buttes, intersecting with our trail near Fort Connor, and Colonel Kidd, commanding Fort Connor, had sent Captain Cole with twenty men as an additional escort for the train to help them through the Arapaho country.

Captain Brown and two companies of California troops were hastily detached from our command and marched west about forty miles to relieve the train. When they reached the train, they found that the Indians had given up the attack, and on the next day, the train pushed on, Captain Brown accompanying them. Our command continued their march fifteen miles down the river.

September 5. Remained in camp all day waiting for some word from Captain Marshall. The general is very anxious to get some news from the column under the command of Colonel Cole. Captain Marshall's guide returned from the Rosebud tonight with no news from Cole's command. Captain Marshall reached camp with his men soon after, having been to the rendezvous and finding no evidence of our supporting column there.

September 6. The command about-faced today and marched back up the river fifteen miles to find better grass for the stock, a scouting party under Captain North having returned from the mouth of the Tongue River on the Yellowstone and reported no grass and no sign of Cole's command.

September 7. Marched upon the river fourteen miles; found good grass and camped.

September 8. Captain Frank North with twenty of the Pawnee scouts left for Powder River this morning. Captain Humphreyville and a part of his company were ordered to the Rosebud. Small scouting parties were sent in every direction to obtain, if possible, some news of Cole's command. No signs of Indians. Weather very cold and disagreeable.

September 9. Still raining and snowing; roads are frightfully muddy; almost impossible to move the train; has been raining and snowing for three days.

September 10. Stopped raining this morning. Several mules and horses have died from the effects of the storm. No news from the other column. Tongue River has risen about two feet, and we find it impossible to cross.

Hauling artillery on Connor's march along the Tongue River.
W. F. BEYER. *DEEDS OF VALOR.*

September 11. Moved the camp one mile up the river to better grass. Captain Humphreyville returned from the Rosebud today, reporting no signs of Cole's command. Captain North also returned from Powder River and reports that he found from five hundred to six hundred dead cavalry horses, undoubtedly belonging to Cole's command; most of them were found shot at the picket line. From that it appears that Cole had been hard-pressed by the Indians and had been compelled to dismount his men and shoot his horses, the Indians giving them no chance to forage. A large number of saddles and other property had been burned. His trail was well marked and showed that he had pushed on up the river in an opposite direction from the course which he had been ordered to take. This startling news gave evidence that we were nearing the end of our expedition, which we feared must end disastrously, and explains the distant report of cannon [on] September 1. As acting commissary of subsistence, as well as quartermaster (Captain Tubbs had remained at Fort Connor), I realized that Cole's command must be out of provisions; that they had provisions until only September 3 or 4, when they were supposed to meet our train. That by this time, September 11, they must be either out of provisions or had been living on half rations for some time.

The situation was, indeed, a critical one. Here a superior force had been attacked by the Indians at a point only fifty miles east of us, had been driven from its line of march to take another route, and had been so hard-pressed by the savages that they were compelled to shoot their horses to save them from falling into the hands of the enemy and to enable the men to do better fighting on foot. Our fighting force was only about three hundred fifty men, counting sixty men with Captain Brown, who was then one hundred miles away; theirs, seventeen hundred—nearly five times our number. What would be our fate should these Indians return from the pursuit of Cole, cross over from the Powder River to Tongue River, and concentrate with the Arapahos in an attack upon us? We knew, or at least Captain North and his Indians knew, that the Indians who were pressing Cole were the Sioux and Cheyennes, and that they numbered thousands—according to the best estimate, five or six thousand Indians. Nearly all the men realized that we must be prepared to do some very good fighting; that our only chance of escape from the country depended upon cautious movements as well as good luck.

Early on the morning of September 12, we took up our line of march for Fort Connor. By doubling teams, as many as thirty span of mules hitched to several wagons, we managed to drag our loads across the river and by hard work made twenty miles today. Saw two very large herds of elk that had been driven into the timber by the storm. Last night General Connor dispatched one white man, Sgt. C. I. Thomas, Company E, 11th Ohio Cavalry, who volunteered to go with two Pawnee Indians at the risk of his life and join Cole's command with dispatches from the general, directing Cole to push on up Powder River to Fort Connor, where he would find supplies for his men, a fact unknown to Colonel Cole. This move was an important one, and the scouts were instructed to travel only by night and to run the gauntlet at all hazards, otherwise Cole and his men might perish within close proximity to the fort, where there was an abundance of food and ammunition. This party made the trip safely. Traveling only by night, they managed to reach Cole's camp and told him—which to his starving troops was glorious news—that if they pushed on rapidly, they would find plenty to eat. (Sergeant Thomas lives at Dwight, Kansas, and is certainly entitled to a Medal of Honor from Congress for this brave deed.)

September 13. Continued our march up the river eight and one-half miles, when the teams were so badly played out that we could march no farther.

September 14. Marched thirteen and one-half miles. Another detachment of scouts, Pawnee Indians under command of Captain North, and also Captain Marshall with a small squad of the 11th Ohio Cavalry, started for Powder River this evening with instructions to fight their way through to Cole's command. The general is risking our entire force for the salvation of Cole's men. If our force should be attacked now, it would be short work for the Indians to massacre the entire party.

September 15 and 16 were spent in recuperating our stock, as we found the mules too weak to pull the wagons.

September 17. Marched up the river fourteen miles and camped. About 3:00 P.M. today, while the train was crossing the river and experiencing a great deal of trouble, I straggled on ahead of the command to the advance guard beyond. I had my Sharp's rifle with me and thought I would push on a little farther and see if I could not shoot an elk. Crossing over a little divide, I found that to reach the next point of timber I had a bottom of about two miles in width to cross. Not seeing any Indians or signs of Indians, I recklessly gave my fast-walking mule the rein and continued on. Soon after reaching the timber, I concluded I was getting too far ahead of the command, led my mule a short distance off the road, tied him to a sapling, took my gun, and sat down on a log, when suddenly I heard the clank of horses' hoofs upon the rocks just ahead of me. Glancing in that direction, I saw just before me a party of Indians. I sprang to my feet and raised my carbine as they pulled their reins, having noticed me. Just at that moment, the face of a white man appeared behind the Indians, and they threw up their hands to show that they were friendly. The white man, who proved to be Lieutenant Jones of the 2nd Missouri Artillery, rode up. He was from Cole's command and had been sent by Cole with Sergeant Thomas and his two Indians to advise General Connor of the safe arrival of our scouts, and that he would push on to Fort Connor. Jones had left Cole's command in an opposite direction from the Indians; had gone around them, striking our trail near Big Piney, and followed down Peneau Creek to Tongue River to the point where we met. I was so rejoiced at hearing from Cole's command that I could scarcely keep back the tears, and when I rode back to the train, the news set the men wild with joy. Cole's command had been found.

Lieutenant Jones reported that soon after passing to the right of the Black Hills, they were attacked by the Sioux and Cheyennes, who had continued to fight them from that time until they reached Powder River. By that time, their stock had become so worn out for want of feed that they were compelled to shoot many of their horses and burn up a large supply of saddles, stores, and accoutrements and to turn from their course towards the Wolf Mountains and the Rosebud, the country before them being so rough that they could not drag their wagons after their command. Colonel Cole, being so early surrounded by Indians, made up his mind that General Connor's command must have been massacred, and that if he ever reached the Rosebud, he would then be in a more dangerous position than he was east of Wolf Mountains; that his only chance for escape now would be in marching up Powder River, making his way if possible to Fort Laramie. Several of his men had been wounded by the Indians, and for several days the men had to subsist on mule meat, being absolutely out of provisions.

September 18 and 19. We continued our march up the river, camping on the nineteenth on Peneau Creek, three miles above our old camp. Large bodies of elk passed the command today, and several of them were halted by our bullets.

September 20. Continued our march up Peneau Creek sixteen miles.

September 21. The command marched twenty-one miles today. Just before we left camp this morning, I prevailed upon the general to allow Lieutenant Jewett, Captain Laurant, and myself, with three men, to ride two or three miles to the right of the command, to the front of the right flankers, to give us an opportunity to kill some elk; the country seemed full of them. The general made us promise that we would keep together, and being well armed, we might fight off the Indians if they should attack us and make our way back to the train. We extended our ride some two or three miles to the right of the line of march and out of sight of the train in the foothills of the mountains. About 8:00 A.M., we ran across a large band of buffalo, and as we were out upon a hunt, we dashed among them to see how many we could kill. I took after a fine bull, one of the best in the herd, which, with a small band of buffalo, struck up a ravine. It was short work to down the fellow and cut out his tongue as a trophy and to remount, when I discovered that there was not one of the party in sight—I was entirely alone. I rode up on a hill, expecting to see the party a short distance away, but saw nothing, except here and there a buffalo, all on the gallop, and here and there an antelope. Thinking I was pretty close to the men, I pushed on in my regular course south, parallel to the train, obliquing a little to the left, expecting soon to come in sight of the wagons. After riding about half a mile and reaching the top of a little ridge, I discovered, just before me, an antelope so close that I could not resist the temptation to chance a shot. Jumping from my pony, which, by the way, was a wild Indian pony captured out of the herd a day or two before, I threw the lariat over my arm, raised the gun, and fired. The pony made a jump and dragged the rope through my hands, blistering them badly, and escaped, galloping off in an opposite direction from the course I was traveling. My first impulse was to fire at the pony to save my saddle and other accoutrements. Turning, I saw that I had shot the antelope and that he was getting onto his feet again. As he was so close by, I dropped my gun to the ground, pulled my revolver, ran up towards the antelope, and fired as I ran. The antelope gained his feet and started down the slope. I had fired the last shot from my revolver and had no time to reload, and as I had wounded the antelope, I continued the pursuit. For nearly half a mile, I followed the antelope in a winding course, until finally he fell to the ground in his death struggles. I cut his throat and took the saddle—the two hindquarters. Started back to the hill to get my gun, but found I was on the wrong hill. Was finally compelled to return to the carcass and retrace my steps to where I fired at the antelope, tracking my way by the blood. This work delayed me fully an hour, but I was rewarded by finding the gun. Then, as I was so far behind the train (it was now 10:00 A.M.), I concluded it would be dangerous to attempt to follow it, and as I was afoot, my only salvation was in keeping at least four miles to the right of the train and to make camp in the nighttime. I hung on to the saddle of antelope and with my gun took up the tramp.

After walking two or three miles, I came to a ridge overlooking a little valley and in the valley saw a horse, which upon closer inspection I determined to be my own, and which had by a roundabout course struck the valley ahead of me. The animal was feeding by himself—not another animal in sight. I resolved at once to make an effort to recapture him. Slipping down to the creek, I deposited my gun and antelope meat in the limb of a dead cottonwood and commenced to crawl through the grass, which was very high, towards the horse. After more than an hour's work, slowly dragging myself along, I just managed to get hold of the end of the rope, but not with sufficient grip to hold the startled pony, who again escaped from me. This only aggravated me and made me resolve that I would have the pony or die trying. One, two, and more than three hours passed before I could again get hold of the rope, and finally it was about 4:00 P.M. when I managed to capture the pony. I had worked up the valley three or four miles above where I had left the antelope meat and my gun, but after I had mounted my pony, it was a short ride back to these articles, and without further incident of importance reached the camp at daylight next morning, having gone fifteen miles out of my way to avoid the possible chance of meeting Indians. The other members of the party had joined the command about 3:00 P.M., and after nine that night, nearly every man in the camp had given me up for dead.

September 22. Captain Marshall and a detachment of his company came from Fort Connor with a letter to General Connor with the news that he had been relieved of the command of the District of the Plains under an order from Maj. Gen. John Pope, commanding the Department of the Missouri, dated at St. Louis, Missouri, August 22, 1865, abolishing the District of the Plains and ordering Connor to Salt Lake. This was the first communication or dispatch received by Connor since August 15, and not a man of our command had received a letter from the states of a later date than July 20. We also learned that Colonel Cole, with his two regiments of Missouri troops and the 16th Kansas Cavalry, had reached Fort Connor in a very destitute condition, half of the men barefoot, and that for ten days they had had no rations at all and had subsisted entirely upon what little game they could get close to camp and on mule meat, and that they had been obliged to burn a large portion of their train, together with camp equipage.

September 23. Camped on Crazy Woman's Fork, and on September 24 reached Fort Connor, having traveled twenty-five miles today. The general and staff reached the fort about 11:00 A.M. The train got in just before sundown.

Cole's men looked as if they had been half starved and are very ragged and dirty; the men resemble tramps more than they do soldiers. They have had little but suffering since they left the Platte River and are as disgusted and discouraged an outfit as I ever saw. They report having fought the Indians six days on the Powder River and claim they killed three hundred or four hundred of them.[24] This day's march ends the story of the Powder River Indian expedition. General Connor will return with a small escort of men, leaving the command of the expedition to Colonel Cole, who will make his way back to the states by slow marches. General Frank Wheaton has been assigned to the command of the District of the Plains, and we expect to meet him at Fort Laramie. I persuaded General Connor to allow me to take back to Fort Laramie the captured stock that we might have credit therefore.

On September 26, the general pushed out for Laramie with three ambulances, Captain North and his Indians driving the stock. The general remained at Fort Laramie until October 4, when I received receipts from Captain Childs, A.Q.M., for 610 horses—all that had been saved of the 1,100 head captured from the Indians. Horses had escaped from us every day on the march, and during the storm on Tongue River several had perished. On our march up Tongue River, at least three hundred or four hundred made their escape—at one time a band of more than fifty in one drove. In the four days' layover at Fort Laramie, I had completed my reports to the Quartermaster and Commissary Departments, receiving the general's approval on all my papers and his thanks for services rendered, and was enabled to accept his invitation to a seat in his ambulance and rode with him to Denver, where we had been invited by the citizens to a reception in his honor. We left Fort Laramie with an escort of twenty men, who accompanied us as far as Fort Collins. From that point, we pushed on to Denver without an escort, arriving there about October 15. We were received with all honors that could be bestowed; a grand feast was prepared for us at the Planter's Hotel, and the best people of Denver, almost *en masse,* turned out to the reception.[25] The next day, we were escorted by more than thirty carriages filled with prominent citizens to Central City, forty miles away in the mountains, where we were again received and toasted in the most hospitable manner.

I returned to Denver in time to leave on the first coach that had been started from Denver for three weeks. Capt. Sam Robbins and Capt. George F. Price (who had been chief of cavalry for the general, and whom he had left at Fort Laramie in charge of the office as adjutant general of the District of the Plains while we were on the expedition), together with Bela M. Hughes (attorney general of Ben Holliday's overland mail line) and two Pacific railroad exploring engineers, with Johnnie Shoemaker as messenger (who had with him $250,000 in treasure), were fellow passengers. We left Denver at 10 A.M., October 19; met with no incidents of an exciting nature until we reached Larry Hay's ranch about daylight the second day out. Just as we were driving up to the station, we heard the rattle of musketry and the infernal yells of the Indians, who had attacked a train camped close to the station. The chief wagonmaster, Wells of Fort Lupton, was killed in this attack. I had just climbed out of the coach to a seat with the driver, Johnnie Shoemaker was in the boot asleep, and everyone in the coach was asleep except the driver and myself. I had remarked to the driver that it was daylight and asked him how far it was to the station. He said it was close by—a mile or two ahead. Just then we heard the firing. The driver whipped his six mules into a run, and away we went pell-mell for the station, expecting momentarily the arrows and leaden messengers of death. Fortunately for us, the Indians were on the opposite side of the station, and before we reached the same had been driven away by the teamsters and wagon men. At O'Fallon's Bluffs, near Baker's ranch, we were again attacked by the Indians and ran into the station, where we defended ourselves until morning.

Next day pushed on with the coach, with all the passengers on foot as an advance guard and flankers. Fortunately two companies of a West Virginia cavalry regiment were on the line of march up the Platte and happened to meet us in the worst part of the hills. Their presence had driven away the Indians, and we were enabled to drive through the bluffs in safety. This is the last incident worthy of record of the Powder River Indian expedition.

As a summary of general results, I can only say that (even with the disastrous ending of Cole's expedition) the Powder River Indian expedition of 1865 was not a failure. The general's plan to "carry the war into Egypt" succeeded admirably. The warrior element, by the movement of these columns, were compelled to fall back upon their villages to protect their families, and during the progress of the campaign the overland line of travel became as safe as before the Indian outbreak. It was not until General Connor retraced his steps, by order of the War Department, back to Laramie with all the soldiers that the Indians, thinking that he had voluntarily retired from their front, again hastened to the road, passing General Connor's retiring column to the east of his line of march, and again commenced their devilish work of pillage, plunder, and massacre.

General Connor's ability, sagacity, and courage and, best of all, his success as an Indian fighter remains unchallenged in all the western country. His early schooling in Indian wars especially fitted him to become, as he was, the "big medicine man" of their hereditary foe. Ben Holliday, the proprietor of the great stagecoach and mail line—Atchison, Kansas, to Sacramento, California—wrote the Secretary of War E. M. Stanton, October 15, 1864, urging the assignment of Connor to the command of the District of the Plains. He was the best Indian fighter in our service at that time. This was General George Crook's opinion as expressed to me by him in 1887.[26]

Raiding a Hostile Village

CHARLES W. ADAMS

National Tribune, February 11, 1898

A detachment of the 11th Ohio Cavalry, numbering about two hundred, in command of Brig. Gen. P. E. Connor, with "old man" Bridger and a half-breed called Popcorn[1] as guides, left Fort Laramie August 8, 1865,[2] on an expedition against hostile Indians then in force some three hundred miles north.

After a few days out, I was detailed on picket, and well do I remember it. I was posted a quarter of a mile from camp (alone) at dark in the sagebrush, with instructions to move some fifty yards after dark, so that if Indians should be watching, they would not know just where to pounce upon me. In case I should see or hear Indians moving toward camp, I was to fire and then do the best I could. Well, I did not see any Indians, but I imagined I could hear everything. I was relieved at midnight, and it appeared to me I had been there twenty-four hours.

There is no fun in sitting alone in the brush half the night, with wolves howling all around and not knowing when a grizzly or some other wild animals may be on one; to say nothing of the rattlesnakes.

On the evening of August 21, we arrived at Fort Connor, on Powder River, and were joined by Company E, 11th Ohio Cavalry, the 7th Iowa Battery, and two companies of Pawnee scouts commanded by Captain North. Two days later, we were joined farther on by two companies of California troops, two companies of Winnebago scouts, and two pieces of artillery, commanded by Captain Brown. After we had been in camp a short time near Bighorn Mountain, we heard the Pawnee scouts yelling and soon saw them coming, driving some twelve or fifteen buffalo right toward camp. We were soon out with our carbines, and as they passed near camp, gave them a volley, which brought down three fine animals, so we fared well for a few days.

On the afternoon of August 27, we were startled by several shots in quick succession. We were soon out in line, but we learned that two of the California boys had been playing cards and had some disagreement and settled it with the ever-ready revolvers. One had been shot through the body, the other through both arms.

On the twenty-eighth, we struck Tongue River in the forenoon and followed it, and next day camped on it. We had just got the horses fed when some of the scouts reported an Indian village forty miles up the river.

The order was to get ready to start as soon as possible. Two hundred men and two six-pounder howitzers were soon ready, and we started at dusk, traveled all night, following the river, and just before daylight, the command was halted.

General Connor made us a little speech, saying we were near the village, and he had no idea what force was there, but had confidence in the men and expected each to do his duty. Should we get in close quarters, the men should group in fours; under no circumstances were we to use revolvers unless there was no other chance, and then be sure and leave one charge for ourselves, rather than fall into the hands of the Indians. We were to avoid killing women and children as much as possible.

The purpose was to get to the village at daylight and take the Indians by surprise; but it was about 8:00 A.M. when we saw an Indian on a high point riding in a circle—their sign of danger. Then the bugle sounded forward, and away we went. As we neared the village, the command divided, some turning to the right, others to the left. Then for an hour or more was an exciting time. The Indians had some of their tepees down and ponies packed, and some were so heavily loaded that when they tried to run, the packs pulled them over and they lay with their feet in the air.

The squaws, papooses, horses, and dogs were all running to save themselves. As we were armed with Spencer carbines, the firing became lively. The first Indian I saw down was an old man, shot through the body. We learned he was the "medicine man." The Indians ran to a high point and rallied, but they could not stand long before the Spencers. We chased them four or five miles, when our horses began to tire and we gave up the chase. I saw two of the scouts run a redskin back to the rocks, shoot him from his pony, and scalp him, although the order was to do no scalping.

After we gave up the chase and turned back, the Indians turned on us, and as our horses were run down and theirs fresh, they might have cut us off from the rest, if they had tried. They followed us back to the village and got in the brush on the opposite side of the river, but a few shells from the howitzers scattered them.

When we all got together, we found seven had been wounded slightly and one scout had been killed. We learned afterwards that sixty-three Indians were killed and wounded. We found all the jerked buffalo meat we could eat and carry, and it tasted good. After plundering the village and burning the lodges and a great many of the finest buffalo robes I ever saw, we began making preparations for return to camp. Some three hundred horses, mules, and ponies were gathered up and taken to Fort Laramie.

About noon we started on the return, a distance of ten miles, arriving at camp about midnight, tired and sleepy. After a few days we went on, arriving at Laramie October 4, without any trouble, men and horses in good condition, having traveled about eight hundred miles.

An Interview with General Connor

OVANDO J. HOLLISTER[1]

Daily Mining Journal (Black Hawk, Co.), October 20, 1865

DENVER, October 15, 1865
DEAR JOURNAL:
 General Connor and staff came in on Thursday, and a complimentary supper was given him at the Planter's last evening, which wasn't near as dull as it might have been. I cannot detail the proceedings at length. There were a military salute, music, toasts and responses, a dining hall tastily fitted up, tables well-loaded, fair women, brave men, and sparkling wine. It was a spontaneous expression of the feeling of the town and of Colorado toward one of the first of gentlemen soldiers.
 You have doubtless noticed the uncommon-like termination of the late campaign against the Indians. The truth is, rather harm than good was done, and our troops were in one sense driven out of their country by the Indians.
 In the first place, the contract for furnishing supplies for the troops on the plains was loosely made by the War Department, and generals in the field had no control over it. The consequence was that the supplies intended for Connor did not reach Laramie until the expedition had returned to that post. For what he did do, the general stripped the posts along the Overland Route and sent to Denver for supplies. Many of his troops were mutinous, had no heart in their duty, chiefly because they considered themselves entitled to their discharge, the war being over. They were poorly armed. One regiment was sent forward with sabers and a very few revolvers. There was no such number of troops at his disposal as has been reported. Two thousand in all, three-fourths of them, the columns commanded by Cole and Walker, failed for some reason to rendezvous as directed at the Panther Mountains, 375 miles from Laramie, whence it was designed to proceed with pack animals on a sixty-day campaign, this again to be followed by a winter campaign if necessary.

Cole and Walker came across the country from Omaha, struck the Indians on Powder River, and punished them severely. Their force numbered five hundred. Many of their horses had already given out. The grass was very poor, and their stock having to be widely herded, the Indians managed to stampede about a hundred head. A cold rainstorm occurred on September 9, and the stock being weak, from three hundred to five hundred head perished. These columns had orders to proceed due west perhaps fifty miles further, across Tongue River, down which Connor had come with five hundred men to the rendezvous at Panther Mountains on Rosebud Creek, not far beyond Tongue River. Instead of doing so, they sent forward a scout, which proceeded about halfway to Tongue River and then returned, having concluded from the abundance of signs and Indians that Connor was destroyed. These columns then moved slowly up Powder River, the Indians following them two or three days, two-thirds of the command on foot and barefoot at that, and living on mule meat. They were not overtaken by Connor's scouts, four of which were successively sent, the last one consisting of ninety men under Captain Marshall, until within twenty-five miles of Fort Connor, a post established by Connor on Powder River, one hundred miles north of Laramie.

Meanwhile, Connor had proceeded north from Laramie with five hundred men, established Ft. Connor as above stated, gone on north to Tongue River, near the head of which his scouts came across an Arapaho encampment. He started for it in the evening, intending to strike it at sunrise, but it was forty miles distant as it proved, and he did not reach it till long after sunrise. The Indians, meanwhile, having detected his approach, had started their women and children into the mountains, and well mounted and armed, prepared to protect their rear. Connor followed them, skirmishing, for ten miles, until in the ardor of pursuit, nearly all the horses of his command had given out and laid down to die. When he halted, he had with him thirteen officers and ten men. He turned back, and the Indians in turn followed him. He destroyed their lodges and all they had, capturing five hundred head of stock, and proceeded down the river, perhaps a hundred miles.

Here he heard that the Niobrara wagon road expedition, from Sioux City, Iowa, to Gallatin, Montana, had been attacked by the Indians at the crossing of Tongue River near the scene of his recent fight, and he was compelled to detail two companies to escort the expedition through. He also learned, by some means, that these pestilent Arapahos wanted peace. He mounted his captives and sent them back with a pass for the Indians into Fort Laramie. When Connor left that fort, they had not come in. By the way, the Niobrara road is impracticable, according to the experience of these men.

Connor moved down the river to the appointed rendezvous, near the Yellowstone, and waited for his main force to join him. This, we have seen, they did not do. Connor sent three successive scouts to open communication with them, and becoming somewhat alarmed at the nonreturn of the third scout, he ordered Captain Marshall with ninety men to go through at all hazards and express word back.

He now had but 150 men to guard a large train of five hundred head of captured stock, with the Arapahos on his left, the Sioux and Cheyennes on his right, and he knew not what in front. He "bout-faced" and moved slowly up the river, until he learned the condition of Cole's and Walker's commands, when he sped his march to Laramie to find positive orders for the return of his troops to Leavenworth to be mustered out, and his own immediate return to Salt Lake. It may be proper to add that two thousand troops were assigned, in the orders, to Utah, two thousand to Nebraska, and about 1,800 to Colorado, so that we are not left defenseless. About five hundred will be stationed at Fort Connor. These orders of course prevented Connor's proposed winter campaign. His troops killed between three hundred and five hundred Indians, captured five hundred head of stock, and destroyed one village. The Sioux and Cheyennes, like the Arapahos, signified their wish for peace.

It will be seen from the above that the Indians escaped subjugation through circumstances over which Connor had no control. He did all that one could do, more than less than five men of a million would have done. At one time he was in the saddle two nights and one day, riding one hundred miles and fighting Indians twenty of them. This is but a specimen of his exertions throughout the season.

It is the general's opinion that the Indians can be whipped into quiet, and that justice to the western people demands that it be done. With others, he believes the treaty system false in theory and pernicious in practice. By the usages of nations, that civilized people which discovers a savage country owns it [by] virtue of discovery. It is the mingling of the Utopian–William Penn policy with this common sense, and common-law policy that causes all our Indian troubles. The Indians should be made to understand that they are subjects of the United States government, not independent nations. This can only be done by military force, but let them once learn to fear a general, as they do Connor, and they could soon be taught their status. Treaties are of no avail, because the red gentlemen have no systematized government, and no one is certain that the action of a chief, so-called, binds anyone but himself. The treaty is impracticable for any good purpose, proven so a hundred times. Why not abandon it for something equal to the object sought?

In conclusion, I never was better pleased than with the demonstration in honor of General Connor. I met him, myself, yesterday, for the first time, and derived the foregoing account of his operations from his own lips. He impressed me as a man of superior good sense, of uncommon sagacity and persistence, scrupulously honorable, and more tender of the honor of the service, if possible, than of his own; an upright, incorruptible, patriotic man, precisely the one to carry on an Indian war, which is so very liable to abuse by all kinds of jobbers. He does not feel sore over the treatment accorded him, personally, but thinks the policy of the government toward the Indians wrong, and very unjust to the western people. I am sorry he was not better supported during the season. He has an extraordinary prestige with the Indians, and is, without doubt, from that reason alone, the best man in the West to deal with them, whether with the sword or pen.

A Fifteen Day Fight on Tongue River

ALBERT M. HOLMAN[1]

Winners of the West 17, no. 1 (December 1939): 10–12

The story of adventure and exciting experiences of the Sawyers expedition, which traversed the Sheridan country in 1865, is likened unto wild fiction, with harrowing tales of Indian fights, distraction wrought by lack of water, and all the other vicissitudes of an overland trip with a wagon train made up of crude prairie schooners and drawn by the slow and easygoing oxen. At times joy filled the hearts of the men, and then again gloom brought on a terrible despondency. The trials and tribulations suffered by the men in this expedition scarcely recompensed them for the pleasure they had of wonderful fishing and hunting.

In 1912, Mr. A. M. Holman, of Iowa, one of the survivors of this trip, was in Sheridan trying to locate the route taken by the Sawyers expedition and related his experiences as follows:

In 1864, the government appropriated $50,000 for the purpose of finding a shorter route to Virginia City, and to establish an emigrant road connecting Sioux City with Virginia City. J. A. Sawyers was appointed commander of the expedition. On May 1, 1865, he crossed the Missouri at Sioux City, near Yankton, and made the final details of the trip. Included in the overland train were fifteen wagons with three yoke of oxen apiece; eighteen double wagons with six yoke apiece; and five emigrant wagons with three yoke each. The expedition was finally on its way June 13. From the initial starting point, it was on the road for six months, arriving at its destination October 14, 1865.

I was nineteen years of age at the time, and I was employed as a driver of the oxen. Most of the command were young fellows, and we all received a salary of forty dollars a month, with the food and other experience thrown in.

As very little of interest of the expedition up to the time of arriving in this country occurred, I will start with the story after arriving on the Cheyenne. We followed up the North Fork of the Cheyenne River to the Belle Fourche country, and then on to Powder River. In the Powder River brakes, we were first harassed by Indians. Two thousand of the red devils swooped down on us and succeeded in killing three men of the expedition.[2] We were annoyed by them for five days, and finally a peace conference was called. We bought them off by making them a present of a wagonload of food.

We found our way out of the Badlands there through Pumpkin Creek, and proceeded to Fort Connor on Powder River, afterwards called Fort Reno.[3] This location is about twenty miles south of Kaycee. We found that General Connor had left a week before for a stockade on the Bighorn, and it was there that we learned from Captain Kidd, commander of the fort, why the Indians on Powder River had desisted in their attacks and were so ready to make peace. They were being followed by General Connor and his troops and were driven down the Powder River, when they ran into us. The Indians communicated with each other by means of signal smokes, and several nights before the peace conference, we saw the skies illuminated by the fires, and in the daytime, smoke. Their purpose, of course, was mystifying to us until we were afterward acquainted with their method of communication. They were kept informed of the approach of the soldiers, and when their proximity was too close for comfort, they hastily declared peace with our expedition and departed. Connor knew of our coming into the country when he left Fort Laramie, but we didn't know of his presence.

At Fort Connor, we made arrangements with Captain Kidd for an escort of cavalry, and parts of two companies of the Michigan cavalry were detailed to us, consisting of about forty men. They were all fresh from the Civil War and had seen active service of three years on the battlefield. Their enlistment had begun to expire, and they disliked the idea of further service, but finally yielded to the inevitable and accompanied us. They were of little use, as they persisted in hunting along the route and at nights would camp by themselves.

We followed General Connor's trail until it diverged into the Bozeman Trail, the route taking us along the base of the Bighorn Mountains.

The events of the trip were written by myself about twelve years ago,[4] and to my recollection, there were sixty-five or seventy-five men in the party, most of whom were employed in driving the oxen, leaving the expedition without adequate protection.[5] We all carried the old-fashioned Springfield army muskets and revolvers and were fully supplied with ammunition. A six-pound howitzer was also included in our arsenal of defense.

Referring back to the trip in the Powder River country, we had followed the course of the Niobrara for about two hundred fifty miles and took up the North Fork of the Cheyenne River at about the location of Edgemont, South Dakota. After following this dry fork for many miles, we turned westward to the head of the Belle Fourche. Between the Belle Fourche and Powder River, we struck a terrible, rough country, and at one place we were three days traveling thirty-six miles. The fourth morning, we drove the cattle loose to the Powder River, sixteen miles distant, and saved them from dying of thirst. Between the Belle Fourche and Powder River, the distance is about fifty miles.

After we left Fort Connor with our military escort, we were bumping over the country until one day were surprised to meet twenty cowboys, mail carriers for General Connor, who had been attacked by Indians and were retreating. Twenty of our escort reinforced the mounted mail carriers so they could again go to the front and through to their mission.

The soldiers were ordered to keep near the wagon train both day and night, but to no avail. They declared they had seen three years of the battlefield and had no fear of the Indians. Consequently, they employed their time according to their own liking, and many times ignored the protection of their charges.

We passed through this country one-half mile west of Lake De Smet, in Johnson County, fording Little Goose Creek in the neighborhood of the present town of Bighorn and reaching Wolf Creek sometime in August 1865.[6] Captain [Osmer F.] Cole, commanding the company of the 6th Michigan Cavalry, preceded the train on the west, or north side of the river. In company with Lieutenant Moore, he rode up the steep bluff on the west side of the river for a better view of the country and rode into a veritable ambush of Indians. The two officers were confronted by a large force of the painted warriors, and with one volley from their guns, Captain Cole fell from his pony, pierced through the heart by a bullet. The lieutenant retreated down the embankment at a mad gallop and escaped uninjured, though no effort was made by the redskins to overtake him. They were evidently satisfied with one death at this time. The next morning, we broke camp and passed over the scene of the tragedy, between Wolf Creek and Tongue River. The distance between the streams at this point was about two and one-tenth miles. We did not bury Cole's body at this time, but thought it would preserve long enough to have taken it back to Fort Connor for interment.

We knew hostile Indians infested the country and so were guarded against any emergency which might arise, and kept our arms ready for instant use. Upon descending into the Tongue River Valley, we saw smoke from numerous campfires rising slowly from the trees, and from indications there must have been a veritable horde of the redskins. From our previous experience, we knew they were not friendly. We trained our howitzer on a spot where the smoke was the thickest and sent a few shells flying into the camp. The result verified our suspicions, for the Indians literally swarmed from the trees and underbrush. They were arrayed in war paint with feathers, bells, and animal skins for their garb. In a double column, our train forded Tongue River, but this task was so arduous that by the time the last wagon was over, the leading wagons were half a mile in the lead. Forty head of loose oxen were bringing up the rear and were still in the water when the Indians, about one hundred in number and of the Arapaho nation, swooped down on them and succeeded in cutting several off from the train. The wagon drivers couldn't use their guns, as their oxen required their entire attention. We formed an irregular corral with our wagons and took the defense against the Indians, who by this time had been increased to about six hundred. They would ride in circles around our corral and shoot at us from under their horses' necks. All were bareback, and the way they yelled would shame the most ardent football rooters of our big colleges.

The Indians were short of powder, so that [the] force of the bullets was insufficient to inflict dangerous wounds. In fact, the marksmanship of the Indians was good, but their bullets didn't hurt either the cattle or men. Had they used more powder and shot less, they would have done far better execution, and the list of fatalities would have been far more, even making it a doubt whether any of us would have escaped.

The Indians swarmed the dense timber along the river, and toward this point we decided to direct a heavy fire from our baby howitzer. We hauled the cannon to a commanding position and dropped a few shells into their midst. The Indians yelled with rage, and we knew the cannon balls had done execution. The Indians did not retaliate, but started building great fires, and a barbecue of the stock captured from us was soon in progress. We thought the Indians would be appeased for the time being with their bellies full, so we broke corral and in two columns entered the low hills beyond Tongue River.

The Indians divined our motive and attempted to cut off our retreat. From there until we reached the river, it was as pretty a skirmish fight as ever occurred, according to our military escort of twenty soldiers. The Indians attacked us from all sides, but seemed to concentrate their strength on our rear. They poured volleys into the wagon train, but the bullets lacked force, and many of them landed on the hides of the oxen with a thud, but failed to even break the skin. We approached the river farther down than our first fording point. Twenty-five Indians circumvented the train and rode ahead to a vantage point along a high bank. We continued toward this bank in two columns with the bullets flying thick and fast, denoting a much superior force than first opposed us. James Dilliner,[7] driving an oxen team in the lead, was killed by a bullet which struck him in the back, and in a few minutes E. G. Merrill, an emigrant of Sioux Falls, was also killed by a bullet while standing near the wheels of his wagon. Both men were placed in one of the wagons, and as no reserve drivers were in the train, Dilliner's wagon followed along without a guiding hand.

For the fifth time since reaching Tongue River, we made corral, but now we were out of rifle range. This point was between Ranchester and Dayton, about the location of the old Seventy-six ranch, or to others known as the Bingham Crossing. Here sixty canvas-covered wagons were arranged in a large circle, with all the oxen and cattle loose in the enclosure. The Indians were encamped one-fourth of a mile up the river. Both forces held these same positions the second night, and the prospect of avoiding a massacre at their hands seemed very slim indeed.

General Connor, with his troops, was fifty miles away on the Bighorn, and that night Colonel Sawyers offered a liberal reward to anyone who would volunteer to locate him and bring reinforcements. Three men with rations stole away that night on this perilous undertaking.

There was no change of position of the Indians or our wagon train the third day. The weather had turned colder, and a severe storm ensued. The Indians began leaving their camps in large numbers and retreated to the canyon. The stock waded around the enclosure in mud up to their knees, and almost every man in the outfit was benumbed with cold. The night of the third day, one of the drivers was restless while trying to sleep, and he became much annoyed at a steer which kept rubbing its side against his wagon. He gave it a punch with a stick and started it on a frightened run. In return, this steer startled others, and in a few minutes all the animals had joined in the movement, which by this time was a regular stampede. The darkness was intense, and the noise of the bellowing animals sickened one's heart. They broke through the wagons and went on their way. Every man in the train had been sleeping on their arms that night, and so all were up at the first commotion. It was the general impression that the Indians had stolen into the camp and had purposely stampeded the animals. Confusion reigned supreme for some time, and dark figures were seen everywhere scurrying back and forth through the cold and clammy mud. Finally the word passed around explaining the cause of the commotion. Nobody followed the animals. We didn't know where they had gone, and we didn't care. We were all dejected in spirits because of the cold and inclement weather and because we seemed doomed to destruction by the superior force of our enemy.

The next morning, we found our cattle quietly grazing in the timber near the camp vacated by the Indians. They had fled before the storm and had sought a retreat in the Tongue River canyon. We built big fires, warmed ourselves, dried our clothing, and then started westward again with our wagons. What was our dismay on getting several miles out to see the pesky varmints again riding down on us. We prepared for a defense, but on their closer approach, we discerned their white flags waving above their heads.

They were flags of truce, so we quietly let the chiefs of the tribe enter our camp without molestation. They wanted peace, and in talking of the affair, they explained their motive in attacking us. They thought we were soldiers, and as the bluecoats were known to be in the neighborhood against them, they concluded we were but a party of the detachment. Upon learning we were an emigrant outfit, they decided to cease war upon us. While the seven chiefs were parleying in the camp, other Indians would stalk bravely into camp, requesting a word with their chiefs. They tried to deceive us, and the move was a fine piece of strategy on their part. At one time they did succeed in placing twenty-seven armed men inside our corral, and the other three hundred braves were drawn up outside. They had planned to annihilate us with one blow but couldn't succeed in getting the proper number of men into our camp at one time.

Considerable objection had been made to Sawyers, and much grumbling and complaint was heard against him in his treatment of the Indians. He was warned repeatedly not to let the savages enter the camp, but he only ignored these protestations. Finally, an indignation was held of everybody in camp, and with a majority vote of about sixty to five, Sawyers was deposed. By a similar vote, the fate of the seven Indian chiefs held as hostages in our camp was decided, and they were released, together with other Indians who had remained both day and night. They were all told to get out and stay away. Some of [the] boys could hardly refrain from shooting them down for their attempted treachery, but they were finally prevailed upon to allow the red devils their freedom without further trouble.

While in this camp, the bodies of Captain Cole, Dilliner, and Merrill were buried in one grave. The next captain of the expedition used diplomacy in the ceremonies, and kept it a secret, else the remembrances of their tragic death would have caused a revolt against the Indians in camp. On that night, in order that the Indians in our tent would not know what was going on, our fiddler took out his violin and, in front of the tent, regaled them with music. To add further to the amusement and divert the minds of our guests from the real purpose, a number of boys danced cotillions, jigs, and reels. In the center of the corral was a much different scene, for there another group was solemnly digging a grave.

As a successor to Colonel Sawyers, we selected one of our number, a brave and fearless leader, and he followed out the wishes of the majority. We had been in camp for thirteen days, and it was the consensus of opinion of all that we should abandon the remainder of the trip and return to Fort Connor, one hundred miles back. Colonel Sawyers was appealed to, but he was determined to push ahead. We knew well our mutiny against him, and we tried to induce him in another plan, to destroy all but thirteen wagons, as the remainder were only superfluous and burdensome. Seven lives had already been lost on the trip, and it was declared that the train could not proceed in such a country without adequate protection. With the wagons reduced to thirteen, the remaining drivers could act as guards. Sawyers would not counsel such an action, so under the new leader we decided to retreat to Fort Connor and left camp in two columns the next morning on the backward trip. We must have been about ten or twelve miles from Tongue River when we were overtaken by the U.S. Cavalry from General Connor's command on the Bighorn. There were about one hundred mounted soldiers under command of Captain Brown, and most of them had enlisted from California. They were accompanied by a great number of Winnebago Indians under Little Priest, all of whom were allied with the soldiers against the Sioux, Arapaho, and other tribes. The sight of the cavalry and their allies was a most welcome one to us, and their arrival was surely at an opportune moment. They had reached our evacuated camp that morning and had correctly guessed we had turned our steps homeward. By following our trail, they came upon us in time to get a good warm meal. Many a cheer was thrown to the farthest echo of the Bighorn Mountains upon their arrival, and even several of our expedition wept with joy on clasping the hands of the fearless and brave soldier boys. The three couriers sent from our camp several days previously had fulfilled their mission, and they returned as heroes to their comrades. After camping for a day and night, we again turned westward and were escorted to the Big Horn River by Captain Brown and his troops. On Pas Creek, two hundred Indians approached our camp, and seeing our superior numbers, declared their mission to be only friendly. They were supplied with guns and ammunition, and undoubtedly would have attacked a force greatly inferior to theirs. It was with great difficulty that the Winnebago Indians were held in check, as they had sworn vengeance on this very tribe. The captain was forced to point his revolver at Little Priest's head before the Indian ally would give the word to his followers to desist their preparations for a fight.

From the Bighorn, the expedition went through to its destination without encountering additional hostile Indians. The fifteen-day fight on Tongue River was the memorable event of the trip, and everyone of the expedition told the story to astonished people on the safe arrival at Virginia City.

Mr. Sawyers kept an incomplete record of the entire trip and never even mentioned any one of the Indian engagements. He never referred once to the Bozeman Trail, although I am confident we followed the same route selected by Bozeman just the year previous to our trip. I do not attempt to say, however, that our trail was the Bozeman Trail, but I have tried faithfully to locate the trail followed by the Sawyers expedition.

We crossed the Tongue River about September 1, 1865, I believe, just a few days before the memorable engagement of General Connor with the Indians at the grove near Ranchester, in which the Indians were whipped and utterly put to rout with loss of many dead and several wounded. It was in this battle also that the soldiers captured about three hundred head of Indian ponies.

The name of the Indian guide who chose our route from Fort Connor was Estes Desfond, who afterwards appeared with General Crook in the campaign of 1876. He was inexperienced at the time he enlisted with us.[8]

PART TWO

Red Cloud's War, 1866–68

A Bloody Prospecting Trip in the Bighorn Mountains

"W"

[Virginia City] *Montana Post,* October 27, 1866

NEVADA CITY, October 15, 1866

EDITOR *POST*: As I have just returned from a prospecting trip to the Bighorn, a few items incident to it might be of some interest to your readers. In company with four others, I left Helena [on] August 6, and after traveling six days, we reached the Yellowstone River at the Bozeman Crossing, a distance of about one hundred forty miles. We laid over there seven days waiting for a man calling his name Wilson, who had promised before our leaving Helena to meet us at this point. This man had told me that he, in company with three other men, had made a very rich and extensive discovery in the Bighorn country, which was all that prompted me and many of my friends to start on this dangerous trip. But greatly to our disappointment, we learned before leaving the Yellowstone that he was an outrageous impostor; consequently, he did not make his appearance among us. Then, not wishing to turn back, we united ourselves with the Jeff Stanford prospecting party.

Our party by this time had increased in numbers to 115. With this number we considered it tolerably safe for us to prospect either in the Bighorn or Wind River Mountains. After leaving the Yellowstone, we left the emigrant road at our left, taking an Indian trail which followed along at the base of [the] Boulder Mountains. This trail crossed seven or eight quite large streams, some of which were very rocky and rapid. The party along the base of the mountains made short drives, often laying over a day at a place for the purpose of prospecting. Very fine colors only could be obtained there. When the Stanford party had traveled together a distance of one hundred miles, we had arrived at a point where we had to either turn up toward the Wind River or down to the Bighorn. Here the party, all not being of one mind, split. Seventy-five (myself being one of the number) went toward the Bighorn, Jeff Stanford, with the remainder, toward the Wind River.

Chief Red Cloud. W. FLETCHER JOHNSON. *LIFE OF SITTING BULL.*

We were three days making the Bighorn River, after leaving Stanford—a distance of about seventy miles. A good part of this three days' travel was over badlands, which was nearly void of grass or water. We rafted the river just above the canyon, fifty-five miles above Bozeman's Crossing, where Fort C. F. Smith stands. Being above and on the right of the mountain, we concluded to travel and prospect on this side about seventy-five miles, then to cross over and prospect back on the opposite side. No favorable indications for gold being discovered by us on the upper side, we crossed over.

After crossing the mountains, our first camping ground was on Goose Creek, an eastern tributary of Tongue River. It was on this creek, about six miles above the Bozeman Road, and eighteen this side of Fort Phil Kearny, where Col. J. N. Rice and J. W. Smith were so horribly murdered by the Indians. I will here give a few of the particulars of this sad occurrence. We laid over one day to rest our horses, which was September 13. Rice, being very fond of hunting, started out with Smith for that purpose, both taking saddle animals along. Night came without their return. This fact caused us extreme anxiety, for we were aware that we were among a numerous and bloodthirsty tribe of Indians, although up to this time we had seen none, yet many fresh signs had been seen.

On the fourteenth, eight men were sent out in search for the missing, who returned at night without success. A search on the fifteenth proved as fruitless, but about 4:00 P.M., two of our men came in from hunting and reported that down the creek about five miles they had discovered three dead horses, two of which apparently had been killed by Indians. From the description they gave, we were fully convinced that two of them were the horses belonging to Rice and Smith.

Early the next morning, fourteen of us went to the spot, and after a few minutes search found both of their remains, which were lying about three hundred yards from their horses. The third horse we discovered to be an Indian horse. The numbers of pools of blood, pony tracks, and other signs that were visible led us to the belief that quite a number of Indians must have been killed during the struggle. The two bodies were awfully cut up by arrows, four or five of which were still remaining in each. One ball had penetrated Rice's chin; this was the only mark of the kind we discovered on either of the bodies. Both were scalped and laying on their backs. The only part of their clothing missing was their hats. Rice's watch was taken, but three finger rings and a small breastpin were left undisturbed. Their guns, saddles, etc., were of course taken away. Both bodies were wrapped in blankets and buried as decently as possible in one grave.

We discovered a hay party the thirteenth, who informed us that we were about eighteen miles this side of Fort Phil Kearny, a new fort, which had been established a few months. We probably would not have visited this fort had it not been for a sick man who we knew must be taken there. On September 17, he was carried to the fort on a litter, escorted by the remainder of the party.

Fort Phil Kearny is a distributing post, containing about six hundred soldiers. The Indians, since its establishment, have stolen nearly all of their stock, only twenty or thirty poor old horses being left, which were so poor that probably the Indians would not take them.

This fort is about one hundred miles from Fort C. F. Smith, on the Bighorn. Between these two forts we saw countless numbers of buffalo, and as a grazing country, it cannot be excelled. Twenty-six of our party hired out at the fort as an additional escort for a party who were cutting hay for the fort.

For seven or eight days previous, the party had been able to cut no hay, but had constantly been employed fighting Indians. There were about sixty of them, and with the best that they could do, they were not able to prevent the Indians from burning large quantities of hay which had been put up in stacks. Our party, then reduced to sixteen, was too small to undertake the hazardous trip back, but to our great joy, we learned that a mail escort of twenty-six soldiers would leave for the Bighorn on September 20, who were anxious to have us accompany them.[1]

We readily accepted their proposition. Early on the morning we left, a large band of Indians made a raid about the fort and came very near getting all of our stock. But we were lucky in getting around them just in time to save them. A good many of the reds were visible at the time of our leaving, and we were satisfied that they would follow us. Eighteen of the soldiers were mounted, and the remainder started out in an ambulance, which when about twelve miles out broke down, leaving six on foot. This left the escort in an awkward shape for fast traveling and fighting Indians.

About twenty miles out, we met the hay party, with which we camped for the night. Happily for us, the "noble red man," the first day out, did not make his appearance. At daybreak the next morning, we left the hay cutters and came on, intending to make a good drive that day. At 10:00 A.M., we stopped about two hours for breakfast, then traveled till 3:00 P.M., stopping about two hours for supper, after which we continued our journey until 9:00 P.M., when we made a dry camp for the night, it being about forty-five miles beyond Fort C. F. Smith, and four miles beyond the Little Bighorn. Picketing the horses closely together, six men were placed on guard, and the remainder retired to their blankets, without divesting themselves of any part of their clothing. No Indians had been seen after leaving the fort up to this time, but we had not been camped more than an hour when they made a fierce attack upon us with guns. At first, confusion prevailed in the camp to some extent; but we soon rallied and returned their fire, driving them back. Keeping them at a distance, we commenced entrenching. After they were driven off, their fire was not so rapid, and all of their balls apparently passed over our heads. In about two hours, the entrenchments were finished, a little before which time the Indians ceased firing, and nothing more was seen of them during the night.

During the fight, a soldier received a flesh wound in the leg,[2] and one horse was slightly wounded and seven missing. At daybreak, the horses were saddled, and as we were about to leave camp, we discovered that the Indians had completely surrounded us. It appeared at first sight that they were numerous enough to eat us up. Our situation at this time looked critical in the extreme. We had but one show, that was to fight them. A small hill about one hundred yards from our camp was selected for our standpoint. They rode up in the small ravines about us, within four or five hundred yards, and from these places, they evidently intended to pick us off by degrees, until our numbers had become so decimated that there would be but little risk in their making a dash upon us as a finishing stroke.

We remained in one body and fought for about thirty minutes, when we were convinced that some new plan must be adopted or the last one of us would be killed. They were in positions where we could do them but little if any damage, while we were standing in showers of leaden hail. It was plainly to be seen that they must be driven out of the nearest ravines. This, if accomplished, would keep them at a distance where they could do but little damage. Twenty or thirty of them were lodged in a ravine at a distance of about four hundred yards. Eight of our men made a cavalry charge upon them, which came so quick and unexpectedly that they fled in wild confusion. At this charge, we captured two fine horses and wounded several Indians, who were taken up by others and carried off.

After this charge, we were not long driving them out of all the nearest ravines. About two hours after the first attack, they ceased firing, apparently satisfied that they could not whip us. At one time during the fight, we saw from two to three hundred, only a part of them doing the fighting, while the others kept at a distance. The soldier that was wounded the night previous, during the morning fight received another slight wound in the head from a glancing ball. One horse was killed and another wounded. This was all that we were damaged in the morning. Our loss of seven horses left ten or twelve men on foot. The sergeant of the soldiers' escort told us (miners) that if we would throw away our mining tools, provisions, etc., and let the men without horses ride our pack animals to the Bighorn, there was no doubt in regard to our getting enough provisions from the commander of the fort to bring us through. Consequently, our packs were thrown away, which left enough horses for all to ride. As soon as horses were provided for every man we commenced traveling, expecting that the savages would follow us, but fortunately they gave up the chase and no more was seen of them afterwards. We reached the fort that night[3] about 10:00 P.M., nearly chilled through, wet and hungry. A violent storm of snow and rain came upon us about noon that day, which lasted until after we reached the fort.

Fort C. F. Smith has about one hundred and sixty soldiers and is commanded by Brevet Lt. Col. N. C. Kinney.[4] Upon our arrival at the fort, we were kindly received by Captain James Marr and A. C. Leighton (both citizens),[5] who furnished us with good and comfortable quarters. To these gentlemen, we owe an extreme debt of gratitude, for had it not been for them, we would probably have suffered, for instead of being received kindly by the commander, he treated us with the utmost contempt. When we first met him, he was beastly drunk, and the citizens told us that he had been in that condition for weeks. There is one thing certain, that he did not draw a sober breath during the few days that we remained there.[6]

I will state a few of his official acts, in order that the public may know what kind of a man our government has sent to the Bighorn country for the protection of its citizens, among the worst savages of America. After our fight with the Indians, we had to bring along the wounded soldier with us, who, when within twenty-five miles of the fort, had become so exhausted from the loss of blood that he could hardly sit on his horse. The sergeant took five of his men and started on ahead for the fort, for the purpose of bringing back an ambulance for the wounded man. They arrived at the fort near night and immediately asked Captain Kinney for an ambulance for the purpose above stated, which he refused them, although there were plenty of them at the fort. With a great deal of effort and trouble, the man was brought through; he had to be held on his horse the last fifteen miles. A week or two before, two men were attacked and killed by Indians, in sight and within two miles of the fort, who would probably have been saved if the commander had been humane enough to have sent them aid. Their bodies lay where they were killed three days, with the chances of being eaten up by wolves, before they were sent for.[7] I state these two cases in order to show the inhumanity of the commander.

Just before leaving, we asked him for ten days' rations, which we thought would take us to Bozeman City, a distance of 220 miles. He said that he wanted us to stop and work for him, and that if we could not obtain provisions, we would be obliged to stay. He went so far as to threaten to press us, in case we did not choose to stop with him. We were told that our wages would be $40 per month, and we asked if the pay would be in Treasury notes. He answered, "No, government vouchers will be your pay. I have no greenbacks." After finding that he would give us no provisions, we asked him to sell us some. His reply was, "You have come to the wrong market to buy grub." We finally managed to purchase enough of private individuals, and left the fort September 27, in company with six men who had three ox teams. These teams we left the fourth day out, our limited supplies compelling us to travel faster. Being then in the Crow country, we considered ourselves comparatively safe. The Crow Indians pretend to be friendly, but they will steal horses whenever there is a chance.

We crossed the Yellowstone at the Bozeman Crossing on October 3. This crossing is about 155 miles this side of Bighorn River. With one exception, we were not molested by Indians after leaving the Bighorn, which was at our last camp on the Yellowstone. At about eleven that night, we discovered quite a large party skulking about, evidently intent on stealing our stock. As soon as they were discovered, they left in a hurry and were not seen afterward. In conclusion, I will state that we prospected all of the most favorable streams in the Bighorn Mountains for a distance of about one hundred miles, during which time not a respectable color of gold was obtained.

The Forgotten Battalion

WILLIAM MURPHY

Annals of Wyoming 7, no. 2 (October 1929): 383–401

I will give my experiences from the time I left Fort Leavenworth, Kansas, April 7, 1866. We marched to Fort Kearny, Nebraska, arriving there May 15, having marched every day, Sunday included. We passed or were passed by all kinds of rigs going in both directions, but mostly immigrants and bull trains. The immigrants were passing the finest kind of land for farming purposes, but one could travel without seeing a settler's house anywhere after the second day out. Buffalo and antelope were plentiful.

On arriving at Fort Kearny, we were issued two days' rations consisting chiefly of seven hardtack. Each hardtack was about four inches square and three-eighths of an inch thick. The balance of the rations were in the same proportion. The explanation given us was that the quartermaster in charge of the stores of rations had run short. A hungry man could have eaten the entire two rations at one meal and asked for more.

On May 18, I was assigned to Company A, 2nd Battalion, 18th U.S. Infantry. We left Kearny the nineteenth and marched to Julesburg, where we built a scow to ferry across the South Platte River, which was running bank full. On trying out the scow, we found it would not work owing to the quicksand and shallows. In places the water would be only two or three inches deep, while a few feet away there would be seven or eight feet of water. Two of our men got caught in the quicksand and were drowned. We finally crossed by having a long rope stretched from man to man, strapping our guns and equipment to our backs and holding to the rope. Some of the men were up to their armpits in water and some traveled nearly dry shod. We were ordered not to stop for anything, for if we did, we would get stuck in the quicksand.

Nothing more of an exciting nature happened until we passed through Scott's Bluffs. There an eight-yoke bull team stampeded with two wagons loaded with parts and equipment for a sawmill, and ran down a steep hill to the North Platte. I do not believe any of the steers were alive when they got to the bottom of the hill. This sawmill was intended for Fort Phil Kearny and arrived a month or six weeks later. This, of course, delayed us some in building the fort.

At this time, at Fort Laramie, army officers and Red Cloud[1] and his warriors held a council but came to no agreement. The report that we men got was that Red Cloud had issued an ultimatum to the officers that he would kill every white man that crossed the North Platte. At that time, there were Indians—Sioux, Cheyennes, and Arapahos—camping for a mile or two along the North Platte and Laramie Rivers, and the government was feeding them—at least to the point of giving them beef steers to kill. They ate them all but the hides, hoofs, and horns without washing. At that time, we were shown samples of their marksmanship with the bow and arrow. The young boys could hit a button, pencil, or any small article at about thirty yards.

After the council, we left Fort Laramie, crossed the North Platte at Bridger's Ferry, and after that we had a picket line outside of the guards. We kept this up till we built the stockade at Phil Kearny. The order of the day was in putting a guard to work building the stockade, and our barracks then went on picket at night. Every other trick had one night in.

We arrived at Fort Reno about July 1. That afternoon, while the stock were grazing near camp, with some of the mules being picketed, some hobbled, and some being herded by a number of the men, a heavy hailstorm came up with hailstones as large as pullets' eggs. Evidently the mules and horses thought it was no fit country for them. We had had some trouble about an hour previously in getting them to ford the Powder River; but they went back over it as though it were dry land. The animals that were picketed pulled their pins; the hobbled ones and even the stock the herders were riding all stampeded. The herders finally stopped their horses two or three miles from where they started. A company of cavalry from Fort Reno, with the herders, trailed the herd all night, and it was overtaken at Pumpkin Buttes, some forty-five miles from the fort. We got the stock back the next evening. If there had been a few Indians with their spears and buffalo robes, they could easily have had a herd of six or seven hundred head of horses and mules, and it is extremely doubtful if Fort Phil Kearny and Fort C. F. Smith would have been built had this happened.

I was detailed the next day to help load some wagons with provisions from the storerooms at Reno. The warerooms were built of cottonwood logs, chinked and daubed with mud and having dirt roofs. Some of the daubing had dropped out and snow had drifted in. The dirt roofs also leaked and added to the dirty mess. (The soldiers made great improvement in that fort in the summers of 1866 and 1867.) We loaded up some sacks of bacon. I do not know how old it was, but the fat had commenced to slough off from the lean, and it was from three to five inches thick. There was a lot of flour in the storerooms, and the mice had tunneled through it and the bacon, evidently for some time. July 3 was payday and we received four months' pay. There was some bootlegging, but very little drunkenness in those days. One method I saw here for punishing drunkenness was on this day, and one of the worst cases of cruelty I saw in the army. At the guard tent, four stakes were driven into the ground, and the drunken soldier was stretched at full length and tied to them. This was called the "Spread Eagle." The sun was beating down on him when I saw him, and I thought he was dead. Flies were eating him up and were running in and out of his mouth, ears, and nose. It was reported that he died, but in the army one can hear all kinds of reports. I only saw that one case, but heard they started the same thing at Fort Reno a month or two later and caused a riot or mutiny. The commander gave the soldier his discharge as a compromise.

Our next camp was "Crazy Woman"[2] and was reached after marching for twenty-eight miles on a very hot day with no water except what we carried. The water was found to be very bad after we reached the North Platte, with the exception of one camp—I believe they called it Brown's Springs. Most of the water was impregnated with alkali, which had a bad effect on lots of the men. Many of the soldiers had bad feet, owing to being forced to wear woolen socks in the hot weather, but no other kind was issued. Add to this the fact that there was only one ambulance available for sick soldiers, as the women and children had all the others in use, and you have a picture of what it meant for a soldier to be sick.

After crossing Crazy Woman, we found a wide bottomland on the north side and the road entered a long ravine, coming out on top of the divide going towards Buffalo Wallow.[3] This was a bad place, and the Indians killed several people there during our stay in the country, stripping, mutilating, and scalping the bodies. They may still be buried there, as we dug holes along the side of the road and then dropped the bodies in, covering them with rocks when possible to keep the wolves and wolverines from digging them up. Sometimes an Indian would dig up the body and drag it down the road.

The next bad place was Buffalo Wallow. Several were killed there—immigrants, citizens and soldiers. We buried them as described above, and at every campground from C. F. Smith on, there are one or more bodies. Buffalo Wallow and Crazy Woman, however, were the two worst places between Fort Reno and Fort C. F. Smith. We arrived at the forks of the Big and Little Piney [Creeks] July 13 or 14. For some reason, they picked out a location about seven miles from the timber and from five to eight miles from any hay bottom. A federal judge who had been a judge of one of the territories was with us. I believe he had something to do with the selection of the location of the fort, as he and his partner had a bull train. There was a man who was surely "on to his job." He was a good diplomat. He made love to men, women, and children and lived at the fort most of the time. His partner ran the teams.

About the middle of July, Phil Kearny was staked out. Up to July 17, we hadn't seen an Indian and had commenced to think the threat of Red Cloud at Fort Laramie was just a bluff, but the rest of that summer, from July 17, 1866, and continuously thereafter until July 14, 1868, he was on the job. There was hardly a day passed at Phil Kearny, up to December 21, 1866—the date of the massacre—that we did not see Indians, and the others at Fort Reno and C. F. Smith had about the same experience. The usual order of the day was to make a forced march to the relief of some immigrant or freight train. In most cases,

Red Cloud's War, 1866–68   67

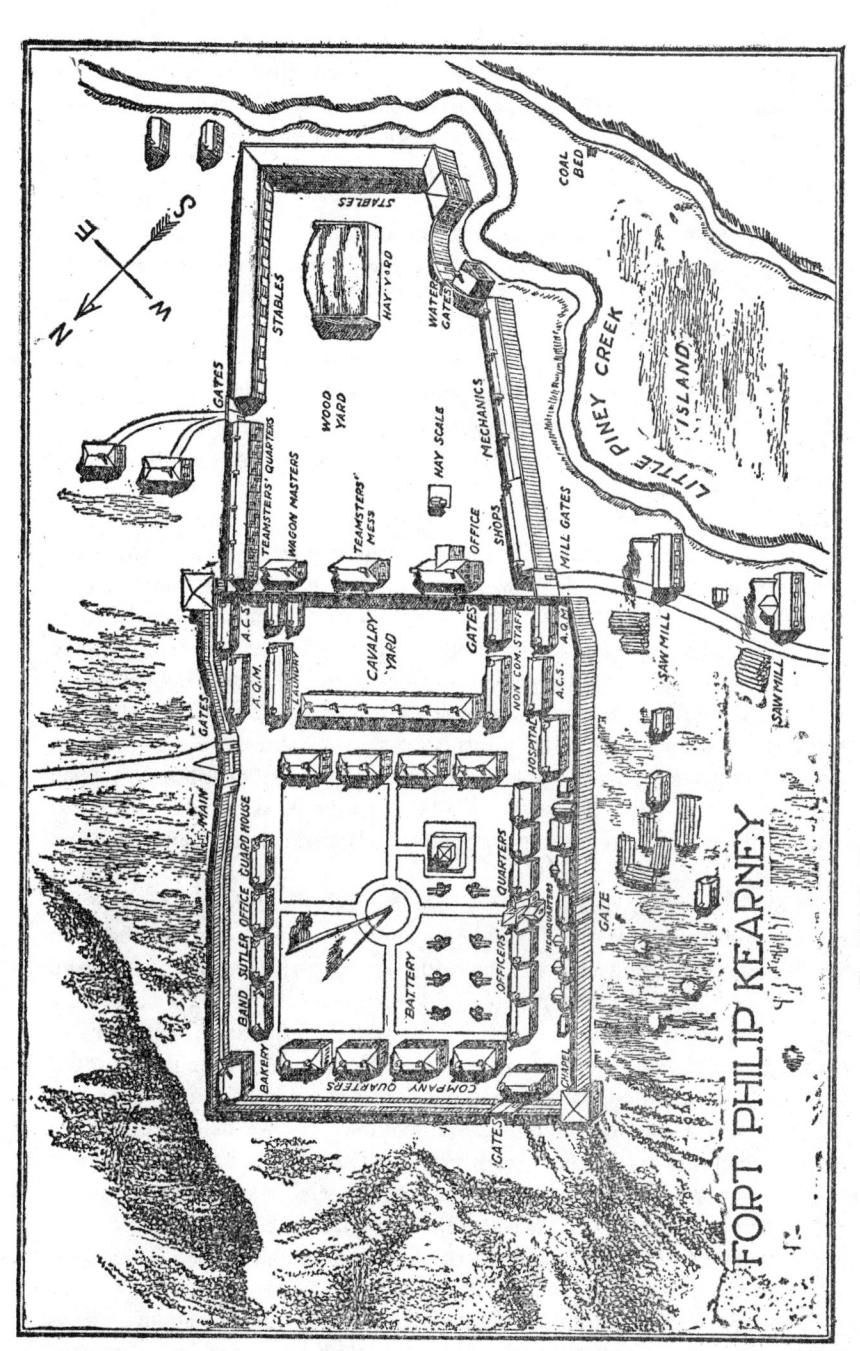

Fort Philip Kearny. CYRUS T. BRADY. *INDIAN FIGHTS AND FIGHTERS.*

the Indians had taken their toll and gone before we arrived. On July 17, the Indians killed an Indian trader at Peno Valley, about four miles north of Phil Kearny. The Indians killed "French Pete" Gayzous and his five men, ransacked his wagons, and stripped, scalped, and mutilated the men. He was married to a Sioux squaw. She hid in the bushes until the soldiers rescued her. She was at the fort for about two months and left one night.

The same day, the Indians ran off what we called our "dead herd." They were mules and horses that had sore necks, sore backs, or were crippled. Some were crippled at the stampede a few days before. It took several men all day to drive them from one camping ground to another fifteen to twenty miles away. That day also three men were wounded and two killed. One man—John Donovan, of my company—was wounded twice, once with a poisoned arrow. One of the men received an arrow wound and another a bullet wound. When the herd stampeded, they ran across the Pineys, and we could scarcely see them for the cloud of dust they raised. The mounted men followed until nearly dark but only found four dead animals.

About July 20, Orderly Sergeant Lang of my company and I bought two fresh cows from an immigrant train. No one wanted to work in the kitchen, so I volunteered in order to be able to take care of the cows morning and evening. It was not known that I had any interest in the cows, or it might have caused some trouble. We had a first-class baker in the company who volunteered to do the baking and cooking. At that time, the government did not furnish cooks or bakers. They simply furnished the rations, and the soldier could cook them himself or eat them raw if he saw fit. They furnished no vegetables. We cooked soup, bacon, and coffee and dished it out to the men in their cups and plates—we had no dining room. We boiled everything. I believed the bacon would have killed the men if it had not been thoroughly boiled. As it was, it surely came near to it that winter.

During the winter of 1866 and 1867, the bacon and flour I had seen at Reno was given to us. The flour had been hauled sixty-five miles and handled several times. The result was that the refuse left by the mice was well mixed with the flour, and we found a number of dead mice in it also. As we could not get a sieve, we manufactured one out of a burlap sack by pulling out some of the strings and nailing it on a wooden frame. We got most of the larger refuse out. The bacon, where the fat had commenced to slough off from the lean, was yellow with age and bitter as quinine. Some of the worst we shaved off, but we could not spare too much. One reason why our rations were so scanty was that flour was worth $100 per sack and bacon, coffee, and beans proportionately. The companies of those times had no quartermaster or commissary sergeants, and two or three men would be detailed to go and get the rations. They were piled out in a heap and you could take them or leave them.

At this time, the 2nd Battalion of the 18th Infantry was divided up by leaving two companies at Fort Reno to relieve two volunteer companies. Four companies went sixty-five miles north of Reno and built Fort Phil Kearny. Two companies went ninety miles farther north and built Fort C. F. Smith on the bank of the Bighorn, which left four companies at Phil Kearny.[4] I was among those left at this place. We started in building the Fort Phil Kearny stockade, which was six hundred feet by eight hundred feet. The logs were set three feet in the ground, projected eight feet, and were hewed on two sides to a touching surface. We built quarters for the officers, warerooms, sutler's store, guardhouse, stockade for the mules, and quarters for the men. There were approximately 250 men at the fort, but I could not vouch for the exact number. I was a member of Company A, of forty-eight men. Company K was the largest and had about sixty-five men, if I remember correctly. Some time after we established the fort, Company C of the 2nd U.S. Cavalry arrived with some sixty men, which made about 300, all told. Some reports stated that we had mounted infantry, but that was a mistake. They were about thirty men who were detailed out of the infantry company at the fort.

On December 6, 1866, the wood train was attacked. In itself, this was nothing unusual, as it was an everyday occurrence. Colonel Carrington,[5] with Company C of the 2nd Cavalry and some mounted men, went to its relief. The Indians retreated and crossed the Pineys, and Carrington followed them and was nearly trapped. This was two or three miles north of where the massacre occurred December 21st, following. It was at this time that Lieutenant Bingham[6] and Sergeant Bowers were killed.[7] Carrington himself had charge of the command. Bingham was on the skirmish line and was on the right flank with Sergeant Bowers and John Donovan. Carrington saw his danger and had the recall sounded. That left Lieutenant Bingham, Sergeant Bowers, and John Donovan cut off by the Indians. They dismounted for a short time, but decided that their only chance was to run the gauntlet, as their commander had retreated to a higher point. Lieutenant Bingham and Sergeant Bowers were pulled off their horses by the Indians. John Donovan was armed with a Colt army revolver and a single-shot Star carbine using a copper cartridge, the same as a Spencer carbine. The revolver, he told me, was all that saved him when the Indians were on each side of him trying to pull him off his horse, for just in the nick of time, he shot one on each side. He was a bunky of mine and a good man and was a Civil War veteran. We both belonged to the same company, 2nd Battalion, 18th U.S. Infantry. He told me that Bingham was unarmed except for a cavalry saber.

THE PHIL KEARNY MASSACRE, DECEMBER 21, 1866

We had a fine fall, with cool nights, and on this day the wood train left as usual, about 7:00 A.M., to go to the timber. As I remember, we mounted guard as usual at 8:00 A.M. I was in the orderly-sergeant's office, giving him the money for the milk, when the Orderly gave him the order to have Company A go to the relief of the wood train. They "fell in" in front of our quarters, which was the men's northwest quarters of the garrison. The main gate was at the north end of the stockade. The road ran by the west end of the quarters and passed by the adjutant's office and all officers' quarters, to the government storerooms and into

70 EYEWITNESSES TO THE INDIAN WARS

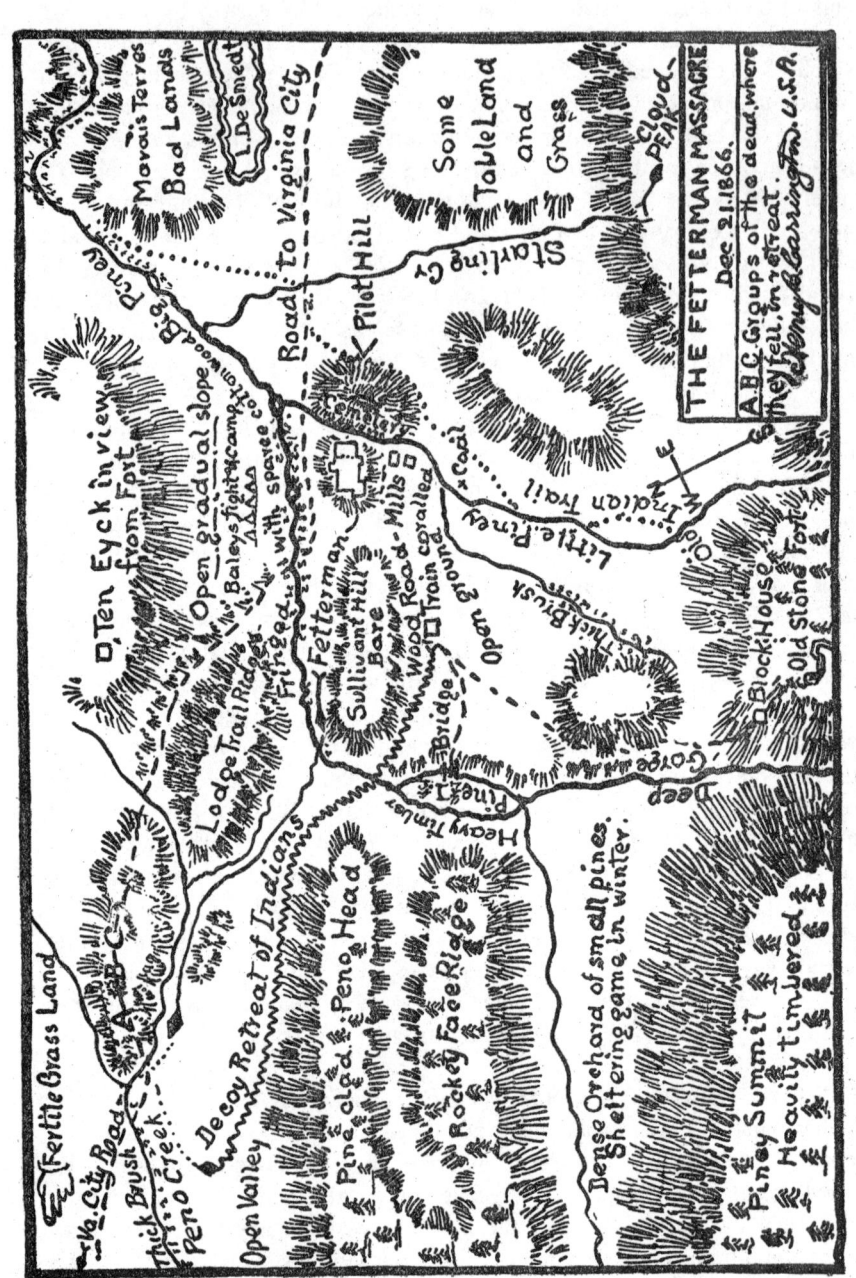

The Fetterman Fight. CYRUS T. BRADY. *INDIAN FIGHTS AND FIGHTERS.*

the stock corral. The bastion of the stockade was at least two hundred feet from where the men fell in in front of the quarters. I was standing right there and saw the men start on a double-quick and go up over Sullivant Hills. From the position of the troops, the guard could not have heard any command given, for he would have had to hear the command through the buildings. Captain Fetterman[8] was the captain of Company A.

I did not see the mounted men go out. They never passed through the main fort, but went out either the east or the west side of the stockade where the stock was kept. At the noon hour, we could hear volleys plainly, and they continued for a long period of time. About two or two-thirty, Colonel Carrington ordered reinforcements of about forty-five men under Captain Ten Eyck[9] to go out. They went at a double-quick, or as fast as they could, until they came to the crossing of the Big Piney. Cool nights had caused ice to form on the edges of the stream, but this stream was hard to cross at any time of the year. The men had to remove their shoes and stockings to get across.

At that time, Colonel Carrington's orderly, a man by the name of Sample, met the reinforcements and told Captain Ten Eyck that the men were all dead and that the Indians were all over the ground where the men had been. Some of the men said that this was Sample's second trip out with information. I could not say, as I saw him out once for certain. In reply to this, Captain Ten Eyck said that there were not enough Indians in the country to kill the men. He advanced along the road with a few men on each side on the ridges as skirmishers. When they got to the top of the divide which separates the Piney Creeks from the Peno Valley, where the men had been stationed, they found that the Indians had withdrawn from where they had massacred the soldiers and seemed to be rehearsing the battle. They were shooting, shouting, and charging up and down the hill over and over again. I suppose the hill must have been as much as a mile away from where the men were massacred.

Our first thought was that the battle was still going on, but a man from my company by the name of McLain, who had been with the haying party and was familiar with the road, said, "There are the men down there, all dead." Sure enough. There was at that time a large stone that had the appearance of having dropped from a great height and thereby split open, leaving a space between the pieces men could pass through, which made a good protection for a small body of men, I should say for about twenty-five or thirty. Around this rock was where the main body of the men lay. There were just a few down on the side of the ridge north of the rock, not more than fifty feet from the main body. Along down the ridge, farther north and east, we found the bodies of Captain Brown, the two citizens, [James S.] Wheatley and [Isaac] Fisher, and also a man of my company by the name of Baeber. They were scalped, stripped, and mutilated. They must have put up a hard fight, as they were all armed with breech-loading rifles, and a lot of empty shells lay all around. The Indians had given Baeber an extra dose. It looked as though they had first stripped him and then filled his body with arrows, as they were sticking out of him all over like porcupine quills. He had straight black hair and looked something like an Indian himself. He had passed through the Civil War, as had three-fourths of the men that were killed. In some reports of the massacre, it was stated that the men were ambushed, but looking over the ground, anyone could see, and can now see, that they had a very good position for the arms that were used in those days. There was no stampede or ambush.

Colonel Carrington sent two empty wagons and an ambulance, and possibly one box of ammunition of one thousand rounds (certainly not more than that). These conveyances were used in bringing in the dead. There was not even one load (twenty thousand rounds) in the three forts. They started out with twenty rounds each and undoubtedly used some of this on their detail work before the massacre. We had known for a long time that we were short of ammunition.

On the ground around the rocks, there were thousands of arrows, a lot of which were picked up by our men.

It was customary, I understood, to have the guards have target practice when they came off guard, but our guns were loaded when we got into the Indian country and were kept so. We had no target practice of any kind. At the time of the massacre, they tried to show that Captain Ten Eyck showed cowardice and took a roundabout way, but this was not true. One thing was sure about Ten Eyck—there was no cowardice in his makeup. He could not have taken a roundabout way if he wanted to do so, as his command was in plain sight of the fort. There was an Indian riding around near where the bodies of the dead were lying. He hollered for the men to come down. Captain Ten Eyck told some of the men to go down and load the wagons and ambulances with the bodies. All of the bodies were stripped, scalped, and mutilated, with the exception of two who were not scalped, but the Indians had drawn a buffalo bag over their heads. We returned to camp without firing a shot. It was dark when the forty-five men under Captain Ten Eyck returned to the fort.

At the fort, all was excitement. The magazine at the fort was a half dugout located on the parade grounds. The men worked all night there building a stockade all around it with green planks and putting water and provisions inside in case of a siege. The next afternoon, Colonel Carrington with about fifty men went after the balance of the bodies. They dug a long trench and put two or three bodies into each box.

A day or two after the massacre, the weather turned bitterly cold, and the men were badly frozen trying to bury the dead. There was a heavy fall of snow, which drifted the roads and ravines badly. The master of transportation had left sometime in November, and with him in his pockets went the money for our supply of wood and hay. It was reported that he went to Canada. We had to go seven miles for pine wood for the officers. The men got green cottonwood from the Piney bottoms and fed the tops to the mules. The poor mules ate holes through the logs in their stables. We had to go to Reno, sixty-five miles away, for corn. The snow was very deep, and it took several days to make the trip. The men suffered terribly, as there was no shelter for men or mules and they were three or four nights out on the road. The mercury dropped to twenty-five and forty below zero and kept that way for about six weeks. Our shoes were made of cheap split leather, and the shoddy clothes that were furnished at that time were not any protection. One thing in our favor was that after the first few days' storm, we had very little wind. Burlap sacks were at a premium and saved our lives. We wrapped them about our shoes to keep from freezing, for there were no overshoes or rubbers to be had at the fort. A few years later, soldiers were furnished fur overcoats and overshoes. Sometime [on] the 1st of January reinforcements arrived, marching on foot from Fort Laramie. They had had to shovel snow all the way. Their arrival made our conditions, if anything, worse, for they had no provisions and no feed for the stock. Two companies of cavalry that came to the relief of the fort returned at once to Fort Laramie. They had brought some extra ammunition with them, which we needed badly. Most of the men were badly frozen.

In the early spring, we were issued some cornmeal, ground at the fort. We were not as badly off as the men at Fort C. F. Smith. They were abandoned from the middle of November 1866 until March 1867, and corn was about all they had to eat. I am of the opinion that the officers thought that the men were all killed at the time of the massacre and no one was left. We didn't have a stick of wood three days after the massacre. The slabs from the mills were used in roofing the barracks, and these were all covered with dirt except the officers' quarters and all of the buildings in the stock stockade. The cull slabs were used by the mills to keep up steam. The wood and hay all went to Canada with the master of transportation. About March 1, two sergeants—two men that should have monuments, but forgotten—volunteered to go to Fort C. F. Smith and see what had become of the men there. The snow was very deep, and they went on snowshoes. They finally returned, bringing some Crow Indians with them and a lot of mail packed on dogs. The men at all three forts were out of tobacco, and some of them seemed to miss that as much as their rations.

In the spring of 1867, Col. John E. Smith[10] arrived with recruits. They had been snowed in all winter on the Platte River where Fort Fetterman was built later. After his arrival, there was a great change at the fort. Men up to this time had worked at all kinds of work. There were all kinds of mechanics in the army, and they had built the fort, driven teams, etc., but had had no drill or target practice. Colonel Smith put all extra men working at extra pay at thirty-five cents per day. We had target practice for the first time. This was expensive, as the government charged twenty-five cents per cartridge to the men if they were short. We received a couple of orders from Omaha, Nebraska, Department of the Platte, never to shoot at an Indian until he shot at you. It was undersigned by General Cooke.[11] He wanted us to save the ammunition, I suppose.

The spring of 1867 also was the time the effects of the spoiled flour and bacon showed up. All of the men that were at the fort at the time it was established got the scurvy. Some lost their teeth and some the use of their legs. In the spring when the grass came up, there were lots of wild onions, and the scurvy gang was ordered out to eat them. The writer had to get out on his hands and knees for some time, and then the general order came not to let the men dig onions, as some of them at Julesburg had been poisoned, but we went out just the same. We thought we might just as well die at once as to die by inches. The government carried these men on the roll until their time was up. There were several of my company discharged at Omaha on March 1, 1869. In this way they avoided the necessity of giving a pension, as would have been compulsory if let out as they should have been. I remember one man they gave a "Bobtail" discharge to because he got drunk a few days before his time to be discharged. I do not know what became of him, as both of his legs were as stiff as posts from the hips down. A lot of men who should have been discharged for disability were thus carried or gotten rid of by some other means and did not get the pension they were justly entitled to.

At Omaha Barracks, I saw another cruelty similar to the one I saw at Phil Kearny in 1866. A member of Company C had broken some of the rules, just what I do not know now, if I ever did. His head was shaved and he was branded with a hot iron and drummed out of the army. At that time, it was suicide to go a mile from the fort, for the Indians watched the road constantly, but this did not seem to matter. The day for carrying out the penalty had arrived, so he was drummed out. About that time, there was a bull train coming in, and I suppose they picked him up. I had thought that this custom was just a way the officers of Fort Phil Kearny had of punishment, but by February or March 1869, there had been four or five men drummed out of the Omaha Barracks. In each instance, the men were branded with a hot iron, their heads were shaved, they were marched around the fort with a fife and drum playing "Poor Old Soldier," and then drummed out. (The cruelty was not all practiced by the Indians.)

Brig. Gen. Philip St. George Cooke.
BATTLES AND LEADERS OF THE CIVIL WAR.

Colonel Smith was a strict officer, but he was just. Our rations were better and things went along smoother. After the massacre, the Indians did not show up again until sometime in May, owing to the condition of their ponies, I suppose. They then commenced to attack the trains again, but we had more men to guard them by that time. In the summer of 1866, a detail of about seven men was the limit. In the summer of 1867, it was about twenty men.

THE WAGON BOX FIGHT

About July 1, twenty men were detailed from Company A to guard the Gilmore and Porter bull train.[12] They had the wood contract and had established their camp about six miles from the fort. They used only the running gear to haul the logs on, so used the wagon boxes to form a corral about two or three hundred yards from the timber. The logs were hauled out to the corral, and the teams circled around the corral, and some loaded and some hauled logs and top-loaded at the corral. They could haul a full load from the corral to the fort, but only a small load out of the timber. These logs were some sixteen to eighteen feet long. August 2, the day of the fight, the Indians charged up to these wood piles, which were fifteen or twenty feet from the corral. The wagon boxes were of the "Prairie Schooner" type, about five feet high, with an extra board about fourteen inches high to go on top of the boxes. These wagon boxes had no lining whatever.

On July 31, the Indians had tried to drive off the cattle that were grazing between the Pineys about a mile from the foot of the mountain. They tried to stampede the cattle, but the men at the corral ran out on each side and stopped the cattle. The Indians tried hard to get a civilian by the name of Brown.[13] Some of the soldiers at the corral managed to give the Indians a hot time, and several were hurt before they abandoned the idea and picked up their men. A boy about fifteen years of age was with the civilian and hid in the brush and was not injured. Both this man, Brown, and the boy were in the Wagon Box Fight, the only civilians in the fight.

I was with a detail of six men and a corporal guarding a train a mile or so from the Gilmore and Porter train. We saw the skirmish, but took no part in it. The corral was burned the day of the Wagon Box Fight, and the Indians followed the men to the timber and tried to burn up some of the oxen. They fastened them to trees, but only killed five or six head. During the years we were there, the Sioux Indians never followed the men into the timber, but seven men were killed by the Blackfeet Indians in the timber.

It was on July 31 that Company C relieved twenty men of Company A. Company C was a strong company, and Colonel Smith knew the Indians would be after revenge. About 8:00 A.M. August 2, the men on the picket hill saw a large body of men (Indians) on the east side of the Big Piney and signaled the fort. The picket hill was south of the fort, and one could see all over the valley and watch the wagon corral and the men from the time they entered the timber or came out and all the way down to the fort. The men at the corral saw the Indians about the time the picket did. They cut portholes through the unlined wagon boxes, scattered the ammunition along the boxes, removed the end gates so they could move freely around the circle, and piled ox yokes and logs at the two ends of the corral, which was circular in form. Smith immediately called out most of the available men to go to their relief, and though he had been sick for some days, he went with his men as far as the foot of Sullivant Hill. The relief got there in time, and the men at the corral were surely glad to see them. They were a hard lot to look at. The day was hot and the sun was beating down upon them in the wagon beds. The smoke from their guns had colored their faces, and they looked as though they had used burnt cork on their faces. Red Cloud was fooled this time. Red Cloud with three thousand warriors could not defeat thirty-eight men.[14]

Up until about June 1, we had been armed with the old Springfield muzzle-loading rifles. The men at the wagon bed were armed with needle guns, single shot, using a copper cartridge. They were good for eight to ten shots, and after that it was necessary to eject the shell with a ramrod, as the ejector cut a groove in the rim of the cartridge. There were thirty-eight men in the corral, and the Gilmore and Porter men that the soldiers were guarding were in the timber—some fifty or sixty men, soldiers and civilians. The Indians did not molest them.

In the summer of 1867, the government built a log cabin some three hundred yards from the fort and on the banks of the Big Piney, also a footbridge for the Indians to cross. There were about two thousand Crow Indians on the east side of the Big Piney. About the same time that the Indians came, there were six government mule teams that arrived with goods for the Indians. There was an Indian agent at the fort whom we called Doctor. I will not give his name, for he is now gone where all good preachers go. The soldiers guarded the cabin, the agent, and his goods. We also had a guard on the end of the footbridge to keep the soldiers from visiting the Indians. The Indians had also put a guard on their end of the bridge to keep the Indians from crossing the Piney.

We thought the goods were to be given to the Indians, but judging from what I saw, the Indians paid several times the value of what they got. For a folding pocket glass about three inches across, a beaver skin or two buckskins was the price. The goods consisted of beads, calico, blankets, and all kinds of trinkets that an Indian would like. Our interpreter, John Sted, was busy for about ten days. The mule teams went back loaded with furs. When the Doctor got back to Omaha, he published a long article in an Omaha paper, stating that a foreigner could travel anywhere on the plains and not be molested by the Indians. I noticed, however, that he had a guard of twenty men all the way to Fort D. A. Russell.

The Crow Indians were not very well pleased with the treatment they had received, and the young ones got quite ugly. When they went away, they passed by Gilmore and Porter's wood train and helped themselves to what they wanted. They got a pile of oxbows, and two of the Indians would pull to see if they could pull it straight without breaking it. The bows were of good hickory, but owing to the dry climate, some of them broke, which made Mr. Porter angry, and he knocked one of the Indians down with one of the broken bows. The Indians then went away. It seemed that they wanted the bows to make a bow.

There were Indian camps scattered about along the Piney all the time after the first winter. The old squaws were inveterate beggars and a hard-looking lot. They were dirty, their hair was matted, and most of them had nearly all of their fingers cut off. I thought at first that they were frozen off, but later learned that this was the way they mourned for their dead. I still believe that they were frozen off, as they were beasts of burden, packing wood through the snow, sometimes for long distances, and with poor tools with which to cut the wood. The men folks and younger squaws burned the wood as fast as they could get it in the wintertime.

Iron Bull was the war chief of the Crows at that time and ruled with an iron hand. Colonel Smith asked him to keep the Indians at their camp. He put a guard at the east end of the bridge, but some of them would ford the Piney and get into the fort. The Indian police, armed with rods six or seven feet long, would get after them, and if they caught any of the squaws or bucks, would give them a good flaying. I saw one Indian at our quarters whom the Indians had whipped with their switches. He got angry, and as he had smuggled a bow and arrow, he stood them off. One of the police hunted up a chief. When the chief got there, he hit the troublesome Indian on the head with his tomahawk, and he was a good Indian, maybe ever after. The Indians dragged him off to their camp.

One day when the Indians were trading at the cabin, they tied an Indian to a tree, and the squaws and children with switches, sticks, and stones punished him severely. I only saw the last part of the show. The Indian broke loose, and the squaws and children scattered. After knocking over some squaws, he lit out over the bluff with very little, if any, clothing. At first we thought he was a Sioux or a Cheyenne prisoner until we saw his head. He had the hair trim of a Crow Indian. We inquired of several Indians as to what he had been doing, and finally one said, "He heap bad Indian. He never come back." The Indian men were looking on but took no part in the performance, unless perhaps they had tied him to the tree.

When the Crows were at the fort, they would hold war dances lasting most of the night. When a war party got to camp, we could tell by the action of the squaws what success they had had. Sometimes the squaws would go up over the bluffs crying. Some may not understand how they scalped the dead. The ran a knife around the edge of the hair and took off all the scalp. Some tribes cut the scalp up in small pieces and braided it in with their own hair, making a "scalp lock." They then are, in their own estimation, heap brave and look pretty, and they smell, oh, so sweet!

The summer of 1867, the 2nd Battalion 18th U.S. Infantry became the 27th U.S. Infantry, and that year a treaty was made with the Indians for the abandonment of Forts Reno, Phil Kearny, C. F. Smith, and the Bozeman road. The Indians were not to molest us and were to be peaceable, but that made no difference to Red Cloud or Spotted Tail. They were never known to keep a treaty.

The great game country along the Bozeman Trail was a myth. All the time we were in that country, I do not believe I saw more than a hundred buffalo. It was a fine grass country; however, I only speak of the country along the Bozeman Trail. There may have been buffalo east of that where Campbell and Crook Counties are now.

About June 1, Colonel Smith was called east, and Captain Hart[15] had command. He was a good man.

We asked Jim Bridger[16] how the Indians lived in the winter, and he replied that only for their ponies and dogs many of them would starve. Some of them also went to the government posts. It has been said that Red Cloud was a great warrior. Here is a typical example of his actions: The picket hill at Fort Phil Kearny overlooked the fort, and one could see a man with the naked eye and could count all the men in the post. The Indians, however, had field glasses and spy glasses so they could easily count the men. After the pickets retired for the night, the Indians would get on the picket hill and copy all of our signals for the enjoyment of those in the fort. After the massacre, we had not more than a hundred men, sick and wounded included, while Red Cloud had six or eight thousand men. The Crow Indians told us the next summer that at the time of the massacre, Red Cloud got his warriors together to take the three forts, changed his mind, and decided to take Phil Kearny first, then divide his warriors and massacre the troops at Fort C. F. Smith and Fort Reno, but the eighty-one men put up such a stiff fight he gave it up as a bad job. Think of it—eighty-one men were too tough to be palatable for Red Cloud and six thousand warriors!

We abandoned the three forts about the middle of July 1868 and marched to Fort D. A. Russell. After living so long away from where there were any vegetables, and having a lot of cripples with the scurvy, we thought the government would furnish vegetables, but not one vegetable did we get. The men chipped in mostly and traded bacon, coffee, and flour for vegetables. During the three years I was in the army, the government never furnished us with any vegetables. Ours was indeed a "forgotten battalion."

Cold Cheer at Fort Kearny

GEORGE WEBER[1]

National Tribune, October 21, 1897

The rescue of the bodies of Fetterman's command, and the incidents of the day at Fort Phil Kearny immediately after the massacre, are worthy of a story of themselves. With the next morning [December 22, 1866] came a meeting of officers, with universal disinclination, generally expressed, to venture a search for the dead. The safety of any small party seemed doubtful, and the post itself might be imperiled by a large draft upon the garrison.

But the colonel had made up his mind and freely expressed his purpose not to let the Indians have the conviction that the dead could not be brought in. Captain Ten Eyck, Lieutenant Matson,[2] and Dr. Ould went with the party. Long after dark they left. The pickets which were distributed on the line of march indicated their progress, and showed that neither the fort nor the detachment could be threatened without such connection of signals as would advise both, and secure cooperation.

Near midnight, the wagons and command returned with the bodies, slowly passing to the hospital and other buildings made ready for their reception. A careful roll call of the garrison was had, and the body of every missing man identified.

Wheatley and Fisher, the frontiersmen, had been discovered near a pile of rocks, surrounded by cartridge shells, proving that their Henry rifles had done good service. All the bodies had lain along or near a narrow divide, over which a road ran,[3] and to which, no doubt, the assailed party had retreated when overwhelming numbers bore down upon them.

Fetterman and Brown[4] had been found at the point nearest the fort, each with a revolver shot in the left temple, and so scorched with powder as to leave no doubt that they had shot each other when hope had fled.

Captain Brown's repeated dashes, and especially his success on September 23,[5] had inspired him with perfect recklessness in pursuit of Indians. On the night before the massacre, he had declared that he must have one scalp before leaving for Laramie, whither he had been ordered. He had inspired Fetterman, who had been but a short time in the country, and already had great contempt

79

for our adversaries, with the same mad determination to pursue the redskins whenever they could, regardless of numbers. Together they had planned the expedition of a week's time to the Tongue River Valley, with a mixed party of ninety citizens and soldiers, to destroy the Indian villages and clear out all enemies. Disapproval of the plan did not change their belief in its feasibility and wisdom; but now [there] were eighty-one officers and men, among them the veterans of a long war, utterly destroyed in their hands, only six or seven miles on the route to the same Tongue River Valley.

The dead were deposited in the spare ward of the hospital, two hospital tents, and a double cabin. Details from each company assisted in their care and identification. Many gave their best uniforms to clothe decently their comrades, and the good traits of the soldier were touchingly discussed as mutilated fragments were carefully handled, arrows drawn or cut out, and the remains composed for the burial. A long line of pine cases, duly numbered, were arranged by companies along the officers' street, near the hospital, and as each was placed in its plain receptacle, the number and name was taken for the future reference of friends.

The detail to dig a grave for this great entombment was well armed and accompanied by a guard, but so intense was the cold that constant relays were required. Over the great pit, fifty feet long and seven feet deep, a mound was raised. Then the ceremonies were performed. From the very night of December 21, the winter became unmitigated in its severity, requiring guards to be changed at least half-hourly, preventing out-of-door inspection, and driving officers, privates, and women to beaver, buffalo, or wolf skins for protection from the cold. The relief, as they hastened to their regular distribution, presented no bad idea of Lapland or Siberian life. The tastes, workmanship, and capital of the wearers were variously illustrated in their personal wardrobes.

The holidays were as sad as they were cold. Lights were burned in all quarters, and one noncommissioned officer was always on duty in each building, so that in case of alarm there could not be an instant's delay in the use of the whole command. Each company knew its place and the distribution of the loopholes. The gunners slept in tents near their guns, and all things were ready for attack. The constant and drifting snow soon lifted itself above the west flank of the stockade, and when a trench ten feet wide was cleared, the next snow would fill it.

The whole garrison shared the gloom. Charades, tableaux, the usual muster evening's levee at the colonel's, and all the holiday reunions were dropped as unseasonable and almost unholy. It was truly a depressing period.

The massacre proved the wisdom of a settled policy not to precipitate or undertake a general war while there was but a handful of men at the post, and the army had not yet received such increase as could promise any considerable support. Kind providence spared many, and the line of road opened in the summer of 1866 was maintained, other regiments having strengthened the garrison.

A Detail of the Fetterman Massacre

JOHN GUTHRIE[1]

Winners of the West 16, no. 8 (September 1939): 6–8

Early on the morning of December 21, 1866, myself and several of the boys were detailed to form a little squad, which had been ordered to run the mail from the fort [Phil Kearny] to Fort Reno, seventy-two miles from Kearny. It was during our trip to Fort Reno, on the banks of the Powder River, the Indians had attacked a wood train in the valley of [the] Bighorn Mountains at Pine Ridge and Sullivant Hills. My comrades and myself arrived at Fort Phil Kearny at daybreak. In the morning, Captain Fetterman had started out for the purpose of protecting the wood train. Middle of the day, before the morning arrival of my comrades of [the] mail detail, [the] Fetterman command did not return to the fort or to the wood train. He had taken the old Holliday coach road.

Lt. John C. Jenness of the 27th Infantry, two soldiers and myself, a driver with four mules and wagon, [and] three boxes of ammunition—it was feared that the detachment did not take enough ammunition with them—started out to find Fetterman command, [the] lieutenant mounted on an Indian pony, [the] soldiers dismounted. A little over a mile from the fort, on the Holliday coach road near Stoney Creek Ford, we found the dead bodies of the whole detachment, including Captain Fetterman, Captain Brown, and Lieutenant Grummond,[2] laying where the Indians had killed them. The scene baffled description; the dead bodies were horribly mutilated. So you see, the detachment had been surrounded by overwhelming numbers of Indians and everyone killed; nothing had life left but a gray horse, Dapple Dave of Company C, 2nd Cavalry, the only horse left on the battlefield, being shot with both bullet and arrow; all the other horses were captured by these Indians.

Lieutenant Jenness returned to the fort with the news and horror of the situation. It was well understood by the garrison that if the Indians were successful in taking the fort, it meant death for each, and everyone realized the fate that awaited them. The fate of Captain Fetterman's command, all my comrades of the detail could see. The Indians on the bluff, carrying away the clothing of the butchered, with arrows in them, and a number of wolves, hyenas, and coyotes hanging about to feast on the flesh of the dead men's bodies.

The death of Lieutenant Grummond. CYRUS T. BRADY. *INDIAN FIGHTS AND FIGHTERS.*

The dead bodies of our friends at the massacre lay out all night and were not touched or disturbed in any way again, and the cavalry horse of Company C those ferocious devourers of bodies did not even touch. Another rather peculiar feature in connection with those massacred is that it is thought by some that those wild animals that eat the dead bodies of the Indians are not so apt to disturb the white victims, and this is accounted for by the fact that salt generally permeates the whole system of the white race, and at least seems to protect to some extent even after death from the practice of wild animals.

Twenty-four hours after [their] death, the doctor at the fort detailed me to start to load the dead on the ammunition boxes. [We] could not tell cavalry from the infantry, all dead bodies stripped naked, crushed skulls with war clubs, ears and noses and legs had been cut off, scalps torn away, and the bodies pierced with bullets and arrows.

We loaded the officers first. Captain Fetterman, Captain Brown, and bugler Footer of Company C, 2nd Cavalry, were all huddled together near the rocks: Footer's skull crushed in, his body on top of the officers; Captain Fetterman with a lot of arrows sticking in him and breast cut open and scalped; Captain Brown's body hacked up and a lot of arrows sticking in him (he had a little tuft of hair back of the ears and was nicknamed by the Indians, "Bald Head Eagle") and scalped; Lieutenant Grummond, head nearly cut off, a lot of fingers off, scalped, and a lot of arrows and balls in him; Sergeant Baker of Company C,

2nd Cavalry, a gunnysack over his head, not scalped, little finger cut off for a gold ring; Lee Bontee, the guide, found in the brush nearby the rest, body full of arrows, which had to be broken off to load him, pet rifle and pony gone. Bugler Metzer of Company C, 2nd Cavalry, we never found; it was thought that Captain Fetterman sent him to the fort for reinforcements and he was cut off by the Indians.

Some had crosses cut on their breasts, faces to the sky, some crosses on the back, faces to the ground, a mark cut that we could not [figure] out. We walked on top of their internals and did not know it, in the high grass. [We] picked them up, that is, their internals, and did not know the soldiers they belonged to. So you see, the cavalryman got an infantryman's guts, and an infantryman got a cavalryman's guts.

We hauled them all into the fort and made the guardhouse at the fort a dead house. We cleaned the bodies to be buried, and buried them two in a pine box, the officers in a single box. The burying ground was outside of the stockade of the fort, near a little creek called in olden times Bridges Bear Creek, named now Little Piney Creek. Although melancholy described the condition of the garrison, the dead received a respectful memorial military funeral, lamented by all sorrowing friends.

Letters from Fort Phil Kearny

ANONYMOUS

Army and Navy Journal 4, no. 24 (February 2, 1867): 380

A correspondent at Fort Philip Kearny, Dakota Territory, under date of December 31, 1866, sends us the following account of the massacre which recently took place near that post:

About 9:00 A.M. of December 21, sharp firing was heard at this post, in the direction of the wood road, over the hills, evidently an attack made by the Indians on our wood train, which had just left the fort. Capt. W. J. Fetterman, 18th U.S. Infantry, brevet lieutenant colonel, U.S.A., was directed by Colonel Carrington to take command of fifty infantry[1] and proceed to the scene of action and rescue the wood train, and if deemed necessary bring it back to the fort, but not to follow the Indians over the bluffs. Capt. F. H. Brown, 18th U.S. Infantry (until recently chief quartermaster of the District of the Mountains), accompanied Captain Fetterman as a volunteer. Lt. G. W. Grummond, 18th Infantry, was then directed to take the cavalry company stationed here (C, 2nd U.S. Cavalry), numbering about thirty men, and join Captain Fetterman's command. This was done with Lieutenant Grummond's well-known promptness, and the united command was seen crossing Piney Creek, evidently with the intention of cutting off the retreat of the Indians, as the firing at the wood train had entirely ceased. Shortly after the command had disappeared round a bluff, sharp firing was heard at the fort, which increased rapidly, and finally a continual volley of musketry.

Colonel Carrington then ordered Captain Ten Eyck, with fifty more infantry as a reinforcement, to hurry to the scene of the conflict, and four wagons with extra ammunition, also to bring in the wounded (should there be any). A large number of mounted teamsters were also sent to Captain Fetterman's assistance.

About four miles from the fort, Captain Ten Eyck saw an immense body of Indians, which he estimated from two to three thousand, on a

The Fetterman fight. HARPER'S WEEKLY, 1867.

bluff, evidently waiting for him. About a mile further, he found the bodies of Captain Fetterman, Captain Brown, and forty-seven soldiers, all dead, stripped, and most horribly mutilated. The surrounding ground was littered with dead horses and Indian ponies, but no bodies of dead Indians.

For a mile further on could be seen dead and naked bodies of our fallen comrades strewn in and along the wagon road.

The wagons were loaded with bodies and returned to the fort, reaching here at dark, the Indians keeping the bluffs and sending out small parties, apparently to cut off the return of the party to the fort, but made no attack on them. Next morning Colonel Carrington, with Captain Ten Eyck and Lieutenant Matson, with a party of soldiers, went to the battleground and recovered and brought in the remaining bodies, including Lieutenant Grummond's and [those of] two citizens who volunteered to accompany the command under Captain Fetterman. The dead numbered eighty-one in all. Not a man lives to tell the history of this terrible disaster, and all we can do toward solving the mystery is merely conjecture. Evidence of a terrible struggle is seen in the numerous spots of blood within rifle range of where the bodies were found; in the long resistance made, as determined by the firing heard at the fort; in the number of shells of metallic cartridges found around the bodies; and the fact that the Indians, although numbering two or three thousand, did not attack Captain Ten Eyck's party while removing the dead bodies. It is supposed that Captain Fetterman's command followed a small party of Indians and were ambushed, and their retreat cut off by this large force. The Indians, from their numbers and arrows found, were a combination of all the Sioux bands in Dakota, the Arapahos, Cheyennes, and no doubt Blackfeet Indians.

They are determined not to give up the route through this country, and unless a large number of troops are sent here at once, this line cannot be maintained. They threaten all the forts on this line, and are strong enough to awaken grave apprehensions. Their treatment of the dead is unparalleled and beyond imagination.

"A"

Army and Navy Journal 4, no. 30 (March 9, 1867): 458

FORT PHILIP KEARNY, Dakota Territory, January 21, 1867
To the editor of the Army and Navy Journal:

SIR—The following is a correct account of the massacre of Bvt. Lt. Col. William J. Fetterman, 18th U.S. Infantry, and his command:

On the morning of December 21 last, a train of wagons was sent out with an armed escort from this post to procure timber for saw logs. They proceeded along the road leading to the spur of the Bighorn Mountains, and about two hours after their departure, firing was heard in the direction they had taken, and it was supposed they had been attacked.

Captain Fetterman was ordered "to take a detachment of forty-nine infantry, composed of details from the different companies, and go to the assistance of the train, and conduct it to the post, but not to pursue the enemy." About fifteen minutes after his departure, Lt. G. W. Grummond, 18th Infantry, was ordered to take command of twenty-seven men of Company C, 2nd Cavalry, and go to the support of Captain Fetterman, and to reiterate to him the orders previously given. Captain Brown accompanied the party as a volunteer.

They took a northerly course over the hills and were soon out of sight. Shortly after they disappeared from sight, perhaps three-quarters of an hour, sharp firing was heard, which lasted about an hour and a half, when Captain Ten Eyck, 18th Infantry, was dispatched with a detachment to their support. He crossed the hills in the same direction they had taken, and after going about four miles, saw the Indians in large force retreating, and found the dead bodies of Captain Fetterman's command scattered over a space of about three-quarters of a mile. The bodies were stripped, and many of them horribly mutilated; all were scalped, and not a man of the whole command escaped. The details of the affair can only be conjectured. It is supposed by many that the Indians showed themselves in very small parties, and drew Captain Fetterman to the place selected by themselves.

It seems that the party were completely surrounded, for arrows were found sticking in the ground, pointing in all directions. Six bodies were found scattered along the ground for a distance of three-quarters of a mile; the rest were all within a space of five hundred yards square. Two citizens, Wheatley and Fisher, were found alone, and the ground around them covered with the empty cases of the cartridges fired from Henry rifles, with which both were armed.

After this, it is to be hoped that the government will take the matter up in earnest and send sufficient force to the frontier to enable the troops to protect themselves and prevent the recurrence of such things.

The numbers of the Indians are estimated at from two thousand to eight thousand warriors[2], mostly of the Sioux nation.

"B"

The Murder of John Bozeman

THOMAS W. COVER[1]

[Virginia City] *Montana Post*, May 4, 1867

Gen. T. F. Meagher,[2] Virginia City:

SIR—On April 16, accompanied by the late J. M. Bozeman,[3] I left here for Forts C. F. Smith and Phil Kearny. After a day or so of arduous travel, we reached the Yellowstone River and journeyed on in safety until the twentieth, when, in our noon camp on the Yellowstone, about seven miles this side of the Bozeman Ferry, we perceived five Indians approaching us on foot and leading a pony. When within say two hundred fifty yards, I suggested to Mr. Bozeman that we should open fire, to which he made no reply. We stood with our rifles ready until the enemy approached to within one hundred yards, at which time Bozeman remarked, "Those are Crows. I know one of them. We will let them come to us, and learn where the Sioux and Blackfeet camps are, provided they know."

The Indians, meanwhile, walked toward us with their hands up, calling "Ab-sa-ra-ka (Crow)." They shook hands with Bozeman and proffered the same politeness to me, which I declined by presenting my Henry [rifle] at them, and at the moment Bozeman remarked, "I am fooled—these are Blackfeet. We may, however, get off without trouble."

I then went to our horses, leaving my gun with Bozeman, and had saddled mine, when I saw the chief quickly draw the cover from his fusee, and as I called to Bozeman to shoot, the Indian fired, the ball taking effect in Bozeman's right breast, passing completely through him. Bozeman charged on the Indian but did not fire, when another shot, taking effect in the left breast, brought poor Bozeman to the ground, a dead man. At this instant, I received a bullet through the upper edge of my left shoulder. I ran to Bozeman, picked up my gun, and spoke to him, asking if he was badly hurt. Poor fellow, his last words had been spoken some minutes before I reached the spot; he was "stone dead."

Finding the Indians pressing me, and my gun not working, I stepped back slowly, trying to fix it, in which I succeeded, after retreating say fifty paces. I then opened fire, and the first shot brought one of the gentlemen to the sod. I then charged, and the other two took to their heels, joining the two that had been saddling Bozeman's animal and our packhorse immediately after Bozeman's fall.

Having an idea that when collected, they might make a rush, I returned to a piece of willow brush, say four hundred yards from the scene of action, giving the Indians a shot or two as I fell back. I remained in the willows about an hour, when I saw the enemy cross the river, carrying their dead comrade with them.

On returning to the camp to examine Bozeman, I found, but too surely, that the poor fellow was out of all earthly trouble. The red men, however, had been in too much of a hurry to scalp him or even take his watch—the latter I brought in.

After cutting a pound or so of meat, I started on foot on the back track, swam the Yellowstone (a cool bath), walked thirty miles, and came upon McKenzie and Reshaw's camp, very well satisfied to be so far on the road home and in tolerable safe quarters. The next day, I arrived at home with a tolerably sore shoulder and pretty well fagged out. A party started out yesterday to bring in Bozeman's remains.

From what I can glean in the way of information, I am satisfied that there is a large party of Blackfeet on the Yellowstone, whose sole object is plunder and scalps.

Yours,
T. W. Cover

Indian Affairs in the Powder River Country

JAMES BRIDGER[1]

Army and Navy Journal 4, no. 45 (June 29, 1867)

To the editor of the Army and Navy Journal:
SIR: I propose to give you, in as few words of possible, my views of Indian affairs in what is called the Powder River country. In June last, a so-called treaty was made at Fort Laramie, Dakota Territory. I was at Fort Laramie at the time the preliminary council was held and told the commissioners that the treaty would not amount to anything, but that all the Indians wanted was to receive presents and procure a supply of powder and lead, and then they would take the warpath and would plunder trains and murder emigrants going over the road. A preliminary council was held, at which most of the principal chiefs of the Sioux and Cheyenne tribes were present. They were dissatisfied with the provisions of the proposed treaty and were unwilling to grant the right-of-way for an emigrant road from Fort Laramie, Dakota Territory, to Virginia City, Montana Territory, and left the fort soon after and returned to their homes. None of the Cheyenne, Arapaho, or principal Sioux chiefs, who live in the country through which the road runs, signed the treaty. The chiefs who signed the treaty, and the Indians who received the principal portion of the presents, were the "Laramie loafers" and "road beggars"—a class of Indians who hang around Fort Laramie and gain their living by begging and stealing.

On June 16, [1866,] Colonel Carrington's command left for Fort Reno, Dakota Territory, the only post then established on the proposed road. On the day after our arrival there, some of these Sioux stole about fifty head of mules and horses from the vicinity of the post.

On July 16 the principal part of the command arrived at the place selected as the site of Fort Philip Kearny, Dakota Territory. The next day these same *friendly* Indians, who were said to have made a treaty, ran off eighty head of government mules, and in trying to recover them, several men lost their lives.[2] Three days later, a small detach-

Jim Bridger. GRENVILLE M. DODGE. *BATTLE OF ATLANTA.*

ment of officers and men—twenty in all—on their way to join the regiment at Fort Philip Kearny were attacked on Crazy Woman's Fork of Powder River, between Forts Reno and Philip Kearny, and one (Lieutenant Daniels[3]) was killed. From this time until emigration ceased passing over the road, nearly ever train was more or less harassed, and mail and other small parties were frequently attacked.

Now as to the Philip Kearny massacre, it has been said that the Indians did not approach with hostile intent, but the commanding officer of the post, mistaking their intentions, fired on them, and thus brought on a fight. This is preposterous. Up to that time, the Indians had been hanging around the fort every day, stealing stock on every opportunity, attacking the trains going to the woods, and even stealing up at night and shooting men connected with passing trains, while they were sitting around their campfires within one hundred yards of the fort. But a few days before the massacre, a train going to the woods was attacked, and in defending it, Lieutenant Bingham, a promising young officer of the 2nd Cavalry, and one sergeant, lost their lives. This may be a sign of friendship, but I don't think so. Every person that knows anything of affairs in this country knows very well that the massacre at Fort Philip Kearny was planned weeks before, and that the Sioux, Cheyennes, and Arapahos had been collecting together, in preparation for it, on Tongue River, until they numbered 2,200 lodges. The intention was to attack Fort Philip Kearny first, and if they were successful, to then attack Fort C. F. Smith. At the present time, the entire tribe of Northern Sioux are collecting on Powder River, below the mouth of Little Powder River, and their avowed intention is to make a vigorous and determined attack on each of the three posts, and on all trains that may come along the road. Friendly Indians report that they are being supplied with ammunition by half-breed traders connected with the Hudson's Bay Company. There is no use sending out commissioners to treat with them, as it will be only acting over again last summer's scenes. They would be willing to enter into any temporary treaty to enable themselves to get fully supplied with powder with which to carry on the war. The only way to settle the question is to send out a sufficient number of troops to completely whip the hostile Sioux, Cheyennes, and Arapahos and make them sue for peace. Unless this is done, the road had better be abandoned and the country given up to the Indians.

I have been in this country among these Indians nearly forty-four years and am familiar with their past history, and my experience and knowledge of them is greater than can be gained by any commissioners during the sittings of any council that may be held. I know that these Indians will not respect any treaty until they have been whipped into it.

            James Bridger,
            May 4, 1867

The Wagon Box Fight

E. A. BRININSTOOL[1] AND SAMUEL S. GIBSON[2]

Teepee Book 1, no. 8 (August 1915): 186–201

Unquestionably the most remarkable battle between Indians and white men fought on the American continent, considering the overwhelming odds against the whites, was what is known historically as the Wagon Box Fight of August 2, 1867, in which thirty-two soldiers and civilians, under Capt. James Powell[3] from Fort Phil Kearny, Wyoming, were surrounded in a corral made of the beds or boxes of wagons, six miles northwest of the fort, by three thousand Sioux under command of Chief Red Cloud, and after a terrific engagement, lasting from 7:00 A.M. until about 3:00 P.M., were relieved by a detachment of soldiers from the fort. The most astonishing part of the combat is the fact that Powell's forces suffered a loss of but three men killed and three or four wounded, while the Indian loss in killed and wounded, as acknowledged years later by Red Cloud, was 1,137 warriors.[4]

But two of the white men who took part in the fighting are known to be alive today. They are Sgt. Sam S. Gibson of Omaha, Nebraska, and [Max] Littman of St. Louis, Missouri.

Fort Phil Kearny was established in July 1866 by Col. Henry B. Carrington on a plateau which lay between the Big Piney and Little Piney Creeks, in the state of Wyoming, and about twenty-six miles south of the city of Sheridan. The site of the fort is on the ranch of George Geier.

The building of the fort was accomplished under the most trying ordeals. Red Cloud, angered at the encroachment of the whites on the favorite hunting grounds of the Sioux, resorted to the most desperate measures to rid the country of the obnoxious soldiery. Scarcely a day passed during the time spent in the erection of the stockade that the Indians did not cut off stragglers from the fort and kill them. Skirmishes were of almost daily occurrence, as it was necessary to go to the pinery, six or seven miles from the fort, for the necessary logs to erect the stockade and buildings. These wood trains were always compelled to go under a heavy guard, and it was almost a daily happening that the trains would be attacked, either going or coming, and forced to go into corral to withstand the attacks of the Indians.

93

During the first six months of the life of the garrison, the Indians killed 154 persons and wounded many more. They also ran off valuable stock and harassed every wagon train that passed under the walls of the fort. On Pilot Hill, a prominent peak about a mile from the fort, Colonel Carrington maintained a lookout, which would signal the fort when Indians were seen approaching. On December 21, 1866, Capt. William J. Fetterman, with seventy-six privates and four civilians, left the fort to go to the relief of the wood trains, which had been attacked and had signaled for help. The entire command was led into ambush and slaughtered, to a man.

In July 1867, a contract was given to a civilian outfit to supply the fort with logs necessary for the winter supply of fuel, and Capt. James Powell was detailed with his company to act as guard for the contractor's party. When Powell and his command reached the place where the camp of the woodcutters had been established, he found that the men had been divided into two parties. One had its headquarters on a treeless, level plain, and the other in a pine thicket about a mile distant, at the foot of the mountains. Twelve soldiers were detailed to guard the camp in the pines, and twenty-six to watch the headquarters camp.

Nothing but the running gear of the wagons was used in transporting the logs to the fort, the wagon boxes being arranged in the form of a semicircle, and inside these were deposited extra guns and one thousand rounds of ammunition, so that in case of an attack, the entire command could retreat to the wagon-box corral and put up a stubborn resistance. It has been reported by some writers that these wagon boxes were lined with boiler iron as a protection against the bullets of their foes. This is an error, for Sergeant Gibson and Mr. Littman both declare that the wagon boxes were the ordinary pine affairs, such as were used on all government wagons at the time.

The writer of this story personally interviewed Sergeant Gibson as to the facts of the fight, and they are given herewith in his own words. Said Sergeant Gibson:

> We were detailed to relieve Company A, which had been on duty guarding the woodchoppers during the entire month of July. We pitched our tents around the outside of the corral, made by the beds of the wagons. All our stock was kept within the enclosure at night to prevent a stampede by the Indians.
>
> On August 1, I was with the detail guarding the woodchoppers at the lower pinery and was on picket all day, and several of us, when questioned by the sergeant in charge of the detail as to whether we had seen any Indians, replied that we had not. After breakfast on the morning of the second, the wagon trains started for their different destinations. One started for the fort with a load of logs, and the other pulled out for the Lower Pinery. I was with this command. Arriving there, I was ordered to relieve the private on picket on the banks of the Little Piney. I fixed up a sort of shade to keep off the hot sun, and had laid

The wagon-box corral on Piney Island. CYRUS T. BRADY. *INDIAN FIGHTS AND FIGHTERS.*

under it perhaps fifteen minutes with Private [Nolan] Deming, when suddenly Private [John] Garrett jumped to his feet and shouted to Deming and me, "Indians!"

Deming and I jumped to our feet. Sure enough, away to the east of us, we saw seven Indians mounted, coming across the divide from the north on a dead run, riding toward the Little Piney. As none of us had fired a shot at an Indian since receiving the new breech-loading Springfield rifles with which we had been armed only three weeks, I sat down, adjusted my sights to seven hundred yards, and fired at the Indian in advance. My bullet struck the ground in front of the Indian, ricocheted off, and wounded his pony. As the pony fell, the Indian rose and got astride the next warrior's horse behind.

Immediately following my shot, we looked toward the main camp and over the Big Piney to the foothills to the north, and there we saw Indians in hordes swarming down the slopes. Hearing shots across the Little Piney, I sent Deming to the other camp to see what was doing there. Deming soon returned and reported that the Indians had run off the herd, and that all the men had started for the mountains to try to escape.

We at once decided it was getting too warm there for us and started for the wagon-box corral, but had gone only seventy-five or one hundred yards when the Indians commenced to come up out of Little Piney Creek by ones, twos, and threes, at different places. The first one I saw was coming up the bank of the creek, and he carried an old Spencer carbine in his hand and was waving it at the others to come ahead. He saw me at once, and we both aimed at the same time. My bullet knocked him off his pony, and I heard his shot whiz past my head.

All of us were now on the dead run, and the arrows and bullets began whistling around our ears until it seemed as if hell had broken loose. The Indians whooped and yelled as they tried their best to surround us and cut us off from the main camp.

We saw one of our men run out from the corral as we neared camp. He dropped on one knee and opened a rapid fire on the advancing hordes of savages, killing several and wounding others. This man proved to be a bright, blonde-headed German boy named Littman,[5] who by his courage in coming out to meet us, and by the rapidity and accuracy of his fire, saved us from being surrounded and cut off.

Upon our arrival at the corral, completely winded, I at once reported to Captain Powell as to why we had left the picket post without orders. He looked me in the eye and replied, "You did nobly, my boy." Then, addressing us all, he said, "Men, find your places in the wagon beds. You'll have to fight for your lives today!"

Much has been said by historians and others who have written short accounts of this fight regarding the wagon boxes in which we fought. Some have contended that the wagon boxes were lined with boiler iron, and others that they were lined with steel and had loopholes thru the sides. All such statements are absolutely without foundation. They were the ordinary government wagon boxes, simply made of thin wood, while some were makeshift wagons belonging to the contractor's bull train, the heaviest of them being only inch boards. There was not a particle of iron about them except the bolts, stay straps, and nuts used in holding the rickety concerns together. I have also read in some accounts that the wagon boxes were a sort of traveling fort, supplied by the government. This is absurd.

I soon found a place on the south side of the corral with Sergeant McQuiery and Pvt. Johnny Grady. Grady was the only one to speak to me, inviting me to come in with them, saying, "You've got to fight like hell today, kid, if you expect to get out of this alive." I was the youngest boy in the company, being but eighteen years of age, and was always called the kid.

Leaning my rifle against the side of the wagon bed, I carried a hundred rounds of ammunition to my place, and then took a walk around among the men who were watching the Indians assemble all around us. I spoke to some of them, but nobody answered me. I saw Pvt. Tommy Doyle piling up some neck yokes on top of one another for a breastworks. I saw old [Sergeant] Frank Robertson take the shoestrings from his shoes, tie them together, and fit one loop over his right foot and the other to the trigger of his rifle. I knew full well that this meant the red devils never would get him alive.

I joined a group of five or six men who were watching Lt. John Jenness[6] as he surveyed the oncoming hordes thru his field glasses. There seemed to be thousands of Indians all mounted on their finest war ponies, riding here and there, chanting their war and death songs. I heard Jenness say to Captain Powell, "Captain, I believe that Red Cloud is on top of that hill pointing to the east." The captain made no reply, but hearing a commotion among the men to the south of us, he saw the Indians beginning to form and exclaimed, "Men, here they come! Take your places and shoot to kill!" And those were the only words of command given by him, save one, during the entire fight.

We all quickly obeyed. When I got to my place, I saw that Grady and McQuiery had both taken off their shoes and fixed the strings into loops to fit over the triggers of their guns for the same purpose that Robertson had done—to kill themselves when all hope was lost, in the event of the Indians passing the barricade by an overwhelming force of numbers, when every man would stand erect, place the muzzle of his loaded rifle under his chin, and take his own life, rather than be captured and held for the inevitable torture.

Resting my rifle barrel across the top of the wagon box, I began firing with the rest. The whole plain was alive with Indians, shooting at us, and the tops of the boxes were literally ripped and torn to slivers by their bullets. How we ever escaped with such slight loss I never have been able to understand, but we made every shot tell in return, and soon the whole plain in front of us was strewn with dead and dying Indians and ponies. It was a horrible sight! The Indians were amazed at the rapidity and continuity of our fire. They did not know we had been supplied with breechloaders and supposed that after firing the first shot, they could ride us down before we could reload.

During a lull in the firing, which now took place, we got a fresh supply of ammunition out of the seven one-thousand-round cases, which had been opened and placed at convenient places around the corral. We had to crawl on our hands and knees to get the ammunition, pushing away as we did so, the arrows which had been shot inside the corral and remained sticking in the ground.

When I got back to my wagon box, I heard somebody ask in a loud whisper for a chew of tobacco. I also heard someone ask if anyone had been shot. I heard a reply, "Don't know." Lieutenant Jenness was leaning over the cover of the wagon bed at the west end of the corral, firing at some Indians on the northwest side, where they lay partially concealed under the brow of the hill where the land sloped down toward Big Piney Valley. It was these Indians who later killed Lieutenant Jenness and Privates Doyle and Haggerty.

The fight had commenced about seven in the morning, and I did not hear any man ask about the time of day during the fight. Most of us were bareheaded, having used our caps to hold ammunition. The sun beat down with a pitiless glare that terrible August day, and it seemed like an eternity to us all.

The line of tents in front of us had been left standing, and we had simply fired through the spaces between them. No one had thought of pulling them down so we could see better, until someone at this juncture suggested it. Then two men leaped out of a wagon box to the east of us, ran to the tents, and began pulling them down.

At this moment, Private Grady, who sat near me in my box, yelled, "Come on kid, let's help." As he jumped out over the box, I followed him, with the bullets zipping about our ears and the arrows swishing past and striking into the ground on all sides of us. We loosened the loops, working together till the last tent dropped, and then, amid a perfect hail of bullets and arrows, leaped into our wagon boxes again, neither of us being hit.

With the tents down, we could see the Indians to a much better advantage and delivered a more effective fire upon them. Our fire was terribly effective and deadly in accuracy. As I crawled back for more shells, I saw the body of Lieutenant Jenness lying where he had fallen, shot through the head and heart, within a few feet of the corpse of a man who had been fighting through it all with bravery never excelled.

About this time, word was passed around that Privates Henry Haggerty and Tommy Doyle had been killed on the north side of the corral. Haggerty had been shot through the shoulder earlier in the fight, and the men in his wagon box wanted him to lie down, but with his left arm hanging useless at his side, he used his good right arm and kept on loading and firing for over two hours, until the Indians on the north ridge finally killed him by sending a bullet through the top of his head. Doyle had been killed some time after the first charge, while fighting behind a breastworks of ox yokes. He was struck in the forehead.

It was now becoming a question of water. Men were everywhere asking for it, and the supply was mighty scarce. The heat was awful, and added to this, the Indians rained fire arrows inside the corral, which set fire to the dry manure, and the stench from this was abominable. I had filled my canteen from Little Piney Creek that morning and had brought it to the corral on the retreat from the picket post.

There was a barrel half full of water standing outside the corral at the west end when the fighting began, but it had been struck by bullets, and the water had nearly all leaked out. Under a covered wagon close to the west end of the corral were two camp kettles, in which our coffee had been made for breakfast, and the cook had filled them with water on top of the old coffee grounds. Pvt. Jim Condon had seen the water leaking from the barrel and had passed around word that it was almost empty. Thereupon we planned to secure the iron kettles of water.

My comrade, Johnny Grady, said, "Kid, let's go and get one of those kettles." We took a careful look about, and then commenced crawling on our stomachs through the dozens of arrows that bristled in the ground inside the corral.

The men on the north side seemed to divine our purpose, and word was passed along to keep up a steady fire on the Indians along the ridge. We crawled through the opening between the wagon beds, hugging the ground as closely as possible, and soon reached the place where the kettles stood, without apparently having been detected. We each grabbed a kettle and commenced crawling back, pulling the kettles along after us. We had got about halfway to safety when bang! bang! bang! went several guns from the Indians to the north of us. There were more shots, and zip! ping! and we heard some of the bullets strike the kettles. We both thought our time had come, fully expecting to feel a bullet or an arrow in our backs, as we sprang back inside the corral with those kettles of dirty black water. When I looked at my kettle, it had two holes clean through!

The time between the charges dragged heavily, yet the savages kept us constantly alert. Along about 2:00 P.M. in the afternoon, as near as I can judge, we heard a loud humming sound, which grew louder and louder, and presently there was a loud cry from the west end of the corral, "Here they come again!"

We all looked to the west and saw a sight I never will forget to my dying day, and it chilled my blood at the time. We saw the naked bodies of hundreds upon hundreds of Indians swarming up a ravine about ninety yards to the west of the corral, all on foot and in the shape of a letter V, led by Red Cloud's nephew.[7] We opened a terrific fire on them, and the leader fell, pierced by many balls. But the mass came on slowly and in great numbers, the places of those who fell being immediately taken by others.

And now the great horde of savages were so close that the heavy bullets that we fired must have gone thru the bodies of two or three

Indians, and it seemed as if nothing could prevent their swarming over the tops of the wagon boxes, in spite of our withering fire. Some of the men, in their excitement, jumped to their feet and hurled sticks and stones in the faces of the enemy, forgetting to reload their guns for the moment, but nothing could stand before that galling fire we poured in upon them, and just as it seemed as if all hope had gone, the great mass of Sioux broke and fled. Not a member of our party was hit in their last charge. The several hundred Indians who were mounted, and who were on the plain to the south of us, intently watching the charge on foot, never offered to assist their comrades by making a mounted charge, but remained out of rifle range.

Just then, someone at the east end of the corral cried out, "Did you hear that?" Everybody ceased firing, and in another moment we heard the boom of a big gun to the east of us. It was the relief from the fort, and the big gun was driving the Indians off the hill, and soon those on the plain to the south could be seen disappearing into the pinery to the west. Suddenly one of the men jumped to his feet and shouted, "Here they come," and as we looked toward the east, we could see our comrades as they appeared in a long skirmish line.

How we jumped to our feet and yelled! We threw our caps in the air. We hugged each other in our joy and laughed, cried, and fairly sobbed like little children in the delirium of our delight. The awful strain was over.

Major Smith[8] was in command of the rescue party, and our post surgeon, Dr. Samuel Horton, was with him. Our rescuers told us they did not expect to find a man of us alive.

When we started back for the fort, we looked back up the Big Piney Valley and saw a long train of Indian ponies, three and four deep, and fully a quarter of a mile long. They were carrying off their dead and wounded.

Chief Rain-in-the-Face told me at Standing Rock agency in 1895, through Johnny Wells, an interpreter, that he did not care to talk about the Wagon Box Fight.

I have served in the army 48 years, taking active part in the Sioux campaign of 1876 and also in the Wounded Knee campaign of 1890–91, during the Ghost Dance excitement, but never before or since have my nerves been put to the test that they were on that awful August 2, 1867, when we fought Red Cloud's warriors in the wagon-box corral.

An Indian Perspective on the Wagon Box Fight

GEORGE B. GRINNELL[1]

Midwest Review 9, nos. 2 and 3 (February–March 1928): 1–7[2]

In the Wagon Box Fight, according to the statement of the Cheyennes, there were engaged on the Indian side about three hundred Sioux and one hundred or more Cheyennes. These seem to have been in two parties, one of two hundred Sioux and a small number of Cheyennes, and the other say of twenty-five Cheyennes and sixty or seventy Sioux. They were aware of the presence and situation of the soldiers, and the night before the fight, they made plans for the attack next day.

Two old men, Wolf Chief and Braided Locks, who were present, have told me something about the fight; Wolf Chief was with the smaller party, and Braided Locks with the larger.

The night before the battle, the chief men of the two tribes got together and determined to try to induce the soldiers to leave the position of defense which they occupied and to come out to the open. Ten young men were chosen who were ordered to charge on the troops and, when they met resistance, to retreat gradually, in the hope that the soldiers would follow them. They were to lead the pursuing soldiers toward the hills, where the other Indians were stationed in concealment. As soon as the soldiers had reached the hills and had got among the Indians, the real fighting would begin. The Indians' plan was to repeat on a much smaller scale the tactics which had brought about the so-called Fetterman massacre, which had taken place about seven months before.

This time, however, the plan did not work out as the Indians had hoped. Perhaps the strategy of the Indians was understood, though this is not likely. It is more probable that the troops realized how slight was the opportunity for a few men on foot to overtake and seriously injure a body of mounted Indians.

When the Indians found the men would not leave their breastworks, they called all the concealed Indians and charged the white men, but without much result. It was no doubt this charge, made by Indians that had not before been seen, that gave rise to the stories by different writers of the great numbers of Indians that took part in the fight. Colonel Dodge[3] says there were three thousand; other writers speak of them as "hundreds and hundreds." There were a

101

great many—perhaps three hundred or four hundred—and the anxieties of the beleaguered men multiplied their numbers. No doubt, they were ten to one against the white men, but as already said, the conditions favored the whites. The Indians charged up close to the barrier but could do nothing—notwithstanding their numbers. They lost three men, two Sioux and one Cheyenne, and did not know that the whites had lost any. Finally from Fort Kearny came a company of infantry, which had a small cannon. On the arrival of these troops, the Indians withdrew.

After the relieving force had come up, the Indians went away from the place and the troops returned to Ft. Kearny.

PART THREE

The Yellowstone Expedition, 1873

Battling with the Sioux on the Yellowstone

GEORGE A. CUSTER[1]

Galaxy 22, no. 1 (July 1876): 91–102

In the early spring of 1873, the officials of the Northern Pacific Railroad applied to the government authorities at Washington for military protection for a surveying party to be sent out the ensuing summer to explore and mark out the incomplete portion of the road extending from the Missouri River in Dakota to the interior of Montana, west of the Yellowstone. This enterprise, which was intended to open a new highway to travel and commerce between the people of the Atlantic and Pacific states, had not then encountered the financial calamities that swept over the country later in that year. It had commended itself to the attention and approval of not only the public, but to the protection and fostering care of the national government. It was seen that the completion of the Northern Pacific road would be a measure which, aside from opening to settlement a large tract of valuable country, and aiding in the development and successful working of a rich mineral region otherwise inaccessible, would produce to the government a large annual saving of money in the way of cost of transportation of troops and supplies. The experience of the past, particularly that of recent years, has shown too that no one measure so quickly and effectually frees a country from the horrors and devastations of Indian wars and Indian depredations generally as the building and successful operation of a railroad through the region overran. Thus, aside from the ordinary benefits and purposes which inspire the building of railroads through the unsettled portions of the West, the government, simply as a measure of economy, has ample reason to extend to such enterprises encouragement and help.

So earnest is my belief in the civilizing and peace-giving influence of railroads when extended through an Indian country that the idea has often occurred to me, laying aside all considerations and arguments as to whether such a road will ever be required in the interests of trade and commerce, that a railroad established and kept in operation from a point on our extreme northern boundary, somewhere between the one hundredth and one hundred fifth meridian, to a corresponding point on the Rio Grande River in Texas, would forever after have preserved peace with the vast number of tribes infesting the immense area of country lying between the Rocky Mountains and the valley of the Mississippi. A more surprising statement than this, however, and one which will bear investigation, is that the avoidance of wars with the tribes which have occupied this region of the plains lying contiguous to the indicated line of railroad, would have resulted in a saving of money to the government more than sufficient to build, equip, and place in running order a railroad from British America to the Rio Grande.

Few of our people realize the immense outlay and expense rendered necessary by an Indian war. As an illustration, take the following extract from a report to the president of the United States, made in 1868 by a commission, of which Generals Sherman, Harney, Terry, and Augur were members. Referring to the alleged "Chivington massacre" and the Cheyenne war of 1864, the report of the commission states, "No one will be astonished that a war ensued which cost the government thirty million dollars."

To extend encouragement and aid to the projectors and builders of the Northern Pacific road, the government granted the application of the road for a military escort, and gave authority to the organization of what was afterward designated as the Yellowstone expedition. The troops composing the expedition numbered about seventeen hundred men, consisting of cavalry, infantry, an improvised battery of artillery, and a detachment of Indian scouts, the whole under command of Bvt. Maj. Gen. D. S. Stanley,[2] an officer whose well-known ability and long experience on the plains and with Indians amply qualified him for the exercise of so important a command. Fort Rice, Dakota, on the Missouri River, was selected as the point of rendezvous and departure of the expedition.

An Indian delegation in Washington. HARPER'S WEEKLY, 1867.

To illustrate how our little army, as occasion demands, is frequently shifted from one remote point to another in order to meet the demands of the service, it may be mentioned that in collecting troops to compose the Yellowstone expedition, most of my command, the cavalry, was transported from the extreme southern states—the Carolinas, Florida, and Louisiana—to within a few days' march of the British possessions. When it is remembered that a portion of the immense journey was by rail, a portion by steam transports, and about five hundred miles by marching, the extent of the preliminary preparations rendered necessary in an expedition of this kind will be appreciated. It was not until July that the Yellowstone expedition assumed definite shape and began its westward movement from Fort Rice. The engineers and surveyors of the Northern Pacific Railroad were under the direction and management of [Maj.] Gen. Thomas L. Rosser.[3] This gentleman deserves a fuller notice than the limits of this article will permit. He and I had been cadets together at the Military Academy at West Point, occupying adjoining rooms, and being members of the same company, often marching side by side in the performance of our various military duties while at the Academy. When the storms of secession broke upon the country in '61, Rosser, in common with the majority of the cadets from the Southern states, resigned his warrant and hastened to unite his personal fortunes with those of his state—Texas. He soon won distinction in the Confederate army, under Lee, and finally rose to the rank and command of major general of cavalry. I held a similar rank and command in the Union army, and it frequently

Construction crews and army guards on the line of the Northern Pacific Railroad. HARPER'S WEEKLY, 1875.

happened, particularly during the last year of the war, that the troops commanded by Rosser and myself were pitted against each other in the opposing lines of battle, and the two cadets of earlier years became not only hostile foes, but actual antagonists.

When the war was ended, Rosser, like many of his comrades from the South who had staked their all upon the issue of the war, at once cast about him for an opportunity to begin anew the battle, not of war, but of life. Possessing youth, health, many and large abilities, added to indomitable pluck, he decided to trust his fortunes amidst his late enemies, and repaired to Minnesota, where he sought employment in one of the many surveying parties acting under the auspices of the Northern Pacific road. Upon applying to the officer of the road for a position as civil engineer, he was informed that no vacancy existed to which he could be appointed. Nothing daunted, he persisted, and finally accepted a position among the axe men, willing to work, and proved to his employers not only his industry, but his fitness for promotion. He at once attracted the attention of his superiors, who were not slow to recognize his merit. Rosser was advanced rapidly from one important position to another, until in a few months he became the chief engineer of the surveying party accompanying the expedition. In this capacity, I met him on the plains of Dakota in 1878, nearly ten years after the date when in peaceful scabbards we sheathed the swords which on more than one previous occasion we had drawn against each other. The manly course adopted by Rosser after the war, his determined and successful struggle against adversity, presents a remarkable instance of the wonderful recuperative powers of the American character.

Scarcely a day passed, during the progress of the expedition from the Missouri to the Yellowstone, that General Rosser and I were not in each other's company a portion of the time, either as we rode in our saddles, "boot to boot," climbed together unvisited cliffs, picked our way through trackless canyons, or sat at the same mess table or about the same campfire. During these strolling visits, we frequently questioned and enlightened each other as to the unexplained or but partially understood battles and movements in which each had played a part against the other.

Passing over all this, and omitting the incidents of the march from our starting point, Fort Rice on the Missouri,[4] we come to the time when we found ourselves encamped on the east bank of the beautiful and swift-flowing Yellowstone, about a hundred miles from its mouth. At this point, the expedition was met by a steamer, sent for that purpose up the Missouri, hundreds of miles above Fort Rice, then up the Yellowstone to the point of juncture. From it fresh supplies of forage and subsistence stores were obtained. This being done, the entire expedition, save a small detachment left at this point to guard our surplus stores, intended for our return march, was ferried by the steamer across the Yellowstone River. Our course for several days carried us up that stream, our tents at night being usually pitched on or near the riverbank. The country to be surveyed, however, soon became so rough and broken in places that we encountered serious delays at times in finding a practicable route for our long and heavily laden wagon trains, over rocks and through canyons hitherto unexplored by white men. So serious did these embarrassments become, and so much time was lost in accomplishing our daily marches, that I suggested to Colonel Stanley that I should take with me each day a couple of companies of cavalry and a few of the Indian scouts, and seek out and prepare a practicable road in advance, thereby preventing detention of the main command. This proposition being acceded to, it was my custom thereafter to push rapidly forward in the early morning, gaining an advance of several miles upon the main expedition, and by locating the route, relieving the troops and trains in rear of a great amount of fatigue and many tedious detentions. One result of this system was that I and my little party, who were acting as pioneers, usually arrived at the termination of our day's march, our campground for the night, at an early hour in the day, several hours in advance of the main portion of the expedition.

This of itself was quite an advantage, as it gave the party in advance choice of campground and enabled themselves and horses to obtain several hours of rest not enjoyed by their less fortunate comrades in rear. We had marched several days after our departure from the point at which we crossed the Yellowstone without discovering any signs or indications of the presence of hostile Indians, although our scouts and guides had been constantly on the alert, as we knew we were traversing a portion of the country infested by savage tribes. On the morning of August 4, with two companies of the 7th Cavalry, commanded by Captain Moylan[5] and [Tom] Custer[6]—who, with my adjutant, Lieutenant Calhoun,[7] and Lieutenant Varnum,[8] composed the officers of the party—and guided by my favorite scout, Bloody Knife, a young Arikara warrior,[9] the entire party numbering eighty-six men and

George A. Custer as a major general of volunteers. CENTURY MAGAZINE, 1892.

five officers, I left camp at 5:00 A.M. [August 10, 1873], and set out as usual to explore the country and find a practicable route for the main column. Soon after we left camp, Bloody Knife's watchful eyes discovered fresh signs of Indians. Halting long enough to allow him to examine the trail, Bloody Knife was soon able to gather all the information attainable. A party of Indians had been prowling about our camp the previous night and had gone away, traveling in the direction in which we were then marching.

This intelligence occasioned no particular surprise, as we had been expecting to discover the presence of Indians for several days. Bloody Knife's information produced no change in our plans. The hostile party of whose presence we had become aware numbered nineteen; our party numbered over ninety. So, sending intelligence back to Colonel Stanley of the circumstance of the discovery, we continued our march, keeping up if possible a sharper lookout than before, now that we were assured of the proximity of Indians in our neighborhood. Over rock-ribbed hills, down timbered dells, and across open, grassy plains, we wended our way without unusual interest, except at intervals of a few miles, to discover the trail of the nineteen prowling visitors of the previous night, showing that our course, which was intended to lead us again to the Yellowstone, was in the same direction as theirs. Bloody Knife interpreted this as indicating that the village from which the nineteen had probably been sent to reconnoiter and report our movements was located somewhere above us in the Yellowstone Valley. About 10:00 A.M., we reached the crest of the high line of bluffs bordering the Yellowstone Valley, from which we obtained a fine view of the river and valley extending above and beyond us as far as the eye could reach. Here and there, the channel of the river was dotted with beautiful islands, covered with verdure and shaded by groves of stately forest trees, while along the banks on either side could be seen for miles and miles clumps of trees, varying in size from the familiar cottonwood to the waving osier, and covering a space in some instances no larger than a gentleman's garden, in others embracing thousands of acres.

After halting upon the crest of the bluffs long enough to take in the pleasures of the scene and admire the beautiful valley, spread out like an exquisite carpet at our feet, we descended to the valley and directed our horses' heads toward a particularly attractive and inviting cluster of shade trees standing on the riverbank and distant from the crest of the bluffs nearly two miles. Upon arriving at this welcome retreat, we found it all that a more distant view had pictured it. An abundance of rich, luxuriant grass offered itself to satisfy the craving appetites of our traveled steeds, while the dense foliage of the forest trees provided us with a protecting shade, which exposure to the hot rays of an August sun rendered more than welcome. First allowing our thirsty horses to drink from the clear crystal water of the Yellowstone, which ran murmuring by in its long tortuous course to the Missouri, we then picketed them out to graze.

Precautionary and necessary measures having been attended to looking to the security of our horses, the next important and equally necessary step was to post half a dozen pickets on the open plain beyond to give timely warning in the event of the approach of hostile Indians. This being done, the remainder of our party busied themselves in arranging each for his individual comfort, disposing themselves on the grass beneath the shade of the wide-spreading branches of the cottonwoods that grew close to the riverbank. Above us for nearly a mile, and for a still greater distance below, the valley was free from timber. This enabled our pickets to command a perfect view of the entire valley, at this point about two miles wide and almost level, save where here and there it was cut up by deep washes in the soil. Satisfied that every measure calculated to ensure our safety had been taken, officers and men—save the trusty pickets—stretched their weary forms on the grassy lawn and were soon wrapped in slumber, little reckoning that within a few rods there lay concealed more than five times their numbers of hostile Sioux warriors, waiting and watching for a favorable moment to pounce upon them. For myself, so oblivious was I to the prospect of immediate danger, that after selecting a most inviting spot for my noonday nap and arranging my saddle and buckskin coat in the form of a comfortable pillow, I removed my boots, untied my cravat, and opened my collar, prepared to enjoy to the fullest extent the delights of an outdoor siesta. I did not omit, however, to place my trusty Remington rifle within easy grasp—more from habit, it must be confessed, than from anticipation of danger. Near me, and stretched on the ground sheltered by the shade of the same tree, was my brother, the colonel,[10] divested of his hat, coat, and boots; while close at hand, wrapped in deep slumber, lay the other three officers, Moylan, Calhoun, and Varnum. Sleep had taken possession of us all—officers and men—excepting, of course, the watchful pickets into whose keeping the safety, the lives of our little detachment was for the time entrusted. Many of the horses even, having lunched most bountifully from the rich repast which nature had spread around and beneath them, seemed to share in the languor and drowsiness of their riders, and were to be seen here and there reposing upon the soft green carpet which to them was both food and couch. How long we slept I scarcely know—perhaps an hour, when the cry of "Indians! Indians!" quickly followed by the sharp ringing crack of the pickets' carbines, aroused and brought us—officers, men, and horses—to our feet. There was neither time nor occasion for questions to be asked or answered. Catching up my rifle, and without waiting to don hat or boots, I glanced through the grove of trees to the open plain or valley beyond and saw a small party of Indians bearing down toward us as fast as their ponies could carry them.

"Run to your horses, men! Run to your horses!" I fairly yelled as I saw that the first move of the Indians was intended to stampede our animals and leave us to be attended to afterward.

At the same time, the pickets opened fire upon our disturbers, who had already emptied their rifles at us as they advanced, as if boldly intending to ride us down. As yet we could see but half a dozen warriors, but those who were familiar with Indian stratagems knew full well that so small a party of savages unsupported would not venture to disturb in open day a force the size of ours.

Quicker than I could pen the description, each trooper, with rifle in hand, rushed to secure his horse, and men and horses were soon withdrawn from the open plain and concealed behind the clump of trees beneath whose shade we were but a few moments before quietly sleeping. The firing of the pickets, the latter having been reinforced by a score of their comrades, checked the advance of the Indians and enabled us to saddle our horses and be prepared for whatever might be in store for us.

A few moments found us in our saddles and sallying forth from the timber to try conclusions with the daring intruders. We could only see half a dozen Sioux warriors galloping up and down in our front, boldly challenging us by their manner to attempt their capture or death. Of course, it was an easy matter to drive them away, but as we advanced, it became noticeable that they retired, and when we halted or diminished our speed, they did likewise. It was apparent from the first that the Indians were resorting to stratagem to accomplish that which they could not do by an open, direct attack. Taking twenty troopers with me, headed by [Tom] Custer and Calhoun, and directing Moylan to keep within supporting distance with the remainder, I followed the retreating Sioux up the valley, but with no prospect of overtaking them, as they were mounted upon the fleetest of ponies. Thinking to tempt them within our grasp, I, being mounted on a Kentucky thoroughbred in whose speed and endurance I had confidence, directed [Tom] Custer to allow me to approach the Indians accompanied only by my orderly, who was also well mounted; at the same time, to follow us cautiously at a distance of a couple of hundred yards. The wily redskins were not to be caught by any such artifice. They were perfectly willing that my orderly and myself should approach them, but at the same time they carefully watched the advance of the cavalry following me and permitted no advantage. We had by this time almost arrived abreast of an immense tract of timber growing in the valley and extending to the water's edge, but distant from our resting place, from which we had been so rudely aroused, about two miles.

The route taken by the Indians, and which they evidently intended us to follow, led past this timber, but not through it. When we had arrived almost opposite the nearest point, I signaled to the cavalry to halt, which was no sooner done than the Indians also came to a halt. I then made the sign to the latter for a parley, which was done simply by riding my horse in a circle. To this the savages only responded by looking on in silence for a few moments, then turning their ponies and moving off slowly, as if to say, "Catch us if you can." My suspicions were more than ever aroused, and I sent my orderly back to tell [Tom] Custer to keep a sharp eye upon the heavy bushes on our left and scarcely three hundred yards distant from where I sat on my horse. The orderly had delivered his message, and had almost rejoined me, when, judging from our halt that we intended to pursue no further, the real design and purpose of the savages was made evident. The small party in front had faced toward us and were advancing as if to attack. I could scarcely credit the evidence of my eyes, but my astonishment had only begun when, turning to the wood on my left, I beheld bursting from their concealment between three and four hundred Sioux warriors mounted and caparisoned with all the flaming adornments of paint and feathers which go to make up the Indian war costume. When I first obtained a glimpse of them—and a single glance was sufficient—they were dashing from the timber at full speed, yelling and whooping as only Indians can. At the same time, they moved in perfect line, and with as seeming good order and alignment as the best drilled cavalry.

To understand our relative positions, the reader has only to imagine a triangle whose sides are almost equal; their length in this particular instance being from three to four hundred yards, the three angles being occupied by [Tom] Custer and his detachment, the Indians, and myself. Whatever advantage there was in length of sides fell to my lot, and I lost no time in availing myself of it. Wheeling my horse suddenly around, and driving the spurs into his sides, I rode as only a man rides whose life is the prize, to reach [Tom] Custer and his men, not only in advance of the Indians, but before any of them could cut me off. Moylan with his reserve was still too far in the rear to render their assistance available in repelling the shock of the Indians' first attack. Realizing the great superiority of our enemies, not only in numbers, but in their ability to handle their arms and horses in a fight, and fearing they might dash through and disperse [Tom] Custer's small party of twenty men, and having once broken the formation of the latter, dispatch them in detail, I shouted to [Tom] Custer at almost each bound of my horse, "Dismount your men! Dismount your men!" but the distance which separated us and the excitement of the occasion prevented him from hearing me.

Fortunately, however, this was not the first time he had been called upon to contend against the sudden and unforeseen onslaught of savages, and although failing to hear my suggestion, he realized instantly that the safety of his little band of troopers depended upon the adoption of prompt means of defense.

Scarcely had the long line of splendidly mounted warriors rushed from their hiding place before [Tom] Custer's voice rang out sharp and clear, "Prepare to fight on foot." This order required three out of four troopers to leap from their saddles and take their position on the ground, where, by more deliberate aim, and being freed from the management of their horses, a more effective resistance could be opposed to the rapidly approaching warriors. The fourth trooper in each group of "fours" remained on his horse, holding the reins of the horses of his three comrades.

Quicker than words can describe, the fifteen cavalrymen, now on foot and acting as infantry, rushed forward a few paces in advance of their horses, deployed into open order, and dropping on one or both knees in the low grass, waited with loaded carbines—with finger gently pressing the trigger—the approach of the Sioux, who rode boldly down as if apparently unconscious that the small group of troopers were on their front. "Don't fire, men, till I give the word, and when you do fire, aim low," was the quiet injunction given his men by their young commander, as he sat on his horse intently watching the advancing foe.

Swiftly over the grassy plain leaped my noble steed, each bound bearing me nearer to both friends and foes. Had the race been confined to the Indians and myself, the closeness of the result would have satisfied an admirer even of the Derby. Nearer and nearer our paths approached each other, making it appear almost as if I were one of the line of warriors, as the latter bore down to accomplish the destruction of the little group of troopers in front. Swifter seem to fly our mottled steeds, the one to save, the other to destroy, until the common goal has almost been reached—a few more bounds, and friends and foes will be united—will form one contending mass.

The victory was almost within the grasp of the redskins. It seemed that but a moment more, and they would be trampling the kneeling troopers beneath the feet of their fleet-limbed ponies; when, "Now, men, let them have it!" was the signal for a well-directed volley, as fifteen cavalry carbines poured their contents into the ranks of the shrieking savages. Before the latter could recover from the surprise and confusion which followed, the carbines—thanks to the invention of breechloaders—were almost instantly loaded, and a second carefully aimed discharge went whistling on its deadly errand. Several warriors were seen to reel in their saddles and were only saved from falling by the quickly extended arms of their fellows. Ponies were tumbled over like butchered bullocks, their riders glad to find themselves escaping with less serious injuries. The effect of the rapid firing of the troopers and their firm, determined stand, showing that they thought neither of flight nor surrender, was to compel the savages first to slacken their speed, then to lose their daring and confidence in their ability to trample down the little group of defenders in the front. Death to many of their number stared them in the face. Besides, if the small party of troopers in the front was able to oppose such plucky and destructive resistance to their attacks, what might not be expected should the main party under Moylan, now swiftly approaching to the rescue, also take part in the struggle? But more quickly than my sluggish pen has been able to record the description of the scene, the battle line of the warriors exhibited signs of faltering which soon degenerated into an absolute repulse. In a moment, their attack was transformed into flight in which each seemed only anxious to secure his individual safety. A triumphant cheer from the cavalrymen as they sent a third installment of leaden messengers whistling about the ears of the fleeing redskins served to spur both pony and rider to their utmost speed. Moylan by this time had reached the ground and had united the entire force. The Indians in the meantime had plunged out of sight into the recesses of the jungle from which they had first made their attack. We knew too well that their absence would be brief, and that they would resume the attack, but not in the manner of the first.

We knew that we had inflicted no little loss upon them—dead and wounded ponies could be seen on the ground passed over by the Indians. The latter would not be satisfied without determined efforts to get revenge. Of this we were well aware.

A moment's hurried consultation between the officers and myself, and we decided that as we would be forced to act entirely upon the defensive against a vastly superior force, it would be better if we relieved ourselves as far as possible of the care of our horses and take our chances in the fight, which was yet to come, on foot. At the same time, we were then so far out on the open plain, and from the riverbank, that the Indians could surround us. We must get nearer to the river, conceal our horses or shelter them from fire, then with every available man form a line or semicircle, with our backs to the river, and defend ourselves until the arrival of the main body of the expedition, an event we could not expect for several hours. As if divining our intentions and desiring to prevent their execution, the Indians now began their demonstrations, looking to a renewal of the fight.

This time, however, profiting by their experience on their first attack, they did not come forth in a body, thus presenting a large target to the aim of their opponents, but singly and alone—their favorite mode of warfare—each seeming to act upon his own judgment, yet all governed by one general plan. The troopers, most of them being thoroughly accustomed to Indian fighting, preserved the most admirable coolness from the moment the fight began. Some even indulged in merry-making remarks, tinctured at times with the drollest humor. When the savages first made their sudden appearance from the wood and came rushing down as if to bear everything before them, and the fifteen troopers were kneeling or lying on the ground, waiting till the Indians were near enough to receive their fire, a trooper addressed his comrade, "Say, Teddy, I guess the balls opened."

"Yis," says Teddy; "and by the way them red niggers is comin', it's openin' with a grand march."

"Teddy, if we only had the band here, we could play 'Hail to the Chief' for their benefit."

"Begorrah, if they'll come a little closer to this little shootin' instrument, I'll play hell with their chief for me own benefit."

Of course it was easy to see what had been the original plan by which the Indians hoped to kill or capture our entire party. Stratagem, of course, was to play a prominent part in the quarrel. The few young warriors first sent to arouse us from our midday slumber came as a decoy to tempt us to pursue them beyond the ambush in which lay concealed the main body of the savages; the latter were to dash from their hiding place, intercept our retreat, and dispose of us after the most approved manner of barbarous warfare.

The next move on our part was to fight our way back to the little clump of bushes from which we had been so rudely startled. To do this, Captain Moylan, having united his force to that of [Tom] Custer's, gave the order, "Prepare to fight on foot." This was quickly obeyed. Three-fourths of the fighting force were now on foot armed with the carbines only. These were deployed in somewhat of a circular skirmish line, of which the horses formed the center; the circle having a diameter of several hundred yards. In this order, we made our way back to the timber, the Indians whooping, yelling, and firing their rifles as they dashed madly by on their fleet war ponies. That the fire of their rifles should be effective under these circumstances could scarcely be expected. Neither could the most careful aim of the cavalrymen produce much better results. It forced the savages to keep at a respectful distance, however, and enabled us to make our retrograde movement. A few of our horses were shot by the Indians in this irregular skirmish; none fatally, however. As we were falling back, contesting each foot of ground passed over, I heard a sudden sharp cry of pain from one of the men in charge of our horses; the next moment, I saw his arm hanging helplessly at his side, while a crimson current flowing near his shoulder told that the aim of the Indians had not been entirely in vain. The gallant fellow kept his seat in his saddle, however, and conducted the horses under his charge safely with the rest to the timber. Once concealed by the trees, and no longer requiring the horses to be moved, the number of horse holders was reduced so as to allow but one troop to eight horses, the entire remainder being required on the skirmish line. The redskins had followed us closely step by step to the timber, tempted in part by their great desire to obtain possession of our horses. If successful in this, they believed, no doubt, that flight on our part being no longer possible, we must be either killed or captured.

Taking advantage of a natural terrace or embankment extending almost like a semicircle in front of the little grove in which we had taken refuge, and at a distance of but a few hundred yards from the latter, I determined by driving the Indians beyond to adopt it as our breastwork or line of defense. This was soon accomplished, and we found ourselves deployed behind a natural parapet or bulwark from which the troopers could deliver a carefully directed fire upon their enemies, and at the same time be protected largely from the bullets of the latter. The Indians made repeated and desperate efforts to dislodge us and force us into the level plateau. Every effort of this kind proved unavailing. Several times, savages were discovered creeping stealthily toward us through the deep grass in our front, but the whistling of a few carbine bullets about their ears changed their determination. The Indians never ceased during the fight to engage in their favorite mode of warfare, dashing at full speed along our front, firing and draining our fire. Thus they continued so long that, fearing to exhaust our supply of ammunition, an object that our enemies had probably in view, directions were given to the troopers to reserve their fire as much as possible consistent with safety.

Rather a remarkable instance of rifle shooting occurred in the early part of the contest. I was standing in a group of troopers and with them was busily engaged firing at such of our enemies as exposed themselves. Bloody Knife was with us, his handsome face lighted up by the fire of battle and the desire to avenge the many wrongs suffered by his people at the hands of the ruthless Sioux. All of us had had our attention drawn more than once to a Sioux warrior who, seeming more bold than his fellows, dashed repeatedly along the front of our lines, scarcely two hundred yards distant, and although the troopers had singled him out, he had thus far escaped untouched by their bullets. Encouraged by his success, perhaps, he concluded to taunt us again, and at the same time exhibit his own daring, by riding along the lines at full speed, but nearer than before. We saw him coming. Bloody Knife, with his Henry rifle poised gracefully in his hands, watched his coming, saying he intended to make this his enemy's last ride. He would send him to the happy hunting ground. I told the interpreter to tell Bloody Knife that at the moment the warrior reached a designated point directly opposite to us, he, Bloody Knife, should fire at the rider, and I at the same instant would fire at the pony.

A smile of approval passed over the swarthy features of the friendly scout as he nodded assent. I held in my hand my well-tried Remington. Resting on one knee and glancing along the barrel, at the same time seeing that Bloody Knife was also squatting low in the deep grass with rifle leveled, I awaited the approach of the warrior to the designated point. On he came, brandishing his weapons and flaunting his shield in our faces, defying us by his taunts to come out and fight like men. Swiftly sped the gallant little steed that bore him, scarcely needing the guiding rein. Nearer and nearer both horse and rider approached the fatal spot, when sharp and clear, and so simultaneous as to sound as one, rang forth the reports of the two rifles. The distance was less than two hundred yards. The Indian was seen to throw up his arms and reel in his saddle, while the pony made one final leap, and both fell to the earth. A shout rose from the group of troopers, in which Bloody Knife and I joined. The next moment, a few of the comrades of the fallen warrior rushed to his rescue, and without dismounting from their ponies, scarcely pulling rein, clutched up the body, and the next moment disappeared from view.

Foiled in their repeated attempts to dislodge us, the Indians withdrew to a point beyond the range of our rifles for the apparent purpose of devising a new plan of attack. Of this we soon became convinced. Hastily returning to a renewal of the struggle, we saw our adversaries arrange themselves in groups along our entire front. They were seen to dismount, and the quick eyes of Bloody Knife detected them making their way toward us by crawling through the grass. We were at a loss to comprehend their designs, as we could not believe they intended to attempt to storm our position on foot. We were not left long in doubt. Suddenly, and almost as if by magic, we beheld numerous small columns of smoke shooting up all along our front.

Calling Bloody Knife and the interpreter to my side, I inquired the meaning of what we saw. "They are setting fire to the long grass and intend to burn us out," was the scout's reply, at the same time keeping his eyes intently bent on the constantly increasing columns of smoke. His features wore a most solemn look; anxiety was plainly depicted there. Looking to him for suggestions and advice in this new phase of our danger, I saw his face gradually unbend and a scornful smile part his lips. "The Great Spirit will not help our enemies," was his muttered reply to my question. "See," he continued; "the grass refuses to burn." Casting my eyes along the line formed by the columns of smoke, I saw that Bloody Knife had spoken truly when he said, "The grass refuses to burn."

This was easily accounted for. It was early in the month of August; the grass had not ripened or matured sufficiently to burn readily. A month later, and the flames would have swept us back to the river as if we had been surrounded by a growth of tinder. In a few moments, the anxiety caused by the threatening of this new and terrible danger was dispelled. While the greatest activity was maintained in our front by our enemies, my attention was called to a single warrior who, mounted on his pony, had deliberately, and as I thought rashly, passed around our left flank—our diminished numbers preventing us from extending our line close to the river—and was then in rear of our skirmishers, riding slowly along the crest of the high riverbank with as apparent unconcern as if in the midst of his friends instead of being almost in the power of his enemies. I imagined that his object was to get nearer to the grove in which our horses were concealed, and toward which he was moving slowly, to reconnoiter and ascertain how much force we held in reserve. At the same time, as I never can see an Indian engaged in an unexplained act without conceiving treachery or stratagem to be at the bottom of it, I called to Lieutenant Varnum, who commanded on the left, to take a few men and endeavor to cut the wily interloper off.

This might have been accomplished but for the excessive zeal of some of Varnum's men, who acted with lack of caution, and enabled the Indian to discover their approach and make his escape by a hurried gallop up the river. The men were at a loss even then to comprehend his strange maneuver, but after the fight had ended, and we obtained an opportunity to ride over and examine the ground, all was made clear, and we learned how narrowly we had escaped a most serious if not fatal disaster.

The riverbank in our rear was from twenty to thirty feet high. At its base and along the water's edge ran a narrow pebbly beach. The redskins had hit upon a novel but to us most dangerous scheme for capturing our horses and at the same time throwing a large force of warriors directly on our rear. They had found a pathway beyond our rear, leading from the large tract of timber in which they were first concealed through a cut or ravine in the riverbank. By this they were enabled to reach the water's edge, from which point they could move down the river, following the pebbly beach referred to, the height of the riverbank protecting them perfectly from our observation. Thus they would have placed themselves almost in the midst of our horses before we could have become aware of their designs. Had they been willing, as white men would have been, to assume greater risks, their success would have been assured. But they feared we might discover their movements and catch them while strung out along the narrow beach, with no opportunity to escape. A few men on the bank could have shot down a vastly superior force. In this case, the Indians had sent on this errand about one hundred warriors. Judging from the trail made along the water's edge, they had already accomplished more than two-thirds of the distance which separated them at starting from the coveted prize, when I saw and observed the strange movements of the lone warrior as he deliberately made his way along the riverbank. He was acting as the lookout for the party of warriors at the foot of the high riverbank and kept them advised of our movements. Of course, when Lieutenant Varnum and his party attempted the capture of the lookout, his comrades instinctively supposed that we had discovered their intentions, and they turned and fled up the river when success was almost within their grasp. Even after the flight of the lookout on the bank, the Indians below could have continued their movement in the direction of our horses unsuspected and undiscovered by our party. We only learned of their designs after the fight had terminated.

The contest had now been going on almost without interruption for several hours. It had begun about noon, and it was now nearly 3:00 P.M. I knew that we would soon be released from all danger by the arrival of the main body of the expedition; but a serious question presented itself. Many of the men who had been firing most incessantly now began to complain that their stock of ammunition was well nigh exhausted. They were cautioned to use the few remaining rounds as sparingly as possible. At the same time, I sent a couple of noncommissioned officers quickly into the timber, instructing them to obtain every round remaining in the cartridge boxes of the horse holders and the wounded. This gave us quite a number of rounds, as this supply had not been touched during the fight.

In this chapter, already extended to its full limit, I fear I must omit many interesting minor incidents. The reader can imagine how longingly and anxiously both officers and men constantly turned their eyes to the high ridge of hills, distant nearly two miles, over which we knew we would catch the first glimpse of approaching succor. Our enemies seemed equally aware of our hopes and fears, and strange to say, their quick eyes, added to better points for observation, enabled them to detect the coming of our friends sooner than did we whose safety depended upon it.

Before we became aware of the fact that succor was near at hand, we observed an unusual commotion in the ranks of our adversaries, and soon after a gradual withdrawal from in front of our right and a concentration of their forces opposite our left. The reason for this was soon made clear to us. Looking far to the right and over the crest of hills already described, we could see an immense column of dust rising and rapidly approaching. We could not be mistaken; we could not see the cause producing this dust; but there was not one of us who did not say to himself, "Relief is at hand." A few moments later, a shout arose from the men. All eyes were turned to the bluffs in the distance, and there were to be seen, coming almost with the speed of the wind, four separate squadrons of Uncle Sam's best cavalry, with banners flying, horses' manes and tails floating on the breeze, and comrades spurring forward in generous emulation as to which squadron should land its colors first in the fight.[11] It was a grand and welcome sight, but we waited not to enjoy it. Confident of support, and wearied from fighting on the defensive, now was our time to mount our steeds and force our enemies to seek safety in flight, or to battle on more even terms. In a moment we were in our saddles and dashing after them. The only satisfaction we had was to drive at full speed for several miles a force outnumbering us five to one. In this pursuit, we picked up a few ponies which the Indians were compelled to abandon on account of wounds or exhaustion. Their wounded, of whom there were quite a number, and their killed, as afterward acknowledged by them when they returned to the agency to receive the provisions and fresh supplies of ammunition which a sentimental government, manipulated and directed by corrupt combinations, insists upon distributing annually, were sent to the rear before the flight of the main body. The number of Indians and ponies killed and wounded in this engagement, as shown by their subsequent admission, almost equaled that of half our entire force engaged.[12]

That night, the forces of the expedition encamped on the battleground, which was nearly opposite the mouth of Tongue River. My tent was pitched under the hill from which I had been so unceremoniously disturbed at the commencement of the fight; while under the wide-spreading branches of a neighboring cottonwood, guarded and watched over by sorrowing comrades who kept up their lonely vigils through the night, lay the mangled bodies of two of our companions of the march, who, although not present nor participating in the fight, had fallen victims to the cruelty of our foes.

With General George A. Custer on the Northern Pacific Surveying Expedition in 1873

LOUIS E. HILLS

Journal of History 8 (1915): 143–60

When a boy fourteen of age, I was employed by a deaf old gentleman by the name of Tyler to drive one of his teams from my hometown, Janesville, Wisconsin, across the state, and into Iowa to a town named Greeley, about forty or fifty miles west of Dubuque. When we reached Greeley, Mr. Tyler found his friends and stopped there, and he, having no further need of my services, advised me to go home by way of McGregor. I struck across the country for McGregor, Iowa, thinking to cross the Mississippi River to Prairie du Chien, Wisconsin, and to return that way to Janesville, my home.

When I reached McGregor, I found there was no bridge, and that I must cross the river by boat. I went down to the boat landing just as a large wheel steamer, the *Muscatine,* came up to the landing. I went aboard this boat and went down the river to Saint Louis. The steamer *Mary McDonald,* plying between Saint Louis and New Orleans, was about ready to start on her trip down the river, so I went aboard and went down as far as Memphis, Tennessee. Here I left the boat and began to look for work, which I found in the Southern Oil works. The foreman, Mr. McNair, took an interest in me, gave me work, and was a good friend to me. I got board a short distance from the works and worked there until in March 1873.

In the latter part of March 1873, a son of a lady where I boarded came in at dinnertime and said a lot of soldiers had just come into town, and asked me to go with him where they were going into camp. We went out east of town, where they were putting up their tents, and one of the first persons I noticed was an officer who seemed to be directing all the work; he had long, yellow hair and a yellow mustache. I learned later it was Colonel Custer, who was in command of the regiment. I had a desire to go with them, so stepping up to this officer, I asked him if I could get work and go along with them. He looked at me intently for a moment, with what I thought were the brightest eyes I had ever seen, then abruptly asked me where I lived. I told him in Janesville, Wisconsin. He then asked me what I was doing in Memphis. I told him that I had been working there but had no relatives in the South. He then asked me if I would like to enlist as a soldier. I answered, "Yes, sir, if I may." He then asked me if I thought my parents would care. I said I did not think so, as I had started out to make my own way in the world. "Come with me," he said. We went a short distance among the tents, when we met another officer, whom I afterwards learned was Lieutenant McDougall.[1] After a short conversation between the officers, in which the bugler was mentioned, the lieutenant took me to a tent, where the surgeon examined me. I was enlisted bugler of Company E, 7th United States Cavalry.

I was given a blue suit of clothes, very much too large for me, and a white cow pony named Frank, having a figure eight upon his shoulder, also a bugle and a large revolver. We remained in Memphis a short time after this, and in the first part of April, we loaded our horses, tents, and baggage upon steamboats (three, I think) and went up the Mississippi River to Cairo, Illinois. Here we left the boats and entrained on the Illinois Central Railway for Yankton, Dakota Territory, about April 7 or 8, 1873. We unloaded about a mile out of town, near a new water tank on the railroad, and went into camp. We had our tents nicely up when it began to rain, a slow, drizzling rain, and kept it up until about April 10, when in the forenoon of that day, I saw coming over the bluff northeast of us what looked like a bank of fog coming rapidly toward us, but when it reached us, my! my! it was the worst blizzard I ever experienced. Every snowflake seemed to have been shot out of a gun at close range. We were ordered to lead our horses to town, then only a small village of wood buildings, and Company E and another company put their horses into a new freight house; and we were given quarters in a hall over a store, where we were supplied at mealtimes with wash boilers full of coffee and rations of meat and bread. The storm soon passed, and in a day or so we returned to the camp, finding most of our tents had weathered the storm, and we soon packed up, preparing for our march of five hundred miles up the east side of the Missouri River, to Fort Rice. About seventy-five miles from Yankton, we passed Fort Randall, located on the opposite side of the river from us and about a week later we reached Fort Sully, where we stayed a day or so to rest. This was quite a large post; a number of companies of infantry and a fine band was stationed here, all making our stay very pleasant.

From here on, our trip was very interesting. A number of Indian reservations were passed, and one night we camped near Medicine Rock and some of us went out to see it. It was a large, flat stone, and on the top of it was the imprint of naked feet made when it was soft clay, no doubt many centuries ago. There were medicine bags on sticks, and lumps of sugar, and lots of other stuff too numerous to mention, scattered around this rock, placed there by the Indians.

When we saw any of the Sioux, they looked at us in a way that made me feel they were no friends of mine. We saw many dead Indians rolled up in buffalo robes and tied up in trees. In one place I counted seven in one large cottonwood tree, and a number in other trees nearby, and the air was foul while passing that place.

From here on, we would see antelope, jackrabbits, coyotes, et cetera, and to see the staghounds and foxhounds chase them was a sight. One of the hounds could catch an antelope by the hind foot and throw him as nicely as a professional wrestler, but the jackrabbit, when the hounds were close, would turn a short corner, and the hounds could not turn so short but would have to make a big circle, thus giving the rabbits quite a start. At one time I saw three of the hounds close to a jackrabbit going at full speed, when the rabbit stopped and flattened out on the ground, and I thought the hounds would break their necks; each one grabbed at the rabbit, but all missed it and turned somersault after somersault before they got stopped.

We reached Fort Rice along in May and were ferried across the river on a steamer. Here we camped near the fort for some time, and a lot of Sioux chiefs visited us and smoked the pipe of peace. They were all powerful-looking fellows, and all they would say in English was "How, how."

Finally the command was given to break camp, and we went north twenty-five miles to Fort A. Lincoln, where we joined the rest of the expedition and turned west, going up Heart River quite a distance. We now had over three hundred six mule wagons, a number of ambulances, et cetera.

The line of march was as follows: A number of companies of infantry would go ahead; then the wagon train, six companies of cavalry on each side; then a lot of infantry in the rear.

Each company of cavalry was supposed to be one hundred strong, three commissioned officers with each company, and a number of noncommissioned officers and two buglers. The buglers would ride at the head of the company, in the rear of the officers; and each day, one bugler would mount guard, and it would be his duty to blow the calls for that twenty-four hours, sleeping with the guard, ready to blow any call as directed by the officer of the day or sergeant of the guard.

Each cavalry company had two of the large wagons for their supplies, and at night the wagons would be placed about one hundred and fifty feet apart, and a large rope would be stretched from the hind wheel of one wagon to the hind wheel of the other, thus making a picket line to tie our horses to, where we would feed them oats in nose bags, nights and mornings. When we first went into camp, we would stake our horses out to feed where there was good grass, then just before dark bring them in, and tie them to the picket line and give them their oats. Our tents would be a rod in the rear of the horses in a long row. One night there came up a storm; it rained hard, then turned to hail; the horses stampeded, tipped the wagons over, ran over our tents, and we had quite a time getting them back and the wagons righted. What a night! Not a dry thread of clothing, and our blankets lying in water—a night long to be remembered.

We found some small streams hard to cross, and one time the crossing was extra bad, the wagons sinking to their hubs in mud. Here they got a long rope and a hundred men would help the mules pull the wagons across.

The Yellowstone Expedition, 1873

After leaving Heart River, we suffered for water, using water out of buffalo wallows and were compelled to drink fearful alkali water. The scouts said it would not be long until we would reach the Little Missouri River, where we would have plenty of water, but oh! such water, alkali, and mud; it was surely a treat when we reached the Yellowstone, where we got good water.

A day or so before we reached the Badlands, we could see them in the distance, and a pretty sight it was. It looked like a great city in the distance, great sand buttes looking like buildings, castles, forts, everything about a great city. We passed trees one hundred feet long lying upon the ground, solid stone. Surely the Badlands are one of the wonderful sights of the world.

Here we found rattlesnakes, and lots of them. I ran into a den of them one night when I was going down the dry bed of a creek, looking for water. I saw Captain French[2] shoot some fine shot with a revolver.

As we found our way through the Badlands, we came upon the remains of a lot of wagons, pieces of boxes, trunks, barrels, et cetera, and on a small white stone butte were a large number of skulls, no doubt of those who had been with the wagons; a mute testimony of a massacre by some of the large bands of hostile Sioux that roamed through this country each summer.

We reached the Yellowstone River about the middle of July. Coming down into the valley, we had to pass through a lot of wild sage, where we started up a large flock of sage hens, the first that most of us had ever seen. We also saw a large prairie dog village, where little ground owls, snakes, and prairie dogs all housed together. Here, upon the bank of the river, we found an old stockade, built of logs set in the ground endwise; it must have been more than one hundred feet square.

Here we camped some time while the steamboats *Far West* and *Josephine* were ferrying the expedition across the Yellowstone River. This must have been somewhere near where the town of Glendive now stands. After all had been ferried to the north side of the river, we started on our march, going up the river. It was here we found lots of beautiful moss agates, on the bluffs and in the Badlands. We had found lots of fine fossils. I still have a fossil nautilus, a fine one. I had so many fossils and moss agates in the saddlebags that it made my horse's back sore.

We passed many dead Indians upon scaffolds ten or twelve feet high, made by placing long posts in the ground with forked ends on top, then put[ting] crosspieces, thus making a strong platform.

The body was wrapped up in a buffalo robe and was then wrapped tightly with green rawhide strips, about a quarter of an inch wide; when they dry, they become as hard as bone. I cut into several of them and found one half of the skull stained red and the other half black; a mystery to me [to] this day.

As we were going north on August 4, I was permitted to go to the river with a number of canteens to fill with fresh water for some of the men of the company. The command was then traveling along the bench, about a mile back from the river. I rode rapidly ahead of the wagon train for about three miles, then stopped at a little grove of cottonwood and brush, and picketed my horse out to eat grass, while I went to the river and filled the canteens. A man from Company F was just below me on the same errand. I saw Mr. Baliran, the regimental sutler,[3] and Mr. Honsinger, the veterinary surgeon,[4] ride up to a large grove, a short distance up the river from where I was. There was a soldier there also from Company K, I think also after water. I thought I would wait until the wagon train came in sight, so laid down near my horse and must have dropped into a light sleep, when suddenly I was startled by yells from the large grove above. I jumped up and went out a few steps where I could see, when I was horrified to see a number of Indians killing Mr. Baliran and Mr. Honsinger. Mr. Baliran was running on foot, and two Indians were shooting arrows into his back; Mr. Honsinger, also on foot, was running, and a big Indian rode up and struck him over the head with the stock of his gun. When Mr. Baliran was found, there was an arrow run clear through his body and into the ground, and he had hold of it with his right hand, his eyes open, dead, and the arrow still in his body. Mr. Honsinger's left hand was at his head as he fell and was brought into camp in that way.

As soon as I got a glimpse of what was going on, I jumped to my horse, unsnapped the lariat, mounted, and guiding my horse with my revolver by touching him on either side of the head, I made for the command as fast as we could travel. The man of Company F, a little below me, was also riding for the command, cap gone, and yelling at every jump of his horse. I remember his white hair to this day.

Colonel Custer, with a scouting party, had gone on ahead that morning, and about the time we reached the command, we heard rapid firing up the river, and the cavalry went quickly to the aid of the scouting party. Company E, under command of Lieutenant McDougall, charged at a mad gallop down a ravine and out into the river bottom, where we could see Colonel Custer and the scouting party in a fight with a large band of Indians, about three hundred. All the rest of the 7th Regiment came down into the river bottom about the same time we did, and when the Indians saw us coming, they fled up the valley and were soon out of sight.

The small party of Sioux who killed Mr. Baliran and Honsinger was led by an Oglala Sioux named Rain-in-the-Face. They were out on purpose to catch stragglers. That night, we buried those killed, and just as the graves were dug, up drove a priest, Father De Smet,[5] in a white, canvas-topped buggy. His appearance was a surprise. From whence he came and where he went, I never knew; but I learned later that he baptized Sitting Bull, so I think he must have been with the Indians.

Three or four days later, we discovered the trail of a very large Indian village, moving up the river; the lodge poles dragging, cut all the grass, leaving a trail of dust over one hundred feet wide.

We were issued a week's rations and ordered to be ready to start in pursuit at 10:00 P.M. We traveled swiftly that night, and the next morning we stopped awhile to let our horses graze and rest while we ate our lunch. We would take our knives and scrape our ration of raw salt pork, then spread it on the hardtack like butter, and it surely tasted good, after our thirty- or forty-mile ride.

A little after sunrise, we saddled up and took up the trail. We found we were getting close upon them, as they dropped camp kettles, axes, and all kinds of stuff in their haste to get away, showing they must have known we were after them.

We stopped at noon in a large cottonwood grove and waited until night, resting men and horses, and giving the horses a chance to graze. Just after sundown, we took up the trail again, and followed rapidly until sometime in the fore part of the night, when we came to where the Indians had crossed the Yellowstone River, bag and baggage.

This was a disappointment, as all hoped that we could teach them a lesson they would not soon forget. This last night I rode with Colonel Custer and the scouts. Colonel Custer's standing orderly, Private Tuttle, was also a member of Company E, and the best shot in the regiment. The principal Indian scout was Bloody Knife, the Arikara; and Charlie Reynolds,[6] the white scout, and a number of Crow scouts.

At daylight we mounted again and forded a small channel of the river, out to a sandbar, but it was deep and swift on the other side. A lot of the men and a young officer succeeded in swimming the river, but they could not get a rope across that was made of lariats. After many efforts were made during the day to cross, the general gave it up, and near sundown we went back to the cottonwood grove, disappointed and tired, yet I have always believed it saved us from a massacre. As it proved the next morning, they were watching for us, and I believe one thousand or more Indians were lying in ambush, waiting for us to come across, when they would have pounced upon us as we came out of the water, and few would have ever gotten back.

A strong guard was placed around the grove, and Tuttle and I slept behind a large cottonwood tree near the bank of the river. I little thought as we lay there that Tuttle would be shot there the next morning, but he was.

At daylight, the Indians began shooting at us from across the river, and one yelled, "You need not try to cross anymore; we will come over to you," and a little later one yelled in broken English, "Long-Hair Colonel Custer, we will get your scalp yet." For about three hours or more, there was heavy firing across the river. Tuttle shot an Indian across the river that exposed himself and crippled another that tried to pull him back into the brush. I laughed aloud when Tuttle shot the Indian, and Colonel Custer, who was only a short distance below where we were, told someone to take that boy and put him behind a tree and make him stay there. Pieces of leaves were then dropping like rain from the bullets passing through the trees overhead. About the middle of the forenoon, as near as I can remember, the river above us and below us was black with the heads of ponies and Indians swimming the river, coming over to our side, and about noon they were all around us, above, below, and back of us. About this time, we discovered a large band of the Indians on the bench above us, several hundred, I should judge, riding right towards us. Colonel Custer then sent me to the bandleader to tell him to take his band up on a little hill, at the west end of the grove, and to play "Garry Owen," the colonel's favorite tune. A skirmish line was on the ridge back of us, and Lieutenant Braden and a small party of men were upon a point of the bluff above us, trying to pick off some of the Indians that were behind rocks on the opposite side of the gulch from where the band was. While I was looking for the bandleader, my company was sent with others to charge the Indians, so I stayed near the band and watched the fight. What a sight it was! As the four companies charged the large band above us, the Indians stopped, dismounted, and fired; then mounted and retreated a short distance, then dismounted again, while the soldiers would ride up near them, then they would dismount and fire a volley into the Indians. Many an Indian was shot, and their ponies also, in that fight, and some of the soldiers, and Lieutenant Braden was also shot.

From the time the Indians began to cross the river, Chief Sitting Bull[7] was upon a high bluff over a mile away, on the opposite side of the river from us, giving commands in a voice truly marvelous. He was also using smoke signals. Along late in the afternoon, the wagon train came in sight, and they took a mountain howitzer up on the hill where the band had been and shot a bomb over the river and up into a large bunch of Indians. The dust flew, and there was an awful scattering of Indians for a few minutes.

Colonel Custer ordered Tuttle's body to be sewed up in canvas and placed in an ambulance, for he thought a great deal of him, and we buried him the next night at sundown, in a cottonwood grove near the river.

Two or three days later, we reached Pompey's Pillar, about August 14, I think, and while a number of soldiers were bathing in the river, the Indians, from some brush on the opposite side of the river, shot into the water at the bathers, but no one was hurt. It was near here where we first saw buffalo. We left the Yellowstone when we left Pompey's Pillar, and struck across the divide, northwest, to the Musselshell River. It was while going across from the Yellowstone to the Musselshell that I killed the first buffalo killed on the expedition, an old buffalo bull.

Colonel Custer had two fine rifles, a Springfield that Tuttle used and carried, and a Remington that he used most of the time himself. After the death of Tuttle, for a short time Colonel Custer let me carry the Springfield rifle, and I had it the day we run on to [sic] three old buffalo bulls. When we got up close to them, I put spurs to my horse and began shooting at the largest one. I followed him quite a ways and shot a number of times before I finally brought him down. I then cut off his tail just as Custer rode up. He was angry at me for going so far from the command, yet he had to laugh when he saw me with the tail in my hands. He told me to mount at once and follow him, as the Indians were liable to get me when I got so far away from the command. Colonel Custer was very good to me, and it was his desire to help me in Memphis that brought about my enlistment. We passed through a great herd of buffalos the same day I killed the old bull. In a day or so we reached the Musselshell River, a most beautiful stream full of whitefish. I had a fishhook and line and caught grasshoppers, and there would be a number of fish jump out of the water before the grasshopper would strike it. I caught enough for the company.

The first night we camped on that river. From here we began our return trip; we went downstream until we reached the place the river turned north, then struck over the divide, northeast, reaching the Yellowstone in the fore part of September, where we waited a week or more for the main wagon train to catch up, and then it took some time to get all across the river ready for our homeward trip, reaching Fort Lincoln in the fore part of October and found that while we were gone, fine barracks and stables had been built for our winter quarters.

The Yellowstone Expedition of 1873

CHARLES BRADEN[1]

Journal of the United States Cavalry Association 16 (October 1905): 218–41

In the spring of 1873, the government decided to send an expedition to guard the surveyors of the Northern Pacific Railroad in their efforts to locate the line west of the Missouri River. The road had been built as far as Bismarck, Dakota, now in North Dakota. Considerable resistance was expected from the Indians, so a large force was to be sent. The 7th Cavalry, to which I belonged, was to form part of the command. The regiment was scattered throughout the South, where we had been since 1871, taking part in suppressing the "Ku Klux" organization.

Our troop (L) was at Jackson Barracks, Louisiana. Lieutenant (now Commissary General) Weston[2] was in command of the troop. It was a fine body of men, nearly every man an old soldier, for the vacancies in the troop, when we reached New Orleans in December 1872, were about all filled by men who had served one or more terms in other regiments in the South, and when discharged drifted to the city, having spent their money, and were ready to enlist again. It was known that we were to go on the expedition, and the prospect of active service was the magnet which drew a number to our ranks.

We were to go on a steamboat as far as Cairo, Illinois. We were ready about the middle of March, but our departure was delayed because there was much floating ice in the Mississippi above Memphis. We started on the evening of April 1, 1873. The trip, lasting about a week, was comfortable and pleasant, but rather tedious. At Memphis, we took aboard several troops of the regiment which had come by rail from their stations in South Carolina. At Cairo, the entire regiment was to be collected. We were all there on the same day, but not together, for two troops (D and I) left in the morning for St. Paul, where they were to form a portion of the escort of the commission to locate the northern boundary of the United States. We arrived at Cairo in the afternoon of the day D and I Troops left.

At Cairo, we took trains for Yankton, Dakota. Traveling in those days for men and horses was not as comfortable as it is now. The regiment, after the expedition's return in the fall, was to be stationed at Forts Lincoln and Rice, the former nearly across the Missouri River from Bismarck, and the latter about twenty-five miles south. It was to be a change of station to another department, so all baggage, public and private, was taken along, and there was a great deal of it.

The trip to Yankton from Cairo was uneventful. Upon arriving at Yankton, we went into camp on a low plain about two miles from the city. The officers' wives, who accompanied their husbands, went, all but two, to the best hotel in the town. The exceptions were Mrs. Custer and Mrs. Calhoun (Colonel Custer's sister). They occupied a vacant house about midway between town and camp.

Most of the officers and men wore the thin clothing which they had used in the South, and no one anticipated the great change in the climate that came upon us. A few days after our arrival, a typical Dakota blizzard set in. It began snowing on a Saturday morning and did not let up until the following Thursday.[3] The strong wind piled the snow into huge drifts and filled every hollow. Sunday morning the scene was extremely desolate. Some of the tents had split open at the top, and the inmates were covered with anywhere from a few inches to a foot of snow. I woke up before dawn and felt the heavy weight. Getting dressed the best way possible, I waited for daylight. I picked some of my belongings out of the snow, put what I could find into my trunks, and covered the trunks with a poncho. I then went out to look around. The snow was so blinding that it was impossible to see twenty feet. I found my way over to the first sergeant's tent. We went along the picket line and found that many of the horses were over half buried in the snow.

What to do was the question. There was no one to give orders, for Colonel Custer was not well, and also could not get over to camp. Before long the governor of the territory, Colonel McCook,[4] and Colonel Forsyth,[5] one of General Sheridan's aides, reached camp and told us to get over to town with our horses as soon as possible, and the best way we could, and to take possession of several large buildings which the quartermaster had had constructed, and also any vacant houses we could find, and to put the animals under shelter.

Colonel McCook said the blizzard would probably continue several days, and that the horses would perish if left outdoors. Fortunately the wind was blowing in the direction of the town. We put no saddles on the horses; each man rode bareback and with the snaffle bit. No semblance of order was possible, each troop getting along as well as he could. Lieutenant Weston was away, and I was in command of the troop. I was the first to receive Colonel McCook's directions. Every little while a rider would be thrown. There was no time to stop and help him, but he had to look out for himself. After great exertions, we finally got the horses under shelter, and then we had to look out for a place for ourselves, as it was impossible to face the storm and go back to camp. Some of us found refuge in the town hotels; other were cared for by citizens in their homes. There were many laundresses and children in camp, and we became very anxious about them. Fortunately the weather was not very cold, so they were in no immediate danger of freezing to death, but we knew they must be suffering from hunger.

On the third day of the storm, several officers, with a number of men, endeavored to reach camp, but were unable to face the driving wind and snow. On the fifth day, we succeeded, after several hours of the hardest work, in reaching camp. We found some of the women and children buried in the snow; a number had frostbitten hands and feet, and all of them were half dead with fright and lack of sustenance. They were put into sleds and dragged to town, where the kindhearted citizens turned out en masse to aid the unfortunates in every way possible.

After the storm was over, we went back to camp with our horses. They were a sorry-looking lot, all gaunt from hunger and thirst, and many without manes and tails, which had been gnawed on by other animals in efforts to obtain a little nourishment. In a day or two, the snow melted and our camp was, for several days, one vast lake.

Mrs. Custer, in *Boots and Saddles*,[6] describes the storm, but her account falls far short of a complete presentation of the sufferings of those who were in the camp.

After the ground became dry, we had an animated camp. It was the first time since the Wichita campaign of 1868 that as many as ten troops had been together. There were squad drills, company drills, squadron drills, and regimental drills daily, ending every evening with a dress parade mounted. To witness this came the people of the surrounding country for miles. Entertainments by citizens of Yankton were given several times each week. With few exceptions, the married officers had their families with them. Time passed rapidly and pleasantly, while we were getting ready for the march to Fort Rice, where the main body of the Yellowstone expedition of 1873 was to rendezvous. General Stanley, colonel of the 22nd Infantry, was in command. I have forgotten the exact composition of the expedition, but there were about all the companies of the 22nd Infantry, six companies of the 9th Infantry, four of the 8th Infantry, one or two of the 6th Infantry, several of the 17th Infantry,[7] besides a detachment of Ree Indians[8] under Lt. Daniel Brush,[9] 17th Infantry. There was an immense wagon train, for supplies had to be carried for the long march to Glendive, on the Yellowstone River, where we were to meet some steamboats with additional supplies for the trip west along the Yellowstone.

In moving up the Missouri from Yankton, each troop was allowed two wagons, enough to carry a few days' rations for the men and forage for the horses. A flat-bottom steamboat went along loaded with supplies. Of course, our march was across the bends of the river, while the steamer had to follow the windings, and probably went at least twice as far, if not more, every day than we did. The families of the officers, excepting Mrs. Custer and Mrs. Calhoun, were on board. Several times each week, the camp was almost alongside of the steamer. The passengers on the boat found it a very monotonous trip, their only consolation being that they were always sheltered from the heavy rainstorms to which we were exposed.

I was caterer of our mess on the march from Yankton to Fort Rice. In the mess were Captain Benteen, Dr. Kimball, Lieutenant West, Gibson, DeRudio, and myself. Before leaving Yankton, I purchased enough eggs to fill two barrels. These eggs were carefully packed in oats, and the last of them were not used till after we reached Fort Rice. They were a welcome addition to our bill of fare. Our cook was a colored woman called "Sam"—abbreviation for Samuela.

One interesting incident, perhaps worth describing, occurred during the march. One night our camp was pitched near an Indian village. We noticed that there were no young men, all the Indians being old, worn-out warriors, women, and children. The absence of the young bucks was due to the fact that they were on the warpath, and we afterwards met them in several affairs. The villagers soon visited our camp and made themselves at home. When our mess was about finishing dinner, which was served on a large box, we sitting around on smaller boxes or camp stools, five squaws (one old and the others from about sixteen to twenty years old) came near. Dr. Kimball had served in the Sioux country and knew a little of the language. He asked them to come nearer, and they sat on the ground. Our dinner consisted of roast beef, mashed potatoes, canned tomatoes, and hot biscuits, baked in a "Dutch oven."

When we had finished, we gave each squaw a piece of beef and some vegetables, with a knife and a fork. They had evidently never seen a fork and did not know what to do with it. After a few minutes' talk among themselves, they laid the forks behind them on the ground and used their fingers to carry the food to their mouths. When nothing more could be gathered with their fingers, they used their tongues and literally licked the platters clean. All the while, they curiously eyed our colored Sam, who returned their stares, expressing at the same time, in language more forcible than elegant, her opinion of the squaws.

The latter, evidently beholding a negress for the first time, seemed to be much interested in her looks, although they said nothing that we understood. As the last course to the dinner, each of the squaws was given a hot biscuit, inside of which had been placed a lump of butter. At first they were suspicious that some trick was about to be played on them (they had undoubtedly never seen hot bread), but as we ate biscuits prepared as were those given to them, their courage came back, and having tasted one of the biscuits, [theirs] could not be buttered rapidly enough. On the whole, it was a unique dinner party. We learned that the squaws were Mrs. Two Bears and the four Misses Two Bears.

At Fort Rice, the department commander, Brig. Gen. Alfred H. Terry, visited our camp, [and] reviewed and inspected the regiment. Afterwards a reception was given him at the quarters of the commanding officer.

When everything was ready, the expedition started on its long journey.[10] Whenever the circumstances were favorable, the wagon train was in four columns. Half of the infantry marched in front and half in the rear of the train. The cavalry was equally divided into left and right wings, and marched on the flanks of the train.[11]

It was not known how long it would require to reach Glendive, and so it was necessary to take as many stores as possible, so officers were restricted in what they could take. Mess chests, cots, and trunks were prohibited. Each officer could take a valise with a change of underclothing, roll of blankets, and each mess a few cooking utensils. An inspection was made to see that no officer exceeded the allowance, but one managed to take his mess chest and a cooking stove. The cooking stove came to grief before long, due to a few peculiar circumstances.

Before the expedition was well under way, a poker club had been started in the cavalry camp. One of the rules was that play must stop at midnight. Reveille was at three, breakfast at four, and advance at five every morning. One morning, the poker players were late at breakfast, and when the advance was sounded, the cooking outfit with the stove was not ready to move on time. I was officer of the guard and received directions to stay behind till this outfit was loaded, and then see that it caught up with its proper place in the column.

Soon Colonel Stanley rode up and asked what we were doing there and why we were not where we should be. The excuse of the soldier in charge of the mess was that the breakfast was late and the stove too hot to handle. Colonel Stanley said a few emphatic words about officers having stoves in violation of orders, and declared that the stove should not again delay the entire command. The next day, there was no stove in camp, and I presume the pieces of it are still rusting somewhere in Dakota.

There had been heavy rains, and the ground was quite soft. Progress was very slow, for the wagons had heavy loads. In about two weeks, we did not go fifty miles, and it was decided to send all empty wagons back to Fort Lincoln for extra supplies of rations and forage. Our squadron, under Captain Yates,[12] was detailed as escort. The return trip was quite rapid, as our train was light. We had to wait several days at Lincoln before we could get enough to fill our wagons. We had heard of the mosquitoes along the Missouri River bottom, but never dreamed that the pests could be so numerous and so troublesome. After our experience, I was ready to believe any mosquito story that could be told, even to that I afterwards heard my West Point roommate tell. After graduation, he served awhile in Alaska and declared that the mosquitoes there were so large and strong that each carried under his wing a small whetstone with which to sharpen his bill. Another of his stories was to the effect that netting was no protection, for the "skeeters" always got through. He had seen them do it, saying that they worked in threes, and when they encountered a net, two stuck their bills into an opening and pulled the mesh apart so that the third could go through. Then this one pulled one way from the inside, one pulled the other way from the outside, and the second one went through. Then the two inside pulled and the last one entered. When they had feasted to their heart's content, they simply reversed the process of entering, and went out.

After getting our wagons loaded at Lincoln, we started after the main command, but did not overtake it until we reached Glendive. Our trip to Glendive was made as rapidly as possible. We followed the trail of the main command and had the benefit of their road making, so that there was no delay to us. Our marches were long, for we endeavored to make daily double the distance gone by Colonel Stanley. Our camping places at night were at every other camp of the main force. There were no exciting incidents on this march, but we passed through a part of the famous Badlands of Dakota and Montana.

At Glendive was the steamer *Josephine,* loaded with supplies. There was great activity in camp. A small earthwork was constructed, and all the supplies that could not be loaded into wagons were to be left with a guard under Captain Pearson, 17th Infantry,[13] to await the return of the expedition after the summer's work was finished.

Some days after our arrival at Glendive, the expedition pulled out for the really difficult part of the journey. We had to pass over some more of the Badlands, and after several days of toilsome and very slow marching, we got clear of them near the mouth of the Powder River. At this place we were again met by the *Josephine,* which brought us the last mail we had until the return in September. In looking over a New York paper, I saw a notice of a disastrous fire in my native city of East Saginaw, Michigan. My father's house was burned in the fire.

We fully expected to meet Indians, and orders were given to be on the lookout for signs. As day after day passed and none were seen, the men became careless, and there was considerable straggling while looking for water. The line of march was along the north bank of the Yellowstone, but every morning the wagon train took to the high lands and cut across the bends. Colonel Custer, with two troops of cavalry, went ahead each day in order to look out for the best route for the train. The troops took turns for this duty, which was far more agreeable than to go with the train.

One day, during a halt, some of the officers thought they saw a few Indians several miles ahead. They supposed the Indians were lying among some rocks. I was the only officer of the regiment who carried a field glass. Everyone present took a turn with the glasses. There were as many opinions as there were lookers. Finally Bloody Knife, the scout and guide, appeared; shading his eyes with his hands, he took a long look and said there were no Indians. Then, using the glass, he confirmed his first idea and said that what we saw was a piece of half-burned log and a few rocks. An hour later, we passed the place. Bloody Knife was correct. His naked eyes were better than ours with the glasses thrown in.

On August 4, we were opposite the mouth of Tongue River. It was the hottest day we had had. Custer had, as usual, gone ahead with Troops A and B. Troop F was part of the escort of the surveyors. Our troop (L) was the rear of the left flank, between the train and the rear. About 2:00 P.M., the train came to a stop at a place where it was necessary for the wagons to go one by one over a gully. Long before this, scores of infantrymen had succumbed to the heat and crawled into the wagons. The horses would not graze; they stood motionless, with their heads lowered and the tongues protruding. We sat in the shade made by the bodies of the animals and found a little relief from the broiling sun. The air was a dead calm, and we afterwards heard that one of the hospital attendants said the thermometer on the shady side of an ambulance had registered 110 degrees. The officers and men were about as languid as the horses.

Suddenly the scene was changed. A few shots were heard to our left and rear. Although we had not seen up to this time any Indians or signs of them, we felt that the shots meant something doing. Everyone jumped up and quickly put the bridle on his horse. At this time the column moved forward, and in another minute we saw coming toward us, as fast as he could urge his horse, a single rider, behind him, his picket pin flying up and down as it struck some obstruction. As he approached us, Weston and I rode out to meet him. As he got within hearing, he yelled, "All down there are killed."

He belonged to F Troop, which was a part of the engineer escort. We at once concluded that the engineers and their escort had been attacked, and that this man had escaped from the supposed slaughter. Such, however, was not the case. The soldier, with another, had straggled and looked for water. They had joined the veterinary surgeon of the regiment and the post trader.[14] The four, finding a spring, had taken the bridles off their horses, picketed them out to graze, and were sitting near the spring, when they were surprised by a small party of Indians. The two civilians fell at the first round, but the soldiers pulled up the picket pins and started to get away. They were pursued, and one was killed, the other escaping unhurt and giving us warning.

Lieutenant Weston at once sent word ahead to the officer in command of our wing and gave orders for the men to go in the direction of the firing. We were on a very high plateau, probably three hundred feet above the river. The descent was very steep and covered with loose stones of all sizes. The men scattered, each going down as best he could, with orders to assemble at the bottom of the hill. I was fortunate in finding the best place for the descent—it was in a little valley—and was the first to get down. The horses were led, and at times fairly slid on their haunches. Loose stones, started above us, came whirling past our heads, and it is a wonder that no one was injured. A few of the men were close behind me.

A minute or so before we reached the bottom, and traveling at right angles to our direction, rode at a trot five or six Indians, leading several horses, one of which I recognized as that of our veterinary surgeon, because of the size of the animal and the red saddle blanket. We could easily have fired on and probably killed some of the party, but we thought they belonged to the Ree scouts with us. They were, in fact, as we afterwards learned, Rain-in-the-Face[15] and a few of his warriors who had killed, as before mentioned, the veterinary and trader and appropriated their horses and other belongings.

In a few minutes more, the entire troop was down the hill and assembled. Saddle girths were tightened, and we moved up the valley of the Yellowstone. Ahead of us was Rain-in-the-Face and party going as fast as they could. We then realized that the Indians were hostile, and we started in pursuit.

Rain-in-the-Face. NELSON A. MILES. *PERSONAL RECOLLECTIONS AND OBSERVATIONS.*

After going probably a mile, we rounded the point of a bluff. A glance up the valley showed that the grass had been set on fire. It was in patches, large and small, and being quite dry, burned readily. Soon we were riding between these burning patches, occasionally dashing across one. It was not possible to keep the men together. For probably half an hour, we were in this situation. Between the heat of the sun and that of the burning grass, it is inconceivable how we escaped loss, but all finally were through the fire.

A stop was made to collect the scattered troopers, and while waiting, I used my glasses to survey the land. Way up the river was more smoke, and as it cleared away, we could see many mounted men riding to and fro. Again the saddles were adjusted, each man loaded his carbine, and in line we moved on. Not long afterwards, a mounted man rode out of a clump of woods and came in our direction. He was one of Custer's party. Custer had in the morning marched rapidly and soon was farther in advance than it was possible for the wagon train to go. Then he stopped in a small grove of cottonwood trees. The horses were unsaddled and picketed out to graze, and most of the men went to sleep. Along in the afternoon, about the time our stragglers were attacked, a large number of Indians attacked Custer's party.

From what we could learn of the affair, it came near being a surprise to Custer, but fortunately the Indians were discovered just in time. While some of the men formed a skirmish line to stand off the warriors, the others brought in the horses. Custer was comparatively safe in the grove so long as his ammunition held out. The Indians, foiled in their attempt to surprise the command and to stampede the horses, set fire to the grass and hoped to burn out the besieged troops, but the grass in the woods was not very dry and did not burn rapidly, so this plan was a failure. It was this fire which, spreading down the valley, caught us in its warm embrace. I have never been in such a hot situation, and I hope I may never again be, either in this world or the next.

We had distanced the balance of the left wing. If they started up the valley, they must have gotten lost, for we did not see them again until night. Our approach caused the Indians attacking Custer to withdraw. When we were near enough to Custer's position to be distinguished from hostile Indians, Custer is said to have remarked, "Ten to one that is Weston and his troop in the lead." "A safe bet, General," said Captain Moylan, "but there are no takers." This remark, surely a great compliment to Weston and L Troop, was well deserved.

When we halted, there was not a man who did not look as black as the ace of spades; the smoke of the burning grass had stuck to our faces; all had perspired so much that we were as wet as if we had been in the river. Perspiration was dripping from the horses, and many a leg was badly singed while galloping through the patches of burning grass. I crawled on all fours far enough into the Yellowstone to get my head underwater. It felt as if ice had been packed around me. The water itself was not so very cold, but it felt so in our overheated condition.

After waiting several hours and there being no indications of the wagon train, Custer retraced his steps and near sundown met the wagons. The veterinary surgeon and post trader, as well as one trooper, were missing. Searching parties were sent out, and the bodies of the two former were found, but not that of the soldier. They were covered with canvas and carried along next day. A month later, when the expedition was on its return, a skeleton was found near where the veterinary and trader had been killed. This was probably the missing soldier.

After this day's experience, there was no more straggling, and everyone was on the alert to discover signs of Indians. We were now in the vicinity of a number of villages. On August 5, 6, and 7, we passed several places where there had been large camps and also noted heavy trains coming from the north. On the eighth, a number of large campsites were passed, in some of which were abandoned articles of value to the Indians. It was reported that a rifle had also been found. Less than twenty-four hours had elapsed since some of these camps had been used.

On the afternoon of August 8, Colonel Stanley directed Custer to take every mounted man, including the Ree Indians, make a forced march, and endeavor to overtake the villages. About three days' rations were carried on pack animals. A blanket and overcoat was allowed each man—soldiers and officers—and about one hundred rounds per man of extra ammunition were taken. No tents were permitted, not even for the commanding officer. An extra feed of grain was given to the horses, and we started as soon as it became dark and with brief halts marched all night. At sunrise, we stopped an hour to graze the horses and let the men get some breakfast. All day of the ninth, we moved as rapidly as we could, being stimulated by fresh signs, and hoped to overtake the village we were following. On the evening of this day, we reached the place of the Yellowstone where the Indians had crossed the river. They had probably taken their belongings over in "bull boats" and made their ponies swim. The boats were made by stretching hides over a wicker framework, and it required skillful navigation to keep them from upsetting.

On the march during this day, we noticed where large accessions to the Indian villages had been made, by the number of heavy trails which joined the main party. By evening the command was tired out. We had been on the go all day and night of the eighth and all day of the ninth—thirty-six hours—with very brief halts. Till darkness set in efforts were made to find a ford, but without success. We bivouacked where we were, and by the next morning were very much refreshed.

Next day, August 10, at sunrise, parties were sent up and down the river to look for a crossing. The main force went to a small island. Someone had discovered a narrow ford to the island capable of holding two or three abreast, but between the island and the south bank, the water was deep and the current strong. Efforts were made to swim some of the horses across, their riders carrying a rope made by tying a lot of picket lines together. The efforts failed, for the long line was too heavy to be dragged through the water with its strong current. Lieutenant Weston and several teamsters succeeded in crossing with mules.

Our men and horses had never been drilled in swimming. When the water reached about halfway between their bellies and their backs, the strong current nearly carried them off their feet, and the animals refused to go further, but turned around and started for the shore. The swimmers were advised to keep on their underclothing, but they did not do so, and long before the day was over, the sun had blistered their bodies, and the next morning they were stiff and sore all over. The men who swam across explored the woods and found many indications that the Indians had been there but a short time before. It was afterwards stated that a few redskins were concealed in the bushes and watched our efforts. They might have killed those of our command who crossed, for the latter were stark naked and without any means of defense. Their danger was very great, for a single armed Indian could easily have killed them all without any risk of injury to himself.

The entire command remained huddled on the little island until night, when it returned to the north bank of the river and went into bivouac. It was decided to move up the river the next day and seek a crossing, but the Indians themselves solved the problem by coming back after getting their village to a place of safety.

The bivouac of L Troop was farthest upstream. It was my turn for officer of the guard that night. Pickets were posted on the bluffs, and some hours after dark, all except the sentinels endeavored to obtain a little sleep. About 2:00 A.M., I felt sure I heard sounds that resembled those made by horses running over hard ground. I thought that some of our animals had become stampeded, but one of our scouts said that the sounds we heard were made by ponies, and that the Indians were undoubtedly concentrating in the woods opposite us and would open fire at daybreak. The scout thought that Colonel Custer ought to be notified. I followed his advice and went to where Colonel Custer was asleep, woke him up, and told him what the scout had said. Custer replied that he did not believe the Indians were coming back. His manner indicated that he was annoyed at being awakened. I also was annoyed at the manner of my early reception and went back to the guard.

The pony sounds continued, and the scout declared that by daylight there would be several hundred warriors in the woods opposite, and that they would make it warm for us, as we had no protection whatever except a few scattered trees, and the width of the river was less than the range of their Henry rifles. It turned out as the scout had predicted.

As the mist on the river became dissipated by the rising sun, a hot fire was opened upon us. The cooks, preparing coffee, were the only ones astir, and for all but the scout and myself, it was a complete surprise. The bottom on which we were bivouacked was about half a mile broad, and orders were given to move back out of range. A number of skirmishers were scattered along the bank of the river and returned the fire of the Indians. I had gone to where Keegan, the cook of our mess, was preparing coffee for Weston and myself. The bullets were flying around at a lively rate. I called to Keegan to take the coffeepot along. Just as he stooped to take it from the fire, several bullets struck the blaze, and some of the live coals fell on his hand. The result was that he dropped the pot, our precious coffee was spilled, and all we had for breakfast was hardtack and water.

One of the horses of the guard had been left behind when we moved out of range. With one of the troops, I went back to get the animal and had barely pulled up the picket pin when the animal leaped into the air and fell dead, a bullet from the other side having gone through his brain. I next went to a high bluff from which could be seen the country for eight or ten miles up and down the river. With the aid of my glasses, I was able to notice that numbers of Indians were crossing and approaching our position from both directions. A report of this was at once sent to Colonel Custer, and he made his dispositions accordingly. To the west were hills, which in possession of the hostiles would render our position in the bottom a very unsafe one. Our squadron commander was directed to occupy this hill with about a third of a troop, dismounted. I was ordered to turn over the guard to the sergeant and go in charge of this detachment. We went as rapidly as possible and, leaving our horses at the foot of the hill, scrambled to the top through a narrow ravine. There were about twenty men with me.

As our party reached the top, spread out before us was a plateau probably a mile or more in extent and not a hundred yards away. Riding in our direction was what looked like the whole Sioux nation to the few of us. There were probably a hundred dressed in their war toggery of paint, feathers, horns, etc. We saw them before they saw us and, hurriedly forming a line, opened fire. Our volley caused them to stop; several ponies were seen to fall, but I do not know if any of the warriors were hit. At any rate, we saw several ponies an instant after scurrying back with two riders each. Our one volley caused them to turn, some to the right and some to the left, but close behind them was another lot of about the same number. Our men had barely time to slup a fresh cartridge into their carbines when the second line was where the first was checked. The second onslaught turned out as did the first. Our men were lying down on the slope, with only their heads above the summit. The fourth charge of the Indians came closer than any of the others, and to me it seemed as if some of them had gotten between us and the river, and would work to our rear. I arose and started to the left to see if this was the case, and had taken but a few steps, my right side toward the hostiles, when a bullet hit my left leg midway between the hip and the knee and, just missing the femoral artery, went clear through the leg, badly shattering the bone. I fell on my left side and rolled down the hill quite a distance. This put me out of business, and I told the sergeant (Hall) to take charge of the detachment. Hall was an old soldier and a very capable one.

As soon as the firing on us was heard in the valley below, the balance of our squadron, under Captain Yates, hurried to our relief, and upon their appearance, the Indians withdrew. They were pursued up the valley a distance, but were not overtaken, as their ponies were in a much better condition than were our horses. Not one of the men with me was hit, but three or four had holes in their hats, and one had his hat rim shot away.

While we were having our little fight, there were more things doing in another part of the field. A party of Indians, who had crossed below us, moved forward and were met by Captain French. In the fight that ensued, several of the Indians were seen to fall, but were carried off the field by their comrades. Another party of warriors attacked the center of our position. They were driven off by Capt. Tom Custer. In this affair Lieutenant Ketchum,[16] 22nd Infantry, the assistant adjutant general of the expedition, had his horse shot under him. Colonel Custer's horse was also shot in this affair.

The pursuit continued about eight miles up the valley, where the Indians again crossed the river at the place where they had come over in the morning.

When the charge of the main body of our men was about to begin, the band was lined up and the regimental favorite, "Garry Owen," struck up as an inspiration to the troopers.

The loss of the Indians in this affair is not known, but as they did the attacking and exposed themselves freely, probably they had quite a number killed and wounded. Our loss, as reported by Colonel Custer, was "one officer badly wounded, four men killed and three wounded; four horses killed and four wounded."

After the fighting on our side of the river was over, the hostiles again concentrated in the woods opposite us. Near sunset, Colonel Stanley arrived; with him were two pieces of artillery, three-inch rifles, I believe. A few shells thrown across the river caused the Indians to abandon the woods.

After this day, we saw no more Indians, except a few who fired into our camp near what is called Pompey's Pillar. They caused a little commotion among the men who were bathing or washing their clothes in the river.

I recall an interesting experience of that summer. One day we were marching along in the bottomland, the officers to one side in order to avoid the dust, when, without warning, my horse went down and I was thrown over his head. It seemed as if the earth had opened under us. We had gotten into a quicksand hole or pit of unknown depth. Luckily it was not more than eight or nine feet across. Horse and rider floundered around, and I felt myself going down. A picket line was thrown to me, and I was pulled out, but a very sorry-looking sight—mud and sand all over from the neck to the feet. The horse was also, after much difficulty, pulled out. My ride the balance of the day was anything but pleasant. The mud got dry, and my clothes became stiff. I suffered no injury from this experience, but lost one of my handsome spurs, which is way down somewhere in the bowels of the earth, I suppose.

One afternoon, in camp, many of the men had washed their underclothing and put the articles on somw low bushes to dry. A sudden whirlwind swept through the camp and carried off a number of the garments. For a few minutes, the air was full of them. Some lodged in the branches of cottonwood trees and were with difficulty recovered; others when last seen were going heavenward, and they were never again seen by their owners. It was a ludicrous sight, but proved a serious thing to those who lost an only shirt, with no way of getting another till the return of the expedition.

On one occasion, we had to cross a stream about forty feet or more wide, and too deep for fording. The banks were nearly perpendicular, and at least fifteen feet high. There were no trees anywhere around that were long enough to reach across. A unique bridge was constructed. Each wagon carried an extra tongue and reach, also a water keg holding about twenty gallons. Wagon bodies were filled with empty kegs. When enough to reach across—placed lengthwise in the stream—were so filled, they were put into the river, kegs underneath, and securely fastened with ropes. A row of stringers was laid on the upturned wagons, and on these a platform was constructed; all parts were lashed together as firmly as possible. The banks of the stream were dug away so that there was about a thirty-degree slope on both sides. To test the bridge, some horses were led over, then some men rode over. The bridge did not sink more than a few inches under their weight and was considered strong enough to bear a half-loaded wagon. The wagons were taken across by hand. Each was halted at the slope; the mules unhitched and driven across, where they were caught; the wheels were locked; and then the wagon pushed till it ran by itself. To the tongue was tied a rope with a hook at the loose end. Two men were at the tongue to guide the wagon, and two others carried the loose end of the rope. At the other side were two harnessed mules and a score of men.

As the wagon was pushed down the slope, it gathered considerable speed. At the beginning of the bridge were two teamsters with spades. As the wagon passed them, each with much skill and dexterity hit the lock with the edge of the spade. One stroke by each was generally sufficient to open the lock. As the wagon shot across the bridge, the hook on the loose end of the rope was inserted into the ring on the whiffletree, the mules were whipped up, and aided by men at the drag rope, the wagon was over and up the bank in less time than it takes to tell of it. The men with the spades rarely missed the first trial at unlocking. At first, the ambulances and light wagons were tried, but it was soon seen that the bridge was strong and would stand more strain. When the heavily loaded vehicles went on the bridge, it sank below the surface, but readily arose as soon as the weight came off. Everything worked smoothly and well; there was not a breakdown, and our entire command crossed without an incident. It was an interesting sight to witness. It required less than a minute to cross each wagon. I believe the bridge was designed and constructed by Lt. P. H. Ray, 8th Infantry.

While we were at Lincoln, I had the good fortune to witness a "Scalp Dance" by the Ree Indians. In a skirmish a short time previous to our arrival, the Sioux had lost one of their number, whose body fell into the hands of the Rees. He was, of course, scalped. It is not possible for me to describe the ceremony, as it was enacted there on the plains amid the great surrounding stillness an hour or so after sunset. Yet in memory it cannot be quite forgotten.

In a circle were the Indian women, young girls, and boys. The warriors, between thirty and forty in number, were gorgeous in all their war paint and feathers, and they formed an inner circle, in the center of which was an old squaw, holding aloft on a long pole the scalp. The warriors were formed one behind the other, and so close together that no one could pass between any two. They slowly moved around the old squaw with the scalp and kept up a continual chant, every few minutes giving vent to piercing whoops, at the expiration of which the squaw, in her turn, violently shook the pole and gave a few wild screeches. Occasionally one of the warriors in the ring turned his face toward us, gave a sardonic grin, shook his fist at the scalp, and yelled, "Sioux, damn —," in language not to be printed, and which evidently was the extent of his English vocabulary.

The chanting of the braves had for its accompaniment the incessant noise of tin kettles and pans, beaten by the squaws and children. Fires were kept going, and it seemed to us, as we stood there, watching through the smoke the moving figures, with their painted faces, and listening to the unceasing noise of their kettles as it came to our ears, that we had been suddenly transported to a scene from the infernal regions.

One brave, who had been shot in the fight when the scalp was taken, was the hero of the occasion. He was mounted on a box nearby and attended by several squaws, and proudly exhibited a severe flesh wound.

I saw this ceremony for two evenings, with no apparent change of the program noticeable to us. On the morning after the last dance, the scalp was, with great ceremony, escorted to a steamer going up the river and taken to the headquarters of the tribe at Fort Berthold, where it was placed with their other trophies.

The Rees were, before the dances, in mourning for the loss of one of their braves killed sometime before in a fight with the Sioux Indians, and the period of their mourning was to continue till a Sioux scalp could be taken in battle and certain ceremonies took place.

Another interesting incident at Lincoln was the case of a sick Indian for whom the post surgeon prescribed. He became worse, much to the surgeon's surprise, and it was hinted that the surgeon's prescription was disregarded and the medicine man was treating the suffering warrior. An investigation brought out the fact that the drugs prescribed by the surgeon had never been taken, but that the medicine man had forced a nail under the skin just behind the ear. This had caused a festered sore. The nail was removed, and the invalid rapidly recovered.

I have written the above from memory, after a lapse of thirty-two years. There may be a few slight errors, but if so, they are trivial. I had kept a diary, in which was entered every night the length of our march; time of going into camp; nature of the country passed over during the day; if good grass, wood, and water were found; and whatever incidents of the day I thought would be of interest later on. After I was wounded, nearly everyone thought I could not possibly survive the long journey ahead. My effects became scattered, and the notebook was lost, together with my saber and remaining spur.

Journal of the U.S. Cavalry Association 15 (October 1904): 289–301[17]

About 8:00 A.M. on August 11, 1873, on the north bank of the Yellowstone River in Montana, in a spirited fight between eight troops of the 7th Cavalry under Lt. Col. George A. Custer, Lt. Charles Braden of this regiment was shot through the upper left thigh. The bullet, from a Henry rifle, fired at a range of not over fifty yards, went clear through the leg, badly shattering the bone and splitting it down to the knee. The lieutenant was dismounted and walking with his right side towards the Indians. The left leg was in the air when struck, and as the wounded man fell, his weight coming on the broken bone caused the ends to pass each other and stick into the flesh, making a very ugly wound. One of the sergeants with his detachment wore a long, black silk scarf. This he took off and wrapped it as tight as he could around the leg, above the wound.

Lieutenant Braden's detachment numbered about twenty men of L Troop and was an advance guard about a mile ahead of the main command. The detachment met a large number of mounted Indians, but succeeded in holding its position until several troops of the regiment arrived and drove off the Indians, pursuing them some distance up the valley.

Lieutenant, now Commissary General, Weston rode to where Braden lay, unstrapped an extra blanket from his saddle, and left four men and a bugler to take charge of the wounded man, ordering them to put him in the blanket and take him to where Custer had established his headquarters. The bugler was to lead the horses and carry the carbines of the four soldiers, who carefully put Braden in the blanket and, each carrying at one corner, started for the field hospital.

It was necessary to go across several large ravines and up and down hills. The bugler, who became scared, could not manage his extra horses and carry the four carbines, and disappeared. This left the party unarmed. Then one of the contract doctors with the expedition appeared and said the Indians were coming back, and the carrying party had better hurry or they would all be killed. This message greatly accelerated the pace, and the party went as rapidly as possible. Some patches of cactus had to be crossed; the prickers were long, dry, and brittle.

For a few minutes, the men carrying the blanket were able to keep it from touching the ground, but they soon became tired, and the injured man frequently hit the cactus. Many of the prickers went through the blanket into the flesh and broke off. It seemed as if every square inch of his anatomy that had come into contact with the cactus had at least a hundred of such broken spears. They afterwards were the cause of much pain and suffering.

After a while, the party reached headquarters. Dr. Ruger, brother of General Ruger, U.S.A., retired, pulled the pieces of bone out of the flesh and made the patient as comfortable as possible. There were no appliances to dress such a wound, and there was nothing to do but wait for the wagon train to arrive, which it did about sundown.

Dr. James P. Kimball, U.S.A., recently deceased,[18] was the chief medical officer of the expedition. There were no splints or plaster bandages in the medical wagon, so the doctors, aided by a blacksmith and a carpenter, having obtained a few pieces of boards by breaking up some boxes used for commissary stores, made a trough long enough to hold the entire leg. The trough, or box, was open at the top; across the bottom was fastened a tourniquet, which held two strips of adhesive plaster about three inches wide, fastened one on the inside and the other on the outside of the leg, and extending up to where the bone was broken. On the left side of the box was screwed an iron rod, reaching along the body and bent at the shoulder so as to pass under the neck. Two other strips of adhesive plaster, about the same width as those used below the break, were put on the leg. One of these strips was stuck to the front of the body, and the other to the back, and both were fastened to the iron rod under the neck.

The object of these strips was to hold the leg in place and keep the ends of the broken bone from rubbing against each other, and to prevent, if possible, shortening of the leg. Before these strips of adhesive plaster were applied, the leg and body were shaved so that a better hold could be had by the plasters. It is unnecessary to say that the pulling in opposite directions of these strips was not one of the pleasant sensations to which humanity is sometimes treated. A cushion of tow and cotton was made for the box, and the leg, prepared as above described, consigned to what many said would be its last little bed.

The work of making the box and setting the injured leg was done after dark. The only light was from candles held by soldiers and was very poor. The doctors said that the pain of setting the broken bone would probably be intense, as no anesthetic could be given because none was on hand.

Two officers (one Lieutenant Godfrey,[19] the other's name cannot be recalled now) were asked to hold the patient's hands so as to keep his fingernails from being sunk into the flesh.

A majority of the five medical officers present favored amputation. Dr. Kimball told the wounded man the result of their consultation, saying that in either case the chances to survive the long journey ahead would be about equal if the leg was cut off or left on. The patient decided to keep his leg.

It was realized by everyone that the task of carrying such a severely wounded man was going to be serious. The expedition could not be delayed on his account. He, with the other wounded, could not be left behind with a small guard, for the command was not to return by the route it was to go. Colonel Custer proposed that a raft of dry cottonwood logs be built, and the wounded man, with two men as escort, be floated on it down the Yellowstone River to the nearest post, Fort Buford. The distance was about two hundred fifty miles, and it was calculated that the current would carry the raft about four miles an hour. The floating was to be done by night, and during the day the raft was to be concealed in the bushes. Lt. Benjamin H. Hodgson, 7th Cavalry, a classmate, afterwards killed in the Little Bighorn fight, asked to go along as one of the attendants.

The scheme was not approved by Colonel Stanley, commander of the expedition, for various reasons. One of his characteristic remarks was that it would be more humane to shoot Braden at once rather than have him captured en route by the Indians or have his raft wrecked and he be drowned in the Buffalo Rapids, which were a short distance above the mouth of Powder River.

When the expedition moved out the morning after the fight, the wounded officer, with a soldier who had a broken arm, was put in an ambulance.

In order to get the benefit of a beaten road, the ambulance was to travel after the wagon train. The jolting of the ambulance was simply awful; the soldier with the broken arm got out and walked. After going about ten miles, the doctor reported to the commanding officer that Braden was rapidly losing strength and could not last much longer, so the expedition halted and went into camp.

The next day, a new plan was tried. It was proposed to carry him on a stretcher. He was put on one, and at first two men carried it. Each pair carried the stretcher till they were tired, when two others relieved them. Progress was slow, fatiguing to the men, and very uncomfortable to the occupant of the stretcher, who had no protection from the broiling sun. After going three or four miles in about five hours, the carriers were exhausted, and camp was pitched.

It was seen that this plan was a failure, and that suggestions were in order. The wagonmaster proposed to rig up a conveyance and was told to go ahead. He used the running gear of an ambulance, took out the reaches, and cut two small cottonwood poles about six inches in diameter and thirty feet long. The ends of the poles were securely fastened to the springs of the ambulance. Four slings, made of rawhide, were attached to the poles. Into these slings were inserted the handles of the stretcher. The slings were of such a length and so placed that the stretcher hung in the middle of the conveyance, about eighteen inches above the ground. Wagon bows were fastened to the poles, and over these bows was placed a canvas wagon cover to keep off rain and sun. The conveyance looked much like what are sometimes, in the country, called "stone boats," where a low platform hangs from the body of the wagon.

The wheels of the rig were wrapped with hide. The object of this was to widen the surface so that the vehicle would run more easily. Wide tires would have been a great improvement, but the rawhide wrapping was not a success. It was all right while the hide was soft and pliable, but when it became dry and hard, there was an uneven surface to the wheels, which caused jolting. On the underside of the stretcher, boards were nailed so that the canvas could not sag. A thin mattress was put on the stretcher, and on this the invalid lay.

The next morning, when all was ready for the start, the handles of the stretcher were inserted in the slings, and Lieutenant Braden was strapped to the stretcher so that he could not fall off. Two mules were hitched on, the driver riding one of them. When the mules started or stopped, there was an unpleasant jerk, and the patient would have been thrown off had he not been tied fast. He did not mind the swaying of the stretcher from side to side, but the longitudinal motion was unpleasant, for at every stop or start, there was a jerk, which seemed to make the ends of the broken bones rub together and cause intense pain. After the first day's trip, it was seen that the conveyance, with a few changes, would work very well.

Ropes were run from the handles of the stretcher to the opposite axles so as to prevent the longitudinal swing; a stick was nailed across the poles in such a position that Braden could hold on to it. The mules were given up, and the wagon was hauled by men. A detail of thirty cavalrymen and three noncommissioned officers was sent, and at Lieutenant Braden's request, Lieutenant Smallwood[20], 9th Infantry, a classmate at West Point, was detailed to take charge of the outfit. The detachment was divided into three reliefs of ten men and a corporal or sergeant. The reliefs were changed every hour. Ropes were fastened along both sides of the vehicle and to the tongue. One man walked alongside each wheel; two were at the end of the tongue to guide; and four others pulled at the rope.

The duty of the men at the wheels was to ease them over ruts and stones in the path. The change from mules to men was a great improvement, for the wagon was started and stopped without any jerking or jolting.

In order to have as good a road as possible, the outfit was made to follow the wagon train. A hospital steward and several attendants accompanied the party. About every half hour, he inspected the condition of the patient. The steward was provided with a keg of water and stimulants, and occasionally gave a small quantity of brandy and water. When Braden became weak and exhausted, word to that effect was sent ahead to Colonel Stanley, and he always stopped for the day at the next good camping place. At first, about one and a half miles an hour could be made under average conditions. One annoyance which could not be avoided was the dust which was thrown up in quantities by the wheels and covered the stretcher and its occupant.

As the party moved along, some wag remarked that the thing resembled the hook and ladder truck of a vintage fire department.

The command marched faster than the men could drag the conveyance, so the escort was usually from one to several hours late in reaching camp. Braden's tent was always ready upon arrival, and the stretcher was lifted from its place and put on the ground, where it remained till the next day's march began.

The trip, for the first two weeks especially, was a severe and trying ordeal. No one expected Braden to live from day to day. On the eighth day, the march was long, hot, and dusty. It was nearly dark when his party reached camp. He was so covered with dust that his features could not be distinguished. A number of officers and men were waiting for him.

Dr. Kimball took hold of his wrist and said, "I can't feel a thing. I guess he is dead."

The report spread that Braden had died, and preparations were commenced to make a coffin for him out of a wagon box.

After a couple of weeks, the end of the broken bone had begun to knit, and mules were again put to the conveyance, but the four men were kept at the wheels till the journey's end.

It was frequently necessary to ford streams. When this happened, one of the men would wade across first. If the water did not reach higher than a certain part of his legs, the conveyance would be dragged over, the bottom of the stretcher sometimes just skimming the water. If the water was too deep, the stretcher was taken out, and six men carried it over their shoulders.

Lieutenant Braden was hauled in this conveyance for twenty-eight days, and in it traveled about four hundred miles, as measured by the odometer.

The last day's journey was on September 10, when the reserve camp at Glendive, Montana, was reached. After remaining there some days, the sick and wounded were put aboard the steamer *Josephine* for a trip down the Yellowstone and Missouri Rivers. The water in both was so low that the boat spent more time on sandbars than in motion, and it was early in October before Fort Lincoln was reached.

The leg was taken out of the box, and adhesive straps were removed, sixty-two days after the fight. It was a long time to be in one position. During the trip, with no proper nourishment, the body became greatly emaciated, and the flesh in several places was worn down to the bone, causing bad sores. To add to the discomfort, the cactus prickers above mentioned caused ugly little ulcers, which festered. The patient could not be turned over, and in order to attend to these sores, he was held up by six strong men, and the doctor, from underneath the raised body, dressed the ulcerations and put on collodion with a camel's hair brush. It felt like hot coals as the liquid touched the raw flesh.

Several incidents, perhaps worth relating, occurred during the long and awful journey. Two soldiers, one a Holland Dutchman named De Geer, and an Irishman named Keegan, were detailed to attend Braden. Their tent was always adjoining his, and he could distinctly hear their conversation and is probably one of the very few persons who have listened to the details of their own funeral. One night, about the third or fourth day, when he seemed to be weakening rapidly, he hard Keegan say, "Well, when the lieutenant dies he will have a decent funeral. He won't be sewn up in a bag as were Honsinger and Baliran, but he is going to have a real coffin made out of a wagon box. It has all been arranged."

Honsinger, the veterinary surgeon, and Baliran, a post trader with the expedition, were killed by the Indians on August 4. Their bodies were recovered before the Indians mutilated them; the redskins had rifled the pockets of the dead men, but were chased away before they could do any scalping. The remains were sewed in canvas and carried one day before being buried. This was done to keep the location of their graves from the Indians, who would undoubtedly have dug up the bodies. They were buried at sundown the night after they were killed. A picket line was put over the burial place, and the next morning the entire wagon train passed over it, completely obliterating every sign of a grave.

Keegan and De Geer were fluent talkers, and their conversation and arguments were the source of much amusement to the wounded officer. The poor, faithful fellows did not attend his "decent funeral" as they expected to do, but were, it is believed, afterwards killed in the "Custer massacre."

One day an early camp was made near "Pompey's Pillar." Several hundred of the men were in the river, and others were washing clothes. Suddenly a small party of Indians, concealed in the bushes across the river, opened fire. The bathers lost no time in getting out of the water. It was a ludicrous sight to see the men, some carrying their clothes, scurrying for camp. Fortunately no one was hit. The Indians quickly mounted their ponies and scampered off before any of our men could shoot at them.

One night Braden's tent was pitched on a patch of dried grass. Early next morning (reveille was at three, breakfast about four, and the advance at five every day), when the striker came into the tent with breakfast, he put his candle on the ground. The candle tipped over and set fire to the grass. The blaze was noticed at once by Braden, who used his lungs to such good advantage that in less than a minute, fifty men or more were there. They cut the tent ropes, threw down the tent, and stamped out the fire. It was a narrow escape for the helpless man.

The last day of the eventful journey was on September 10, just thirty days after the fight. The steamboat *Josephine* was in sight, and the end of a tedious journey was within an hour of its close. Suddenly the mules hitched to the conveyance started to run, and ran a mile before they could be stopped. In crossing some patches of cactus, the hoofs had knocked off some dry pieces; a number of these had hit the bellies of the animals, and the pain caused a stampede. No damage was done, but imagine the feelings of the helpless occupant of the wagon, who expected an upset or a breakdown when the promised haven of rest was so near.

Dr. Kimball took personal charge of Lieutenant Braden's case. He was taken from the regiment and kept with the headquarters of the expedition. About ten days before Glendive was reached, on the return trip, the 7th Cavalry, under Custer, was directed to cut loose from the main column and take a short route to Glendive through the Badlands. The infantry, with the wagon train, was to go where it was known they would have a good trail.

An exceedingly pretty and thoughtful incident happened the day Custer separated from the main command. It may best be described by the following extract of a letter written by him to Mrs. Custer and published in her book entitled *Boots and Saddles:*

> Our mess continues to be successful. Nearly every day we have something nice to send to Lieutenant Braden. Only think of him with his shattered thigh, having to trail over a rough country for three hundred miles! He is not transported in an ambulance, but on a long stretcher arranged on wheels about thirty feet apart, pulled and pushed by men on foot. They carry him much more steadily than would horses or mules. It requires a full company of men each day to transport Mr. Braden in this way. He is with the main command, but was doing well when we left. The day the command divided, I had the band take a position near the route where the rest of the expedition would pass, and when he and his escort approached, they struck up "Garry Owen." He acknowledged the attention as well as he could.

The acknowledgment consisted of reaching out under the cover and waving a handkerchief.

All of the officers of the 7th Cavalry assembled to greet their wounded comrade and wish him a safe and pleasant journey. The day Custer left the main column, it turned toward the Yellowstone River. The march continued till after dark. No water was found, so a dry camp had to be made. Only a few tents were pitched, and the mules were not harnessed. Some miscreant stole Braden's water keg. It was a contemptible thing to do under the circumstances, and he would have fared badly, with no water to bathe the inflamed wound, had not a small quantity of this necessary liquid been husbanded by the hospital steward. The thief, had he been known, would have been roughly treated by the attendants.

Colonel Custer had taken his cook, a colored woman named Eliza, along. Late at night the day of the fight, when the doctors were busy dressing the wound, Eliza came to the tent. She brought a lemon, saying it was the last one left to the colonel's mess, and that it would do Mr. Braden more good than anyone else. Kindhearted Eliza! It surely was a very thoughtful act on her part.

Afterwards, whenever the cavalry camp was near headquarters, Eliza always made some good nourishing soup and sent it over. Had it not been for her kindness, Braden might have starved.

Capt. Andrew Burt,[21] 9th Infantry, now brigadier general, retired, was with the expedition. He was a great hunter, and whenever he succeeded in getting some game, always sent a generous share to Braden. Another gentleman to whom Braden was indebted for a number of kind acts was a Mr. [S. J.] Barrows,[22] correspondent of the New York *Tribune*. Mr. Barrows is, it is believed, now a clergyman and editor of a religious journal published in Boston.

Upon arriving at Fort Lincoln, Lieutenant Braden was taken to the post hospital, a ramshackle wooden structure situated on the high bluff where the infantry post was located. The only ward was occupied by enlisted men, so Braden was taken to the attic, where there was no heat. Through holes in the roof, the stars could be seen at night and the sky in the daytime. Between the rafters, where they rested on the frame, was an open space. The place was cold, extremely desolate, and dreary.

A few days after being put into this attic, a driving snowstorm came up during the night. By morning, several inches of snow had drifted in through the openings, and it covered Braden's bed with a shroud like a mantle. He was then taken downstairs, and his bed placed in the dispensary. There was some warmth there from an old stove, but it was not a pleasant place for an invalid, as it was also the doctor's office, and sick call was held there.

When wounded, he weighed about 180 pounds. After being able to hobble on crutches, the commissary scales at Lincoln showed his weight to be only 125.

Could Braden have been taken to a hospital soon after the fight, he might have recovered with quiet and proper care, but the wound completely disabled and unfitted him for further active service. He was subsequently retired as a first lieutenant. The leg became shortened nearly two inches and partially stiff at the knee, but part of the knee stiffness was probably due to an accident at West Point six months before graduation, when a horse fell with him in the riding hall and injured the kneecap. For eight years, there were two running sores on the leg, from which, before final healing, several pieces of bone, several chips of lead, and fragments of clothing were taken. An x-ray picture made at West Point some years ago shows that many more pieces of bone never came out, but were caught in the callous that formed around the ends of the broken bone.

Crossing the Big Muddy [Creek]

SAMUEL J. BARROWS[1]

Army and Navy Journal 10, no. 52 (August 9, 1873): 328–29

From a letter to the New York *Tribune*, we condense the following account of an episode in the history of the Yellowstone expedition:

Colonel Custer, whom Colonel Stanley had sent with the 7th Cavalry and a few light loaded wagons to afford relief to the hail-pelted engineers, had arrived at this stream the day before [July 1, 1873]. He had found the water too high to cross and built a bridge in the afternoon, on which he had crossed his troops and wagons. Through a mistake of our guide and the wretched condition of the roads, our heavy train did not arrive at this stream until the following day. Our mules were almost exhausted by their pulling. It was deemed inadvisable to attempt a crossing that night. It was doubtful whether we could cross without building another bridge.

The stream that night decided the question for us. The heavy rains swelled it considerably. Its level rose higher and higher. Somehow it seemed to take a fancy to Colonel Custer's bridge. The bridge seemed to reciprocate it. There was a collusion and finally an elopement. I saw the water creep up closer and closer, and at last lift the bridge from its feet and carry it off on its bosom. We had no objection to the amours of this bridge, but it was unkind in it to desert us just as we needed it most. The stream had risen so high that it was impossible to bridge it again on account of its increased width. We had no timber long enough.

It is a fact known, I suppose, to the United States Quartermaster's Department that any army wagon laden with five thousand pounds will not float in ten feet of water. It is unreasonable to expect six mules to swim with such a weight. It was with reference to this want of levity in loaded army wagons that pontoons were invented. But notwithstanding this fact, the largest expedition since the war started off on a journey of several hundred miles across a new country without a single pontoon. The reason is that the country has a dry reputation. This year, however, it has belied its name. A few pontoons would have neutralized the falsehood. They were asked for, but there was a knot in the red tape somewhere, and we did not get them. With pontoons, our whole command might have crossed in three or four hours.

How should we get over the Big Muddy? It was a problem for an engineer. The problem was there, but not the engineer—I mean a member of the engineer corps. I find, however, that army officers as a general thing do not place a very high estimate on our engineer corps. "Why did not a regular army engineer accompany this expedition?" I asked of an officer. "Oh, he'd be afraid of getting sunburn. Besides, we can get along better without them. They can't work unless they have everything just so. They are good to stay in the office and make maps, and that is about all they are good for."

Be this true or not, we happily have two men with us who are better than a dozen desk engineers. I refer to Colonel Stanley and Lieutenant Ray, of the 8th Infantry, our chief commissary. Colonel Stanley is a thoroughly educated officer and has had a wide experience on the plains. He has a natural talent for his profession, and unites excellent powers of observation with rare judgment and ability to command men. Lieutenant Ray[2] is eminently a practical man. He has seen life on the plains in all its aspects and served with great credit during the war. He has passed through many trying expeditions, and never but once was caught in a place that he could not get out. This happened near New York and brought him worthily into public notice. While stationed at David's Island, he went out in a boat one stormy night to rescue a party who had been caught in the ice. He reached them, but was unable to return to the fort. The floating ice carried him far out into the sound. It was not until the next day that they were taken off, with frostbitten hands and feet.

Major Baker,[3] the quartermaster, and Lieutenant Dougherty,[4] commanding the pioneers, make up the other members of our unorganized engineer corps.

The first thing to do was to get forage and commissary stores over for Major Townsend.[5] This difficulty in a stream twenty-five or thirty feet wide did not present the magnitude that the transit of our wagon train did. If we could get the forage on the other side, Major Townsend could send back some wagons for it.

A wagon body was dismounted. It was wrapped on its bottom and sides in a heavy tarpaulin, which was firmly secured by ropes. It was the work of a few minutes to make it and launch it. The heavy canvas effectually kept out water. It was safely navigated to the other side. Colonel Stanley and Lieutenant Ray were among the first to cross the rapid stream. A number of men, stationed on each side, easily pulled the boat across, receiving no little aid from the current. On this little craft we could safely put one thousand pounds of forage. It solved one element of the problem. In five or six hours we had ferried enough stores and forage to supply the company of cavalry and two companies of infantry that formed the surveyor's escort.

The next question was, how should we get over our heavy train and teams? The commissary, Lieutenant Ray, once more solved the problem. He offered to build a bridge and cross the command. But how could he build a bridge without timber, pontoons, or lumber? We have in this expedition over one hundred water kegs. Nearly all of them are reformed whiskey kegs. When they contained whiskey, the bung always leaked. They finally leaked dry and became hopefully converted. These temperance kegs have been heretofore carried on the wagons. Lieutenant Ray now proposed to carry the wagons on the kegs.

Ninety-six empty kegs were accordingly ordered to report at the stream. Four wagon beds were dismembered of their covers and wheels. Twenty-five or thirty men were then set to work to bung and plug the kegs. Only those thoroughly coopered were accepted; the dry and unserviceable ones were rejected, and their places supplied by others. Each of the wagon beds just held twenty-four kegs, placed on their ends side by side in three rows. Some timber was, meanwhile, cut into poles, and one pole placed lengthwise over each row of kegs to keep them in place. Ropes and chains were passed over the poles and completely around the wagon beds, so that the booms and kegs were firmly secured. The wagon bodies were then dragged down the bank and launched in the water bottom-side up—that is, with the kegs down. Each wagon bed was then floating, upside down, upheld by twenty-four airtight kegs. These extemporized floats were then moored lengthwise in the stream. The next trouble was to lash them securely side by side. This was no easy matter, but Mr. Ray met it as he did every other difficulty in the construction, with a ready brain and a ready hand. He had one man on the first float with him, and with his coat off and sleeves rolled up, lashed them together with his own hands. The shores were lined with officers and men watching the experiment. Very little confidence was expressed in this structure by the wagonmasters and teamsters.

By means of some wagon reaches and plenty of picket rope, the floats were finally fastened together. If we had had some plank now to place across the inverted wagon beds, one bridge would have been complete. If we had only brought one plank to each wagon in our train, we should have had ten times as much as we could use. But we had not a single available plank or board. We were compelled to fall back on our extra wagon tongues and reaches. These were placed side by side across the wagon beds; they did not make a very even floor, but it was the best we could do. The bank had been previously cut away to form a gradual descent. It was easy to connect the float with the shore.

The bridge was done. I imagine that Lieutenant Ray watched with considerable interest the crossing of the first wagon. To secure great safety, the mules were detached and led down the bank and over the bridge. The wagon wheels were locked, and the wagons gently let down to the bridge. A detail of men on the other bank then took the rope and pulled the heavy-laden vehicle across the float and up the opposite bank. Under the great weight, the bridge sunk to the water's edge, but no further. The wagon crossed in safety. The success was repeated two hundred fifty times. When finally all our teams and men were safely landed on the other side without a single accident, without losing a pound of forage or a single piece of hardtack, the bridge had published its own triumph, and the doubters were silent. Such a bridge was not a new undertaking or achievement for Colonel Stanley. In his twenty years of army life, all of which have been spent in active service, he has become familiar with every known device for managing a train. I doubt if there is an officer in the service better qualified for the difficult work of conducting a train through almost impassable places. There are few who have such resources of judgment and experience. On this trip, he is fortunate in being seconded by a competent staff. The mechanical success of the work was due to the perseverance and ingenuity of his chief commissary, who constructed it mainly with his own hands. Our little bridge shows what may be accomplished by putting this and that together, brain-wise and otherwise.

PART FOUR

The Black Hills and Beyond, 1874–76

The Black Hills Expedition: Dispatches and Letters

GEORGE A. CUSTER

Army and Navy Journal 12, no. 2 (August 22, 1874): 26–27

HEADQUARTERS BLACK HILLS EXPEDITION,
PROSPECT VALLEY, DAKOTA, July 15, 1874
Lon. 103 46 W., lat. 45 29 N.
Assistant Adjutant General, Department of Dakota, St. Paul, Minn.:
   This expedition reached this point yesterday, having marched since leaving Fort Lincoln, 227 ½ miles. We are now 170 miles in a direct line from Lincoln and within five miles of the Little Missouri River, and within about twelve miles from the Montana boundary, our bearing from Fort Lincoln being south, 62 degrees west. After the second day from Lincoln, we marched over a beautiful country; the grazing was excellent and abundant, wood sufficient for our wants, and water in great abundance every ten miles. When we struck the tributaries of Grand River, we entered a less desirable portion of the country, nearly all the streams flowing into Grand River being more or less impregnated with alkali, rendering the crossings difficult. We found a plentiful supply of grass, wood, and water, however, even along this portion of our route. Upon leaving the headwaters of Grand River, we ascended the plateau separating the watershed of the Little Missouri from that running into the Missouri, and found a country of surpassing beauty and richness of soil. The pasturage could not be finer, timber is abundant, and water both good and plentiful. As an evidence of the character of the country, we have marched since leaving Fort Lincoln on an average over seventeen miles per day, one day marching thirty-two miles; yet our mules and beef cattle have constantly improved in condition, the beef cattle depending entirely upon the excellent grazing we have marched over.
   The health of my command is something remarkable, not a single man being on the sick report. Everyone seems not only in good health, but in excellent spirits.

Between the forks of Grand River we discovered a cave, to which the Indians attach great importance. The cave extends about four hundred feet underground, beyond which point it was not practicable to explore it. Its walls and roof are covered with rude carvings and drawings, cut into the solid rock, apparently the work of Indians, although probably by a different tribe than either of those now roaming in this region. Near the cave was found a white man's skull, evidently perforated by a bullet. It had been exposed to the atmosphere for several years. As no white men, except those belonging to this expedition, are known to have passed anywhere near this locality, the discovery of this skull was regarded with unusual interest.

The cave was found to contain numerous articles of Indian equipment, which had been thrown into the cave by the Indians as offerings to the Great Spirit. I have named the cave "Ludlow's Cave," in honor of the engineer officer of the expedition.[1]

Our march thus far has been made without molestation upon the part of the Indians. We discovered no signs indicating the recent presence of Indians until day before yesterday, when Captain McDougall, 7th Cavalry, who was on the flank, discovered a small party of about twenty Indians watching our movements; the Indians scampered off as soon as discovered. Yesterday the same or a similar-sized party made

"*To Horse!*" HARPER'S WEEKLY, 1888.

its appearance along the line of march and was seen by Captain Moylan, 7th Cavalry, who was in command of the rear guard, and soon after, several signals of smoke were sent up, which our Indian guides interpret as carrying information to the main body of our presence and movements. As I sent pacific messages to all the tribes infesting this region before the expedition moved and expressed a desire to maintain friendly relations with them, the signals observed by us may have simply been made to enable the villages to avoid us. Our Indian guides think differently, however, and believe the Indians mean war; should this be true, they will be the party to fire the first shot.

Indians have been seen near camp today. Mr. Grinnell of Yale College, one of the geologists accompanying the expedition, discovered on yesterday an important fossil. It was a bone about four feet long and twelve inches long, and had evidently belonged to an animal larger than an elephant.

Beds of lignite of good quality have been observed at various points along our route by Professor Winchell, one of the geologists of the expedition.[2] I do not know whether I will be able to communicate with you again before the return of the expedition or not.

      G. A. Custer,
      Brevet Major General, U.S.A.,
      Commanding

HEADQUARTERS BLACK HILLS EXPEDITION,
8½ MILES SOUTHEAST OF HARNEY'S PEAK,
August 2, 1874

Assistant Adjutant General, Department of Dakota:

My last dispatch was dated July 15 and sent from Prospect Valley, Dakota, longitude 103 degrees 46 minutes, latitude 45 degrees 29 minutes. Two of my Indian scouts left as bearers of the dispatch as soon as their departure could be concealed by the darkness. After leaving that point, this expedition moved in a southwesterly direction until it reached the valley of the Little Missouri River, up which we moved twenty-one miles. Finding this valley almost destitute of grazing along our line of march, I ordered the water kegs filled and a supply of wood placed on the wagons, and left the valley in search of a better campground. During our passage up the valley of the Little Missouri, we had entered and were about to leave the Territory of Montana. Our course was near due south.

After a further march of about nine miles, we arrived before sundown at a point capable of furnishing us good grazing and water for our animals, having marched over thirty miles since breaking camp in the morning. From this point to the valley of the Belle Fourche, we found the country generally barren and uninviting, save in a few isolated places.

We reached the Belle Fourche on the evening of July 18, encamping where good grass, wood, and water were abundant, and at a point just west of the line separating Dakota from Wyoming. The following day was spent in camp.

On the twentieth we crossed the Belle Fourche and began, as it were, skirmishing with the Black Hills. We began by feeling our way carefully along the outlying ranges of the hills, seeking a weak point through which we might make our way to the interior. We continued from the time we ascended from the valley of the Belle Fourche to move through a very superior country, covered with the best of grazing and [an] abundance of timber, principally pine, poplar, and several varieties of oak. As we advanced, the country skirting the Black Hills to the southward became each day more beautiful.

On the evening of the twenty-second, we halted and encamped east of, and within four miles of, the base of Inyan Kara. Desiring to ascend that peak the following day, it being the highest in the western range of the Black Hills, I did not move camp the following day, but taking a small party with me, proceeded to the highest point of this prominent landmark, whose height is given as 6,600 feet. The day was not favorable for obtaining distant views, but I decided on the following morning to move due east and attempt the passage of the hills. We experienced considerable delay from fallen timber which lay in our pathway. With this exception, and a very little digging, rendered necessary in descending into a valley, the pioneers prepared the way for the train, and we reached camp by 2:00 P.M., having marched eleven miles. We here found grass, water, and wood of best quality and in great abundance.

On the following day, we resumed our march up this valley, which I had explored several miles the preceding evening, and which led us by an easy ascent almost southeast. After marching nearly twelve miles, we encamped at an early hour in the same valley. The valley in one respect presented the most wonderful as well as beautiful aspect. Its equal I have never seen, and such too was the testimony of all who beheld it. In no public or private park have I ever seen such a profuse display of flowers. Every step of our march that day was amidst flowers of the most exquisite colors and perfume. So luxuriant in growth were they that men plucked them without dismounting from the saddle. Some belonged to new or unclassified species. It was a strange sight to glance back at the advancing columns of cavalry and behold the men with beautiful bouquets in their hands, while the headgear of their horses was decorated with wreaths of flowers fit to crown a queen of May. Deeming it a most fitting appellation, I named this Floral Valley. Lieutenant Colonel [J. W.] Forsyth, at one of our halting places, chosen at random, plucked seventeen beautiful flowers belonging to different species, and within a space of twenty feet square. The same evening, while seated at the mess table, one of the officers called attention to the carpet of flowers strewn under our feet, and it was suggested that it be determined how many different flowers could be plucked without leaving our seat at the dinner table. Seven beautiful varieties were thus gathered. Professor Donaldson, the botanist of the expedition,[3] estimated the number of flowers in bloom in Floral Valley at fifty, while an equal number of varieties had bloomed or were yet to bloom. The number of trees, shrubs, and grasses was twenty-five, making the total flora of the valley embrace 125 species. This beautiful valley may well bear comparison with the loveliest portions of Central Park.

Favored as we had been in having Floral Valley for our roadway to the west of the Black Hills, we were scarcely less fortunate in the valley which seemed to me to meet us on the interior slope. The rippling stream of clear cold water, the counterpart of that we had ascended the day before, flowed at our feet and pointed out the way before us, while along its banks grew beautiful flowers, surpassed but little in beauty and profusion by their sisters who had greeted us the day before.

After advancing down this valley about fourteen miles, our course being almost southeast, we encamped in the midst of grazing [and], whose only fault, if any, was its great luxuriance. Having preceded the main column, as usual, with our escort of two companies of cavalry, E and C, and Lieutenant Wallace's[4] detachment of scouts, I came upon an Indian campfire still burning, and which with other indications showed that a small party of Indians had encamped there the previous night, and had evidently left that morning in ignorance of our close proximity. Believing they would not move far, and that a collision might take place at any time unless a friendly understanding was arrived at, I sent my head scout, Bloody Knife, and twenty of his braves to advance a few miles and reconnoiter the valley.

The party had been gone but a few minutes when two of Bloody Knife's young men came galloping back and informed me that they had discovered five Indian lodges a few miles down the valley, and that Bloody Knife, as directed, had concealed his party in a wooded ravine, where they awaited further orders.

Taking E Company with me, which was afterwards reinforced by the remainder of the scouts and Captain Hart's company, I proceeded to the ravine where Bloody Knife and his party lay concealed, and from the crest beyond obtained a full view of the five Indian lodges, about which a considerable number of ponies were grazing. I was enabled to place my command still nearer to the lodges undiscovered. I then dispatched [Louis] Agard, the interpreter, with a flag of truce, accompanied by two of our Sioux scouts, to acquaint the occupants of the lodges that we were friendly disposed and desired to communicate with them.

To prevent either treachery or flight on their part, I galloped the remaining portion of my advance and surrounded the lodges. This was accomplished almost before they were aware of our presence. I then entered the little village and shook hands with its occupants, assuring them through the interpreter that they had no cause to fear, as we were not there to molest them. I invited them to visit our camp and promised presents of flour, sugar, and coffee to all who would accept. This invitation was accepted. At the same time, I entered into an agreement with the leading men that they should encamp with us a few days and give us such information concerning the country as we might desire, in return for which service I was to reward them with rations. With this understanding I left them. The entire party numbered twenty-seven.

Later in the afternoon, four of the men, including the chief, "One Stab," visited our camp and desired the promised rations, saying their entire party would move up and join us the following morning as agreed upon. I ordered presents of sugar, coffee, and bacon to be given them; to relieve their pretended anxiety for the safety of their village during the night, I ordered a party of fifteen of my command to return with them and protect them during the night. But from their great disinclination to wait a few minutes until the party could saddle up, and from the fact that two of the four had already slipped away, I was of the opinion that they were not acting in good faith. In this I was confirmed when the two remaining ones set off at a gallop in the direction of the village. I sent a party of our scouts to overtake them and request their return; not complying with this request, I sent a second party with orders to repeat the request, and if not complied with, to take hold of the bridles of their ponies and lead them back, but to offer no violence. When overtaken by our scouts, one of the two Indians seized the musket of one of the scouts and endeavored to wrest it from him. Failing in this, he released his hold after the scout became dismounted in the struggle and set off as fast as his pony could carry him, but not before the musket of the scout was discharged. From blood discovered afterwards, it was evident that either the Indian or his pony was wounded. I hope that neither was seriously hurt, although the Indians have their own bad faith as the sole ground for the collision.[5]

One Stab, the chief, was brought back to camp. The scouts galloped down the valley to the site of the village, when it was discovered that the entire party had packed up their lodges and fled, and the visit of the four Indians to our camp was not only to obtain the rations promised them in return for future services, but to cover the flight of their lodges. I have effected arrangements by which the chief One Stab remains with us as guide three days longer, when he will take his departure and rejoin his band. He claims to belong to both Red Cloud's and Spotted Tail's agencies, but has been to neither for a long time. He has recently returned from the hostile camp on Powder River and represents that the Indians lost ten killed in their fight with the Bozeman exploring party.

The creek which led us down into the interior of the Black Hills is bordered by high bluffs, on the crests of which are located prominent walls of solid rock, presenting here and there the appearance of castles constructed of masonry. From this marked resemblance, I named this stream Castle Creek. The direction of Castle Creek having commenced to lead us more to the northwest than we were prepared to go, and the valley having become narrow and broken, I left this watercourse and ascended the valley of a small tributary, which again gave us a southeasterly course. After a march of fourteen miles, we camped on a small creek,[6] furnishing us an abundance of good water and grass. The direction of this creek was nearly west.

On the thirtieth, we moved in the continuation of our previous course and through a fine open country, covered with excellent grazing. After a march of over ten miles, we encamped early in the day about five miles from the western base of Harney's Peak, finding water, grass, and wood abundant, with springs of clear, cold water running through the camp.

On the following day, the command remained in camp, except the exploring parties sent out in all directions. With a small party, I proceeded to Harney's Peak and, after great difficulty, made the ascent to its crest. We found this to be the highest point in the Black Hills. From the highest point, we obtained a view of Bear Butte in the north and of the plains to the east, five miles beyond the Cheyenne River. Our party did not reach camp until nearly 1:00 A.M., but we were amply repaid for our labor by the magnificence of the views obtained. While on the highest point, we drank the health of the veteran out of compliment to whom the peak was named.

On August 1, we moved camp a few miles simply to obtain fresh grass, still keeping near the base of the hills to the east of us. This morning I dispatched two companies in a southeasterly direction to extend our exploration with the South Fork of the Cheyenne River. Tomorrow at 5:00 A.M., I will set out with five companies of cavalry and endeavor to reach the same stream in a southwesterly direction from Harney's Peak.

Reynolds, the scout who is to carry this dispatch to Fort Laramie, will go with us as far as we go in that direction, when he will set out alone to reach his destination, traveling mainly by night. The country through which we have passed since leaving the Belle Fourche River has been generally open and extremely fertile. The main portion of that passed over since entering the unexplored portion of the Black Hills consists of beautiful parks or valleys, near or through which flows a stream of clear, cold water perfectly free from alkali, while bounding these peaks or valleys is invariably found unlimited supplies of timber, much of it capable of being made into good lumber. In no portion of the United States, not excepting the famous bluegrass region of Kentucky, have I ever seen grazing superior to that found growing wild in this hitherto unknown region. I know of no portion of our country where nature has done so much to prepare homes for husbandmen and left so little for the latter to do here. The open and timbered spaces are so divided that a partly prepared farm of almost any dimensions, from an acre upwards, can be found here. Not only is the land cleared and timber, both for fuel and building, conveniently located, with a stream of fine water flowing through its length and breadth, but nature often times seems to have gone further and placed beautiful shrubbery and evergreens in the most desirable location for building sites. While on Harney's Peak I could contrast the bright green verdure of these lovely parks with the sunburned and dried yellow herbage to be seen on the outer plains. Everything indicates an abundance of moisture within the space enclosed by the Black Hills. The soil is that of a rich garden, and composed of a dark mold of exceedingly fine grain. We have found the country in many places covered with wild raspberries, both the black and red varieties. Yesterday and today I have feasted on the latter. It is no unusual sight to see hundreds of soldiers gathering wild berries. Nowhere in the states have I tasted cultivated raspberries of equal flavor to those found growing wild here, nor have I ever seen them larger or in as great profusion as I have seen hundreds of acres of them here. Wild strawberries, wild currants, gooseberries, two varieties of pine berries, and wild cherries are also found in great profusion and of exceedingly fine quality. Cattle could winter in these valleys without other food or shelter than that to be obtained from running at large.

As there are scientific parties accompanying the expedition who are examining into the mineral resources of this region, the result of whose researches will accompany my detailed report, I omit all present reference to that portion of our explorations until the return of the expedition, except to state, what will appear in any event in the public print, that gold has been found at several places, and it is the belief of those who are giving their attention to this subject that it will be found in paying quantities. I have upon my table forty or fifty small particles of pure gold, in size averaging that of a small pinhead, and most of it obtained today from one panful of earth. As we have never remained longer at one camp than one day, it will be readily understood that there is no opportunity to make a satisfactory examination in regard to deposits of valuable minerals. Veins of lead and strong indications of the existence of silver have been found. Until further examination is made regarding the richness of the deposits of gold, no opinion should be formed. Veins of what the geologists term gold-bearing quartz crop out on almost every hillside. All existing geological and geographic maps of this region have been found incorrect. This will not seem surprising when it is remembered that both have been compiled by guesswork and without entering the country attempted to be represented.

The health of the command continues excellent. I will begin my northward march in four days from this date. I do not expect to arrive at Fort Lincoln until August 31.

G. A. CUSTER,
Brevet Major General,
commanding expedition

Army and Navy Journal 12, no. 3 (August 29, 1874): 38

HEADQUARTERS BLACK HILLS EXPEDITION,
BEAR BUTTE, Dakota, August 15, 1874
To Assistant Adjutant General, Department of Dakota, St. Paul:

My last dispatch was written on the second and third instant and sent from the South Fork of the Cheyenne, from a point on the latter nearest to Fort Laramie. On the morning of the fourth, I began my return march to our main camp near Harney's Peak, arriving there by a different route on the sixth.

On the morning of the seventh, the expedition began its march northward, Bear Butte being our next objective point. We advanced without serious obstacle until within ten or twelve miles of Bear Butte, when we found our further progress barred by a high range of impassable hills. We attempted to effect a passage through some one of the many valleys where the watercourses ran directly through the hills in the desired direction, but in every instance we were led into deep, broken canyons, impassable even to horsemen. Through one of these I made my way on foot from a high point and obtained a view of the plains outside.

Retracing my steps, I placed the command in camp in a fine valley in which it had halted, and converted the remainder of the day to a further search for a practical route through the hills. The result decided me to follow down a watercourse, which led us first towards the south and afterwards towards the east. This stream proved to be Elk Creek, the valley of which, as well as the stream itself, proving to be at least equal in beauty and extent to any passed through during the march. We camped twice on this stream, and as far as we proceeded down its course, we had a most excellent road; but finding that, like nearly all other streams leaving the hills, its course would take us into a canyon which could be barely made practicable for wagons, I searched for and discovered a narrow gap in the rocky wall which forms the northern boundary of the valley, and which was large enough to allow our wagon to pass conveniently through.

A march of an hour up a gradual ascent and through a pine forest brought us to a beautiful park, containing thousands of acres, from which we obtained a fine view in the distance of our old acquaintance, the plains. Here we pitched our tents for the last time in the Black Hills, nearly everyone being loath to leave a region which had been found delightful in almost every respect. Behind us the grass and foliage were clothed in green of the freshness of May. In front of us we cast our eyes over the plains; below we saw nothing but a comparatively parched, dried surface, the sunburnt pasturage of which offered a most uninviting prospect both for horse and rider, when remembering the rich abundance we were leaving behind us.

A march of twenty-six miles, gradually bearing northwards, brought us to the Bear Butte, at which point I concluded to remain one day before beginning our return march. I proposed to return by a different, although perhaps not shorter, route than that adopted in coming to the Black Hills. I am induced to make the change in order to embrace a large tract of unexplored country within the limits of our explorations, and particularly to enable us to locate as much as possible of that portion of the Little Missouri of which nothing is known. I expect the expedition to reach Fort Lincoln about August 31. The health of the command has been most excellent.[7]

This expedition entered the Black Hills from the west side, passed through the eastern and most southern ranges, which form the boundary of the Black Hills. From the fact that in all our principal marches through the Black Hills, we have taken without serious obstacle a heavily laden train of over one hundred wagons, it may be inferred that the Black Hills do not constitute the impenetrable region heretofore represented. In entering the Black Hills from any direction, the most serious, if not the only, obstacle we encountered [was] near the outer base. This probably accounts for the story which has so long existed regarding the character of the interior. Exploring parties have contented themselves with marching around the exterior base, and from the forbidding aspect of the hills, as viewed at a distance, inferred that an advance toward the interior would only encounter increased obstacles. In regard to the character of the country enclosed by the Black Hills, I can only repeat what I have stated in previous dispatches. No portion of the United States can boast of a richer or better pasturage, purer water, the natural temperatures of which in midsummer, as it flows from the earth, is twelve degrees above the freezing point, and of greater advantages generally to the farmer or stock raiser than are to be found in the Black Hills. Building stone is found in inexhaustible quantities, and wood, fuel, and lumber sufficient for all time to come. Rains are frequent, with no evidence of either drought or freshets. The days are perhaps too short and the nights too cool for corn, but I believe all other grains could be produced here in abundance. Wheat particularly would yield largely.

There is no doubt as to the existence of various metals throughout the hills. As this subject has received the special attention of experts who accompanied the expedition, and will be reported upon in detail, I will only mention the fact that iron and plumbago have been found and beds of gypsum of apparently inexhaustible extent. I referred in a former dispatch to the discovery of gold. Subsequent examinations at numerous points confirm and strengthen the fact of the existence of gold in the Black Hills. In some of the watercourses almost every panful of earth produced gold in small yet paying quantities. Our brief halts and rapid marching prevented anything but a very hasty examination of the country in this respect, but in one place, and the only one within my knowledge where so great a depth was reached, a hole was dug eight feet in depth, and the miners report that they found gold among the roots of the grass, and from that point to the lowest point reached, gold was found in paying quantities. It has not required an expert to find gold in the Black Hills, as men without former experience in mining have discovered it at an expense of but little time or labor. As an evidence of the rich pasturage to be found in this region, I can state the fact that my beef herd, after marching upwards of six hundred miles, is in better condition than when I started, being now as fat as consistent with marching condition. The same may be said of the mules of the wagon train. The horses of the command are in good working condition. I have never seen as many deer as in the Black Hills. Elk and bear have also been killed. We have had no collision with hostile Indians.

G. A. CUSTER,
Brevet Major General U.S. Army,
Commanding the Expedition

Army and Navy Journal 12, no. 22 (January 23, 1875): 373

HEADQUARTERS, MIDDLE DISTRICT,
DEPARTMENT OF DAKOTA,
FOR ABRAHAM LINCOLN, D.T.,
September 10, 1874

To. Rev. S. D. Hinman.

MY DEAR SIR: As the services of the Santee[8] scouts are no longer required—they having been employed in connection with the Black Hills expedition—and as they are about to set out on their return to their reservation, I desire to express to you, as their missionary, my hearty approval of their conduct during the brief period they have been under my command. As soldiers, I have found them faithful, obedient, and trustworthy, always ready to perform their duty. It gives me still greater pleasure to testify to their deportment as men. I doubt if the same number of young men belonging to the white race could be collected in any community of the same size, whose moral bearing would excel that of the Santee young men who accompanied the Black Hills expedition. They seemed to be generally free from the prevailing vices found among young men. As a class, they neither indulge in profanity or strong drink.

One pleasant incident among the many which characterized my visit to the Black Hills, I now recall. It was during one of our resting days in camp. I was seated alone in my tent, when suddenly, as if from the rocks and forests of that beautiful region, I heard the familiar air "Old Hundred" roll forth from a score or more of many voices. Then followed the equally familiar hymn "Rock of Ages," and others not less known. Cavalrymen are not noted for their hymn-singing qualities, and I stepped outside my tent to discover from whom this music came. It was from a group of Santee young men, and I shall long remember the pleasing effect produced by hearing these good old hymns sung, as I then heard them, by men or the sons of men who, but a few years ago, roamed over this country in a state of barbarous wildness.

So much for the labors of Christianity and civilization; and to you, and through you to the Santees under your charge, I express my gratification that so much has been achieved. May the good work go on, is the sincere wish of

Yours truly,
G. A. Custer, Brevet Major General,
U.S. Army, Commanding District

Cavalry on the march. HARPER'S WEEKLY, 1889.

Army and Navy Journal 12, no. 22 (January 9, 1875): 341–42

FORT ABRAHAM LINCOLN, DAKOTA,
December 13, 1874

To the Editor of the [New York] World.

SIR: In your issue of November 18, 1874, which I have just seen for the first time, there is published the annual report of the commissioner of Indian affairs, in which there occurs the following statement:

> A military reconnoitering expedition to the country in southwestern Dakota, known as the Black Hills, occasioned great excitement among the whole Sioux people. They regard it as a palpable infraction of their treaty stipulations, and were filled with the apprehension that it might lead to their exclusion from a country held sacredly their own, and highly prized their home and last refuge from the encroachment of settlements. The exaggerated accounts of rich mines and agricultural lands given in the dispatches of the commander and explorers and correspondents of the expedition intensify the eagerness of the people along the border to take possession of this country, notwithstanding the subsequent correction of these exaggerations by statements on reliable information that

no indication of mineral wealth were found, and that the lands were undesirable for white settlements, etc.

If the other statements and opinions with which the report of the commissioner is made up are equally devoid of truth, and I know some of them to be so, the entire document is not worth the paper upon which it was written.

In assailing the correctness of the "dispatches of the commander and explorers and correspondents" of the Black Hills expedition, the commissioner endeavors to controvert the statements contained therein regarding the mineral and agricultural wealth of the Black Hills by simply putting forth his individual assertion, based either on ignorance or a willful perversion of facts, to the effect that "no indications of mineral wealth were found, and that the lands were undesirable for white settlements." I repeat that in putting forth the last quoted statement, the commissioner was either guided by ignorance or by a failing even less excusable. He cannot refer to a single statement "on reliable information that no indications of mineral wealth were found, and that the lands were undesirable for white settlements." On the contrary, I assert that the dispatches of the correspondents and the explorers who accompanied the expedition were, so far as they touched upon these points, generally accurate and just. Furthermore, the official dispatches forwarded from time to time while the expedition was in progress, and describing the country of the Black Hills as rich and inviting, and particularly well adapted to white settlements, were in strict accordance with the facts, and were in substance repeated in my preliminary report, made after the return of the expedition, and these statements have never been contradicted by any person or persons competent to do so, or having knowledge of the country.

Lieutenant General Sheridan, in his annual report, also asserts that gold was found in the Black Hills. I fear the commissioner will have difficulty in naming his "reliable" information. Professor Winchell (brother of the distinguished geologist of that name), who accompanied the expedition as one of the geologists invited to examine the country, did make a preliminary report, in which he did not say there was no gold found, but that he saw no gold, a statement in which no doubt the commissioner could consistently join.[9] Why Professor Winchell saw no gold was simply due to the fact that he neglected to look for it, and why he failed to look for it I have explained in my report, rendered since the return of the expedition, but which I need not repeat here, further than to say that the commissioner, sitting in his comfortable chair in Washington, might, in a similar manner and upon equal grounds, assert that there are no wrongs heaped upon the Indians at remote agencies by the representatives of the Indian

Department; that they have not been deprived of large portions of the annuities intended for them, and that they have not been in reality robbed by being forced to trade, where ten times the market price is taken from them.

That the commissioner may or may not know of these wrongs does not affect the truth of the statement that they exist. If, instead of assailing representatives of other departments of the government upon false grounds supported by false accusations, the same time and attention were devoted to his own department, which, by the way, is a glass house of huge dimensions, great benefit might result to the Indians.

Within the past ten days, I have been appealed to by a delegation of prominent chiefs asking that the military would exert its influence to protect them and their people against the unjust demands, as they believed, of their agent. This is but one of many incidents of the same kind. To this appeal, as to others of the same nature, I replied that the military had nothing to do with their grievances; that they must represent the facts to their agent and ask to have the matter forwarded to the Great Father in Washington. To which they replied that the agent (as might be inferred from the glaring report of the commissioner based on the statements of agents) only tells his own side of the story, while there is no one to speak for the Indian. I then assured the chief who acted as spokesman that the Great Father had the interest and welfare of the Indians at heart, and in selecting men for agents endeavored to select only good men. The reply of the chief is well worth considering by the commissioner. He said, "The Great Father may choose only good men, as you say, and they may be good men when they leave Washington, but by the time they get to us they are damned thieves, and we would like a change."

I have quoted the chief's reply literally, and have referred to this matter more as an illustration than under the belief that by doing so I would invite the attention of the commissioner to the affairs of his department.

As another illustration of the beautiful working of the Indian Department, by which the government feeds and clothes during the winter the Indians who make unprovoked war upon its citizens during the summer, a party of one hundred men has been dispatched from this post within the past few days to arrest one or more of the Indians, now known to be at Standing Rock agency, who were engaged in the killing of Dr. Honsinger and Mr. Baliran during the Northern Pacific survey of 1873. One of these Indians has been at the agency referred to since last summer, has openly and repeatedly acknowledged his participation in the killing of the two parties named, and has exhibited articles taken from them after having killed them.[10] Yet the agent, who no doubt can see no harm in an Indian killing a white man, has practically kept the matter a secret, and it has only been by accident, and not through the Indian Department, that the matter has been made public. Perhaps the agent remembered the experience of his brother agent in Southern Kansas recently who, because of his stating that the Indians were in the wrong and deserved punishment, was at once requested to resign.

Officials connected with or representing a particular department or bureau of the government have always exercised great care not to meddle with or unnecessarily comment upon the management or details of another department. In this case, however, the commissioner of Indian affairs, departing from this rule, has seen fit in an official report to call in question the correctness of officials' statements made in a department with which he is in no way connected, and for which he is in no manner responsible. If he had either truth or justice on his side, he might furnish a plausible excuse for his conduct, but he has perverted the truth to the extent of stating in an official document that which is not only not true, but which he had no "reliable information" even upon which to base his voluntary misstatements. If the commissioner will confine his attentions to his own department and correct such evils as a conscientious discharge of duty might find therein, he will have no time left to interfere with other departments, much less to publish unwarranted, because untruthful, statements concerning the official conduct of others.

G. A. CUSTER,
Brevet Major General, U.S.A.

The Black Hills Expedition

WILLIAM LUDLOW[1]

Army and Navy Journal 12, no. 6 (September 19, 1874): 31

ST. PAUL, MINN., September 7, 1874
To the Assistant Adjutant General Department of Dakota:
SIR: The expedition was organized for the purpose of exploring the unknown territory lying principally in the western and southwestern portion of Dakota and the eastern portion of Wyoming, with the view of discovering practicable interior military routes between Fort Lincoln in the Department of Dakota and opposite the terminus of the Union Pacific Railroad and Fort Laramie in the Department of the Platte, with that railroad for its base. In case circumstances should require the establishment of military posts in the region referred to, more knowledge of its resources than we possessed would also be required to guide in the selection of suitable sites.

I was directed by the department commander to accompany the expedition and act as engineer officer. Unable to obtain funds which would be available for the payment of salaries, I nevertheless secured the valuable services of Prof. N. H. Winchell of Minneapolis to act as geologist for the expedition, and of Mr. G. B. Grinnell, representing Professor Marsh[2] of Yale College, who kindly agreed to report upon the paleontology and zoology of the region traversed. Professor Winchell would also make such report as his time afforded upon the botany of the Hills, and Dr. Williams, assistant surgeon, U.S.A. and chief medical officer of the expedition,[3] promised to aid in the same department. A photographer[4] was fitted out with apparatus and chemicals, and a spring wagon, [as] constructed for similar use on the Yellowstone expedition of 1873. In the surveying, I had a detachment of engineer soldiers consisting of two sergeants[5] and four men, who were to keep two sets of notes of the route with prismatic compass and odometer, while my assistant, Mr. W. H. Wood,[6] and myself would attend to the general topography and the astronomical observations for latitude and longitude.

The expedition left Fort Lincoln on July 3 and consisted of ten companies of the 7th Cavalry, one company of the 20th Infantry, and [one] of the 17th Infantry, with a battery of three Gatlings and one three-inch Rodman gun, and a detachment of Indian scouts, guides, etc. The train consisted of over one hundred wagons. We were assured by the guides of two things in advance: first, that the expedition would be strenuously opposed by a hostile force of Indians and secondly, that we could never penetrate the fastness of the Black Hills. They represented the difficulties in our way as being formidable for cavalry, and for wagons insuperable. Both predictions failed. The expedition returned to Fort Lincoln on August 30, the sixtieth day out, with a loss of only four men, three from sickness, and one killed in a quarrel, having seen no hostile Indians during the whole trip of nearly one thousand miles, and having explored the Black Hills from east to west and from north to south.

The route pursued led us up to the south side of Heart River, thence in a west, southwesterly direction, across the Cannonball and up the North Fork of Grand River; thence southwesterly to a point which we named Prospect Valley, in about latitude 45 degrees, 30 minutes, and longitude 103 degrees, 40 minutes; thence up the east side of the Little Missouri River, and southerly to the North Fork of the Cheyenne River, Belle Fourche. This point we reached on July 18, in about longitude 104 degrees, after sixteen marches and three hundred miles of travel. Hitherto the country had much resembled other portions of Dakota—an open prairie; wood scarce, and only found in river valleys; water not always to be met with in sufficient quantity, and frequently impregnated with salts, making it both disagreeable and injurious; but still, a fair amount of grass, and no serious difficulties presented to the traveler. All the country bordering on Heart River is good, that on Cannonball is fair; Grand River country is poor, as well as that near the headwaters of the Moreau or Owl River.

All the streams flow eastward, and head close up to the Little Missouri, which, running northward at right angles to the others, has but a narrow and barren belt tributary to it on the east side. Its main support is from its branches heading in the Powder River range of hills. Our route led us in view of Slim Butte (which is rather a high, steep coteau than a butte), of Slave and Bear Buttes, and many others not hitherto located. The Black Hills, as we approached them, looked very high and dark under their covering of pine timber.

We crossed the Belle Fourche on July 20 and found ourselves in a new country. The whole character of our surroundings was changed. There was an abundance of grass, timber, small fruits, and flowers, and what perhaps was better appreciated than all, an ample supply of pure cold water. These advantages, with a few exceptions, we enjoyed until we left the Hills for the return journey. Our course lay up the valley of the Redwater—a large branch of the Belle Fourche—to Inyan Kara [Creek], thence easterly and southeasterly into the heart of the Hills. Valley leads into valley, to the beautiful park country, always until now marked "unexplored" on the maps, of which we had heard so much, but hardly hoped to reach with our wagons. After arriving near Harney's Peak—a lofty granite mass with an altitude of over eight thousand feet above the sea, and surrounded with craggy peaks and pinnacles—a rapid reconnaissance was made to the South Fork of the Cheyenne, nearly due south of us, with five companies of cavalry, and the exit from the interior was ascertained to be not difficult on that side.

Returning, the course lay northerly and northeasterly, looking for an exit near Bear Butte. Failing to find an easy one, we went southerly a short distance and discovered a pass near Elk Creek which let us out on the prairie.[7] The change to the hot dry air and yellow grass of the prairie was wonderfully sudden and anything but pleasant. From Bear Butte the return journey led back past Slave Butte, touching the headwaters of the Moreau, crossing the down trail in Prospect Valley, thence tapping the head of Grand River and following roughly the east side of the Little Missouri northward and eastward to where the trail of the Yellowstone expedition crosses it, and thence into Lincoln, on the north side of Heart River. The return route was a much better one for a large force than the other. We had no difficulty in finding good camps, with plenty of water and grass. The country passed over, tributary to the Moreau, is barren, but the river valley itself is more favorable, and at the head of the Grand River is much better country than lower down. From Grand River to above Heart River, the grass had been thoroughly burned by the Indians. It caused some inconvenience, but we were always fortunate in finding a camp in some locality which the fire had spared.

With regard to the geology of the Black Hills, Professor Winchell's report will be nearly exhaustive. Both Mr. Grinnell and he were as industrious as possible in collecting information, and I can only regret that the want of time prevented much opportunity for study. I call attention to the preliminary reports from both gentlemen. Their detailed reports will be prepared as soon as possible, as well as one from Dr. Williams on the flora of the Hills. It is a region admirably adapted to settlement, abounding in timber, in grass and flowing streams, with springs of pure cold water almost everywhere. The valleys of South Slope are ready for the plow; the soil is of wonderful fertility, as evidenced by the luxuriance of the grass and the profusion of flowers and small fruits; the climate entirely different from that of the plains, giving evidence of being much more agreeable—cooler in the summer and more moderate in winter; not subject to drought, for the nightly dews are very heavy; not liable to excessive snowfall, for in narrow valleys containing a large creek no indications of overflow could be detected.

The creeks confine their favor to the Hills. Upon reaching the exterior range, they pass through rocky canyons, sometimes of great depth, and arriving at the outer foothills sink into the ground and disappear.

Upon the mineral resources of the Hills, Professor Winchell's report will throw full light. No coal was found. Extensive deposits of iron ore of good quality exist. Immense beds of gypsum were met with. Specimens of gold were washed from the soil in the vicinity of Harney's Peak, and quartz in bed and boulder was visible in large quantities. Any amount of excellent building stone, limestone, sandstone, and granite are present. Some of the limestone, particularly in the vicinity of Inyan Kara [Mountain], were fine enough for marble and handsomely colored. The timber is mainly red pine and spruce of large size. Oak, ash, and elm are found on the exterior slopes. Game is abundant: bear, elk, and deer of two kinds were found, and many killed. On the prairies, antelopes were found in large numbers.

The complete report, accompanied by the reports of Professor Winchell, Mr. Grinnell, and Dr. Williams, will be transmitted at the earliest possible day, together with a map showing the route pursued, with bordering country, from Fort Lincoln and return, and a special map on a larger scale of the Black Hills proper.[8]

The photographer secured negatives for about sixty views, a set of which will accompany this report.

       Respectfully submitted,
         WM. LUDLOW,
      Captain of Engineers, U.S.A.,
      Chief Engineer Department of Dakota.
ST. PAUL, MINN., September 7, 1874

Reminiscences of the Black Hills Expedition

WILLIAM H. WOOD[1]

W. H. Wood Reminiscences, Small Manuscripts Collection, State Historical Society of North Dakota, Bismarck

In 1874, I went to the Black Hills with Custer. We outfitted at Fort Lincoln, near where Mandan is now, and struck southwest across the prairie. We had with us the War Department maps of the explorations up to that date. Captain Hardy of the Engineer Corps said he had heard of the Black Hills—he didn't go into them, but he had marked them on his map. We were on the lookout for signs of his party, but we didn't hit the trail all the way out. He had half a dozen army wagons with him, and they would make quite a trail because they follow one right after the other.

One day, I think it was Ludlow who said, "Look at that!" There were two rows of sunflowers, just the gauge of the wagon apart, and as far as we could see, just an unbroken line of sunflowers. We didn't follow the line of the flowers; we were crossing it at right angles. The horses and the wagons had broken the sod, what little sod there is out there. The sod on that prairie isn't like ours; they probably went out in the time when the sunflowers were in bloom and scattered their seeds. The seeds that fell on the unbroken sod dried up, but the seeds that fell in the wagon trails sprouted. It was a pretty sight, the two lines of sunflowers.

We crossed this line in the northeast corner of the Black Hills on the prairie. We went into the Black Hills at the north end, and we went through them to the south end, and it was pretty slow travel. We had a big train; we had about twelve hundred soldiers—cavalry, infantry, and artillery. My impression is that we had twelve hundred men,[2] and all their supplies for a two months' trip. It made a pretty big trail. I think we had one hundred army wagons. We didn't have time to hunt a trail, we just went in, and we had loads of trouble. Sometimes we didn't make more than four or five miles a day; we had to stop and pick a way for the wagons to get through. I have seen them go all night long, once or twice—there was no letup with Custer. He went ahead and picked out a camping place and said, "I guess they can come this far." They didn't get there until 4:00 A.M., then they fed the horses and went right on.

Custer was a typical soldier—he looked every inch a soldier, except that he wore his hair in long curls. He was a young man still, a man of about thirty, a fine-looking man—very tall and erect, carried himself very well. He was pleasant, but of course I didn't get to know him well. There were some young men in the party when we went to the Black Hills. I made friends with one or two of them. I think Ludlow had a small opinion of Custer, and he had a better chance of knowing what sort of man he was than I did.

During that afternoon [August 7, 1874], Colonel Ludlow said, "Wood, let's go out and see if we can find a grizzly." There were plenty of them there; we had seen signs of them. So he and I went out, and we took his orderly with him. The three of us were mounted, and we took rifles and went hunting. We left camp, where there was considerable noise, and went down a little coulee where we thought there might be a spring, and in just a short time we found it—just at the foot of two hills, where the two hills came together. There was scarcely enough space for the horses to stand, the hills came together at such a steep angle. Sometimes we had to jump some fallen trees. Ludlow was in front, I was in the middle, and the orderly was behind. When Ludlow's horse jumped over a little place about two feet high, we were surprised to see a bear come out from under a tree to the left of us. He was surprised to see us too, and just stood looking. I was right beside the bear, so close to him that if he had reached out with his paw he would have hit me. I saw Ludlow fingering his gun, and I said, "For God's sake, Ludlow, don't shoot." I was nearest the bear, and I was afraid if Ludlow did shoot, the bear would have thought I was the aggressor. The bear stood still for what seemed like a few minutes, I suppose it really was only ten seconds, then he just turned and went up the hill.

Our horses could not get up that hill, but we tried to find the bear again when we got to level ground. We were several miles from camp, and though we looked for him all the way back to camp, we couldn't find him. But when we got back to camp, there was our bear, lying on the ground dead. Custer and some of his friends had gone hunting bear and got him. Before we got back to camp, Ludlow said, "Wood, Mike, remember this: We have seen no bear."

Col. William Ludlow was in the Spanish-American War; he was governor of Havana after we conquered Cuba. He was captain of the engineers and then a brevet major when I knew him—he was a fine man.

We went on for some time toward the south end of the Black Hills. The engineer[3] whose trail we saw had located Harney's Peak. He had estimated its height. It was a real peak, and the only peak in the Black Hills. It was a granite peak, standing up above the rest of the mountains. One day [July 31], Ludlow and three or four other men and myself decided to climb Harney's Peak. It was quite a climb. We took out horses as high as we could, then tethered them and went the rest of the way on foot. Custer went too, but he took his horse a great deal higher than we did. Harney's Peak has a [7,242] foot elevation, and we got a wonderful view of the surrounding country. I took a good many compass bearings of permanent places, and then we turned around and went down. Custer's horse had a hard time getting down the steep peak—it was cruel, the horse's knees were bleeding, and he had a hard time to make the grade.

We came out of the Black Hills at the southern end, not far from Harney's Peak, and went parallel on the prairie to go north and strike home again. We came back on the east side of the Black Hills, so we were south and east of our going trail.

There was a captain in the cavalry, I wish I could remember his name, he was such a nice man. We two struck up quite a friendship. We rode parallel with the wagon trail, a little farther up. I suppose they were a quarter or half a mile on our left. While we were riding along one day, we saw, not far away, a blacktail buck. We both exclaimed, "I believe we could get a shot at him." I told the captain to take the first shot at him, and he got down on his knees and shot, and missed. Then it was my turn, and I got down on my knee and shot. I knocked the buck over, and took a second shot. That killed him. I thought that was pretty good shooting. We measured the distance later, and it was just one hundred yards. We had a Colt .45 revolver. Well, we cut his head off and took him back to camp and had his antlers cut off. They were still in the velvet, and it was a nasty job. I kept those antlers for years, but they have finally disappeared.

I suppose that trip took six weeks or two months, from Fort Lincoln to Fort Lincoln.[4] The purpose of the trip was to explore the Black Hills. There were rumors that the Black Hills had gold in them. Custer took several gold hunters on that trip, and they found some gold. I saw those fellows pull up a bunch of grass, and you could see the gold sparkling in the roots. It's a rich country; they are still mining gold there.

I made astronomical observations of the camp and kept a log with compass and odometer findings of all the windings of our trail so we could map the country. The map I made, showing our trip and all the hills and streams, is now in the War Department files.

Col. Fred Grant was a guest of Custer on that trip. Fred Grant was the son of General Grant and was drunk nearly all the time.

We used to start early in the morning, about 6:00 A.M., and stopped anywhere from 12:00 P.M. to 4:00 P.M. The sutler had a wagon with liquor, which we sold to the soldiers and everybody who wanted to buy it. Colonel Grant was a guest of Custer. He went along to see the country and have a good time. He was in the army then, but he must have got a leave of absence.

Story Told by Strikes Two and Bear's Belly of an Expedition under Custer to the Black Hills in 1874[1]

ALFRED BEAR[2]

Collections of the State Historical Society of North Dakota 6 (1920): 163–70

The scouts on the expedition were as follows: Bloody Knife and Lean Bear, as leaders; Bear's Ears, Horns-in-Front, Crow Bear, Standing Soldier, Red Horse, Bear's Arm, Strikes Two, Bear's Belly, Enemy Heart, Young Hawk, Red Bear, Little Sioux, Bear's Eyes, Left Hand (different in his discharge papers), Goose, Angry Bear (Mandan name, He-ra-ta-ke), Red Angry Bear, Crooked Horn (Arikara), Elk Face, Angry Bull (half Dakota and half Arikara), Left Hand (Dakota), Spotted Horse Eagle (Dakota), Shoots the Bear (Dakota), two Blackfoot, and twenty-five Santee scouts.

They started from their camp at the bottom of a hill on the present site of Mandan and joined Custer at his fort [Abraham Lincoln]. They went south on the hill, crossing the Cannon Ball at the sacred stone or the stone with the holy writing on it. After two or three nights [July 11, 1874],[3] they camped at a place they called the cave or den. The Arikara were told by the Dakota scouts that they were near the big den or cave, so that they camped and went to look for it. The walls were covered with painted designs, and toward the interior were carved figures on the walls. On the ceiling, a flash of lightning was figured. The dung of deer covered all the floor to the opening into the interior. Here the ceiling was out of reach, and it was wholly dark. At the opening of the interior were offerings of beads in a heap and bracelets. From here they picked up a flintlock and took it to Custer. Beyond the cave were two piles of stones put up by the Dakotas, and still farther on from the opening was a large flat rock. When they first found this cave, they saw on the flat rock a woman taking the hair off a deer hide with an old-fashioned scraper. She ran away, and they could not find her. They thought she hid in the cave, far in. Beyond the flat rock was a spring. Here was a large hollow rock full of water like a trough in a pasture, and the tracks of the deer were all about like cow tracks at a watering place. The soldiers came after this to explore the cave. They had three candles and a pick and shovel. The Arikara scouts went in till the cave floor slanted steeply down, and then they went back. The Mandan scout was with the soldiers and stayed after the other scouts left. But he turned back too after he was about halfway down.

Scouts on the march. HARPER'S WEEKLY, 1887.

The next morning, their interpreter for the Dakotas, Baker (his sons are Lewis and James), told them that the soldiers found it wet and muddy and had to turn back after going knee-deep without reaching the end. The next morning, they broke camp and came to a butte shining with selenite, and large pieces at the bottom.

The next place was Black Butte; heavy cedar timber was all over it. Here Custer sent two scouts back with mail, Bull Neck and Skunk Head. They now entered the timber; it looked like a prairie that had been burned, it was so black. They camped at a river, shallow like the Little Missouri. They called it the Big River, and the Dakotas call it the Beautiful River. There was pine timber on both sides of the river. Across the river was the Cut Butte, with two high points, and they camped here. The scouts were on a hill, and the soldiers were in a valley [Prospect Valley, July 14]. Their interpreter told them that two soldiers were quarreling, and one of them asked Custer for permission to finish the fight. Custer said, "I don't care," and one of the soldiers got his gun out. The scouts heard someone call, "Hold on, hold on," and then a shot, and then another. The soldier shot his comrade through the arm and then through the heart. The dead body was carried on in a wagon. Custer came to the scouts and told them that the doctor was planning to cut up the body to see why he was so quarrelsome. The scouts saw the doctor cut the body open, put salt in the body, put all the parts back, and then the body was buried. The soldiers fired a salute over the grave.[4]

The next morning, they set out through the timber, and they tried to keep track of the number of days they were in the woods. When they came to a butte, they went up and saw only timber, no earth at all. They found an old Dakota camp [July 26] where they had been preparing tepee poles, peeling bark and leaning the poles up on trees nearby. The camp was old, but presently they struck a fresh Dakota trail. Custer told them to go on duty, and a few scouts went ahead to scout. A fresh Dakota camp was reported by the scouts, and they all went on to the place and found coals of fire not yet out, deer bones freshly gnawed, dried meat still hanging here and there.

All the scouts lined up under Custer's orders, and he picked out the best of them to scout ahead to look for the Dakota camp. Strikes Two was one of these and two white men—soldiers, not officers. At a place where there was a junction of two ravines, they saw at their right up the ravine the Dakota camp. There were five tepees, and it was as far as from Bear's Belly's house to Red Bear's house. They sent the two white soldiers back to Custer to notify him. They stood together at the top of the hill and looked across the ravine. They could hear scattered shots from the Dakota hunters. The soldiers came up, and Custer sent one party of scouts to surround the camp and the others were to charge straight in. Strikes Two was with the first party, and Bear's Belly was with the second. The first party surrounded the camp and waited for the others to charge. Then they heard the horses charging in, and they ran out of the woods. They saw two boys with a yellow blanket on, and they were afraid and cried and ran up where there was a creek. They threw away their blanket, and the scouts saw the fish they had. Then a naked warrior ran out with a gun, which he held up against the charging scouts. Red Angry Bear reached him first and struck him with his whip, and the others did the same. The women ran out and tried to get away into the woods, but the scouts told them to go to their tent. They found out the warrior's gun had no hammer, and he [Slow Bull] was the only man there. Then he went inside and came out with a pipe, which he held towards the scouts as a peace sign.

Custer then came up with his men and called up the Dakota scouts, and they told Custer that the camp would follow, as they were prisoners. He left one white man in the camp to see that they came on and one white man on a hill to watch them. When three Dakota hunters came back, they told the man in camp they were going to buy a gun of the soldiers, so he went with them to the other white soldier, and they all came on to Custer's camp. One Dakota came to where the scouts were and by signs told them that he wanted to get a gun in exchange for a horse. He said he would go and get his horse, and Custer said all right but told the other two to stay behind. The other Dakota scouts went along with the Dakota captives, but one lagged back and ran away to a creek. Then they saw the other Dakota [Long Bear] wrestling on horseback with his captor. The Dakota scout drew his revolver and fired, but the two Dakotas got away. The Arikara scouts fired one shot apiece, and the Dakota scouts held one of the Dakota captives, the old man [One Stab]. They all rode on to the old camp, but all the Dakotas were gone. They followed hard on the trail till dark and then gave it up.

They returned and found the old Dakota tied outside to an iron picket pin. His feet were hobbled, he had a string around his waist, and his leg was bandaged, but his hands were not tied. Custer came to the Arikaras and made signs that he at first planned to have them kill this Dakota captive, but that now he was to be guide. The captive tried to tell them that they were coming to more Dakotas than their whole number and all would be killed.

At last [July 30] they came to the Shell River [Ruby Creek]. Here the Dakota guide pointed out distant smoke on the prairie and said it was a train and a town. Custer said he was to stop and give up and return on the back trail. The officer the Arikaras called the Lucky Man (Charley Reynolds) was given papers by Custer and he went on alone. He was a good hunter and a dead shot. He was to go to the town in the direction of the smoke. The Dakota captive cried in the night and by signs said that his children would cut their hair as for his death, since he was as good as dead. At one place, Custer signed to the scouts that he proposed to let the Dakota captive go. He gave the Dakota a good suit, hat, and other things, and though the Arikaras planned to kill him, Custer got him off in the night, and they never saw him again.

From this they camped at a broken place [Golden Park, August 1]. Red Angry Bear found some gold in a spring, and word was sent in the Arikara language that they were all to come and get some of the pretty yellow stuff to trim their bridles with. They all got some, and their arms were sparkling with the golden dust. Custer asked them where they got the gold, and they showed him. He sounded a bugle and called the soldiers and put pickets out to keep all others away. Then Custer came with some gold in a cloth and opened it before the Arikaras saying, "You scouts have found this, which is money, and you shall have your share"; as he said this, he picked up and threw down gold by handfuls. "You shall have it like this," he said. The soldiers had gotten this gold from the spring, digging where the Indians had first found it. He said this land would be marked, and it was marked so they could find it again. Piles of stones were put up, and the soldiers went about putting up marks or signs.

They marched to the Bear Butte [August 15], and six scouts were sent with mail to Fort Lincoln. Three of these were Arikara scouts, Strikes Two, Angry Bear, and Left Hand. The other three were Dakota scouts, one of them was called Goose. Strikes Two had a horse with mailbags, and Custer gave him a flask of whiskey. They rode off at sunset and rode all night, and after a rest they rode on all day and reached the Beautiful River. After crossing the river, they traveled one-half the night and all day. They took six days to get to Fort Lincoln. They were here a day when the Lucky Man got in. He had delivered his papers and had come on to Fort Lincoln by rail. After twelve days, Custer's party came in.

A Winter March to the Black Hills

GUY V. HENRY[1]

Harper's Weekly 39 (July 27, 1895)

The story of this ride has often been told, but only a plainsman knows what it is to face a norther. It is more dreadful than fire or shipwreck: When the ice god turns on his blizzard and drives the thermometer down to forty degrees below zero, no human being can live in the open air, and many of the toughest and hardiest animals succumb to the intense cold. Deer have been found huddled together in groups of five and ten, dead and frozen stiff by a norther, and even wildcats, lynx, buffalo, and Rocky Mountain lions have died of cold on the plains. The day before Christmas 1874, an Indian courier rode into our camp near Red Cloud agency, Nebraska, bringing orders from the department commander for troops to be sent to the Black Hills to remove miners who were supposed to be there in violation of treaty stipulation. Complaint had been made that the white man was stealing the Indian's gold. To penetrate into this unknown country beyond Badlands at this season of the year was to put one's life at the risk, not only of the cold storms which swept the country, but of the attacks of hostile Minneconjou Sioux. If the proper authority had known as well as we of the character of the service required, it is probable that the order would never have been issued; but it had come, and it was not ours to question why.

The day after Christmas, the command, consisting of Troop D, 3rd Cavalry, of which I was captain, about fifteen men of the 9th Infantry, under Lieutenant Carpenter,[2] with wagons, rations, and forage for thirty days, bidding adieu to families and friends, started on our march into the wilderness. Camp Robinson (now Fort Robinson) at this time was a mere shelter for its small garrison of one troop of cavalry and four companies of infantry. It was near Red Cloud agency, whose thousands of Indians were far from friendly and were liable to break out at a moment's notice. The knowledge of all this made our farewell a sad one and increased the dreariness of our already desolate surroundings. The evening of the first day's march was comparatively mild; ice had to be cut in order to procure water for our animals, some one hundred and forty in number, but they, under the shelter of a bank, with blanket covers, and the men in their tents, with stoves, were comfortable. The second day's march brought us to Spotted Tail

Guy V. Henry. COURTESY OF PERRY FROHNE.

agency, or Camp Sheridan, where we were to obtain our guide, an Indian called "Falling Waters." He, after the manner of his race, refused to go, as his suggestive name indicated to him that the weather was not suitable for travel. We succeeded, however, in obtaining the services of one Raymond, a white man and at one time a soldier, who joined us in response to an impulse of his early training. He was also well acquainted with the country and with the risks which we were to encounter. The third day we pushed on, passing the old agency and camping on White River, treating that night some of the men for frosted fingers. Continuing our march, we arrived at Wounded Knee Creek, so called because a French trapper had been wounded in the knee by Indians and left to die. Here we left the White River, which was frozen almost solid, and a very unusual thing it was for this river to freeze at all, and commenced our march across the Badlands. It would be impossible to properly describe this region of desolate country. Immense bald bluffs of chalky whiteness confront you. There is not a sign of vegetation, except as here and there a solitary pine tree stands its lonely watch, making by contrast the desolation more wretched. In summer, you are suffocated with clouds of alkali dust; in winter, or when the ground is wet, your wagons sink to their axles. Nature seems to forbid approach. A green deposit or strata here and there marks what is supposed to have once been the bottom of a lake. Here are found what scientists regard as the richest deposits of bone, backs of turtles, et cetera. It may easily be imagined, however, that under the circumstances, this subject did not occupy our thoughts.

This vast region of desolation can be best compared to the picture which our imagination makes of the "lower regions" with the fires extinguished. It is in fact Dante's "Inferno" reproduced. In this Inferno, camped on the frozen surface of a lake to obtain shelter from a howling wind, with the thermometer forty degrees below zero, we spent the New Year's Eve of 1874. 'Twas truly a cheerful place, and as we wrapped ourselves (Lieutenant Carpenter and myself) in our buffalo robes, we felt thankful we had wood and shelter from the storm. On this same place, Harney Springs (named after General Harney), I camped during the Pine Ridge troubles just sixteen years after the experience I am now relating. Our next camp, New Year's Day, was made on the Cheyenne River, and we were thankful for an abundance of wood. Raymond, our guide, had said the day before that when we got to the Cheyenne, he would "prospect" a little, as he thought that if there was gold in the Black Hills, it would show in the Cheyenne, receiving as it did so many streams from the supposed El Dorado. Seeing him sitting by an air hole in the ice, I found his prospecting consisted in "thawing out" a couple of frozen fingers. The next day, we crossed to a stream supposed to have been followed by the miners. We entered the hills, but found no sign of a trail, so we started back on the homeward march. It was afterward ascertained that the miners were brought out of the hills in the spring of the year in an almost starved condition. The Black Hills are so called not because of their color, but of the contrast of color, green or brown, with that of the chalky whiteness of the Badlands.

Nothing of particular importance occurred on our return march except the intense cold, ranging from twenty to forty degrees below zero. Fortunately the little wind we had was on our backs, and when once in camp, we could make ourselves and our animals comfortable. The delay in pitching and striking tents or in preparing and breaking camp was the most disagreeable part of the march. The ground was so hard that driving a tent pin, which had to be iron, was almost impossible, and the removal of it was so difficult that we had often to tie our tent ropes to trees or bushes. All food was frozen solid and had to be thawed before cooking, bits had to be warmed before being placed in the mouths of the horses, and any teamster who touched a trace chain or iron part with bare hands would quickly drop it or be blistered. We had to abandon some wagons owing to bad roads, but as we were nearing the end of our journey, our loads were as light as our hearts. On the last day's march, we broke camp early in the morning in gay spirits, as we thought that evening would bring us to Camp Robinson and the end of our two weeks' march of 300 miles, useless as it had been, with its hardships and sufferings. But, alas! sunset of that memorable day told a far different tale. At 7:00 A.M., an hour out from camp, a strong, piercing wind arose, a norther, cutting like a razor. If we could have found shelter, it would have been the part of wisdom to camp, but there was no shelter to be found, and a return to our old camp was out of the question, as our wagons had followed the road while we had taken a trail. Indeed, the chance that they could be quickly found, if at all, in this blinding snow-drifting storm was very slight, and the search could not have been made without risking the lives of the searching party. So to push on was our only alternative. The cold was so intense that it was impossible to ride. Dismounting, we led our horses, and they, poor brutes, in their sufferings, struggled to escape from their riders, who in their frozen condition had trouble to prevent them.

Our trail was lost, or obliterated by the snow; our eyes were absolutely sightless from the constant pelting of the frozen particles. And thus we struggled on. A clump of trees or a hill for a shelter from the killing and life-sapping wind would have indeed been a sweet haven. With frozen hands and faces, men becoming weaker and weaker, many bleeding from the nose and the ears, the weakest lying down and refusing to move, a precursor of death; with them the painful stinging bite of the frost had been succeeded by the more solid freezing, which drives the blood rapidly to the center and produces that warm, delightful, dreamy sensation, the forerunner of danger and death. They had to be threatened and strapped to their saddles, for if they were left behind, death would follow, and an officer's duty is to save his men. Ours now was a struggle for life; to halt was to freeze to death, to advance our only hope, as Red Cloud could not be far away, and some of us might be able to reach camp with life, though with frozen limbs.

Weakened till we could no longer walk, in desperation the command "mount" was given. Stiffened and frozen, we clambered into our saddles. "Forward, gallop!" and we all knew this was a race for life. We were powerless. Brain nor eye could no longer help us. The instinct of our horses would alone save those who could hold out. So on we rushed, life and home in front, death behind. Suddenly turning the curve of a hill, we came upon a ranch inhabited by a white man and his squaw, and we were saved. Had the sun burst forth with the heat of summer, our surprise and joy could not have been greater than they were to thus find this place of refuge and safety in the wilderness, and to be saved from the jaws of death by a "squaw ranch"! I have since passed this ranch, and nothing has ever awakened stronger feelings of gratitude than the sight of that hovel. The horses were put in the corral. Those that were running wild with their powerless riders were caught. Men were put under shelter, and the process of thawing out frozen parts commenced, with its attendant pain and suffering.

Every officer and man was frozen; some suffered more than others; and to this day, many are still suffering from the effects of this march by the loss of members. Even where there is no physical disability, freezing leaves a nervous prostration from which one never recovers. We found ourselves about fifteen miles from our post, and so great was the cold that we could not persuade an Indian to carry a message to Red Cloud asking that wagons and ambulances be sent to our assistance. The next day, we received medical attention, and the helpless were carried to the post. There could not have been a greater contrast between our departure and return. Entering my own quarters, I was not recognized owing to my black and swollen face. All my fingers were frozen to their second joints; the flesh sloughed off, exposing the bones. Other flesh gradually grew afterward, except on one finger, the first joint of which had to be amputated, while the joints of my left hand are to this day so stiffened by freezing and extraneous deposits that I am unable to bend or close my fingers. The above narrative shows what many other officers and soldiers in the past have had to undergo on the plains in the performance of duty, and not a winter but has had its maimed and suffering victims, who have borne their share in this battle of civilization, rendering victory possible through the protection of settlers, the building and extension of railroads, and the peopling of the "Great West."

The Black Hills

PHILIP H. SHERIDAN[1]

Army and Navy Journal 12, no. 34 (April 3, 1875): 533

HEADQUARTERS MILITARY DIVISION OF THE MISSOURI,
CHICAGO, March 25 [1875]
General W. T. Sherman, Headquarters of the Army, St. Louis.
GENERAL: In reply to your question, "What do you know of the Black Hills?" I respectfully submit the following remarks: My first knowledge of the Black Hills was derived from the late Father De Smet, a noted Catholic missionary, whom I met many years ago on the Columbia River in Oregon,[2] from whom I heard an Indian romance of a mountain of gold in the Black Hills, and his explanation of that extraordinary and delusive story of the Indians, frontiersmen, and explorers. The Black Hills country is much more extensive than that particular locality brought to the notice of the public by the recent explorations of Colonel Custer, and gets its name from the black, scrubby character of the timber which grows on the sides and tops of the mountains and hills. It comprises the whole of the country bounded on the east by longitude 102 degrees, on the south by the Sweetwater and Laramie Rivers, on the west by the Bighorn and Wind Rivers, and on the north by the Yellowstone River.

This is really the country of the Black Hills, but embraced in it are several localities called Black Hills; for instance, Black Hills of Laramie, Black Hills of Powder River, and Black Hills of Cheyenne River, the latter being the locality in which Colonel Custer made his reconnaissance last summer, and about which there is so much speculation at the present time, and within the bounds of which it is supposed by a large number of people is to be found Father De Smet's mountain of gold.

Father De Smet's story was that while living with the Sioux Indians, he was shown by them nuggets of gold, which they informed him had been obtained at different points in the Black Hills, supposed to be from the beds of the Bighorn, Rosebud, and Powder Rivers, and from branches of the Tongue River,[3] and on his representing that such yellow metal was of great value, they told him that they knew where a mountain of it was to be found. Subsequent investigation, however, proved that the Indian mountain of gold was nothing more than a formation of yellow mica, such as may be found in a number of places in the above-described country. I had scarcely given the story a thought after this until about three years ago, when I happened to be in New York, and it was there brought to my recollection by some prominent gentleman, who asked me where Father De Smet was to be found and insisted that someone should be sent at once to get from him the secret of the gold mountain, which would pay the national debt. After I had informed him that it was an old and exploded story, his ardor cooled, and the excitement about the mountain of gold again subsided.

It so happened, however, that the Black Hills country was embraced in my military commission, and two years ago it became apparent to me that a military post in the Black Hills of the Cheyenne would soon become necessary for the proper protection of the settlements in Nebraska from the raids of Sioux warriors, who always, before they commenced depredating on the frontier, secured a safe place for their families and villages in the locality mentioned.

Believing that these Indians would never make war on our settlements as long as we could threaten their families and villages in this remote locality, abounding in game and all that goes to make Indian life comfortable, and with this purely military object in view, an order was given for Colonel Custer's reconnaissance. The discovery of particles of gold by alluvial washing near Harney's Peak, on the eastern slope of the Black Hills of Cheyenne, followed and brought to the surface Father De Smet's story for the third time.

The Black Hills of [the] Cheyenne described by Colonel Custer are situated between the north and south forks of that river, one of which is known as the Belle Fourche, the other as the South Fork; although I have the utmost confidence in the statements of Colonels Custer and Forsyth,[4] of my staff, that gold was found near Harney's Peak, I may safely say there has not been any fair test yet made to determine its existence in large quantities. There is not a territory in the West where gold does not exist, but in many of them the quantity is limited to the color, which is as much as has yet been obtained near Harney's Peak. The geological specimens brought back by the Custer expedition are not favorable indications of the existence of gold in great quantities. Still, it may be there. But as the treaty of 1869, duly ratified, virtually deeds this portion of the Black Hills to the Sioux Indians, there is no alternative but to keep out trespassers.

But to go back to Father De Smet's information. There is not much doubt of the correctness of his statement that gold exists in the Black Hills, but much further west than the Black Hills of the Cheyenne. I

Trespassing prospectors on the lookout for Indians. HARPER'S WEEKLY, 1875.

have seen nuggets from the Bighorn and Tongue Rivers, and many specimens from near Fort Stambaugh, in the Upper Wind River country, where the mining has failed for want of water for alluvial washing, and from the hostility of the Indians. I have good reason to believe, in fact it is quite certain, that gold exists in the Owl Creek Mountains, on the headwaters of the Powder River and the Rosebud, all the localities being, under the general meaning, in the Black Hills, and outside of the treaty of 1869, except so far as the privileges to hunt game. It has been my intention to communicate much information this coming summer to the government on the above-described country, and as the Indians have no absolute right to the soil, there may be little difficulty in extinguishing their hunting privileges.

    I propose, if you do not object, to open up the Yellowstone River by sending Lieutenant Colonels George A. Forsyth and [Frederick D.] Grant,[5] of my staff, up the Yellowstone to the mouth of the

Bighorn as soon as the ice breaks, which will give the lowest tidewater, having already secured a steamboat to make this exploration. If Colonel Forsyth is successful, I will send Colonel Custer with a command from Fort Lincoln across the mouth of Powder River, thence up on the south bank of the Yellowstone, crossing Powder River, Tongue River, the Rosebud, and on to the mouth of the Bighorn. This country is as yet entirely unexplored, and the expedition may develop a very valuable auriferous section and make the Father De Smet story to some extent true, but I am of the belief that a mountain of mica has not changed to gold. I will also send an expedition down the Wind River, through the Owl Creek Mountains, from Fort Stambaugh, via Fort Brown,[6] to the mouth of the Bighorn, and will bring it back through the parks, about the headwaters of the Powder River, visited by Captain Mills[7] and his command last summer. These parks are, for beauty, fully equal to those described so graphically by Colonel Custer as existing in the Black Hills of [the] Cheyenne.

I may also say, from my own knowledge, that the valleys of the Big and Little Popooge, Little Wind River, and Main Wind River can scarcely be excelled in beauty and fertility, while the student of nature will find there the most extraordinary upheavals of the earth's crust probably to be found on this continent. I am of the opinion that this country is gold bearing, but of its abundance there can only be conjecture. At present, I feel quite confident of our ability to prevent the intended trespass on the rights of the Indians, and the cavalry and infantry of the Department of Dakota are being moved at the present time to the most available points to carry out my directions of September 3 of last year.

Were it not for these precautions on the part of the government, there might be a repetition of California's gold beach and gold lake humbugs, with still greater suffering, as many of the persons now crazy to go to the Black Hills never think of how they are to exist after they get there, or how they could return in case of failure. If they will wait for further information from the government, which now seems to be desirous of making concessions to meet these new interests, there will be no one more willing than myself to aid in ascertaining their value.

So far as troops are concerned, I will promise activity in the present emergency and the conscientious performance of duty. Should the points from which the miners start be so remote as to make it impossible for our scanty force to watch them, we can occupy the two or three gaps in the Black Hills and effectually exclude trespassers.

                Very respectfully,
                P. H. SHERIDAN,
                Lieutenant General Commanding

The Sun Dance of the Sioux

FREDERICK SCHWATKA[1]

Century Magazine 39, no. 5 (March 1890): 753–59

A few years ago, it was the good fortune of the writer to witness, at the Spotted Tail Indian Agency on Beaver Creek, Nebraska, the ceremony of the great Sun Dance of the Sioux. Perhaps eight thousand Brule Sioux were quartered at the agency at that time, and about forty miles to the west, near the head of the White River, there was another reservation of Sioux, numbering probably a thousand or fifteen hundred less. Ordinarily each tribe or reservation has its own celebration of the Sun Dance; but owing to the nearness of these two agencies, it was this year thought best to join forces and celebrate the savage rites with unwonted splendor and barbarity. Nearly halfway between the reservations, the two forks of the Chadron Creek form a wide plain, which was chosen as the site of the great sun dance.

In general, it is almost impossible for a white man to gain permission to view this ceremony in all its details; but I had in Spotted Tail, the chief, and in Standing Elk, the head warrior, two very warm friends, and their promise that I should behold the rites in part slowly widened and allowed me to obtain full view of the entire proceedings.

It was in June that the celebration was to be held, and for many days before the first ceremonies took place, the children of the prairies began to assemble, not only from the two agencies most interested, but from many distant bands of Sioux to which rumors of the importance of this meeting had gone. Everywhere upon the plains were picturesque little caravans moving towards the level stretch between the branches of the Chadron—ponies dragging the lodge poles of the tepees, with roughly constructed willow baskets hanging from the poles and filled with a confusion of pots and puppies, babies and drums, scalps and kindling wood, and rolls of jerked buffalo meat, with old hags urging on the ponies and gay young warriors riding. Fully twenty thousand Sioux were present, the half-breeds and the "squaw men" of the two agencies said, when the opening day arrived. Probably fifteen thousand would be more correct. It was easier to believe the statement of the Indians that it was the grandest Sun Dance within the memory of the oldest warriors; and as I became fully convinced of this assertion, I left no stone unturned that would keep me fast in the good graces of my friends, Spotted Tail and Standing Elk.

When all had assembled and the medicine men had set the day for the beginning of the great dance dedicated to the sun, the "sun pole" was selected. A handsome young pine or fir, forty or fifty feet high, with the straightest and most uniformly tapering trunk that could be found within a reasonable distance, was chosen. The selection is always made by some old woman, generally the oldest one in the camp, if there is any way of determining, who leads a number of maidens gaily dressed in the beautiful beaded buckskin gowns they wear on state occasions; the part of the maidens is to strip the tree of its limbs as high as is possible without felling it. Woe to the girl who claims to be a maiden, and joins the procession the old squaw forms, against whose claims any reputable warrior or squaw may publicly proclaim. Her punishment is swift and sure, and her degradation more cruel than interesting.

Spotted Tail.
JOHN G. BOURKE. *ON THE BORDER WITH CROOK.*

The selection of the tree is the only special feature of the first day's celebration. After it has been stripped of its branches nearly to the top, the brushwood and trees for a considerable distance about it are removed, and it is left standing for the ceremony of the second day.

Long before sunrise, the eager participants in the next great step were preparing themselves for the ordeal; and a quarter of an hour before the sun rose above the broken hills of white clay, a long line of naked young warriors, in gorgeous war paint and feathers, with rifles, bows and arrows, and war lances in hand, faced the east and the sun pole, which was from five to six hundred yards away. Ordinarily this group of warriors numbers from fifty to possibly two hundred men. An interpreter near me estimated the line I beheld as from a thousand to twelve hundred strong. Not far away, on a high hill overlooking the barbaric scene, was an old warrior, a medicine man of the tribe, I think, whose solemn duty it was to announce by a shout that could be heard by every one of the expectant throng the exact moment when the tip of the morning sun appeared above the eastern hills. Perfect quiet rested upon the line of young warriors and upon the great throng of savage spectators that blacked the green hills overlooking the arena. Suddenly the old warrior, who had been kneeling on one knee, with his extended palm shading his scraggy eyebrows, arose to his full height, and in a slow, dignified manner, waved his blanketed arm above his head. The few warriors who were still unmounted now jumped hurriedly upon their ponies; the broken, wavering line rapidly took on a more regular appearance; and then the old man, who had gathered himself for the great effort, hurled forth a yell that could be heard to the uttermost limits of the great throng. The morning sun had sent its commands to its warriors on earth to charge.

The shout from the hill was reechoed by the thousand men in the valley; it was caught up by the spectators on the hills as the long line of warriors hurled themselves forward towards the sun pole, the objective point of every armed and naked savage in the yelling line. As they converged towards it, the slower ponies dropped out, and the weaker ones were crushed to the rear. Nearer and nearer they came, the long line becoming massed until it was but a surging crowd of plunging horses and yelling, gesticulating riders. When the leading warriors had reached a point within a hundred yards of the sun pole, a sharp report of rifles sounded along the line, and a moment later the rushing mass was a sheet of flame, and the rattle of rifle shots was like the rapid beat of a drum resounding among the hills. Every shot, every arrow, and every lance was directed at the pole, and bark and chips were flying from its sides like shavings from the rotary bit of a planer. When every bullet had been discharged, and every arrow and lance had been hurled, the riders crowded around the pole and shouted as only excited savages can shout.

Had it fallen in this onslaught, another pole would have been chosen and another morning devoted to this performance. Though this seldom happens, it was thought that the numerous assailants of this pole might bring it to the ground. They did not, however, although it looked like a ragged scarecrow, with chips and bark hanging from its mutilated sides.

That such a vast, tumultuous throng could escape accident in all that wild charging, firing of shots, hurling of lances and arrows, and great excitement would be bordering on a miracle, and no miracle happened. One of the great warriors was trampled upon in the charge and died late that evening, and another Indian was shot. The bruises, sprains, and cuts that might have been spoken of in lesser affairs were here unnoticed, and nothing was heard of them.

Later in the day, the sun pole was cut down and taken to the center of the great plain between the two forks of the Chadron, about a mile away. Here a slight excavation was made, and into it the butt of the sun pole was put, and the tree, the bushy top having now disappeared, was held upright by a number of ropes made of buffalo thongs diverging from its top. At their outer ends, probably from seventy to eighty feet away from the sun pole, they were fastened to

Selecting the sun pole. CENTURY MAGAZINE, 1890.

the tops of stakes seven or eight feet in length. These, with a large number of stakes of similar size driven in close together, formed a circular cordon around the sun pole, and over these stakes were stretched elk skins and buffalo robes, canvas and blankets, and a wattling of willows and brush. Sometimes canvas, blankets, and light elk skins are thrown over the supporting ropes to ward off in a slight way the fierce rays of the noonday sun. To one approaching by the road that led over the winding hills which hem in the broad plain between the two forks of the Chadron, the affair looked not unlike a circus tent, the top of which has been ruthlessly torn away by a cyclone.

All day, from the closing of the ceremony of shooting at the sun pole, the attention of the Indians was occupied in constructing this enclosure, where, within a day or two after its completion, they performed those barbarous rites and ceremonies of cruelty and self-torture that have placed the Sun Dance of the Sioux on a level with the barbarisms of any of the far more famed devotees of Juggernaut.

Early on the morning of the third or fourth day, the true worship of the sun, if it can be strictly so called, was begun. So far, all that that luminary had done was to signal the charge of the young warriors on the sun pole. It now entered into the calculation of every minute, almost of every second, of the barbarous proceedings. Those who were to torture themselves, probably forty or fifty in a Sun Dance of this size, were, as near as I could judge, young warriors from twenty to twenty-five years of age, all of them the very finest specimens of savage manhood in the great tribe.

I was told that these fine fellows fast for a number of days before they go through the self-torture, one informant saying that before the ordeal takes place, it is required of them to abstain from food for seven days and from water for two. While their condition did not indicate such abstemiousness as this, I think it true that some fasting precedes the more barbarous ceremonies.

The third day was mostly consumed in dancing and in exercises that did not vary greatly from the dances and exercises usually seen at any time in large Indian villages. On this day, however, the Sun Dance began. Within the arena were from six to twelve young warriors, still in war costume of paint and feathers, standing in a row, and always facing the sun, however brightly it shone in their eyes; with fists clenched across the breast, like a foot racer in a contest of speed, they jumped up and down in measured leaps to the monotonous beating of the tom-toms and the accompanying yi-yi-yi-yis of the assembled throng. The dancers occasionally vary the proceedings with savage music or with whistles made of bone. Now and then a similar row of young maidens would appear in another part of the arena, and their soprano voices would break in pleasantly on the harsher voices of the men. The dancing continued for intervals of from ten minutes to a quarter of an hour, broken by rests of about equal length, and lasted from sunrise to sunset.

Many trifling ceremonies took place while the important ones were proceeding. Horses and ponies were brought into the arena, and the medicine men,

The charge on the sun pole. CENTURY MAGAZINE, 1890.

with incantations, dipped their hands into colored earth and besmeared the sides of the animals with it. As these animals were evidently the best war ponies, the ceremony was doubtless a blessing or a consecration to war.

On the fourth day of the Chadron Sun Dance, the self-torture began, and I was told that those who were to submit themselves to the great ordeal were the same young warriors who had been dancing the day before. Those who began the dance on the fourth day took the final ordeal on the fifth, and so for four or five days, the dancers of one day became the sufferers of the tortures of the next.

The row of dancers took their places promptly at sunrise, but it was not before nine or ten that the tortures began.

Then each one of the young men presented himself to a medicine man, who took between his thumb and forefinger a fold of the loose skin of the breast, abouthalf way between the nipple and the collarbone, lifted it as high as possible, and then ran a very narrow-bladed but sharp knife through the skin underneath the hand. In the aperture thus made, and before the knife was withdrawn, a stronger skewer of bone, about the size of a carpenter's pencil, was inserted. Then the knife blade was taken out, and over the projections of this skewer, backwards and forwards, alternately right and left, was thrown a figure-of-eight noose with a strong thong of dressed skin. This was tied to a long skin rope fastened, at its other extremity, to the top of the sun pole in the center of the arena. Both breasts are similarly punctured, the thongs from each converging and joining the rope which hangs from the pole. The whole object of the devotee is to break loose from these fetters. To liberate himself, he must tear the skewers through the skin, a horrible task that even with the most resolute may require many hours of torture. His first attempts are very easy and seem intended to get

A Sun Dance devotee. HARPER'S WEEKLY, 1891.

him used to the horrible pain he must yet endure before he breaks loose from the thongs. As he increases his efforts, his shouts increase, huge drops of perspiration pour down his greasy, painted skin, and every muscle stands out on his body in tortuous ridges, his swaying frame, as he throws his whole weight wildly against the fearful fetters, being convulsed with shudders. All the while, the beating of the tom-toms and the wild, weird chanting of the singers near him continue. The wonderful strength and extensibility of the human skin is most forcibly and fearfully displayed in the strong struggles of the quivering victims. I have seen these bloody pieces of bone stretched to such a length from the devotee that his outstretched arms in front of him would barely allow his fingers to touch them.

I know it is not pleasant to dwell long upon this cruel spectacle. Generally in two or three hours the victim is free, but there are many cases where double and even triple that time is required. Oftentimes there are half a dozen swinging wildly from the pole, running towards it and then moving backwards with the swiftness of a war horse and the fierceness of a lion in their attempts to tear the accursed skewers from their wounded flesh. Occasionally some overambitious youth will erect four stakes within the arena and, fastening skewers to both breasts and to both shoulders, will throw himself backwards and forwards against the four ropes that hold the skewers to the stakes.

Faintings are not uncommon even among these sturdy savages; but no forfeit, opprobrium, censure, or loss of respect in any way seems to follow. The victim is cut loose and placed on the floor of some lodge nearby and left in charge of his nurses. The only attempt I saw to break loose from double skewers in front and behind terminated in this manner. Whether the men ever afterwards enter the cruel contest after having thus failed I do not know. It may be possible that some exceedingly ambitious warrior may enter the lists year after year to show his prowess, but I understand that it is supposed to be done but once in a lifetime. It is not obligatory, and by far the greater number grow up sensibly abstaining from such savage luxuries. When the day is almost over, and the solar deity is nearly down in the west, the self-tortured warriors file from the enclosed arena, one by one, and just outside the doors, deeply covered with handsomely painted buffalo robes, they kneel and, with arms crossed over their bloody breasts and with bowed heads, face the setting sun and rise only when it has disappeared.

Many other horrible variations have been reported to me, such as tying a saddle or a buffalo's skull to the end of the long rope fastened to the skewer and running over the prairie and through the timber, the saddle or skull bounding after the victim until he liberates himself; or, when fainting, to draw the tortured man clear of the ground by the ropes until his weight overcame the strength of the distended skin. My informants told me that no two of the ceremonies were alike, the self-torture in some form being the one common link in all. The consecration of the sun pole, much of the dancing and singing, the double efforts of ambitious youths, and other ceremonies might be left out entirely or others substituted. I describe it only as I saw it. I will add that this Sun Dance was called the greatest the Sioux had ever held; the greatest self-sacrifice of the greatest native nation within our boundaries. Within a year they had checked, at the Rosebud Hills in Montana, the largest army we had ever launched against the American Indians in a single fight; had retired successfully to the Little Bighorn, a few miles away, and there, a week later, had wiped Custer's fine command from the face of the earth; had held Reno for two days upon a hill; had never lost a battle worthy of the name in the war which led to their subjugation; and had proved the utter worthlessness of victory to a savage race contending against civilization.

"Alter Ego" on the Powder River Expedition

ROBERT E. STRAHORN[1]

(Denver) *Rocky Mountain News,* February 28, 1876

CHEYENNE, Wyoming, February 23, 1876
Although there is still a tantalizing air of mysteriousness about some of the details and objects of General Crook's[2] suddenly organized expedition, enough is now known in military circles to at least foreshadow its earlier operations and some of its results. As early as last December, an order was issued by proper authorities, the disobeying of which by the Indians was the direct cause of this campaign. The order was to the effect that all the tribes of the Sioux then off their reservation should immediately repair thereto, and if they failed to obey by January 31, they would be considered common enemies and thoroughly chastised.[3] Lying north and northwest of Fort Fetterman is a vast scope of country known as the "unceded lands," to which the Indians have no right or title, but in which the most warlike of them have sought refuge, rest, and succor ever since the general abandonment of that region by military and settlers during the massacre of 1866.[4] Since the date just mentioned, those bands of the Sioux who bid defiance to all attempts at reconciliation have marauded north, south, and east from this, their natural stronghold, and then, with the swiftness that characterizes an Indian on retreat, have plunged back and regaled themselves upon plunder, thoughts of their isolation, and plans for future incursions. These tribes were included in the order referred to above; but not only have they treated the order with a supreme contempt,[5] [they also] have made redoubled efforts in the way of replenishing their supplies of arms, ammunition, etc.

This, then, is one of the secrets of General Crook's movements. The reasons given for the hasty and quiet manner in which he has thus far proceeded are, simply, first, that he is determined to strike a blow at once, which will demoralize the savages from the start; second, that a winter campaign, although terribly arduous in that region, will have thrice the terror that one would be likely to influence two

General Crook's headquarters at Fort Fetterman. HARPER'S WEEKLY, 1876.

months earlier; third, because everything points to a general Indian war in the section adjacent to the Black Hills, even in advance of the advent of spring, and to make the small force at his command adequate to the demands of next summer's serious task, General Crook sees the prime necessity of immediately crushing out the more western tribes, at the same time showing all others that the Bighorn and Powder River regions are not to be made the hiding place of the whole Sioux nation in case of its general defeat.

Now, as to the relative strength of troops and Indians in the present campaign. As far as we can determine at present, General Crook's force will consist of but ten companies of cavalry, averaging fifty men each. Five companies belong to the veteran 3rd, and five are from the well-known 2nd Regiment. [Brevet Maj.] Gen. Joseph J. Reynolds, colonel of the 3rd, will have immediate command. It is expected that one or two light Gatlin guns will cover the armament in the way of artillery.[6] All of the troops have seen more or less of this kind of service, and as they go splendidly equipped and mounted, under a commander who will give them as much fighting in as short a time as they could wish, they are wonderfully pleased that they have been thus detailed.

It is a hard matter to estimate the number of Indians who will oppose the advance of this miniature but gallant division. The best authority places the number at from twelve to fifteen thousand, including men, women, and children. Of these, at least three thousand can be counted upon as being first-class fighting braves, almost as well armed as troops could possibly be.[7] Knowing their country thoroughly, and with an attachment for it second only to the love of life itself, they certainly are not to be despised as enemies, and it needs no prophet to foretell serious times, if they fight as they can reasonably be expected to.

As the readers of the *News* have already been informed by telegraph, General Crook left for Fort Fetterman—his present rendezvous—yesterday. He goes by way of Fort Laramie, there to reinforce from the garrison, and then proceeds northwest to the point of concentration referred to, by the regular government trail. Tomorrow morning, Maj. T. H. Stanton[8] and myself, who have cast our fortunes with the expedition, take the shortest trail for Fort Fetterman, and as we go in light marching order, with small escort, we expect to arrive there about the same time as the commander and his troops.

ALTER EGO

(Denver) *Rocky Mountain News,* March 5, 1876

FORT FETTERMAN, Wyoming, February 27, 1876

Leaving Cheyenne at dawn of the twenty-fourth for the purpose of joining General Crook in his northwestern campaign, our small party and escort made a forced march of 54 miles before sunset, and tarried at night at the ranch of Portugee Philips on the Chugwater. During the evening, we gained several items of interest in regard to the country in which the present expedition is to operate, in conversation with Mr. Philips, who is a pioneer in the true sense of the word; he has been in government employ as scout and guide for many years, and among other thrilling experiences, he was an eyewitness of the Phil Kearny massacre. He pronounced the region to be traversed of unusual interest, both on account of the many natural wonders in the way of scenery and on account of the wealth of the country in mineral and agricultural area. The Indians, known to be scattered over its vast extent, he said would number at least eighteen thousand or twenty thousand, and could muster nearly four thousand warriors; that they would fight he considered there would be no reasonable doubt, as he witnessed their prowess in that line on more than one occasion when there was not as much to arouse them as at present. Unless the savages were thoroughly demoralized at the first encounter—which could result in the event of their being concentrated—he was of the opinion that it would require more than one campaign to force them to the extreme of suing for peace.

Early on the morning of the twenty-fifth, we were again on the trail which for 25 miles descended Chugwater Valley. Signs of late improvements were noted at many points, plains and valley were covered with well-conditioned stock, and our occasional meeting a ranch man suggested a new state of affairs in spite of [Indian] incursions. During the forenoon, a superlative bright and pleasant one, we overhauled several pack and transportation trains. The former consisted of over two hundred stout mules, laden with supplies for the expedition, in charge of a large corps of professional packers, and the latter were the usual huge and heavily laden army wagons with six-mule teams for motive power. Later in the day, a high grassy divide literally covered with cattle was crossed, and after fording the main Laramie River, we ascended to where it receives the waters of the North Laramie and made camp.

Though in our estimation the finest stream in southern Wyoming, with a wide, comparatively well-timbered valley, the North Laramie has scarcely yet begun to be utilized by settlers. But the reason is quite plain. On a fertile bench overlooking our riverside camp, a too venturesome pioneer was scalped only a few months ago, and recent advices tell of the successful entry of several plundering bands of Indians within as many weeks just passed. Cattle and horses were carried off in each instance, but thus far this season no loss of human life has occurred. In the course of a little hunt up the valley during the evening of our stay, I came upon the ranch of T. A. Kent, of Cheyenne—the only one for a number of miles up and down the river. Passing through a strong cordon of dogs and finally gaining the single entrance to the little fortress of a cabin, I had an excellent opportunity to see how men live who are in momentary danger of an attack by Indians. Guns of the most approved pattern were more numerous than chairs and all other articles of furniture combined. A window hardly designed for "transit observations" commanded a wide view of the plain and valley and was flanked on either side by general piles of robes and blankets, where quite undisturbed repose, mayhap, is oftener thought than found—for to be a ranchero here is to be a man on the constant alert, and on the tiptoe of expectant intrusion, and in perfect preparation to extend the warmest of warm greetings.

About noon of the third day out, we commenced overtaking the long column of picked cavalry headed by the gallant officer whose hardships and duty we were to share in the very near future. Men they looked and men of the best stamp they are, whom General Crook has detailed for this difficult undertaking. Rank and file are in excellent trim, mounted upon the best horses the department affords, and everything in their appearance betokened "business" from the start.

As we entered camp at the Elkhorn, it was discovered that several companies had already pitched their tents by the side of that pretty little stream and were comfortably fixed for the night. Before dark, six companies had their quarters arranged up and down the creek on either side, and these, with their horses, a large pack and transportation train, and the mounted sentries on surrounding bluffs, quickened the quiet neighborhood into a life that it seldom and perhaps never will ever again see. Snow commenced falling about the middle of the afternoon and continued through the night, the temperature in the meantime falling low enough to make the weather absolutely cold as well as unusually disagreeable. We were compelled to undergo a general "shoveling out" next morning, by the last relay of guards, and the order to mount and march, in the face of fast falling snow and piercing winds, was obeyed with that peculiar vim which characterizes the undertaking of unpleasant necessities rather than the accomplishment of coveted duties.

From officers met at the camp above referred to, we had learned that some unruly renegades were having about their own way down along the North Platte, just above Fort Laramie. A few nights ago they cut a valuable cavalry horse out of the band belonging to one of the companies now approaching this fort and were successful in getting across the river with him almost under the noses of the command. Next day a soldier was sent back to Fort Laramie armed to the teeth, and whom it was supposed the bandits would hardly attempt to intercept in broad daylight, when four or five miles above the fort he saw two men crossing the river and making their way toward him, but as they did not display any arms and seemed otherwise peaceable, he did not think it was necessary to show signs of distrust by preparing himself for an attack. Upon overtaking him, one rode up on one side and one on the other, and the audacious and rascally pair almost instantly whipped out revolvers and presented them at the head of the unfortunate bearer of dispatches, at the same time requesting him to "Git down off that hoss!" He obeyed, as a great many men have done before in such emergencies, and then was relieved of the possession of a splendid new Sharps rifle, revolver, etc., and told to carry another message to the officers at the fort, to wit, "Tell them fellers down there that infantry ain't calculated to follow us, and that as General Crook has got all the cavalry, we jest politely request them to go to Hell!" The soldier recognized one of the horses ridden by the highwaymen as the one stolen from his command the night before.

We rode in the face of one of the most severe storms of the season until 2:00 P.M. today, when we reached this post, considerably in advance of our transportation, having accomplished 170 miles in less than four days. Major Stanton, his secretary, Mr. Chase, and your correspondent were at once requested to report at the quarters of [Maj. Alexander] Chambers, commandant of the post, where General Crook and Reynolds also have their headquarters. The remaining hours of the day, as well as those of the evening, have been most delightfully spent in the company of officers named and the accomplished and entertaining hostess, Mrs. Chambers.

We find many changes in rank and file have occurred here during our visit of a year ago, some of the most familiar of the officers having been assigned to other posts of duty. But a greater and far more noticeable change is that which marks their new departure to the northwest.

Long lines of tents are pitched on the banks of the quiet and peaceful La Prelle nearby; hundreds of men are crowding around the campfires—which tonight lead me in fancy back to Denver's lamp-lit streets—cleaning their arms, looking up the few necessities that a soldier is allowed to possess, and speculating, as a soldier will, upon the campaign and its results; horses, mules, and pack animals, to the number of a thousand or more, are pawing and neighing a loud refrain to the hum of masters' voices; the fort is flooded with commissary supplies, arms, ammunition, etc., and officers are galloping back and forth with the orders that bring system out of all this din and chaos.

ALTER EGO

FORT FETTERMAN, Wyoming Territory, February 29, 1876

The Bighorn expedition is now thoroughly organized and will push out early tomorrow morning for the wilderness of the Northwest. That it is the most important movement ever undertaken in this section of our unceded territory is admitted by all who understand its expected results, and who are conversant with its very probable bearing upon the vexatious Indian problem.

The entire command is to proceed in one body in a northwesterly course, taking in old Fort Reno and old Fort Phil Kearny en route. Beyond this, nothing is definitely known, save that where Indians are ascertained to be by the scouts, there the command will be. When impracticable to be longer retarded by the wagon train, and swift marching is necessary, wagons, mules, and every pound of commissary stores, save the barest necessities, will be dropped behind and suitably guarded until the first campaign is practically decided. The two companies of infantry, teamsters, etc., are detailed to guard this miscellaneous equipage. Every man in the expedition, no matter under what auspices he goes, has been thoroughly armed by order of the commander and is expected to do active field duty at any time. Six weeks at least will be required, and beyond this we can merely speculate as to the time to be consumed by the operations of this expedition.

It is quite evident, from the movements of peaceably disposed Indians, that hostile bands have an inkling of the fact that a demonstration is to be made against them. Several days ago Plenty-of-Bears, an Arapaho chief, with ten or a dozen lodges of followers, came here and said he was anxious to always be at peace with the "Great Father," that he was then on his way over to Red Cloud agency to attest his sincerity in the matter. When questioned about the Indians against whom we are to proceed, he replied, "Minneconjou heap braves. Many lodges. Mak'um tired count'um." Black Crow, another Arapaho chieftain with thirty-six lodges, also came in a day or two ago and is now encamped nearby on the Platte. He too is very much afraid something unpleasant is about to happen and says he is on his way to the agency. He intimates that Indian runners have already conveyed intelligence of an anticipated move by the military from this point to the northern tribes. In addition to these facts pointing to the arousing of the Indian suspicion, we have positive information that the Minneconjou and other tribes are already overrunning the northern frontier, and that numerous depredations have recently been committed by them.

General Crook therefore discovers that instead of taking the Indians by surprise, they have almost anticipated him by first opening the ball thus early in the season. The unusual mildness of the winter, now almost over, and the consequent excellent condition in which they have been enabled to place their ponies, together with their reasonable supposition that their more eastern brethren are just in the right mood to cooperate with them, accounts for such an unusual activity now reigning up north.

ALTER EGO

(Denver) *Rocky Mountain News,* March 23, 1876

HEADQUARTERS BIGHORN EXPEDITION,
CAMP ON SOUTH CHEYENNE, WYOMING,
March 3, 1876

A bright and cheering omen attended the cause of our hardy little division as it filed out of Fort Fetterman and forded the icy Platte on the morning of March 1. When tattoo sounded the night before, and the troops looked up toward the little sky that Fetterman needs for a cover, it was found that even that little was hid by clouds that hung black and heavy as a pall. A northeastern wind—which brings the worst storms here—whistled a refrain to that tattoo, which did anything but lighten spirits and unburden hearts. Snow came down in great thick flakes and promised faithfully to gather to the depth of a foot before ceasing, and then came up the declaration of General Crook, which drowned all hopes of camping until the storm was over, in this wise: "The worse it gets the better; always hunt Indians in bad weather."

The [North Platte] river was crossed without the slightest mishap, though the current flowed deep and strong, and then, being considered on Indian ground, we took a look at our strength. Closed up nicely in line of march, we found that there was just a little over two miles of us. A rollicking, keen-eyed band of scouts—in whose first ranks I have had the pleasure of dashing along from the start—were first; ten long companies of cavalry were next, two of infantry following; then the ambulances, transportation wagons, pack trains; and in the rear of all, our herd of beef cattle, sixty or seventy head in number, which were to be slaughtered along the way as occasion demanded. Perhaps I ought to mention that the Medical Department is represented and has three or four ambulances for the accommodation of medical stores and wounded men—ominous affairs at best, which we have earnestly hoped might be rendered conspicuous for their disuse, but which, alas, have been needed even this early in the campaign.

A short march was the order for the first few days; consequently, at 1:00 P.M. on our initial day, we made camp fifteen miles from the fort, on Sage Creek. There, as over all the region preceding, we found an abundance of grass, but water only in a few pools, and no fuel except sagebrush. During the forenoon, we met a fine lot of Arapahos, who were badly frightened and making tracks for the agency. Their band of two or three hundred ponies were among the finest we have ever seen, and as fat as stall-fed cattle. Next morning, breaking camp quite early, we were on the road at sunrise. Ten or a dozen miles from camp, we found abundant croppings of slate and other indications of coal. Near the same point were obtained fine views of the Black Hills of golden promise, some seventy miles to the northeast; Pumpkin Buttes, four large elevations resembling in shape the good, old-fashioned vegetable of the same name, forty miles north; and Laramie Peak, long since left behind, to the southeast. The stream upon which we are now camped, commonly called the South or Dry Fork of the Cheyenne, cuts its narrow bed through hills and bluffs so rugged that at many points it cannot be approached. There is plenty of cottonwood and other soft timber, but the valley is too contracted to ever make desirable locations for farming. Grass, however, is abundant on every side, and good stock ranges could be found at several points. Cropping out of the bluffs near camp are two veins of bitumous coal, from which several fine specimens three or four inches in diameter were secured. There are indications of immense deposits of coal almost everywhere here.

At about two o'clock this morning, when the entire camp was wrapped in deepest slumber, and when all but the sentinels and herders were sleeping in as fancied security as though yet at Fetterman, we went through the novel sensation of a modern Indian stampede. There were a number of unearthly yells, as if from a man surprised, several rifle shots in quick succession, an Indian whoop, a cloud of dust, and a man was dangerously wounded, a herd of fifty cattle and a horse vanished, and that is what we know of a stampede. The wounded man, a herder,[9] who is shot through the lungs, says he saw two or three Indians creeping toward him through the sagebrush, and his yells and the rapidly succeeding shots were the result. The entire command was instantly aroused, and the order to "fall in" came almost upon the heels of the alarm from several captains. But immediate pursuit was not allowed, as that would have been next to a hopeless undertaking. At break of day, however, a company of cavalry, headed by two or three of our best trailing scouts, took the track and were soon going at high speed over a neighboring plateau. A very short time has elapsed, and now, as the sun has reddened the east and is just peeping out upon the scene of its widespread blush, the pursuers enter the almost deserted camp with the information that the cattle are on their way back to Fort Fetterman, where, it is to be hoped, their safe arrival will be as greatly appreciated as would have been their onward march with us. We have less now to retard us, but, alas for the rarity of Indian charity, we are out of beef and have a wounded man on our hands—all this, too, within thirty-two miles of the fort. It is thought that the Indians, observing the sudden alarm of the camp, were fearful that in trying to get away with so much booty, they might lose their own scalps, and so made tracks in another direction with their stolen horse.

Indian signs were numerous and fresh in almost every direction, and that they—the savages—are watching our every movement in spite of all precaution is indisputable. Some of our half-breed scouts say that Crazy Horse, the chieftain who rode stark naked and armed to the teeth through the grounds of the peace commission last summer and lifted up his voice for war, is only about seventy miles ahead with a large number of warriors. To take his camp would almost of itself be worth the trouble of the present campaign, and it is earnestly hoped that ere a week has rolled by, himself and band will be treated with for all time to come.

ALTER EGO

(Denver) *Rocky Mountain News,* April 6, 1876

CAMP ON CRAZY WOMAN'S FORK, Wyoming,
March 7, 1876

Following the old government trail to the northwest, on March 3, we found everywhere signs of Indians, from one to three days old. The principal trail made by the red men was believed to be of a party of about a dozen, and also that they were identical with our stampeders of the very early hours of the same morning. Eight miles of travel brought us to the Middle Fork of the Cheyenne, seven miles more to the North Fork, and six miles, which completed the day's march, to Buffalo Wallow. The water at all of these points is scarce and badly diffused with alkali. Timber, consisting of cottonwood and willow, is also quite scarce. The whole surface of the country is covered with a generous growth of the common upland grasses, and a finer pasturage could hardly be wished. Should the country be settled up, the lack of water would be the greatest drawback, as the fuel question is virtually put to rest by the existence of numerous beds of coal.

The principal item of the day was our first view of the Bighorn Mountains, which occurred from the top of a prominent mesa during the forenoon. We could see almost the whole of the resplendent range, stretching off for over a hundred miles along the northwestern horizon, its loftiest peaks appearing white, fleecy, and ethereal enough to belong to cloudland—yet too beautifully grand to be spared by even a beautiful earth.

From evidence everywhere visible, the fact is apparent that we are certainly tracked and watched by runners of the tribes we are so anxious to meet. On the night of the fourth, after a twenty-three-mile march over country similar to that already described, one crept up through the grass and was discovered by a sentry, who immediately fired. Next morning it was found that three or four had been taking observations on the outskirts of the camp. As we were descending the Dry Fork of Powder River, about ten o'clock the same morning, several were seen scampering off to our right, and subsequently in the day, others were seen on one of the flanks near the rear of the command. It could scarcely have been called a nice day for the Indians, either, as it commenced snowing before daylight and continued snowing and blowing cold and disagreeable blasts in our faces all the way down to the main Powder River. Their camp was made on a well-wooded stretch of bottomland just across the river, and in sight of which lay the ghostly relic of old Fort Reno. We had followed and crossed the trails of moving Indian villages during the entire day, but we were not even allowed to follow those we saw, as the commanding officer said he was not after the small fry, and that by paying no attention to these less important movements of the enemy, we might possibly mislead and even surprise him in his stronghold.

At about 8:00 P.M., a sentry belonging to the command of Captain Coates[10] discovered three mounted Indians approaching him, and as he had orders to challenge no one coming in that direction, he commenced firing upon them. They returned the courtesy with their usual spirit, and almost instantly a brisk fusillade from their secreted comrades commenced on two sides of the camp. There were bright campfires with groups of soldiers gathered about them at many different points of the camp, and numerous tents being also lighted, the Indians for the first moment or two had an excellent chance to distinguish themselves as moonlight marksmen. But a very few moments had elapsed before the entire scene changed; lights were snuffed out in a twinkling, campfires were kicked to smithereens, men were in their ranks, and rifle pits were sunk in an incredibly short space of time.

Of course, the loud whoops of the savage foe, the cracking of guns, and whizzing bullets produced commotion among horses and mules, but being admirably arranged, a stampede of them was rendered almost impossible. As trees and sagebrush were plenty, the Indians did their usual skulking and rendered the whole affair very tantalizing, and all that could be done in the way of returning their fire was to watch the flashes of their guns and send a bullet after the flash; it was about as sure a thing of hitting the flash as the Indian. Shooting and yelling were kept up quite regularly on the part of the foe for half an hour or more, bullets whizzing about our heads and sometimes lower, in a manner that was a little more interesting than agreeable, especially to those of us who had never been under fire until then. Fortunately, however, but one man was wounded, Corporal Slavey of Captain Ferris' command,[11] who received a bullet through a cheek.

Considering that many of the privates were green and an attack in the evening was entirely unlooked for, the sudden onslaught was met with remarkable coolness—a coolness that saved us the stampede which the foe would certainly have attempted, had he been met by confusion. The whole affair lasted but little more than half an hour, and nearly all prepared for and expected a repetition, but we heard no more of Indians that night.

It was no less amusing than it was suggestive to note the bearing of General Crook, whose tent was situated at the point where the two lines of fire converged. Being located by his side, and having the crossfire of the foe concentrated in an alarming proximity to my head, I could appreciate with a peculiar zest the imperturbable spirit of the veteran. He was reclining quietly upon a few robes, evidently in deep thought, when the firing commenced. Without glancing upward to see where it came from, he waited until excited officers commenced rushing forward with versions of the affair and asking for instructions. He coolly replied that the plan of the Indians was simply to stampede a portion of our stock by sending in the three braves, who appeared on our front, through camp with their usual whooping and flinging of blankets, while the force upon our right was to add to the confusion by their volleys and then swoop down through the straggling bunches of stock and make off with all they could. He said the early firing of the sentry had completely frustrated their scheme by placing our entire command in a state of preparation, and concluded by remarking that we would hear no more of the Indians that night. To all who were upon the ground, these explanations seemed the best that could possibly be given, and as the general suggested, there was not another shot fired during the night.

On the sixth, we broke camp on the Powder and, after crossing to the west, rode over the site of old Fort Reno. Its ruins are still well enough preserved to give the visitor an idea of its extent and uses in the days of its occupation.

Thus far, game of all kinds had made itself conspicuous only by its absence, but during the day our scouts killed three fine blacktailed deer and saw a solitary buffalo. Small and straggling bands of antelope were also quite frequently visible, but they generally hugged the horizon in a manner that displayed even more discretion than they are usually credited with possessing.

Here on Crazy Woman's Fork of Powder River, we have had one day of comparative rest. We have had not only a snug little camp on the prettiest stream yet encountered, but have also been blessed with three or four hours of actually pleasant weather. The stream runs swift and clear under a twelve-inch cover of ice, and the valley is so narrow and broken as to be of little consequence, except, perhaps, eventually for stock raising.

Another hour will hardly elapse before one very important move of the expedition will be inaugurated—that of the cavalry and pack trains cutting loose from the infantry and heavy transportation, and commencing the forced night marches and the active campaign.

The battalion and company officers have just been receiving their last instructions preparatory to marching. Gathered in a semicircle around General Crook and [Colonel] Reynolds, the ten or a dozen veterans listening respectfully to their leaders, with the confusion and bustle incident to the move all about, furnished a picture long to be remembered. In a few plain sentences, General Crook made known his wishes and expectations from each one in authority. Above all things, he required that nothing cumbersome in the way of luggage should be taken along, and to indicate clearly what he meant, said that only two blankets to the man and no tents should be taken, and only the clothes that were worn. Hardtack, coffee, and bacon—only half rations of the latter—were to constitute the diet, officers to mess with their men. One-sixth rations for the horses, for the fifteen days we were to be out, consisting of twenty-five thousand pounds of grain, were to make use of a large share of the pack train transportation.

We are to start north at dark, our scouts having already picked a trail. The battalion of infantry under command of Captain Coates will return to Reno tomorrow with wagons, there to entrench and await our return.

ALTER EGO

(Denver) *Rocky Mountain News,* April 4, 1876

CAMP ON TONGUE RIVER, MONTANA, March 13, 1876

At dark on the evening of March 7 commenced the first night march of that portion of the Bighorn expedition detailed to carry the war into the home of the Sioux. The moon was at its full, the stars shined their brightest, and the five squadrons of cavalry, with their attendant pack trains, moved away from the murmurs of hundreds of farewells and good wishes under auspices as pleasant as they were novel. Swiftly and silently the long dark column moved off northward across the plains, over rugged hills, through dark gulches, and occasionally winding around the brinks of dangerous precipices, its men groping carefully for footholds and wondering what the next few hours would bring forth.

At 8:00 A.M. of the eighth, the command was halted on the banks of Clear Fork of Lodge Pole Creek, having accomplished thirty miles of distance during the night. Only two or three hours were allowed for rest, however, and by 10:00 A.M. the half-refreshed troops and animals were descending the valley in the face of a furious snowstorm. At the mouth of the Piney, five miles down, the scouts came in with information that wood, water, and grass were not so abundant further on, and on account of these conveniences and the rest that both men and animals required, it was thought best to camp. Although the storm gathered in force, and the cold was more noticeable than at any previous halt, the tentless, shelterless troops complained but little of their snowy mattress, and none the less snowy covering next morning. Before daylight of the ninth, all were again astir and soon on the trail of the indefatigable scouts. After ascending the valley of the Piney a few miles, we crossed over a high, badly broken divide some fifteen miles further, the snow and piercing blasts opposing every forward step. The fleecy element had covered the ground to a depth of five or six inches; in many places it was drifted to great depths, and the precipitous hillsides presented little less than faces of ice. Horses and men could only brace themselves and slide as they descended into the gullies, and the ascent beyond was always more difficult, if not so dangerous. Occasionally an animal would turn a somersault and find a shorter way to the bottom than had been bargained for. Such drawbacks as these rendered travel not only aggravatingly slow, but fearfully wearing on both man and beast.

The command finally halted near the head of Prairie Dog Creek, fifteen miles from the last camp. Twenty scouts were sent ahead at nightfall to further prospect the way, and also to guard against our alarming an Indian encampment, which might be found at any moment. Seven miles to our left was the spot upon which occurred the never-to-be-forgotten Phil Kearny massacre.

On the morning of the tenth, we more than ever realized what campaigning in the heart of winter without tents or adequate bedding meant. We were practically snowed in, mercury was tumbling, and still the bitter storm of wind and snow sought us at every point.

Marching due north twenty-two miles against a severe storm, we found Prairie Dog Valley, whose company we kept all day, quite picturesque at many points. The luxuriant growth and grasses and brush gave evidence of a very fertile soil, and the numerous fine belts of bench and bottomlands suggested the eventual probability of sturdy and valued homes in spite of the present reigning solitude.

The scouts came in at nightfall and reported Indian signs plentiful and quite fresh, but the flesh and blood Indian had taken his departure for more congenial grounds, or else was hanging around unseen, ready to snuff out campfires and stampede stock under his favorite cover—darkness. Trails and other signs indicated that the fleeing red men had gone down Tongue River, and numerous freshly picked buffalo skeletons suggested that they emigrated on full rations of good meat at least. On the morning of the eleventh, with the mercury at twenty-six degrees below zero—the lowest temperature our sole thermometer was constituted to register—we descended Prairie Dog Creek to its confluence with Tongue River and during the day's march crossed into the territory of Montana. The bluffs on either side rapidly assumed the proportions of foothills, and from the best maps, we learned that we were passing in full view of the southeastern base of the Rosebud Mountains, on our left, and of the southwestern end of the Panther Mountains, on our right.

Of all crooked streams we have ever explored, Tongue River certainly bears off the palm, although its general course is as direct from source to mouth as any. In descending the river some fifty miles, we have crossed the river thirty-two times—crossings so precarious, too, on account of the polished surface of the ice, that many smooth-shod horses and impatient riders have cause to remember them. The usually narrow valley is often limited to canyon dimensions, although it occasionally swells to the width of a mile or more.

At almost every well-wooded and sheltered turn of the valley, we find relics of old as well as of recent Indian camps. There are rudely constructed corrals, commodious enough to hold hundreds of ponies each, some of them evidently occupied less than three months ago. Then there are scores of drying poles perched from six to ten feet above ground and used for drying buffalo and venison; numerous roughly built shelters for man and beast, tepee poles, tanning apparatus, freshly picked skeletons of animals, and occasionally the remains of their own dead, lashed to wickerwork and perched high among the limbs of trees. A fine mule, evidently a stray from the camp of Crazy Horse, was picked up by our scouts today. All of these items point to the conclusion that some important hostile band must be near, and the scouts have orders to move forward tonight and to thoroughly and expeditiously scour the country for a distance of twenty-five or thirty miles in front and on either side.

Yesterday mercury dropped into the bulb of the thermometer and then further aggravated us by taking to itself that curdled appearance which denotes very bad cases of frostbite; men could only use their bacon by slowly splintering off pieces with axes; the few loaves of soft bread yet to be found in the command were frozen solid as so many rocks; arms and knives adhered to fingers as though each had been freshly coated with adhesive plaster; and ice on the river was from eighteen inches to three feet thick.

During the night, two men belonging to one of the pack trains grew as uncomfortable as the balance of the shivery command, and singularly enough each blamed the other for his discomfort, never dreaming that mercury was congealing and that spirit thermometers would have registered forty or fifty degrees below zero beneath his blanket. After fighting around an hour or two, and wasting a vast amount of scientific profanity, the two freezing packers, after years of warmest friendship, agreed to part. Their scanty supply of blankets was divided, each took up his portion and moved some twenty paces in an opposite direction, the frozen ground and snow creaking underfoot like a rusty hinge, and the air thick with frost. Again lying down in plain view of each other, the divorced packers, every moment growing colder, commenced thinking of how beautiful it is for brethren to dwell in unity together—or something to that effect—when it is so unmercifully cold. Then each would wonder how long the other would "grin and bear it," whether it would be better after all to commence making overtures looking to a speedy consolidating of personal effects—especially blankets. Soon there was a rolling and cramping, and unmistakable grunting, and finally at 2:00 A.M., both sat bolt upright; for fear of freezing a good intention by undue procrastination, they then rose to their feet as one man, icy blankets were lifted from the icy ground, and the twain came to right shoulder shift with military precision; without a word, they strode rapidly toward each other and when they met as they had parted, Hans threw down his blankets, Pat and Hans lay down in one time and two motions, and Pat pulled his offering in the shape of blankets up very carefully up over both. Then, for the first time since the pangs of parting, the intensity of feeling broke out in words for each. Pat said, "Hans?"

"Wot?"

"It's damned cold, ain't it?"

And then Hans said, "Pat?"

"What?"

"Ve has peen damt fools, ain't we?"

They are about as good judges of cold weather now as any other men on the expedition. Hans, evidently a sacrilegious wretch, upon leaving Fort Fetterman marked on his knapsack the words, "Big Horn or Hell," but after breathing the Montana atmosphere for a few days, defaced the inscription and wrote underneath, "Hell Froze Over!"

ALTER EGO

(Denver) *Rocky Mountain News,* April 5, 1876

CAMP ON OTTER CREEK, MONTANA, March 16, 1876

As indicated in my letter of the thirteenth, a detachment of our best scouts made a final and complete examination of lower Tongue River Valley, and of much of the country lying between our camp of that date and the Yellowstone. They returned on the night of the fifteenth to our last camp on Tongue River, near the mouth of Otter Creek, with the information that the tribe of Crazy Horse must undoubtedly be located further east, and recommended that we immediately cross the country in a northeasterly direction to Powder River. Their reasons for this advice were that all of the more recent trails led that way, and that all the buffalo seen, as well as the fresh game trails, were pointing in an opposite direction. Acting upon this and other suggestions, the command accordingly turned its back upon Tongue River this morning, and after a twenty-mile march over pine-covered mountains and through pretty alternating valleys, has made camp here on the banks of the Otter.

As we were descending a steep mountain overlooking this valley, an hour ago, two horsemen were seen trotting their ponies leisurely down along the creek, and by the aid of glasses, the welcome intelligence soon passed along the line that they were Indians. At the first sight of the mounted savages, half a dozen of our best mounted scouts started in hot pursuit and endeavored, by crossing the valley a short distance below, to cut off the attempted escape. To catch a single Indian alive and, by virtue of a threatening noose or, mayhap, good promises, to learn all about the homes of his brethren, has been one of our most eager desires, but this, our first opportunity, resulted only in an unsuccessful chase. The Indians, of course, plunged into the mountains and soon disappeared under cover of the gigantic rocks and dense forest which here gird their summits. Upon an examination of their back trail—the direction from whence they had come—it was found that the red men had been following buffalo, and for this and other reasons, it was very evident that they had not the slightest idea of an approach by a hostile force. It was also apparent that their home camp was not far distant, because, during the present rigorous winter weather, they would be careful not to rove over the distance of a day's march from their tepees on such an unimportant errand as a hunt. Misgivings as to an early encounter can now only arise from the fear that the two escaping Indians will make their way back to the village, inform their chief of our coming, and that when we arrive, the coppery birds will have flown. However, orders have already been issued for a forced march, and scouts are "prospecting" the first few miles of the route to learn whether—as they anticipate—the Indians came across from Powder River.

Three squadrons of cavalry, consisting of two companies each and officered as follows, are to start as soon as horses can be fed and men partake of a hearty repast: 1st Squadron, Companies M and E, 3rd Cavalry, Capt. A. Mills; 3rd squadron, Companies I and K, 2nd Cavalry, Capt. H. E. Noyes; 5th Squadron, Companies E, 3rd, and E, 2nd Cavalry, Capt. A. Moore; entire force numbering about three hundred men.

The 2nd and 4th squadrons, under command of Capt. William Hawley and Capt. T. B. Dewees, respectively, are to remain in charge of the pack trains and camp equipage. It now being taken for granted that a swift march of one night will overtake Crazy Horse somewhere on the Powder, arrangements have been made for the two divisions to meet on that stream at the mouth of the Lodge Pole. Of course, the smaller division will remain encamped with the pack train here for the night, and the force first reaching the point of rendezvous will await the other's arrival. The troops composing the force now about to advance are to carry nothing but their arms and an extra supply of ammunition, besides lunch for tomorrow; there will thus be no dead weight to retard the most expeditious movements.

With his keen appreciation of the strong desire of subordinates for honors in such matters, combined with his perfect faith in the ability and willingness of Colonel Reynolds and other officers to execute this important aggressive movement, General Crook has for once in his history subdued that most striking of his characteristics—"to be there"—and will remain with the lesser force. He can, however, partially console himself with the view that an attack by the Indians themselves upon the reserve is not unlikely, considering that the force is scarcely sufficient to prevent a stampede of the large number of animals left in charge, to say nothing of repulsing a midnight assault by the redskins.

The scouts have just returned and report that the trail of the Indians referred to above leaves this valley about two miles farther up and strikes across the country directly toward the Powder. Frank Grouard, our most efficient guide,[12] who was long a prisoner among these northern Indians, says he believes he can follow the trail in spite of the almost impenetrable darkness and the usual storm that is coming on. At any event, from his knowledge of the country and of the habitats of the red men, he is quite confident he can lead the column into the village of Crazy Horse[13] by daylight tomorrow. The distance to the Powder is about thirty miles, and the country intervening is described as being extremely high and rough; we therefore look forward to a night march, which every participant will have cause to remember.

ALTER EGO

(Denver) *Rocky Mountain News,* April 7, 1876

CAMP ON POWDER RIVER, MONTANA, March 18, 1876

Without doubt, the most remarkable event of General Crook's present campaign was the night march commenced early on the evening of the sixteenth. As a matter of history, it well deserves a place by the side of any similar incident known to frontier service; and if the three hundred gallant and uncomplaining spirits who participated in its thrilling scenes had nothing more whereof to tell in future bivouacs around more peaceful fires, this would be enough. A hard day's march had just been accomplished, men and beasts had earned the hearty fare and the bed of frozen ground that usually were their lot; but the circumstance narrated in my last changed the aspects of affairs.

A leader like General Crook was in search of just such circumstances, and if there were any complaints heard in connection with the swiftness of his movements, they came from those whose lot it was to remain behind. Therefore, about two hours after reaching Otter Creek, with darkness already shadowing the gulches, the three squadrons pushed silently forward. A cutting breeze, with its usual perversity in these parts, drove the falling snow directly in our faces. The storm, without even a moonlit sky above, served to deepen the gloom so rapidly that we were little more than out of sight of the campfires left behind until the blackest of nights was upon us.

Riding at the head of the scouts in company with Major Stanton and Lt. J. G. Bourke,[14] the latter aide-de-camp to General Crook, I had, during the night, an excellent opportunity of witnessing the truly remarkable achievement of Frank Grouard, our principal guide and trailer. His knowledge of the country had been noteworthy ever since the opening of the campaign, but the duty he was now called upon to perform was of just the nature that would have bewildered almost anyone in broad daylight. He had orders to follow the back trail of the two Indians we had seen early in the evening, lead where it would. This he did through the entire night in the face of a storm that was constantly rendering the pony tracks of the two savages less distinct, while it was also hourly increasing the tedium of travel.

Over rugged bluffs and narrow valleys, through gloomy defiles and down breakneck declivities, plunged the indomitable Frank; now down on his hands and knees in the deep snow, scrutinizing the faint footprints, then losing the trail for an instant, darting to and fro until it was found, and again following it up with the keenness of a hound and a fearlessness that would have imbued almost anyone with fresh vim and courage. Nor should we forget his valuable assistants, Baptiste Garnier, Jack Russell, Baptiste Pourieer, Louis Gringos, and others of our keen-eyed scouts who were practically indispensable. With such unfailing celerity was the trailing accomplished that during almost every hour of the long night, order would come from the rear to halt in order that the command might be kept closed up.

Towards morning, the clouds commenced breaking, and soon the sky was almost clear; but with the change came the most intense cold we had ever experienced, and were it not that the almost exhausted men were compelled to walk and lead their horses much of the way, on account of the roughness of the country, many cases of freezing must have been recorded.

The worst was yet to come. At 4:00 A.M., we halted upon what seemed the apex of the entire region. We had at last been ascending quite rapidly nearly all night, and now by the aid of the dim starlight, and through the thick, frosty atmosphere, we could look down, down, as far as the strained vision would reach, into a wilderness of mountains, forest, and vale. How to get down, and at the same time be morally certain of striking the Indians at once, was the question—for we knew that somewhere through that mass of rocky upheavals must flow the Powder. Again the ever ready scouts were to show us their true worth, and with Frank in the lead, off they bounded, to find or make a way.

Near the summit upon which we had thus briefly halted was a deep, narrow ravine. In order to have his men as well sheltered as possible while waiting, Colonel Reynolds ordered the command to take position therein and dismount. Here a scene was presented which we cannot forget. The cold grew in intensity, and exert ourselves as we would to keep up a circulation, it seemed almost unbearable. The fatiguing marches of the day and night, the great strain upon the nerves caused by the loss of sleep and the continuous cold, the hunger, too, making itself felt, and our not being permitted to enkindle a single fire, however small, on account of the danger of alarming the foe—all of these influences combined tolled severely upon the strongest physiques. Stalking my way up and down the gulch in which the shivering men and horses were crowded like bees in a hive, I had no trouble in discovering how they were bearing up under such difficulties. There were very few complaints, but every few moments some poor fellow would drop into the snow, "just for a minute, you know," and when at once shaken up by his more determined comrades, would make all sorts of excuses to be allowed to enter that sleep which, if undisturbed, would have known no waking. Officers were everywhere on the alert to keep their men upon their feet, and thanks to this general watchfulness, no cases of amputations are yet known to be necessary on account of freezing, although nearly all of us are now nursing frostbitten feet, faces, or ears. At daylight, the returning scouts reported the discovery of a trail leading down to the river, and the stream was yet some three or four miles distant. An advance was ordered—an order that was obeyed with more than usual willingness.

In less than an hour, the scouts, who had again been pushed far in advance, came back with the pleasing intelligence that the encampment of Crazy Horse, consisting of over a hundred lodges, lay under the shelter of the mountain we were then descending. They described its situation as best they could and advised that in making the attack the command separate, as two gulches leading down into the valley admitted of an approach from two directions. A short consultation was held, which resulted in plans for an immediate attack, Colonel Reynolds detailing the Egan Grays, Company K, 2nd Cavalry, Capt. James Egan, to charge through the village from the upper end to, if possible, thoroughly demoralize the foe from the start and drive him out of the brush; Companies F, 3rd, and E, 2nd Cavalry, Captain Moore, battalion commander, and Lt. W. C. Rawolle, to dismount, take a position on the left of the village, and thus prevent the escape of the savages; Company I, 2nd Cavalry, Capt. H. E. Noyes, to cut out the ponies and drive them from the field; and Companies M and E, 3rd Cavalry, Capt. A. Mills and Lt. J. B. Johnson, to act as reserve. These preliminaries being arranged and a thorough understanding arrived at by the various officers, they at once proceeded toward the positions assigned, each headed by about an equal number of the fifteen or twenty scouts. Major Stanton, having virtually finished his duties as chief of scouts by piloting the command to the camp of the foe, could have consistently remained at headquarters, but dismounting, shouldering his long rifle, and advancing at the head of Captain Moore's column, it was quite evident that he didn't propose to stop until the fight ended, at least. Lieutenant Bourke, also detached from any command, and myself cast our fortunes with Captain Egan,[15] by whose side we remained during the continuance of the fight.

Separating a mile or more from the village, both divisions had an extremely serious time of it getting over the ground—more especially the one with which we were connected, because we were compelled to take our horses while the others left theirs behind under a suitable guard. The Indians had good reason to wonder at the idea of a command of cavalry coming from that direction, considering the terrific plunges our horses were compelled to make down icy canyons, through fallen timber, and over dangerous rock-strewn chasms. However, Captain Egan does not believe in impossibilities, and in less than thirty minutes, we had floundered to the bottom.[16] Here, securely hid by a low bluff, we could look over and see the village spread out in full view, yet nearly a mile distant. Its position was such as a more civilized chieftain might have selected, and crafty Crazy Horse rose considerably in our estimation as with one long, eager look we took in those points which particularly interested us now—its adaptability for speedy abandonment rather than its strength. Looking down the valley, between us and the camp, lay a long, wide stretch of benchland, a natural pasturage; meeting this, and with an elevation from ten to twelve feet lower, was a narrow belt of bottom-land, with the river washing it on the right. At the limit of this view, where the river swept quite closely around the base of a high and very rugged mountain, and on our side of the stream, lay the object of so much toil and search. The hundred and odd tepees were nestled quite cozily in a grove of large cottonwoods and on the lower and river side were sheltered by a dense growth of willows. Scattered here and there, quietly feeding along both banks of the stream, were bands of hundreds of ponies.

Not the slightest mistrust or alarm was apparent in this forest home, and it was undoubtedly as clear a case of surprise as there is on record. Arms were hastily inspected, belts filled with cartridges, overcoats and other impediments to ease of movement strapped to the saddles, and after a thorough inspection of the ground lying between us and the village to aid an undiscovered approach, the eager little squad was ordered to creep forward to cover, a little further on, before mounting. That point reached, a few brief instructions were given by Captain Egan to the effect that the horses should be trotted slowly over the ground until it was certain that we were discovered, then, drawing our revolvers, we should put the steeds to the full gallop, dash into the village with as much force and with as terrific yells as possible, and when once among the savages, to empty our six-shooters "where they would do the most good." Obtaining cover by winding down around the back of the benchland referred to, and securing good ground on the edge of the river bottom, the order to "fall in for charge" was soon given by the clear-headed captain. In a twinkling, the company, with only half its complement of men, swung beautifully forward with one solid front for the charge.

Revolvers were drawn with a grip that meant something more than parade, the pace was slightly accelerated, and when within less than two hundred yards of the nearest tepee, the first terror-stricken savage was seen to run and loudly whoop the alarm. "Charge, my boys!" came like an electric flash from the dauntless leader,[17] and giving their magnificent gray steeds rein and spur, and yelling like so many demons, the gallant "forty-seven" bounded into the village with the speed and force of a hurricane. With the savages swarming out of their tepees and scattering almost under our feet, we fired right and left at their retreating forms, our horses meanwhile worked into such a frenzy by the din of whoops and yells and discharging arms that they fairly flew over the ground. The demoralization of the foe seemed to last but an instant. A majority of the redskins snatched their arms as they ran, dropped as though shot, behind a log or stump, in the tall grass, or took temporary refuge in the thickets of willow and plum. Bullets and casualties were then bestowed upon us with a will that showed plainly we were not to sweep the field without paying a penalty. The beautiful gray horses were a splendid mark for the Indians, and four or five dropped before we got through the village, Captain Egan's own animal being among the number.[18] Then, with the desperate foe pouring in bullets from behind every convenient cover in the shape of rocks, trees, thickets, etc., we were ordered to dismount, turn our horses over to every fourth man, and continue the fight with our carbines.

Our position was now indeed a critical one. In vain did we scan the faces and foot of the bluffs which Captain Moore[19] was ordered to occupy. No troops were in sight, and the savages, evidently believing no other force at hand, must have thought it an easy matter to annihilate us in a very short course of events. But Captain Egan did not seem to think the case quite so desperate and soon ordered a charge through the brush on foot. While advancing, the savages resisting at every step, a small detachment of troops was seen coming down the hill to the left of where we had looked for the command of Captain Moore, but instead of that officer, we afterward learned that it was Major Stanton, who, finding that Captain Moore was not endeavoring to get into position, secured half a dozen men and advanced to the scene of action. Soon after, Captain Mills and Lieutenant Johnson,[20] with companies M and E, 3rd Cavalry, came forward and did excellent service in assisting to drive the enemy from the field and in destroying the village. I am informed that Captain Moore also finally followed in the wake of Captain Mills, after the Indians had taken advantage of the loophole left in their rear and escaped.

The Indians, severely punished and driven from their village, took refuge in the mountain thus unguarded, and from that time forward, aside from the destruction of their property, had a positive advantage over the troops. Scattered all over this almost impregnable mountainside, and secreted behind its numerous walls of rock, they could pick off our men without running the slightest risk of losing their own lives. Therefore, the more the engagement was prolonged after the prime object of the expedition was accomplished, the more serious and useless were our losses. Realizing this, Colonel Reynolds, at 2:00 P.M., after a five hours' engagement, ordered the command to abandon its position and to at once proceed toward the mouth of Lodge Pole—the rendezvous appointed by General Crook—some twelve miles up the river, which point was reached at dark.

With all the scenes of native splendor and luxury our fancy had pictured, this Powder River reality yet excels, yet astonishes. In the more than one hundred large tepees totally destroyed were beds of furs and robes that, to a soldier, looked simply fit for savage gods; war bonnets and squaw dresses, regal in their construction and decoration, requiring months for making and worth from five to ten ponies each; cooking utensils that an ordinary housewife would not need be ashamed of; tons of dried and fresh meats, and occasionally dried fruits; every tepee an arsenal within itself, with its kegs and canisters of powder, its large supply of bar lead, caps, and fixed ammunition; and then piles of such miscellaneous articles as axes, knives, saddles—over 125 of these—buckskin clothing of every description, moccasins, beautifully ornamented saddlebags, sewing outfits, and really everything any frontiersman would need to insure his comfort. With the exception of a few robes and other trinkets removed by the troops, these vast stores, in many instances the accumulation of a lifetime, were piled upon the dismantled tepees and the whole reduced to ashes. In the case of the generous piles of nicely dried meat, this action was particularly unfortunate, as the troops needed such provender badly, and General Crook had especially impressed upon the minds of the officers the importance of saving it.

But the grand item in this connection was the capture of a herd of seven hundred ponies, horses, and mules, many of which were of the best class and identified as belonging to various stock men on the Colorado and Wyoming frontier. These were gathered and driven a short distance from the battlefield by the command of Captain Noyes,[21] assisted by the scouts. However, this triumph was of comparatively short duration, as a few of the never-sleeping Indians swooped down upon the herd this morning and recaptured nearly the entire band. Leaving no orders for the disposal of the ponies yesterday on the field, Colonel Reynolds also neglected to place a guard around them last night when Colonel Stanton—who, with a few scouts, had taken it upon himself to drive them twenty miles to their camp—turned them over to him. Also, when at daylight this morning the ponies were reported as being driven off by the Indians, the general declined sending a force in pursuit, although they could easily have been recovered.

The loss of the savages in killed and wounded cannot even be approximated, although men who were on the skirmish line during the engagement state it all the way from thirty to fifty. Retreating slowly, as they did after our first onslaught, and nearly always close to cover of some kind, they had no difficulty in removing every body from one position to another.

The command suffered a loss of four killed and four wounded. The killed were Pvt. Peter Dowdy, Company E, 3rd Cavalry; Michael McCannon, Company I, 2nd Cavalry; Lorenzo E. Ayers, Company M, 3rd Cavalry; George Schneider, Company K, 2nd Cavalry. Wounded: Patrick Goings, artificer, Company K, 2nd Cavalry, seriously; Edward Egan, private same company, seriously; John Lang, corporal, Company E, 2nd Cavalry, slightly; Charles Kaminski, sergeant, Company M, 3rd cavalry, seriously. It was noticed that at the opening of the fight, the shooting of the Indians was very wild, but a marked improvement in their aim was manifested toward the close. Bows and arrows were used in exceptional cases, but no wounds inflicted by them.[22]

In charging into one of the tepees, a man received a bullet through his cap. It just grazed his head, and as himself and a comrade or two rushed in to wreak their vengeance on the redskin who had fired, what was their astonishment at seeing three or four squaws, armed with revolvers, in the act of slipping through the opposite side of the wigwam by way of a hole they had just carved with butcher knives.

These Indians may be cowardly, but they have a queer way of showing it. While in the extreme front, we noticed a small band of ponies on our right that had been overlooked by the men detailed to gather them in. The main body of Indians was then on our left, and we were amazed to see a gaudily dressed warrior, well mounted, emerge from behind a clump of bushes, tauntingly brandish his weapons, and start with breakneck speed toward the ponies with the evident intention of making off with them. To accomplish this, he was compelled to ride within two hundred yards of fifteen or twenty of us, and just before reaching the goal, faithful horse and reckless rider fell riddled with bullets.

Steward [W. C.] Bryan, of the Fort Fetterman hospital, who was with us on the charge, just after dismounting discovered a young warrior but a few yards distant with revolvers leveled over the top of a stump and in the act of shooting at him. The steward dodged behind his horse's head, and the poor animal received the bullet in his brain. That Indian, it is generally believed, belonged to Lieutenant Bourke—although he denies the soft impeachment—as he was seen to look over the sights of his revolver in that direction about the time the audacious brave disappeared.

The village contained about seven hundred people, of whom the greater number were Sioux,[23] who steal ponies from the frontier, go to the northern agencies and draw supplies, and also trade ponies there for arms and ammunition. There were also a few lodges of renegade Arapahos.

Pvt. [Theodore] Gouget, a Frenchman, of Captain Egan's company, while charging over rough ground on foot, fell unnoticed into a deep narrow pit. He was just tall enough to level his gun over the edge, and although the position was swept by the enemy's fire from three directions and there was no one to keep him company, he thought that a good place from which to fire some sixty rounds.

Private [Jeremiah J.] Murphy, Company M, 3rd Cavalry, had his gun stock shattered in his hands and a pair of pantaloons ruined by the same ball. He now prefers carrying that broken gun and wearing those punctured pantaloons to getting a new outfit. We failed to see the white girl who is known to be with this tribe. She was captured when only two or three years old, from Mormon emigrants, it is believed, and is now about twenty years of age. Frank Grouard, who while a prisoner here saw her daily, says she is quite handsome, has a very pleasant disposition, and is esteemed and guarded as the richest treasure by her dusky companions. He never knew them to insult or maltreat her, and she is not obliged to perform any of the common labor of the squaws, most of her time being spent in doing fancy beadwork, embroidery, etc. Yet, not knowing a word of English, and having no knowledge of a more convenient sphere, she often, by her listless and unsatisfied manner, betrays a desire to leave the tribe, or at least to make some changes for the better.

Among the domestic animals about the village, we noticed several broods of chickens and a number of fine dogs. The conduct of several of the latter seemed particularly strange. Lying by the sides of their masters' tepees when we arrived, they would not change their position one iota. As the domicile was torn down, and it with its effects set on fire, the great faithful fellow would still remain motionless as a statue, heedless of coaxing, gazing wistfully and without a growl at the bands of destroyers.

General Crook, in ignorance of what has transpired, has failed to meet us here as yet, and while waiting, we have time to take a hasty glance at the work of the last twenty-four hours. In spite of the fact that we have, in the midst of winter, thus found and routed from his own stronghold the second savage chieftain in importance, perhaps, in the whole western country, and have utterly wiped out his village and supplies, a number of very unpleasant conclusions here force themselves upon us. And it is only due the people who support the army and pride themselves in its efficiency, as well as to the brave and true soldier, who otherwise would suffer with the coward and the pretender, that these conclusions take the shape of words. Disguise it as we may, the fact still remains that owing to the failure yesterday of Captain Moore to take the position assigned him, a large proportion of the Indians were permitted to escape, thus rendering the victory incomplete in its most important detail; further, that through this same tardiness, the situation of his brother officer, Captain Egan—who had charged into the heart of the enemy, in obedience to orders, with but a handful of men—was greatly imperiled. Then, in view of the fact that the troops were on half rations of meat, and that General Crook had instructed the officer in command to save all that could be carried off, the destruction of the large quantities of buffalo and venison not only deprived the troops of that which rightfully belonged to them, but also withheld from them that of which they now stand in great need. Also, the leaving of the bodies of the dead and one wounded man upon the field to fall into the hands of the red monsters, who no doubt immediately swept over it after our departure, seems utterly inexcusable, as there was no obstacle in the way of their prompt removal that could not have been surmounted by a battalion of troops. This grave oversight sounds all the worse from the fact that during the latter part of the engagement, one battalion or squadron was permitted to unsaddle its animals, make coffee, and partake of lunch in the very sight of the battlefield. Another point and I am done. After having captured some seven hundred ponies—by all odds the most important fruits of the victory—Colonel Reynolds, in neglecting to either place a guard over them or to order their recapture when informed that the Indians were driving them away, certainly allowed the savages to equip themselves with the most important auxiliary to their future predatory incursions upon our frontier.

ALTER EGO

(Denver) *Rocky Mountain News,* April 1, 1876

CHEYENNE, March 31

General Crook, his aide Lieutenant Bourke, with Major Stanton and the *News* correspondent, arrived from Fort Fetterman today. The general left for Omaha tonight and will at once proceed to organize a second campaign. The present expedition has been disbanded, and the companies composing it are now on their way from Fort Fetterman to their respective posts.

The next expedition is to consist of about fifteen companies, composed largely of cavalry. It will start for the Northwest May 15 and will proceed to the neighborhood of old C. F. Smith. There they will locate a permanent summer camp, from which swift detours are to be made over a large scope of country adjacent to the Bighorn Mountains, the Indians to be pursued and chastised as long as one is found in the country.

ALTER EGO

A Review of the Reynolds Campaign

THADDEUS H. STANTON[1]

New York *Tribune,* April 7, 1876

CHEYENNE, W. T., April 1

General Crook, with Lieutenant Bourke and Major Stanton, returned yesterday from the Bighorn expedition, and the general set out at once for Omaha.[2] The troops comprising the expedition returned to their posts. They could not remain at Fort Fetterman, as forage supplies were very short at that post, and the animals had been on short allowance so long that they were much reduced in flesh. During the last two days before Fetterman was reached, many gave out and had to be killed.

Seven companies of cavalry are to return to Fort Russell and will remain here until General Crook is ready for another attack upon the Indians, which will probably be early in May. The troops will arrive at this place in a few days and go into quarters. It is possible that the movements of other expeditions now in the field[3] may render further operations from this point against the Indians unnecessary, but if they should not be successful, General Crook is not the man to remain idle while there is work to be done. For the present, the Indian Department is not ready to order the immediate removal of the Red Cloud and Spotted Tail agencies[4] to the Missouri River. Congress has not voted money for supplies during the next year, and until there is a reasonable prospect of this being done, so that food will be ready for them when they arrive on the Missouri, Indian affairs will be in confusion. Summer is near, and many of the young Indians will leave their agencies and join the hostile bands, so that their fighting strength will be materially increased.

Now that the expedition is over, and while the troops are permitted to take a breathing spell, it is proper to review its work. First, it made a march of nearly nine hundred miles through a hostile country, in a terrible inclement season, much of the time on half rations.

Maj. Thaddeus H. Stanton. NATIONAL ARCHIVES.

As for shelter or warm clothing and bedding, there was none. The frozen, snow-covered ground, with such shelter as brush and banks could afford, was all they had from the time of leaving the train on Crazy Woman's Fork until they returned to old Fort Reno. That more was not accomplished than the destruction of Crazy Horse's village[5] cannot be charged to the discredit of the troops. When General Crook took upon himself the burden of caring for the pack train and sent Colonel Reynolds forward with the real fighting strength of the command, to attack and destroy any camp of savages to be found on the Powder River, he acted generously and gave his subordinate officer an opportunity which many an officer might serve a lifetime and not get. That greater results were not obtained is due to the fact that Colonel Reynolds failed to do his work as thoroughly as he should have done.[6] Upon his success depended other movements, which would have in all probability resulted in the subjugation of all the hostile savages south and east of the Yellowstone River.

General Crook was particular to inform Colonel Reynolds of the importance of securing the ponies of any band he might attack, and also of loading all the meat, and provisions of every kind that might be found in case of capturing a village, upon the ponies and bringing it away for the use of the command.[7] With rations thus replenished, and with plenty of mounts to replace those of our own that were breaking down, General Crook proposed to push boldly down the Powder River to its mouth and attack Sitting Bull's band before the latter could possibly escape him.[8] This would have ended the war and prevented the necessity of sending other expeditions. Colonel Reynolds neglected to obey these injunctions when he captured the village of Crazy Horse and burned, destroyed, and left enough meat there to have fully enabled General Crook to carry out the plan of the campaign. But with this failure, and only partial rations for four days left, it was impossible to take the command further, and the only thing left to do was to return to Reno. Moreover, the substantial fruits of the victory—the captured herd of between seven hundred and eight hundred ponies—Colonel Reynolds permitted to escape, after it had been driven into his camp, twenty miles from the battlefield; when informed by the chief of scouts, Major Stanton, on the next morning that the herd had escaped and was only two or three miles away, having been driven away by the Indians, he made no effort whatever to recapture it. When General Crook came in in the afternoon, it was too late to recapture the ponies, and there was no meat in the command, so that General Crook's plan was completely frustrated.[9]

The fact is that Colonel Reynolds left the battlefield, taking with him a battalion, which he kept most of the time on a trot, paying no attention to what was going on in the rear, not knowing whether the herd was coming or not, and leaving his dead and one wounded man to fall into the hands of the Indians. The fact of a wounded man being left on the field was reported to him by Captain Mills, but he would not order anything to be done about the matter.

When Major Stanton found that no one had orders to bring off the herd and that it was about to be abandoned, he got together such scouts as Colonel Reynolds had not taken and drove it away. As it was large, unwieldy, and hard to manage, he applied to Captain Moore, whose battalion formed the rear guard, for a few men to assist him, but this officer declined to furnish a man.

Further, there is every probability that if Moore's battalion had taken the place assigned it, covering the rear of the village before the attack was made, not an Indian would have escaped. Colonel Reynolds failed to call this officer to account for his noncompliance with orders and virtually sustained him. Captain Moore's failure jeopardized needlessly the lives of the members of the company that made the charge under Captain Egan. He did not arrive upon the ground until half an hour after the attack was made, and came in

An attack on a hostile village.
NELSON A. MILES. PERSONAL RECOLLECTIONS AND OBSERVATIONS.

then upon the same path that Egan charged over, firing wild volleys at the flying Indians, who were fast hiding among the rocks and bluffs overlooking the village. General Crook was not nearer than twenty or thirty miles to the scene of the attack at the time it took place. He had remained in the rear with the pack train, purposely to give his subordinate every opportunity possible to make a brilliant reputation, and cannot, therefore, be charged in any manner whatever with the blunders committed by Colonel Reynolds—errors which were of such a nature as to completely frustrate General Crook's plans for bolder movements.

The country lying east of the Bighorn Mountains, along the Rosebud, Tongue, and Powder Rivers, is extremely uninviting. It is generally a badland country, with high buttes of indurate clay and sandstone, attaining almost the magnitude of mountains. But in this entire region there are no auriferous strata, and no rock harder than that above described. I feel compelled to make this statement in opposition to the statements of many maps of that country which are being scattered throughout the land, upon which gold is represented as among the minerals to be found in the Panther and Wolf Mountains (the highest badland buttes above described), and where there not only is no gold, but where the country has not a single gold-bearing strata or feature. The Bighorn range of mountains, one of the finest on the continent, doubtless is rich in precious metals, and this region is large enough to give room for a large mining population. The Black Hills country does not compare with it in extent, and probably not in the amount of concealed treasure. But between the Black Hills and the Bighorn Mountains there is no gold, and no gold-bearing country. Neither is there any land that would bear the hardiest grain or vegetable. There is no timber worthy of the name; the water is scarce and of bad quality usually, and grass is poor and thin. Altogether, nearly the entire region lying south and east of the Yellowstone River, from the Bighorn range to the Black Hills, is utterly worthless. A military post established at the mouth of the Tongue River would enable the soldiers to control the country from the Rosebud to the mouth of the Powder River, and would have a good effect upon the Indians of that region. A force could attack the Indians in any direction, and as this is the last stronghold of the hostile savages, they could not long resist the active blows that the troops could inflict upon them. Such a post could be supplied by river transportation at less cost than is now required for most inland posts.

Omaha *Daily Herald,* April 13, 1876

Correspondence of the Washington *Chronicle*[10]

CHEYENNE, W.T., April 3, 1876

I returned here three days ago, after a hard campaign with Crook against the Sioux. Major Stanton went out as chief of scouts, had about thirty-six men, chief half-breeds, under him, and led the column, always having the post of danger. Our route of march was from Fort Fetterman to old Fort Reno, on Powder River, at which place the Indians made a night attack upon us, which was easily repulsed but made things very lively for a while. We paid no attention to this, however, and pushed on to Crazy Woman's Fork, from which place the wagon train was sent back to Reno with two companies of infantry and one hundred armed teamsters, to entrench itself and wait for us. Taking fifteen days' rations of sugar, coffee, hardtack, and half rations of bacon, all loaded on pack mules (of which there were twenty to each of the ten companies of cavalry with us), we made a night march to Clear Fork of Powder River, and thence over to Tongue River. From that stream, we marched almost to the Yellowstone, covering with scouts the Rosebud and adjacent streams. Finding no Indians there, we started eastward for Powder River.

March 16, left Tongue, marched twenty-nine miles to head of Otter Creek, where at 2:00 P.M. saw two Indians, who lit out toward Powder. A halt was called, supper gotten, and Colonel Reynolds was ordered to take six companies and push ahead by a rapid night march to Powder. Major Stanton took fifteen scouts and went with this column. General Crook stayed behind with four companies and pack trains, ordering Reynolds to follow and strike any body of Indians he could find.

The night was terribly cold, thirty below zero, and snow on the high mountain ridges from one to three feet deep. Stanton led the column, and we marched till 4:00 A.M., when we thought we must be near the river.

A halt was made, and we stood here two hours, not even a match being lighted. It was as much as we could do to keep from freezing to death. We sent out scouts, who came in at 6:00 A.M., reporting a large fresh trail heading down the Powder, which was about four miles distant. Command started at once, and when near the high bluffs overlooking the stream, the scouts saw a large herd of ponies and, close under the bluff, a village of over one hundred lodges.

Preparations were made to attack at once. One battalion (two companies) was ordered to descend a gorge, and while one company charged the village, the other was to cut out the herd and drive it away. Another battalion (two companies) was ordered to dismount and proceed along the bluffs to a point covering the rear of the village, and close in when the charge was made, and keep the Indians from decamping. One battalion (two companies) was held in reserve. The dismounted battalion was under command of Capt. Alexander Moore, 3rd Cavalry.

Imagine my surprise, after going with it about half a mile, to find that Moore was not going to the place assigned him by at least one thousand yards, leaving a gap for the Indians to get away through. He was urged to go to his place in vain.[11] After cursing everything at a fearful rate, Stanton walked off and told him he was going there himself, if not another man went. Stanton picked up a sergeant [Lewis Gilbert] and four men, who were a little ahead of their command, ordered them to come with him, and went on to the place the battalion should have reached, or as near as so small a force dare go, and when the charge was made, poured in a sharp fire on the Indians as they ran out. But, of course, we could not keep them from escaping.

The whole command then rushed into the village, and it was completely destroyed, with immense quantities of powder and all sort of ammunition, together with robes, blankets, provisions, arms, etc. It was very rich in plunder.

The Indians, who had escaped by Moore's cowardice, numbering about six hundred, soon opened sharp fire on us from the sides of the mountain, and kept it up all the time we were there, from 9:00 A.M. to 2:30 P.M., making one or two fierce assaults on the camp. We lost four men killed and eight wounded. Don't know how many Indians were killed. Reynolds seemed to have lost his head and finally stampeded from the field, leaving his dead and one wounded man to fall into the hands of the Indians.

General Crook had ordered him to bring away all meat and provisions he might find for the use of the troops. This Reynolds failed to do. When he left, he gave no orders about the herd of ponies. Stanton found no one had orders about it and sent his orderly to Reynolds to ask for orders. He gave none, but kept on his march up the river as fast as he could go. Stanton then got five or six scouts and started it out himself, and drove it twenty miles from the battlefield to the mouth of Lodge Pole, where Reynolds had gone into camp.

Got in at 9:00 P.M. with about eight hundred ponies. Turned these over to him, and he put on no guard over them, so that next morning they were gone. The scouts reported Indians driving it away, and only about two miles from camp. He wouldn't send a man to bring it back. So we lost the most substantial fruits of our victory right there, for the ponies were everything to the Indians.

When Crook came up in the afternoon, he was terribly incensed at the blunders made by the imbecility of Reynolds. I was nearly worn out. Had slept on the snow without covering, after the night, with nothing to eat. There was little to eat anywhere, and Reynolds had disobeyed Crook's order in not bringing away provisions from the captured village. We were four days from our wagons at Reno, so we pulled out for them as fast as we could, eating ponies before we got in.

We got back to Fetterman March 23, and I arrived home the thirty-first. Altogether, it was a hard campaign. We beat the Indians badly, but nothing like we should have done if it had not been for the imbecility of Reynolds, to call it by no worse name. Crook has preferred charges against him for disobedience of orders for leaving dead and wounded on the field, and letting the herd go, etc. So there will soon be a big-court martial here.

PART FIVE

The Summer Campaign of 1876

Military Notes, 1876

DANIEL C. PEARSON[1]

Journal of the United States Cavalry Association 12, no. 63 (September 1899): 295–312

The field of encounter—the arena, lay midway on east and west line between the Mississippi River and the shores of the Pacific, and embraced the following territory: the central northern part of Wyoming, the southeastern quarter of Montana, and the middle western and southwestern portions of the Dakotas. At the time in question, no railroad passed through this territory. Here, whatever was useful in forest, stream, and mountain, or upon the prairie, was monopolized by the Indians. Here, that continued recession from the advancing, irresistible wave of a stronger race, which began in America four hundred years ago, had stranded a big bunch of nature's copper-colored children, who, instead of banding all together for mutual safety, were broken into hostile elements amongst themselves.

Strange perversity in human affairs; crowded to the wall by the whites, the long inherited hatred amongst these red men had sprinkled battlefields thickly over the territory hereinbefore described. In the westerly portion were the Crows. To the east, the Sioux, Cheyennes, the Rees were friends. When events had ripened, under providence, for the governing race to strike the weaker [a] more heavy blow, when the restrictions upon the autonomy of the latter had reached a point no longer to be endured, and when, in his own peculiar methods with respect to white settlers along the Pacific railroad, to his south, and with respect to farmers and miners in the Black Hills, to his east, he made his protests plain not for the first time to the world—then it was that the two great neighboring military departments of the government, the Dakota and Platte, took the field against the unfortunate Indians.

The Indians in arms were the Sioux and Cheyennes, the former in the larger numbers; the latter not excelled for bravery by any race of men, which accords with the fact that more Cheyennes met death on the field of battle than did Indians with whom they were allied. The number of Indians arrayed against the troops cannot be stated, and it is doubtful if the Indians themselves knew their own number. That they largely exceeded the troops, not counting squaws and children, was an undoubted fact. Those of us who had the fortune to see one of

Cheyenne warriors. HARPER'S WEEKLY, 1891.

their old camping grounds, and likewise the trail of their combined numbers, must remember the barren, trodden earth, stripped of all vestige of vegetation, than which nothing could be more expressive of desolation, or more significant of the almost unprecedented multitudes of men, women, children, and ponies who had preceded us in the occupancy of those places. Of course, it will be understood that no trails of this description blazed the way for us generally throughout the campaign in question. Only when it suited their convenience, or when abundantly able to encounter the troops, or when comparatively near their point of concentration on the Little Horn, did the hostiles offer such signs of themselves.

    That portion of the United States forces destined to come up with the concentrated Indian camp, and which had opportunity to know the most about the size, composition, and numbers, paid dearly for that knowledge. I refer to the more than decimated 7th Cavalry, and to those fatal days, June 25 and 26. In the month of March preceding, the Department of the Platte sent forth ten troops of cavalry and two companies of infantry, with wagon train and pack mules. Debouching to the north from Fort Fetterman, Wyoming, this command for one week, during which it was favored with the brightest possible skies for the time of year, marched intact. Then the wagons and infantry were left in camp. The cavalry and packs were pushed out at the beginning of the second week, with rations and forage and blankets cut down to the lowest notch, leaving camp after dark one night. That night was the longest, without exception, that I ever passed. The most intense desire for sleep asserted itself, chiefly, no doubt, because sleep was among the impossibilities, and altogether out of the question. An officer comrade, to whom a night march was not so much of a novelty, remarked interrogatively to me and, as I thought, with an unnecessary reach to his voice, that that was probably my first night march. At this date, I do not mind admitting that it was. In that night, one of the sudden changes of weather occurred for which Montana is noted. A blizzard struck us, locked the streams up solid, and lay a carpet of snow. What success in escaping the observation of Indians had attended our night march was threatened to be of no avail by our conspicuous trail in the snow. Our belief at the time, corroborated by subsequent events, was that the Indians just then were comfortably quartered in their tepees.

At daylight, whose coming that cloudy and snowy morning was greatly belated, we dropped down into a camp of ice and snow, with the thermometer twenty degrees below zero. This temperature held night and day for the following two weeks, at the close of which period we were back with our wagons. I will state that the ten troops of cavalry were commanded by a brigadier general, with a colonel second in command. After the first week away from the wagons had passed, during which no signs of Indians appeared, two were one day suddenly observed riding rapidly away from us. A halt was immediately ordered. The brigadier general sent forward at nightfall the colonel and six troops to take up the trail, remaining himself with the other four troops. It being my fortune also to remain with the latter, I know only from hearsay concerning the fate of the six troops that night, the next day, and the night following. An Indian village on the Powder River, commonly described as Crazy Horse's village, was attacked and destroyed by the six troops on March 7. A large herd of ponies was captured, but fell again into the hands of the Indians. The cold, the reduced rations and bedding and forage, broken sleep, and the unaccustomed exposure had seriously crippled both men and horses for active, vigorous work. But a severe blow had been inflicted upon the Indians. The return march to the wagons, and thence to Fort Fetterman, rounded out a month's absence from that post, and finished an expedition in which no one claimed or received much credit, although there was quite as much ground for the claim, undoubtedly, as has often sufficed to render men illustrious in Indian warfare.

The rank and file had borne well all the hardships of the expedition, but received scant credit. The subjugation of the northern hostiles had not been accomplished. A larger contract had been undertaken than had apparently been anticipated. Summer was coming, when the Indians were regarded as less vulnerable. The attack on Powder River had not sent them into the agencies, suing for peace. The prospect of a speedy and rich harvest of renown was far from encouraging. As if to make some amends, the colonel was court-martialed for destroying dried meats and robes in the Indian village, which "might have" otherwise been used by the troops in further prosecution of the campaign; also for failing to hold on to the Indian ponies, which "might have" been substituted for exhausted cavalry horses; also for generally failing to secure all the fruits of victory.

This winter expedition from the Department of the Platte was followed in early summer by a second, from the same department, at which time, also, an expedition set out in the Department of the Dakota. The total in the field, from first to last that summer, from the first named department was thirty-five companies of cavalry and infantry, with an aggregate of 1,512 officers and men. The total from the Department of Dakota was forty-one companies, with an aggregate of 1,853 officers and men. Crow, Ree, and Cree Indians were allied with the Dakota column; Crows and Shoshones with the Platte column. These two columns were commanded in the field by their respective department commanders. The two expeditions set out from widely separated points, and with a very vague knowledge of each other's whereabouts, until in midsummer a most appalling disaster overtook the 7th Regiment of Cavalry in the Dakota column. The disaster, commonly know as the "Custer massacre," was but the outcome of a brave and successful effort of the Indians to save themselves, their families and all they owned in this world from death and destruction. There they had congregated in self-defense; and there they did thoroughly the duty which devolves upon all men, when all they hold dear is threatened with destruction. Some concert of action then suggested itself, the first essay in this direction coming from the column which had experienced this crushing blow from the common enemy.

Let us go back from this particular date, June 25 and 26, to the latter part of May, and again to Fort Fetterman, where the Platte column was outfitting. Below, and near at hand to the fort, swiftly ran the North Platte River, bank-full at that time of the year. The command was, with the exception of horses that could be made to swim, taken over on a ferry boat, which was propelled to and fro by presenting sides, alternately, obliquely to the current, with the help of ropes, blocks, and pulleys operating upon a cable that was stretched from bank to bank.[2] The process of swimming the horses was interesting, more particularly when it came to those of one troop which positively refused to take [to] the water. With that mount, as was the case with all, the men of the troop formed a semicircle about the horses, the ends of the circle resting at the water's edge, to force the horses into the river. The particular mounts referred to were young and new to the service. They broke through the line of men; they turned tail to the river; they sailed past the fort like the wind, and then they disappeared in the mountains southward, the most of them never to be recovered.

This column, having collected on the north bank of the river, was then inspected. As a result of this inspection, a carload of the personal effects of officers and men had to be sent back to the fort, to be left in the quartermaster's storehouse. In fact, many of those effects were yet on the riverbank as the column pulled out to the north. Every pound that could be dispensed with was left behind. Currycombs and brushes were not allowed to the cavalry. Clothing, blankets, and equipage were closely scanned and reduced by an inflexible rule in the case of every individual. Herein the infantry suffered most. Many nights were spent by them hovering over campfires, while the cavalryman was sleeping well under the additional cover afforded by saddle blanket and another extra blanket, which was carried beneath the saddle in the daytime with no detriment to the horse.

With considerable dispatch, the first of our long series of marches began. The rule adopted was for the infantry to start ahead each morning at about 4:00 A.M., the cavalry, their horses having grazed since daylight, between two and three hours later, by which arrangement, the infantry averaging two and a half miles an hour, got into camp with least fatigue, and the entire command arriving practically at the same time. Before the expedition came to an end the following October, the infantry had acquired splendid marching capacity, while the cavalry, cheated of its forage, was at a disadvantage by comparison.

The formation of camps habitually approximated to a circle. High points in the vicinity were occupied as lookouts. The main circle at night had an outer circle of bunches of men within earshot of one another, one man in each bunch constantly awake by turn, and all lying close to the ground with arms at hand. More than once during those months was the wisdom of this method of guarding the command demonstrated. The theory was that when one or more of our wily foes should reconnoiter us at night, not only should we have our cordon of sleepless men on the watch, but this fact discovering itself to the unequalled eye and ear of the savage, the latter, after noiseless contact at one point and another, and worst of all, finding himself between the two circles, would return to his starting point with all speed, lucky to escape a bullet.

It is said that we never know what a day may bring forth. Never was there a keener realization of the saying than throughout the period from May to October, of which I write. Each night, as one's head lay down, sound and whole, on the saddle of a cavalryman, or upon whatever pillow could be improvised if an infantryman, there was no certainty that that head would be sound and whole the next night; death, or starvation, or sickness was almost constantly forced upon the contemplation. Perhaps the most trying factor was the very general state of uncertainty. In camp, June 8, toward evening, the enemy without notice gave us a few volleys from an overlooking eminence. Two troops of cavalry charged up the declivity and drove them away. Some holes here and there in our canvas were all that was left to tell of the encounter. A circumstance in this camp is recalled which impressed upon all the necessity of careful handling of firearms. One of our men, upon taking off the belt to which his pistol was attached, tossed it upon the ground, fetching the pistol sharply onto a rock, discharging a cartridge into his body, and receiving his death wound. A very impressive burial service was had, and the grave was secured from savage disinterment by collecting above it, with teams of mules, immensely heavy rock.

Eight days later, June 16, our command, stripped of tentage and other impedimenta, accompanied by Crows and Shoshones with four days' rations, our infantry mounted on our wagon mules, set out. On the morning of the second day, June 17, our antennae, the Indian scouts, saw buffalo running, evidently pursued by somebody outside of our command. They also came upon hurriedly abandoned breakfasts of buffalo meat. And shortly they actually laid eyes upon their red brothers with whom they and we were at war. They lost no time in conveying the news to us. The news was electrifying in the extreme. When I say "electrifying," I use the most literally opposite word. The whole atmosphere—the air we breathed—became charged with intense excitement. The scouts stripped. They frescoed their bodies. They vaulted onto their ponies. With rifle in one hand and coiled end of lariat in the other, they steered their ponies at a mad gallop, now in straight lines, now in circles, all the time uttering deafening, fiendish, confusing cries until, like a flash, off they go by ones and twos to square up old feuds. No one should pretend to be able to tell all that occurred that day on the upper Rosebud.

It subsequently transpired that upon that identical day, the Dakota column was scouting within easy reaching distance of the Platte column upon this same Rosebud Creek. About this same date, also, it became known to the Dakota column almost exactly where the hostiles had concentrated upon the Little Bighorn. Concert of action between the two columns at this time must certainly have produced more creditable results for the troops. In our June 17 affair on the upper Rosebud, our Indian allies, of whom the Crows were in their own familiar country, proved of great assistance. The evidences we had of their wonderful eyesight were constantly with us. The 2nd Cavalry squadron was first in contact with the Indians. I recall the strange and unaccustomed sensation of that target practice, in which the bullets whizzed thick and close to my firing point instead of safely away at the three, five, and six hundred yard target butts near garrison. I recall, too, the fact that at one time more than my share of bullets, apparently, struck the ground nearby, and that I afterward discovered that the motion of my horse had inverted my open cartridge box and pitched a large percentage of my cartridges upon the ground. Does it not rank high among comical events of this world to think of a soldier creating a battlefield all by himself, and being dismayed by the sound of his own bullets as he unconsciously fires them at the ground? I am not proud of the occurrence, and hasten attention to the fact that, yielding to contact with the 2nd Cavalry, seeking our left flank and rear, the enemy found themselves confronted with the rifles of the infantry. They then tried flanking the infantry, but found more cavalry coming up on the infantry left. Here the hottest part of the engagement took place. Here ten of our men were killed and twenty wounded. Here, on one part of the skirmish line, were recruits doing their first service. Here the enemy charged boldly into close quarters. One of the recruits handed an Indian his carbine in token of surrender. The Indian, acting with dispatch in such close proximity to our line, grasped the carbine, smashed the soldier's face with the stock, and then dashed away. For one on the ground, it was impossible to tell of the duration of that fight. Thoroughly convinced that our foes were in multitudes, although for the most part concealed from our sight— momentarily assured by Crow or Shoshone, who, with gesticulating hand, indicated the hostiles, that never in the world were quite so many Indians assembled before—no conclusion was so apparent as our defeat.

Finally, orders came to move down the Rosebud to the supposed Indian village. Nine troops of cavalry were disengaged from the fight and started in that direction. Not to leave the dead of those troops behind, they were swung across saddles for their last ride, head down on one side and feet depending from the other, blouse and trousers strained to parting above pommel and cantle; with rollicking comrade—not so rollicking at heart—leading the dead trooper's horse among the rear twos. That was no time for moralizing or for tender sensibilities. The nine troops had rapidly passed some seven miles into the canyon, whither our Indian allies refused to go. At this point, an aide overtook us with an order to retire from the canyon by the quickest route. The reason stated by the commanding general in his report for countermanding the order for us to go down the canyon was that he desired to use us elsewhere. The very evident fact to us was that we certainly would never have been of use elsewhere, except for that countermanding order. If of any immediate subsequent use on that day, it was not apparent. Turning short to the left hand in the canyon, our path was up a steep, thickly wooded declivity. My part at that time was to be messenger to communicate directions to succeeding troops, to overtake the head of the column, and to be bearer of messages to the rear again until, breathless and leg weary, as the ascent was too steep for riding, I was the last to clamber out of that canyon, fully persuaded that the whole Sioux nation was at my heels. Upon reaching the high and level ground, there were the balance of the command and the wounded. In aiding the wounded, much skill was manifested by our Indians. The first thing that struck me was the sight of our wounded prone upon the ground, in the hot summer sun, without protection. At the same time, there were the wounded of our friendly Indians with hastily constructed tripod and shelter over them. In all their treatment of the wounded, they displayed a certain skill that was born of familiarity with life and death contests.

And so here we were with two of our four days' rations gone, with which we had left our wagons. Two days' march from our wagon base of supplies, with just sufficient rations to return. We had not then learned the practical operation of going a week or more with no rations at all. On June 19, however, we were back with our wagons and made good connection that time, so far as rations were concerned. The remainder of June, the whole of July, and a few days in August were passed in inactivity, mostly, in camps skirting the northern base of the Bighorn Mountains. The wagons, with infantry escort, were sent to Fort Fetterman, then two hundred miles to our south, for more rations and for more troops. Meantime, camp was changed at intervals from one point to another, from mountain stream to mountain stream, there being a succession of such at from about five to eight miles apart, all cool and crystal, emerging from canyons opening northward from the Bighorn range.

About July 10, the first news of the Custer fight, by way of Fort Fetterman, came to us by courier three weeks after the event. The effect upon the command may be imagined. It dawned upon us that Custer and his men had met the fate in store for us had we followed up the gentlemen with whom we had the argument of bullets a week in advance of the Custer fight. The impression made upon our commanding general, who had not been suspected of overrating the northern hostiles, was such that he immediately sent couriers back for more reinforcements, beyond those already ordered, before making another advance.

About this time, also, the memorable expedition was made in which one of our regimental officers did distinguished and gallant service. The general belief prevailed that Custer's destroyers had moved up the Little Horn River, to a point west of us, and also near the Bighorn Mountains. To get information of them, the commanding general desired his leading scouts to explore in that direction, but the scouts demurred to go alone. Accordingly, Lieutenant [Frederick W.] Sibley[3] and twenty-five picked men and horses were ordered to accompany the scouts. It is my opinion, with all deference to that of Captain Sibley, who certainly had the best opportunity for judging, that for purposes of observation, the usual method in the Indian country of sending but one or two, or at the most three, individuals would have been better tactics. The circumstance which enabled Captain Sibley's party ever to return to us—not forgetting the courageous action and excellent judgment displayed—was their finding their way, after enforced abandonment of their horses, into the heavily wooded mountains, where the Plains Indians with whom we were at war were loath to go. So far as the opposition to be expected from the enemy was concerned, they were in such warlike mood and equipment as to render a detachment of twenty-five men a mere fleabite for them. So I say that the rule of minimum vulnerability with maximum excellence of powers of observation should not have been departed from. I fail to find in published official records any allusion to this hazardous service of Lieutenant Sibley's detachment. It certainly deserved conspicuous and honorable mention, which it received, I am glad to say, in all other quarters. I congratulate the captain that the Indian scalping knife, which he and his detachment so narrowly escaped, had nothing to do with the scanty field of operations for the tonsorial artist which the top of his head now presents.

That was a most interesting day in camp when, toward evening, two infantrymen arrived with dispatches from the Dakota column, our first definite information of the whereabouts of that column, and also of the full details of the Custer fight. The Dakota was senior to the Platte commander [Brig. Gen. George Crook]. In these dispatches, he waived his rank and offered to cooperate with the latter in any plan of operations he might have. About this time, also, orders were received from the Division Commander that the Platte column should join the other. A regiment of cavalry coming to our reinforcement early in August, a start was made to the Dakota column. Abandoning the wagons, which we were not to see again for two months, and stripped once more of everything that could be left behind, we emerged again to the north. In a few days, after crossing trails which denoted that our Indian foes had gone eastward in the direction of their agencies in a broken and scattered condition, the two columns came together, each at first mistaking the other for the enemy, and making dispositions accordingly. Junction was made on the historic Rosebud.

There was tardy wisdom in uniting the two columns. The Dakota troops had abundant supplies, which had been facilitated by the navigation of the Yellowstone and Missouri Rivers. The Platte troops had been insufficiently and poorly supplied throughout.

If this difference between the two bodies of troops should be attributed to the differences in the means of transpiration, the inquiry is suggested, Why should the Platte column have deliberately turned its back, as it did early in September, upon twenty days' forage and rations, which the Dakota commander [Brig. Gen. Alfred H. Terry] had conveniently placed for it. And in consequence of which action on the part of the Platte commander, the latter's men were almost starved to death; horses had to be abandoned by the hundreds, while other scores of horses, emaciated as they were, were made to simulate beef cattle for issue by the Subsistence Department. In fact, dry and tasteless horsemeat, straight, for days constituted the sole rations for the Platte column.

And so it was that the Dakota column was not permitted to continue its hospitable and generous provision for us, which it showered upon us so long as we remained together. The joint command marched eastwardly, crossed Tongue and thence to Powder River, where the latter empties into the Yellowstone. Our stay at the latter place was for about a week,[4] during which time we were frequently drenched by night rains. Much skill was acquired in the selection and preparation of the spot of ground upon which we individually slept, to avoid in particular the formation of rivers and pools of water during the night. In the absence of tents, and as late summer was blending with early autumn, the nights grew cold, and the rainy season was on. It would surprise the uninitiated to know what comfortable nightly shelter was had. Camping places at that time usually abounded in trees and bushes, from which small withes and saplings could be had for the framework. Six or eight withes, each sharpened at the heavier end and forced into the ground in two parallel rows at, say, two and a half feet asunder, the tapering ends brought together and interlaced, formed a support about three feet in height for a blanket, whose sides came to the ground and were fastened down with wooden pegs. A blanket so placed with reference to a man asleep on the ground at night was more efficacious, as a second blanket to the one which came next to the body, than if the man slept with both blankets next to him, especially if it rained or snowed. One end of the semicylindrical tepee so constructed was closed by an overcoat, or a saddle blanket, or a piece of shelter tent. Into the other open end you entered, headfirst, in a prone position, and gradually squirmed into your bed for the night—headquarters always in the saddle. It was while so reposing one night that there came thunder, lightning, rain, hail, wind, in terrible violence, sounds and shapes—a wretched, unhappy, tormenting night. Lying flat on my back, with hands grasping and holding down the sides of my blanket roof, I was ashamed to have passed the night so comparatively comfortable when I learned of the general experience. The great majority were drowned out and had absolutely no resource but to stand or sit in the water and mud till morning. All attempts to light pipes or firewood were out of the question. The expletives, the lamentations, the objurgating, the deep resentments against the fate of that night [August 23] have seldom been paralleled.

When the time arrived at which it had been foreordained that the two columns should separate, the commander of the Dakota column (who, being senior to the other brigadier, supposed he had something to say on the subject), upon rising one morning, was informed, to his amazement, that the Platte column had decamped—a most astonishing proceeding it has ever seemed. Without any pretense of courteous leave-taking, our Platte commander skipped out with his 1,500 men one fine morning [August 24] in the mud. The senior brigadier who had been treated in this way ordered up his horse and, with an escort of twenty-five men, overtook the junior commander at his first camp from the Yellowstone, in order to have a mutual understanding as to the future movements of their respective commands. The Dakota column was to move east on the north bank of the Yellowstone; the Platte to the east, but along a line some distance to the south of the Yellowstone. At the mouth of Glendive Creek, on the Yellowstone, it was arranged to leave the twenty days' supplies, before referred to, for the Platte troops. In due time [August 31], the latter reached their nearest point to these supplies. A march of forty miles would have reached them, and there were two days' rations on hand, which would nicely have sufficed for the necessary two days' march, and little or no grain for the animals. A field officer interceded with the general commanding that we should go for our supplies. The general commanding demurred, on the ground of uncertainty of there being any supplies, in spite of the promise of the Dakota commander. As a concession to the situation, our commander sent scouts to see if there were any supplies. The scouts returned and reported no supplies, notwithstanding that there were supplies at the appointed place, and as there was abundant subsequent testimony.

The march determined upon, as an alternative, with but two days' rations, led us further east and then south to the Black Hills, in Dakota, over a stretch of two hundred miles. As we journeyed onward, I must not omit to mention the growing corn on a portion of our trail where the 7th Cavalry had passed in early summer and dropped the seed corn from their wagons—a suggestive reminder of the changing fortune of the soldier's life. Early summer had been bright and bonny for them. Autumn now had come, and horses and riders had heard their last bugle call, had made their last march, and had paid the debt of nature far from home and friends.

But let us push on and see what was in store for us before the business of that season was over. There we were with hardtack and bacon fast disappearing. Maps were constantly in requisition, to inform ourselves where we were, and where we were going. The maps gave most meager information, barring distances, which were discouragingly plain and accurate in their formidable aggregation. Our march became an exploration under difficulties. Infantry began to receive reinforcements from the dismounted cavalry. The horses of the latter were shot at first, but later were simply abandoned along the trail to their fate.

Excellent grazing abounded, but it being necessary to get to food for the men, delay for the recuperation of horses was not permissible. The superiority of grass-fed Indian ponies for rough and long-continued service has often been noted. Demonstration to the contrary was afforded us. Our Indians had two ponies apiece, some of them more. Each Indian had at least one led pony for riding, for a change. It became finally a pitiful spectacle to see those unshod, footsore, emaciated little beasts marching, day by day and side by side, with our cavalry horses, toward the latter part of the time the Indians remained with us, and at a period much in advance of the exhaustion of our horses.

One long stretch of our journey in those starvation days was over a treeless country with no fuel for warmth or cooking. Wild onions and cactus fruit were sparsely scattered here and there, and ministered triflingly to the pangs of hunger. The need at this time may be truly described as awful. In one place, the trail had to be corduroyed with boxes of ammunition, there being absolutely nothing else at hand, and the threatened starvation of the command made the ammunition, which was unrecovered, an inconsiderable loss that was not taken into account. Saddles from abandoned horses accumulated beyond the capacity of the pack train, and so finally were burned in one big bonfire. The texture and odor of horse meat had become so familiar as the bill of fare for our two daily meals as to generally alter the sensation customary in using them as saddle animals, besides suggesting an injustice in making them do double duty as food and transportation. It is a satisfaction for me to know that the chestnut sorrel I rode in those days is today enjoying life in the bluegrass region of Kentucky.

Although the demands made upon that animal in those days of which I have been writing, in our own and in other regiments, were so excessive, it must be remembered that our men were subjected to corresponding hardships. I recall very vividly the lines in the horses' flanks, which sank deeper and deeper in as the period of trial was more and more drawn out. One troop in our whole twenty-five troops of cavalry had the credit and the distinction of not losing a single horse on that trip. In my possession is a letter from the captain of that troop, now a major upon the retired list. It is as follows:

THE ARMY AND NAVY CLUB,
WASHINGTON, November 11, 1895
MY DEAR CAPTAIN: It affords me pleasure to notice receipt of your esteemed favor of the twenty-eighth ultimo. I find it difficult to tell you how Troop B, 5th Cavalry, at the ending of the campaign of 1876 had not lost a single horse, when hundreds were left upon the trail by other commands. I have only this to say: My troop was in fine shape to enter the field when called to Dakota. I had few recruits. Most of my men were in second and third enlistment, and we had passed through a long and arduous campaign in Arizona. My non-commissioned officers were capable and fit for higher positions. The men were never allowed to leave the ranks when marching without

the knowledge and consent of the troop commander, and then only on the most urgent circumstances. I made every trooper feel an ownership in his horse that was assigned to him. No other person could use the animal without his consent. In this way, I found my men often cutting grass with a pocket or other knife, in places where his horse could not get at when grazing at the length of the lariat, to supplement his feed and perhaps give him a tidbit. I wish you were here, that we might go over the field again. I often meet men in the club that were with us.

Yours truly,
MONTGOMERY[5]

The exhaustion of our command proceeded from bad to worse. Having reached the North Fork of the Grand River, Dakota, 150 men, mounted on the strongest horses, were sent forward with orders to proceed as rapidly as possible to Deadwood for rations, starting at 7:00 P.M. of September 7. Having gone eighteen miles, the detachment camped until morning, and then again took up the march, and in the afternoon of that day unexpectedly came upon an Indian village of thirty lodges. This village was destroyed and all it contained, excepting about five tons of dried meat, which eked out our rations of horse.[6] Owing to the peculiar and not very choice way the Indians have in curing game, it is not, of course, a popular article of commerce. The main command arrived upon the scene before the destruction of the village was completed, and later, upon the day of arriving, was deployed in an immense skirmish line, making a circle about three or four miles in diameter, to meet the attack of the Indians, who had returned with reinforcements, and with the expectation of having only to contend with our first attacking body. The size of our firing line and its heavy fire was greatly more than a match for our foes, who permitted us to retire from the historic ground of Slim Buttes without serious damage to either party.

But few marches more sufficed to bring us to the point where we were met by rations and grain. Enterprising citizens also came up with wagonloads of breadstuffs, the average profits of which were not bad. It is true that starving men besieged the wagons and caused a miraculous disappearance of loaves and cakes, the responsibility for which no man could find out. But then there were loaves upon loaves that brought a dollar each.

About this time, a contractor's beef herd came in sight and in a surprisingly short time was killed, cooked, and eaten. Five hearty meals a day was the rule for a long time. It was not until the inner man was somewhat rehabilitated that the outer man received attention. Ragged, patched, and worn-out coats, shirts, and trousers had, for a long time without change, been the covering for the bent-over, hollow-cheeked, sunken-eyed men.

At the close of the last day's march of twenty-seven miles, in rain and mud, before getting rations, the number of stragglers who had not been physically able to keep up was 125. It became my duty to go back the following morning over the trail and pick up those men. One after another came along, with too evident signs of exhaustion and emaciation. To those who were on the point of utter exhaustion, I caused men of my detachment, one by one, to give up their horses. Some declared it was useless to go farther. I gave them the good news that they would find rations in camp. Then they had the courage to go on, struggling still in the mud, barefooted, with boots slung over their shoulders. By some merciful providence, hostile Indians had not hovered upon our trail at that time. The slaughter of our weak and starving men would have been small glory to our arms.

Finding ourselves soon after this in Deadwood and Custer City, we had the pleasure of seeing our wagons once more, which had been sent to us by a detour. Tents seemed like palaces then. Camp bed and bedding, positive bliss. Ordinary necessities of life, real luxuries. The newspapers of Deadwood and Custer City spoke a hospitable welcome to us. It was a matter of regret, however, that from some source they had procured such unreliable information of our comrades of the Dakota column. Comparisons were made which were very erroneously intended for our gratification. The Dakota column was denominated the "rocking-chair brigade." Contact with the Dakota column had been such a "serious hindrance" to the Platte commander. Had the Platte commander been left to himself, the Indians would all have been "wiped out"; and more such deplorably false and partisan reports were brought to the newspapers.

I regret that I am not equipped with the facts that would enable me to do a measure of justice to the medical department of our column. The services they rendered to the wounded, the sick, and the exhausted would make a most instructive and interesting chapter. While the outdoor life tended, in the main, to the preservation of health, or at least counteracted largely the effects of poor diet and of other untoward hygienic environment, there were cases of severe sickness, notably that of Huntington[7] of our regiment, who was prostrated with fever and was transported for days upon a travois constructed by men of his troop. Most skillful surgery was done in the case of another officer at Slim Buttes, whose right leg was amputated above the knee, in consequence of a shattering of the joint by a ball.[8]

Prompt, faithful, skillful attendance was prominently characteristic of our medical officers, in keeping with the habitual efficiency of their department. Even to the unprofessional mind, their ingenious improvisation of substitutes for appliances necessarily absent in the field was interesting. Ready resource was in daily evidence. Copper cartridge shells, relieved of their deadly contents, their open ends stopped with wooden plugs, were transformed into very timely and useful receptacles for remedies constantly needed on the march. The infantry column has reason to remember the good doctor who lightened the day's burden often for many of its weak and famished men by carrying as many rifles as could be fastened to either side of the pommel and cantle of his saddle; or, relinquishing his horse to some sick man, plodded on foot, although in the same worn and weak condition himself as was the majority of the command.

I have two thoughts born of the experience of 1876. First, as to clothing: It should be warm without unduly cumbering the body. Rapid motions and good circulation of the blood are often seriously impeded by too great a load of clothing. Fur garments are indispensable. Second, as to food: Feed full rations to men and full forage to horses and mules. Condemn all unnecessary reduction and diminution in this regard as maladministration in its worst form. The physical endurance, the good heart, and the nerve and muscle of the components of an army form its indispensable working capital and should be prized somewhat as the miser does his treasure. It is a lamentable thing when a want of foresight, a jealous disposition, misguided judgment, or selfish ambition sit at the helm. If for adequate object, and with good results, men are put to the test of their supreme abilities, they may be expected to make light of hardship and privation. It is then that proud and heroic conduct may be confidently looked for. The bearing of these observations was made plain by the morale of the Platte column, the last days preceding the relief which came to us in the Black Hills. Discipline had become strained. A condition akin to mutiny was smoldering. Fortunately, relief came to hand when it did!

The War Path

HENRY W. DALY[1]

American Legion Monthly 3, no. 9 (April 1927): 16–18, 52–56

The Bozeman Trail, or Montana road, as we called it mostly, branched off from the Overland at Fort Casper in Wyoming Territory. The Overland was the Forty-niner route to California. The Montana road veered north to the new gold country.

In the spring of 1876, it was merely a string of wagon tracks across the grass—not so wide or so much used as the Overland, which was three times the width of Fifth Avenue, New York, or Market Street, San Francisco, and muddy in wet weather and dusty in dry. The Montana road was pleasanter traveling, but more lonesome. But on the trip I speak of, we had plenty of company.

There were twelve hundred of us—the biggest collection of white men ever in that country in one party, I guess, since Brigham Young took his Mormons out to Utah in the forties. The cavalry led the column—ten troops of the 3rd and five of the 2nd. After that came three companies of the 9th Infantry and two of the 4th Infantry. Bringing up the rear were the wagon trains—four of them, consisting of twenty-five six-mule teams each. One of these was driven by the famous plainswoman the West knew as Calamity Jane.[2]

So we made quite a procession. I was with the pack trains. There were nine of these, and our mules moved in single file alongside the column of troops, about fifty yards off the trail. We were always on the lee side, so the troops didn't get our dust, but we got theirs. The chief packer was Tom Moore,[3] and his assistant was Dave Mears.[4] Both were old-time frontiersmen. They had gone to California in 1849, making the voyage around the Horn. Tom came from Kansas, where in later years his sister, Mrs. Carrie Nation, made prohibition conspicuous, if not particularly popular with the liberal element. Kansas had a dry law, but it made little difference in the life of the frontier towns until Carrie began calling attention to it with a hatchet. She must have broken thousand of dollars' worth of bar mirrors and glassware. Tom introduced Mrs. Daly and myself to her at Camp Carlin in 1889. I noticed that she did not attempt to carry on her reformation that close to home, for Tom had a jug of whiskey handy and said he was never without it in his house. Smoking also was one of

Mrs. Nation's aversions, but you would have to get up early in the morning to see Tom without his pipe, big as a Ben Davis apple. Still, brother and sister were very fond of each other.

Our expedition was under Brig. Gen. George Crook, one of the greatest Indian fighters the army ever had. We were one of three expeditions in the field, comprising the grand offensive of 1876 to exterminate the bands of Crazy Horse, the Sioux, and of Dull Knife, the Northern Cheyenne, chieftains. The other contingents were led by Colonel Gibbon and Lt. Col. George A. Custer.

Custer and Crook were about as different as two men could be and still be members of the same profession. I shall never forget the first time I saw General Custer, as they still called him, from the rank he had held during the Civil War, in which he had served with great distinction. It was during a cattle drive from Texas to Kansas City, before the advent of the Texas Pacific Railroad, in 1868. He wore a bleached buckskin suit of fancy cut, and lavishly ornamented with fringes. His yellow hair hung in long ringlets over his shoulders and was crowned by a broad, white hat. His hands were encased in gauntlets, and his feet in boots as soft as a lady's dancing slippers, and as spotless. He carried himself with the air of a lion.

In a populous place, General Crook would have worn the regulation uniform, but it probably would have needed pressing. A battered slouch hat would have been carelessly thrust on his head, and his boots would have been dusty. In the field, except that everyone knew him, he might have been taken for a Montana miner. The only part of the uniform he wore was an old overcoat. Except in wet weather, he wore moccasins, and his light, bushy beard would be gathered in a series of braids. He was a silent man, but good-natured and philosophically humorous. I have seen him walk up to a cook fire where the troops were getting their coffee, take his turn for a cup, and then walk away and sit down on the ground, and blow it off and drink it without saying a word.

The forces of Crook, Gibbon, and Custer were to converge upon the hostiles from different directions. General Terry had come west to supervise the three forces and direct the campaign.[5] Sheridan was in Chicago awaiting the outcome.

Our command halted at old Fort Reno, at the three forks of the Powder River in Wyoming.[6] There we expected to be reinforced by Crow and Shoshone scouts, who were hostile to the Sioux and Cheyenne. But our Indian allies were not on hand, and General Crook sent his chief of scouts, Frank Grouard, with Baptiste Pouriee, on ahead to see if they could find out what had become of them.

Frank Grouard was one of the strangest characters I knew in the West. He was a Sandwich Islander, or Hawaiian as they call them now. As a child, he had been captured by Crazy Horse's band and brought up by them. He spoke Sioux as well as, or better than, he did English. Baptiste Pouriere, or Big Bat, as we called him, to distinguish him from Little Bat, who was named Baptiste Garnier, was a French-Canadian and an old-time trapper for the Hudson's Bay Company.

Frank Grouard. FRANK LESLIE'S ILLUSTRATED NEWSPAPER, 1876.

These two went ahead to look for Indians, friend or foe, and the command followed on. At Clear Creek, a branch of the Powder, in northern Wyoming, we met a party of sixty-five miners en route from the Black Hills in South Dakota to the Bighorn range in Wyoming. They had seen no hostiles but were glad enough to join us. We continued westward to the Tongue River and turned north down that watercourse. The march was uneventful except for a slight attack in which we had two men wounded.[7] But we were apprehensive of more serious trouble and anxious for word from the scouts.

The scouts returned on June 14 with parties of Crow and Shoshone. They brought information concerning Gibbon, Custer, and the enemy. The Sioux, they said, were encamped in force along the Rosebud River.[8]

We made a base camp and the next morning set out with four days' rations and plenty of ammunition to force the fighting. The night of the sixteenth, we reached the Rosebud and slept on our arms. On the morning of the seventeenth, with the friendly Crows and Shoshones, we began a rapid but alert descent along the east bank of the Rosebud. It was hard going. The Rosebud is as crooked as a corkscrew, and the country is very rough. Now we would be hugging the bluffs through the narrow, winding valley, unable to see fifty feet ahead; now passing through an open glade, which, though difficult underfoot, presented fewer perils of surprise.

Shortly before noon, our scouts reported the valley a few miles ahead alive with Sioux and Cheyennes, who were coming our way on our side of the river.[9] Just below this point, the Rosebud enters a canyon. If we could drive the hos-

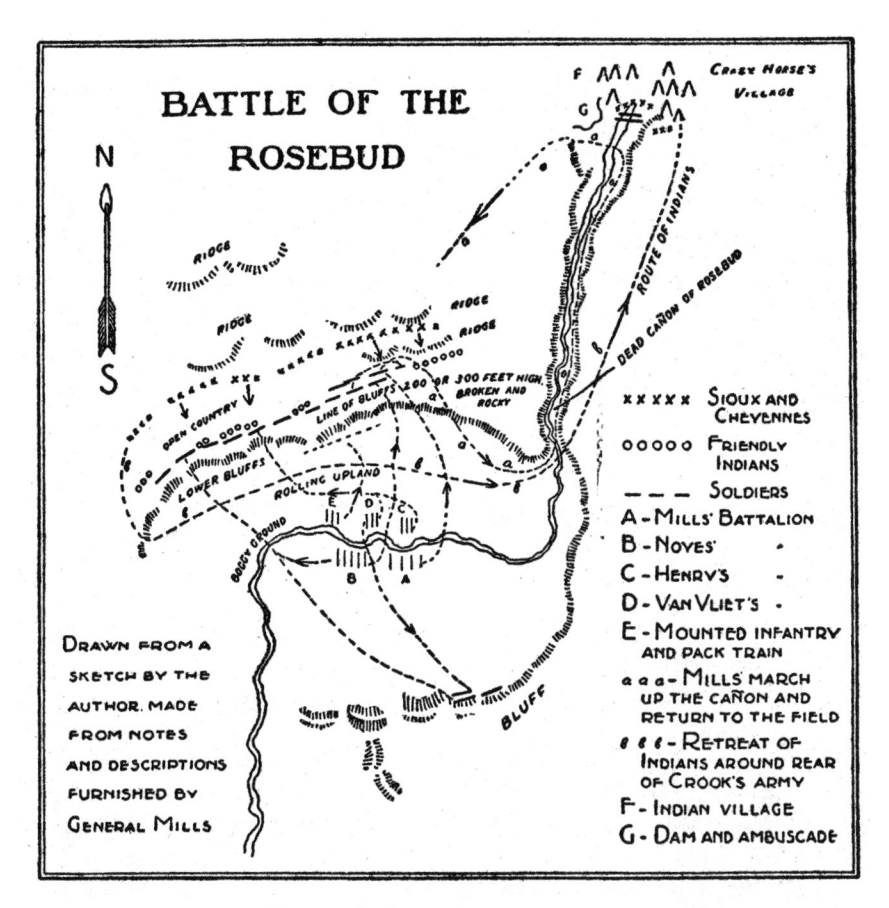

The Battle of the Rosebud CYRUS T. BRADY. *INDIAN FIGHTS AND FIGHTERS.*

tiles in there, there would be a chance of exterminating them. But if they should prove the superior tacticians and drive us into the canyon, their chances of doing the exterminating would be equally good. They outnumbered us three or four to one, but Crook matched his wits against those of Crazy Horse and got us ready for battle.

The battlefield was about 150 yards wide and was bounded on one side by the river and on the other by a line of bluffs that defined the valley. Crook arranged his forces in two columns. On the riverside, he placed the friendly Indians in advance, mounted on their ponies, and supported by two companies of infantry and two troops of cavalry, dismounted. The second column, which paralleled the bluffs, consisted of cavalry on their horses.[10]

In approximately the center of the field, midway between the bluffs on the right and the stream on the left, was an upthrust ledge of rock that would accommodate about eight men and give them room to fight. There Crook posted the sixty-five Black Hills miners and about fifteen packers, of whom I was one. This ledge was thirty-five feet high in places. It afforded a perfect view of the battlefield and of the battle.

I have seen few more exhilarating sights in my time than the picture that vantage point present. It was just past noon and the sun was out.[11] On our left streamed our painted Crow and Shoshone allies, naked except for breechclout and moccasins, singing the war song of the Ab-sa-ra-ka and gesticulating. Their ponies were spirited ones, with plaited manes and tails adorned with eagle feathers, and small bells, which tinkled like those of an old-fashioned sleigh. Before them they held shields of buffalo hide, gaily ornamented with colored quills and feathers. On their glistening backs were strapped bows and arrows in quivers. Their lances, carried aloft, sported eagle feathers. Rifles were held in front, across their elk-horn saddles.

On our right swept the cavalry under Colonel Royall,[12] and beyond them some Shoshones under Chief Louissant were posted on the sides of the bluff that dominated the approach of the hostiles from downstream. General Crook stood under a scrub pine tree on the riverbank, waiting for the action to begin.

Up the valley came the Sioux and the Northern Cheyennes—a solid phalanx from stream's edge to bluffs. There were no handsomer Indians and no better riders. The chiefs rode in front. From the forehead to the waistline, each warrior was painted with stripes of black and red. Their gorgeous headdresses fanned the breeze like the tails of a boy's kite. They chanted a war song in unison and in perfect time. They attacked with great fury and with the precision of trained cavalry. The Sioux under Crazy Horse struck to the right front of the ledge from which I was firing over the heads of our forces. The Cheyennes under Dull Knife[13] struck our left column, which was on the riverside. At first they shouted to our Indian allies, "You go home! We want to kill only white men!" But the Shoshones and Crows were loyal, and they, with the supporting troops, were hotly engaged. Meantime, the Sioux on the right attempted to dash between our cavalry and the bluffs and gain our rear.

The shock of the first onrush sent both of our columns back. The ledge from which the miners and we packers were fighting was surrounded. The hostiles charged it. We fired pointblank, but on they came. Several reached the top of the ledge, and one of them came at me with a tomahawk. A scar over my right eye, which is still visible, enables me to recall the incident the more distinctly.

The attack was progressing satisfactorily for Crazy Horse. His Sioux were working around the right flank to our rear. Their object was to drive us forward into the canyon ahead, which would have been our death trap. But Crook, who did not underestimate Crazy Horse as a tactician, had anticipated this maneuver and had held five troops of cavalry and two companies of infantry in reserve. At the right moment these charged the Sioux, who, caught between two fires that were punishing in their intensity, were driven back in some disorder. This retreat exposed the flank of the Cheyennes, who also fell back.

But Crazy Horse was not beaten. He endeavored to transform his enforced retreat into a strategic one, designed to coax us and box our pursuing troops in the canyon. General Crook saw the danger of this and the futility of pursuit in any event. He sent his aide, Lieutenant Bourke, with Trumpeter [Elmer A.] Snow, forward to sound recall. While Snow rode along the line of fire, he was severely wounded,[14] and Bourke saved him from capture.

That ended the fight. It had last an hour.[15] It was a draw, neither side being in a humor to continue the engagement or to remain on the field. Crazy Horse crossed the Rosebud and retreated over the ridge separating that stream from the Little Bighorn River, fifteen miles away. In this valley, he encamped to nurse his wounded and replenish his ammunition. We retired to our base camp for the same purposes, and to learn of the movements of the cooperating forces under command of Colonels Gibbon and Custer.

We had lost ten killed and twenty-six wounded. The losses of the Indians were not ascertained as, according to custom, they carried their casualties from the field, with the exception of eleven dead who had fallen during their farthest advance into our lines. To recover these bodies was too dangerous.[16]

The first three weeks in camp were uneventful and are remembered principally for our rich living for campaigners. The streams were filled with fish, the hills plentiful with buffalo, deer, elk, and mountain sheep. We had two good meals every day.

In this connection, I was once asked concerning an incident on the march, whether it had happened before or after our noon meal. In those days there was no noon meal on the march, and seldom one in camp in the field. We ate morning and night. Even this was a strain on the cooks, whose equipment was as scanty as possible. We had to travel light when fighting Indians, but we could never travel as lightly as they did. Indians could march and fight for days without eating or apparently sleeping. We cooked only once a day—in the evening. When supper was out of the way, breakfast was prepared and kept over until morning. If a man wanted anything between breakfast and supper, he had to save it out for himself. Troops often did this, but with the pack train, it was considered too much bother. We were seldom hungry, though. Eating three times a day is simply a habit.

The tranquility of our life was interrupted one day when one of our reconnaissance parties was attacked by a large band of Sioux, which lost its leader, White Antelope, at the first exchange of shots and pursued our men to the verge of the encampment to avenge his death.[17] Three days after that, on July 10, scouts Louis Richard and Ben Arnold rode into camp with dispatches which threw the camp into the wildest commotion I have ever witnessed among United States soldiers.

Eight days after our fight with him on the Rosebud, Crazy Horse had fallen on Custer and destroyed his command. We only knew there had been a great disaster. No details. Groups of men rushed about to learn the particulars. How many killed? How many had escaped? A party galloped off to find General Crook, who was on reconnaissance.[18] No sooner had they gone when a party of prowling Sioux set fire to the grass about the camp.

General Crook came in that night, and on the following day three enlisted men of the 7th Infantry arrived with more dispatches confirming the news of the previous day. Two days after that, on July 13, four Crow scouts came in with the same story, but in detail.[19] These Crows had either witnessed the fight from places of concealment on overlooking bluffs or had talked to others who had. At any rate, they had the whole story as completely and exactly as it has ever been put together after fifty years of investigation. Moreover, they put in some details which I have never seen in print. I wrote their story down as they related it.

It was in the evening of the day of the Crows' arrival. We had finished supper, and with some others, I walked over to the campfire of the Crows to find out what I could about what had happened to Custer. Baptiste Pouriere was along. The Crows were sitting in a circle about the fire, discussing the fight with some of their tribesmen and with the Shoshones who were standing about. Big Bat addressed them in their language and asked them to tell us what had taken place.

One of the Crows squatted down and smoothed off a space on the ground about a yard square. Across the center of this, he drew a crooked line and said something to Big Bat, who explained that the line represented the stream of the Little Bighorn. Then the mapmaker drew another line to the right of the stream and roughly parallel with it, and held a stick in a horizontal position about three feet from the ground. This meant that the new line represented the bluffs which followed the stream. Then he drew a series of lines from the bluffs toward the stream. These were little ravines which ran from the crest of the heights toward the river.

The battlefield topography was complete. Our informant peopled the scene.

He made a series of imprints on the ground along the right bank of the stream. At each imprint, he would say, "Sioux, Sioux," or "Cheyenne, Cheyenne," bringing his right hand from the crown of his head to his left shoulder, and again in a curving manner in front of his body. This indicated that the lodges of the squaws and children were placed along the edge of the stream.

He then took a handful of ashes from the fire and distributed it along the ravines that ran from the bluff tops to the stream, saying, "Sioux, Sioux," and "Cheyenne, Cheyenne." This meant that the Sioux and Cheyenne warriors were concealed in the ravines. Then, back of the line of bluffs, he placed twelve twigs and said, "Soga," at the same time placing the first two fingers of his right hand astride the four fingers of his left. The Shoshones standing by grunted their understanding. This pantomime meant that Custer, with twelve troops of soldiers, mounted, was approaching the line of the bluffs, behind which the Sioux and Cheyenne warriors were in ambush.

Then our narrator indicated the bluff line and, shading his eyes, as if from the glare of the sun, looked from right to left, saying, "Tash-unco-nitco," which in Sioux means Crazy Horse. Thus we learned that from the top of the bluffs, the Sioux chieftain was observing the approach of Custer and his twelve troops of cavalry.

Again saying, "Tash-unco-nitco," he picked up a pinch of ashes from each ravine and put them in one pile in the center of the series of ravines. He drew lines from each ravine to this spot. This meant that Crazy Horse had called his subchiefs to a council of battle. Next he placed the back of his right hand against his mouth and, touching the thumb and second finger, opened and closed the hand in a series of jerks. This was the sign for a talk. Then he retraced the lines running from the council spot to each of the draws. This conveyed that Crazy Horse had communicated his plan of battle to his lieutenants and sent them back to take charge of the warriors hidden in the different ravines. Then our narrator indicated the tepees along the bank of the stream, and drew a series of lines from them in the direction of the flow of the river. This meant that the women and children had been moved to places of safety. Crazy Horse's dispositions for battle were now complete. Our historian now transferred his attention to Custer.

Directing attention to the twelve twigs representing the troops of Custer's 7th Cavalry, he placed his thumbs to his ears and moved the fingers back and forth, making the expressive and easily interpreted sign of a mule's ears in action. Then he drew a circle and placed a twig beside it. From this we knew that Custer had left his pack mules behind, with a troop of cavalry to guard them.

The twigs representing the other eleven troops were then advanced to the crest of the bluff. Then three twigs were taken up and transferred across the stream and marched down a piece and halted. Three other twigs were likewise swung across the stream, in the rear of the first three. They were made to describe a wide circling movement toward downstream. This was the fatal division of Custer's forces. It was perfectly plain to Crazy Horse, who watched every move from his place of concealment, what his adversary proposed to do. He had sent three troops under Major Reno to cross the river and follow the bed of the stream down and deal with any hostiles on that side. He had sent Captain Benteen with three other troops across to swing out in a large semicircle and then come in, driving before him any hostiles in that region. With five remaining troops, Custer stayed on the right bank. The three forces, reuniting, intended to round up the hostiles in the narrow valley and annihilate them.

Custer had simply played into the hands of Crazy Horse. The Sioux strategist's insurmountable advantage lay in the fact that he had exact information as to the strength and disposition of Custer's troops and had correctly surmised his plan of battle, while Custer was completely in the dark concerning his adversary.

On reaching the crest of the bluff, Custer saw the deserted wigwams on the bank of the stream below. He knew the hostiles were near, but the small number of tepees led him to underestimate their numbers. With his five troops, he rode boldly down the slope of the bluffs toward the stream. Our narrator indicated this by moving the twigs representing the five troops remaining with Custer after the division of his force. Then, raising his hands to his mouth, our relator uttered a piercing, "Aye-hee-yah!" That was the Sioux war cry. I have heard an Indian yell it so it could be heard for three miles. Grasping a small handful of ashes from a ravine directly in the path of Custer's approach, the narrator scattered them rapidly in front of the troops, making a trail downstream. The troops followed the trail of ashes.

This was the trick that sealed the fate of Custer. Crazy Horse had ordered about fifty braves to ride up from one of the ravines, fire a volley, and flee pell-mell down the valley. As he had anticipated, the troopers dashed after them—and to their destruction.

When the troops were well into the valley, with the stream on one side and the bluffs on the other, our narrator picked up the ashes from each ravine and, shouting "Sioux, Sioux! Cheyenne, Cheyenne!" scattered the ashes in a semi-circle about the five twigs which indicated the troops. Shouting and striking his palms together with a great noise, he scattered and broke the twigs. Finally he ceased his shouting and clapping, and raised his right hand to indicate that the battle was over, his story finished, and Custer and his force dead to a man. One young Crow scout, called Curley, got away by fleeing before the battle really began.

It was perfectly clear to us what had happened. We had fought Crazy Horse only twenty-seven days before this recital, and eight days after Custer had fought him, I was still nursing a gash in my head. It required little imagination to see Custer, with his yellow hair flying to the wind, leading his men in pursuit of the decoys. Then an ear-splitting "Aye-hee-yah!" A veritable tidal wave of Sioux and Cheyennes pouring down the bluffs. Outnumbered five, maybe ten, to one—cut off on the front, the rear, and the river sides—Custer was driven against the bluffs and annihilated. Then the women came out to scalp and mutilate the bodies—all except Custer's: an Indian's tribute to a brave man.[20]

Crazy Horse had attempted exactly the same tactics with us. He had failed because, in the first instance, our scouts had been as good as his. There was no surprise. We knew where he was and had a good idea of his numbers. This prevented our commander from dividing his force, if he had ever entertained any such intention. Neither was he deceived by the strategic retreat by which Crazy Horse, after his first assault had failed, attempted to lure us into a trap as he had lured the impetuous Custer.

Having finished with Custer, we persuaded the narrator to tell us what had happened to the forces of Reno and Benteen that Custer had sent across the river. Reno, we were informed, had been engaged by a greatly superior number of hostiles, but after hard fighting and heavy losses had managed to retreat back across the river. Benteen encountered no Indians and eventually returned across the river, uniting with Reno.

The question is still an open one whether Reno should have gone to Custer's rescue after Reno knew Custer to be engaged and probably in need of support. Some army men say one thing and some another. Reno was tried for cowardice and neglect of duty, but acquitted. Nevertheless, my personal feeling

Sitting Bull. NELSON A. MILES. *PERSONAL RECOLLECTIONS AND OBSERVATIONS.*

is that he should have made the attempt. It was a slim chance and possibly a forlorn hope, but such things are a part of the profession of arms. Custer would have done as much had the situations been reversed.

The following winter, I was with the escort that was marching two or three hundred Cheyenne and Arapaho prisoners of war from Camp Robinson to old Fort Crisper on the North Platte. In the band were several Cheyennes who had participated in the defeat of Custer. There was also an Arapaho whom I knew. His name was Friday. He had been educated in St. Louis and spoke English like a college student. He had heard the story of the Little Bighorn from the Cheyennes, and he relayed it to me as we marched along. This story contains amplifications of the Crow's version, some of which I have never seen in print. He said Chief Gall, of the Teton Sioux, was the warrior that killed Custer, and that one enlisted man on a white horse nearly escaped alive. This trooper somehow managed to ride through the encircling attackers and dash upstream. He was pursued for a distance and, believing capture inevitable, deliberately shot himself after the hostiles had abandoned the chase.

He also told me a few things about Sitting Bull which do not agree with most recorded history. Sitting Bull was not a warrior, as many suppose, but a medicine man, or priest, of Chief Gall's band. It was the duty of medicine men to accompany their warriors into battle and invoke the aid of the Great Spirit to bring victory. At the Little Bighorn, Gall assigned Sitting Bull to the Cheyennes, whom he thought to be in need of spiritual assistance. But on seeing the size of Custer's command, Sitting Bull took his family across the stream and was well on his way to safer places when he saw that the whites were getting the worst of it. Then he turned around and joined the Cheyennes in the mad rush to be in at the death.

The Cheyennes hooted him for his cowardice, and when the fight was over, Gall tongue-lashed Sitting Bull and slapped his face and kicked his backsides. I believe this story implicitly, although I know it may come as a shock to many believers of the numerous legends that surround Sitting Bull. Perhaps no Indian of his generation is better known. In the popular mind, he is given credit for the defeat of Custer. He was quite a character, certainly, but I think that he was a coward at heart, which was a rare thing among Indians of that day and time. On the other hand, one scarcely ever hears of Crazy Horse. He has, I mean, left no impression on the popular mind. Yet Crazy Horse was the greatest strategist among the western Indians, and Dull Knife and Gall, who are likewise devoid of popular reputations, were the equal of any combat leaders, white or red, of that period—a statement which is not intended to depreciate the ability or valor of our army leaders in the least. But other writers, and very justly, have given them their due.

Brave Boys are They: The Newspaper Correspondents with Crook's Army

ANONYMOUS

(Denver) *Rocky Mountain News,* August 8, 1876

In order to correctly estimate the news we receive from the commands now operating against the Sioux, the following personnel of the correspondents now with General Crook's command will be useful. It will be observed that they are mentioned alphabetically, and an artist who furnishes the material from the spot claims that in neither white nor black paint has he been too profuse. The sketches are from life, and the peculiarities of each are set down faithfully so far as they go, though necessarily brief.

[Reuben B.] Davenport of the New York *Herald* is an American by birth, about thirty-five years of age, and five feet six or seven inches in height, black hair and whiskers, gray eyes, regular features, and rather light complexion. Davenport represents the *Herald,* and when we say represents, we mean all that the word implies. His saddle, bridle, blankets, haversack, canteen, etc. are all marked conspicuously, "New York *Herald.*" He has not branded his horse "*Herald,*" but he has got him so he looks like a *Herald* horse. In fact, everything about him goes to herald the fact that he represents the *Herald.*

Davenport is always hungry. Not for food, but for news. Whenever he talks with you, you are impressed with the fact that he is suffering for news, and if you fail to tell him anything out of which he can frame an item, the look of disappointment that comes over his face is painful to behold. The temptation, then, to give Davenport news, though it is manufactured out of whole cloth, is very great, and the young men of the command have occasionally perpetrated "whoppers" on him.

In writing about the Rosebud fight, he (and probably through the representation of some storyteller) states to his journal that General Crook sent a column in pursuit of the Indian village, which he recalled after he found that the village was located in exactly the opposite direction, and upon the basis of this and other statements, the *Herald* berates General Crook with column after column of abuse. The facts were that General Crook did not discover, nor was he informed, that the village was located in the opposite direction, nor any other direction than that in which the column was marching, and the change in direction was made by the flank and not the rear, the column moving on the flank of the Indians for the purpose of relieving the pressure brought to bear on Colonel Royall's command.[1] Probably Davenport did not mean to misrepresent, but he took this, as he does other cock-and-bull stories, for news, and the world will read the lie before the truth gets started.

[John F.] Finerty of the Chicago *Times* is an Irishman, and about thirty-six or thirty-seven years of age. It has been alleged by some that he is seven feet in height, but this is not credited. It is not believed that his altitude is more than six feet two, but his great lack of longitude and circumference gives him the appearance of greater height. He is undoubtedly a tall man, so tall in fact that it is difficult to tell just the color of his hair and eyes, though the latter are believed to be brown and the former the rich auburn so common in the Emerald Isle. In complexion, he is decidedly rosy. He will go anywhere for news. When the first skirmish with the Sioux took place on Tongue River, and a couple of companies of cavalry were ordered across to dislodge the savages from the bluffs, Finerty rode at the head of the column, his coat off, carbine on his pommel, pipe in his mouth, and his tall form looming up like that of the mythical Don Quixote when he set out to regulate the affairs of the world.

When Finerty is on horseback, he has to bend his knees to keep his feet off the ground, so when he got back from Sibley's last scout,[2] minus his horse, hungry and thirsty, it was freely asserted, and by many believed, that the way he lost his horse was when the Cheyenne chief White Antelope got after him, he forgot himself, straightened his legs, and his horse walked out from under him. How he came to get away after that is a mystery. But when he writes about the troops being willing to storm the gates of hell, he means it, and if they ever do so rash an act, Finerty will be there, and he won't be in the rear of the command, either.

[Andrew S.] Burt, an army officer who writes for the Chicago *Tribune,* is an American by birth and a captain of one of the infantry companies serving with the command, a short, rugged man about five feet seven in height, thirty years of age, black hair, gray eyes, dark mustache and goatee, and regular features. With his short, solid figure in field costume, and mounted on a stout-built white pony, he appeared more like Sancho Panza than any other celebrated character mentioned in history or romance that we can think of.

During the march from Fort Fetterman north, Burt had a penchant for riding about the country with a single orderly, hunting for game, signs, etc., and it was current to the command that the Sioux would get him some morning, though he insisted that no Sioux pony could catch his white pony. He was generally known in the command as "Burt's cow," until he got into camp on the Tongue River, where Burt created no little amusement by challenging any pony in the command to run against his, for corn or coin. Ponies were forthcoming at once, Colonel [Alexander] Chambers's being selected as the fleetest, and coin being scarce, a can of corn was wagered, and the race came off. Betting on the outside was freely indulged in, and the odds against the white pony were three to one. Great was the surprise when the white pony not only won the race, but distanced his competitor and beat all the others they could bring against him, fully establishing the reputation of being the "liveliest cow" in the herd.

The triumph, however, was of short duration, for less than an hour after the race, the Sioux made an attack on the camp, and the only casualty in the infantry was Burt's white pony, killed by the side of his master's tent. As an officer, Burt is brave, attentive to his duties, jolly, and withal popular with his fellow officers. As a correspondent, he is clear and conscientious, his letters from the Black Hills last summer being among the best.

[T. C.] MacMillan of the Chicago *Inter-Ocean* is a Scotchman, about thirty-two or thirty-three years of age; five foot eight in height, fair hair and eyes, a slender, pale-faced man in very poor health. How he came to stay with the command as long as he did can only be accounted for by a nervous energy that will hold out long after his slender physique gives way.

MacMillan is a solid writer and can be relied upon. It is not believed that any inducements of possible gain to himself or the paper he represents could be strong enough to persuade him to write anything he does not believe to be true. He left the command immediately after the Rosebud fight and is universally regarded as a fair, impartial correspondent.[3]

[Robert E.] Strahorn (Alter Ego) of the *Rocky Mountain News* is the youngest Bohemian on the list, being not over twenty-eight years of age. He is about five feet nine in height, solid built, dark hair and whiskers, black eyes, regular features, and an American beyond no doubt. Though young, he has spent a great deal of time in the West and has become thoroughly familiar with frontier life. As a correspondent, he ranks with the best, his letters being not only correct in detail, but also choice bits of literature, whether he essays the serious or lighter words.

[Joseph] Wasson of the New York *Tribune* is a genius. He is an American, about thirty-nine years of age, five feet nine inches in height, sandy complexion, light red hair and moustache, gray eyes. Crossing the Great Plains to California when a mere boy, he has wandered around on the Pacific Coast as an editor, miner, and correspondent; thence back to the States, and across the sea to Europe. He is by nature, inclination, and education a model Bohemian.

Though good-natured and affable, he is a man of positive opinions and character, and as stubborn as a mule. The reason we say stubborn as a mule is that we know of where we speak. One day on the march, Wasson's horse gave out, and he was obliged to ride a mule. Now, that mule was possessed with all the qualities that grace the mule family, and when Wasson wanted him to go in one direction, he wanted to go to the opposite. The march was a long one, and officers offered to loan him a horse, told him to ride in the ambulance, and all to no purpose—the irrepressible conflict went on. Night came, and when camp was reached and the orderlies came for the riding animals, Wasson was seated on a log, the bridle rein in his hand, and the mule facing him, both completely used up, made a picture not easily forgotten. He had ridden the mule into camp, "You bet your life."

Wasson is a clear, able writer; he gives you facts, boiled down and in language than can be easily understood. Take them all in all, the correspondents with General Crook's command are able men, Finerty and Davenport being about the only ones who imagine themselves to be military geniuses, and the former generally takes his out in talk, while the latter, in committing what the young officers of Colonel Royall's staff stuff him with and tells how, if the command had moved thus and so, and the column had deployed thus, then the Sioux would have been annihilated, etc., he simply demonstrates that correspondents are rarely good military critics. Besides, in matters of this kind, correspondents are apt, by careless handling of professional topics, to inure the reputation of officers unjustly; reputations that have been acquired by years of hard and faithful service, and that should not be soiled by the careless shedding of too much ink from a correspondent's pen.

From Fort Fetterman to the Rosebud

JAMES E. H. FOSTER[1]

Chicago *Tribune*, July 5, 1876

Journal of Our Correspondent with the Expedition
May 29 — Marched from our camp on the north bank of the Platte River, opposite Fort Fetterman, at 1:00 P.M. today, the column being composed of troops commanded by Brig. Gen. George Crook. One hundred wagons accompany us, together with 205 pack mules, the latter under charge of chief packer Moore, who has served with General Crook in Oregon and Arizona.

The march was for about twelve miles over a miserable country, the only vegetation being composed of sagebrush and cactus. The sand was deep in places, making it severe work on the mules to drag the wagons through. We reached our camp on Sage Creek in due time, and found that the creek was a succession of mud holes, not very well supplied with surface water. The weather has been hot and sultry, and the dense clouds of fine dust thrown up by the hoofs of the two thousand and odd animals did not add materially to the delights of the day's journey.

May 30 — Marched from Sage Creek to South Fork of the Cheyenne, where the last expedition issued all their fresh beef to Sitting Bull, the herd being captured and a herder killed on the night of their arrival here.[2] In view of the fact that we have some fifty beeves with us, our poet-laureate has propounded the following conundrum:

> *If Sitting Bull doth steal our meat,*
> *What shall we do for grub to eat?*

Echo answers — that is to say, Lieutenant Bubb, our commissary[3] — half-rations of bacon.

The country passed over today is a barren waste of sand, sage, and cactus, and fit for nothing but for a place of punishment for those very wicked men for whom orthodox Hell would be too good. Weather uncomfortably chilly all day, and decidedly cold after sundown.

May 31—Marched to the Dry Fork of the Cheyenne River. Its desolation is complete beyond all description, and for "pure cussedness," it will discount the Desert of Sahara. Weather in keeping with the country.

June 1—Marched on this glorious summer's day, with blinding drifts of snow in our faces, to the Dry Fork of Powder River. Pumpkin Buttes in sight all day, which was a consolation, as it gave us something to talk about.

June 2—Reached Powder River at old Fort Reno, coming on the north side of the river quite near to the site of the old post; a few chimneys and broken-down adobe walls are all that is left of this station, which was abandoned early in 1869 by request of the great, unterrified Sioux nation, who said that they would not love the peace commissioners unless all the soldiers were taken south of the North Platte River.

A squadron of the 3rd Cavalry, consisting of C and G Troops, had left Fetterman on May 26, under command of Captain Van Vliet,[4] with orders to come to this point and meet the Crow Indians, who were expected to be here by the latter part of May. The troops came through by rapid marches, but found no Crows. Frank Grouard, a noted guide, was started out tonight with Louis Richard (pronounced Reshaw) and one other to push through to the Crow agency in Montana and try and procure the services of a couple of hundred of the Indians, as they are valuable auxiliaries in fighting the Sioux. Their natural qualities as trailers, and in finding the whereabouts of Sioux villages, cannot be equaled by the most experienced white man on the plains. The trip of our messengers is one fraught with danger, but they are brave men, and full of grit and endurance. May they get through safely and succeed in their mission is the heartfelt wish of every heart in the command.

June 3—Marched 27 miles today to Crazy Woman's Fork of Powder River. A signal smoke was seen to our right; and in the same direction, but so far off as to render it out of the question to tell with certainty whether they were buffalo or men and horses, moving objects were seen on the hills. We know that the buffalo and Indian both roam in this country, and every man in the column is at liberty to take his individual choice in the matter and suit his fancy as to whether the objects seen are the hostile savages, or only a portion of the aforesaid hostiles' commissary train. The country improves perceptibly as we march northward.

June 4—Marched to the Clear Fork of Powder River today. It is a beautiful stream of clear, cold water, which comes leaping and bounding over its rocky bed from the venerable, snow-clad mountain range which we have admired so much as we marched along today. Fish are plenty, but being suckers, the baited hook has no temptations for them. General Crook shot quite a number, and his example was followed by others. A party of miners who are with us report that they found good prospects on this stream. Two white men reported to General Crook this evening, representing that they belong to a party of sixty miners who are on their way from the

Crook's command crossing Crazy Woman's Fork, June 3, 1876.
HARPER'S WEEKLY, 1876.

Black Hills to the Bighorn Mountains, having given up the former "goldfields" as worthless. We passed through a camp of sixty-five miners the other day, who left a written paper stating that they were en route from Montana to the Black Hills. So honors are easy between the two mining districts. The two who came into camp reported to the general that they had seen no Indians, but had crossed large numbers of pony trails, all going north. They had no lodge-poles with them, and it is thought that they are going to interview Colonel Gibbon's column, and have sent their families into the agencies to be fed and clothed by the government while the war continues. A very convenient arrangement for them.

June 5 — Marched to old Fort Phil Kearny today, a post admirably situated to be harassed by Indians, as it can be approached on almost any side, under good cover, to within easy rifle range. There is perhaps no military post in the country west of the Missouri around whose short but eventful history more tales of blood congregate in crimson clusters than around this. Established in the early summer of 1866 and abandoned in the spring of 1869, over two hundred dead that now sleep in this abandoned post cemetery all lost their lives in its immediate vicinity. During the time that Colonel Carrington was in command, the garrison were in a state of siege all the while. Men were shot and killed within a few hundred yards of the flag. The advance wagons of supply trains leaving the post were hurriedly going into park to resist the enemy before the rear of the train had left the quartermaster's corral; while, within two miles of the post, Captains Fetterman and Brown of the 18th Infantry, and Lieutenant Grummond of the 27th, together with eighty-one soldiers, were killed by a large band of Sioux led by Red Cloud, Red Dog, and Red Leaf on December 22, 1866.

The story of Fetterman and his ill-fated band is too well known to need repetition here. Their bodies lie buried in a trench in the graveyard, and over the remains of our gallant and unfortunate comrades rise the ruins of a brick pillar, half destroyed by the accursed hands of their murderers, who are too utterly lost to all the attributes of humanity to respect the corpse of a brave foe. Would it not be a fitting mark of respect to the memory of the departed brave, to remove their bones to some fitting place where the coyotes do not delve and the wild red man cannot cast continually upon his dead enemy.

The graveyard at Old Phil Kearny is but one more sad commentary on the gratitude—or absolute want of it—of this our model republic. I saw within the ruins of the old enclosure, which once surrounded the burial place, human bones lying unburied and bleaching in the sun, having been doubtless exhumed by the coyote, a small, cowardly cross between the fox and the wolf that infests this country . The ghoul of the Western Plains, he will eat carrion and offal of all descriptions, and positively enjoys the old bridle or piece of mule harness. He always looks hungry and savage, but is too cowardly to attack anything more formidable than a dying antelope. They will collect by legions around an old buffalo bull that is dying of old age and, as the doctors say, lack of vitality; and, instead of attacking the poor old wretch, although he has not got enough strength left to wag his head, they will circle around him and howl and yell at a respectable distance, until the breath is out of his body.

When we came into camp today, the frame of a wickiup was found near which still burned a fire, that had evidently been abandoned as the head of our column came into the valley. An ax on which were fresh bloodstains, and which had, to all appearances, been used in butchering some animal, was also found nearby. How these Indians must have agitated the gravel when they saw our command coming.

Within about six miles of our camp today, we passed within a short distance of Lake De Smet, a sheet of water very beautiful to look upon, but remarkably unpleasant to take, as it is composed mainly of Glauber salts. The lake, which is about 2 $1/2$ miles by 1,200 yards in size, is named in honor of the famous Father De Smet, a French missionary of the early days who devoted his whole life in an endeavor to lessen the moral turpitude of the American savage—with what success, the high moral Indian agents and the people who live on the frontier each have their own opinions.

June 6—As usual, the reveille sounded off at 4:00 A.M. After marching about 2 $1/2$ miles, we came to the exact spot where the massacre of December 21, 1866, occurred, and saw the identical pile of rocks around the base of which were found the bodies of Fetterman, Brown, and Grummond, and from among which Wheatley, the guide, fired over a hundred shots from his Henry rifle before he, too—the last of the unfortunate detachment—

gave up his life. A few yards farther down the hill, covered carefully with a buffalo robe, was found the corpse of Trumpeter Metzgar, C Troop, 2nd Cavalry, who, when his ammunition gave out, fought the enemy with his trumpet. He was the only one in the whole command that was not scalped and otherwise mutilated. Red Cloud said afterward that they spared him the indignities lavished on the others by reason of the great courage displayed in one so young. On all sides of the scene of the massacre are ravines overgrown with brush, and in these lay concealed all but thirty or forty of the Indians, who acted as a decoy to lead the soldiers into the trap. But the story of Fetterman's sad fate is too well known to bear repetition. Suffice it to say that the ground is admirably adapted for an ambush; five thousand men could be completely hidden from view within five hundred yards of the road, at the point where it occurred.

Marched through a magnificent country, admirably adapted for grazing, and camped on Prairie Dog or Peno Creek—nobody is absolutely certain which.[5] We have left the C. F. Smith road to our left and are now supposed to be on Jim Bridger's "cutoff," which is principally distinguished by the fact that after one train has passed over it, no one else could ever be induced to try it again. We had a fine thunderstorm this evening, lasting for about two hours.

June 7—Marched down the creek and found that we were on the trail of the column which struck Crazy Horse's village last March.

The first death in the command occurred this morning in camp. Pvt. Francis Tiernay, B Troop (Meinhold's), 3rd Cavalry, accidentally shot himself with his pistol some days ago. It appears that just after the command had reached camp, Tiernay was engaged in chopping wood and, finding his pistol in the way, took it off and threw it carelessly on the ground. The hammer, striking a stone or other hard substance, exploded a cartridge, which struck him in the thigh, and the ball, ranging upwards, lodged in his bowels. The body was brought with us to our camp on Tongue River, near the mouth of Prairie Dog Creek, and buried at retreat with all the honors of war. All the officers and soldiers off duty, from General Crook down, attended the funeral, which altogether was an impressive affair. A huge stone that required the united strength of ten men to lift was placed over the grave, and a suitable inscription carved thereon. The deceased was a native of New York.

Our march down the creek was more difficult than any that preceded it. I Troop, 3rd Cavalry, was in the advance and marched two hours and a half before the balance of the command. We all put this up as the permanent camp, but nobody knows but General Crook, and he won't tell. The general doesn't make any confidants. If an officer asks him a question, he doesn't "sit on" him, as we call snubbing out here, but just looks pleased at the interest manifested in affairs by the inquiring officer, and sometimes gives him an answer which leaves the querist more completely in the dark than before, but generally simply says, "I don't know," which answers the purpose just as well.

June 8—In camp, waiting for the guides who left us at Reno, and who are expected to bring with them our Crow allies.

Last night, a small party of Indians came to the opposite side of the river and signified a desire to "talk." A half-breed who is employed as packer[6] accommodated them, and his translation of the conference is as follows:

Noble Red Man—"Have your Crows come into camp yet?"

Packer—"No."

(How in the world did those rascals know that we expected any Crows?)

N.R.M.—"Where are your half-breeds?"

No answer from our half-breed. Then they wanted to know where General Crook's tent was; how many soldiers and wagons we had; and wound up by suggesting that we had better not cross Tongue River if we ever wanted to see our families again. The latter remark might be construed into a threat.

Since last night's affair, a great deal of anxiety is felt for Frank [Grouard] and his companions, as it is said that the inquiry in regard to our "Crows" and "half-breeds" was made in a mocking tone, seemingly to imply that they knew more about their whereabouts than we did. This afternoon, a hunting party discovered the trail of five Indians crossing the river above the camp and going in a southeasterly direction. A party of I Troop, 2nd Cavalry, got a pony from this party, which they triumphantly conducted to camp. Just before retreat, quite a little excitement was produced in camp by the report that large numbers of Indians were seen coming up the river. A field glass exposed the cheat, however, it being found that the supposed war parties were simply clumps of bushes. The originators of the report were thoroughly laughed at, and quiet and monotony were again restored.

Tonight Captain Dewees,[7] with a troop, 2nd Cavalry, was sent over the river and ambuscaded, in order to capture any Indians of a conversational turn of mind that might approach. At about 9:30 P.M., when everybody had turned in, or was just about to, three shots were heard from over the river, and we all turned out to see the fireworks and hear the serenade. Something being the matter with the orchestra, the celebration was postponed. We waited half an hour patiently, but all remained quiet.

June 9—This morning we learned that one of the men could not resist the temptation to fire upon a deer that was approaching the river to drink. He will probably be able to resist better next time.

It is getting very monotonous in camp, and we use up a good portion of the time discussing the general plan of the campaign and the whereabouts of the Sioux. The most generally accepted opinion appears to be

Signaling for a talk. EDGAR B. BRONSON. *REMINISCENCES OF A RANCHMAN.*

that all the Indians have left this part of the country and are now on the Yellowstone watching Gibbon and skirmishing after Terry. Supporters of this theory base their opinion mainly on the fact that we have not been molested; that none of our camps have been fired into; and that our column, starting from Fetterman so long after Gibbon and Terry had taken the field, concentrated the vigilance of the savages on them alone, and consequently they are not yet aware of our invasion of their country, which, by the way, is not their country but "Ab-sa-ra-ka," or the country of the Crows, from which tribe the Sioux have taken it.

At last they have come. At about 6:30 P.M., the infantry picket on the heights across Prairie Dog Creek was seen to manifest considerable emo-

"A number of Indians were seen running about the crest."
FRANK LESLIE'S ILLUSTRATED NEWSPAPER, 1876.

tion, displaying it by firing his piece and running around in a circle in the approved manner always practiced when Indians are seen approaching. We had not time to even express and form an opinion as to what was the matter with the picket, when a rattling volley was fired into the camp from the heights on the other side of Tongue River, and a number of Indians were seen running about the crest of the cliff, firing their breechloaders and making themselves especially unpleasant and remarkably noisy, while one who appeared to be principal musician in the serenade kept galloping up and down as though he had lost something and was in a great hurry to find it. The packers and teamsters, of course, opened a perfect fusillade on the rocks and crevices across the river, laying a first-class foundation for a lead mine in the face of the cliff, while the soldiers got their arms and quietly awaited events, not being allowed to fire by their officers, as the distance was too great to make it effective.

It being found that the Indians evidently liked the fun, and as the bullets were "zipping" and "swishing" around in an unpleasant manner, it was determined to clear the heights in a manner that would keep them cleared permanently. A battalion of the 3rd Cavalry, consisting of M, E, I, and A Troops of that regiment, and accompanied by Captains Mills, Sutorius, and Andrews, and Lieutenants Lawson, Schwatka, and Foster, was designated for this duty. They saddled up promptly, and riding straight for the river, crossed it and gained a grove of heavy timber. Here they dismounted and, leaving their horses, pushed up the cliff on foot, deployed as skirmishers—M on the right, I on the left, A right center, and E left center, Captain Mills commanding the battalions. When halfway up the heights, the Indians abandoned their original position and retreated to a crest that flanked the original line of our skirmishers. The battalion swung around to the left and carried this position, as did those following, driving the enemy for over a mile across a rocky country, cut up with ravines and admirably calculated for a strong defense. The line came up on the last crest as thoroughly dressed as though on parade or drill. As night was closing in, and the Indians had gone home to tell all about it and send runners in to the agencies with flaming accounts of how they had killed a great many soldiers and whipped the whole command, the troops were withdrawn, and the heights opposite the camp occupied by B Troop, 2nd Cavalry.

Our total loss in the whole affair was two men slightly wounded; one man seriously shot through the tail of his blouse, but it is thought he will recover; several mules and horses shot, among which was a troop horse of E Troop, 3rd Cavalry, seriously in the leg; a private horse of Major Burt's, which had to be shot and killed, as its leg was broken; and one of Lieutenant Robertson's, which will recover.

Officers of the 9th Infantry, who occupied the heights across Prairie Dog Creek, as an attack was expected from that quarter, variously estimate the number of Indians all the way from one hundred to two hundred. As the position which they occupied overlooked the whole ground, they are better able to judge than anyone else. Take it altogether, it was a very lively little affair, and as a picket of the 2nd Cavalry knocked an Indian off his pony as a party were attempting to cross the river above camp, we feel that we are a little ahead of [the Indians] in that line; but he has the honors as far as mules and horses are concerned. Quite a number of tents were perforated, and Captain Luhn of the 4th Infantry was seriously injured in the ridge pole of his tent. Captain Mills of the 3rd Cavalry was hurt in his stovepipe and very nearly lost his dinner, as his cook was just engaged in his culinary duties when the ball came along. A number had their feelings hurt because the Indians could not be induced to give the battalion who went after them a respectable fight. If they had done what everybody had expected, they could have inflicted serious loss on us as the line ascended the hill; but they appeared to have a pressing engagement farther back.

Some of the younger officers, for a moment forgetting the whistling of the balls, went for their army registers, when they saw three captains and the senior lieutenant in the regiment going up the face of the cliff then occupied by the Indians, and stood, pencil in hand, ready to make all necessary corrections. One of them immediately applied for admission into the very independent order of grumblers and growlers and said that this thing was about played out; he had lost seven files since he left Fetterman, just by not having senior officers shot when in all reason they should have been. Remarkable as it may appear, the captains do not look on it in this way.

June 10—A troop of cavalry is now kept on the bluffs from whence the attack of yesterday was made, and we are all discussing today the probabilities of having a "serenade" from the south side of camp tonight. Orders issued this evening to break camp in the morning.

June 11—At 6:00 A.M., E Troop, 3rd Cavalry, under the temporary command of Lieutenant Foster, crossed the river and relieved Captain Vroom,[8] who had occupied the bluff all night. E Company remained there, with pickets out, until the last soldier had marched out of camp, and then, descending the cliff, remounted and followed, joining the other troop of the rearguard squadron on the east side of the river. The command moved back over their old trail about eleven miles to the last crossing of Prairie Dog Creek; then, striking westward, crossed over the divide to Goose Creek, where they are now encamped, with plenty of wood, water, and grass, all of the best quality.

Everybody again supposes that we are to leave the infantry and wagon train here and start out with pack mules; but nobody knows anything about it but General Crook, and he has a faculty for silence that is absolutely astonishing. There is one thing very certain: None of the general's plans will ever be discussed until after they are executed—a priceless quality in a commanding officer. Grant is loquacious when compared with him.

June 12—A young officer asked General Crook last evening whether it would not be as well to wait until the wagon train went in, and send letters by it instead of intrusting them to a messenger who had to ride almost two hundred miles through an Indian country. "How do you know that the wagon train is going in?" asked the general. The result is that today we all doubt whether the train is going back at all, or whether it was ever intended it should go back. It is generally believed that we are waiting for the arrival of either the Shoshones or Crows, who should be here now. It is part of the plan to use the friendly Indians to find where the hostile villages are, and then the whole cavalry command will pull out at dark some evening, and if they can't reach the point by daybreak, march within a night's travel of the point to be struck, lay up all day, and push on the next night, surround the enemy by daybreak, and "scoop them in," as it were. We have all made up our minds that we have got to stay here until Sitting Bull's wives are all widows, and Crazy Horse and Little Bad Man have both gone to join their distinguished ancestors. We will have to do this if it takes all summer, and next winter too, and we could do it in a very little while with good guides and trailers. We can trust the Crows and Shoshones, for they hate the Sioux and love to steal.

June 14—At about 5:00 P.M., the Crows, numbering 175, came into camp; two hours afterward, eighty Shoshones arrived. All during the night, they kept

In the camp of the Crow and Shoshone scouts.
FRANK LESLIE'S ILLUSTRATED NEWSPAPER, 1876.

up a fearful racket, beating their tom-toms and howling in a manner calculated to aggravate the most even-tempered individual, provided he wanted to sleep. It appears that the Indian who came down the opposite bank of Tongue River on the night of the seventh was a Crow, but being replied to in the Sioux dialect, he became alarmed and left. When the main party reached this camp, they found our trail leading back toward the south, and supposing that we had left the country, wanted to return to their villages, but were induced to return by Captain Burt of the 9th Infantry, who was known to many of them. Grouard having come into camp and represented the state of affairs, the captain volunteered to go after them.

June 15—We learn today that a Sioux village of seven hundred lodges—which means 2,500 warriors—is on the Rosebud about forty-five miles from here.[9] We march tomorrow at 5:00 A.M., the infantry accompanying us on pack mules. Each man carries one hundred rounds of ammunition and four days' rations. We expect to have the biggest Indian fight, about the eighteenth, that has ever taken place west of the Mississippi, and finally settle the business for the Sioux Nation, or else.

The only pack animals allowed with the column will be two mules laden with medical supplies and surgical instruments. All the doctors, and sixteen volunteers from the packers, go along.

June 16—Reveille at 3:30 A.M. Marched down Goose Creek ten miles to Tongue River, crossed it, and struck across the worst country that it has fallen to my lot to travel in, always excepting the Badlands. It is broken by barren ridges, and its only vegetation is cactus and sagebrush.

At about 2:00 P.M., the country began to improve, and at three o'clock the column was halted and closed up in a well-sheltered valley, it being reported that a large body of Indians were ahead of us. Finding that it was nothing but a herd of buffalo, the command was unsaddled and rested for an hour and a half.

At 7:30 P.M., we went into camp in a hollow square—animals in the center—on the Rosebud.

June 17—Reveille at 3:00 A.M. Marched at six o'clock. We marched down the stream, the 3rd Cavalry on the left flank, and the infantry and 2nd Cavalry on the opposite. About three miles down the creek, the Indians evidently had discovered something, and after some little delay, the whole command was halted, unsaddled, and ordered to graze their animals. We all expect a night's march and a fight in the morning, as we are told that we bivouac here. The men, with the promptness to use any materials at hand that may promote their comfort, are cutting sticks on the bank of the creek and erecting frames upon which they hang their saddle blankets, affording excellent shade. Everybody is speculating on the probable result of tonight's march and the morning's fight, when a dropping skirmish fire is heard on our right, and the battle of Rosebud Hills has begun.

The Shoshones and Crows dash about madly on their ponies, and the firing increases in volume every moment, coming nearer and nearer, until at length our allies break over the ridge. The 2nd Cavalry, dismounted and deployed on the right, and the infantry on the left, move up in beautiful order, occupying the crest. D and I of the 2nd each have a man wounded, while Cain,[10] of the 4th Infantry, away to the left, loses three of his best men in as many minutes.

The firing is now a continuous rattle, and having saddled, the 3rd are ordered over at a sharp trot. The 1st Battalion, Brevet Lieutenant Colonel

Mills commanding, and consisting of Troops I, A, E, and M, 3rd Cavalry, were led by Colonel Royall, at a rapid gait, through a depression in the ridge to the left of the position just carried by the infantry and, debouching into a broad valley with a ridge on either side, went by company left-front into line at a gallop. Andrews[11] was ordered to deploy and carry the ridge on the left, which he did in gallant style, driving a strong force of the enemy before him, Mills, Sutorius, and Lawson carrying the ridge on the right in like manner. Sounding the charge, the gallant fellows dashed forward, their impetuous onslaught driving the enemy like chaff before the winds of heaven, the officers leading with a pluck that deserves all praise.

Mills was soon ordered to halt and hold ground taken, whilst Andrews, having detached Lieutenant Foster to clear a ridge with the second platoon of I Troop, pressed on under a galling fire and drove the enemy from a strong position among some rocks, which he occupied and held until positively ordered to fall back.

Foster's platoon, making a left half-wheel, plunged down the side of the hill, across the valley, and were on the crest opposite in less time than it takes to write it. The enemy, although superior in force, position, and arms, broke before the gallant little party and were driven pell-mell from the ridge, occupying a crest further on. Halting at the end of the ridge, having changed his direction so as to conform to the general direction of the line, the horses were allowed a moment's breath, and again charging on their second position, he carried it and, swinging to the right, dashed at a party of the enemy who were running down the valley, giving them the pistol as they rode. In a moment, a volley was fired from a body of Sioux on a point to the left and front, and seeing that to farther follow would bring his command under the point and expose them to great loss, the chief of platoon wheeled to the left and took position under cover about three hundred yards from the point whence he was last assailed. Thinking that the forward movement so well begun by Mills's battalion would be continued, Foster charged and carried this point also, sweeping the ridge as usual.

Finding that the balance of the battalion were not up with him, the command was halted, occupying a strong position at the farther end of the crest, with the intention of holding it until the line came up. Observing a body of Indians, some two hundred in number, moving around on his right, with the evident intention of cutting off the party, the officer in command withdrew the platoon slowly, being assailed as he did so by an uncomfortably hot fire from his rear. Continuing the retreat slowly, occasionally firing on the enemy as they rode, the platoon had fallen back about six hundred yards to another hill, when an orderly from Colonel Royall and Pvt. [Herbert] Weaver of I Troop, 3rd Cavalry, who had gallantly run the gauntlet of a sharp fire to carry the message, reached the platoon with positive orders to fall back at as rapid a gait as possible to our lines, as the enemy were trying to surround them. In order to do this, a steep hill had to be descended, an eight-foot dry ditch at the bottom to be passed, and a plain of seven hundred yards to be crossed. Starting down the hill at a trot, the party had gotten halfway to the ditch, when the crest just abandoned was occupied by the enemy, who at once commenced firing rapidly. Taking the charging gait, the ditch was passed and the open plain gained, when a sweeping discharge came from the left and right, wounding Private [Charles] Stuart through the hand and forearm and Private [James] O'Brien in the arm, and hitting a horse in the hock joint. In a moment more the platoon had rejoined the troop, and the wounded were en route to the field hospital.

Royall's forward movement had been checked by General Crook,[12] who desired to concentrate the whole command and move upon the Indian village, which was said to be seven miles down the Rosebud. The 2nd Cavalry, with M, E, and a part of A Troops, 3rd Cavalry, twenty men having been detailed to operate with the Crows—all under the command of Captain Mills—were ordered to march at as rapid a gait as the horses could endure down the creek to the village, carry it, and hold it until the remainder of the command came up.

Following the creek for 6 miles, being accompanied by Lieutenant Bourke, aide to the general, and Frank Grouard, the guide, Mills was overtaken by an order from General Crook, carried by Captain Nickerson,[13] and ordered to change direction to the left and, making a detour, return to the main body. In the meanwhile, C and G of the 3rd, under Van Vliet and Crawford, who had driven the enemy from the ridge back of camp and occupied it, were drawn back, and B (Meinhold's) of the 3rd, taken from Royall's line and concentrated on the hill now occupied by the infantry and the field hospital, with Colonel Royall, with D, L, and F, of Henry's Battalion, and I Company of the 3rd, of Mills's Battalion, now held the ridge along which A, E, and M had charged earlier in the day.

It is estimated that from five to seven hundred Indians were pressing this battalion from the front and left flank, a number of shots coming from their left and rear. This fire was especially annoying to the left of the line, which, being held by a part of Andrews's troop and a few men who had become separated from their proper commands, induced a small number of men to break away, saying that they could stand a fire from the front, but, when it enfiladed them and came from the rear, it was rather rough. The officer in charge appealed to them to go back, saying, "Men we must hold the hill." "All right, sir," replied one of them doggedly; "if you say so, we'll hold it till hell freezes over," and they went back and stayed until the order came to abandon the position. As soon as abandoned, the crest was at once occupied by the enemy, who poured in a terribly strong fire on the troops as they hastened across the intervening valley. This line was held for ten minutes, and again the order came from General Crook to fall back, as he wished these four companies to join him in one grand rush for the village.[14]

The Indians, seeing the soldiers retreating, imagined they were beaten and, being encouraged by the thought, displayed a dash and courage not before seen on that day, and seldom seen in Indian warfare. Occupying a position farther to the rear, on a crest that was destined to be the scene of the hottest encounter that had ever taken place between Indians and soldiers, the gallant little battalion, now reduced by wounded, details necessary to carry them back to the hospital, and horse holders to not more than seventy men all told,[15] firmly awaited the onslaught of the enemy, who were now pouring in a rolling, continuous fire from rocks, ravines, and cover of all descriptions. The company officers—Henry, Vroom, Andrews, Reynolds, and Foster—remaining still mounted as they had been all day, and being ably and gallantly assisted by 1st Sgt. John Henry of I Troop of the 3rd, rode up and down the line, encouraging the men and cautioning them to waste no ammunition, but wait for the charge. And soon it came.

With "Yip! Yip! Hi-Yah! Hi-Yah," they dashed at the line at a gallop. The skirmishers gave back a few paces, but instantly returning, poured a withering volley into the rascals, repulsing them with considerable loss.

The horses were about one hundred yards farther back, in a ravine, and the enemy getting on the right flank, poured an enfilading fire into the troops and threatened the safety of the animals. At about this time, Col. Guy V. Henry, captain 3rd Cavalry, was shot through the apex of both cheekbones; men were dropping and, it being necessary to send them back out of the way, the gallant little line already too small, was rapidly thin-

Dismounted—the fourth troopers moving the lead horses. CENTURY MAGAZINE, 1872.

ning, and evidently knowing that an order to mount would be followed by a dash of the enemy, who would charge the moment they saw the skirmish line give way, and catch the men at a disadvantage when mounting, Colonel Royall, who gallantly stayed with the battalion throughout, sent Lieutenant Lemly[16] to ask General Crook for reinforcements.

Again the Sioux advanced. Pressing up a ravine which ran toward our right, they charged in on the right of the line. In an instant, the men broke to the rear and front, and facing to the right flank, gave them a withering volley, driving them back as fast as they came, many of them holding to their ponies' manes, showing how that fire had told. Hoping for reinforcements that came not, the gallant little band fought on with a desperate courage hardly to be believed if not actually seen. There was a season of this scorching enfilading fire, while all the while the bullets came thick and fast from the front. One man said to another, "Jack, it's only a question of cartridges"; while an officer to another remarked coolly, "Well I guess were done for. Better die right here, facing the rascals, than give way an inch, and go down with a lance in the back further to the rear." An occasional grim joke about cleaning out old Sitting Bull was passed, as such things will happen even in the face of death itself.

Now come the last onslaught, the supreme effort of the day.[17] Massing under cover, the Sioux rushed on with a wild yell, receiving the first volley unchecked. Our line broke and gave way, and for a moment it looked as though the end had come at last. But the worried, harassed, and worn-out little band of heroes still had a reserve of soldierly pluck. Spurring their horses forward, the officers appealed to the men. Sergeant Henry's stentorian voice was heard above the rattle of the small arms, crying, "Face them, men! On them, face them!" Some officer called out to the men, "Great God! Men, you are going to go back on the old 3rd. Forward!" A cheer swelled up; a rolling puff of smoke issued from the rallied line; and onward, down the hill for two hundred yards, pressed the battalion, in close pursuit of the flying enemy.

Falling back, they formed again on the old line, and held it until positive orders came to mount and retreat to the hill to the right and rear—the one carried by the infantry in the morning. Fortunately, at this moment, Burt and Burrowes of the 9th Infantry had come down this hill within eight hundred yards of the position and, having gotten the range, prepared to cover the retreat which was ordered by volley firing. This they did excellently well, knocking a number of Indians from their ponies, killing several horses, and checking the advance of the mass that swarmed from every rock and arroyo the moment the line had finally given way.

The loss in the companies who were in this part of the line—"Royall's line," as it is generally called here now—is 11 killed and 28 severely wounded; add to this 33 slightly wounded and not reported at the hospital.[18] As to the loss of the enemy, it must be estimated, as they

An artist's conception of the charge of Crook's cavalry at the Rosebud.
COLLECTION OF PETER COZZENS.

always carry off their dead if it is within the bounds of possibilities. Our Indian allies have 14 scalps, whilst the ground in the immediate front of Colonel Royall's last position was found to be thick with pools of clotted blood. Every rock had its bloodstain showing where an Indian had dragged himself, while on the march up the creek, a dead Sioux was found shot through the body. Those best capable of judging, who saw the gallant fight made on Royall's last position, say that they must have had fully fifty killed right there.

As soon as D, L, F, and I [Troops] had rejoined the main body, the whole command moved out, except the infantry who were left to guard the wounded. No results followed, as Sitting Bull, in his effort to "scoop" us all in, had gotten enough of it and abandoned the field. The command, having buried their dead, bivouacked on the ground occupied in the morning, and the next day started back to the camp on Goose Creek with the wounded, who are all doing as well as can be expected.

The train which takes this [dispatch] in to Fetterman carries with it our wounded and will return with five more companies of infantry and Russell's[19] troop of the 3rd Cavalry. The campaign has only opened, but before the leaves turn yellow on the trees, it will close with the end of the power of the Sioux nation.

Custer's Last Battle

CHARLES KING[1]

Harper's New Monthly Magazine 81 (August 1890): 378–87

It is hard to say how many years ago the Dakotas of the upper Mississippi, after a century of warring with the Chippewa nation, began to swarm across the Missouri in search of the buffalo, and there became embroiled with other tribes claiming the country farther west. Dakota was the proper tribal name, but as they crossed this Northwestern Rubicon into the territory of unknown foemen, they bore with them a title given them as far east as the banks and bluffs of the Father of Waters. The Chippewas had called them for years "the Sioux" (Soo), and by that strange sounding title is known to this day the most numerous and powerful nation of red people—warriors, women, and children—to be found on our continent.

They were in strong force when they launched out on their career of conquest west of the Missouri. The Yellowstone and its beautiful and romantic tributaries all belonged to the Ab-sa-ra-kas, or Crows; the rolling prairies of Nebraska were the homes of the Pawnees; the pine crested heights of the Black Hills were claimed as the headquarters of the Cheyennes and Arapahos; the western slopes of the Bighorn range and the broad valleys between them and the Rockies were owned by the Shoshones, or Snakes; while roving bands of Crees swarmed down along the north shore of the Missouri itself.

With each and all of these, with the Chippewas behind them, and eventually with the white invaders, the Dakotas waged relentless war. They drove the Pawnees across the Platte far into Kansas; they whipped the Cheyennes and Arapahos out of the Black Hills, and down to the headwaters of the Kaw and the Arkansas; they fought the Shoshones back into the Wind River Valley, with orders never again to cross the "dead line" of the Bighorn River; and they sent the Crows "whirling" up the valley of the Yellowstone (which they proceeded to call the Elk); and when our great war broke out in 1861, they lent valuable aid and comfort to the rebellion by swooping down on our settlements in Minnesota without the faintest warning, and slaughtering hundreds of defenseless women and children, from whom they were begging or stealing but the day before. General Sully,[2] with a strong command, was sent to give them a severe

Charles King as a young lieutenant. COURTESY OF PERRY FROHNE

lesson in payment for their outrages, and he marched far into their territory and fought them wherever they would assemble in sufficient force to block his way, but it did no lasting good. When 1866 came, and our emigrants began settling up the West, they found the Sioux more hostile and determined than ever. The army was called on to protect the settlers and to escort the surveyors of the transcontinental railways. Not a stake was driven, not an acre cleared, except under cover of the rifles of the regulars, and while the nation seemed rejoicing in unbroken peace and increasing prosperity, its little army was having anything but a placid time of it on the frontier. In the ten years that immediately preceded the centennial celebration at Philadelphia, the cavalry regiments had no rest at all; they were on the warpath winter and summer; and during those ten years of "peace," more officers of the Regular army were killed or died of wounds received in action with the Indians than the British Army lost in the entire Crimean War with its bloody battles of the Alma, Balaclava, Inkerman, and the assaults on Sebastopol. The Indians were always scientific fighters, but when, in '74 and '75, they succeeded in arming themselves with breechloaders and magazine rifles, the Sioux of the Northern Plains became foemen far more to be dreaded than any European cavalry.

Treaties had been made and broken. A road had been built through the heart of the country they loved the best—the northeastern slope and foothills from the Bighorn to the Yellowstone; and far up in this unsettled region, surrounded by savages, little wooden stockaded forts had been placed and garrisoned by pitifully small detachments of cavalry and infantry. From Fort Laramie down on the Platte, far up to the rich and populous Gallatin Valley of Montana, only those little forts, Reno, Phil Kearny, and C. F. Smith, guarded the way. One day, vast hordes of Sioux gathered in the ravines and canyons around Phil Kearny. Red Cloud was their leader. They sent a small party to attack the woodchoppers from the fort, who were working with their little escort. Two companies of infantry and one of cavalry went out to the rescue. These were quickly surrounded and hemmed in, then slowly massacred. After that, for ten long years, the Sioux held undisputed sway in their chosen country. Our forts were burned and abandoned. The Indian allies of the Dakotas joined hands with them, and a powerful nation or confederacy of nearly sixty thousand souls ruled the country from the Bighorn River on the northwest down to the Union Pacific Railway.[3] No longer dared they go south of that. Taking with them the Cheyennes and Arapahos, who had intermarried with them, the Sioux fell back to the North Platte and the territory beyond. From there, they sent raiding parties in every direction. One secretary of the interior after another had tried the experiment of feeding, clothing, bribing them to be good. Agencies and reservations were established at convenient points. Here the old chiefs, the broken-down men, and the noncombatant women and children made their permanent homes, and here the bold and vigorous young chiefs and warriors, laughing at the credulity of the Great Father, filled up their pouches and parfleches with rations and ammunition, then went whooping off on the warpath against the whites wherever found, and came back scalp-laden to the reservation when they needed more cartridges or protection from the pursuing soldiery, who could fire on them only when caught outside the lines.

Two great reservations were established southeast of the Black Hills in the valley of the White River. One of these was the bailiwick of the hero of the Phil Kearny massacre, old Red Cloud, and here were gathered most of his own tribe (the Oglalas) and many of his chiefs; some "good," like Old-Man-Afraid-of-His-Horses and his worthy son, but most of them crafty, cunning, treacherous, and savage, like Red Dog, Little Big Man, American Horse, and a swarm of various kinds of Bulls and Bears and Wolves. Further down the stream, twenty miles away, were the headquarters of the Brules, Spotted Tail's people, and "Old Spot" was loyal to the backbone, though powerless to control the movements of the young men. Other reservations there were along the Missouri, and into these reservations the Department of the Interior strove to gather all the Sioux nation, in the vague hope of keeping them out of mischief.

But the young Indian takes to mischief of that description as the young duck to the water. The traditions of his people tell of no case where respect was accorded to him who had not killed his man. Only in deeds of blood or battle could he hope to win distinction, and the vacillating policy of the government enabled him to sally forth at any time and return at will to the reservations, exhibiting to the admiring eyes of friends and relations the dripping scalps of his white victims. The fact that the victims were shot from ambush, or that the scalps were solely those of helpless women and children, detracted in no wise from the value of the trophies. The perpetrator had won his spurs, according to the aboriginal code, and was a "brave" henceforth.

But there were those who never would come in and never signed a treaty. Herein they are entitled to far more respect than those who came, saw, and conquered—by fraud; and one of those who persistently refused, and whose standard was a rallying point for the disaffected and treacherous of every tribe, was a shrewd "medicine chief" of the Hunkpapas, a seer, prophet, statesman, but in no sense a war chief, the now celebrated Tatanka-Yotanka—Sitting Bull.

Far out in the lovely fertile valleys of the Rosebud, the Tongue, the Little Bighorn, and the Powder Rivers, Sitting Bull and his devoted followers spent their days. Sheltered from storm and tempest by the high bluffs through long, hard winters, living in the midst of untold thousands of buffalo, elk, mountain sheep, antelope, and deer, rejoicing in the grandest scenery on the continent, and in a climate that despite its rigor during the midwinter months is unparalleled for life-giving qualities, it is no wonder they loved and clung to it—their "Indian story-land"—as they did to no other. But here flocked all the renegades from other tribes. Here came the wild and untamable Oglala, Brule, Miniconjou, Sans Arc, Hunkpapa, Blackfoot; here were all warriors welcomed; from here time and again set forth the expeditions that spread terror to settler and emigrant, and checked the survey of the Northern Pacific Railroad.

1875 found trouble everywhere. White settlers swarmed in the Black Hills in search of gold. Oglalas and Brules stole their stock and killed their herders, claiming that the land was theirs and the whites were invaders. Sitting Bull's ranks swarmed with recruits from far to the southeast. The Interior Department found it useless to temporize. Orders were given to the army to bring him in or "snuff him out." Early in March 1876, [Brig.] Gen. George Crook, famous for his successes with the Indians in Oregon and Arizona, was started up into the Sioux country with a strong force of cavalry and infantry. On "Patrick's Day in the morning," long before he was anywhere near Sitting Bull himself, his advance struck a big Indian village deep in the snows of the Powder River. It was thirty degrees below zero; the troops were faultily led by the officer to whom he had entrusted the duty, and the Sioux developed splendid fighting qualities under a new and daring leader, "Tashunka-uitco"—Crazy Horse. Crook's advance recoiled upon the main body, practically defeated by the renegades from the Red Cloud and Spotted Tail agencies.

Early in May, warned by this lesson, three great expeditions pushed forward into the Indian story land, where by this time full six thousand warriors had rallied around Sitting Bull.[4] From the south came General Crook, with nearly twenty-five hundred men. From the east marched General Terry, with almost as many infantry and cavalry as had Crook, and a few light pieces of artillery. Down the Yellowstone from the west, Colonel Gibbon led a little band of long-trained frontier soldiers, scouting by the way, and definitely "locating" the Indians over on the Rosebud before forming his junction with General Terry near the mouth of the Tongue. If Sitting Bull had been alive to the situation, Gibbon's small force could never have finished that perilous advance, though they might have stood and defended themselves; but Bull was not a general; his talents lay elsewhere.

Early in June, Crook's command was on the northeast slope of the Bighorn, and General Sheridan, planning the whole campaign, saw with anxiety that vast numbers of Indians were daily leaving the reservations south of the Black Hills. The 5th Regiment of Cavalry was then sent up by rail from Kansas to Cheyenne and marched rapidly to the Black Hills to cut off these re-enforcements. The great mass of the Indians lay uneasily between Crook at the headwaters of Tongue River and Terry and Gibbon near its mouth, watching every move, and utterly cutting off every attempt of the commanders to communicate with each other. They worried Crook's pickets and trains, and by mid-June, he determined to pitch in and see what force they had. On June 17, the general grappled with the Sioux on the bluffs of the Rosebud. He had several hundred Crow allies. The stirring combat lasted much of the day; but long before it was half over, Crook was fighting on the defensive and coolly withdrawing his men. He had found a hornets' nest and knew it was no place for so small a command as his. Pulling out as best he could, he fell back to the Tongue, sent for the entire 5th Cavalry and all his available infantry, and lay on his arms until they could reach him. He had not got within sight of the great Indian village—city, it should be called—of Sitting Bull.

Meantime, Terry and Gibbon sent their scouts upstream. Major Reno, with a strong battalion of the 7th Cavalry, left camp on the Yellowstone to take a look up toward the Wolf Mountains. Sitting Bull and his people—men, women, and children—after their successful defense of the approaches to their home on the Rosebud on June 17, seem to have bethought themselves of roomier and better quarters over in the broader valley of the Little Bighorn, the next stream to the west. Their village had stretched for six miles down the narrow canyon of the Rosebud; their thousands of ponies had eaten off all the grass; they were victorious, but it was time to go.

Coming up the Rosebud, Major Reno was confronted by the sight of an immense trail turning suddenly west and crossing the great divide over toward the setting sun.[5] Experienced Indian fighters in his command told him that many thousand Indians had passed there within the last few days. Like a sensible man, he turned about and trotted back to report his discovery to his commander. Then it was that the tragedy of the campaign began.

At the head of Terry's horsemen was the lieutenant colonel commanding the 7th Regiment of Cavalry, Bvt. Maj. Gen. George A. Custer, United States Army, a daring, dashing, impetuous trooper, who had won high honors as a division commander under Sheridan during the great War of the Rebellion, who had led his gallant regiment against the Kiowas and the Cheyennes on the Southern Plains and had twice penetrated the Sioux country in recent campaigns. Experience he certainly had, but there were those, superiors and subordinates both, who feared that in dealing with so wily and skilful a foe, Custer lacked judgment. All had not been harmonious in his relations with his commanders in the Department of Dakota, nor was there entire unanimity of feeling toward him in the regiment itself, but all men honored his unquestioned bravery, and when General Terry decided to send his cavalry at once to "scout the trail" reported by Reno, the command of the expedition fell naturally to Custer.

Terry had promptly arrived at the conclusion that the Indians had simply moved their villages over into the valley of the Little Bighorn, and his plan was to send Custer along the trail to hold and hem them from the east, while he, with all his own and Gibbon's command, pushed up the Yellowstone and Bighorn in boats; then, disembarking at the junction of the Big and Little Big Horn, to march southward until he struck the Indians on that flank. His orders to Custer displayed an unusual mingling of anxiety and forbearance. He seems to have feared that Custer would be rash, yet shrank from issuing a word that might reflect upon the discretion or wound the high spirit of his gallant leader of horse. He warned him to "feel" well out toward his left as he rode westward from the Rosebud, in order to prevent the Indians slipping off southeastward between the column and the Bighorn Mountains. He would not hamper him with positive orders as to what he must or must not do when he came in presence of the enemy, but he named June 26 as the day on which he and Gibbon would reach the valley of the Little Bighorn, and it was his hope and expectation that Custer would come up from the east about the same time and between them they would be able to soundly thrash the assembled Sioux.

But Custer disappointed him in an unusual way. He got there a day ahead of time, and had ridden night and day to do it. Men and horses were well-nigh used up when the 7th Cavalry trotted into sight of the city on the Little Bighorn that cloudless Sunday morning of the twenty-fifth. When Terry came up the valley on the twenty-sixth, it was all over with Custer and his pet troops (companies) of the regiment.

He started on the trail with the 7th Cavalry, and nothing but the 7th. A battalion of the 2nd was with Gibbon's column; but luckily for the 2nd, Custer would [have] none of them. Two field guns, under Lieutenant Low,[6] were with Terry, and Low begged that he and his guns might be sent, but Custer wanted only his own people. He rode sixty miles in twenty-four hours. He pushed ahead on the trail with feverish impatience, and he created an impression that it was his determination to get to the spot and have one battle royal with the Indians, in which he and the 7th should be the sole participants on our side, and by consequence the sole heroes. The idea of defeat seems never to have occurred to him, despite his experience with old "Black Kettle's" bands down on the Washita.

Only thirty miles away on his left, as he spurred ahead with his weary men that Sunday morning, over two thousand soldiers under Crook were in bivouac on Goose Creek. Had he "felt" any great distance out there the scouts would have met, and Crook would eagerly have reinforced him, but he wanted nothing of the kind. At daybreak, his advance under Lieutenant Varnum had come upon

Indian scouts watching Custer's advance. CENTURY MAGAZINE, 1892.

the scaffold sepulchers of two or three warriors slain in the fight of the seventeenth, and soon thereafter sent back word that the valley of the Little Horn was in sight ahead, and there were "signs" of the village.

Then it was that Custer made the division of his column. Keeping with himself the five companies whose commanders were his chosen friends and adherents, and leaving Captain McDougall[7] with his troops to guard the mule pack train in rear, he divided the six remaining companies between Major Reno and Captain Benteen, sending the latter some two miles off to the extreme left, while Reno moved midway between. In this order of three little parallel columns, the 7th Cavalry swept rapidly westward over the divide.

Unlike the 2nd, 3rd, or 5th Regiment when on Indian campaign, Custer's men rode into action with something of the pomp and panoply of war that distinguished them around their camps. Bright guidons fluttered in the breeze; many of the officers and men wore the natty undress uniform of the cavalry. Custer himself; his brother, Capt. Tom Custer; his adjutant, Lieutenant Cook; and his old Army of the Potomac comrade, Capt. Myles Keogh, were all dressed nearly alike in coats of Indian-tanned, beaver-trimmed buckskin, with broad-brimmed scouting hats of light color and long riding boots. Captain Yates seemed to prefer his undress uniform, as did most of the lieutenants in Custer's column. The two Custers and Captain Keogh rode their beautiful Kentucky sorrel horses, and the adjutant was mounted on his long-legged gray. The trumpeters were at the heads of columns with their chiefs, but the band of the 7th, for once, was left behind; Custer's last charge was sounded without the accompaniment of the rollicking Irish fighting tune he loved. There was no "Garry Owen" to swell the chorus of the last cheer.

Following Custer's trail from the Rosebud, one comes in sight of the Little Bighorn, winding away northward to its junction with the broader stream. South are the bold cliffs and dark canyons of the mountains, their foothills not twenty miles away. North, tumbling and rolling toward the Yellowstone in alternate swale and ridge, the treeless, upland prairie stretches to the horizon. Westward, the eye roams over what seems to be a broad, flat valley beyond the stream; but the stream itself—the fatal "Greasy Grass," as the Sioux called it—is hidden from sight under the steep bluffs that hem it in. Coming from the mountains, it swings into sight far to the left front, comes rippling toward us in its fringe of cottonwoods and willows, and suddenly disappears under or behind the huge, rolling wave of bluff that stretches right and left across the path. For nearly six miles of its tortuous course, it cannot be seen from the point where Custer drew rein to get his first view of the village. Neither can its fringing willows be seen, and—fatal and momentous fact—neither could hundreds of the populous lodges that clustered along its western bank. Eagerly scanning the distant tepees that lay beyond the northern point where the bluff dipped to the stream, and swinging his broad-brimmed hat about his head in an ecstasy of soldierly anticipation, he shouted, "Custer's luck! The biggest Indian village on the continent!" And he could not have seen one-third of it.

But what he saw was enough to fire the blood of any soldier. Far to the northwest and west, huge clouds of dust rose billowing from the broad valley. Far across the hidden stream could be seen the swarming herds of ponies in excited movement. Here, there, and everywhere, tiny dots of horsemen scurrying away could be readily distinguished, and down to the right front, down along what could be seen of the village around that shoulder of bluff, all was lively turmoil and confusion; lodges were being hurriedly taken down, and their occupants were fleeing from the wrath to come. We know now that the warriors whom he saw dashing westward were mainly the young men hurrying out to "round up" the pony herds; we know now that behind those sheltering bluffs were still thousands of fierce warriors eager and ready to meet "Long Hair"; we know that the signs of panic and retreat were due mainly to the rush to get the women and little children out of the way; ponies and dogs, hastily hitched to the dust-raising travois, dragged the wondering papooses and frightened squaws far out over the westward slopes; but seeing the scurry and panic, Custer seems to have attached only one meaning to it. They were all in full retreat. The whole community would be on the run before he could strike them. Quickly he determined on his course. Reno should push straight ahead, get down into the valley, ford the stream, and attack the southern end of the village, while he with his pet companies should turn into the long, winding ravine that ran northwestward to the stream, and pitch in with wild charge from the east. To Reno, these orders were promptly given. A courier was sent to Benteen, far off to the left, notifying him of the "find"; and another galloped to McDougall with orders to hurry up with the pack trains where the extra ammunition was carried. Custer knew it would be needed.

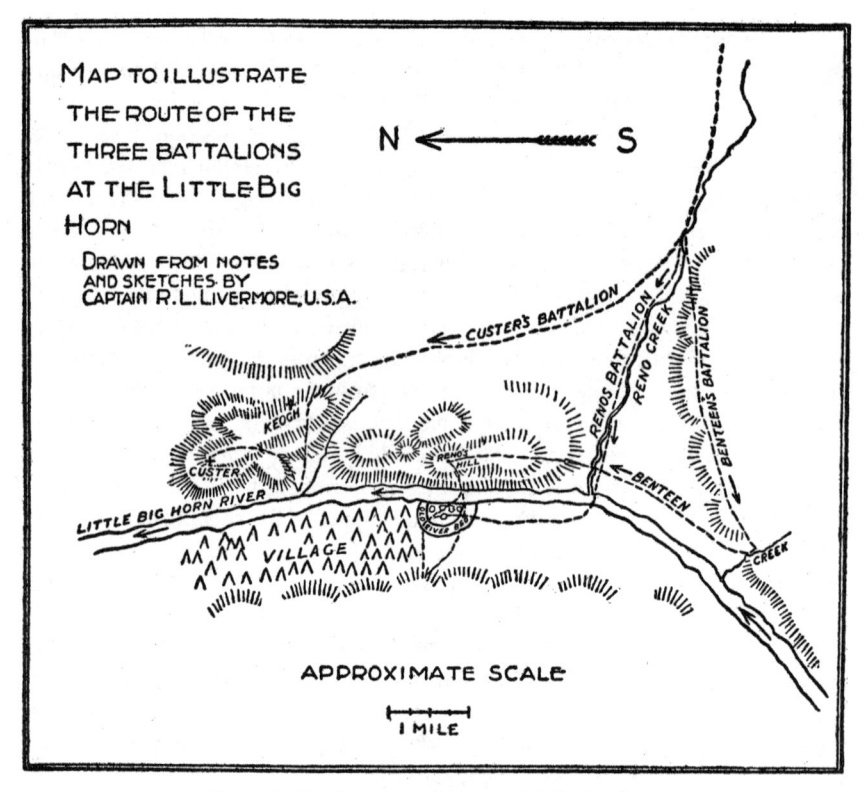

Custer's final approach to the Little Bighorn.
CYRUS T. BRADY. *INDIAN FIGHTS AND FIGHTERS.*

Then the daring commander placed himself at the head of his own column, plunged down the slope and, followed by his eager men, was soon out of sight, perhaps out of hearing of what might be taking place over in the valley behind the bluffs that rose on his left higher with every furlong trotted. The last that Reno and his people ever saw of them alive was the tail of the column disappearing in a cloud of dust; then the cloud alone was to be seen, hanging over their trail like a pall.

Pushing forward, Reno came quickly to a shallow coulee (frontierism for gully) that led down through the bluff to the stream. A brisk trot brought him to the ford; his troopers plunged blithely through and began to clamber the low bank on the western shore. He expected from the tenor of his orders to find an open, unobstructed valley down which, five miles away at least, he could see the lodges of the Indian village. It was with surprise, not unmixed with grave concern, therefore, that as he urged his horse through the willows and up to the level of the low "bench" beyond, he suddenly rode into full view of an immense township, whose southern outskirts were not two miles away. Far as he could see, the dust cloud rose above the excited villages; herds of war ponies were being driven in from the west on a mad run; old men, squaws, children, draught ponies, and travois were scurrying off toward the Bighorn; and Reno realized that he was in front of the assembled warriors of the whole Sioux nation.

What Custer expected of Reno was, is generally believed, a bold, dashing charge into the heart of the village—just such a charge as he, Custer, had successfully led at the Washita, though it cost the life of Captain [Louis M.] Hamilton and eventually of many others. But Reno had no dash to speak of, and the sight that burst upon his eyes eliminated any that might be latent. He attacked, but the attack was nevertheless spiritless and abortive. Dismounting his men, he advanced them as skirmishers across the mile or more of prairie, firing as soon as he got within range of the village. No resistance of any consequence was made as he pushed northward, for the sudden appearance of his command was a total surprise to the Hunkpapas and Blackfeet, whose villages were farthest south. Their scouts had signaled Custer's column trotting down the ravine, and those who had not rushed for safety to the rear were apparently rushing toward the Brule village in the center as the point which Custer would be apt first to strike. Reno could have darted into the south end of the village, it is believed, before his approach could have been fairly realized. As it was, slowly and on foot, he traversed the prairie without losing a man, and was upon the lodges when a few shots were fired from the willows along the stream, and some mounted Indians could be seen swooping around his left flank. He had had no experience in Indian fighting. He simply seemed to feel that with his little command of two hundred men, he could not drive the whole valley full of warriors, and in much perturbation and worry, he sounded the halt, rally, and mount. Then, for a few moments that to his officers and men must have seemed hours, he paused irresolute, not knowing what to do.

The Indians settled it for him. They well interpreted his hesitation. The "White Chief" was scared; now was their chance. Man and boy, they came tearing to the spot. A few well-aimed shots knocked a luckless trooper or two out of the saddle. Reno hurriedly ordered a movement by the flank toward the high bluffs across the stream to his right rear. He never thought to dismount a few cool hands to face about and keep off the enemy. He placed himself at the new head of column and led the backward move. Out came the Indians, with shots and triumphant yells, in pursuit. The rear of the column began to crowd on the head; Reno struck a trot; the rear struck the gallop. The Indians came dashing up on both flanks and close to the rear; and then—then the helpless, horribly led troopers had no alternative. Discipline and order were all forgotten. In one mad rush, they tore away for the stream, plunged in, sputtered through, and clambered breathlessly up the steep bluff on the eastern shore—an ignominious, inexcusable panic, due mainly to the nerveless conduct of the major commanding.

In vain had Donald McIntosh[8] and "Benny" Hodgson,[9] two of the bravest and best-loved officers in the regiment, striven to rally, face about, and fight

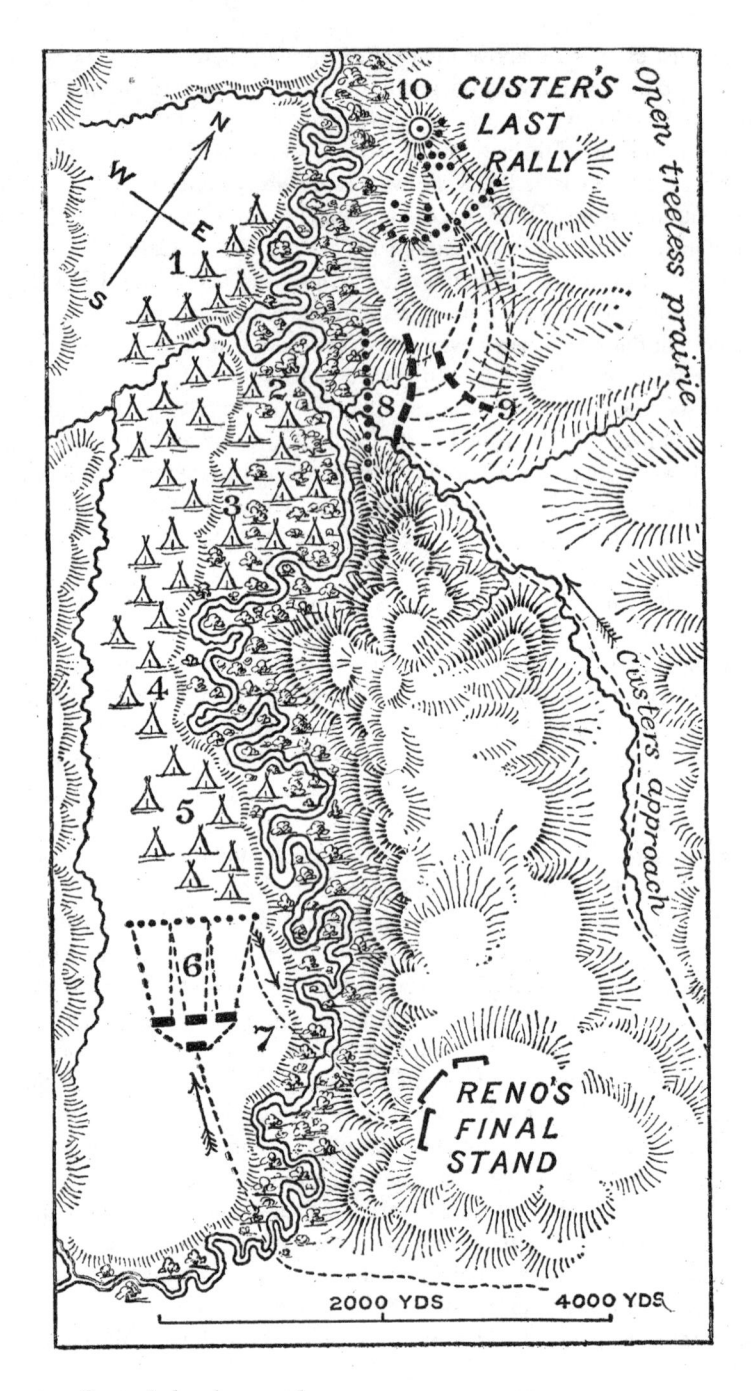

Custer's battleground. CYRUS T. BRADY. *INDIAN FIGHTS AND FIGHTERS.*

with the rear of column. The Indians were not in overpowering numbers at the moment, and a bold front would have stood off double their force; but with the major on the run, and foremost in the run, the lieutenants could do nothing but lose their own gallant lives. McIntosh was surrounded, dragged from his horse, and butchered close to the brink. Hodgson, shot out of saddle, was rescued by a faithful comrade, who plunged into the stream with him; but close to the farther shore, the Indians picked him off, a bullet tore through his body, and the gallant little fellow, the pet and pride of the whole regiment, rolled dead into the muddy waters.

Once well up the bluffs, Reno's breathless followers faced about and took in the situation. The Indians pursued no further, and even now were rapidly withdrawing from range. The major fired his pistol at the distant foe in paroxysmal defiance of the fellows who had stampeded him.[10] He was now up some two hundred feet above them, and it was safe—as it was harmless. Two of his best officers lay dead down there on the banks below; so, too, lay a dozen of his men.[11] The Indians, men and even boys, had swarmed all around his people and slaughtered them as they ran. Many more were wounded, but, for the present at least, all seemed safe. The Indians, except a few, had mysteriously withdrawn from their front. What could that mean? And then, what could have become of Custer? Where, too, were Benteen and McDougall with their commands?

Over toward the villages, which they could now see stretching for five miles down the stream, all was shrill uproar and confusion; but northward, the bluffs rose still higher to a point nearly opposite the middle of the villages—a point some two miles from them—and beyond that they could see nothing. Thither, however, had Custer gone, and suddenly, crashing through the sultry morning air, came the sound of fierce and rapid musketry—whole volleys— then one continuous rattle and roar. Louder, fiercer, it grew for a full ten minutes. Some thought they could hear the ringing cheers of their comrades and were ready to cheer in reply; some thought they heard the thrilling charge of the trumpets; many were eager to mount and rush to join their colonel, and with him to avenge Hodgson and McIntosh, and retrieve the dark fortunes of their own battalion. But almost as suddenly as it began, the heavy volleying died away; the continuous rattle broke into scattering skirmish fire, then into sputtering shots, then only once in a while sonic distant rifle would crack feebly on the breeze, and Reno's men looked wonderingly in each other's faces. There stood the villages plain enough, and the firing had begun close under the bluffs, close to the stream, and had died away far to the north. What could it mean?

Soon, with eager delight, the little commands of Benteen and McDougall were hailed coming up the slopes from the east.

"Have you seen anything of Custer?" was the first anxious inquiry.

Benteen and Weir had galloped to a point of bluff a mile or more to the north, had seen swarms of Indians in the valley below, but not a sign of Custer's people. They could expect no aid from Custer, then, and there was only one thing left—entrench themselves and hold out as best they could till Terry and

Gibbon should arrive. Reno had now seven troops and the pack train, abundant ammunition and supplies. The chances were in his favor.

Now what had become of Custer? For him and his, there was none left to tell the story except the Crow scout "Curley," who managed to slip away in a Sioux blanket during the thick of the fight, and our sources of information are solely Indian.[12] The very next year, a battalion of the 5th Cavalry passed the battleground with a number of Sioux scouts who but twelve months previous were fighting there [against] the 7th Cavalry. Half a dozen of them told their stories at different times and in different places, and as to the general features of the battle, they tallied with singular exactness. These fellows were mainly Brules and Oglalas. Afterward we got the stories of the Hunkpapas—most interesting of all—and from all these sources, it was not hard to trace Custer's every move. One could almost portray his every emotion.

Never realizing, as I believe, the fearful odds against him, believing that he would find the village on the run, and that between himself and Reno he could double them up in short order, Custer had jauntily trotted down to his death. It was a long five-mile ride from where he sighted the northern end of the village to where he struck its center around that bold point of bluff, and from the start to the moment his guidons whirled into view, and his troopers came galloping front into line down near the ford, he never fairly saw the great village—never dreamed of its depth and extent. Rounding the bluff, he suddenly found himself face to face with thousands of the boldest and most skillful warriors of the prairies. He had hoped to charge at once into the heart of the village, to hear the cheers of Reno's men from the south. Instead, he was greeted with a perfect fury of flame and hissing lead from the dense thicket of willow and cottonwood, a fire that had to be answered at once. Quickly he dismounted his men and threw them forward on the run, each fourth man holding, cavalry fashion, the horses of the other three. The line seems to have swept in parallel very nearly with the general course of the stream, but to no purpose. The foe was ten to one in their front. Boys and squaws were shooting from the willows ("Oh, we had plenty guns!" said our storytellers); worse than that, hundreds of young warriors had mounted their ponies and swarmed across the stream below him, hundreds more were following and circling all about him. And then it was that Custer, the hero of a hundred daring charges, seems to have realized that he must cut his way out. "Mount!" rang the trumpets, and leaving many a poor fellow on the ground, the troopers ran for their horses. Instantly, from lodge and willow, Oglalas and Brules sprang to horse and rushed to the ford in mad pursuit. "Make for the heights!" must have been the order, for the first rush was eastward; then more to the left, as they found their progress barred. Then, as they reached higher ground, all they could see, far as they could see, circling, swooping, yelling like demons, and all the time keeping up their furious fire, were thousands of the mounted Sioux. Hemmed in, cut off, dropping fast from their saddles, Custer's men saw that retreat was impossible. They sprang to the ground, turned their horses loose, said the Indians, and by that time, half their number had fallen. A skirmish line was thrown out down the slope, and there they dropped at five-yard intervals; there their comrades found them two days after. Every instant the foe rode closer and gained in numbers; every instant some poor fellow bit the dust. At last, on a mound that stands at the northern end of a little ridge, Custer, with Cook, Yates, and gallant "Brother Tom," and some dozen soldiers, all that were left by this time, gathered in the last rally. They sold their lives dearly, brave fellows that they were; but they were as a dozen to the leaves of the forest at the end of twenty minutes, and in less than twenty-five—all was over.

Keogh, Calhoun, Crittenden, had died along the skirmish lines; Smith, Porter, and Reily were found with their men; so were the surgeons, Lord and DeWolf;[13] so, too, were Boston Custer and the *Herald* correspondent;[14] but two bodies were never recognized among the slain—those of Lieutenants Harrington and "Jack" Sturgis. Down a little coulee some thirty men had made a rush for their lives; the Sioux had simply thronged the banks shooting them as they ran. One trooper—an officer, said the Sioux—managed to break through their circle, the only white man who did, and galloped madly eastward. Five warriors started in pursuit—two Oglalas, two Hunkpapas, and a Brule, all well mounted. Fear lent him wings, and his splendid horse gained on all but a Hunkpapa, who hung to the chase. At last, when even this one was ready to draw rein and let him go, the hunted cavalryman glanced over his shoulder, fancied himself nearly overtaken, and placing the muzzle of his revolver at his ear, pulled the trigger and sent his own bullet through his brain. His skeleton was pointed out to

The end of Custer's command. W. F. BEYER. *DEEDS OF VALOR.*

the officers of the 5th Cavalry the following year by one of the pursuers, and so it was discovered for the first time. Was it Harrington? Was it Sturgis? Poor "Jack's" watch was restored to his father some two years after the battle, having been traded off by Sioux who escaped to the British possessions; but no mention was made by these Indians of a watch thus taken. Three years ago, there came a story of a new skeleton found still farther from the scene. Shreds of uniform and the heavy gilding of the cavalry buttons lying near, as well as the expensive filling of several teeth, seem to indicate that this too may have been an officer. If so, all the missing are now accounted for. Of the twelve troops of the 7th Cavalry, Custer led five that hot Sunday into the battle of the Little Bighorn, and of his portion of the regiment, only one living thing escaped the vengeance of the Sioux. Bleeding from many wounds, weak and exhausted, with piteous appeal in his eyes, there came straggling into the lines some days after the fight Myles Keogh's splendid sorrel horse Comanche. Who can ever picture his welcome as the soldiers thronged around the gallant charger? To this day, they guard and cherish him in the 7th. No more duty does Comanche perform; no rider ever mounts him. His last great service was rendered that Sunday in '76, and now, sole living relic of Custer's last rally, he spends his days with the old regiment.[15]

But I have said that Sitting Bull was not the inspiration of the great victory won by the Sioux. With Custer's people slaughtered, the Indians left their bodies to the plundering hands of the squaws and once more crowded upon Reno's front. There were two nights of wild triumph and rejoicing in the villages, though not one instant was the watch on Reno relaxed. All day of the twenty-sixth, they kept him penned in the rifle pits, but early on the twenty-seventh, with great commotion, the lodges were suddenly taken down, and tribe after tribe, village after village, six thousand Indians passed before his eyes, making off toward the mountains. Terry and Gibbon had come; Reno's relic of the 7th was saved. Together they explored the field and hastily buried the mutilated dead, then hurried back to the Yellowstone while the Sioux were hiding in the fastnesses of the Bighorn.

Of the rest of the summer's campaign, no extended mention is needed here. The Indians were shrewd enough to know that now at least the commands of Crook and Terry would be heavily re-enforced, and then the hunt would be relentless. Soon as their scouts reported the assembly of new and strong bodies of troops upon the Yellowstone and Platte, the great confederation quietly dissolved. Sitting Bull, with many chosen followers, made for the Yellowstone and was driven northward by Colonel Miles. Others took refuge across the Little Missouri, whither Crook pursued, and by dint of hard marching and fighting that fall and winter, many bands and many famous chiefs were whipped into surrender. Among these, bravest, most brilliant, most victorious of all, was the hero of the Powder River fight on [Saint] Patrick's Day, the warrior Crazy Horse. The fame of his exploit had reached the Indian camps along the Rosebud before this young chief, with his followers, Oglala and Brule, came to swell the ranks of

Sitting Bull. Again on June 17, he had been foremost in the stirring fight with Crook, and when the entire band moved over into the valley of the Little Bighorn, and the Brules, Oglalas, and Sans Arcs pitched their tepees in the chosen ground, the very center of the camp, it is safe to say that among the best and experienced fighters, the tribes from the White River and their neighbors the Cheyennes, no chief was so honored and believed in as Crazy Horse.

In pitching the new camp, the Blackfeet were farthest south—upstream; next came the Hunkpapas, with their renowned medicine man, Sitting Bull; then the Oglalas, Brules, and Cheyennes, covering the whole bottom opposite the shoulder of bluff around which Custer hove in sight; farthest north were the Minneconjou; and the great village contained at least six thousand aboriginal souls.

Now up to this time, Sitting Bull had no real claims as a war chief. Eleven days before the fight, there was a Sun Dance. His own people have since told us these particulars, and the best storyteller among them was that bright-faced squaw of Tatonka-he-gle-ska—Spotted Horn Bull—who accompanied the party on their eastern trip. She is a cousin to Sitting Bull and knows whereof she speaks. The chief had a trance and a vision. Solemnly he assured his people that within a few days, they would be attacked by a vast force of white soldiers, but that the Sioux should triumph over them; and when the Crows and Crook's command appeared on the seventeenth, it was a partial redemption of his promise.

Wary scouts saw Reno's column turning back down the Rosebud after discovering the trail, and nothing, they judged, would come from that quarter. All around Crook's camp on Goose Creek, the indications were that the "Gray Fox" was simply waiting for more soldiers before he would again venture forth. Sitting Bull had no thought of new attack for days to come, when, early on the morning of June 25, two Cheyenne Indians who had started eastward at dawn came dashing back to the bluffs and, waving their blankets, signaled, "White soldiers—heaps—coming quick." Instantly all was uproar and confusion.

Of course, women and children had to be hurried away, the great herds of ponies gathered in, and the warriors assembled to meet the coming foe. Even as the chiefs were hastening to the council lodge, there came the crash of rapid volleys from the south. It was Reno's attack—an attack from a new and utterly unexpected quarter—and this, with the news that Long Hair was thundering down the ravine across the stream, was too much for Sitting Bull. Hurriedly gathering his household about him, he lashed his pony to the top of his speed and fled westward for safety. Miles he galloped before he dared stop for breath. Behind him he could hear the roar of battle, and on he would have sped but for the sudden discovery that one of his twin children was missing. Turning, he was surprised to find the firing dying away, soon ceasing altogether. In half an hour more, he managed to get back to camp, where the missing child was found, but the battle had been won without him. Without him, the Blackfeet and Hunkpapas had repelled Reno and penned him on the bluffs. Without him the Oglalas, Brules, and Cheyennes had turned back Custer's daring assault, then rushed forth and completed the death-gripping circle in which he was held. Again had Crazy Horse been foremost in the fray, riding in and braining the bewildered soldiers with his heavy war club. Fully had his vision been realized, but Sitting Bull was not there.

For a long time, it was claimed for him by certain sycophantic followers that from the council lodge he directed the battle; but it would not do. When the old sinner was finally starved out of Her Majesty's territory, and came in to accept the terms accorded him, even his own people could not keep straight faces when questioned as to the cause of the odd names given those twins— "The-One-That-Was-Taken" and "The-One-That-Was-Left." Finally it all leaked out, and now "none so poor to do him reverence."[16]

Of course, it was his role to assume all the airs of a conqueror, to be insolent and defiant to the high joint commission, sent the following winter to beg him to come home and be good; but the claims of Tatanka-Yotanka to the leadership in the greatest victory his people ever won are mere vaporings, to be classed with the boastings of dozens of chiefs who were scattered over the northern reservations during the next few years. Rain-in-the-Face used to brag by the hour that he had killed Custer with his own hand, but the other Indians laughed at him. Gall, of the Hunkpapas, Spotted Eagle, Kill Eagle, Lame Deer, Lone Wolf, and all the varieties of Bears and Bulls were probably leading spirits in the battle, but the man who more than all others seems to have won the admiration of his fellows for skill and daring throughout that stirring campaign, and especially on that bloody day, is he who so soon after met his death in a desperate effort to escape from Crook's guards, the warrior Crazy Horse.

The Indian Version of Custer's Last Battle

CHARLES A. EASTMAN (OHIYESA)[1]

Chautauquan 31 (July 1900): 353-58

Nearly half a century has elapsed since the Sioux people took up arms against the whites. For over twenty-five years, they almost continuously defied the westward progress of American civilization. The world will never know all the truth concerning many of their battles upon the plains and among the mountains.

After the treaty of 1868 had been concluded with the western Sioux, it was hoped by the Indians that they might be let alone. The sixteenth article of that treaty declared the country of the North Platte and the Bighorn Mountains to be "unceded Indian territory" and provided that no white man should settle upon it or travel through it without the consent of the Indians. But no sooner was the agreement made than gold was found in the Black Hills district, which is within the unceded territory. The cry was "Remove the Indians to Indian territory!" It was feared that the Sioux could not be prevailed upon to consent to this scheme. However, a commission was sent to labor with them. Meanwhile, the whites were pouring into the Black Hills.

All the western Sioux then determined to defend their rights at any cost. At this time, a tremendous pressure was brought to bear upon Spotted Tail and Red Cloud to induce them to yield to a new agreement by which their grievances might be adjusted by the "Great Father." The real scheme was to get their consent to go to Indian territory. Spotted Tail was easily won over, but the position of Red Cloud was not fully understood, although in reality he desired the peaceful adjustment of their difference with the government. On the other hand, Crazy Horse and his lieutenants, and Sitting Bull and his associates, charged the other chiefs with treason, and in unmistakable terms declared their intention to kill any white man who might be found in their country without authority from them.

At this point, I might say that there were already ten thousand Sioux located on reservations east of the Missouri River, who had no sympathy with the hostiles west of that river, and whose occupation was that of farmers and not of hunters. After examining the census of the Sioux from that time to the present, I am convinced that there were not over 28,500 Sioux in the country, both in and out of the reservations. This leaves about 18,000 of these people, known as the Tetons, who lived on the west side of the Missouri. According to the official reports of the year 1876, there were 16,000 of these accounted for at the various agencies. That leaves only about 2,000 unaccounted for.

	POPULATION	
EASTERN SIOUX	1876	1898
Crow Creek Agency, Dakota	1,213	1,061
Devil's Lake, Dakota	1,071	1,046
Flandreau, Dakota	361	296
Lower Brule, Dakota	1,800	914
Santee, Nebraska	973	1,019
Sisseton, Dakota	1,745	1,871
Yankton, Dakota	1,992	1,728
In Minnesota (nonreservation)	300	800
Renegades in Eastern Montana	1,000	1,000
Total	10,455	9,735
WESTERN SIOUX		
Cheyenne River Agency, Dakota	2,280	2,557
Red Cloud, or Pine Ridge, Dakota	6,000	6,000
Spotted Tail, or Rosebud, Dakota	2,315	4,451
Standing Rock, Dakota	2,205	3,726
Renegade Sioux at Fort Peck, Montana	4,000	1,239
Total	16,800	17,973
Grand Total	27,355	27,608

It is generally supposed that a great number of the reservation Indians joined the hostiles. This is true so far as concerns the 4,000 renegades who were about Fort Peck, Montana; but I am certain that there was nothing like as many as Capt. E. S. Godfrey claims in his article published in *The Century Magazine* for January 1892, and by General Fry in his comment thereon.[2] These two gentlemen place the number of Indians encamped upon the Little Bighorn at from 12,000 to 15,000. This would take nearly all the Indians then upon reservations west of the Missouri River.

All of the Indian agents in charge of the various agencies say in their official reports that the Indians under them were uneasy because of the hostiles, but that they were loyal. Only two agents reported the departure of any Indians. One of these was James Hastings of Red Cloud agency, but he states that those who had gone were Cheyennes. The other was J. Burke of Standing Rock. He placed the number of Indians who left his agency at not over one hundred, and further states that if certain young men were to be found in the hostile camp, they had gone there during the winter, not with hostile intentions, but "for the sake of trade, novelty, and curiosity." The same agent states that the people were encamped around the government buildings within an area of fifteen miles, and he gave them a weekly ration; therefore, he was in touch with them continuously.

The agent at Fort Peck, Montana, where there were over four thousand of the renegade Sioux, states in his report for the same year that he was in close touch with them until the last of May, when they went away on their summer hunt. He places them along the country north of his agency, and as far west as the Little Rocky. I found that a good portion of this consolidation of renegades was on the Little Bighorn on June 25 and participated in the battle. I estimate that there were not over five thousand Indians encamped there when Custer attacked them. I have been investigating this matter for the past ten years, but I find no evidence to show that there were more than this number present.

In all my wild life, I know it to be the habit of Indians never to camp in too large numbers. It was impossible to feed three thousand on the daily hunt for any length of time, and the water question was also very important in that dry country. Such a great number would have to follow the river at all times. Besides, the buffalo was the most wily animal in the world. He was likely at any time to leave in a body for other plains.

Who, then, were the people on the Little Bighorn on June 25, 1876? I answer, nearly all the Hunkpapas under Sitting Bull, Gall, Crow King, and Black Moon; about half of the Minneconjous under Hump, Lame Deer, and Iron Star; that portion of the Oglalas under Crazy Horse, Big Road, and No Water; the Brules under Low Dog and Little Hawk; the San Arcs under Spotted Eagle and Elk Head; the Northern Cheyennes under Two Moon, Little Horse, and White Bull; and a small band of fifteen tepees under old Inkpaduta of Clear Lake massacre fame,[3] who came across the country from Manitoba and joined the hostiles in the fall. Among this band was my own uncle, White Foot Print, who is still living in Canada.

The camp was in the following order from south to north down the river:

Hunkpapas	224 tepees [lodges]
Sans Arcs	85 " "
Inkpadutas	15 " "
Brules	140 " "
Minneconjous	190 " "
Oglalas	240 " "
Cheyennes	55 " "
Total number	949 tepees [lodges]

If we allow five persons to the [lodge], we have 4,945 Indians, and counting one-fourth of this number [as] warriors (which is altogether too large an estimate), there will be 1,211 warriors. Suppose we add to this number 200 war-

Two Moon, chief of the Northern Cheyennes. MCCLURE'S MAGAZINE, 1898.

riors who may possibly have come from the various agencies in Dakota, the number of fighting men all told will be 1,411. This will bring it within the number that Colonel Custer had expected to meet. In fact, if we exclude the boys of under eighteen years of age and the old men over seventy (a majority of whom had not sufficient weapons), the number of warriors would be about 800 to 900, and that was about the estimate General Sherman made before the expedition was sent out.[4]

It may be of interest to the reader to know where these different bands were during the previous winter. The Cheyennes were on the Powder River; Crazy Horse was not far from them; while Sitting Bull, with the Hunkpapas and the Sans Arcs, was on the Little Missouri, and the Minneconjous and the Brules were on the Yellowstone, near the mouth of the Tongue River. Both the Cheyennes and the Oglalas, under Two Moon and Crazy Horse respectively, had been attacked during the winter by General Crook's command.

As these two bands proceeded from their winter camp, they soon met, and a little later they overtook the other bands. It is a fact, as Two Moon stated in Hamlin Garland's interview, which appeared in *McClure's* Magazine for September 1898,[5] that they were all trying to get as far away from the military as possible, in order to hunt in peace. Game was more abundant in the Bighorn region, so all the bands were converging toward that point, without any idea of making a united stand there. It is true that the Indians were better armed than they ever were before, but this cannot be taken as meaning one hundred rounds of cartridges to each warrior. While they had many of the latest improved guns, the majority had no such weapon; indeed, many had nothing more than the usual bow and arrows and a war club.

As this large village of tepees was moving leisurely up the Rosebud River, they were ready at any time to separate into smaller parties, and waited only for the promised Sun Dance, until they learned of the expedition of General Crook. At midnight on June 9, there was great excitement in the Minneconjou camp. Heralds were soon galloping around all of the camps announcing the coming of the soldiers in great numbers. A party of forty warriors who went to Fort Reno had seen Crook's trail on their return. They followed it up and finally gave him a running battle. Here was a band of only forty young men who dared to attack a command of over one thousand. The army reports represent this attack as made by a large number of warriors.

When these men brought the news, there was a great council of war. It was agreed to meet General Crook when he came within a day's march. It was also planned that only half of their forces should meet him, and that they would use all of their tactics to take him at a disadvantage, and to stampede his horses if possible.

Accordingly, on the evening of June 16, just as the hunters were returning with their meat, the scouts reported that Crook was now upon the Rosebud, a short distance from them. The warriors ate their supper hastily, and fresh ponies were saddled for the attack. Crazy Horse volunteered to lead the Brules as well as his own men. Gall, Rain-in-the-Face, and Lone Bull led the Hunkpapas, while Spotted Eagle, Iron Star, and Fearless Bear (the latter was killed there) were at the head of the Minneconjous and Sans Arcs. The Cheyennes were led by Little Horse and American Horse—not the well-known Sioux by that name; that man was killed later in the fall.

Up the Rosebud, fully seven hundred strong, the warriors went. There were some belated hunters who straggled after the main body. Four of them started after dark and missed the trail, so they ascended a hill to view the country beyond. The gray dawn appeared over the eastern hills as they neared the summit. But it happened that there were several Crow scouts who were at that moment ascending the same hill on the other side for a similar purpose—only they were looking for the Sioux camp. Both parties, being greatly surprised, exchanged two or three hurried shots and parted. The Sioux came down the hill yelling. They found the main body of their friends at the foot of this same butte, where they had lain with the intention of watching Crook's movements from behind it. Aroused by the war cry of their comrades, they quickly pursued the scouts into Crook's camp.

They tried hard, but failed to stampede or draw him out. Only once did the wary general nibble their bait. He sent an officer, Captain Mills, with his command, to follow up the Indians with the hope of capturing their camp. But the quick eye of the wily braves had seen the movement, and they had already nearly surrounded him when he was recalled. Crook stood his ground, but he acted on the defensive throughout. The Sioux were satisfied that they had thoroughly scared the white soldiers, and they returned to their camp.

They, however, kept a close watch of his movements, and they saw him return to Goose Creek. It was then that they raised their camp and moved across the divide to the Little Bighorn. They had lost only a few men in the battle. Crook had been practically defeated and repulsed. The game was still abundant enough in the vicinity to warrant their continuing together for a few days longer, and they intended meanwhile to celebrated some of their usual summer dances. They had as yet no suspicion of General Terry's approach or the advance of Colonel Custer on their trail. One day's hunt drives all the buffalo far off, so that on the following day they usually go much farther to find him.

On June 25, the early starters among the hunters had already brought in their game by a little after midday, but as usual there were many who had not yet returned; fortunately for them, not all the warriors joined in the daily hunt. There were hundreds of young men and boys upon the flats, playing games and horse racing. Anyone who knows at all about the natural life of the Sioux upon the plains would know that these young men were armed as far as they had the weapons. These are their ornaments in times of peace—weapons of defense and offense in time of trouble.

Many were in the midst of their meal when, from the south end of the camp, came the warning cry, "Woo, woo! Hay-ay, hay-ay! Warriors to your saddles! The white soldiers are now upon us!"

The Sioux who gave the warning was mounted upon a swift pony. Each leading chief was quick in calling upon his respective warriors to fight to the utmost. Some cried out to let the old men and the women move the children beyond the reach of the bullets; others loudly advised to remain still, "for," they said, "if you do not, the soldiers will believe we are confused and demoralized."

By this time, the bullets were whistling through the Hunkpapa camp, and the excitement was great. The young men who had been playing upon the flats were the first to meet Major Reno. Led by Sitting Bull's nephew, Lone Bull, they rushed forward and would have forced him back, had it not been for the prompt interference of Gall, Rain-in-the-Face, and Spotted Eagle.

"Wait—wait!" they said. "We are not ready. Many of us have not our ponies at hand. Hold them there until there are warriors enough upon their ponies!"

In the midst of the confusion, Sitting Bull stood by his tepee and addressed his people thus, "Warriors, we have everything to fight for, and if we are defeated, we shall have nothing to live for; therefore, let us fight like brave men."

Major Reno now dismounted part of his men and continued his fire upon the fleeing women and children. A large number of warriors had all but surrounded him, but had not yet charged. Their position was along a dry creek [Shoulder Blade Coulee] that goes off from the river at this point.

Gall, Crow King, Black Moon, and Rain-in-the-Face now joined the young men; this encouraged the latter so much that no sooner had Lone Bull given the war whoop for the charge than the soldiers retreated. The first company endeavored to return the way they came, but they were forced to the east, almost at right angles with their trail.[6] Just as the Indians made their general charge, the second company of the soldiers turned to flee.[7] They were closely pursued. The Indians, having full knowledge of the ground and the river, were greatly encouraged. The leaders shouted, "We can drown them all—charge closer!"

The first company of soldiers fared tolerably well, but the second lost many men.[8] Many of the horses became unmanageable, and as their riders had no opportunity to choose a safe crossing, they were compelled to jump over the high riverbanks into the stream. The Indians say there were several who never appeared again.

The opposite hill was equally steep and dangerous, but the soldiers scrambled up in a most unwarlike manner. Here some of the privates showed fine presence of mind and uncommon bravery. One officer of the fleeing command aroused the highest admiration of the Indians. He emptied his revolver in a most effective way and had crossed the river when a gunshot brought him down. There were three noted young warriors of three different lodges (Indian young men have lodges corresponding to white men's clubs or lodges) vying with one another for bravery. They all happened to pursue this officer; each one was intent upon knocking him off with a war club before the others, but the officer dispatched every one of them. The Indians told me of finding peculiar instruments on his person, from which I thought it likely that this brave man was Dr. DeWolf, who was killed there.

The pursuing braves soon saw that the soldiers were reinforced and occupied a good ravine for defense, so they concluded to hold them until more warriors could arrive; besides, they did not know how much of a force there might be behind. At this moment, word was brought that a large body of soldiers had already attacked the lower camp, and they were advised to hold Reno's men. The forces that repulsed Reno numbered not over five hundred. This was all that they could muster up in so short a time. Of this number, probably one hundred went over to the Custer battle, but they were a little late.

Just as the forces under Gall, Rain-in-the-Face, and Crow King made their famous charge, the lower (north) end of the camp discovered Colonel Custer and his men approaching. The two battles were fully two and a half miles apart.

"Woo, woo! Here they come!" shouted the Indians, as Custer with his formidable column appeared on the slope of the ridge. They knew well he could not cross the river at that point. He must go down half a mile. The crossing, therefore, became at once of first importance.

As Crazy Horse started down to the ford, Custer appeared upon the riverbank. Having discovered that it was impossible to cross, he began to fire into the camp, while some of his men[9] dismounted and were apparently examining the banks. Already Crazy Horse with his men had crossed the river, closely followed by Little Horse and White Bull with their Cheyenne warriors. Two Moon was still loudly urging the young men to meet the soldiers on the other side, and as he led the remaining Cheyennes in the same direction, the Minneconjous and the Brules were coming down at full speed.

The forces under Crazy Horse and Little Horse followed a long ravine that went east from the crossing until it passed the ridge; it then took a southerly direction parallel with and immediately behind the said ridge [Custer Ridge]. Iron Star and Low Dog, on the other hand, turned southward immediately after crossing the river. The firing from the camp still continued, and as the later forces arrived, they at once opened fire upon the soldiers, who were gradually retreating toward the ridge half a mile back from the riverbank.

Up to this time, Colonel Custer did not seem to comprehend the danger before him. But when one company of his command reached the summit of the ridge, it was quickly forced behind the brow of the hill by the Indians. The soldiers now took up three separate positions along the ridge.[10] But they were practically already hemmed in.

At first the colonel kept his men intact; but the deafening war whoops and the rattling sound of the gunshots frightened the horses. The soldiers had no little trouble from this source. Finally they let go of their horses and threw themselves flat upon the ground, sending volley after volley into the whirling masses of the enemy.

The signal was given for a general charge. Crazy Horse with the Oglalas, and Little Horse and White Bull with the Cheyennes, now came forward with a tremendous yell. The brave soldiers sent into their ranks a heavy volley that checked them for the moment. At this instant, a soldier upon a swift horse started for the river, but was brought down. Again the Indians signaled for a charge. This time the attack was made from all sides. Now they came pell-mell upon the soldiers. One company[11] was chased along the ridge to the south, out of which a man got away. A mighty yell went up from the Indians as he cleared the attacking forces, as if they were glad that he succeeded. Away he went toward Reno's position. The rest of the company were now falling fast, and the ridge was covered with the slain.

"Hay-ay, hay-ay! Woo, woo! The solder who escaped is coming back!" The man now appeared again upon the ridge where he had just escaped death, closely pursued by fifteen warriors. He was more than halfway down to Reno's stand when the party set upon him. They were coming up from the other battle. Some say that this soldier took his own life when he was driven back to the main body of the Indians.

The soldiers found near the spot where the big monument now stands [Last Stand Hill] fought best and longest. The Indians used many arrows and war clubs when the two forces came closer together. There was one officer and his attendant who fought their way almost through, but they were killed at last.

"Crazy Horse with the Oglalas came forward with a tremendous yell."
COSMOPOLITAN, 1911.

The last of Custer. CYRUS T. BRADY. *INDIAN FIGHTS AND FIGHTERS.*

They fell farthermost toward the east at the head of the ravine. It is said that the private stood over the wounded officer, and when two warriors attacked him, he killed one of them, but the other lassoed him and dragged him away.

Thus ended the last battle and the career of a daring American officer. It was a surprise to the Sioux that he held his men together so well.

The Indian forces were now directed against Reno's position. The young men, encouraged by the total annihilation of Colonel Custer's command, desired to rush upon him and force him from his protected stand, but the more experienced warriors advised otherwise. It was thought that so long as they had pinned them down, the soldiers would sooner or later give up; therefore there was no need of sacrificing any more young men. Many of the chiefs had not reached the battlefield until now. They did not participate except in counseling as what should be done.

The Sioux occupied every available point around Reno, so that he could not escape. However, on the afternoon of the next day, the scouts brought word that a large boat and a great number of soldiers were coming up the Bighorn River not far away. It appeared to them not practicable to hold Reno any longer; therefore, that afternoon the camp was raised, and the people departed in several smaller parties in different directions.

The battle of the Little Bighorn was a Waterloo for Colonel Custer and the last effective defense of the Black Hills by the Sioux. It was a fair fight. Custer offered battle and was defeated. He was clearly outgeneraled at his own stratagem. Had he gone down just half a mile farther and crossed the stream where Crazy Horse did a few minutes later, he might have carried out his plan of surprising the Indian village and taking the Indian warriors at a disadvantage in the midst of their women and children.

Was it a massacre? Were Custer and his men sitting by their campfires when attacked by the Sioux? Was he disarmed and then fired upon? No. Custer had followed the trail of these Indians for two days and finally overtook them. He found and met just the Indians he was looking for. He had a fair chance to defeat the Sioux, had his support materialized and brought their entire force to bear upon the enemy in the first instance.

I reiterate that there were not twelve thousand to fifteen thousand Indians at that camp, as has been represented; nor were there over a thousand warriors in the fight. It is not necessary to exaggerate the number of the Indians engaged in this notable battle. The simple truth is that Custer met the combined forces of the hostiles, which were greater than his own, and that he had not so much underestimated their numbers as their ability.

On the Little Bighorn with General Custer

THEODORE W. GOLDIN[1]

Army Magazine 4 (June and July 1894)[2]

Over seventeen years have passed away since the sun sank to rest behind the Montana hilltops one hot June day in the centennial year, shedding its last rays on a little detachment of regulars, bravely battling for their lives against ten times their number of frenzied, bloodthirsty savages, while only a few short miles away, their old-time leader, with some two hundred gallant comrades—stripped, mutilated, and ghastly—lay cold and mute in the soldier's last sleep.

In this length of time, one would naturally suppose all the facts connected with that long to be remembered chapter in our frontier military history would have been given the public. But through magazines, books, and newspapers, we find the battle being fought over anew, in some instances by officers and ex-soldiers who were with the command, in others by officers and even civilians who were not there, while the "last survivor" of Custer's gallant command is getting more numerous as the years roll along, and striving to rob Trumpeter Martin of "H" Troop (the only living white man entitled to the appellation) of the honors so justly his due.[3]

When orders were received to join the regiment at Fort Lincoln, D.T., in the spring of 1876, the troop of the 7th Cavalry to which I then belonged was enjoying, for the time being, a somewhat inactive existence in permanent camp near Shreveport, La. But no time was lost in getting under way for our new location, and shortly before midnight on April 30, Troops B, G, and K rolled into the yards at Bismarck, tumbled out of our cars, and by the light of a flickering campfire and a stable lantern or two, hurried through the form of the regular bimonthly muster.

The following morning, our company property was loaded into a waiting wagon train and went trundling off down the valley of the Missouri to the post, some five miles distant. "Boots and Saddles" soon sounded, and by noon the battalion was in camp about half a mile below the post, with the balance of the regiment reunited again for the first time in several years.

Our first night in camp was one long to be remembered. To those of us just from the south, Dakota spring weather was a revelation. Early in the night we

Romance on the Hudson—reality on the Plains. HARPER'S WEEKLY, 1876.

woke up, our teeth chattering and the very marrow in our bones seemingly congealed. We tried more blankets, but that didn't work, and at last, chilled through and through, we crept out of our tents, wrapped a blanket over our overcoats, and spent the remainder of the night crouching over the cook fires and relieving our minds in language only proper on the frontier in times of great emergency.

Soon after the first of May, we began active preparations for the summer campaign. Forage caps and natty uniforms gave place to broad rimmed [*sic*] scouting hats, and riding breeches heavily reinforced with tent canvas or "Stark A" bags; glistening cartridge boxes and fancy leather belts were consigned to our boxes and replaced with the less elegant, though far more serviceable "prairie belt," and in a very few days the command was ready to take the field.

As we have said, for the first time in several years the entire regiment was in camp, looking forward to one of the biggest Indian campaigns ever known in the history of the Northwest.

Colonel Gibbon, of Iron Brigade renown, was already creeping down the valley of the Yellowstone, with a small infantry force and the Montana Battalion of the 2nd Cavalry, bound to the rescue of the beleaguered traders at Fort Pease, just below the mouth of the Bighorn River; while far away to the southward, that prince of Indian fighters, [Brig.] Gen. George Crook, the old "gray fox" of Arizona fame, was completing preparations to take the field with a large force of cavalry and infantry, composed of regiments and detachments known throughout the army for their gallant service records in many a hard campaign.

Just as our preparations were about completed, word was received at the camp that Colonel Custer had been ordered under arrest at Chicago by order of the president (Grant),[4] and that the regiment would take the field under command of Maj. Marcus A. Reno, an officer not generally liked among the enlisted men who had soldiered under him, and an officer for whom even the "commissioned" force of the regiment had no unbounded love or admiration. The reader can therefore imagine that it was with unconcealed feelings of pleasure the rank and file heard the news "Custer will be here tomorrow."[5] With this information came the news that the Fort Lincoln column would take the field in the command of Brig. Gen. Alfred Terry, at that time department commander of the Department of Dakota.

The reason for this change in commanding officers was freely commented on at the time, and it was pretty generally conceded that it was perfectly proper for the general commanding the department to go out in command of the expedition, in order that he might be close at hand in case of an emergency. Both during and since the time of that fatal expedition, we have often heard it said, both by army officers and others, that Colonel Custer's arrest and detention at Chicago, and the treatment accorded him at Washington, had far more to do with his course of action after he left the mouth of the Rosebud than might be generally supposed. Proud, sensitive, and brave even to rashness, Colonel Custer must have felt his seeming disgrace very keenly, and when he was placed at the head of the regiment he had so long and ably commanded, and was temporarily freed from the restraint occasioned by the presence of his immediate superior, his desire to clear himself from the cloud hanging over him led him to place a very liberal construction on the suggestions made to him by General Terry, at their council on the *Far West*. But be that as it may, those of us who followed him along that fated trail know that he died with his face to the foe, making no cowardly retreat, even before half his regiment were in action.

At daybreak on the morning of May 17, we rolled out from under our blankets to the stirring notes of the reveille, swallowed our hardtack and coffee, finished our packing, and then lounged around, smoking and chatting, waiting for the hour to move.

Just as the sun peeped over the eastern hilltops, the ringing notes of the "general" sounded from headquarters. In an instant every tent was down, and leaving them to be packed and hauled away by a detail from the garrison at the post, we hurried out to the herd as the bugles were sounding "Boots and Saddles," horses were led in, saddled up, and in a brief space of time the whole regiment was led into line. Five minutes later, we clambered rather than swung into our saddles, owing to the large amount of baggage and equipment we were compelled to carry on our saddles, and at the command "Right forward, fours right, march!" we broke into column, and the expedition of 1876 was in the field.

As we moved slowly up the valley, we drew near the shacks occupied by the families of our Indian scouts. Grouped along the roadside were the mothers, wives, and sisters of the men who were to guide us on our journey, and as we approached them, our ears were saluted with the mournful notes of one of their peculiar chants; louder and louder the weird, wailing notes rang out on the clear morning air. Try as we would, it seemed impossible to banish a feeling of depression as we listened and wondered how many times this same band, gathered in their distant village, had chanted this same dirgelike song for fathers, brothers, husbands, and sons, who, going forth to battle, as we were now, had never returned.

We soon left this strange scene behind and drew near the quarters occupied by the married enlisted men of the regiment. Gathered along the outskirts of these rude frontier homes were the wives and children who were to be left behind; every moment some bronzed, stalwart trooper would rein out of line for a farewell handclasp from wife and child, while up and down the dusty road, all unconscious of the true meaning of the scene before them, astride brooms, clothes poles, and other convenient articles, pranced dozens of urchins in mimic imitation of their sires. This scene too was soon left behind, as with a ringing "Column left, march!" the band at the head of the regiment struck up the familiar air "The Girl I Left Behind Me," and we marched rapidly across the southerly side of the parade, then turned northward at the old adjutant's office, and here it was the last sad partings took place. Here and there at the windows along officers' row, we could see the tear-stained faces of officers' wives and children, striving eagerly for a last farewell glimpse of the loved husband and father, who, at the head of his troop, was striving by unusual sternness of demeanor to conceal the grief filling his heart to overflowing, and with impatient hand brushing away the unaccustomed tear. Here a loving wife, more courageous than her sisters, had ventured as far as the gate for a parting handclasp or a kiss, but the effort was too great, and with burning tears coursing down her cheeks, she fled to the solitude of her doubly deserted fireside, there to master her grief alone.

Pausing for a moment on the brow of the hill near the infantry guardhouse to readjust our saddles a trifle, the whole scene was spread out before us like a mammoth panorama. Far out to the front fluttered the red and blue headquarters flag of Colonel Custer, and near it, the white star on the blue ground used by General Terry to designate department headquarters; off to the left of the trail, the column of sturdy infantry was plodding along, arms "at will," while lumbering along the trail and stretching its creeping length over hill and valley like a mighty serpent, rolled the long line of heavily laden white covered army wagons. Winding in and out among the ravines and over the rolling prairie, just lengthening out into column of twos, was the cavalry command, the morning sun shining on their arms and equipment and flashing back from the glossy coats of their well-groomed horses, while off to the left and near the wagon train, the little artillery detachment ambled along at a steady walk. Thus it was we started.

After a thirteen days' march, enlivened only by a hailstorm, some heavy pioneering, and the incidents usual to the first days of the campaign, we reached the Little Missouri River, where we went into camp[6] and remained for a day or two, while a scouting party under Colonel Custer scoured the country for some distance up the valley in search of a possible enemy. On May 31, we forded the river, made a march of about ten miles, and went into camp near Sunset Peak, where we were compelled to remain until the morning of June 3, owing to a heavy snowstorm.

Leaving this camp, we struck out for the mouth of the Powder River, and on the afternoon of the seventh, after five days of hard marching and harder pioneering over a rough and hilly country, we found ourselves in the summit of a range of high bluffs. Looking downward, far below us, we could see, winding in and out through the distant valley, the rushing waters of the Powder River, but it required several hours of hard work ere we succeeded in getting our wagon train safely into camp. We remained in camp here for two or three days, and in the meantime, General Terry, with a cavalry escort, went down to the mouth of the river, distant some twenty miles.

On his return, it was decided to send out a scouting party, and on the afternoon of June 10, Major Reno with six troops of the regiment, equipped with pack animals, broke camp and started up the valley, with orders, as we understood, to carefully scout the country as far up as the forks of the Powder River, and from thence by way of the valley of Mizpah Creek to the Tongue River, and down that stream to its mouth, to which point it was then understood the remainder of the regiment would proceed. To enable Major Reno to comply with this order, all the rations and forage of the remaining six troops, save one day's supply, were turned over to the 1st Battalion.

This, of course, necessitated a move on our part, and on Sunday morning, the eleventh, we broke camp and with the entire wagon train pushed downstream toward the Yellowstone, where we arrived the same afternoon. Soon after our arrival, the steamer *Far West* put in an appearance, and we replenished our depleted commissary.

The time spent in camp at the mouth of the Powder River was far from being wasted; arrangements were made for the establishment of a supply camp; the wagon train, band, and dismounted men were to be left behind; pack saddles and aparejos were issued to the several troops, mules were taken from the wagon train, and details from each troop were carefully instructed in the work of packing.

On the afternoon of June 14, we received orders to "Leave everything not absolutely necessary with the wagon train, as at daybreak tomorrow the cavalry command will move toward the mouth of the Tongue River." For the first time since we left Fort Lincoln, it began to look as though there was stirring work ahead, and everyone in camp seemed anxious for the move.

Soon after daylight on the fifteenth, with the band on an adjacent knoll playing "Garry Owen," we clambered into our saddles, waved a cheery goodbye to the comrades unwillingly left behind,[7] and twenty minutes later were out of sight of the camp and, with pack train well closed up, were pushing northward for the Tongue River, distant about forty miles. Owing to the fact that neither the packers nor the mules were well hardened to the work, our progress was slow and we were a day and a quarter in covering the distance, passing on our way several abandoned Indian camps and arriving at our destination on the forenoon of the sixteenth.

Our camp was pitched on the site of an abandoned Indian village, near where Miles City, Montana Territory, was afterward first laid out. Broken tepee poles, branches of cottonwood stripped of their bark by hungry ponies, and numerous other evidences of savage occupancy were scattered through the timber, while out on the prairie in our immediate front, wrapped in their gaudy blankets, were the bodies of perhaps half a dozen Sioux or Cheyenne warriors, serenely sleeping their last sleep, all unconscious of the fact that their recent habitation was peopled with their hated enemies the pony soldiers.[8]

As yet, no word had reached us from Major Reno's command, and some anxiety was felt, even though we knew the time for which they were rationed had not yet expired. We at this time knew nothing of the fact that on the very day of our arrival at this point, the column under General Crook was fighting practically a losing battle with the hostiles far over on the Rosebud. All the long afternoon of the eighteenth, the command lay within the shelter of the timber, officers and men eagerly watching every dust cloud that whirled across the distant prairie, hoping, but in vain, that it was the harbinger of the approach of the absent ones. During the afternoon, it was reported that unless news reached us during the night, our command would move up the river the following morning.

On the morning of the nineteenth, General Terry having passed on up the stream with the steamer, we too broke camp and moved up the valley of the Tongue River. By 10:00 A.M., the heat was intense, and we finally sought the shade of the timber and went into camp; our horses were soon on lariat, and the cooks were busily preparing soup for our dinners; all else was dead. Far out on the surrounding hills, we could see the pickets keeping lazy watch, but we knew them well enough to feel that no sign, however slight, indicating the presence of an enemy would escape their vigilance. Out on the prairie where our herds were picketed, the usually active herd guard, sheltered from the burning sun behind a saddle blanket spread over a convenient sagebrush, kept nodding watch over his charges, most of whom were lying down, while a few lazily cropped the juicy buffalo grass.

Dinner was almost ready, and officers and men were rousing up and stirring about in the edge of the timber, when word was brought in by one of the pickets that a big cloud of dust had been discovered moving down the valley on the other side of the river. "Boots and Saddles" was at once sounded, and pausing only long enough to seize carbine and belts, the men dashed away for the herd, and in less than ten minutes the whole command was saddled up and in line, but just before we received the order to mount, Major Reno's battalion, tired, dust-covered, and hungry, came riding into sight. While their leader was making his report to Colonel Custer, we divided our dinners with hungry comrades and soon learned that the command had discovered a trail over toward the Tongue River, the second or third day after they left us, and had followed it across to the Rosebud, where they struck an abandoned camp, estimated to have contained some eight hundred fifty lodges. Some of the Indian scouts told us they could have overtaken this party in less than two days, judging from the way they seemed to be moving, a statement substantially repeated to the writer by Charley Reynolds, one of our most reliable scouts, who also said that some of the officers of the battalion claimed at the point where the command turned back the trail was fully a week old, but that he knew better than that.

After a brief halt, the entire regiment again took up the march and struck square across the country for the mouth of the Rosebud, to overtake General Terry and in hopes of making a junction with Colonel Gibbon's command. Sunset found us miles on our journey, but there was no indication of a halt; darkness came over us and we were still marching; mile after mile was covered in almost utter silence, save for the steady tramping of the horses and the rattle of equipments. Sometime after dark, the writer was sent back with instructions to hurry up the pack train; the message delivered, we dropped back with the rear guard and followed along the trail.

Half an hour later, we began the ascent of a range of hills bordering on the Yellowstone; a few moments of stiff climbing and we were at the top; far below us, winding in and out among the trees, gleaming like a thread of silver, rippled the waters of the Yellowstone; here and there along its banks, tiny campfires were breaking into a blaze; the moon just appearing above the eastern hilltops shed a soft light over the valley; off to the left, a white tent fly shone out in bold contrast to the deep shadows of the timber; moving in and out among the campfires, scores of troopers were busily preparing for the midnight bivouac; over on the left, near the camp of the scouts, the ringing strokes of an ax sounded for a few moments on the clear night air; the fires were growing brighter and brighter, and the moon, now sailing in unclouded majesty across the heavens, was bringing into bold relief the entire camp; the soft summer winds gently rustling the treetops; the river murmuring in the distance; the trampling of the horses and the tinkle of the bells on the pack animals now rapidly moving into the valley, all came to us softened and subdued by the distance.

From our elevated position, it was hard to realize that the gathering below us was one of friends and comrades; it seemed rather that we were gazing on a beautiful picture which, through some supernatural agency, had been stirred into sudden life. Every passing moment added new beauties to the scene, and we sat on our horses and gazed at it, lost in silent admiration, until the appetizing smell of coffee brought us to a realizing sense of the earthly character of the scene before us, and we lost no time in getting into camp. Our hurried supper was soon over, and after a social smoke about the embers of the campfire, we rolled ourselves into our blankets and were sound asleep, our heads pillowed on our saddles, and the starry canopy of heaven our only tent.

We were in the saddle soon after daybreak of the twenty-first, and about 10:00 A.M. caught a glimpse of Colonel Gibbon's command moving slowly up the opposite side of the river, and a few moments later the *Far West* steamed into sight around the bend. Couriers were sent forward to overtake them, and by noon the two commands were in camp on opposite sides of the river, near the mouth of the Rosebud.

Active preparations were at once commenced for a forward move. Many of our pack animals were exhausted or disabled, and we replaced them with fresh ones from the wagon train of Colonel Gibbon's command. Fifteen days' rations were issued and prepared for packing; additional ammunition was issued throughout the command until every man was supposed to have not less than one hundred rounds of carbine and twenty-four rounds of pistol ammunition.

A council was held on board the steamer between General Terry, Colonel Gibbon, and Colonel Custer, and a plan of action mapped out. This council was a short one, and as soon as it was over, the final orders were issued for our advance.[9]

Some general instructions were given Colonel Custer by the department commander on the morning of June 22, a few brief extracts from which we desire to quote:

> The brigadier general commanding directs that as soon as your regiment can be made ready for the march, you will proceed up the Rosebud in pursuit of the Indians whose trail was discovered by Major Reno a few days since. It is, of course, impossible to give you any definite instructions in regard to the movement, but were it not impossible to do so, the department commander places too much confidence in your zeal, energy, and ability to wish to impose upon you precise orders which might hamper your actions when nearly in contact with the enemy.
>
> He thinks that you should proceed up the Rosebud until you ascertain definitely the direction in which the trail above spoken of leads. Should it be found as it appears almost certain that it will be found, to turn toward the Little Bighorn, he thinks you should still proceed southward perhaps as far as the headwaters of the Tongue, and then toward the Little Horn, feeling constantly to your left so as to preclude the possibility of the escape of the Indians to the south or southeast by passing around your left flank. The column of Colonel Gibbon is now in motion for the mouth of the Bighorn. As soon as it reaches that point it will cross the Yellowstone and move up at least as far as the forks of the Big[horn] and Little Bighorn. Of course, its future movements must be controlled by circumstances as they arise, but it is

hoped that the Indians, if upon the Little Bighorn, may be so nearly enclosed by the two columns that their escape will be impossible.

Nothing was said in these instructions as to the time when Colonel Gibbon's column would probably reach the forks of the Big[horn] and Little Bighorn, but it was understood and generally talked in our command that it could not be earlier than noon of the twenty-sixth.

During the forenoon of the twenty-second, it was rumored in camp that Colonel Custer had been offered the battalion of the 2nd Cavalry but had declined it, whether from a feeling of confidence in his own regiment or an idea that there might be a latent feeling between the officers of the two commands that might interfere with his plans at a critical moment, we do not know. He also declined to take the Gatling gun section, as he thought it might interfere with rapid movements, owing to the extreme roughness of the country along the proposed line of march.

At noon of the twenty-second, the twelve troops of the 7th, in column of fours, passed in review order before the department commander and were soon lost to sight in the hills. Our march the first day was between fifteen and twenty miles, and we went into camp about 4:00 P.M. in the afternoon.[10] Only the smallest of fires were allowed, and those only long enough to prepare our meals; extra herd guards were posted; bugle calls, except under circumstances of great necessity, were prohibited; strict injunctions were given against hunting while on the march, and every possible precaution taken to conceal our movements and guard against surprise.

Five o'clock on the morning of the twenty-third found us ready to move, and all day long we pushed ahead on the trail discovered by Major Reno, passing a number of abandoned camping places, and finding the ground littered with evidences of the recent presence of the Indians. Along the banks of the little streams and under the shelter of the timber, we found many "wickiups," a species of rude shelter built by entwining willow branches and small tree limbs into the form of a rude tepee; these when completed were usually covered with a blanket or a buffalo robe or something of that sort, sometimes with grass or the boughs of trees. Our Crow scouts, on seeing these, at once said they were used by the young warriors who had only recently joined the camp.

That night, we camped in a broad valley along the banks of a clear, running stream [Greenleaf Creek], and only a short distance from a recent camp of the enemy, our day's march having been something over 35 miles.[11] Morning of June 24 dawned bright and clear and found us already on the trail. About noon, we halted near an abandoned camp, one of the largest we had yet seen, and while coffee was cooking, "officers' call" was sounded, the first bugle call, as I remember it, since we had sighted the trail. While we were drinking our coffee, one of the orderlies at headquarters stopped near our halting place, and through him we learned that our Crow scouts had discovered recent Indian signs, and that some of the officers had found a white man's scalp in a deserted Sun Dance lodge near the center of the Indian camp.

Our halt here was very brief, and we were soon pushing forward down the widening trail, every mile coming across additional signs of the recent presence of a considerable number of the hostiles. Just before sunset, the head of the column diverged from the trail, wound up the valley of a neighboring stream [Busby Bend of the Rosebud] for a short distance, and went into camp under the shelter of a high bluff, after a march of about thirty miles. A few small fires were kindled in the bottom of an adjacent ravine, over which we hurriedly cooked our bacon and coffee, after which the fires were at once extinguished.

Upon our arrival in camp, we had received orders to keep our saddles packed and have our equipments ready for a possible night march. Ever since leaving the Rosebud, most of the men had been carrying, in addition to their other equipments, small sacks each containing twelve quarts of oats; but fully convinced that the coming twenty-four hours would call for the utmost endurance on the part of their faithful steeds, many of the boys emptied the forage out in front of them and rounded out the forage sacks with their spare clothing. Somewhere about 9:00 P.M., the officers were summoned to headquarters, and soon after this we learned that the trail seemed to lead over the divide and probably down into the valley of the Little Bighorn; that it was deemed desirable for the command to cross the divide under cover of the darkness if possible, and if not, to at least get the command well concealed in the foothills along its base. The officers' council did not last long, and in a few moments they were groping their way back through the darkness to their several commands. Lieutenants Hare and Varnum had been assigned to duty with the scouts, who had been directed to push forward at once and make their way as near the camp of the hostiles as was possible, rejoining the command at daybreak. Striking a match, I looked at my watch and saw that it was nearly 11:00 P.M. A few moments later, word was passed down the lines to "saddle up quietly." The men sprang to their feet, hurried their horses in from the herd, and in a very few moments had completed the work and led into line, where they stood at their horses' heads in anxious expectation. "Mount" was the next command, and swinging lightly into the saddle, we moved out in column of fives, crossed the stream, regained the trail, and were once more pushing ahead on our march.

The darkness was intense. Canteens, sidelines, and everything liable to make a noise had been carefully secured. Colonel Custer was well out to the front with a force of expert trailers; the necessary changes of direction were from time to time indicated from the head of the column by the flickering light of a match, seen but for an instant. Scarcely a word was spoken, but every eye was peering to the front and every ear on the alert for the slightest sound.

So we marched, hour after hour with only the briefest halts, and just as the first rosy tinges of approaching day began to light up the eastern sky, the command halted after a march of somewhere from ten to fifteen miles.[12] Pausing only long enough to slacken their saddle girths and slip the bits from their horse's mouths, the weary troopers threw themselves on the ground and were soon asleep. Just after daybreak, the cooks undertook to prepare some coffee, but the water was so strongly alkaline the attempt was abandoned, as the stuff was not fit to drink.

During our halt, Colonel Custer had pushed on to the point [Crow's Nest] where Lieutenant Varnum had spent a portion of the night of the twenty-fourth with the Indian scouts, and on his return, he told the officers that the scouts had told him they could see the location of the village, some tepees and some ponies, but that he (Custer) didn't believe it; that he had looked through a field glass they had and couldn't see anything and didn't believe they could. Notwithstanding this, the scouts still maintained they had located the village in the valley of the Little Bighorn, distant perhaps twenty miles from where we then were. And I heard several of the officers of the command express the opinion that the Indians had seen, and could see, all they had claimed.

About 8:00 A.M., the command moved out and marched steadily and as rapidly as the rough and broken condition of the country would admit, for perhaps two hours, when we found ourselves well sheltered in the ravines at the base of the divide. Here we halted and remained concealed for some little time, just how long I am not able to state.[13] While here, it was reported that one of the troops had lost a pack during the night, and a detail sent back to recover it had run across several Indians in the valley in our rear. This was at once reported to Colonel Custer; "officers' call" was sounded, and the several troop commanders ordered to make a detail of one noncommissioned officer and six men as an escort to the pack train, which was placed in charge of Lieutenant Mathey. Just before we mounted, the writer was ordered to report at once to Lieutenant Cooke, the regimental adjutant, and on reporting was ordered to keep as close to him as possible and be ready to perform any duty for which he might be needed.

Just previous to moving out, the regiment was divided into three battalions, one under Major Reno, consisting of Troop A, Captain Moylan and Lieutenant DeRudio; Troop G, Lieutenant McIntosh and Lieutenant Wallace; and Troop M, under Captain French. With this column was Lieutenant Hodgson, acting battalion adjutant, and two surgeons, Dr. DeWolf and Dr. Porter.

Troop D, Captain Weir and Lieutenant Edgerly; Troop H, Captain Benteen and Lieutenant Gibson; and Troop K, Lieutenant Godfrey and Lieutenant Hare, were placed in command of Captain Benteen. The last orders Captain Benteen received came to him through the sergeant major of the regiment and were in substance as follows: "If from the furthest line of bluffs you now see you cannot see the valley (no particular valley mentioned), you will keep on until you come to a valley (or perhaps *the* valley); pitch into anything you come across and notify me at once."[14]

Troop B, Captain McDougall, was detailed as rear guard. Troop C, Captain Custer and Lieutenant Harrington; Troop E, Lieutenants Smith and Sturgis;

Troop F, Captain Yates and Lieutenant Reilly; Troop L, Lieutenants Calhoun and Crittenden; and Troop I, Captain Keogh and Lieutenant Porter, were commanded by Colonel Custer in person. This assignment was made while we were yet some twelve or fifteen miles from the village.

Major Reno was ordered to draw out of the column and continue the march along the trail, and in doing so marched for some distance parallel with and only a short distance from the column under Colonel Custer.

A ride of several miles, a climb up the almost perpendicular sides of a towering bluff, and we came out on the edge of a rolling prairie, undulating away for several miles to the foot of a range of bluffs bordering on a stream, which we afterward learned was the Little Bighorn. Away over to the left, we could get an occasional glimpse of Captain Benteen's battalion, moving rapidly across the broken country to the southward, trying their best to carry out the orders they had received.

Soon after striking the edge of the prairie, a heavy dust cloud was discovered moving down the valley of the stream, and evidently on the opposite side. As soon as this was noticed, Major Reno was ordered to move forward as rapidly as possible until he came up with the Indians, when he was to charge them and drive everything before him. With a rousing cheer, the men of the three troops settled themselves in the saddle and galloped rapidly down the trail.

For some distance, perhaps a couple of miles or more, Colonel Custer with his column followed the same general direction taken by Major Reno, but finally swung off to the northward.[14] Just after this change of direction, Colonel Custer rode up to the head of the column and called out to the captain of the advance troop, "Keogh, those Indians are running; if we can keep them at it, we can afford to sacrifice half the horses in the regiment." This remark served to firmly fix in my mind the idea that Colonel Custer intended to convey the idea that the Indians had discovered our approach and were seeking safety in flight.

Very shortly after our column headed to the northward, I received a hurriedly scrawled order from the hands of Lieutenant Cooke, with the order, "Deliver that to Major Reno, remain with his column until a junction is effected, then report to me at once."

A moment later, I saw the rear of our column go sweeping by, thundering on down the valley. Not at all in love with my position, I delayed only long enough to drop a cartridge into the chamber of my carbine, draw my revolver around within easy reach, and then, touching my horse lightly with the spurs, I struck out to overtake Major Reno, then perhaps a mile away.[16]

I overtook his command just after they had reached the west bank of the river and under shelter of the bluffs were readjusting their saddles and allowing their tired horses a moment's breathing spell. I at once delivered my message to Major Reno; he read it hurriedly, asked me where I had left Colonel Custer, and then handed the message to Lieutenant Hodgson and walked away. I did not read the message save the last three or four words, which were, "We'll soon be with you."

In a very short time, Major Reno reformed his battalion and moved on down the valley with two troops in line of battle, the third troop being held in reserve. When nearly halfway to the point where we finally halted, the third troop was brought up on the line and we moved forward again, first at a trot and then at a gallop, covering a distance of perhaps two miles. We were then dismounted and prepared to fight on foot. Instead of finding the village on the run, as we had been led to expect while with the other column, we saw stretching out before us an immense village of tepees and wickiups, the lower end of which was lost to sight down the valley. We could see there was intense excitement in the upper end of the village, and it was only a few moments when considerable bodies of Indians appeared in our vicinity, and the fight soon became general all along the line.

Soon after we dismounted, someone on our left called out, "There's Custer on the bluffs." Looking up, I saw him, but only for an instant, as he raised his hat and rode down out of sight.[17] The Indians in our vicinity made a determined resistance to our advance toward their village and soon made a determined advance on our right flank, as we faced up the valley, stampeded our Cree scouts, and were soon making vigorous efforts to stampede our led horses.

Soon after this, the skirmish line was drawn into the timber, followed by the horses; here we renewed the fight, remaining in this position possibly twenty-five minutes. All at once we noticed a commotion over toward the left, and could see that some of the men had left the skirmish line and were moving toward our horses; this was at once brought to the attention of Lieutenant Wallace, who called to Captain French, who was in command of the center troop and only a short distance away, asking what it meant. Captain French replied that he did not know, as no orders had been received by him. A few moments later, he called to the lieutenant, saying, "Wallace, I understand they are going to charge." We thought this rather a strange proceeding, inasmuch as no general understanding of the move or its purpose seemed to exist among the officers, and in view of the further fact that our position seemed an excellent one.

We were protected in our front by a bank of considerable height and some small timber, while in our rear was the heavy timber and the river, furnishing us both shelter and water. A few moments later, Lieutenant McIntosh ordered us to get our horses, and those of us still fortunate enough to possess one lost no time in obeying the order; but there were some dozen or fifteen of our men whose horses had been killed, severely wounded, or stampeded; these men were left behind to struggle for their lives as best they could. It is said that one of the officers, just as we commenced the retreat, discovered a guidon, abandoned by someone in the command, and dismounted to recover it and in the attempt lost his horse and was left behind. I cannot vouch for the truth of this statement, but I do know that this officer [Lieutenant DeRudio] did not succeed in reaching the command until late the next night.

In the hurry of mounting, Lieutenant McIntosh took a sorrel horse belonging to trooper McCormick, his own horse either having been shot or stampeded.

Unhorsed. CENTURY MAGAZINE, 1892.

Soon after we left the timber, I noticed that his lariat was dragging its full length; several of the men near him tried to call his attention to it, but he did not seem to hear them, and the next I saw his horse was on his knees and the lieutenant was rolling on the ground several feet ahead of him; I thought then, and still think, his horse was thrown either by another horse stepping on the dragging lariat, or else by the picket pin catching on a sagebrush or some other obstruction. So far as I know, he never regained his feet, as later on we found the body apparently at the point where he stopped rolling.

Well out to the front on this "gallant charge," we could see Major Reno, closely followed by the leading troop commander [Captain Moylan], both seemingly doing their level best to put as much distance as possible between themselves and the Indians, a proceeding none of us were at all slow in imitating. It was currently reported at the time that Major Reno, after exhausting the shots from his revolver, threw the weapon away; I know this to be a mistake, however, as that identical weapon is now in possession of a former officer of the regiment.

My own horse, a big rawboned sorrel formerly ridden by Lieutenant Aspinwall,[18] and with a first-class record as a runner, was doing his level best, but just as we were in sight of the ford, down he went, pitching me over his head very unceremoniously. Luckily I was on the side of the column nearest the timber and, scrambling to my feet, but little the worse for my involuntary circus performance. I proceeded to obey to the letter the order "rush for the brush" shouted at me by Lieutenant Wallace as he passed, and I was soon burrowing my way out of sight under a pile of driftwood. In the meantime, the "charge" had developed into a very respectable "go as you please" race. The officers were utterly powerless to check the mad rush; the Indians were crowding in on their flanks, and from where I was hidden, I saw several of our men pulled from their saddles and cruelly butchered. Notwithstanding the general panic, the men did not cease the fight, and carbines and revolvers did splendid execution.

As the head of the column reached the riverbank, the foremost men urged their horses into the stream and forced them, staggering and stumbling, toward the opposite shore. Here it was that gallant "Benny" Hodgson, the battalion adjutant, was killed. I saw him for the first time just as his horse leaped from the bank; the animal seemed to have been wounded, as he stumbled, fell, rolled, and struggled for a few moments and seemed unable to regain his feet. The plucky little officer cleared himself from the stirrups and, with rare presence of mind, grasped the stirrup strap of the nearest trooper, and with this aid floundered across the stream and out upon the opposite side. The trooper[19] dared not stop, but while in motion, strove to assist the lieutenant to clamber up behind him; twice he tried but failed; a third attempt, almost successful, when with a cry of pain the gallant trooper relaxed his hold, reeled for a moment in the saddle, and fell heavily to the ground. For just an instant, Lieutenant Hodgson lay where he fell, then struggled to his feet, and I could plainly see that he too was either wounded or badly hurt in some way, but with revolver in hand, he staggered forward—stumbled—fell—rose again—staggered forward a few steps more—fell again—crawled on his hands and knees for a few yards, then desperately turned and faced his pursuers; a shot or two from his revolver, a merciless volley from the savages, and he fell back dead—one more sacrifice to the mistaken Indian policy that so long disgraced our government.

In the meantime, the remainder of the little battalion had scrambled up the steep hillside as best they could, Dr. DeWolf being killed when halfway up the hill. As it was afterwards reported, the loss in Major Reno's command up to this time was three officers and some thirty men killed, and nearly as many more or less severely wounded, and one officer and some eighteen men missing.

From my hiding place I could see the Indians moving about the valley along the line of our retreat, shooting arrows into our wounded, and otherwise cruelly torturing them and finally either scalping them and/or crushing their skulls with stone hammers. A short time after this, I noticed a considerable commotion among the Indians in the vicinity of the upper end of the village, large numbers of them hastily mounting up and galloping down the valley in a state of great excitement; a few moments later, after setting fire to the grass in the river bottom, the remainder departed in the same direction. Almost immediately after this, I heard firing over toward the northeast; at first it was almost incessant, with once in a while something that sounded like a volley and seemed to be drawing nearer to the village; but in a short time, it slackened perceptibly; then increased again for a few moments; then became more scattered and sounded farther away.

The Summer Campaign of 1876 325

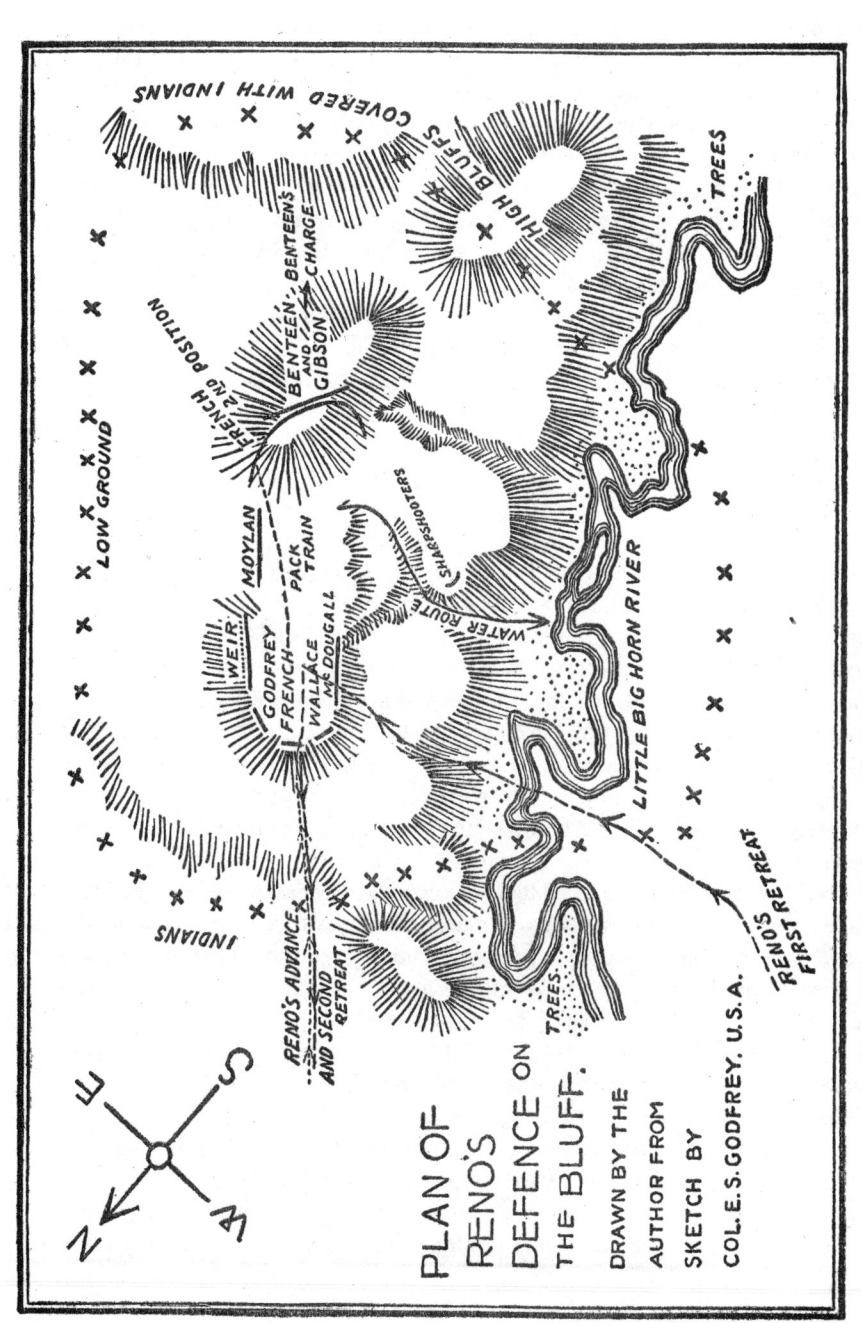

Plan of Reno's defense on the bluff. CYRUS T. BRADY. *INDIAN FIGHTS AND FIGHTERS.*

Up to the time the Indians moved down the valley, I could hear considerable firing on the bluffs in the direction taken by Major Reno's command, but with the departure of the Indians from the valley, this slackened very considerably, although there were occasional shots.

After hugging my pile of driftwood very closely for some time, I saw what looked like a chance to get out of the river bottom by working over toward the right, and made the start, but just as I crept out of my shelter, Captain Benteen's battalion appeared on the bluffs moving rapidly northward, and big Sgt. [James] Flanagan of D Troop took a long-range shot at me, which brought about the display of a very dirty pocket handkerchief on the end of my carbine barrel in the shortest possible order. With this as a sort of protection, I pushed ahead and forded the river, made my way up the steep hillside with the assistance of Half Yellow Face, one of our Crow scouts, and soon found myself in the midst of Reno's command.

Even after I reached the command, we could still hear scattering shots down the river, but nothing indicating heavy firing; that had practically ceased before I came out of the river bottom.

Soon after my arrival, I learned that Captain Benteen's battalion, obedient to the last orders received from Colonel Custer, obliqued off to the left of the trail for several miles, and soon found themselves in a section of country so rough that even an Indian would not travel over it unless forced to. Seeing no possibility of finding Indians, Captain Benteen finally moved back obliquely in the direction of the trail, striking it somewhat in advance of the rear guard and pack train, and after watering his horses, pushed forward in the direction of the river. Hearing the firing on the bluffs in the vicinity of Reno's command, he headed down the river and came up with Reno in time to render him valuable assistance and materially aid in restoring the confidence of the men in the stampeded command.

A short time after I reached them, someone over near the edge of the bluffs called out, "There's a white flag down near the edge of the timber, coming this way." Sure enough, creeping along under the edge of the timber and at times concealed by the eddying smoke rolling up from the burning valley, we saw fully a dozen men, with a white flag at their head. At the risk of his life, Lieutenant Hare crept down to a point of bluffs overhanging the river and signaled them to "come on," remaining there until the whole party under the lead of Herendeen, one of our scouts,[20] had crossed the river.

Just as we were congratulating them upon their successful escape, the pack train came trotting into the corral, followed a few moments later by Captain McDougall with the rear guard; they reported having had a running fight with quite a body of Indians, but came through with the loss of a single pack animal.[21]

Soon after the pack train arrived, I walked over toward the edge of the bluffs with Lieutenant Wallace, trying to point out to him the location of the body of Lieutenant McIntosh. Near where we were standing, quite a group of officers had gathered and stood looking down into the valley, talking earnestly together. Just who made up this party I am not certain, but as I now recollect it, Major Reno, Captain French, Captain Weir, Captain McDougall, and possibly some of the other officers were in the group. While Lieutenant Wallace and I were still talking, Captain Weir hastily left the group, and as he passed us, I heard him say something like "By God, if you don't go I will, and if we live to get out of here, somebody shall know of this." To whom he addressed his remarks, or the particular occasion for them, I never heard, as I never heard the matter mentioned after that.

A few moments after this, I saw Captain Weir mount his horse and move rapidly down the river toward a high bluff that hid our view of the valley to the northward, followed by Lieutenant Edgerly, with D Troop. This move on the part of Captain Weir was, as I afterward learned, unauthorized by his battalion commander and came very near costing us the lives of Lieutenant Edgerly and the whole troop. Just as soon as this move came to the knowledge of Captain Benteen, he mounted the two remaining troops of his battalion and, accompanied by Captain French, with M Troop and detachments from other troops of the command, moved out toward the high point of bluffs, behind which Captain Weir and his troop had already disappeared.

After Captain Benteen and his command moved out, Major Reno had his trumpeter repeatedly sound the halt, but no attention was paid to it by the advancing column, which continued its forward move in column of fours, until they reached the high point above referred to. Here we had a fair view of quite a portion of the Indian village, though, as we afterward discovered, only a portion of it was visible from this point; but as it was, we saw enough to fully convince us, as one of our officers expressed it, that we had "bitten off all we could comfortably chew, this trip."

On reaching this high point, Captain Benteen ordered the guidon of his troop stuck up on top of the hill, thinking, as he said, that the fluttering of the guidon might attract the attention of Custer's command, if any of them were in sight; he also directed Captain French to put his troop in line on a bluff near at hand, running at right angles to the river, saying that possibly the massing of a line on top of the bluffs might catch the eyes of the other column.

While this movement was being executed, Major Reno came up, and a few moments later, D Troop came in sight, moving rapidly by a ravine in our front followed a moment later by hordes of howling Indians. Quick to see that unless something was speedily done, Captain Weir's retreat might precipitate a second stampede, Benteen ordered Captain French to dismount his troop, keep his dismounted men on the bluffs, send his led horses to the rear, let Captain Weir's troop through, then slowly fall back with his dismounted men, winding up by saying, "I'll tell you more when I find it out myself." As it seemed to me, instead of fully obeying these orders, Captain French only held on long enough to let Captain Weir through, and then the line seemed to break slightly and fall back, the men on the run. Seeing this, Captain Benteen directed Lieutenant

Chasing down a runaway pack mule. W. F. BEYER. *DEEDS OF VALOR.*

Godfrey with his troop, to take position at once and drive the Indians back, and then fall back on the main body; this Lieutenant Godfrey did, and after checking the advance of the enemy, by the aid of part of Captain Weir's troop and some of the dismounted men, he gradually fell back. In the meantime, the remainder of the command, under direction of Captain Benteen, most of them dismounted and leading their horses, were slowly falling back, firing whenever they saw a chance, searching for a tenable spot on which to form their line of defense.

In the meantime, the Indians were rapidly increasing in numbers and aggressiveness; word was sent to Lieutenant Godfrey to hold his place for a little while and all would be well. Seeing that further retreat was useless, Captain Benteen turned to the nearest officer, who happened to be Lieutenant Wallace, saying, "Wallace, put your troop, right here, facing the Indians." Lieutenant Wallace grimly replied, "I have no troop, only two men." Benteen replied, laughingly, "Then put yourself and your twos here, and don't let any of them get away—I'll look out for you." This was the nucleus of our final line of defense, Lieutenant Wallace for the time holding the right of the line. As fast as possible, Captain Benteen deployed the troops as they arrived, around the arc of a circle; and in the meantime, Major Reno had undertaken a similar work on the other flank, though, so far as I have ever been able to ascertain, there was no previous understanding as to what was to be done. My own troop, or what there was of it—several of the men having joined us in the meantime—was stationed on the open ground near the top of the ridge to the northward of the point where the corral and hospital were later established. We had no shelter save the inequalities of the ground and an occasional sagebrush. Captain French was on our right; next to him was Lieutenant Godfrey, with Captain Weir on his right, Captain Moylan's troop being on the extreme right facing northward, while on our left and stretching out toward the river was Captain McDougall with B Troop. Just in rear of our position ran a shallow ravine leading down to the north, or northeast; here the hospital and corral were established, and on top of a knoll some little distance south of this ravine, Captain Benteen had posted his own troop; in his immediate front, there was a network of coulees and ravines leading away in all directions, making his position one of great importance, and perhaps the most dangerous one on the field, though the Lord knows any of them seemed dangerous enough.

While Captain Benteen was forming the lines and locating the corral, it is said that he personally rounded up and returned two pack mules, each loaded with two thousand rounds of ammunition, they having been allowed to stray away, and when discovered were making a beeline for the river. I did not see this myself, but do know that later on Captain Benteen gave one officer of the regiment a pretty thorough "dressing down" for his neglect of duty, in the presence of other officers and enlisted men of the regiment.[22]

During the time we were forming our lines and until quite a little after darkness settled over the valley, the Indians kept up an almost incessant fire on us, all along our front, but they finally drew off toward the river in the direction of the village, and all night long we could see the glare of the huge fires blazing in the valley, and hear the howling and screeching of the painted demons.

Shortly after the firing ceased, the position of the several troops on our part of the line was somewhat changed; Captain Moylan's troop was thrown across the shallow ravine to the left and rear of the pack mules and horses, and facing up the river, and the other troops were drawn in closer to the corral. Captain Benteen's troop alone remaining in its original position.

As soon as this change was made, we began entrenching ourselves and preparing for a renewal of the struggle on the morrow. For this work, we called into use tin cups, tin plates, frying pans, hunting knives, hands, what few shovels and spades we could find, and in fact anything with which we could dig and throw dirt, and it goes without saying that the half dozen fellows lucky enough to secure a spade or a shovel were more envied than a Gould or a Vanderbilt.

During the early part of the night, quite a number of the officers were gathered near Major Reno's "dugout" talking over the situation, and in the course of this talk, Major Reno advanced the idea of abandoning the wounded and dismounted men and skipping out with all who could ride, but for the honor of the old regiment, let it be said that it took less than a minute to effectually "sit down" on that cowardly suggestion.[23]

Pretty thoroughly tired out, we abandoned our digging a short time before daybreak, and as we lay there in the dim, misty light and looked into the determined, bearded faces near us, we could see nothing but a grim purpose to fight to the death, and I found myself wondering how many of us would be able to answer roll call by another sunset.

Just about daybreak, the enemy opened fire upon us from all sides, and as it grew lighter, we could see their lines being strengthened by howling contingents from the villages. Over to the south, Captain Benteen, in his exposed position, was bearing the brunt of the attack from the south, and in fact from two or three directions, and the wounded came drifting in from his lines with alarming frequency. Benteen stood it just as long as he could, and then hunted up Major Reno and demanded reinforcements. After some delay and a vigorous use of plain Anglo-Saxon, he succeeded in getting M Troop under Captain French sent over to the south side, and located them, facing up the river, along the southerly side of the ravine and between McDougall's left and the hill occupied by his own troop, and shortly after this, we saw Benteen's command make a fierce charge on the Indians, driving them back some distance; after this, for a short time, there was a cessation in the firing, but we could see the enemy massing to the north and northwest of us in a considerable force, and a few moments later, Captain Benteen came over on our side of the line, and we were ordered to prepare for a charge. It has been said this order was issued by Major Reno; it may be that the original direction was given by him, but I know that Major Reno did not give the order to advance; that was given by Captain Benteen, who stood only a few feet from me. Our only preparations were to shove a cartridge into our carbines, take a hitch in our trousers, sailor fashion, and when we received the word, we tumbled out of our rifle pits with a yell that could have been heard for miles, and proceeded to go for those Indians in a manner not wholly to their liking, for they broke and ran in great disorder almost at our first fire. We advanced on them perhaps a hundred yards or so, and then hurried back to our shelter.

Just before this charge, mounted Indians rode up almost within rifle shot of us, wearing the uniforms of members of Custer's command and waving in their hands guidons and battle flags taken from Custer, all the time taunting us in the most offensive manner.

Soon after we returned to our rifle pits, word came from the hospital that the wounded were begging for water, in fact the whole command was suffering, as many of the men had not tasted water since our first halt on the night of the twenty-fourth, except it might have been some of the alkali stuff where we halted and attempted to make coffee on the morning of the twenty-fifth. It didn't take long to organize a party of volunteers, and Captain Benteen sent us word that there was a ravine just to the west of his position which seemed to offer us a chance to reach the river without discovery, provided we could once gain its shelter. Each man gathered up as many canteens as he thought he could carry, someone brought along a camp kettle to dip the water with, and loading our carbines, we crept well up to the top of the ridge near the head of the ravine and watched our chance to slip over. A moment later, someone called out, "Now's the time, men, skip." And we did skip with a vengeance, and in a moment were practically safe under cover in the ravine. Just as we were congratulating ourselves that for the present, at least, we were reasonably safe, little Campbell of D Troop (now quartermaster sergeant at Jefferson Barracks, Mo., and severely wounded in the fight at Wounded Knee, December 29, 1890) dropped his carbine and canteens and executed a very commendable "Ghost Dance" among the sagebrush. A hasty examination revealed the fact that he had been shot in the shoulder. Picking up his carbine, the plucky little fellow bade us never mind him and made his way back to the corral alone. The balance of the party crept on down the ravine to the river, where it was decided that the best and safest plan would be to make a dash from behind a sheltering bluff, fill the camp kettle, and rush back, and then fill the canteens at our leisure. If discovered, we would of course be liable to be fired upon from three directions, up, down, and across the river; but the detail was after water, and meant to have it, so seizing the camp kettle, two of the men made a dash for the river, filled their kettle, and scurried back in safety with nearly water enough to fill a third of the canteens; two others tried it with equally good success, and a third dash was made, but this time several shots were fired, which whistled uncomfortably close to their heads. Concealing the camp kettle in the brush, the detail got out of there as rapidly as possible, hastily making its way back to the corral, where they divided the supply of water between the wounded in the hospital and the panting men on the skirmish line.

Later in the day, a second attempt was made, and on reaching the river, the same tactics were employed. The first pair to try the rush regained shelter in safety, although a few shots were fired at them. After the kettle was emptied, Mike Madden of K Troop and a man whose name I did not get made the attempt. They succeeded in filling their kettle and were almost under cover when some Indians in the trees on the opposite side of the river fired upon them, and Madden fell, loosing his hold on the kettle, which his partner brought under cover in safety. Two of the detail sprang forward, and at the risk of their lives pulled Madden behind the sheltering bluff; his leg was badly shattered below the knee, and he insisted on his companions leaving him and seeking safety in flight, as the Indians would doubtless be over in a few moments.

It goes without saying that there was a prompt refusal to listen to any such plan as this, and after much hard work, and a vast deal of suffering on the part of poor Madden, they succeeded in getting him to the hospital. Poor "Mike," he won the chevrons of a sergeant, but they cost him his good right leg. This was the last attempt to get water, and notwithstanding the supply we had secured on the two trips, many of our men suffered severely, and it was not until quite late in the afternoon that we succeeded in securing anywhere near an adequate supply.

Somewhere about 4:00 P.M., the firing practically ceased, and it was reported that there was a big commotion in the village. About 5:00 P.M., the Indians again fired the river bottom, and about 6:30 P.M., the whole Indian outfit moved southward up the valley of the stream, but just out of rifle range of our position. The immense cavalcade spread clear across to the western side of the valley, a solid mass of horses, ponies, travois, and mounted men, women, and children. Our men forsook the shelter of their rifle pits and clustered on the knolls bordering on the river, exchanging an occasional shot with the few Indians still hovering around our lines. The Indians kept on up the valley for several miles, finally disappearing behind the distant bluffs, but as long as it was light, we could see their watchful scouts on the distant hilltops. Our men at once set about ministering to the comfort of the wounded and caring for their horses; these, together with the pack mules, were led down to the water, and an ample supply of that necessary article was brought up for the command. A new position was selected, and after a hurried supper, we proceeded to dig new rifle pits and prepare for a general siege; as soon as these were completed, those of us fortunate enough to escape being on guard rolled ourselves in our blankets and slept soundly for the first time since the night of the twenty-third.

The following morning, for the first time in sixty hours, we refreshed ourselves with plenty of good hot coffee, and fried our bacon and hardtack with no sense of immediate hurry or danger.

Soon after breakfast, a number of the men forded the river and scattered out over the line of Major Reno's retreat, some of them even going down as far as the location of the village of the Hunkpapas, the southernmost village of the hostiles. We had only been there a short time when we heard the bugles sounding the "recall" from the rifle pits, and it can be imagined we made some lively moves in that direction. When we reached there, we found our men anxiously watching a big dust cloud advancing up the valley from the direction of the mouth of the river, and in an hour we knew it to be the command of General Terry and Colonel Gibbon, and from them we learned that Colonel Custer and his whole command had undoubtedly been "wiped out."

The new column went into camp in the river bottom, and the day was spent in rigging up stretchers and travois for our wounded, and in the afternoon we carried them across the river into the shade of the timber, our fighting force spending the night in our rifle pits on the bluffs.

On the morning of the twenty-eighth, we burned and destroyed all property for which we lacked transportation, killed all horses and mules unavailable for immediate use, and as soon as this was completed, we mounted and moved down the valley to the scene of Colonel Custer's fight, where we spent the forenoon in burying the dead. This completed, we went into camp on the river bottom near the 2nd Cavalry, where we remained until evening, when we moved, with our wounded, toward the mouth of the Little Bighorn, where the steamer *Far West* was in waiting to receive the wounded. We reached this point sometime in the night of the twenty-ninth, and our wounded were hurried on board, and gallant Grant Marsh, her captain, had started on his long run toward the old home post, where he arrived on the night of July 4, bringing to the widowed and the fatherless the first news of that awful slaughter.

As to any history connected with the final struggle of the command under Colonel Custer, we are to a great extent compelled to rely on the statements of Indians who were in the hostile camp, coupled with such facts and theories as became apparent in a somewhat hurried trip over the battlefield. This, however, I do know, that after separating from Major Reno, or rather after branching off from the trail followed by Reno's command, Colonel Custer's trail followed the general direction of the river for a considerable distance, in fact until nearly opposite the position occupied by Major Reno after his retreat. At this point, the trail bore away from the river into the broken country to the north and east until it reached a high hill or divide; this brought the command some two miles from the village, and fully a mile and a half from the river at its nearest points. Here the trail turned abruptly westward, and as I gathered from the talk of Trumpeter Martin later in the summer, it was at or near this point that he started back on his perilous ride to find Benteen with the packs and deliver to him the last order ever received from Custer to come on quick and bring packs. Notwithstanding all claims to the contrary, every officer and enlisted man in the regiment who survived that fight knows that Martin was the last white man, if not the last living person, to leave Custer's column and get through to our column alive. All others are mere pretenders.

For some years, it was the generally accepted theory that one "Curley," a Crow scout, succeeded in leaving Custer at or about the time he formed his lines for the last stand on the point of the bluffs. But many of us who were in the fight have always been inclined to question the truth of this statement. However, Curley did join General Terry's column, and if the statements of officers and men in that command are to be relied upon, he was about the worst scared Indian ever seen in the Northwest.

Judging largely from appearances, it was near the point where the trail turned westward that the Indians made their first determined attack on the battalion, as from there to the point of bluffs where we found and buried the body of Colonel Custer, a distance of considerably over a mile, there was ample evidence of the hardest kind of fighting. On the top of the ridge, distant possibly half a mile from the point where the trail changed direction, we found the dead of L and I Troops, and still farther to the west, perhaps a quarter of a mile, we found some of the men of E Troop. The indications were that Colonel Custer, with the two remaining troops, C and F, had moved forward a little distance and taken position on and around the knoll at the point of this divide, as it was here we found most of their men; it also appeared to us that Lieutenant Smith and some of the men of this troop, sometime during the engagement, had endeavored to change their position, as we found the body of the lieutenant on the hillside, not a great way from that of Colonel Custer, while in a ravine leading from Colonel Custer's position, down toward the river, we found a number of bodies of men and horses, and knew that some of the men must have belonged to E Troop by the color of their horses, E being the gray horse troop. But just how and when they got there, we have never been able to determine.

Another thing which caused considerable comment at the time was the fact that so few dead horses were found on the battlefield. On and around the knoll where Colonel Custer made his final stand were perhaps half a dozen, evidently shot for breastworks. In the ravine above mentioned were perhaps a dozen or fifteen more. These, with perhaps fifteen or twenty lying in various parts of the field, were all we saw. It was talked of considerably at the time, and the conclusion we reached was that the Indians must have stampeded the horses while the men were fighting on foot, and if so, had undoubtedly deprived the men of a considerable share of their ammunition, as it was the common practice throughout the regiment to carry all ammunition, except enough to fill our belts, in our saddle pockets.

Another thing that surprised us at the time was the fact that the attack on Colonel Custer's column came not from the direction of the villages, but from the northward and eastward, making it evident to us that one of the first moves the enemy had made had been to cut off all chances of a retreat along the trail, or of breaking out and escaping to the northward down the valley in the direction of the Bighorn. This seemed to us a reasonable theory, as the same tactics had been adopted by the Indians on the twenty-fifth when we went into the river bottom, the Indians crowding past our flanks and coming in on the trail behind us.

In going over the battle ground, we found but very few bodies between the ridge and the river, and these were evidently men who had sought to escape and been cut off and killed by parties moving out from the villages to participate in the fight.

The official reports show that some 215 bodies were buried on or near the scene of Colonel Custer's struggle, and there were doubtless a considerable number who were never found. In fact, it was only during the summer of 1891 I learned through an officer of the 3rd U.S. Infantry that a skeleton was found near the scene of the battle and identified as that of Dr. Lord, the medical officer with Colonel Custer's column.

As we moved about from place to place, performing the last sad offices for gallant officers and loved comrades, the campaign and its results were freely discussed among both officers and men, It seemed to be the general idea that there were at least four causes tending to bring about this sad result; named and discussed in the order of their happening, if not of their importance, they were as follows:

1. Arriving in the presence of the enemy fully twenty-four hours in advance of the time indicated by General Terry.
2. Failure to give due consideration to the report of the scouts as to the location of the village on the morning of the twenty-fifth.
3. The division of the regiment into practically four separate and distinct commands, before anything was certainly known as to the location of the village or the Indians, without some arrangement whereby at least two of the four detachments should, at all times, be in supporting distance of one another.
4. Major Reno's disastrous retreat from the river bottom before Colonel Custer had time to engage the enemy.

The instructions issued to Colonel Custer at the mouth of the Rosebud, among other things, said, "Should it (the trail) be found, as it appears almost certain that it will be found, to turn towards the Little Bighorn, he (General Terry) thinks you should still proceed southward, perhaps as far as the headwaters of the Tongue, and then turn toward the Little Bighorn." Our command did not go as far as the headwaters of the Tongue; on the contrary, we scarcely deviated from the trail of the hostiles, from the time we struck it near the Rosebud until the squadrons of Colonel Custer and Major Reno separated in the valley on the forenoon of June 25.

It is very true their orders were not peremptory, but had we followed the plan outlined by the department commander, and proceeded southward as far as the point indicated, we would have arrived in front of the enemy to the south about the time Colonel Gibbon reached a similar position to the northward, and in all probability would have discovered the trail of the large body of hostiles which led in from the southward, and which we did not discover until after the battle was over. What the result of this might have been is, of course, largely speculative.

As has been said, the approximate location of the village had been reported early on the morning of the twenty-fifth by our scouts, and it was a fact known to officers of the regiment, as well as to many of the enlisted men, that Mitch Boyer, the half-breed interpreter and guide accompanying the Crow scouts,

A bitter commentary on Congressional parsimony in the wake of the Little Bighorn. A dead Custer, a hostile Indian, and a Congressman join hands in agreeing, "We stand here for retrenchment, and reducing the Army of the United States." HARPER'S WEEKLY, 1876.

informed Colonel Custer that he would find more Indians at the point where the scouts had located the village than he would care to handle with the force he then had; and it was equally well known that the reply was that he didn't believe there were any Indians at the point indicated by the scouts, and that the command was then pushed ahead without any further investigation.

It has always been generally conceded by military men that when Colonel Custer found himself in the immediate presence of the enemy, there was but one course open to him, and that was to attack at once; but it was freely said that the plan of dividing a command of seven hundred men into four distinct columns and sending them out on widely diverging trails, while yet twelve or fifteen miles distant from the point where the Indians had already been located with reasonable certainty, and this too without any arrangement for supporting either of the columns in case of a sudden attack, was not the best possible military policy.

Take for instance the orders issued to Captain Benteen: "If from the furthest line of bluffs you now see you cannot see the valley, keep on until you come to a (the) valley. Pitch into anything you may come across and notify me at once." In talking over these orders, one of our officers propounded the question, "Suppose Captain Benteen had found up that valley what Major Reno and Colonel Custer found lower down the river, and even supposing he had succeeded in getting word through to Colonel Custer, how in the name of common sense would Colonel Custer ever get back there in time to keep Benteen's battalion from being chewed up by the combined force of the Indians?"

It was also said that had Major Reno kept his head and maintained his position in the river bottom, there was little doubt but that the battalion of Captain Benteen, together with the pack train, could have forced their way through to him, and enabled him to divide the forces of the enemy, and in this way materially aided in saving Custer's command from entire annihilation, as with these two commands menacing the village from opposite directions, the chances were largely in favor of the Indians moving out and leaving us in possession of the field. It has always seemed to me that the division of our command, made at the time it was, was the main cause of our defeat. Under ordinary circumstances, a division of forces was perhaps good Indian policy, but in this case, such a division ought not to have been made until we were better informed as to the strength and disposition of the forces of the enemy.

As to the conduct of Major Reno, the less said the better. I think even the officers of our own regiment would hardly deny now that he was scientifically whitewashed in the second paragraph of the seventh finding of the Chicago Court of Inquiry, as published in General Orders, Number Seventeen, Headquarters of the Army, A.G.O., Washington, March 11, 1879, a quotation from which is as follows: "While subordinates in some instances did more for the safety of the command, by brilliant displays of courage, than did Major Reno, there was nothing in his conduct which requires animadversion from this court."

Reminiscences of the Reno Fight

JOHN SILVERSTEN[1]

Teepee Book 2, no. 6 (June 1916): 579–82

After we had forded the Little Bighorn above the Indian village, Major Reno gave the command, "Right front into line! Load pistols! Gallop!" And away we went down the valley, the men shouting like Indians, "Hi-yah, Hi-yah!" Reno yelled, "That's right boys!"

We rode until we got pretty close to the Indian camp. By this time we saw Indians on every side, the bluffs on the left being crowded with them. The command was given, "Dismount and fight on foot," and we did so, forming in skirmish line, five feet apart. The Indians were shooting at us from all sides. Then we went into a clump of timber. I was the tallest man in the troop—they called me "Big Fritz"—and I was Number One in the line. When we dismounted in the timber, I gave my horse to Number Four, who held it with his own and two others.

The fight in here was very hot, and men were falling fast. We could not see the Indians, but they were signaling all the time to each other with their little bone whistles, and they seemed to be on all sides. Major Reno got alarmed about the horses and ordered a retreat, but Captain French changed the command to "Fall back with faces to the enemy!"

I could find neither my horse nor the horse holder when this order to fall back to the river was given, and so, with about twelve or fourteen others, I stayed in the woods. Lieutenant DeRudio was with us and took command. Firing was still going on all around us, and we could hear the shots and shouts in the pursuit of our comrades to the river and up the bluffs. We hid ourselves in the timber as best we might and succeeded in keeping out of sight of the Indians, but they kept on firing and were whistling all around us. Later, I can't tell how long afterward, things got quieter, and Lieutenant DeRudio said we must try to get upon the bluffs to the command, so we crept down to the river.

It looked rather deep, and as I was the tallest man there, I was ordered to cross first and show the way. Sergeant White, who was done out,[2] asked me to take his gun, which I did, and waded the stream carrying two guns and two canteens. I got over all right and was the first to reach the other shore.[3]

A short distance up the hill, [I] came across the body of an Indian. He was lying on his back with a carbine in one hand and a whip in the other. I felt his head and found that he had been scalped, so I suppose he was one of the Crow scouts that had joined us some days before, as none of our men had time to scalp a Sioux if they had killed one in their flight up the bluffs.

The first man I met on the top of the bluffs was Captain French. He was very much astonished and pleased. They had had a roll call when they got on the bluff, and all who were not present were marked dead or missing. He shook my hand and said, "Fritz, I am glad to see you. You are on the list of dead, and here you are back to life again. You're wet from fording the river. Go to the sergeant and get a blanket and sit down by the campfire." So I found my troop, got a blanket and some food, partly dried my clothes, and got straightened out a little.

The men knew nothing about Custer, but they had heard heavy firing after reaching the bluffs. I was put on the firing line. With my butcher knife, I dug a little hole behind the sagebrush and fought from there. The bush wasn't two feet high, and I was the biggest man in the troop, but somehow that bush seemed to be a protection.

We were attacked many times that night and the next forenoon, but we held them off, and once charged and drove them down the bank with a hurrah. The second day, about noon perhaps, we saw a body of men coming up the river valley. At first we thought it was more Indians, but as they came nearer, we saw that they marched in order like soldiers, and soon the cry arose, "It's Terry, it's Terry!" The few Indians that were still hanging around went off in a hurry, and in a little while General Terry and his command were up on the bluffs beside

On Reno Hill. W. F. BEYER. *DEEDS OF VALOR.*

us. He came forward, and Reno's remnant formed a circle around him and his staff and gave him three cheers. The gray-haired commander took off his hat and wept like a child.

Well, of course that ended the fighting there, and we were soon making friends with the relief party. And one more thing. After we left the battlefield and went into camp, I saw my horse out on the prairie and went and caught him. He was just as I had left him when I dismounted in the woods the first day of the fight. My blouse was still strapped across the saddle, and the saddle pockets were filled with ammunition. Evidently the Indians had not got hold of him. I tell you, I was glad to see him.

Captain Benteen's Command

EDWARD S. GODFREY

Army and Navy Journal 14, no. 4 (September 2, 1876): 58

CAMP 7TH CAVALRY, SIOUX EXPEDITION,
ROSEBUD, M.T., August 7, 1876
To the Editor of the Army and Navy Journal:
SIR: At the battle of the Little Bighorn, June 25, the opinion seems to prevail among military men as well as civilians that Captain Benteen's column of three companies was organized to constitute a reserve, including Captain McDougall's company with the pack trains, for the support of the other columns under Colonel Custer and Major Reno. Such was not the case. When some fifteen miles from the Indian village (just as we were crossing the divide between the Rosebud and Little Bighorn Valleys), the command was divided as follows: Major Reno, with three companies, was ordered in the advance; Colonel Custer, with five companies, followed on his trail to where Reno crossed the river; Captain Benteen, with three companies, was ordered to go to some high bluffs for observation. If he could not see anything from the ones pointed out to him, to go on to the next, and so on, and thereafter to use his discretion whether to continue on that route or return and follow the main command; but to strike whatever came in his way and send word to the commanding officer of any enemy; Captain McDougall, commanding the rear guard and pack train, [was] to follow the main command as closely as practicable.

Reno and Custer pushed down the valley, on the village trail, at a rapid pace. Benteen carried out his orders, but after several miles' travel across a succession of high hills and deep gullies, at no time able to see far ahead of him, much less the village or river or enemy, and no prospect of a near change in the character of the route, he found he was falling rapidly to the rear; that the horses, already jaded, were becoming exhausted by the strain; and changed his course towards the trail of the main column. Soon after, he received an order from Lieutenant Cooke, adjutant, to push ahead with the packs. He was some six miles from the scene of action when he received this note; he had no intimation that the battle had begun, of the force of the Indians or plan of attack. Benteen pushed ahead; the packs followed, and not until he reached the high bluffs overlooking the river valley and near to where the troops afterwards were besieged did he know of the battle or immediate presence of the troops to the enemy; he could only hear occasional shots, not enough to intimate that a battle was going on.

Soon after reaching this point, two volleys were heard down the river where Colonel Custer was, but his force was not in sight. Soon after this, Reno and Benteen joined. By accident, Benteen's column constituted a reserve. It was well it was so. As soon as dispositions were made on the bluff, Weir's company was sent to look for Colonel Custer.[2] He went to a high point about three-quarters of a mile down the river, from which he had a good view of the country. From it could be seen Custer's battlefield, but there was nothing to indicate the result. The field was covered with Indians. He was recalled from the place; the packs closed up; ammunition was issued; and the command moved down the river to, if possible, join Custer. Upon reaching the high, point we could see nothing, hear nothing, to indicate Custer's vicinage. But immediately the Indians started for us.

Very respectfully,
EDWARD S. GODFREY,
first lieutenant, 7th Cavalry

Thrilling Experience Near the Custer Battlefield

WILLIAM D. NUGENT

Winners of the West 3, no. 6 (June 1926): 6

Two days without water, the sun almost blistering hot, and the ground like an oven. The wounded tortured with severe pain, their tongues in many cases swelled until it was impossible to close their mouths. Water, water was the agonizing cry of all the sufferers.

On June 26, 1876, near 4:00 P.M., permission was given to go for water. To get to the river, we had to cross a place that was open and would give the Indians the best chance in the world to shoot us. Very few cared to commit suicide by crossing over at that time.

When I reached safety in a gulch leading to the river, I found four others: Harmon of Troop F, and Easley, Johnson, [Howard] Weaver, and myself of Troop A, 7th U.S. Cavalry. Between ourselves and the river were many crooks and gulches opening into the one we had to follow to reach the river. Our expectations were to find Indians concealed in such places, but happily for us, our expectations did not materialize, and we reached the river safely.

We paused before stepping out on the bank to take a general observation of the lay of things. On the other side of the river were between fifty and one hundred mounted Indian bucks, awaiting our appearance on the bank. They were nearly five hundred yards from the river, but looked much less.

We laid aside our guns [and] prepared ourselves for the rush for water by uncorking our canteens and shortening our hold on the straps, that all might be submerged at the same time. For some time, I knew nothing of the others, as I fell into the water and drank until suffocation broke my hold on that river. I guess my comrades were occupied in like manner. After resting and gaining sufficient breath, I would return to my interrupted drinking. In lowering my head to continue, I received a rap on my head, accompanied by a deluge of water. I carefully examined my head and found out I was not dead, had not suffered the loss of any blood, and was not even shot by a bullet.

We returned to the place where we had left our guns and took a few shots at the Indians, but were deceived in the distance and did not hit any of the redskins.

We made more trips to the river by turns, and our most useful vessel for carrying water was our camp kettle, until a playful Indian put a bullet through it.

We raised our sights to five hundred yards and once more turned loose on the Indians. This time our shooting was effective, and the Indians started on the run. I had a real grouch against them, and when I saw one cut away from the rest, and he would have to ride about a thousand yards before he could get out of range, I made that Indian do some tall riding. Every time a chunk of lead passed him, he wigwagged a signal back that he disliked such close shooting. Before he went over the hill, I had sent about a dozen shots after him, and I felt that I was at least even with one Indian for the grief they had dealt me at various times.

We filled our canteens, returned to the barricade on the bluffs, and the water was then given to the wounded.

Never were there four braver or more loyal comrades than those who were with me. Harmon I never met again. He had a brother in Troop L of the 7th who was killed with Custer on the hill. I was informed Harmon failed to identify his body, as many were so badly mutilated that identification was impossible. Easley in his deportment was a perfect gentleman. Johnson was a man as near without fear as any man I have ever known. He proved it at different times and was given the nickname of Swede. Weaver was our historian or encyclopedian, and all disputes and arguments were referred to him for a decision. He was the only one of my comrades whose given name was known by me. Surely his was a heart of gold.

I will never forget these four true blue comrades of mine, and will always remember them as heroes. The world may never know them, there will be no medals or citations, but in the heart of one old comrade, their names will always occupy the front seat.

Terry and Crook

THEODORE W. GOLDIN

Ours, a Military Magazine 3, no. 3 (March 1888): 37–38

For reasons best known at Washington, it had been deemed best that General Terry should take the field in person as commander-in-chief of all the forces in his department then in the field engaged in operations against hostile Sioux Indians, and our first acquaintance with him was when we escorted him from the railway station at Bismarck to the post at old Fort Lincoln. Up to this time, the knowledge of the rank and file of the regiment as to General Terry's ability as a commanding officer was derived mainly from the acquaintance we had with the promptness with which he could approve the findings and sentences of the numerous courts-martial required to be submitted to him, no matter how severe the sentence.

So that when he joined us early in May 1876, we were inclined to look upon him as a martinet in discipline and utterly void of any feeling of humanity or friendship for the enlisted men in his command. In addition to this, there were many in the regiment only too willing to consider him as in a measure, if not wholly, responsible for the treatment our gallant leader, Colonel Custer, had received when hurrying home from Washington to take command of his regiment, already ordered into the field. We had fondly hoped that Colonel Custer would command the expedition, as he had done in previous years. This feeling against General Terry we even yet think was shared in, not by the enlisted men alone, but gained strength among some of the junior officers of the regiment. How erroneously subsequent events have amply proven. But be all this as it may, he was with us and in command.

Pursuant to orders soon received, the expedition started.

It took but a few days for the dullest man in the command to discover the fact that Terry and Custer were, so far as duty and the success of the expedition was concerned, in perfect sympathy. We also discovered that far from being the strict disciplinarian we had supposed, he was kind and considerate for the welfare of his men and endeavored, so far as lay in his power, to render the hardships and discomforts necessarily attending an expedition of this kind as light as possible.

Brig. Gen. Alfred H. Terry. NELSON A. MILES. *PERSONAL RECOLLECTIONS AND OBSERVATIONS.*

Of the march from Fort Lincoln to the Rosebud, there is nothing new to say. The incident that most impressed us and endeared our leader to the hearts of his men occurred later on in the campaign, in the valley of the Little Bighorn.

The first rays of the morning sun, peering over the tops of the Bighorn Mountains on the morning of June 27, 1876, shone down into the Little Bighorn Valley and wakened into life the disheartened remnant of the once gallant 7th [Cavalry], who for thirty-six long hours, without rest, food, or drink, had been stubbornly contesting for their lives against the overwhelming force of Indians hurled against them, but now worn out and discouraged, their idolized leader gone, they knew not where, they were grouped together around their rifle pits, speculating on the sudden departure of the enemy late the preceding afternoon. No signs of the enemy being apparent, details descended into the river bottoms in the vain hope that they might run across some poor wounded comrade who had in some manner escaped the clutches of the savages, but not one could we find. We were able, however, to recognize many of the dead, and the men were engaged in giving them a decent burial, when suddenly the shrill notes of the recall sounded across the valley, causing a hurried retreat, which was not checked until the last straggler was safe within the shelter of the entrenchments. In the camp, everything was the wildest excitement; everyone was watching a cloud of dust far down the river which seemed to be moving rapidly in our direction. Conjectures as to whether it was made by friends or foes were freely offered, and hurried preparations were made to renew the battle. All this time the cloud had been drawing nearer and nearer until, with the aid of our glasses, we could distinguish the darker outlines of a large body of mounted men. A few moments later and the blue flag, with the single white star in the center, which we knew to designate the headquarters of General Terry, could be seen in the advance. Like lightning, the news flashed down the line, "Terry is here!" Cheer after cheer rose from the entrenchments, feebly echoed from the poor wounded fellows in the hospital. Hurriedly throwing themselves into the saddle, an excited group of officers and men dashed down the hillside, forded the river, galloped across the river bottom, and were soon exchanging greetings with the reinforcements. In a few moments, General Terry and his staff galloped up from a hurried inspection of the lower battlefield, where they had found the remains of Custer and his brave troopers.

A few hurried questions and answers, and we were in possession of the details of that terrible struggle, so far as they were then known. The share of our division of the regiment was explained to the general as he rapidly pushed his way forward in the direction or our entrenchments. His face looked anxious and careworn; his manner was abstracted. He was seemingly paying but little attention to the details of the battle as they were told him; his eyes were on the opposite side of the river. Ordering his command into camp in the river bottom, he pushed on to the ford and was soon on the other side. Reaching the top of the hill, he stopped for a few moments for a few words with our officers, and then rode rapidly away to the hospital. Quickly dismounting, he moved from cot to cot among the sufferers, speaking words of cheer and dispensing hearty hand clasps. Not a man was missed; he had a kind word and a sympathetic grip for all. As the full extent of our loss became more and more evident, and as the poor, wounded fellows, cheered by his presence, feebly tried to smile their thanks for his visit, tears coursed unheeded and unchecked down his bronzed and bearded cheeks. As he completed the rounds, he turned away from the scene, hastily brushed his hand across his eyes, choked down what seemed to be a sob, and turning again, his hand fell on the shoulder of Dr. Paulding, who stood near him, and with a tremor in his voice he said, "Good God, Doctor, this is terrible—what can we do for them?"

In a moment, however, he was the soldier again. Ordering up all the medical supplies from his camp below, he at the same time sent his own orderly for his private pack animal, and on its arrival he personally unloaded the panniers of what few articles it contained that could be of service to the wounded, and busied himself in preparing them for the use of the poor fellows who lay with patient suffering depicted on their faces, following his every movement with their eyes. This was but one of the many instances of the tender watchful care he evinced for those poor fellows until he saw them safe on the steamer *Far West,* bound down the river for the comfortable hospitals at the Missouri River posts. From that hour on, it is safe to say that there was nothing but words of praise and every token of love and respect for the commanding general.

The expedition over, the regiment at home again, we found that the general had not forgotten us. Finding after finding of the various courts-martial were returned with the endorsement that if a man had been a good soldier in the past, he should be released and restored to duty, or else the punishment was materially lessened. It was only where all the evidence went to show that the guilty one possessed no qualifications as a soldier that the full severity of the sentence was allowed to be carried into effect.

Ours, a Military Magazine 3, no. 5 (May 1888): 72–73

After the reorganization of General Terry's expedition on the Rosebud, we moved off across the country with the intention of discovering and attacking the hostiles who were known to have been in force on our front during all the days of preparation.

After several days of hard marching, we reached the vicinity of Tongue River. Early that morning [August 10, 1876], we had been sent to the front with a detachment of Indian scouts, with orders to examine carefully the country over which we marched and to report at once any signs of the recent presence of the enemy.

For several hours, we had been galloping from place to place in the valley but without finding what we all desired, a fresh trail, and at last, tired and hungry, we lit our pipes and jogged along the road, watching our savage allies as they trotted at our side or went madly galloping away at the shrill call of a comrade. Suddenly we were aroused from our meditations by a commotion among the Indians; looking up, we saw some of them gathered in an excited group a few rods in advance, while those near us were hurrying forward to join the throng; a moment later and we could see that they were stripping for a fight. Galloping up, we asked the interpreter for an explanation of this strange move. Scarcely pausing in his work of removing his surplus clothing, he pointed out to us a faint, hazy cloud arising from the opposite side of a range of hills a few miles distant, with the laconic answer, "Heap Sioux, damned big fight." Sending one of our soldier comrades back to the command with the news, we pushed forward to where our now thoroughly excited allies were galloping madly back and forth across the narrow valley, uttering their shrill war cries and brandishing their weapons.

Watching the cloud in our front, we could see that it was dust, and from its size, evidently caused by a large body of animals of some kind. Steadily it kept increasing and seemed to be drawing nearer and nearer, but was still beyond our view.

All this time we had been pushing on up the valley. Looking back over our shoulder, we could see the command rapidly coming up on the trail and already in line of battle. Just in our front was a high bluff, and it was on the other side of this that we could see the dust cloud; a half mile more and we crept around the point of bluffs, and there, sure enough, were Indians, and plenty of them, engaged like our own in startling feats of horsemanship. But what was that dark mass in the background, that long, black column winding down from the hills? Was it possible these were Indians too? Our glass was at our eyes in an instant, but we could not see what they were; a few moments later, and we saw a little group of horsemen detach themselves from the main column and come galloping over the prairie toward us.

Eagerly we watched them until we were suddenly aroused by the voice of General Terry as he called out to some member of his staff, "Why, Colonel, that is Crook; where in the world are the Indians?" and putting spurs to horse, and followed by his staff, he galloped forward to meet the advancing squad. Joining the group of noncommissioned attaches, we too galloped after them, and a few moments later found us dismounted and eagerly greeting strangers of our own rank on the other side.

Looking over the staff of General Crook, we could find no one who wore a single star; in fact, we were struck by the entire absence of any uniform or insignia of rank. Prominent among the group we noticed William F. Cody, "Buffalo Bill," who was at that time acting as General Crook's chief of scouts. We were anxious, however, to see General Crook, and turning to a noncommissioned officer standing near, we asked which one was the general. "Why, there he is, talking with General Terry," was the answer.

Turning, we looked with eager eye for the man who for years had been the terror of the hostiles wherever he had served. What did we see? A man of medium height, dressed in a pair of heavy cavalry boots, with a heavy beard braided closely and tucked beneath the bosom of the shirt, who, with his hand resting on the neck of a strong active mule, was eagerly talking with General Terry, looking shyly up at intervals to answer the enthusiastic greeting of some officer. For a few moments, they conversed alone; then, with his customary brevity, General Crook ordered his command into camp, and seated on the ground, he and General Terry resumed their conversation; the result was that hardly were the horses of the cavalry on herd before we saw Colonel Miles and his sturdy column of infantry trudging down the back trail on their way to guard the crossings of the Yellowstone. Already Crook was planning the campaign that ended in the fight with Crazy Horse, and that never-to-be-forgotten march from the Powder River to the Belle Fourche, on which officers and men alike were compelled to subsist on their own horses.

With Crook's Expedition

FREDERICK SCHWATKA

Chicago *Inter-Ocean,* August 3, 1876

CROOK'S BIGHORN EXPEDITION,
IN CAMP ON MIDDLE GOOSE CREEK, W.T.
July 23, 1876

The command under General Crook, camped as above, is now awaiting the coming of Colonel Merritt[1] with eight companies of the 5th Cavalry, upon whose arrival, about the twenty-sixth, it is expected that we will move northward as far as South Tongue River and, uniting with General Terry, will proceed again about August 1 against the Sioux and Cheyennes.

Four Crow Indians, scouts from General Terry's command, arrived in camp the other night and seem to be of the opinion that, should too large a column unite against the enemy, they will scatter, the Cheyennes returning to Kansas, the agency Sioux to the Spotted Tail and Red Cloud agencies, while the primitive hostile bands of Hunkpapas, Minneconjous, and other Sioux bands under Crazy Horse will find ample hiding room in the vast plains between the Missouri and Bighorn Rivers or, if badly pressed, even take refuge in the British possessions north of Montana.

A Bannock Indian found a trail of lodge poles a few days ago leading toward the agencies. He gives it as his belief that it was made by the wounded from the fights of General Crook and Colonel Custer. This is a very great consolation to our wounded, who have to travel, on an average, about two hundred miles farther to reach permanent medical assistance furnished by the same government.

A bad omen for our frontier states and territories was presented to us the other day while moving camp for a short distance to procure better grass. Myriads of grasshoppers filled the air, appearing like an immense drifting snowstorm, trending toward the southeast and apparently taking advantage of a northwest wind to favor their fight to the same fields that they have so effectually devastated for two consecutive years. In 1874 and 1875, they swept over Kansas, Nebraska, and kindred western states, from the elevated plains of Montana, Wyoming, Colorado, etc., and the present swarms may reiterate the destruction and suffering of those years.

The different parties of Montana miners that are taking the advantage of the large scouting parties now in the field to prospect the Bighorn Mountains have been with us off and on, and generally, from their endeavors, we may safely state that there exists no gold in paying quantities in the eastern spurs or slope of the Bighorn Mountains. When its western slope and the Granite Ridges (or Rattlesnake Hills) on its southern border, north of the Sweetwater country, have been equally well prospected, the subject of gold in this country, second only in excitement to the Black Hills, will be reasonably settled.

An immense fog of smoke has been hanging over the country for several days. This fact, coupled with the attempt of the Indians to burn the grass near our camp on South Goose Creek, would indicate that the Indians are now burning off immense tracts of grazing, prairie land, for the purpose of crippling the stock of our command.

From fifty to one hundred Ute Indians will arrive about the same time that the 5th Cavalry is expected under Lt. J. H. Spence, 4th Infantry, and, in conjunction with the 225 Snakes now with us, will form a scouting party not to be despised when we reflect how the Snakes and Crow Indians saved us from a severe surprise in the canyons of the Rosebud, at the battle of the Rosebud Hills.

Chicago *Inter-Ocean,* August 16, 1876

BIGHORN AND YELLOWSTONE EXPEDITION,
In Camp on Tongue River, W.T., August 2, 1876

The usual inactivity has characterized our camp since the last intelligence I sent the *Inter-Ocean.* We have had as yet no news from General Terry's command, which it was expected would meet us here about August 1. Colonel Merritt, with the 5th Cavalry, will reach this camp tomorrow with ten companies of that regiment, and from present indications we will move against the Sioux immediately upon his arrival. There are orders to draw twenty days' rations and to be prepared to march in three days.

Louis Richard,[2] who left this command and camp a few days ago with ten other scouts on an extended reconnaissance northward, returned yesterday, having found a deserted Sioux village of about five hundred lodges at the junction of Ash Creek with the Little Bighorn River, above the scene of Custer's and Reno's fights of June

25–26. He infers the ponies of the hostiles must be very poor, as the dead ones left in the village would show, and they had also ben kept so closely picketed to their tepees that no grass could be found. The Sioux have evidently been guarding well against any surprise. Dog bones were numerous, showing that they are very low in point of rations, which is confirmed by the fact that the buffalo have entirely deserted this tract of Indian country. The trail followed eastward, in the direction of the Rosebud.

Frank Grouard, our principal guide and scout, started yesterday with other scouts to scour the country of the Rosebud and Tongue Rivers and determine the whereabouts of these Indians. He now thinks they have gone as far east as the Little Missouri River, toward which the main herds of buffalo at this season annually migrate. Late last night he returned, much to our surprise, having found another deserted village farther north on the Little Bighorn, the trail leading eastward toward the Rosebud.

His Shoshone scouts, in regular column of fours, entered the camp with the peculiar yells and war songs that we had heard upon the battlefield of the Rosebud, which, soon taken up by the entire tribe of friendly Indians, numbering about two hundred fifty, made night hideous in a manner perfectly indescribable. Hearing that the cause of all the commotion was the fact that the Shoshone scouts had brought in two Sioux scalps, and that they would indulge in a Shoshone scalp dance, I repaired to the Indian village with Dr. [Charles R.] Stephens to witness that which is so often written about and so seldom seen—a real Indian Scalp Dance.

In the center of their camp, the warriors had formed a large circle, about fifty feet in circumference, in many places in two ranks, and so close as to lap shoulder to shoulder. In the center were five squaws in line, the even numbers holding the scalps suspended from the tops of long, slender poles, which, bending beneath their weight, swayed with every motion of the holders, showing, in the light of the full moon, a bloody clotted mass of hair that looked more like two pieces of black rags than the capillary ornament of a Sioux warrior. In that portion of the circle directly facing the squaws were five warriors wearing black blankets, their faces blackened, and who seemed to be the leaders of the orchestra that held their seance that night. The other warriors were dressed in their ordinary white government blankets or in fancifully painted and well-tanned buffalo robes, while a motley crowd of lesser lights—warriors yet to be soldiers, teamsters, herders, etc.—made up the background of the picture. The scalp song commenced with a low, guttural, measured cadence from the five black devils, which, slowly increasing, and as slowly joined in by the circle, soon swelled to a fearful chorus that no pen, nor musical scales, with all its sharps and flats, could dare describe or portray. The cadence was measured by a swaying of their bodies from side to side, which, sandwiched in so compactly, seemed like one solid mass of pendulating flesh. The squaws, in the meantime, as the song ran up the scale, slowly approached the black-faced warriors and, while keeping time to the wild music with their feet, gradually dropped their hideous standards to the faces of the ebony-like warriors to their front, until its touching seemed to be a signal that stopped the song, and every warrior in the camp joined in a perfect yell when the circle sent up the war whoop of the Shoshones as a closing of the scalp song. The squaws rapidly retreated to the center and there remained quiet for five or ten minutes, when the same scene was reenacted.

These orgies only closed as the morning broke, although I must confess I left long before that time. These Scalp Dances are much enhanced by the Indians being at their proper agencies, where all the paraphernalia of war is obtainable and where all warriors, squaws, and papooses may participate.

August 3—The command broke camp early and marched to our old camp at the junction of the Main and Middle Goose Creeks, from whence we debouched previous to the Rosebud fight. This will probably be the permanent camp where our wagons will be packed to await the issue of the next campaign.

In the afternoon of the day, the long-expected ten companies of the 5th Cavalry arrived. The organization is as follows:

Col. Wesley Merritt, commanding the regiment.

Lt. Col. Eugene A. Carr.

Maj. J. J. Upham, commanding 1st Battalion; Maj. J. W. Mason, commanding 2nd Battalion.

Lieutenant [William C.] Forbush, adjutant.

Lieutenant [William P.] Hall, assistant quartermaster.

By companies: A, Lieutenant [Calbraith P.] Rogers and Lieutenant [George O.] Eaton; B, Captain [Robert H.] Montgomery; C, Captain [Emil] Adam and Lieutenant [Edward L.] Keyes; D, Captain [Edwin V.] Sumner and Lieutenant [Robert] London; E, Captain [George F.] Price and Lieutenant Parkhurst; F, Captain [John S.] Payne and Lieutenant [Alfred B.] Bache; G, Captain [Edward M.] Hayes and Lieutenant [Hoel S.] Bishop; I, Captain [Sanford C.] Kellogg and Lieutenant [Bernard] Reilly; K, Captain [Albert E.] Woodson and Lieutenant [Charles] King; M, Captain [Edward H.] Leib and Lieutenant [Satterlee C.] Plummer of the 4th Infantry.

Companies H and L are at present at the Sioux agencies of Red Cloud and Spotted Tail. The rest of the command, having been previously mentioned in detail, will only recapitulate: 2nd Cavalry, five companies; 3rd Cavalry, ten companies; 4th Infantry, three compa-

William F. "Buffalo Bill" Cody. W. FLETCHER JOHNSON. *LIFE OF SITTING BULL.*

nies; 9th Infantry, three companies; and the 14th Infantry, four companies. The cavalry companies average about fifty-five men to the company, the infantry about forty, or a sum total for the present campaign of 1,400 cavalry, two hundred fifty friendly Indian scouts; in all, 2,050. Ute Indians to the number of two hundred fifty from the White River agency are daily expected, which swells our force to 2,300 effective men. We also have about two hundred packers, but as they have to look after their animals in a fight, they cannot be considered effective, unless our next fight, should we have one, be of the nature of a desperate resistance—a scene not at all likely to happen.

"Buffalo Bill" (W. F. Cody), the celebrated scout and guide,[3] comes with the 5th Cavalry and has early distinguished himself by already killing a Cheyenne brave on Sage Creek while en route to join us.

August 4—Orders have just been received to take four days' rations in the saddlebags, fifteen to be taken on the pack mules, or nineteen in all, to move at daylight tomorrow.

Chicago *Inter-Ocean*, September 11, 1876

BIGHORN AND YELLOWSTONE EXPEDITION, IN CAMP ON ROSEBUD RIVER, AUGUST 10, VIA FORT BUFORD, D.T., August 19, 1876

On the fifth, General Crook's command, organized as explained in my last communication, broke camp from Main Goose Creek and, marching along Prairie Dog Creek, camped on Tongue River five miles below the mouth of Prairie Dog, making a distance of twenty-two miles. On the sixth, the command marched northward along Tongue River twenty-one miles.

The valley of Tongue River is here much contracted, and overlooked by high red sandstone bluffs, covered with a stunted growth of pine and cedar. The river bottom, however, though narrow, is well supplied with ash, cottonwood, willow, etc. The soil is unproductive, being covered only with the well-known sagebrush and greasewood, interspersed with a poor quality of bunch and buffalo grass, affording a slim reliance for forage for our animals. So winding is the river, and so contracted its valley, that during the day's march we crossed the stream, averaging about fifty yards wide and a foot and a half deep, twenty times. No signs of Indians were found, but signal fires near the mouth of this river and the Powder River, near the Yellowstone, could be plainly seen from the picket posts around our camp.[7]

Late in the evening, the scouts returned, having been fifteen miles further down (north) the river, and reported that it was evident that no Indians had passed eastward, as no trails leading in that direction could be found. Supposing that the enemy were still on the Rosebud or Little Bighorn River, it was determined to move westward in that direction. A messenger came in late from General Terry's command, stating that it was at the mouth of the Rosebud. On August 7, after following down the river a short distance, we crossed in a northwest direction to the Rosebud and camped on that stream eight miles further down than the point where General Crook had his fight of June 17.

About a mile up the river, our scouts found where timber had been felled by the Indians to protect their village, which began about a mile below camp, and by its size showed that it must have contained a great many warriors. A large number of willow wickiups, used only by the warriors when on the war trail or hunting expeditions, were interspersed among the round, bare spots that indicated where the lodges had stood and, no doubt, were the abodes of the Cheyennes whose squaws and papooses are safely lodged and fed at the Cheyenne agency in the Indian Territory. Only one mile further on beyond the felled timber is the point on the Rosebud where Mills's battalion of the 3rd Cavalry and Noyes's battalion of the 2nd Cavalry, under Captain Mills, had turned to the left to attack the Indians in flank and rear at the battle of the Rosebud.

Many conjectures naturally arise among us as to what would have been the fate of that cavalry charge had only that one mile been traveled. As shown by its trail, the village is the same charged by Custer eight days later on the Little Bighorn, fifteen miles from here. The village was well situated for a charge, being on a level river bottom about one mile and a half wide, with only one small wooded ravine making perpendicularly through its situation [*sic*]. One thing was very noticeable: The grass was completely eaten up in the immediate vicinity of their tepees, or lodges, while but a short distance from them the grazing was excellent, showing that in daily anticipation of an attack, they had kept their ponies well in hand.

A recent Indian grave, constructed in their style, the body elevated on poles, was found by the Shoshones, or Snakes, and the first intimation we had of its presence was its desecration by our Indian allies. Its contents and surroundings were curious and interesting. A Colt's breech-loading pistol of the most recent pattern, about one hundred rounds of ammunition, and many empty shells ready for reloading, a steel tomahawk, with many minor knickknacks of an Indian's fancy, were found rolled up with his body in his buffalo robes and other wrappings. Among the latter was a very nice patched quilt that at some day had no doubt passed through the dexterous hands of some busy housewife, whose long hair may have been that which dangled in thin skeins from the hollow extremities of a polished bone, which our Indians told us was also human. The poles which held his body in midair were painted red, or rather smeared with red clay, and one was ornamented with the flowing tail of a horse, no doubt the favorite of the dead warrior. On the ground were two reddened buffalo heads, indicative of some unknown superstitious burial rites. The grass in the immediate vicinity had been closely shaved, and his favorite horses had been killed nearby the grave. He was evidently a victim of the Rosebud fight, two bullet holes being found in his chest, and the age of the grave showing about six weeks standing. Eight other fresh graves were found by our Indians, the scalps still intact, which, taken with the thirteen scalps that the Crows and Snakes obtained in the fight, slowly swelled the numbers that our enemies lost in that engagement. The reports from Red Cloud and Spotted Tail agencies, wherein the Sioux and Cheyenne acknowledge a loss of eighty-six killed, may yet be verified, for these Indians, in order to disguise the numbers killed in action, will often scatter the graves of the slain over an immense district, so that but few will be seen by any force going directly through their country. A chief or medicine man, or any important man of the tribe, is entitled to have a lodge over his grave, while the squaws, papooses, and lesser lights are often ruthlessly laid aside in the most convenient tree.

The Rosebud Valley at the point where we struck it is far superior to the Tongue River, being an excellent grazing country. Its hills were well wooded with good pine, and its soil doubtless fairly productive. The stream is sluggish and its banks muddy, but the valley is well timbered with nearly all varieties of valley timber.

On the eighth, the command moved down the river about five miles to good grass and bivouacked, awaiting some definite intelligence from the scouts, who returned about noon, reporting that an immense trail had been found seven miles distant down the river, which, following the river, eight miles farther turned eastward in the direction of the Tongue River. Orders were received to move at 6:00 P.M. and to march as far down the Rosebud as the point where the trail left it—fifteen miles. The trail was about five or six days old. At 6:30 P.M. commenced that bugbear of a cavalry soldier's experience, a night march. The weather, however, was splendid, the moon full, and better than all, the road we were to follow led over an old, well-beaten Indian trail, and with the exception of the loss of sleep, we had but little to complain of. We went into camp on the Rosebud at 12:30 A.M., and the men, tired and sleepy, were soon asleep, with a single blanket over them and their saddle blankets for a mattress, the only bedding allowed a soldier on the plains when in active service after Indians.

At 9:00 A.M. on the ninth, the march was resumed, but contrary to expectations, we continued down the river for twenty miles, making the trip in a cold, driving rain that pelted us in the face during the whole march and until late in the afternoon.

The night was bitter cold, ice forming in a thin sheet over vessels of water, and, considering our scanty bedding, was cheerless enough. Natural ice in August no doubt sounds strangely enough to our eastern friends, but one of the peculiarities, and we might add blessings, of our Great Plains are the cool nights of summer. However warm may be the day, and I have seen it 107 degrees in the shade, the nights are never sultry, but the minute that the sun sets, a notable decrease of temperature begins, and often, as on the night spoken of, sinks so low as to make this opposite extreme equally unpleasant.

On August 10, we resumed the northward march down the Rosebud, and after traveling about four miles, the remnants of an immense Indian village were come upon. The lodges, showing that they had been banked—that is, a small ditch dug around their bottoms—proved the village to be a semipermanent one. It was about two miles to two and a half long and probably filled the entire valley, about a mile and a half wide. Near the center of its length were the [remains] of a large amphitheater, where the Sioux and Cheyennes had had a Sun Dance during the last spring.[8]

Shortly after passing through the village, we were drawn up under cover of a hill on the east bank of the Rosebud, as Indians were expected ahead. A few minutes sufficed to show that it was General Terry's command, and a junction and a common camp was soon formed.

Smokes are seen burning on Tongue and Powder Rivers, and the combined command will no doubt soon move in that direction.[9] As a courier leaves immediately, I am compelled to curtail many little items that I could insert.

Chicago *Inter-Ocean*, September 26, 1876

BIGHORN AND YELLOWSTONE EXPEDITION, IN CAMP ON THE YELLOWSTONE RIVER AT THE MOUTH OF POWDER RIVER, M.T., August 18 via Bismarck, September 18, 1876

After my last communication of the tenth,[4] briefly announcing the junction of the forces of Generals Crook and Terry on the Rosebud, about twenty miles form its mouth, the two commands marched on August 11 to Tongue River, twelve miles, following an Indian trail leading in that direction. The wagon train of General Terry's [command] returned to the Yellowstone, down the Rosebud, while Colonel Miles,[5] with six companies of the 6th Infantry, returned by the same route on a forced march to take the steamer and patrol the Yellowstone River to prevent the crossing of the hostile bands.

After arriving in camp on the eleventh, the dead body of a white man was found about a mile above the camp. He had been killed about six or eight months and was no doubt a stray prospector from a party of miners that crossed westward from the Black Hills to the Bighorn Mountains late last fall. He had a shot through the back of his head and one through his shoulders. His scalp had been completely ripped from the head. He had formed a small barricade of logs, and whether he made a good defense, no one will probably ever know. His remains were properly interred.

The night of the eleventh was cold, cheerless, and rainy; the entire command was soaked, for even a dog tent, you must remember, has been denied both officer and soldier in this campaign, where we have been put to our utmost to obtain pack-mule transportation sufficient to make a respectable scout. The trail was very much washed out by the night's rain; while, to add confusion to our scouts, the trail also divided into several, one leading up, the other down, the river, while two or three diverging tended toward Powder River on our east.

The Tongue River Valley, where we struck it, is much finer than where we left it sixty miles south of here. Should the Northern Pacific Railroad ever be completed along the Yellowstone, it is perfectly evident that these smaller valleys will soon be occupied with stock ranches and farms, the country offering better facilities for grazing, protection, and all other essentials of a stock farm than the lands along the Union Pacific, where such immense herds are annually raised for the eastern markets.

About noon of the twelfth, the scouts having reported that the largest trail had been found downriver, the command was soon on its way in that direction in a drizzling rain, which had continued from the last night. The distance marched was about ten miles, the valley of the river appearing finer as we approached the Yellowstone. During the whole night the rain kept falling, and the "clerk of the weather," as if to add insult to injury, gave us a bitter cold morning in which to enjoy our wet clothing. We started about 7:00 A.M. and made a march of twenty-five miles along the river, which brought us in plain sight of the blue line of the Yellowstone, about five or six miles further on. Our night's camp was a repetition of the last on the rainy score.

On the fourteenth, after continuing down the river, we turned sharply to the eastward, up a large creek called Pumpkin Creek, the main Indian trail leading in that direction.[6] We were all still disappointed in not seeing the Yellowstone and General Terry's steamboats, not having seen any signs of civilization for over three months.

The want of forage and the severity of the march commenced to tell on our stock, several of the horses having played out during the day, and four the day before. The condition of the animals will certainly be one of the worst state of affairs against which we will have to contend. We camped on Pumpkin Creek, six miles from its mouth.

During the night, a courier from Colonel Miles came in from the Yellowstone, reporting that the Indians had not yet crossed that river, which he had patrolled thoroughly from the mouth of the Rosebud to the Yellowstone Shoals. Entrenchments had been thrown up at the mouths of the Tongue and Powder Rivers, guarded by infantry, making it impossible to get northward at these favorable points of crossing.

Two hundred and fifty of the Crow Indians are also at the mouth of the Rosebud, making strenuous efforts to join us. These Indians, as stated in my last, we expected to find with General Terry, but they hung back to await the actions of the Snakes, who, having united with us, decided the minds of our northern Indian allies.

On the fifteenth, the command marched twenty miles to Powder River, at the mouth of the Mizpah Creek. Here we found good water in small springs along the river, which was a great relief to us, as the water in the clay-bank creeks had the consistency of thick cream, with a fine mud, which it was impossible to settle while the rains continued. The Powder River Valley is very fine indeed where we first encountered it.

The marches of the sixteenth and seventeenth were along the river of the Yellowstone. As we journeyed on the bluffs overlooking the Powder River, we had a fine view of its valley, which certainly improves as we descend it. In fact, we might say without hesitation that the Rosebud, Tongue, and Powder River Valleys, in their lower half or two-thirds, will make some of the finest stock ranges in the United States, and that the Bighorn, Little Bighorn, and Little Missouri Valleys, from their close proximity, must partake of the same general character, we have no doubt.

We arrived at the Yellowstone at 4:00 P.M. of August 17 and were greatly disappointed in not finding the steamer, but before long she came in sight from the westward, and we hoped for a relief from the over-perpetual hardtack and bacon, but we were again doomed to disappointment, for her commissary department contained only the time-honored rations.

The Yellowstone Valley at this place is not very prepossessing, the valley being covered with cactus and sagebrush, the whole being overlooked by bare sandstone bluffs.

The command has just received (August 18) orders to take four days' rations in their saddlebags, ten on their pack mules, the destination no doubt being the Little Missouri, and from thence to the Sioux agency at Red Cloud, where you will probably hear from me again. The trail we have been following since our junction with General Terry, and which we dropped a day ago, leads down the Yellowstone, and from there to the Red Cloud agency. This information comes through the Ree Indians, who, being left by General Terry on this river, have busied themselves in trailing, with the above conclusions.

As a courier leaves soon for Bismarck, D.T., I am restricted in time, but have embodied above about all of importance that has occurred since my last.

Chicago *Inter-Ocean,* October 4, 1876

BIGHORN AND YELLOWSTONE EXPEDITION, IN CAMP ON WHITEWOOD CREEK, BLACK HILLS, September 16, 1876

After my last communication from the Yellowstone River, General Crook's command separated from that of General Terry and made two short marches up the Powder River, where General Terry personally joined the command and had a short conference with General Crook, and returned to his steamboats at the mouth of Powder River. Our course was then due eastward, crossing the Elm, Cabin, and Beaver Creeks, the scouts seeing a small war party of Indians on the latter stream. We reached the Little Missouri on September 1 and were certainly agreeably disappointed in the character of the country. This section of the territories is marked on all the authentic maps in our possession as a portion of the Badlands.

The Little Missouri, where we cut it, is in fact a beautiful stream, well wooded, with a fine surrounding country, and is no doubt destined to support a considerable population when the Indian question is fairly settled. The next few days' marches through this unknown country did not shake our belief in its general fertility, for, to say the least, it will support innumerable herds of stock when a railroad or proper steamboat navigation of the Yellowstone makes this branch of industry profitable.

On reaching Heart River, about due north of the Black Hills, our command was placed on half rations. Messengers were sent to Fort Abraham Lincoln, instructing, by telegraph to Fort Fetterman, our train to reach us with as little delay as possible in the Black Hills, and then we turned our face in that direction and home. On reaching the extreme north fork of Grand River, which was rather a series of pools than a stream, it became evident that even half rations would not get us to provisions in the Black Hills, either at Deadwood or Crook City, and Captain Mills of the 5th Cavalry, with fifteen picked men and horses (especially the latter) from each company of the ten companies of the 3rd Cavalry, with three officers of that regiment and Lieutenant Bubb, acting commissary of subsistence, with a pack train, were sent forward to reach either of the above places by forced marches and bring relief to the command.

Captain Mills's command left camp on the evening of the seventh and marched all night, made a short halt for breakfast, and continued forward early on the eighth. The heavy rains made the alkali flats almost impassable for the nearly broken-down horses of the cavalry. A few ripe wild plums and bull berries (a berry similar to the large red currant) were found and greedily devoured by the command. As

Capt. Anson Mills. ANSON MILLS. *MY STORY.*

Lieutenant Crawford's[10] detachment, which was leading, was going over a small hill near the north branch of Owl Creek, our guide, Frank Grouard, galloping back, called attention to a small herd of Indian ponies about two miles to the south. Lieutenant Crawford was soon out of sight, and after a more careful survey, it was concluded that we had an Indian village of unknown extent before us. Frank Grouard believed it to be the village of Roman Nose, a Brule Sioux, that had left the Spotted Tail agency early in the spring to indulge in the coming fights with Sitting Bull and Crazy Horse, and that Spotted Tail had refused the right to return to his agency.

After a short consultation, it was decided to attack at daylight on the morning of the ninth. The plan of attack was to approach the head of the village in the morning with three parallel columns, the outer two being dismounted; the right, numbering fifty-seven men, under Lieutenant Crawford, 3rd Cavalry, and the left, numbering fifty-three, under Lt. A. H. von Leuttwitz, 3rd Cavalry, to diverge respectively to the right and left, with extended intervals as skirmishers, and surround the village. The center column of twenty-five men, mounted [and under the command of Lieutenant Schwatka], as soon as the daylight was sufficient to see the front sights on the carbines, or sooner if the Indians discovered our presence, was to charge with pistols and stampede the herds of Indian ponies. The herd being well away, a sufficient number could dismount at the further end of the village and close the gaps between the columns of Lieutenants Crawford and von Leuttwitz. At nightfall, the command, having remained concealed from the discovery of the herd until then in a small basin surrounded by bluffs, retraced its footsteps about a mile to wood, water, grass, and a safe place of concealment, and bivouacked in a drizzling rain until 2:00 A.M. of September 9, when we started for the village with the entire outfit. After a mile's journey, the pack train under charge of Lieutenant Bubb [and] the lead horses of the dismounted companies of Lieutenants Crawford and von Leuttwitz were left in a safe place, with orders to join the column rapidly as soon as the first shot was heard indicating that a fight was going on.

The column then resumed its course in three lines, as explained, and after several small mistakes as to the probable place of the village, Frank Grouard brought in a herd of about six or eight Indian ponies that he had quietly "gobbled" from the outlying herd of the village without creating any disturbance whatever. Several such small captures were repeated, the column meantime advancing, when the remainder of the herd, alarmed at its approach, stampeded toward the village, now only a few yards distant. The further prosecution of the plan was now changed in a flash, and the mounted party, pistols in hand, yelling and firing into tepees, rushed through the little town and soon depopulated it of ponies, and gave the human population such a morning reveille as they did not have to awaken them at every daylight. The dismounted men followed up the mounted charge rapidly with a deadly fusillade into the village. The night having been very rainy, the Indians had securely fastened the openings in their lodges, and it was with evident impediment that they made their exits. Many were seen to fall, and in the approaching daylight, it was often hard to tell whether the burdens carried were children or the slain and wounded. The village was deserted sooner than it takes to relate the fact, and Captain Mills's command then held a large hill west of this place and overlooking it. The pack train and stampeded herd of Indian ponies soon joined him at the village, and except [for] a few stray shots, the battle of Rabbit Creek [Slim Buttes] had ended, and the first Sioux Indian village that had been "scooped" in the present campaign was in our hands, through the fighting of the 3rd Cavalry, the same regiment that cleared Tongue River heights and had fought the Rosebud in June.

The following is the list of killed and wounded:

Killed—Pvt. John Winzel, Company A, 3rd Cavalry.

Wounded—1st Lt. A. H. von Leuttwitz; Sgt. John H. Kirkwood, Company M; Sgt. Edward Glass, Company E; Pvt. Edward McKlernan, Company E; Pvt. William B. DuBois, Company C; Pvt. August

Doran, Company D; Pvt. Charles Foster, Company D—all of the 3rd Cavalry.

Probably the most exciting incident of the fight was the retreat of several Indians to a large hole in a ravine at the head of the village. It was here that Sergeants Glass and Kirkwood were wounded and Private Winzel of Company A was killed. In the bed of the ravine, the earth had caved in, forming a natural fortification, except in one small place on the south, which the Indians soon completed with their hands. Here American Horse, with four warriors and a number of squaws and papooses, made good their retreat, and not only held us at bay, but made it unsafe to approach the northern end or head of the village. The guides Grouard and "Captain Jack"[11] thought that we were in the vicinity of larger villages, and Captain Mills deemed it expedient to send a courier to General Crook, informing him of events, who promptly responded, the head of his column appearing about noon. In the afternoon, the Indians, to the number of about one hundred fifty, reappeared and tried to retrieve the misfortunes of the morning, but were no match, of course, for our now strong command.

American Horse, mortally wounded, and his family were induced to surrender, and from them we glean the following: The tribe was that of Roman Nose, Brule Sioux, with American Horse in direct command. They know nothing of the killed and wounded, but suppose them to be large. Crazy Horse, with his Cheyenne allies, was about ten miles distant with about three hundred lodges.

During the skirmish of the afternoon, the leg of Lieutenant von Leuttwitz was amputated in the lower third of the thigh, the knee joint having been laid open by the wound. Two days' full rations of dried buffalo meat for the command was captured and, the rations being nearly out, was doubly acceptable, as we did not know where we were in the geography of the Dakota land.

On the tenth, the rear guard, composed of the 1st Battalion, 5th Cavalry, was severely pressed for about five miles of the day's march, losing two men wounded, and no doubt inflicting a more serious loss on the Indians.

On the eleventh, Captain Mills, with fifty men of the 3rd Cavalry mounted on the captured Indian ponies, proceeded on to Deadwood City for the needed relief. Captain Upham[12] was sent with his battalion of the 5th Cavalry on an Indian trail, supposing that it led to some village in the vicinity. We camped that night on Owl Creek, half starved, with a diminished ration of jerked buffalo meat, horse meat without salt, and a pelting, cold rain to add to all our discomforts.

The march of the twelfth was one long to be remembered in the sufferings of American soldiery. With nothing to eat but pony meat, with no salt, a disagreeable, cold, rainy day, the weary and starved command launched itself over the miry alkali flats that separate Owl Creek from Crow Fork of the Belle Fourche—a long, long thirty-five miles. The horses fell out exhausted by dozens, the men were too weak to lead any distance, the halts were only sufferings taken at a standstill—far more annoying than the march, bad as it was. Camp was reached late at night, and weary and broken down, many a man slept that awful night as if he was but a drunkard in the slums of a city, prostrate on the wet ground. Stragglers continued to come in until late the next day.

At noon the next day, we marched seven miles to the Belle Fourche, or North Fork of the Cheyenne River, and there found provisions awaiting us that Captain Mills had collected hurriedly in Crook City. We had hardly expected them so soon, and too many thanks cannot be given Captain Mills for the able and untiring manner in which he had worked during the last week. The provisions of the Indian village and the second succor were like heaven itself to the starved command.

On the fifteenth, we moved to Whitewood Creek, where I now write you, General Crook leaving the troops to proceed to Fort Laramie, where General Sheridan is now reported to be. Captain Upham joined us on the march of the fifteenth, having seen nothing further of the Indians, beyond losing one man, whose scalped and mutilated remains were brought into camp and decently interred. Of the further progress of the command, I will give you due notice.

Chicago *Inter-Ocean,* October 11, 1876

BIGHORN AND YELLOWSTONE EXPEDITION, IN CAMP AT CUSTER CITY, D.T., September 26, 1876

After my last letter, when we had just received our supplies from Crook City, in the Black Hills, and General Crook had just left us for Fort Laramie, we continued by very slow marches southward, giving our stock and footsore men plenty of time to recuperate, our destination, no doubt, being Fort Laramie, where we are to await the action of the present peace commission lately appointed by the president, should a winter campaign be not decided upon before that time.

Sutler wagons from Crook and Deadwood Cities became more numerous, and the first fabulous prices for supplies slowly declined. Butter, for which we first paid from $3 to $5 a pound, fell to fifty and seventy-five cents; potatoes from $10 a bushel to a corresponding price. I simply give these items to show how much it took a command in money to once "fill up" to that degree necessary to satiate an appetite bordering on ravenous. The citizens in the [Black] Hills, however, have responded nobly and generously to our demands, and the prices paid by the government were certainly very fair under the circumstances. The line of sutlers' wagons seemed to convert our encampment into a big county fair and formed a strange contrast to our camp a few days ago when we were half starving.

Dispatches from Crook's Column

ANDREW S. BURT[1]

Cincinnati *Commercial,* September 11, 1876

IN BIVOUAC ON PUMPKIN CREEK,
August 14, 1876

Since Terry's and Crook's columns effected a junction on the Rosebud, our march has followed the route taken by the Sioux; we have "slept on the trail," as a scout said the other day, "and that is good medicine."

The commands met on the tenth, at noon, and by night General Terry, taking a leaf out of General Crook's book, had stripped down from wagons to pack mules, from tents to bivouac, from luxuries to bacon and hardtack, and the next day found us crossing the rough divide between Rosebud and Tongue Rivers. Eight miles marching brought us to the latter stream, which we crossed, thence down for four miles to camp.

So on for four days, reaching this creek today, which puts in from the east, a tributary of the Badlands. Here the trail turns eastward again. Starting from the Little Bighorn, it seems to make slips, first to the east, and then south, the former crossing the divides, and the latter down some river or creek. Evidently the enemy is making for the Yellowstone, and it was the general opinion among the officers before reaching here that Sitting Bull (if he still lives) would cross.

A courier met us at noon with dispatches from Colonel Miles's[2] reconnaissance up and down the Yellowstone, and no trail of Indians has been discovered. This settles the British possessions theory, one which seems to have taken quite a hold on the command. General Terry's frequently expressed belief that we would see the forty-ninth parallel before we were through with our work is a good one, arguing from precedents, and it may be that the Indians have crossed further down, or have concealed their trail in such a way that Colonel Miles has been unable to find it. That the Sioux consider the Northwest Territory as a safe harbor of refuge there can be no doubt, and more, have used it as such. Still, it is questionable if they have made for that country for many reasons; but this is mere speculation and conjecture. It is enough that each night we will sleep on the trail, whether it leads to Canada or some more disagreeable place.

We of the infantry are camped in a beautiful grove of cottonwood trees. The grass is tall and thick. It will make a good mattress for our bones. Each "thigh-bone hole" will not have to be so deep for a comfortable night's rest. The cool shade is grateful after the hot sun of today's march. Altogether, we have the best of the campground this day anyhow. So our Shoshone Indians think; for coming to this grove, they stop in disappointment and surprise to find us with a squatter's title—a preemptive claim, which nothing but an order from General Crook could or would effect.

The Indians have to camp just back of us on the sagebrush, much to their disgust, which we share heartily, for the reason that we can hear their howling late into the night. The commissary has slaughtered a steer for issue to the cavalry. The infantry are to have none tonight, much to their disappointment, but the Snakes (Shoshones) have attended the butchering, and some of the more fortunate bucks have dragged the entrails free of the butcher's muck, and they are to have a feast and sing. Lucky dogs that they can "enjoy that sort of thing, you know." One may not sigh for such a feed, but still, hardpan fare, bacon, and coffee is not an extensive menu, and any little addition is a variety. I do not believe I regret my education, nor assert that I have a desire for this Indian feast, but still, the monotony of our duty at least makes me think perhaps that to take part in one of Crook's campaigns, my early training has been neglected. The Ab-sa-ra-kas, like their namesakes, the Crows, have smelt the meat, and not knowing the quantity the Snakes have obtained, have come ostensibly to give a serenade, but to my thinking, it is with a hope that their brother Indians will be generous and share—at least give them the head and hoof of the beast slaughtered.

They appear at the outer edge of our Indians' camp (the Crows are with Terry) mounted—about twenty young fellows. They ride in line, their ponies being jammed close to one another, with two bucks in some cases on one horse. The song is begun by one of the leaders sending a keynote, and then all join in a two-three chant, descending from a high note to a low one by steps, or rather, sounding each note of the scale twice in a short, jerky method as the tone is lowered. At the end, every fellow yells his peculiar howl, something after the manner of a tiger, only it is not a continuous sound, but a "yip, yip," an "ow, ow," ending in a "oo-ah." These Crows ride slowly round the camp, then to the center, stopping before old Washakie's wickiup; here they dismount in a circle around a buffalo robe, each grasping it

A conference with the Indian allies. FRANK LESLIE'S ILLUSTRATED NEWSPAPER, 1876.

to give a tautness, making a kind of drumhead. This they strike with sticks to keep the time and make an accompaniment to their singer. Louder and louder grow their yells; the singing gets fiercer; they perspire, and the air, not of the song, is odoriferous with moistened beaver medicine; but no meat is forthcoming. In the crowd, I recognize a Crow chief whom I had known some years ago, and stepping close behind him, said, "Ab-sa-ra-ka as-shoo-me-noon; Sho-sho-ne errukee ma-jook-die bar-rel."

"Ko! tuck," and he laughed heartily. By rights, according to the Indian man in the East, I ought to have been scalped then and there for daring to trespass on the grave warriors' ceremony. These fellows [back] East, who know all about the India, are telling George Crook what he ought and what he ought not to have done at this or that stage of this campaign. By the way, it may be as well to translate what I said. My words were, "The Crows are fools; the Snakes ain't going to give meat." He replied, "You bet."

Tongue River, down which we have marched, is a fine stream, though muddy at this point, where we are camped, and for some distance back, owing to recent rains. This stream drains the whole northern face of the Bighorn range. It is about one hundred fifty miles long and runs with great velocity, averaging in depth and breadth three feet by one hundred to one hundred fifty. Its headwaters issue from a chain of little frozen lakes on the highest point of the Bighorn, at an altitude of one thousand feet above the timberline, or 12,500 feet above ocean level. Thence they course down through snow drifts, on through forests of spruce pine and fir or under beetling crags of granite, the home of mountain sheep and elk. In a great portion of its waters, trout are found in astonishing abundance. From one of its minor tributaries, Goose Creek, our command caught, with very rude appliances, much on the pin-hook order, over 1,300 in less than three weeks; while the greater part of these were fine panfish, not over half a pound in weight, there were many that weighed two and three pounds.

Immense herds of elk are found in these wild recesses, with blacktailed deer, mountain sheep, and grizzly bear. The lower slopes are matted thick with grama and buffalo grasses, which keep stock in fine condition all the year round. The Rosebud, with its banks fringed thickly with the wild bushes that give its name, waters another fine pasturage. Its waters are not as pure and clear as those of its neighbor, the Tongue River, and indeed, do not represent any of the drainage of the Bighorn proper, but have their origin in the higher grassy foothills. Near its head, this creeks runs through a deep canyon with precipitous walls and miry bottoms. It was on this stream that Sitting Bull, with nearly three thousand warriors,[3] awaited, last June, the approach of General Crook's command of nine hundred men, expecting to annihilate them. Under other leadership, our soldiery might have been decoyed into an ambuscade, but General Crook was too shrewd to allow himself to be outmaneuvered. He not only frustrated Sitting Bull's design, but inflicted upon that chieftain a severe loss in warriors. We have abundant evidence of this, and many graves of the chiefs and warriors killed in that fight now line the banks of the Rosebud. Those found in a lodge by Custer before his fight, eight of them dressed in state for their final journey, were killed on the Rosebud.

It is confidently believed by many that the Sioux loss was greater then than in the subsequent fight of the twenty-fifth. Remembering this, and that our command numbered on June 17 only about nine hundred men all told, and you must concur that Crook displayed good generalship and quick perception not to try and force his way down through the canyon country beyond his first line of action. His objective was the village, after the battle had been developed, it is true, but only when it could be attacked on other terms than those on which the Indians were willing to allow. He saw what perhaps not another man in the field saw, and though simple, it was the inspiration of genius. He saw that the Indians were not only willing, but anxious for the battalion of cavalry of eight companies, which had started to go towards the village, should continue on its way to certain envelopment and destruction, and the cavalry was ordered back. We slept on the field.

And now about our stay on Goose Creek, and why Crook did not fight the Indians. To have advanced and fought would have produced no positive results, and definite results are what a good general strives for. To use Crook's own words to me, "I could fight and satisfy this clamor, but what would be the results? A lot of my good people killed, and a few dead Indians. But I am not out here to make a reputation or satisfy a foolish personal pride. I am here to do my duty to others, and to knock the bottom out of these Sioux when I do hit them."

In justice, only give Crook and his men a little time, and let them be judged by the results.

A curiosity of our march has been the Indian graves. Quite as curious and horrible is the ghoul-like manner of the Shoshone when he sees one of these graves. These Indians at once become possessed with a savagery revolting in the extreme; the grave is attacked at once, torn to pieces, the dead body beaten and shot and in bits scattered to the four winds. Their excuse is that any one of them striking a dead Sioux counts a coup and has done a boastful deed. It is the same as if they had killed an enemy in an open fight. The "coup" means a strike, and each one is added to the record of a warrior, the list of which he may tell over in the council lodge or harangue to the village when the occasion suits him. The graves of the Plains Indians are built on scaffolding nine or ten feet high. On these, wrapped in the finest blankets, furs, and bead-wrought robes and feather trappings, the corpses of the dead warriors are left to repose. When of prominence in his tribe, the chief or warrior has buried with him his best rifle and pipe, and one of his fleetest war ponies is killed to waft his spirit swiftly to the land of the Great Hereafter.

On the march down the Rosebud, over on the right, we passed a large, circular space with a tall pole in the center. This was the arena reserved for the Sun Dance, a ceremony celebrated with the recurrence of the summer solstice to initiate young bucks into the ranks of the warrior class. The tortures voluntarily undergone during this rite are almost too horrible to relate. The back and arms of the candidates are slit open, and small sticks inserted to which are attached the ponderous heads of buffalo bulls. The young aspirant struggles desperately until he succeeds in tearing himself loose from all encumbrances and is borne fainting away in the arms of applauding friends. After such dances, the Sioux frequently partake of feasts of all the delicacies known to their cuisine. Of these, choked dogs or puppies are most highly esteemed. The strangled animal, without being skinned or eviscerated, is thrown into a kettle of water and boiled to a pulp. The young warriors, half frenzied, rush to the fire and pluck out from the seething mass with their naked hands fragments of meat, which they distribute among the circle of their friends, who crowd forward, eager to be made the recipient of their bounty.

The march tomorrow will be a long one, and my firelight is nearly burned out, and the dipper in the heavens is so far turned as to be spilling its contents, and it must be late, so to bed and dream of rattlesnakes, home, and a square meal.

IN BIVOUAC AT THE MOUTH OF POWDER RIVER,
August 23, 1876

We are on the Yellowstone at last. The Sioux have gone eastward, and the trail was, when we left it, ten days old, with no evidence yet that this had split up, thus still presenting an objective which may yet give us battle. The command turned down the Powder to this point to shore up the infantry, give a few days' rest, and get an additional supply of rations. The incidents of the march from the fourteenth to the eighteenth, from Pumpkin Creek to the Yellowstone, you have in my last letter.[4] Severe as it was in many respects—the heat, rain, bad shoes, played-out horses, and thin fare—still, everyone appears impatient of this delay, though one would think the rest desirable, mentally and physically. This impatience comes more probably with a desire to be moving, hoping it will take us homeward.

The general impression is that we are to have no fight, that the Indians have gone to the agencies, and there is nothing to do but be getting nearer our quarters and something good to eat. "Belly battles" are the only ones seemingly in store for us, judging from the interesting campfire gossip. There is one man in the command, though, who still has hope, who still thinks there is a chance to catch some, if not all, [of] the hostile Sioux. General Crook still believes we may have work to do before going into winter quarters, before we reach any agency; before, in fact, this campaign is over for us. The details on which he bases this belief I do not know, but conjecture that it turns on the probability of the hostile Sioux being able to supply, temporarily, their want of food from the immense bands of migrating antelope to be had between the Little Powder and the Little Missouri, and that they will camp there for meat, and most likely send their squaws and a few bucks to the agencies for supplies. It is likely that now these are making their appearance, and hence the rumor that the Indians have come in.

Our Indian allies have gone home. They, at least, have given up hope. Much of this, however, was owing to the poor condition of their ponies, and that they had been so long and were so far away from home.[5] This is a loss not appreciated by many, simply because of their ignorance.

The cavalry horses, which needed so much the rest given them, have recuperated wonderfully in these few days' stay. Col. Wesley Merritt, chief of cavalry, thinks his cavalry command will be able, on the coming march and in the possible fight, to do all the work required of it now. Moreover, it is the belief of the soldiers amongst us that the inspiration of his energy and ability will add much to that end.

We march this afternoon, going about twelve miles eastward toward the Little Missouri. Part of the command will keep on the trail, and the rest follow the Fort Lincoln road; thus we will be able to take twenty wagons, as the two routes run parallel and not far apart. This train will give us a good sendoff of rations when we turn to our agencies—Spotted Tail and Red Cloud—or Fort Fetterman, should the Indians be found to have separated. Then the two commands will divide, General Crook marching for his department, and General Terry for the Missouri River. At what point this division will take place is of course unknown even to those gentlemen, other reports to the contrary notwithstanding. Whenever it may be, we part with General Terry with regret, saying good-bye to the gentleman, scholar, and soldier.

Judging by the supplies which we shall be enabled to take, it cannot be far from the middle of September when Crook's column will put in an appearance somewhere south of the Black Hills. Just where that may be is hard to tell. It is possible that our work may continue in such a way that we may put into the Black Hills for something to eat, alighting on the poor, honest miners like a swarm of locusts, causing famine and starvation prices for flour.

Cincinnati *Commercial,* September 14, 1876

IN BIVOUAC, HEART RIVER, September 5, 1876

We finished today the four-hundredth mile on our hunting the hostile Sioux out of his trysting place. We have chased them from the Little Bighorn to the Rosebud, out of Tongue River Valley, down the Powder to the Yellowstone, back again, across to Beaver Creek, out of that to the Little Missouri, where, almost hunted down, weary with fleeing, the great Indian village has split up. The trails still lead south and eastward, but only indicating that the hostile Sioux are tired of being pushed from place to place with never a time when they could catch a detached party to slaughter. Steadily the command has moved onward, hoping that the propitious moment would arrive when by a forced march we could reach them. But it seemed as if all the unlucky combinations of a lifetime have culminated on this campaign. We have reached Heart River with two days' rations and two thousand people, a hundred miles away from any supplies, and the Indians most likely housed safely in their agencies. Although this is the alternate objective of the operations of this summer, it is hardly human to be satisfied with what appears to be a tame conclusion. To have met and worsted Sitting Bull, to have terribly punished him and his butchers would be a satisfaction to any man calling himself an American; but since it may not be so, there is the other fact that part of the American army, under difficulties the most trying, have driven these Indians from their haunts, which heretofore have been secure to them. These soldiers have done this, and [Brig.] Gen. George Crook has been their leader.

Here let me say [that] under no other general of our army would we have accomplished as much. I suppose, in fact know, there are opinions strongly to the contrary; that possibly the majority of the papers of the country have (perhaps have expressed) adverse opinions to this, but my belief is this is an injustice to us and to him, which will be acknowledged. However, I shall discuss this question in a future letter, from a military standpoint, when I have more time, but now some of the details of our march from the Yellowstone here are to be told, if the rain will let me do it.

To explain, and give at the same time some idea of the pleasures of our summer jaunt, you must know we have just come into camp, more properly bivouac, meaning without shelter, the arms stacked. I am writing, and it comes on to rain. How to continue is the question? The problem is solved. I throw over my head my blanket and write in the questionable shelter, my knee for a desk, guessing whether the lines are straight. The paper on which I am writing, being of a peculiar nature, is thin, wrinkly, and perverse. My blanket will be wet, and I shall have a cold night bath, but then you will hear from Crook's column and know that it is not yet slaughtered.

We left the Yellowstone on the twenty-fourth, moving up Powder River a short distance. This change of camp was of Christian benefit, for had we remained a day at the scene of our drowning out of the night before, I verily believe some few of the command would have stored up a sufficiency of bad words uttered loudly, deeply—every way, in fact—enough to sink a whole shipload of our prayerful Pilgrim fathers in the past, present, or future. Drowned out? Do you know what it means? No! Well, suppose you have laid yourself down in your luxurious couch of one blanket and an overcoat, and it comes on to rain. You defy the elements. The gradual wetting on top disturbs you not, and you dream, "Let him rest."

That's all very well, but when your hips become gradually and surely immersed, your pants are more than damp, and finally you can count the inches the water has risen up your back, you look toward where the stars ought to be, utter a silent prayer, rise, and say, "I am drowned out." This, my friend, has occurred to us, not once, but many times. And yet Colonel Hazen has said this is a desert. "Hazen's Sahara!" It rains in deserts, then.[6]

On August 25, we moved still further up Powder River, waiting for General Terry to join us. His command did not move from the river the day we did, and as we were still to cooperate, we delayed. In the afternoon, General Terry came to our camp with two of his staff, and we learned that Indians had made their appearance on the Yellowstone and had fired on the boats coming up. Here was a difficult question to decide. The Indians there—did it mean the whole village, or a party on a raid or a *ruse de guerre* to cover a crossing of a few Indians going north with their families, stealing away from the main camp? General Crook, being still under General Terry's orders, could only suggest that the commands separate, one to keep the main trail and run it to a definite conclusion, and the other to go down the Yellowstone and engage any force of the enemy that might cross.

This was accepted as the plan, and to us was given the difficult and arduous task of striking off eastward on the trail into a country with which, saving Frank Grouard our guide, not one of the column was familiar. This compliment to our command was due, I judge, to the superior mobility of our command. It must have been intended as such, for certainly the interior line of operations was the more difficult because of the enemy, the logistics, and other possible contingencies coming with the enemy's retreat. But this letter is not to be so much a military one as "what the boys did in camp and on the march." There can't be much of that, as already my lookout says, "Hurry up, that Indian is saddling up." "What Indian?" "The Ree who rides courier tonight."

We left Powder River behind us, crossed to the Little Missouri over Stanley's route of 1872–73, parallel to which the trail ran. At that stream, where we arrived yesterday, we found the evidence upon which I base the assertion that the village of two thousand lodges and wickiups have broken up in squads of ten lodges to two hundred, going to the agencies probably. But to be sure of that fact, we must move on. And then comes the question of how? We have two days' rations and four days' march to make to reach the Black Hills. It certainly will be a question of eating mules. Will we go there? An officer just passing tells me the general has decided it. So here we go—and here comes that Indian, red hot, and says, "No stoppee."

Cincinnati *Commercial,* September 17, 1876

CROOK'S EXPEDITION ON RAPID CREEK,
September 9

Part of Crook's command attacked and captured a hostile Sioux village of forty-one lodges this morning. The fight was a sharp and decisive one, with not a severe loss on either side, thus vindicating the unerring judgment of Crook. Captain Mills, commanding a battalion of the 3rd Cavalry, who did this good work, had been sent for rations. Our command had marched eighty-three miles and was reduced to horseflesh, but the trail still leading south, threatening the Black Hills and settlements, Crook would not give it up, although opposed by nearly all of his rank officers. In spite of the difficulties appearing, his determination was to keep on and do his imperative duty. The rain beat down each day and night on the unsheltered officers and men. Mud was ankle deep for the plodding, dogged infantry; men going sixty-three miles without wood to cook horseflesh and drinking rain from muddy pools. Horses were left staggering by the way, played out, the dismounting cavalrymen joining the infantry. Accouterments were abandoned by the wayside, but no ammunition.

On the morning of the ninth, two horsemen appeared amidst the mist and rain, to the head of the column galloping, and as they shot past all we could hear is that Mills had a fight. Soon General Crook comes from the rear, and we learn that Mills had charged on a village of forty-one lodges, capturing two hundred ponies and plunder of a rich Indian character. After marching about fifteen miles over the buttes, through gorges and defiles, mounted men and footmen hustling and crowding onward, we at last find ourselves in a Sioux camp no longer hostile, but very peaceable. Soon it is filled with soldiers wandering about, muddy, tattered, lean, and gaunt, rather sleepily lounging around looking for plunder, scattering over prized paint and porcupine quills, nosing about robes. This was not what they have worked for. It seems they had not been in the affair.

Even the shooting at the other end of the village caused no excitement until the fact is known that several Indians are concealed in a narrow ravine. Twenty detailed men are advancing to drive them out. This ravine is only about thirty feet long and a few feet down at its deepest; so narrow and insignificant one could cross it without thinking it was the grave of eight beings in the end.

In the fight of the morning, twenty bucks, squaws, and papooses had fled into this little ravine and hid. How, is a marvel. They had discovered themselves by killing a passing soldier, and now twenty men, led by Lt. Philo Clark, are assaulting the stronghold. Already White and Kennedy have been killed. It is miserable and desperate work, for the soldiers have to go it blind and shoot anywhere into the ravine. Clark stands at the edge shooting. Several men are knocked over by his side, and still the answer comes from the ravine slowly, but each time a soldier is carried off from the foot of this hellhole. A gradual advance is made, when the cry is, "There are some squaws and children!" The fire is ordered stopped, but the maddened soldiers think only of their dead comrades. Clark controls his squad, but a hundred others have gone in for revenge.

In the midst of this melee, an officer rushes between the fire and drags out the children and squaw.[7] The child screamed, "Woman dead." Other officers beat back the men, and there is a pause. The squaw runs to Crook and seizes his coat and would not release him. The general learns from this one that there are more squaws in the ravine and only two live bucks. Then, judging rightly that two Indian lives are nothing to that of any of his men, he makes the squaw go in and induce the rest to come out, which they do, and now it is seen how a few men who are determined to sell their lives dearly in such a position can make a defense successful.

Whilst most of us are at supper of horse and dried meat recently captured, there is another alarm. It is those who have escaped in the morning, returning from another village twenty miles away, [that of] Crazy Horse, with numbers increased to about one thousand warriors. They think probably to find only Mill's command of one hundred fifty men. Mistake, for doughboys are up, and lots of critterback. The matter is soon settled, and the Indians are driven off, wiser men. Night coming on prevents pursuit. There was little loss on either side.

IN BIVOUAC AT OWL CREEK, September 10

The command marched eleven miles today. Men are weary and hungry; one can see looking at the infantry line that the men stagger and are weak. They are trying to buy pieces of buffalo robes to keep warm these cold nights. The excitement is over. They are marching to the [Black] Hills for rations, where we expect meeting our train and the supplies of vegetables which Crook has asked Sheridan to have forwarded. The last act of this summer's campaign ends there.

Crook has landed his army at this point on the circle originally intended. He has proven his hard and long-earned knowledge of Indians to be sound, and had he been footloose instead of compelled to meet Terry, there would have been his oft-repeated "definite results." When at Heart River, his judgment told him the Indians had gone south and the settlements were endangered. His will carried this command through without rations, ambulances, or wood, over a line of country known to none of us, and not a man dying from disease, and found an Indian village as he had predicted, never once giving up the purpose to its present conclusion.

The Battle of Slim Buttes

JOHN G. BOURKE[1]

John G. Bourke Diary 1: 868–85, United States Military Academy Library, West Point, New York

My pen writes freely the routine chronicle of wet, foggy and cheerless morning. We awakened early and delayed but a few moments ere resuming the march, which would at least restore the circulation to benumbed limbs. Our men were much more cheerful today, having had the exhilarating influences of a good, warm fire and good, invigorating coffee last night and this morning.

Five miles out from bivouac, crossed the South Fork of the Grand River, a meandering, lazy branch of muddy water, similar in volume, dimensions, and general characteristics to those described within the past few days. A half dozen stunted willow and cottonwood trees intensified the monotony and loneliness of its otherwise perfectly barren banks. Directly in front of the point where we crossed, a confluent came in from the south, and this we ascended, getting into rugged hills with a thin fringe of cedar and juniper in the ravines near the summits.

Here we met a courier riding back from Captain Mills with the information he had captured a village of over twenty-five lodges, with all the plunder contained, and some two hundred horses. Most of the Indians had escaped, and Mills was fearful they might return with reinforcements and sweep down upon him before General Crook could arrive with the main body. On our side, Lieutenant von Leuttwitz, 3rd Cavalry, and five men had been wounded and one man killed; the Indian loss was reported at six killed. A small party of the hostiles had taken refuge in a ravine near the village and were hemmed in by our soldiers. It was also believed they were anxious to surrender.

General Crook immediately directed Surgeon [Benton A.] Clements to designate the necessary medical attendants to push to the front and sent word to Colonel Merritt, the chief of cavalry, to hurry forward with his command. The infantry battalion, upon learning the enemy had been encountered in front, became very eager to participate in the expected engagement and pressed on through the drizzling mist, determined not to be passed by the mounted troops. So well did they succeed that in the long stretch of ten miles intervening, they marched fully as quickly as the cavalry, and came in right behind them to the scene of the action.

This we found to be a narrow ravine, well hidden by its own steep banks and the adjacent high hills, with a flowing stream of pretty good water and plenty of grass and fuel within convenient reach. Mills had discovered the village the evening previous but had not sent back word, as he should have done, to General Crook. Hence, when he attacked at daybreak, he found himself unable to surround the village, the majority of whose occupants made their escape by cutting their way through the canvas of their tepees, and just barely strong enough to maintain himself against the reinforcements they would certainly return with, until the arrival of General Crook, for whom he was now only too glad to send. Mills's conduct in this feature cannot be commended, but he is entitled to praise for the plucky manner in which he attacked and carried, in the darkness of morning, a village of unknown strength and resources.

The village comprehended thirty-seven lodges, not counting four that did not yet have canvas stretched over them. Several of the lodges were of unusual dimensions; one, probably that occupied by the guard Frank [Grouard] calls the "Brave Night Hearts," containing thirty saddles and equipment. Great quantities of furs, almost exclusively untanned buffalo, antelope, and deerskins, wrapped in bundles, and several tons of meat, dried after the Indian manner, formed the principal part of the spoil, though mention must not be overlooked of the almost innumerable tin dishes. blankets, cooking utensils, boxes of caps, ammunition, saddles, horse equipment, and other supplies that will prove a more serious loss to the savages than gain to us.

The herd of ponies, of more than four hundred, was stampeded early in the attack; not quite two hundred fell into our hands; many of them were fine-looking little animals, of good form and full of life.

A cavalry guidon of silk, nearly new and torn from the staff, an overcoat once the property of an army officer, a noncommissioned officer's blouse, cavalry saddles of the McClellan model, covered with black leather, after the latest pattern of the Ordnance Bureau, a glove marked with the name of the late Captain Keogh, a letter addressed to a private soldier of the 7th Cavalry, horses branded U.S. and 7th Cavalry were the links of circumstantial evidence upon which we rested the conclusion that the inmates of these tepees had assisted in the butchery of Custer and his gallant comrades on the Little Bighorn in June last.

The first thing done by our commanding general was to have a detail made to secure all the plunder and arrange it in large piles for

Lieutenant Schwatka's charge through the village at Slim Buttes.
LIBRARY OF CONGRESS.

future disposition. The condition of our wounded was also examined into, and everything possible done for its amelioration. Captain Mills had already pitched a lodge in a cool, shady spot near the stream [Gap Creek] and sheltered from the annoyance of random shots still fired by the scattered Indians from the distant hills.

The next task was to dislodge those holding the little gulch, fifty or sixty yards outside the line of lodges. Mills had reported the number as two only; the disclosure of the real state of affairs astonished him as much as it did us.

Frank Grouard and Big Bat [Pouriere] were ordered to crawl as close to the ravine as they could do, consistently with safety, and open up a conversation with those imprisoned there. The colloquy was not satisfactory. The Indians declined to accede to any terms and seemed determined to fight it out to the last. Accordingly, a small band of volunteers was picked out and placed under Lt. W. P. Clark, 2nd Cavalry,[2] with instructions to clean out the ravine. A very heavy firing attracted a crowd of idlers, who swarmed up the hill in such numbers that Clark's movements were seriously embarrassed. It was easy for the imprisoned Indians to pick off a man for every shot; in such a throng, the only wonder was that each bullet didn't claim a billet of three or four killed and wounded.

The ravine was so narrow, not over ten feet, and so deep, from fifteen to twenty, with a growth of box-elder trees inside that veiled them from our aim, and soft, loamy banks the Indians dug into and thus speedily sheltered themselves against the great majority of our volley shots—the advantages of position rested with the Sioux entirely. "Buffalo Chips" [White], a sort of guide and scout following the command, a poor, harmless, good-natured liar who played the role of "Sancho Panza" to Buffalo Bill's "Don Quixote," was the first on our side to die, shot through the heart.[3] His dying exclamation of' "Oh Lord! Oh Lord! They've got me now, boys!" was blood-curdling. He fell from his position thirty feet to the bottom of the ravine. About [the] same instant, one of the soldiers, [Edward] Kennedy, a private of Company C, 5th Cavalry, was shot in the leg, the deadly missile carrying away the whole calf; and another, whose name I did not learn,[4] was shot through the ankle joint. The line of soldiers was, ere this, upon the crest of the ravine, which, through the interlacing branches of the trees within, seemed to be alive with Indians, but mostly women and children.

I don't know how it happened, but Captain Munson[5] and myself found ourselves in the ravine on one side, while, similarly, Big Bat and another guide, Carey, occupied the other. Alongside was a pile—the term is the only accurate one I know of—of squaws and little papooses covered with dirt and blood and screaming in a perfect agony of terror. The oaths and yells of the surging soldiers pressing in behind us made the scene truly infernal. Just in front, three or four dead bodies lay stretched, weltering in their own gore. As is usually the case, what would seem from the description to have been a most perilous position really enjoyed a greater exemption from danger than any other within rifle shot. The elbows of the narrow gulch prevented the Indians from molesting us, or even noticing us, at least as long as so many others were in places so much more conspicuous. So when, in response to Bat's encouraging call of "Washte-helo" ("all right," or "very good"), the women and children came up to us, it did not take much time to get them out, following down the bends of the ravine to a place of safety, and in communication with General Crook, who came over to them and spoke pleasantly. The squaws divined at once who he was, and clung to his hand and clothing, their little ones meantime clutching their skirts and yelling piteously. When somewhat calmed and reassured, the women said their village belonged to the Spotted Tail agency and was commanded by two chiefs, Roman Nose and American Horse, or Iron Shield, the latter still in the ravine. General Crook bade one of them go back and say he would treat kindly all who surrendered; the squaw complied and went back to the edge of the ravine. There, holding a parley, as the result bringing back a young warrior, named Charging Bear, afterwards a corporal in General Crook's company of Indian scouts, about twenty years old. To him, General Crook repeated the assurances already given the squaws, and this time the young man went back, accompanied by Big Bat, whose presence, unarmed, convinced American Horse that General Crook's promises were not written in sand. The interest felt about this moment was almost painful in its intensity; for the first time, almost, in the history of American Indian warfare, hostile savages were about to lay down their arms on the open field.

American Horse, supported on one side by Big Bat, on the other by one of his warriors, approached the little nucleus of officers clustered about General Crook.[6] The reception accorded the captives was gentle, and the wounded ones made the recipients of necessary attentions. Out of this little nook, twenty-eight Sioux, little and great, dead and alive, were taken. The corpses were suffered to lie where they fell, a lesson in significance not lost upon their comrades. A little girl, not over five years old, attracted my attention by her beauty and grace. I had her brought to headquarters, in spite of her vociferous screams, which quieted down very soon after she saw our dinner set out upon the piece of buffalo robe made to do service as a table.

In other ways, too, our mess had benefited by the capture. We had secured more than a score of tin cups and a great many articles of table furniture: knives, forks, spoons, plates, dishes, etc. Our cook, Phillips, had possessed himself of a considerable amount of dried buffalo meat, pony meat, buffalo tongue, and one or two parfleche panniers of fresh and dried buffalo berries, wild cherries, plums, and other fruit, a small trifle of salt, and a little flour. Our meal was marked by a comparative sumptuousness and a good humor, somewhat in contrast with the gloomy forebodings crowding upon our minds only a day or two ago.

In such an atmosphere, our little Indian child speedily recovered her composure and ate as heartily as the rest of us. Buffalo meat is not nearly so nutritious or palatable as beef, and I now speak advisedly, having tried them both, dried as well as fresh. Buffalo tongues, dried, are esteemed a delicacy; so is the ordinary dried flesh of the animal, pounded up with dried cherries, bull berries, or plums. This mixture is called "Toro." It is very pleasant eating, by far the most agreeable food of the aborigines I have tasted.

As we were discussing the events of the day, congratulating ourselves upon the good luck of capturing a village with so much food, criticizing the culinary arts of the Sioux, and condoling with the misfortune of Lt. von Leuttwitz, who had had his kneecap knocked off by a bullet and whose leg had been amputated early in the morning, Mr. Wasson produced a couple of certificates of good character given Indians of this village early last spring. One was to "Stabber," signed by [E. A.] Howard, the agent at Spotted Tail agency; the other to "Charging Crow," with the name appended of one [F. C.] Boucher, an infamous scoundrel since detected trading ammunition to the hostiles. Soldierlike, we had almost completely forgotten our recent discomforts in the light of actual excitement; the food we had captured was not the best in the world, but much superior to none at all, and then it was the "Spolia Opima" of a Sioux encampment, and as such relished most keenly.

To fully analyze and discuss the situation was not at this moment granted us, for the sharp cracking of rifles and carbines roused [us] to a new danger in the onslaught Crazy Horse, with a large band, was making upon our line of pickets. The Sioux, thinking that Mills was alone, and not believing General Crook was within striking distance, advanced very determinedly to avenge their disaster and disgrace of the morning.

In expectancy of this event, our horses and mules had been picketed very close to camp and at the first rattle of musketry were driven into camp, saddled, bridled, and kept under the cover of the ridge, in an open space in the creek bottom. The Sioux came very close to our skirmishers, who received them with a fierce roll of carbines and rifles. For a few moments, the enemy wavered. Their doubts were colored by the charge of our infantry battalions, which, commanded by Captains Burt and Burke,[7] lost no time in taking the ridge on our left and front, where the enemy made their strongest demonstration. From the summit of the little rounded knob where General Crook's headquarters were established, the view of the field was unobstructed and very inspiring. The skirmish itself was not of much consequence, but it is rarely [that] so free a view of a scene of action is obtainable. The Indians withdrew under cover of approaching darkness, taking with them their dead and wounded; our losses were very slight, five or six wounded, none seriously. Ten or a dozen broken-down cavalry horses, too weak and sore to get into camp before the skirmish began, were congregated in a small herd nearby, but driven within full sight of our men and of the Indians; the latter, imagining they were some we could not get inside our lines, made a gallant dash to effect their capture. They were allowed to approach so close that it was as easy for them to continue on towards the herd as it would be to retreat; then, when they were committed to the rash act, our skirmishers opened on them a very dangerous fire. The disgust and consternation of the Indians, when they arrived in the midst of our broken-down plugs, were very amusing to our soldiers, who hooted and yelled in derision, as they resumed with increased vigor the fusillade, [which] the more thoroughly scared Indians sought to avoid by scattering and scampering in every direction.

Lt. von Leuttwitz's leg was amputated above the knee this evening [*sic*]. Patient bore the operation extremely well, so the surgeons said.

Lt. A. B. Bache, 5th Cavalry,[8] suffering from a severe attack of rheumatism in the ankles and wrists, insisted upon being hoisted into a saddle and there remained until the termination of the skirmish. We tried to sleep at night, but failed very signally. The Indian ponies fretted and neighed until daylight, and the curs left behind in their lodges barked unintermittently in reply to the howling of wolves and coyotes outside.

Men were detailed under commissioned officers to gather up all the property taken from the Indians; the ponies, some of them very fine ones, were divided among the soldiers of Mills's battalion; the buffalo robes and other furs, after what officers and men needed had been separated, were consumed by fire, and the same fate was reserved for the accumulation of fruit and meat these people had laid by for the winter. Twenty-eight mules were packed with meat, and fully as great a quantity was destroyed in one way or another. Of berries, not so much use was made as should have been, in my opinion; they were exactly what our men needed, but the company commanders somehow didn't seem to realize their value. Instead of gathering them up and issuing them to the different battalions, they were suffered to be tramped underfoot, except where some of the soldiers felt inclined to help themselves. The destruction was complete; the smallest articles were burned or broken with as sedulous care as the largest. Ammunition and caps were exploded, guns broken, robes cut to pieces and then burned, and lodge poles hacked to pieces before being committed to the flames. This little village seemed to be greatly encumbered with baggage, probably was guarding supplies for a greater number than its own members. The lesson of neglect taught us at Crazy Horse had not been forgotten; this time our work was done thoroughly. As our forces numbered all told nearly two thousand men, and as the dried meat taken was abundant rations for all three days, some idea can be gathered of the quantity of stores these Indians had accumulated.

The Fellows in Feathers: An Interview with General Crook

JOHN F. FINERTY[1]

Chicago *Times,* November 4, 1876

RED CLOUD AGENCY, October 26

Pertinent to the movements of the late expedition against the Sioux and the one now being organized by General Crook, your correspondent had a conversation with him yesterday and noted many of the most salient points. Most of these are of general interest to the country at this time and will be found also very plain and outspoken.

The conversation began with the question: "What are your opinions concerning the recent campaign against the Sioux, and why was it not as successful as you had hoped it might be?"

General Crook—The obstacles to that complete success, which the country deemed possible, if not probable, of attainment, are so numerous that no one can be said to be much more prominent than another. In the first place, when the campaign opened, the army was not in charge of the agencies from which the hostiles have drawn supplies and recruits. It was impossible to get from the agencies correct information as to the number of warriors that had joined the hostiles. The Indians themselves asserted none had gone, and the agents and inspectors, without taking the trouble to verify these assertions by an accurate census of the Indians, joined in making the same untruthful statements and published them to the country. The result was what I expected it would be, namely, that when my command reached its field of operations, instead of finding one thousand or fifteen hundred warriors, it found itself confronted with five or six times that number of well-armed and thoroughly agency-equipped Indians.[2] Notwithstanding this disparity of forces, the troops under my command, about one thousand in actual strength, at the battle of the Rosebud thrashed these Indians on a field of their own choosing and completely routed them from it.[3] Scarcely a week elapsed before the same force of Indians I had beaten at the Rosebud met and defeated a column of troops nearly as large as mine in the engagement with

385

Colonel Custer on the Little Bighorn. The Indians constituting the larger part of those in the field against us were agency Indians, armed with guns and ammunition obtained at the agencies, wearing clothing and blankets procured from the same places, and many of them, as subsequent events proved, bearing letters from the agents themselves testifying as to their good character and friendly purposes.

In the second place, few people are aware of the arduous character of the work and the amount of endurance required to overtake and punish Indians in a country as large as that in which we were campaigning. When the Indians thought themselves able to whip us it was easy enough to find them. On the other hand, when my command had been reinforced by the addition of another thousand men, and I felt myself able to beat any force of Indians liable to be brought against it, the entire savage army fled rapidly from the Bighorn Mountains toward the Little Missouri, and their villages disintegrated and scattered in every direction.

Correspondent—It has been stated that you endeavored to get Indians from the Red Cloud agency last spring to go out with you against the hostiles and were prevented by the interference of Agent Hastings[4] and Inspector [William] Vandever.

General Crook—In May last, I came to Red Cloud for the purpose of obtaining the services of such friendly Indians as could be found, to cooperate with me in the approaching campaign. A considerable number were willing to go and so expressed themselves, but the agent and inspector, by means of bribes and threats, prevented them. My plan was to test the pretended friendship of these people whom the government was feeding, and by enlisting them against the hostiles, to draw the dividing line so distinctly that the agency could no longer be used as a base of supply for those on the warpath. If this could have been effected, and it was perfectly easy of accomplishment with the assistance of the agent, it would have very materially lessened the number of warriors to contend in the field. Indeed, it is not at all improbable that the disaster which befell Colonel Custer and his command would have been averted but for the interference of the agent and inspector in this matter. It would also have prevented the numerous murders of white people along the frontier during the summer and rendered the lines of travel to and from the Black Hills perfectly safe. In other words, instead of having hostiles in both front and rear, I wished to leave the latter safe beyond a doubt and secure safety for the people along the frontier, while perfectly willing to take my chances with those in front.

In this I was entirely defeated, and those Indians who were not with Sitting Bull of the north, fighting us, were murdering people and plundering the settlements behind. Even the splendid rifle presented to Sitting Bull of Red Cloud's band[5] by the Interior Department was used against our troops during the campaign. All this time, too, the agent and inspector were deliberately falsifying their reports concerning the friendly character of the Indians at Red Cloud and issuing to about eleven thousand when only about three thousand to four thousand were present during the summer.

Correspondent—Was the force you had in the field sufficient to carry on the campaign against the hostiles successfully?

General Crook—It would have been better if I could have taken a stronger force into the field in May, but the troops were scattered over a large extent of country, and time was required to concentrate any considerable portion. When additional troops were sent, other departments, where troops were also much needed, were almost stripped to give me what was considered a command strong enough for the work to be done. The army is too small at best, and when scattered as it is obliged to be, its efficiency for any sudden emergency is very greatly impaired. I believe it is wrong for a government as great and powerful as ours not to protect the frontier people from savages. I do not see why a man who has the courage to come out here and open the way for civilization in his own country is not equally as much entitled to the protection of his government as anybody else. The army should be strong enough, certainly, to protect our people throughout their whole domain. I am not one of those who believe, as many missionaries sent out here by well-meaning eastern societies do, that the people of the frontier are cutthroats, thieves, and murderers. I have been thrown among them for nearly twenty-five years of my life and believe them to compare favorably in energy, intelligence, and manhood with the best of their eastern brethren.

I do not make the mistake of supposing their side the popular one. On the contrary, I have always found it otherwise. Their representation in Congress is scarcely more than nominal; great and powerful states have little time to devote to, and less interest in, their welfare; they are mercilessly plundered by Indians without any attempt being made to punish the perpetrators, and when they ask for protection, they are told by some of our peace commissioners sent out to make further concessions to the Indians that they have no business out here anyhow. I do not deny that my sympathies have been with the frontier people in their unequal contest against such obstacles. At the same time, I do not wish to be understood as the unrelenting foe of the Indian. I am ready to admit that I am no friend to bad Indians, nor to a policy which encourages them in indolence, vagabondage, and plundering. I think they should be taught to earn their own living, be made amenable to law, and be encouraged to do something for their own support. It would not only be an important step in civilizing them, but would also relieve the country of the burden and expense of maintaining them. To support them as at present is folly and a positive injury. It would degrade and demoralize far more enlightened races to hold them perpetually as objects of charity.

Correspondent—Is there any truth in the report that there was a lack of cooperation between General Terry and yourself on account of jealousy as to command or other reason?

General Crook—None in the world. I found General Terry to be a high-minded, honorable gentleman, and I believe him to be a good soldier.

We never disagreed for a moment as to the main objects to be accomplished. I was following the trail of the Indian villages down the Rosebud, and he was approaching the trail from an opposite direction when the commands joined. They marched and cooperated together as long as cooperation was thought necessary, and then they separated. I was perfectly satisfied to serve under General Terry as long as the public interests could be benefited thereby. When it was considered expedient to divide the commands, they were divided. Each column was still strong enough to whip the Indians wherever found, and independent, could cover a greater extent of country and consequently increase the chances of punishing the enemy.

Correspondent—The movement of your command from the head of the Heart River to the Black Hills, with only two days' supply of provisions, instead of going to Fort Lincoln, a shorter distance, was made, it is stated, in opposition to the views of many of your officers.

General Crook—I am not aware that there was any opposition on the part of the officers in my command to that movement.[6] To have taken the troops to Fort Lincoln to rest and recuperate would have been a very unfortunate move, in my judgment. The trail of a large body of Indians led toward the Black Hills, and there was none leading toward Fort Lincoln. It was impossible to tell what depredations these Indians might be committing on the miners and settlers, and I considered it my duty to march in that direction, notwithstanding the shortness of supplies.

I do not enjoy hardship, horse meat, and starvation more than other men, but when it is necessary to submit to these things, with the prospect of rendering adequate service to the country before me, I am ready to stand my chances. Fort Lincoln is out of my own department and hundreds of miles from the points threatened by Indians. To have gone there would have been to abandon to the Indians the Black Hills settlements, the roads leading to them, and the frontier farther south. Whatever may have been the opinions of other officers as to this movement, I made up my mind to adopt it after a full consideration of all the circumstances, satisfied to leave the approval of my course to my superior officers. The command endured this trying march with great patience and fortitude, and evinced soldierly qualities of the highest order. It enabled us to destroy an important village and to seriously cripple the Indians, whom we found, as I expected, swarming around the entire Black Hills region. Moreover, when supplies were at length obtained, the troops were just where they were needed, and where they could strike in any direction required without having first to march two hundred miles to reach the haunts of the Indians.

Correspondent—It is stated by the correspondent of the New York *Herald* who accompanied the expedition[7] that while the troops were confined to one blanket per man, and living on horse meat, you had extra blankets from the hospital and were messing with the packers, living much better than the rest of the command.

General Crook—One's reputation would scarcely be worth the effort to preserve if it could be tarnished by the word of such men. I have not seen the article you refer to, and if I had, should have paid no attention to it. Every officer and man in the command knows the statement to be untrue. I did not take a meal with the packers during the entire trip, principally because I was not invited to do so. Not that I think there would be anything improper in it, but it so happened that I did not. The fare allotted to the soldiers was all that I had myself, or allowed my staff officers to have.[8] Extra blankets were carried for the use of sick and wounded men, and it may be that the medical officers sometimes used these for themselves when they were not required for the hospital. To this I certainly had no objection, but I never used one myself. Newspaper correspondents have always accompanied my expeditions, if they chose to do so, and I have always treated them courteously. With what they wrote I had nothing whatever to do, nor did I care, further than that, as to matters of fact, I preferred they should tell the truth, while as to matters of opinion, they could exercise every possible freedom. The correspondents who accompanied this expedition were, with the exception of the *Herald* man, so far as I know, fair and thoughtful in their statements of its operations, but the representative of the *Herald,* for what reason I am unable to say, persisted to the last in misrepresenting it, and stating as facts things that never occurred or were utterly distorted and untrue. It is hardly reasonable to suppose that the propriety of a paper of the character and influence of the *Herald* would knowingly countenance its representative in such a course.[9]

General Crook also gave his reasons for surrounding and disarming Red Cloud's band here.[10] It was impossible to tell what mischief these people were plotting. Their position was that of a menace. They were holding communication with the hostiles constantly, and evidently meant to go on the warpath. He resolved to take the bull by the horns in time, and while his prompt action has a salutary effect upon those that were pretendedly friendly, and prevents that number of warriors from taking part against the troops in the approaching campaign, it also leaves affairs here in such shape that the agency cannot possibly be used as a base for the hostiles. He made Spotted Tail head chief because he has shown more ability, friendship, and nerve in doing right than any other man in the nation, and that is the kind of a man he likes to deal with.[11] The whole complexion of affairs here is changed under the new rule. Spotted Tail and Little Wound[12] voluntarily come forward and proffer their warriors to go out with the general against the northern hostiles, and the policy of the government will no longer be thwarted by prevaricating agents and inspectors.

Terry's Tribulations

CHARLES S. DIEHL[1]

Chicago *Times,* August 9, 1876

FORT ABRAHAM LINCOLN, VIA BISMARCK, August 1

A little more than two years have passed since the lamented Custer, at the head of the 7th Cavalry, left this grim old fort on the Missouri to explore the hitherto unknown Black Hills region, to return after several months with reports of the wonderful mineral wealth of the country. To the result of this expedition is attributed by a great many army officers all the troubles which have accumulated in the meantime with the Sioux Indians, and is the real cause of our present war. To this sort of reasoning, the answer is given that the same gallant commander who opened the Sioux sore was the first to strike them in their northern stronghold, and his bones and those of his brave followers rest among the lonely hills of Montana as an evidence that he has paid the full penalty of his first error. Custer left Fort Lincoln on June 25, 1874. He met his death at the Little Bighorn, June 25, 1876. If there be reason in this, make the most of it.

Fort Lincoln was constructed in 1873, soon after the completion of the Northern Pacific Railroad to Bismarck, and is situated a few miles below that point, on the opposite shore of the Missouri. It resembles all of our frontier posts, which by some inscrutable custom in the service are called forts. There is nothing about them to indicate places of defense, and they are of such a temporary character that the term barracks would seem more appropriate when mention is made of them. No frowning piece of ordnance greets the vision to indicate that you are approaching army grounds, and were it not for the blue-coated sentinel covering a weary beat, and the sight of the American colors floating high in the air in the center of the enclosure, there would be little to signify that it was a government post. It is situated on a slight prominence overlooking the black waters of the Missouri, and is chiefly interesting from the fact that it has been the headquarters of the 7th Cavalry, which, under Custer, has always taken an active part in all the Indian campaigns since the close of the Rebellion. It was with him during the Washita campaign in 1868, and figured prominently in a number of raids under their daring leader between that date and the opening of the existing war.

Custer took with the Black Hills expedition the same command that met disaster among the northern Sioux. No changes have taken place among the line officers since that time, with two minor exceptions, and in the meantime the young Lieutenant Sturgis, who was killed, and another West Point graduate have been attached to the regiment. Since that awful encounter, however, the army register has been scored, and at the present time, by the process of promotion among the line officers, the regiment now has but two second lieutenants out of twelve, and a young graduate of 1875, who just joined the command a month since, has through means of that awful slaughter attained a first lieutenancy, which through the ordinary routine would have taken years.

In wandering about the officers' quarters, many evidences are seen which bring to mind the dead commander. Relics are shown, reminders of his campaigning on the plains. Since the slaughter of the main body of the 7th Cavalry, a number of the wives of the dead officers have remained at the post, and recently a number of the wounded of Reno's command were brought here. There is everything therefore to remind one of that chapter of the war.

Mrs. Custer, in company with Mrs. Calhoun, a sister of Colonel Custer, and Mrs. Yates, all of whom lost their husbands in the fight, have remained here during the past month and only left for the home of the dead general at Monroe, Michigan, on yesterday. They will first go to St. Paul and remain a few days. Mrs. Custer has exhibited the deepest grief since the death of her husband, and it is feared that the shock will seriously affect her health. Her nervous system has received a very severe strain, and since her residence at the post, she has maintained a strict seclusion, permitting but a few of her nearest friends to see her.

Your correspondent leaves tonight on board the steamer *Far West* to join General Terry's command on the Yellowstone. The boat has on board a large number of supplies for Terry and a quantity of material for the new post to be located at the confluence of the Yellowstone and Little Bighorn Rivers, the location of Terry's supply camp at the present time. The boat will be under military surveillance during the trip, to guard against any attack that may be made. The senior officer on board will be in charge, and the usual army forms will be observed in camp. The guard from Fort Buford will be nearly two hundred strong, which would seem to be an unusual force, but when it is considered that the command is badly in need of stores, and the grave possibility that the boat will be attacked by some insurgent band, it will not be at all too large. It has seemed strange to a great many officers connected with the department that the Indians have not made an effort before this to impede the progress of the boats and delay the movement of the supplies, and it is only accounted for on the ground that they have not yet discovered the means employed. Some of the boats have been fired into before this, and the rumor reached Fort Lincoln as early as last week that one of the steamers had been burned on the Yellowstone. From the advices received by the owners of the boats, there can be no doubt that they are false. It would be no difficult matter, however, for the savages to make a deadly attack on the boats at some points on the Yellowstone, where the stream is barely wide enough to allow the passage of the steamer, and the high, overhanging bluffs would permit them to exercise any amount of deviltry without fear of retaliation on the part of the troops.

The steamer will probably reach Fort Buford, at the mouth of the Yellowstone, on the fourth, which will be about six days' journey to Terry's camp. The trip up the Yellowstone will be slow and hazardous, owing to the character of the stream. The boat will run during the day only, as it has been found unsafe to attempt to navigate the river after night. On board the vessel is Col. W. B. Hazen,[2] commanding the 6th Infantry, stationed at Fort Buford, who is just returning from Washington, having been called to testify in the Belknap impeachment trial.[3] Captain Weston of General Terry's staff is also on board to join the main column. A number of junior officers are also on board, having received marching orders while on leave of absence. Some have been on the frontier before, and with the comforting assurance that nearly all the available force of the entire army is either going to the front or is being sent to the agencies, there are none who have any decided inclination to return.

In consequence of the order transferring the management of the agency Indians to the War Department, the entire force at all the interior posts that is available is being withdrawn, and is going forward to assist in enforcing the order taking away the arms and ponies of the savages. Several companies of the 20th Infantry passed through here today for Standing Rock agency, where are located between four thousand and five thousand Indians. A force of six hundred infantry is being centered there, and from conversation with the officers, they appear to think that considerable work has been laid out for them in carrying out the orders, and that some trouble may be expected.

Nothing has been received from Terry's command during the past week, but it is probable that I will be enabled to communicate something concerning the movements of the command at Fort Buford. It is reported that he will move south on the arrival of the 22nd Infantry, which will be on the fifth, leaving Colonel Miles with the 5th Infantry to remain in charge of his supply camp. It is understood that facilities will be afforded to allow all officers arriving to follow him, so that I hope to reach the main column by the tenth or twelfth.

Chicago *Times,* August 16, 1876

FORT BUFORD, DAKOTA, MOUTH OF YELLOWSTONE,
August 5

The last reinforcements have gone forward to join General Terry, and so far as it is possible, his command has been strengthened to the utmost. There is now no reason why the campaign should not be prosecuted in earnest, and it is presumed that during the two months that yet remain of the fighting season, an effort will be made to retrieve some of the failures of this inglorious campaign. Four months have now elapsed since the two commands took the field, and thus far no engagement has occurred in which an advantage has been won by our troops. Instead, we have the awful disaster which overtook Colonel Custer's command to ponder over, and judging from the inactivity which has been manifested during the past six weeks, are forced to consider the possibility that the summer may wear away before anything is accomplished by the army.

Since the disaster at the Little Bighorn, which resulted in the overwhelming defeat of the 7th Cavalry, General Terry has been slowly moving east. He first entered into a camp at the confluence of the Bighorn and Yellowstone, 130 miles from the scene of Custer's engagement, and it was presumed that this would be made the base of supplies during the remainder of the campaign. The Indians having become troublesome on the river, and in order to be in closer communication with the supply steamers, he removed his camp eighty miles further east, and his command is now in camp at the mouth of the Rosebud, which it is presumed will continue to be his base of operations during the remainder of the summer. During the absence of the main column, a detachment of three companies of the 17th Infantry will remain to garrison the camp, who will throw up defenses to guard against any attack that may be made by the savages. A battery of light artillery will also be left behind to ensure the security of the camp. But little is definitely known concerning the proposed movements of the command, beyond the fact that General Terry will follow the course of the Rosebud south until a junction is formed with Crook. The plan of the campaign thereafter will depend upon the movements of the savages in the meantime. General Terry will probably make his first dash in light march order, and will take supplies for several weeks' campaigning only. It is believed that it will be impossible to take a heavy wagon train into the mountains.

The defeat of Custer has done much toward demoralizing Terry's command. The officers and men recognize that the entire summer has dwindled away without accomplishing anything, and the war fever has in a measure died out. Men have been compelled to endure all the discomforts of camp life in a desolate region, surrounded by hostiles, and dependent upon such supplies as are brought by slow steamers a distance of one thousand miles. They appreciate that at the best, there is no glory in the war, and shorn of this last impulse, there is no surprise in knowing that the morale of this command has been to a certain degree broken. Aside from the discouragements of the campaign and the repeated defeats of the troops, the enforced monotony of the camp life has tended to destroy any esprit de corps that might have existed. The army has had to subsist upon marching rations, and the constant use of salt meats has occasioned considerable sickness in camp. Scurvy has broken out among the men, and the disease has been spreading to such an extent as to alarm some of the officers. Several men have already died, and a number have been sent to the hospital unfit for duty. To put it mildly, the long confinement in camp and enforced inactivity has destroyed the spirit which actuated the command at the opening of the campaign. In spite of all these discouragements, however, it is believed that the army is in a good humor to win a victory if they are given the opportunity. It is hoped, for the good name of the army and to aver the possible failure of the entire campaign, that it will be afforded them.

In the event of Terry's failure to strike the Indians before fall, the prospect of a winter campaign has been considered, but it is the opinion of old army officers that such a course will be impossible in this northern latitude. Winter sets in early, and there is no forage for the cavalry horses except such as can be brought by steamers and wagon trains. To house the cavalry would also necessitate the construction of the proposed new army posts, which have been practically abandoned for this year. At the best, winter quarters can be provided for several regiments of infantry, taking up the campaign early in the spring. Otherwise the force now in the field under General Terry will be withdrawn, and the campaign will go down as an utter failure.

The grass, which has been depended upon for the cavalry horses, has given out, and they are now fed upon forage supplied to the command. Thus failure of the campaign, in addition to the failure of the cavalry to do any effective work in the field, has urged army officers to consider whether the infantry should not be depended upon almost entirely in the prosecution of the campaign. They have shown their superiority in several instances as effective fighters, owing to the character of the firearms used and the fact that they are almost entirely unencumbered. They are prepared for a fight on the shortest notice and are not liable to be stampeded by a sudden surprise. With the use of their trowel bayonets, breastworks can be thrown up within a very short time, compelling the Indians to take the offensive to make a successful attack. The heavy fighting is bound to be done in the mountains, making cavalry charges impossible. It is asserted that if Custer had not been encumbered by his horses, he would have made a successful defense against the Indians several days until the arrival of reinforcements, as Reno's command succeeded in doing.

Another of the marked failures of the campaign is the abandonment of the construction of the two new army posts on the Yellowstone sanctioned by Congress. Elaborate preparations have been made for their building, for a month past, a large force of mechanics employed, seven hundred carloads of lumber purchased and shipped to Bismarck for transportation up the river, and a quantity sent up the river as far as this point. It has been asserted that if an appropriation had been made for the construction of these posts a year since, the present Indian troubles should have been averted. This was not made public, however, until after the Custer disaster. Soon after the appropriation was made, one of General Sheridan's staff officers, Lt. Col. James W. Forsyth, proceeded up the Yellowstone to select sites for the posts, and after consultation with General Terry, it was determined to locate one at the mouth of the Bighorn, and the other at the confluence of the Tongue and Yellowstone. The partial close of navigation has caused a suspension of operations, and owing to a recommendation which will be made by Colonel Forsyth, it is presumed that the buildings will be delayed until next year. To abandon these posts entirely will of course necessitate the withdrawal of all the troops early in September, leaving the country in possession of the Sioux.

The Indians have recently become very bold and have appeared in large bodies in close proximity to Terry's camp. Their scouts have evidently watched the river closely and have reported the arrival of reinforcements by the steamers. In several instances they have fired on the boats, but thus far they have made no attempts to capture them, which is only accounted for on the ground that it is contrary to their mode of warfare. In anticipation of an attack, however, the boats have been strongly guarded of late, and from two to three companies of infantry have been placed on board each steamer passing up and down the river, for its protection. Several sharp engagements have already taken place between the troops on board and the Indians during the past week, with but slight results. They have tended to show, however, that in the reinforcements recently sent General Terry are numbered several regimental commanders with good fighting records, who will not lose an opportunity for a dash at the savages. An incident is related of Col. Nelson A. Miles, commanding the 5th Infantry. When passing up the river, it was reported that a large band of warriors had been seen crossing the Missouri River near Fort Buford, heading north. Anticipating that they might possibly be a party of Sioux bound for the British possessions, Colonel Miles had the rare good luck of overtaking them, and found them numbering between three hundred and four hundred. He did not hesitate to land his small command and immediately surrounded them. Of course, they were good Indians, but also possibly the worst frightened crowd ever seen on the American continent. They proved to be a hunting party of Mandans, Gros Ventures, and Rees, and after showing their papers were allowed to proceed. This same commander, who has the reputation of having marched several cavalry regiments off their feet in the southern Indian country, did not lose an opportunity of improving the drill of his battalion while en route. It is stated that when within forty miles of the camp on the Rosebud, he succeeded in impressing a detachment of the 17th Infantry bound down the Yellowstone onboard the steamer *Far West,* with the idea that a heavy engagement was in progress. Heavy and continuous firing was to be heard a distance up the river, and the troops on the *Far West* prepared for a fight. They discovered, on reaching a bend in the river, Miles's entire command deployed as skirmishers and firing like mad. His steamer had stopped for some wood, and he was not losing the opportunity. Some of his officers complain that he is altogether too energetic, but if you hear of a fight, look out for Miles.

Lt. Col. Elwell S. Otis, commanding the 22nd Infantry,[4] also evidently came into this region to have a fight, and sighting a war party near the mouth of Powder River, he landed his small command and, after throwing out a skirmish line, prepared to engage the savages. The Indians were evidently surprised and, after firing a few shots, retired into the mountains. The soldiers succeeded in killing several ponies, but no casualties were reported among the Indians. Several soldiers of the 22nd were slightly wounded.[5] At this point on the river, a large quantity of forage had been left behind by General Terry, and the Indians had been engaged in destroying it.

When the engagement was reported, the steamer *Far West* was sent to secure the property, and several companies of the 17th Infantry accompanied the boat. The Indians were seen hovering in

Buying cavalry horses for the Indian War. HARPER'S WEEKLY, 1876

the region, and preparations were made to attack them. The Sioux again retired to the neighboring bluffs, and the command was so small that no attempt was made to follow them. Some of the scouts attached to the command, however, went beyond the skirmish line and exchanged a few shots, killing one Indian, who was left on the field. A scout named [Wesley] Brockmeyer, known as "Yank," was mortally wounded and died soon after being taken on board the boat. The soldiers scalped the dead Indian. Beyond these skirmishes, no engagements with the savages have been reported.

 The navigation of the Yellowstone has suddenly closed, so far as boats of ordinary draught are concerned, and in the transportation of supplies hereafter, General Terry will be compelled to depend upon the two small steamers, *Josephine* and *Far West*. Supplies will be brought as far as this point and shipped. The sudden fall in the Yellowstone is contrary to all reports which have been made by military expeditions during the past three years, which have represented that a good stage of water could be depended upon for a distance of four hundred miles during six months of the year. The water commenced falling a week since and is navigable now for boats not drawing more than eighteen inches. There have been no heavy rains in the Yellowstone for months past, which will account for the sudden fall, but those acquainted with the stream state that the water usually gives out at this season of the year. As an evidence of the treacherous character of the river, a boat of the ordinary draught went up the river during a high stage of water last year and became stranded, and was compelled to remain three months. Owing to this, the steamboat companies will not operate up the river, except under government charter, and as they receive $350 a day while on the river, the government will pay handsomely for its transportation before this war is ended.

General Terry's command will move down the Rosebud on August 7 or 8, and will make a stand after traveling south about seventy miles, and will send out scouting parties in order to discover the trails of any large parties of Sioux, and from that point will move south and west into the Bighorn Mountains, where, by common consent, the fighting will take place if the Indians will make a stand. If they do not, as seems to be probable, the time will be employed scouting among the mountains, until the cold weather compels the withdrawal of the troops, when they will undoubtedly be sent east to the agencies to remain during the winter. No provision has been made by Terry for winter quarters in the northern region, which indicates the withdrawal of these troops after another month's campaign.

Chicago *Times,* August 19, 1876

> FORT BUFORD, MOUTH OF YELLOWSTONE, August 15, via BISMARCK, Dakota, August 18

The steamer *Far West,* having on board eighty recruits for the 7th Cavalry and 22nd Infantry and a quantity of government stores, arrived here yesterday from Bismarck. While thirty miles below this point, the steamer was fired into by a party of Sioux, who were evidently traveling north. Between thirty and forty shots were fired into the boat, but none of those on board were injured, and no attempt was made to follow them, as the recruits were unprovided with arms. This carries out the theory that the northern hostiles are breaking into small parties and gradually traveling north, and there is no indication that they will make a stand against the troops. The wild rumors of an engagement with the Indians by Terry's command up to the present date are groundless. Two scouts arrived at Fort Buford today with news from Terry's command two days after his departure from the mouth of the Rosebud, who report that a junction has been formed with Crook, but that no indication had been seen of any large parties of Indians. The steamer *Josephine,* with four companies of the 5th Infantry, goes up the Yellowstone tomorrow and will endeavor to get to the supply camp at the mouth of the Rosebud.

Chicago *Times,* August 26, 1876

YELLOWSTONE EXPEDITION,
ON BOARD STEAMER *JOSEPHINE,*
NEAR MOUTH OF YELLOWSTONE, August 20,
via BISMARCK, Dakota, August 25

The junction formed by Terry and Crook on August 10 has caused a marked change in the character of the campaign. Everything which could retard the progress of the column has been left behind, and by a rapid movement, it is hoped to overtake and force a fight with the Sioux. The heavy wagon train which accompanied Terry's command was sent back to the supply camp at the mouth of the Rosebud under escort of the 5th Infantry, Colonel Miles commanding, and after two days' delay the combined forces, with fifteen days' rations and a large pack train, left the temporary camp on the Rosebud, thirty miles south of its mouth, moving west into the Bighorn Mountains. No Indian signs were seen till the morning of the fourteenth, when a large trail was found leading north. The trail was five or six days old and is described as being one of the heaviest ever seen on the prairies, being over two miles in width.[6] It showed that the Indians had been fully advised of the movements of the troops and had moved at the same time that Terry had left his camp on the Yellowstone. After following the trail for a day, it was found that the band had broken up, one large party moving toward the Badlands of the Missouri, and the other north toward the Yellowstone. The Indians were in full retreat. It is presumed that they do not intend to make another stand against the soldiers. The northern band were headed in the direction of the British possessions and it is believed will cross the line. The other band will move south along the Little Missouri and cross the Missouri River at a point above Fort Berthold. In any event, they will lead the soldiery a sorry chase.

There is every indication that the hostile band has been heavily reinforced by Indians from the agencies, who, from fear of having their ponies and arms confiscated, have determined to link their fortunes with those of the outlawed tribes. They are accompanied by their wives and children and evidently intend remaining in the northern region during the winter. The task laid out for the army is not an easy one. Their supplies are limited, and though they may make rapid marches, little less than a miracle will enable them to overtake the savages at this stage in the game. The savages are well mounted, and the infantry, upon which everything depends, cannot accomplish at the best over twenty miles a day. When the supplies are exhausted, a return to the main camp on the river will be necessitated, and any extended campaigning will be impossible thereafter, owing to the near approach of cold weather.

Colonel Miles returned to the camp at the mouth of the Rosebud on August 12, with instructions to patrol the river north of Fort Buford and intercept any bands that might attempt to cross the Yellowstone moving north. He was also instructed to commence the construction of winter quarters at the mouth of Tongue River for the accommodation of one regiment of infantry. In carrying out this plan, the steamers *Far West, Josephine, Carroll,* and *Yellowstone* have been placed at his disposal, and supplies for the command are being rapidly shifted up the river from Fort Buford. The steamers *Carroll* and *Far West* will be employed in patrolling the stream. Colonel Miles's command has been reinforced by two companies of the 17th Infantry and about one hundred fifty recruits for the 7th Cavalry and 22nd Infantry, giving him about seven hundred men. Terry's supply camp has been moved to the mouth of the Tongue River, which will be the base of supplies during the remainder of the campaign. In anticipation of an attack, the steamers are well guarded, and strong defenses have been thrown up about the supply camp. The garrison is already supplied with three Gatling and several Rodman guns, and the steamer *Josephine,* on her way up the Yellowstone, in addition to two companies of the 5th Infantry under command of Lt. Col. J. N. A. Whistler,[7] has on board three additional Gatling pieces to be used at the garrison.

Marauding bands still continue along the south bank of the Yellowstone, and some sharp work from this portion of the command may be expected before the war is ended. The main column was moving on the northern trail on the fifteenth and, unless an engagement occurs, will return to the camp on Tongue River about the last of this month. It is believed that a rapid movement on the part of Terry's command immediately after leaving his camp on the Rosebud would have brought on a fight with the Indians, but the delay has allowed the savages to show a clean pair of heels, and unless we have some very sharp work, the fighting is probably over for this season.

YELLOWSTONE EXPEDITION,
NEAR MOUTH OF POWDER RIVER, August 22,
via BISMARCK, Dakota, August 25

The practical failure of the campaign thus far had caused another general change in the plan of operations, and there is now indication that this war will be prosecuted until the Indians are subdued or compelled to return to their reservations. It was the announced intention of General Terry to withdraw all the troops from the northern country after September 15, which would have marked the entire campaign worse than a failure. The blunders which have led to the death of so many brave men would have been placed somewhere, and to have abandoned the northern country to the hostile tribes would have been little less than acknowledging the supremacy of the Sioux. It is almost assured that the scout which is now making by the combined forces under Terry and Crook will prove unsuccessful, and the troops will probably return to the mouth of Tongue River on August 25. The command will then refit for another dash, which, it is hoped, will prove more successful. The winter quarters now in process of construction by Colonel Miles's command will be made to accommodate one thousand men, and if a successful engagement does not occur with the savages before September 15, this number of men will probably be left on the Yellowstone for the winter. It is learned that the 5th Infantry under Colonel Miles and the 5th Cavalry under Col. Wesley Merritt, two of the finest regiments in the service, will both remain in winter quarters, and if necessary an additional number from both arms of the service will remain during the winter months. By this means the campaign can be extended late in the season, and if necessary taken up early next spring. This will allow the Sioux no time to renew for the war and will bring about their subjection. Some trouble was expected to be found in transporting forage and supplies for the command, but all the steamers that can navigate on the river are being pressed in the service, and it is thought that sufficient supplies for the command can be sent forward before winter sets in. This is the first indication that an active and relentless campaign would be made against the Indians and has given new life to the command, as the repetition of this year's work next season was to be dreaded, when the outlawed tribes would be reinforced by thousands from the agencies. The fall campaign will be full of hardships for the troops, but it can better be borne than another season's murderous work, such as has characterized the campaign thus far. There are evidences of Indians along the Yellowstone, but thus far the troops have not engaged them. Colonel Miles has, however, stationed the steamer *Far West* between the mouth of the Rosebud and Tongue Rivers, and the steamer *Carroll* between Wolf Rapids and Fort Buford, and with the aid of his scouts is kept well advised of the movements of the savages, and a fight with them is not an improbability. Strong defenses are being thrown up at the mouth of Tongue River, and the quarters for the troops will be ready for occupation by September 20.

YELLOWSTONE EXPEDITION,
NEAR MOUTH OF POWDER RIVER, August 23,
via BISMARCK, Dakota, August 25

The combined forces under Terry and Crook, after following the trail discovered on the twelfth, moved down the Rosebud for a distance of thirty-eight miles. The northern trail was abandoned on the fourteenth, and the command took up the southern trail, crossed the

Tongue to Goose Creek, and from Goose Creek returned to the Powder River and followed it down to the mouth, reaching there on the night of August 18, where they went into camp, waiting for supplies, and will remain until the morning of the twenty-fourth. The wagon train and all the supplies at the mouth of Tongue River are being shipped to the mouth of Powder River, and it is expected that the wagon train will reach there tomorrow morning.

The Indian trail diverged from the east bank of Powder River, about twenty miles from its mouth, south again toward the Little Missouri, and on taking up its march, the command will follow them into that region. The entire command is short of supplies, and unless he receives other instructions, Terry will march such of his command as are not left to winter on the Yellowstone over the country to Fort Abraham Lincoln. General Crook's command will scout toward the Black Hills and via Fetterman home. The arrival of the steamer up the river with supplies may change the plan of the campaign again, but it is not thought possible. It is the opinion of both Terry and Crook that it is too late for extended field operations. It is thought that the Indians of the southern trail are moving down to the agencies, and it is General Terry's intention in moving south to intercept them if possible. Unless the instructions of the lieutenant general [Philip H. Sheridan] directing a further prosecution of the campaign, as indicated in my telegram of the twenty-second, are respected, the campaign is practically closed.

Chicago *Times,* September 5, 1876

YELLOWSTONE EXPEDITION,
ON BOARD THE STEAMER *JOSEPHINE,*
MOUTH OF POWDER RIVER, August 25,
via BISMARCK, Dakota, September 4

The steamers *Josephine* and *Carroll,* loaded with supplies for the command in the field, left Fort Buford on the twentieth, reaching this point at noon today. The *Josephine* had on board a detachment of the 5th Infantry under the command of Colonel Whistler, and the *Carroll* one company of the 6th Infantry as a guard. The steamers were not molested till within one hundred fifty miles of the mouth of Powder River, but beyond this point the savages kept up an irregular fire on the boats.

On the forenoon of the twenty-third, when nearly one hundred miles below Glendive [Creek], the Indians fired into the steamers, and one soldier named Dennis Shields, Company G, 5th Infantry, was instantly killed. The firing was kept up for several minutes without cessation, when it suddenly subsided, and soon after, the Indians appeared on the bluffs and rode rapidly away.[8] The soldiers sent back an answering volley and killed one Indian. During the remainder of the voyage, the troops remained behind barricades, but beyond a few stray shots, the boats were unmolested. The force on board the steamers was considered too small to follow the savages. On the morning of the twenty-third, the steamers passed a small redoubt near the mouth of Glendive Creek, which had been thrown up by a company of the 5th Infantry under the command of Lt. Edmund Rice.[9] This commander reported that the Indians had been very troublesome, appearing in large bodies in the adjoining woods, and on the bluffs, and had made several attempts to steal the stock. His command is provided with a three-inch Rodman, with which he could shell the woods, which alone prevented the savages from making an attack. The steamer *Josephine* picked up a white man named Charles Pickens below Glendive Creek at noon on the twenty-fourth, who, with a companion, had deserted from Terry's command a few days previous. When two days out, they had been overtaken by Indians, and his companion, named Henry Piquet, of the 6th Infantry, had been killed. He had received an ugly wound in the arm, but by hiding in the bushes had escaped the savages, but was almost dead when found. The Indians had horribly mutilated the body of Piquet and had left it exposed on the riverbank. There is every indication that large bands of Indians are in the country east of the Powder and south of the Yellowstone Rivers, having been attracted by the game which abounds in the region.

Chicago *Times,* September 7, 1876

TERRY'S COLUMN IN THE FIELD,
CAMP ON DEER CREEK, MONTANA,
August 30, via BISMARCK, Dakota, September 6

This command left the Yellowstone River, near the mouth of O'Fallon's Creek, on August 27, moving due north. After proceeding ten miles, the command went into camp for the night and took up the march at 4:00 A.M. the next morning. The country is dry and parched, and long marches have been impossible, owing to the uncertainty of finding water. The beds of a number of streams have been crossed which have long since become dry, and the command has been compelled to depend upon such pools as could be found in the beds of some of the largest streams.

After the first day's march, we entered the buffalo range, north of the Yellowstone, and hunting parties were detached, which have brought in sufficient game to provide the command with fresh meat for some days to come. Yesterday afternoon the command went into camp on the north fork of Rush Creek, about fifty miles north of the Yellowstone, which borders on the divide between the Yellowstone and Missouri Rivers. Capt. Edward Ball,[10] in command of a detachment of the 2nd Cavalry, composed of four companies, left the main column with instructions to move north along the divide in search of any Indian trails leading in the direction of the Big Dry Creek, or Musselshell River. The battalion made a night ride of it, proceeding thirty miles. The main column, in the meantime, moved east and is now in camp on Deer Creek, a tributary of the Yellowstone. Captain Ball returned tonight, reporting that no heavy trails have been discovered, showing that thus far no large body of Indians has crossed the river to move toward the region of Fort Benton. A few small trails were discovered some days out, and the carcasses of a few dead buffaloes were found, showing that a small hunting party had been in the region. Our present camp is within twelve miles of the mouth of Glendive Creek, where a junction, if any, was to be formed with Crook. A courier starts tonight with dispatches to Crook, upon the result of which will depend the general movement of the troops from this time forward. General Terry is convinced that the Indians have not crossed the river in any force west of us, and if they have gone north at all, have moved in the direction of Fort Peck. Tomorrow he will accordingly send out several cavalry detachments to make a further reconnaissance to the east of us, in order to endeavor to discover their trail. The direction of the infantry column is not known tonight, but it is announced that we are to move to the eastward in order to support the cavalry, provided they should make any important discoveries. Our ultimate destination is known to be Fort Peck, on the Missouri, provided Crook has found that the Indians are not south of the Yellowstone and supplies for the entire command have been sent to this point. General Terry's command will at least assist in discovering the Indians who have returned to this agency this fall. It is positively known that a considerable number of the Yanktonais, a branch of the Sioux, which have been located at this agency for several years past, have formed a part of the hostile band under Sitting Bull this year.[11] "Buffalo Bill," the scout, returned tonight from the redoubt near the mouth of Glendive Creek, occupied by a company of the 5th Infantry under Lieutenant Rice, after a continuous ride of one hundred miles, and reports that the Indians have not been seen during the past three days and undoubtedly left at the same time that the command crossed the river. There is everything to indicate that they have been kept fully advised of the movements of the troops. The command will undoubtedly remain in the field until about October 1, and will scout the region north of the Yellowstone and east of our camp before the troops are finally withdrawn. If no heavy bands are found south of the river, the 5th Cavalry, which has been ordered to remain at the mouth of Tongue River this winter, will be attached to this command, and General Crook will proceed south to his old camp on Goose Creek. There appears to be no possibility of a further junction of the two forces for work in the field.

Chicago *Times,* September 12, 1876

TERRY'S CAMP ON THE YELLOWSTONE, MOUTH OF GLENDIVE CREEK, Montana, September 2, via BISMARCK, September 11

Having completed a four days' scout in the country north of the Yellowstone, this command has returned again to the river and is now in camp at the mouth of Glendive Creek, having discovered no trace of the Indians. The whereabouts of any hostile band is a greater mystery today than at any previous time during the year, and in their endeavors to elude pursuit, they are exhibiting the marked superiority over our troops that has been shown throughout the campaign. The problematic position of the Indians, as General Terry puts it, makes it very uncertain that we are to engage them again this year.

On the morning of August 31, Major Reno of the 7th Cavalry left the camp on Deer Creek to make a reconnaissance to the east to ascertain whether the Indians had crossed the river at any point below here. He sent a courier back this morning with the report that he had scouted the entire region within forty miles of Fort Buford, but had failed to discover signs of any large bands. He reports, however, that almost the entire country has been burned by the Indians. He has been instructed to rejoin the main column. General Terry is now convinced that the Indians have not crossed the river at any point below the Rosebud, and is forced to believe that they are either encamped on the Little Missouri or have again sought refuge in the mountains.

Colonel Miles leaves here tomorrow morning with his entire command for the mouth of Tongue River, where he will commence the immediate construction of winter quarters for the troops to be stationed there. He will move overland with a wagon train. This reduces the command under General Terry at the present time to less than one thousand men. We have had no word from General Crook since August 17, and nothing is known of his whereabouts by any portion of this command. It was understood he would return to the mouth of the Glendive or report by September 2, and his failure to do so has confused General Terry all the more concerning his future intentions.

Concerning our future movements, nothing is known. It is announced that we are to make a detour south toward the Little Missouri, but this will depend entirely upon the reports made by General Crook. The impression prevails here that the opportunity to gain any advantage over the Indians has been lost for this year. We needed a general commander when all the troops were in the field who, with the force at his command, could have secured the entire northern country. Instead, the columns under Terry and Crook operated independently while they remained together, and the grand movement by the combined forces culminated after an eight-day scout, after which the forces were to be withdrawn from the country and were only withheld from doing so by the opportune arrival of an order from the lieutenant general. Upon receipt of this, and the arrival of additional supplies, General Terry determined upon a further prosecution of the campaign. The report made by General Crook will now probably influence Terry as to the time he will withdraw his troops from the field.

TERRY'S COLUMN IN THE FIELD,
CAMP ON YELLOWSTONE,
MOUTH OF GLENDIVE CREEK, Montana, September 5,
via BISMARCK, Dakota, September 11

The campaign has suddenly closed. Tomorrow will witness the disbanding of all the troops under General Terry, and all further operations in the field are of course abandoned. The recent advices from General Crook indicate that the Indians are scattering or are moving west into the mountains, and under the circumstances, General Terry feels compelled to devote his entire attention to supplying the new post on the Yellowstone for the winter, and to do this he finds himself unable to keep a consuming army in the field. The instructions of General Sheridan are that a force of 1,500 is to be quartered at the mouth of Tongue River during the winter, which will require the transportation of three thousand tons of supplies overland from Fort Buford, as the water in the river has become so low that steamers cannot ascend above this point at the present time, and no attempt will be made from this time forward to keep boats in the river. Under the circumstances, General Terry will make no further attempt to follow the Indians and has ordered a disbandment of his forces. The Montana column under Brig. Gen. John Gibbon, including the four companies of the 3rd Cavalry and the six companies of the 7th Infantry, will move overland toward Fort Ellis tomorrow morning. The 22nd Infantry, under Colonel Otis, will construct a stockade at this point and aid in forwarding supplies to the new post. The battalion of the 6th Infantry under Major Reno will be kept on the river between this point and Fort Buford for several weeks for patrol duty. The personal staff of General

Terry will return to St. Paul without delay, but the general himself will remain and personally superintend the forwarding of supplies.

A courier arrived from General Crook yesterday morning with dispatches of the second, when he was in camp near the head of Beaver Creek, a tributary of the Little Missouri. He reports that he was delayed two days scouting the trail, it being very dim, but had at last found it going down the stream, apparently about the same size as when it left the Powder, which he thinks indicates that no number of those have crossed the Yellowstone. Two small bands had already chipped off and led in the direction of Red Cloud. He then states, "I will push on the main trail, and should they separate will endeavor to follow the largest, and in case of there being no larger one I shall go toward the southern agencies. Should I get near Fort Buford when my rations are exhausted, I will replenish them." His command had encountered one severe storm since the force separated, which, with the cold nights, had developed considerable sickness and some cases that ought to be sent in.

A late dispatch, dated at his camp on Beaver Creek opposite Sentinel Buttes, states that his march on the second showed that the Indian trail has been scattering for seven or eight miles, the larger portion going in the direction of the Little Missouri, while about one hundred fifty lodges still continued down the Beaver. About seven miles below his camp, about fifty pony tracks were found, the Indians having crossed there two days since, going in the direction of the Sentinel Buttes. He states, "It is my intention to follow this fresh trail in the morning. It is impossible to tell whether this separation is to be final or whether they intend coming together again. I shall do my best to solve the question in the next few days, letting the ration question take care of itself."

General Terry sent a courier last evening to communicate with General Crook, advising him of the disbanding of his command and the fact that there are no supplies at Fort Buford for his command, but that he should return to this point to be provisioned. Under the circumstances, it is thought that he will probably head directly for the old camp of Goose Creek by way of the Black Hills.

A tremendous wagon train is being pressed into service to be used in forwarding supplies up the river, and it is hoped that by great exertion, a sufficient amount can be placed at the mouth of Tongue River by December 1, beyond which date it will be almost impossible to move wagons. Already cold weather is setting in, and snow will be following before the end of the month. Thus our campaign closes. Whatever is accomplished will, of course, now remain with General Crook. General Terry expressed a great regret that he could not make a scout along the Little Missouri.

Chicago *Times,* September 16, 1876

TERRY'S COLUMN, IN THE FIELD,
CAMP ON YELLOWSTONE,
MOUTH OF GLENDIVE CREEK, Montana,
September 6

The news spread rapidly through camp yesterday morning that the campaign had been abandoned. The troops had remained in camp five days, during which time nothing was known of our future movements. It was understood that on receipt of intelligence from Crook, the command would move south of the Yellowstone and scout the country north of the Little Missouri in a final effort to discover the savages, but it was not believed that the pursuit was to be abandoned so suddenly. During the past two days, cavalry detachments have been moving up and down the river in an endeavor to discover a shallow place for their troops to cross without the use of steamers, and it was believed that on the arrival of dispatches from Crook, showing his position, a movement into the country south of the Yellowstone would at once be made. The advices from Crook indicated the presence of Indians in the Badlands along the Little Missouri, but in the face of this, it is now known that we are to return, and the disbandment of the troops is already taking place.

Now that all active operations have been abandoned for the year, the utter failure of the campaign is felt by everyone. This feeling extends throughout the army. The humiliation of defeat is shared by the soldiers and officers alike. The campaign has been prolonged and severe. Tremendous marches have been accomplished through a desolate and broken country. The troops have at times been poorly led, and at no time have they been properly sheltered. As it was originally planned, the campaign was not to extend over three months. Inside of that time, the Sioux would be corralled and a sufficient number of them killed to cause their subjection. This policy has caused universal misery and a considerable loss of life, and can only be attributed to the fact that the several commanders knew nothing of the work to be accomplished or the character of the country to be traversed.

The summer picnic of the Regular army has been shorn of its holiday air. Of the 1,600 troops who took the field so proudly, 1,200 have returned. The remainder have either been killed or have died from exposure or disease. It is one of the terrible peculiarities of an Indian war that there are few wounded men. The Indian never wounds an enemy. He kills.

The troops, on taking the field, were not allowed to carry any tents and but few blankets. This was even more marked with Crook's command than with this, and on forming a junction with Terry, it was learned that the men had been limited to one blanket to each man. No rubber covering of any kind was carried. The presumption, of course, was that it was necessary to thus limit the luggage in order to facilitate the rapid movement of the troops, but the policy that actuated it was cruel. For a light-marching cavalry command, covering a scout for several weeks, it would have seemed a proper thing, but in cutting loose from his supply camp for an indefinite period, there seems to have been no military necessity in thus exposing the men.

General Crook's command included a considerable number of infantry, and to have increased his pack train would not have retarded its progress. When the two columns went into camp at the mouth of Powder River on August 18, after the conclusion of the scout along the Tongue, Rosebud, and Powder Rivers, the suffering of the men was intense. During the seven days in which the troops remained in camp, it rained incessantly, and the cold nights which followed left the men with but little or no protection. In consequence, a considerable number of sick were left behind when the commands again left on the twenty-fifth to move south.

It appears from the recent dispatches from General Crook that he has encountered several heavy storms, which have increased the sickness throughout the command, and is mainly due to the continued and needless exposure of the troops. In this latter instance, the condition of the invalids is all the more intensified from the lack of any accommodation for the sick. No ambulances accompany his command, and his sick are dragged across the rough country in mule litters, a rude contrivance that is somewhat slower than an Indian bullet, but is almost as sure. A heavier pack train accompanied this command, sufficient clothing was allowed, and in consequence but little sickness has occurred. Some few tents were carried, but in following out his instructions to the men, General Terry could not be induced to enter one, and during all the severe weather that occurred shared the same privations as the troops.

On the division of the forces, which occurred on August 26, General Crook gave his word that he would communicate or report with his command at the mouth of the Glendive Creek on September 2. General Terry, with his command, was to move north of the Yellowstone, and after scouting that region, was to return to the same point. He accordingly had supplies shipped here for all the troops. Our command went into camp on September 1, but nothing was learned from Crook until yesterday, at which time he was moving in the direction of the Black Hills. His supplies were nearly exhausted, but he reports having found an old trail, which he intended to follow, and in his own words, "I will let the ration question take care of itself." It is feared this same reckless policy will cause increased suffering among his troops, which appears heirless, when at the date of his dispatch he was but little more than a day's march from this point.

The final dissolution of our command took place this evening. The 7th Cavalry and the 6th Infantry started in an easterly direction along the north bank of the Yellowstone for Fort Buford at an early hour, and at this writing the Montana column is moving slowly over the hills to the west of us. After striking the Stanley trail, they will follow it west for nearly two hundred miles, and then move through the Bighorn country home. The 22nd Infantry, under Colonel Otis, will remain at this point until about November 1, when it will proceed to the mouth of Tongue River and enter into winter quarters with the 5th Infantry. All of yesterday was spent in making preparations for the morrow. There was a great deal of hand shaking, and considerable chaffing over the failure of the campaign. A grim old veteran who had passed through a dozen Indian campaigns remarked to his companion-in-arms, "Well, Hack, I'll see you next spring."

Someone wanted to know what had become of the Regular army, and Captain Weir of the 7th Cavalry was heard to remark, "As the Sioux have failed to find us, we are going home." During the evening, word was passed through the camp, and by 9:00 P.M., nearly one hundred officers gathered about a fire near General Terry's headquarters. The old campaign songs were sung with ringing choruses, and by 11:00 P.M., the farewells had all been spoken. Throughout all the evening, although the officers were in close proximity to General Terry's headquarters, the general kept up a weary beat before his own campfire and seemed unconscious of the presence of his officers. He would stop and bid someone good-bye as he came up, and then resume his beat.

Since the opening of the campaign, the face of General Terry, once full and round, has become careworn and has now a troubled look. He has felt the failure of the campaign keenly, and knows that the result cannot but be cast as a reflection on his entire military record. Loath to enter the field, and with a knowledge that his original plans were disarranged through disobedience of orders, he has felt that whatever blame is attached to the failure of the troops will have to be borne by him. General Terry is by nature one of the kindest of men, and has been willing to accept the odium of the campaign. This has been shown throughout his official reports, in none of which has he cast a reflection upon any of his subordinate officers. In defiance of a sentiment throughout the army, he placed no blame upon Custer for the Little Bighorn disaster. It is to this characteristic of the man that the nature of the expedition is charged by many. In several notable instances, his explicit orders have been disregarded, as in the case of Major Reno, who had been instructed to scout the Tongue River and return to its mouth previous to the affair at the Little Bighorn, but who followed a trail along the Rosebud for some days, literally delaying the movement of the entire column three days. But for the loss of this time, Terry could have entered the mountains three days earlier than he did, and the result of a fight with the Indians might have been a different one.[12] As it was, no charges have been preferred against any officer in the command.

Your correspondent called on the general during the last night in camp and learned from him his reason for the disbanding of the command. He said that he was compelled to send the troops home against his inclination and expectation, as he had hoped to scout north of the Little Missouri before closing operations, but the necessity had become so great that he was compelled to abandon this idea in order to forward supplies up the river for the troops which were to remain in winter quarters. "My instructions are," said he, "to provide for 1,500 troops for the winter, and as a portion of this command is to be cavalry, it will require every effort to forward the necessary supplies, and I am now certain that it will be impossible to forward the amount required. Under the circumstances, I cannot keep a consuming army in the field." Concerning his plan for the battle to have been fought on the Little Bighorn, he remarked, "The plan of the fight was my own, and I considered it a good one. It was the only one in which I could bring my infantry into action as far as it was possible. I felt assured the Indian village was on the Little Bighorn, and in my endeavor to cooperate with Colonel Custer, the troops made a most difficult march to reach the point selected for the junction of the troops." In reply to a query concerning the disobedience of orders on the part of Major Reno, he merely remarked, "That is a matter of record." He felt confident that the campaign would have to be taken up again next year, at which time it would be necessary to place a sufficient number of troops in the field to allow five or six columns to operate independently of each other.

The steamer *Josephine* leaves for Fort Buford today, with General Terry and staff on board. The river has become very low, and it is expected that after the two steamers, *Josephine* and *Far West,* accomplish another trip, no further attempt will be made to navigate the river. All supplies for the command at Tongue River will be forward overland by wagon train from Fort Buford in that event.[13]

PART SIX

The Winter Campaign of 1876–77

The Dull Knife Fight

JERRY ROCHE

New York *Herald,* December 11, 1876

>CAMP ON CRAZY WOMAN'S FORK
>OF THE POWDER RIVER,
>Thursday, November 30, 1876

Since my last writing from old Fort Reno, one arm of the Powder River expedition has had a brisk and successful brush with hostile Indians camped in a wild and almost inaccessible canyon of the Bighorn Mountains. An accidental circumstance led to the discovery of the hostile camp. By that discovery, we were enabled to surprise its inmates, and to it we owe not only our success in routing the band of savages who found shelter there, but also the lives of a large proportion of those composing the column that operated under Colonel Mackenzie in this fight. To our Arapaho and Sioux scouts the credit of utilizing this accidental circumstance belongs, as well as leading us to the village, after they had found it, through a country with the topography of which our white guides were wholly unacquainted. Without their assistance, we might have searched months and then not found the den of the hostiles, so securely was it concealed among the hills.

On our arrival at old Fort Reno, Saturday, November 18, General Crook sent out some Sioux and Arapahos to take a scout in the neighborhood of Crazy Woman's Fork with four days' provisions, his intention being to move in time to meet them on their return.

During their absence, two parties of miners moving eastward from the Black Hills to prospect in the neighboring hills arrived in our camp and had a talk with General Crook. From this interview, the general concluded that Crazy Horse's camp must be located somewhere on the Rosebud. He then determined, instead of moving at once toward Crazy Woman's Fork, to await the return of the scouts. At the appointed time, they came, bringing with them a hostile Cheyenne they had captured a little outside of Crazy Woman's Fork. It was this capture which led to the discovery of the village. In going out, our Indian scouts had left their soldier clothes behind them, and the captive wandered into their camp. Believing himself among friends, he told them that there were some Cheyenne lodges in a ravine on the south side of the mountain, near Crazy Woman's Fork, but that the main body of the tribe had crossed the mountains.

After obtaining all the information he possessed from the Cheyenne, they covered him with their pistols, held under their blankets, and said, "We are white soldiers now and we want your gun; if you don't give it up, you know what will happen." The surprised hostile submitted and was brought to Fort Reno, where General Crook had another talk with him. His statements after his arrival in our camp were confused and contradictory of his first assertions. He did not dare, however, to wander too far from his first story, and in consequence of the intelligence he brought us, General Crook concluded to go at once after Crazy Horse.

In pursuance of this determination, we struck camp at Fort Reno on daybreak on Wednesday [November 22] and arrived at Crazy Woman's Fork late in the afternoon. Immediately orders were promulgated to prepare for a ten days' march toward the Rosebud with the pack train only, our wagons to be left where they were until our return. We got everything ready that night for an early start, determined to take with us only such clothing as we could wear, no tents, and a small allowance of bedding, two blankets each—rather cool covering for such nights as we have had of late, but still all that could be permitted with the transportation at hand.[2]

The camp was astir far into the night preparing for the morrow's march, but by sunrise on Thursday all was changed. At daylight, our pickets on the hills surrounding our camp saw an Indian approaching with a large white flag, which he waved above his head. Some of our enlisted Indians went out to meet him and brought him into camp, where he was recognized as Sitting Bear, a friendly Indian sent out by Colonel Mackenzie from Red Cloud agency to warn those still out that they must come in and give up their arms and ponies, or the soldiers would pursue them and compel them to do so. Sitting Bear had left Crazy Horse's village several days before and was slowly drifting back toward the agency. The day before his arrival in our camp, he ascertained that the five Cheyenne lodges which our captain had spoken of had discovered our approach and set off toward Crazy Horse's camp. They would give him the alarm and doubtless set him also moving.

General Crook then determined to pursue the Cheyennes supposed to be camped beyond the mountains first, and ordered Colonel Mackenzie, with the cavalry and Indian scouts, to start as soon as possible. Meanwhile, fourteen Pawnee and Shoshone scouts were put out with instructions to cross the mountains at the passes to scout for signs of Indians beyond.

We marched thirty-five miles on Thursday, and that evening we sent out on our side of the mountain seven or eight Sioux and Arapaho scouts to search for indications of the village ahead.

At sunrise on Friday [November 24], we resumed our march, and by 1:00 P.M., the head of the column reached a grassy vale completely sheltered in front by a semicircular range of hills. Here our Indians, most of whom traveled ahead, halted to give the cavalry time to catch up with them. In about three-quarters of an hour, the whole command was in, the men dismounted and the horses unsaddled and being led to water at a little stream that wound through the valley. Meantime, the pack train had also come up and was going into camp on the left just as our Indian outposts on the hills in front commenced to circle about on their horses in a wild, excited sort of way.

A moment afterward, a shrill Indian yawp went up from the farthest Indian on the hill in front. This was echoed by two or three of our Indians farther down toward us, and then reechoed a hundred times by our wild irregulars scattered through the valley. Wrongly interpreting this savage signal, our cavalry captains, with nervous haste, rushed their men forward, throwing out skirmishers all along the hillside. One company had resaddled and was at the front, mounted in less than three minutes from the first alarm.

This movement, commendably quick as it was, proved wholly unnecessary. The hostiles were not approaching to attack us, as was apprehended, and the savage yell we heard merely indicated that some of the scouts we had sent out the night before were coming in, having discovered the location of the hostile village. They had communicated their discovery by signals from a distant hill to the outposts, and the howl we had heard was but a shout of triumph. But it had a marvelous effect on the auxiliaries too. With a promptness that would have been creditable to any regular cavalry, they had caught and mounted their war ponies and were galloping back and forth on a little knoll to the right at full speed. Inquiring what was the object of this movement, I was informed that when about to enter a fight, the Indians invariably give their ponies a preliminary canter to improve their wind.

When the alarm subsided and the first of the scouts arrived, we learned that the camp was some distance off—how far the Indian could not say with any degree of accuracy, Indian ideas of time and distance as we view them being rather indefinite. Colonel Mackenzie learned enough, however, to determine at once upon a night march, so as to be ready to strike the village at daybreak the next morning. From this time forward, extreme caution was observed, so as to guard as much as possible against alarming the village. Our pickets were sent out dismounted while we rested here, and no fires were permitted lest the smoke should betray our presence.

After a cheerless meal of hardtack and cold bacon, and about three hours' rest, we started on our night march. As we emerged from the little basin where we had been resting, we entered a wildly picturesque pass in the mountain. The head of the column, at which were moving in irregular form and with varied colors our Indian auxiliaries, wound about the base of a steep conical hill, which commanded a full view of the entire command as it stretched out in double file behind. "What a splendid picture," exclaimed all who saw the advancing column from this point. And so it was a pretty sight for the moment, but its form was changed and its beauty vanished as we passed the crest of the second hill. For about a mile, the land now spread out level to our view, and as we advanced, 'Sharp Nose,' one of our Arapahos, called attention to two black specks away to the left. Before any white man present could do more than barely discover their existence, he told us they were the two Sioux scouts who had remained behind to learn something more about the village. About the same time that we noticed their approach, they discovered our advance and guided their course so as to head us off.

In about twenty minutes they joined us, and just as they reached us, the pony ridden by 'Jackass,' one of the Sioux scouts who was a little in advance of the other, stumbled and fell over, completely exhausted. Jackass himself—who, by the way, is a brave, bright eyed, handsome young Indian—was about as tired and hungry as the pony and could not tell us what he had seen until after he had eaten a few mouthfuls of hard bread and bacon. Then, with flashing eyes and in eager haste, he said he had seen some of the ponies and counted eleven of the lodges from a hill overlooking the village. He said we could reach the village at midnight by marching onward steadily. He could not give us any idea, however, of the size of the village, either from the number of tepees he had counted or the number of horses he had seen.

We continued our march along into the night, over jagged hills, through deep ravines, across rapid mountain streams, miry and deep, but the sky was clear and cloudless, and the moon rose to light up our narrow and difficult pathway.

Before entering the roughest country on our road to the camp, we passed through a beautiful valley about half a mile wide and over three miles long, level as a racecourse all the way. When we emerged from this, we were obliged to move very slowly, and the cavalrymen had to dismount at least twenty times during the night and lead their horses in single file, passing through ravines, with which the country lying between us and the mouth of the canyon where the camp stood was cut up and crossed in all directions. If we could have gone in a direct line from the point where we halted in the afternoon to the camp, the distance would not have been over ten miles, but along the route [on which] we were obliged to move, we must have marched over twenty miles, a march more difficult and exhausting than one covering three times the distance would have been in a tolerably level country. Scouts were kept ahead constantly, and from time to time they came back to guide our movements and assure us that we were gradually approaching the village.

Shortly after midnight, the moon set and left us to grope our way in comparative darkness through a part of our road where it was impossible to find or follow a trail; where brush grew so tall as to hide the foremost horseman from his followers, and a stream wound its course beneath banks so steep that we could not find a way to cross until we had wandered and groped a long way through the darkness. Patiently and persistently we pressed along in this way until just before the dawn of day, when we approached the mouth of the canyon. At this time we knew the village was not far off, but we knew nothing about its location or the nature of the ground hereabouts, and we feared that any efforts to enlighten ourselves on these points, however useful, might alarm the village and defeat our intention to surprise the hostiles. Two or three Indian scouts were again sent forward by Lt. W. P. Clark, who commanded the entire detachment of scouts, to make a reconnaissance and report before the order was given to charge. Meanwhile, every effort possible was made to close up the column, now strung out considerably in consequence of the number of deep cuts through which we had to pass as we approached and entered the mouth of the canyon. At this time, all our Indians were being hurried to the front to make ready to sweep through the village.

While waiting to get them into column ready for action, one of our scouts returned and reported that the bucks were having war dances in four places in the village. He also located two or three herds of ponies and said there were tepees on both sides of the river. With all possible haste, Colonel [Ranald] Mackenzie hurried his command into form.

The Indian scouts were busy now casting off superfluous clothing and relieving their horses of every additional weight that threatened to check their speed or impair their usefulness in the field. This done, they crowded forward, all eager to have the foremost place, more like racehorses coming to the score than warriors entering the field of battle. When the cavalry had almost all crossed the last deep cut near the mouth of the canyon, Colonel Mackenzie got everything in readiness for the charge. Major Gordon's battalion was at the head and Captain Mauck's behind.

Major Gordon[3] had with him one staff officer, Lieutenant [Augustus C.] Tyler, 4th Cavalry, battalion adjutant, and the following companies of cavalry: H, 5th Cavalry, Capt. John M. Hamilton, 2nd. Lt. [Edwin P.] Andrus; L, 5th Cavalry, Capt. A. B. Taylor, 1st Lt. E. H. Ward, and 2nd Lt. Homer Wheeler; H, 3rd Cavalry, Capt. H. W. Wessels and 2nd Lt. [Charles L.] Hammond; K, 3rd Cavalry, Capt. Gerald Russell, 1st Lt. O. Elting, 2nd Lt. [George A.] Dodd; M, 4th Cavalry, 1st Lt. John A. McKinney, 2nd Lt. [Harrison G.] Otis; F, 4th Cavalry, Capt. Wirt Davis and 2nd Lt. J. W. Rosenquest.

Captain Mauck's[4] 2nd Battalion was composed as follows: 1st Lt. W. C. Miller, 4th Cavalry, adjutant; Company B, 4th Cavalry, 1st Lt. Callahan; Company D, 4th Cavalry, Capt. John Lee, 2nd Lt. S. A. Mason; Company E, 1st Lt. F. L. Shoemaker, 2nd Lt. H. H. Bellas; Company I, Capt. W. C. Hemphill, who had with him two young officers who volunteered for the occasion, 2nd Lt. J. M. Jones, 4th Artillery, and 2nd Lt. J. N. Allison, 2nd Cavalry.

While we rested here a moment to make ready for the dash, I dismounted, tightened my saddle girths, and moving a little in advance of the Indians, I distinctly heard the drum and the war song of the hostiles. But the sequel showed that this demonstration was not gotten up in anticipation of our approach. Possibly some venturesome miners or an unfortunate party of Snake Indians furnished the scalps that were the occasion of so much joy in the hostile Cheyenne household.

The light of the rising morning star had been blazing for some time from behind a hill on our right flank during the hurry of preparation, and now the first streak of dawn appeared, to the chagrin of our leader, who had hoped to strike the blow in time to get his men placed as the day was breaking. But the delay was unavoidable. The column could not have been advanced more rapidly with any degree of safety.

At last it was ready to move. At the same moment, Lieutenant Dorst,[5] Colonel Mackenzie's adjutant, was sent forward to Lieutenant Clark to tell him to let loose the Indians, and Lt. John G. Bourke, aide-de-camp to General Crook and a volunteer on this occasion, went back to Major Gordon with an order to charge. We were now, though unaware of the fact, just about three-quarters of a mile from the nearest tepee, and we galloped forward with all the speed possible, wholly unacquainted with the ground we were entering, and not knowing what sort of a reception we should get. The Indians swarmed about the field in front and on either flank of Colonel Mackenzie and staff, Lieutenants Clark and DeLany[6] leading, the Sioux and Arapahos, Major North and the Pawnees, and Lt. W. S. Schuyler,[7] an aide-de-camp to General Crook and a volunteer also, at the head of the Shoshones. Our only music was furnished by a Pawnee Indian who blew on a pipe a wild humming tune that rose above all other sounds and smote the ear with strange effect. It reminded me forcibly of the prolonged shriek of a steam whistle. Added to this were the shouts of our foremost line of scouts as they dashed forward to run off the herds of ponies. Then there were a few flashes here and there in the dusk of morning, a few sharp rifle and carbine cracks, and rising above all other sounds, the thunder of our advancing column resounded from the side of the canyon.

This thundering noise it was that first alarmed the hostile savages and made them cut short the war dance and the song of victory for the grim reality of war itself. On a big bass drum, afterward found in the village, which they had as a present from the Great Father in Washington, those already awake sounded the alarm in the village and then fled through the ravines toward the hills with a rapidity born of mortal terror.

We now found ourselves on a little plain running nearly parallel with the village and elevated about twenty feet above the bottom, on which the lodges stood. The village was in a canyon running from west to east, the lodges numbering nearly two hundred, ranging along both sides of a clear, rapid stream[8] that wound along close to the base of the range of hills forming the south wall of the canyon. The canyon was nearly four miles long and from about a third of a mile to a mile wide from base to base of the hills forming its side walls. It was the narrowest at its eastern end and sloped downward considerably from this point, from which we entered it, for two miles or more to about the beginning of the village, which was fully three-quarters of a mile long. North of the village, the ground rose a little, and about a third of a mile west of it, the canyon terminated in a succession of flat-topped hills, cut up by ravines, which ran in every direction. The lodges were completely hidden in thick brush. The northerly wall of the canyon was an almost perpendicular mountain, averaging some eight hundred to one thousand feet in height for more than half its length.

Once after entering the canyon and before reaching the village, we were obliged to cross the stream that ran through the village. Four or five dry ravines also intercepted our way before reaching the little plain overlooking the lodges. Between this plateau and the tepees were a low bluff and a red sandstone butte about thirty feet high, and nearly opposite these, about half a mile to the northward and a little in advance, were two single and one double red sandstone broken ridges under the shadow of the north wall. A few hundred yards west of these, and running irregularly from north to south, were several deep gulches, accessible from the village by intersecting ravines not quite so deep. This much I deem necessary by way of description before attempting an account of the fight.

By the time Major Gordon's battalion had got on a line with the center of the village, the hostiles, in large numbers, had taken possession of the ravines in front of us, and had also secreted themselves behind the bluffs to the left of the village. The hill on the south side of the canyon terminates abruptly near the western end of the village and is perhaps five hundred feet high at the point where it ends. Lieutenant Schuyler went with the Shoshones to this point and, sheltered by a few loose rocks, remained there all day and through the night. As the different companies of the 1st Battalion arrived on the little plain parallel with the village, they moved toward the ravines and were met by a heavy fire from different points behind the brush and rocks a few dozen yards in front. At this time the hostiles were trying to run off a herd of ponies from the plateau over the village into which our men were trooping, and word of their intentions was taken to Colonel Mackenzie, who sent an order to Lieutenant McKinney,[9] by Lieutenant Lawton, 4th Cavalry, to charge up toward the ravines and cut off the progress of the hostiles.

Lieutenant McKinney dashed forward with his company. The hostiles halted and, dropping into the ravine just ahead, waited until the company came up and then fired, mortally wounding him and also wounding his first sergeant, five of his men, and his horse. Before falling, he exclaimed to his company, "Get back out of this place; you are ambushed." Subsequently he asked the doctor to tell his mother how he died. He lived about twenty minutes. As he fell, the first fours of his company faltered, and Colonel Mackenzie, beside whom I stood, about fifty yards behind Lieutenant McKinney's company, seeing the break, ordered Major Gordon to send Captain Hamilton's[10] company, then just behind us, forward to the same position.

In the charge, two of Lieutenant McKinney's men got cut off from the company and were corralled in the rocks all day, being obliged to defend themselves as best they could until nightfall.

On receiving the order to advance, Major Gordon himself went forward with Captain Hamilton, and as they advanced, the breaking company, re-formed under Lieutenant Otis,[11] returned to the spot and drove the hostiles from the ravine. The pony herd was split, each side getting a share. In this second dash, Lieutenant Otis's cap was turned about on his head by a bullet from a fleeing hostile. Both companies then sheltered themselves behind a bluff to the right. Meanwhile, Captain Hemphill's company was moving forward to take a position to the left, which they were subsequently obliged to abandon, and Captain Taylor[12] was ordered to charge right through the village. He did so and had four of his horses killed. One man named [John] Sullivan, belonging to the other company, was killed and scalped on this dash. This was the only soldier scalped in the fight, while among the tepees, a bullet passed through the lapel of Captain Taylor's coat, just over his heart. Captain Mauck's battalion was pouring into the field, meanwhile, dismounting and running forward toward the west of the village and to the shelter of some bluffs on the left that commanded the ravines west of the village. All this while these ravines were full of hostiles, who had the advantage of the advancing troops to the extent of being in a position to fire at the approaching masses while comparatively secure themselves.

It was still the gray dawn of morning, and the moving figures of men and horses seen at any considerable distance appeared more like shadows than living things. But time sped quickly, and very soon broad daylight broke upon the busy scene. The engagement now became general, and no single spectator could possibly keep a record of the events in progress, although concentrated in a narrow space. I candidly confess I was wholly unequal to the task, especially as I found it necessary to discover some care for the safety of myself and my horse. For a while, the fire of our men was deafening, and its roar reverberated along the hillsides with thunderous sound. From the rocks and ravines in front, the hostiles answered back at first vigorously, but afterward with more caution, and always at an animated object. Many of our troops—among which were several recruits—were not paying much attention to what they fired at, so long as their fire was discharged in the general direction from which the balls of the hostiles came. Indeed, it very soon became apparent to these officers whose attention was not otherwise occupied that we were having a sad waste of ammunition on our side.

This was no unimportant matter, viewed in the light in which we then contemplated the situation. We were not routing the hostiles as fast as was desirable. They had entrenched themselves in the hills in pretty secure nooks from five hundred to one thousand yards off and were pegging away at our troops wherever they could get in a good shot. Anyone who crossed the little plateau above the village was especially made a target of, as I found out more than once during the fight. When the battle had proceeded for an hour, or perhaps longer, the rapid and wasteful firing of our recruits was checked, for Colonel Mackenzie began to think, about this time, that he was in for a long fight. The nature of the country and the ferocity and stubbornness with which the hostiles contested for possession of every ridge and rock and ravine naturally led to this conclusion. For a while, Lieutenants Clark, Bourke, Lawton, and Dorst were kept moving briskly from point to point to caution company commanders that they must not permit their men to waste any ammunition. The hostiles were wasting none, and were continually shifting their position to try and bring our men within range of their long guns, as well as to go beyond the range of our carbines.

It did not take them many minutes to determine the character and range of our weapons and to utilize the discovery to the best possible advantage. One of their tricks was ingenious in its way. A party of braves would creep behind some projecting ledge of rock or hospitable ridge far enough to get just beyond range of our guns, and then would make a wild charge forward, howling savagely, to draw out our fire, from whose bullets they considered themselves safe, but whose exposure would give them the very chance they sought. A somewhat similar plan was once put into successful operation against them by Captain Davis.[13] The captain's company was suddenly withdrawn from a bluff fronting some rocks, behind which eight or nine hostiles were securely concealed. When they saw the men break and run away from them, as they supposed, they jumped up and ran out after them, and in their excitement, familiar as they were with the ground, forgot for the moment that there was a deep, dry ravine just in the rear of the retreating men. Into this cut the soldiers jumped and delivered a volley at the elated savages as they advanced, killing some and sending the rest back to the rocks in dismay. Some of them found shelter in a cave to the right, where they were pursued and killed, every one.

In my endeavors to watch and trace the course of action, I crossed the field I should say a dozen times during the first hour of the fight. I had carried my gun in one hand from the moment of entering the field, but had not discharged it once. I dismounted once during this time behind the red sandstone butte on the left, and in remounting discovered that my overcoat was considerably in the way. On getting into the saddle, I galloped across once more to a ridge where Frank Grouard, Baptiste [Pouriere], Billy Hunter, and one or two other scouts and interpreters were shooting at some hostiles on the hills to the left. There I shed my overcoat, attached a picket rope to my bridle, and crept to the crest of the bluff next to Frank Grouard, who was evidently too much interested in the work at hand to pay any attention to fresh arrivals at his side.

"What are you firing at, Frank?" I inquired.

Without turning to see who spoke, he opened the breech of his gun, pressed in another cartridge, and answered my inquiry in the Sioux language. Again I asked him where the particular Indian was that he was trying to knock over, and again he replied in Sioux and kept on shooting. Then I reminded him that I didn't happen to understand the Indian tongue and should be obliged if he would answer me in English, and suddenly recollecting himself, he laughed and pointed to a hill about eight hundred yards in front, from which bullets were

Mackenzie's attack on Dull Knife's village. CYRUS T. BRADY. *INDIAN FIGHTS AND FIGHTERS.*

coming in quick succession to the crest of the bluff we occupied. A moment afterward, someone on my left knocked over one of the Indians on this ridge, and the others crept to safer quarters. Frank did not get his man that time, but he did before the battle closed, and he now rejoices in the possession of a scalp of a hostile Cheyenne.

Frank and myself then rode across the field again to the village and found that some of the lodges had been set on fire already. On entering the village, we found the body of a squaw, just freshly scalped, lying near one of the lodges. A Pawnee scout was moving off from the prostrate body, bearing with him the dripping scalp. This unfortunate squaw had been found in the village hidden in a tepee after the troops had passed through it by Private Butler of the 2nd Cavalry, who told the Pawnees, many of whom were in the village, not to kill her. Butler's back was scarcely turned, however, before the old squaw was shot and scalped. We then walked through a portion of the village and counted about 175 lodges, and still had not counted all. We went into several and found in every one two or three packages of dried meat. The lodges were mostly lined on the inside to the height of two or three feet with undressed hides, and everything remained as if the inmates had stepped out for a few moments. In some the fires were burning and kettles of water stood on them, as if in preparation for the morning meal. A number of the Pawnees were systematically going through the village and securing large quantities of plunder. We were both very hungry now, and Frank Grouard helped himself to some of the meat. After a hasty glance through the village, we returned to the field again, where the battle still progressed with considerable animation.

A corporal and private had just had a close fight with two hostiles at an advanced position on the right. The men met within a few yards of each other. At the first fire, the corporal fell. Then the private fired, killing the Indian who had killed the corporal, and the other Indian fled. I scoured through the field for some time again, and fire came from twenty different points in the hills beyond. Dead horses were lying about at different points, but the men were now all dismounted and the horses securely sheltered from the fire in the ravines and behind the bluffs. The killed and wounded were now being taken to the right of the field, where Doctors Wood and Le Garde were attending to the wants of the living and sheltering the dead. Meantime, the hostiles had gotten their women and children into the mountains beyond the western end of the canyon. I came back again to the village and found a number of our Indians, some soldiers, and civil employees of the expedition going through the lodges, searching for relics. At one point, I met a soldier who told me he had just seen a silk guidon of the 7th Cavalry, which was found in a tepee. In others were found the guard roster of Company G, 7th Cavalry; saddles, canteens, nosebags, currycombs, and brushes; shovels and axes, marked with the letters of different companies of the 7th Cavalry; a memorandum book with a list of names of the three best marksmen at target practice in Capt. Donald McIntosh's company, 7th Cavalry; rosters of other companies of the 7th; a letter written by an enlisted man of the 7th Cavalry to a young lady, the letter already stamped and directed. This will be forwarded. Several horses of the 7th Cavalry were found among the herds captured. Photographs of several white men were also found; a gold pencil case, a silver watch, pocketbooks with sums of money; some gold pieces; the hat of 1st Sgt. William Allen of Company I, 3rd Cavalry, killed in the Rosebud fight, with the company stamp and his initials in it; an officer's overcoat of dark blue army cloth; an officer's rubber coat and two officer's blouses; a buckskin coat of American make, with a bullet hole in the shoulder, and supposed to be the coat worn by Tom Custer in the Little Bighorn fight; bullet moulds, field glasses, etc.

Among the Indian trophies in the possession of our troops now are three beaded necklaces, ornamented with human fingers. One has depending from it ten fingers, one seven, and one shown me by Lieutenant Bourke has eight fingers strung around it.

We have a belt, found in the village, full of cartridges, with a silver plate marked "Little Wolf," given this doughty chief at Washington a few years ago. We also found a pass for Roman Nose from Red

Cloud [agency], giving him permission to leave the reservation a few days to search for lost mules.

After going through the village the second time, I again crossed the field and took shelter with Major Gordon, Captain Hamilton, and some other officers behind the double bluff to the right. I had some broken hardtack in my saddle pockets, and I found some gentlemen here who gladly accepted the crumbs. It was no easy matter to arrive at or leave this point without getting hit; still, some of the soldiers and some orderlies were continually passing back and forth, and Colonel Mackenzie made this point his headquarters for a while. The hostile fire came over this ledge from three points. Bullets came in just over our heads from the crest of the mountain on the north, from a mound almost directly in front, and others fell near our feet, shot from behind some rocks on the hills to the southwest of us. A soldier who tried to leave just after I arrived had his hat shot off. He calmly picked it up again, put it on, and as he moved slowly away, looked very angry as he glanced toward the point from which the ball came. One soldier was lying dead on the side of the bluff just above us.

Soon after I arrived, the order was given the men at this point to cease firing altogether. It was well, for most of the Indians on the hills had crept beyond range of the cavalry carbines and were watching their chances to pick our men off.

After I had been here half an hour or so—indeed, I cannot definitely say how long, for it is not easy to take note of time on such occasions—Lieutenant Bourke came up and said the pack train had arrived. Instantly I determined to risk another crossing, for I was getting very hungry.

About the same time, the horses of Captain Hamilton's company were ordered across to water, and most of them had been taken over before I mounted my horse. When I did so and moved out into the field, I saw a soldier just ahead of me riding one horse and leading another. This man had not gone fifty yards from the bluff before his led horse fell, hit by a ball from the hills, and he was wounded himself. Before I had crossed the field, though going at full speed, at least a score of balls whistled past my ears. I found the pack train just camping in the willows near the middle of the village and soon was engaged in disposing of a late breakfast. It was about 2:00 P.M. now, I should judge, and the pack train had been in the canyon over two hours but was only just going into camp. The mules had their packs on for twenty-three hours. It just occurs to me that most of us had been in the saddle about the same length of time.

As I arrived at the pack train, Colonel Mackenzie was sending out a dispatch to General Crook, then over two days' march by the shortest route, to bring up the infantry. This looked as if Colonel Mackenzie expected that the Indians would fight him from the hills until he was reinforced. The extreme caution exercised by the hostiles early in the fight in the use of ammunition indicated either a scarcity of the article or a determination to save it for a long battle. At first we did not know which way to interpret their action, but just after eating, I learned that they had left nearly all their ammunition behind, and that considerable quantities of it were being destroyed in the lodges already set on fire. A keg of powder also exploded with a loud report in one of the burning tepees. Doubtless this deprivation made them all the more determined to make every shot tell.

One Indian had found a secure place in the hills and played sharpshooter nearly all day with one of the Sharp's long-range rifles. The gun must have shot a cartridge containing about 120 grains of powder. Every time he fired, the report seemed to rend the very walls of the canyon, echoing like the roar of cannon from hill to hill. Late in the afternoon, a cheer went up from some of our boys in front, and the big gun was silent thereafter. I subsequently heard the fellow was killed by one of Captain Davis's men, but the other Indian near him got away with the gun.

Gradually the Indian fire ceased until toward sundown, when it had stopped altogether. All our killed and wounded but one man, who fell on an exposed bluff near the end of the canyon, had been got in before this time, and just after sundown his body was brought in. As twilight fell on the scene, some of our Indian soldiers kept popping away at hostiles, who in the cover of darkness were creeping from their hiding places in the rocks, but I do not think they fired with much effect. Numerous pickets were posted on the hills before nightfall, for we apprehended a renewal of the fight by sundown or a little afterward. But night fell upon the battlefield, and with it came peace and silence about the hostile village.

Our killed and wounded had been transferred from the north side of the field to the shelter of the bluff on the right, and here I found the extent of our loss was one officer and five men killed and twenty-five men and one Indian wounded. The small proportion of Indians shot in the fight is traceable to their familiarity with the manner of fighting of their own people, and the shrewdness with which they evaded fire. Their chief usefulness, however, consisted in their employment as scouts and in leading the first dash at the hostiles to capture their ponies and demoralize them by showing them that their own people were arrayed against them. They cannot be disciplined to fight like white soldiers. Two of the Shoshones and one of the Sioux had horses shot under them and yet escaped unhurt. During the fight,

Three Bears had his horse shot under him and rode back past me mounted behind another Indian, in search of a pony on which to renew the fight.

In the evening, I saw some scalps that had been taken from the lodges, and among these was the scalp of a white girl. I saw also a number of blank books taken from the tepees, on the leaves of which had been sketched the exploits of several of the Cheyennes braves. After nightfall, an effort was made to count up the Indian loss, and the lowest figure at which it was placed was twenty-five killed outright.[14] I saw the Pawnees parading six scalps early in the evening; two soldiers showed me six scalps they had secured. Frank Grouard got a scalp, Lieutenant Allison[15] killed an Indian, Captain Davis's company killed six or eight, the Shoshones killed four, a one-eyed frontiersman with one party of our Indians killed one, and the Sioux and Arapahos killed about a dozen but did not take any scalps. Others, too, were killed and severely wounded, of which no account has been yet received, so on the whole I should say the hostiles had fully fifty killed and mortally wounded.

The following is a complete list of the killed and wounded on our side:

KILLED

Lt. John A. McKinney, commanding Company M, 4th Cavalry.

Cpl. Patrick F. Ryan, Company D, 4th Cavalry.

Pvt. Joseph Mengis, Company H, 5th Cavalry.

Pvt. Alexander Keller, Company E, 4th Cavalry.

Pvt. John Sullivan, Company B, 4th Cavalry.

Pvt. Beard, Company D, 4th Cavalry.

Pvt. Alexander McFarland, Company L, 5th Cavalry, died on the twenty-eighth.

WOUNDED

Cpl. William Lynn, Company M, 4th Cavalry, hip joint fractured.

Pvt. G. H. Stickney, Company H, 5th Cavalry, flesh wound.

Sgt. Daniel Cunningham, Company H, 3rd Cavalry, foot fractured.

Pvt. J. E. Tallmadge, Company H, 3rd Cavalry, flesh wound.

Pvt. Isaac Maguire, Company M, 4th Cavalry, flesh wound.

Pvt. Charles Folsom, Company H, 5th Cavalry, fracture of thigh.

Sgt. Thomas H. Forsyth, Company M, 4th Cavalry, flesh wound.

Pvt. James McMahon, Company M, 4th Cavalry, flesh wound.

Pvt. Charles F. Lurig, Company F, 4th Cavalry, flesh wound, thigh.

Pvt. Henry Holden, Company H, 3rd Cavalry, flesh wound, shoulder.

Pvt. Patrick Reardon, Company M, 4th Cavalry, flesh wound, arm.

Pvt. Charles Thompson, Company F, 4th Cavalry, flesh wound, shoulder.

Pvt. E. H. Ivison, Company M, 4th Cavalry, flesh wound.
Pvt. E. L. Buck, Company E, 4th Cavalry, ball lodged in thigh.
Cpl. W. H. Poole, Company I, 4th Cavalry, flesh wound.
Pvt. August Strick, Company E, 4th Cavalry, flesh wound.
Pvt. Edward Fitzgerald, Company D, 4th Cavalry, flesh wound.
Cpl. Jacob Schanfler, Company I, 4th Cavalry, fractured arm.
Pvt. William Morrison, fractured foot.
Pvt. George Kenny, Company I, 4th Cavalry, flesh wound in neck.
Pvt. Daniel Stephens, Company I, 4th Cavalry, wounded lung.
Anzi, Shoshone Indian, wound of the abdomen.

Besides these, there were three or four very slightly wounded by having their horses fall on them or being scratched by bullets glancing from the rocks.

Late in the afternoon, I learned that one party of hostiles on a hill to the right showed a white flag three or four times during the night but would shoot at an exposed head after its exhibition, just the same as ever.

When the fight was over, Colonel Mackenzie sent out some Indians with Roland, the Cheyenne interpreter, to talk with the hostiles on the hills. They saw old Dull Knife in the distance, and he said to them that his three sons had been killed in the fight and that he was willing to surrender, but the others were not. They had been told, he said, that the whites were coming to make a treaty with them, but instead they came and fired into their village; consequently, they could not trust the whites. A heap of their people, he said, had been killed in the fight, and the rest were ready to die.

During the night, the hostiles camped within four miles of the village, and in the morning, they were obliged to kill six or seven of their ponies for food. The carcasses were found by our Indians in the hills. The night was very cold and windy, and next day we were enveloped in a heavy snowstorm. After burying Private Beard on the battlefield, the rest of our killed and wounded were placed on litters, hitched at one end to mules and with the other end dragging on the ground, and we prepared to leave the canyon by noon of Sunday. Before starting, the colonel sent out the interpreters and Indians once more to talk with the hostiles, but they had a "big mad" on in the morning, and their pride would not permit them to answer our men at all.

The principal chiefs of the hostile village, I have been told, were Dull Knife, Little Wolf, Roman Nose, Gray Head, and Old Bear, and among the two hundred lodges were forty that have been in all the recent fights with the troops.

Before leaving, we burned everything in the village that our Indians did not want. There were 165 fires going in the hostile camp on Sunday morning, and in the blaze were consumed large quantities of dried meat, undressed skins, axes, saddles, tin-ware frying pans, snow moccasins, strychnine in large quantities, used to poison wolves; the tepees and tepee poles, medicine, and herbs. The destruction was complete—nay, even artistic. Not a pin's worth was left unburned. We captured between five hundred and six hundred ponies.

Sunday evening [November 26], we camped about eight miles from the canyon on our return to the supply camp, and next morning we learned that the infantry was on the way to join us, fully convinced that they would soon have to take a hand in the fight. They were turned back on Monday and arrived here Tuesday, the cavalry, with killed and wounded, getting back last night.

I find that Lieutenant McKinney's death, though he fell in action at the head of his company, as a soldier must be prepared to fall, is very generally regretted by the officers of the command. He was a dashing, brave young officer, whose manly qualities had endeared him to his comrades, and his death has cast a shadow on our victory. His body, I understand, is to be forwarded to his friends.

The nature of the land about the hostile village would have enabled our savage foes to cut the head of the column to pieces, if aware of our approach, and if we had not so thoroughly surprised them, someone would have to record a second edition of the Custer massacre. Had a smaller force, of whose approach the Indians had been apprised, attacked the village, not a man would have escaped.

Rounding Up the Red Men

NELSON A. MILES[1]

Cosmopolitan 51, no. 1 (June 1911): 105–14

The cause of the Indian war of 1876–77 may be briefly stated. In consideration of the Indians giving up a large part of their country and remaining at peace, the government granted them reservations and a large range of country for hunting grounds, and also agreed to give them stated annuities and to keep white people from trespassing upon the Indians' lands. In the main, the Indians adhered to the conditions of the treaty, but the government did not. The pressure of advancing civilization was very great on all sides. It was believed that the Black Hills country possessed rich mineral deposits, and miners were permitted to prospect for mines. Surveying parties were allowed to traverse the country for railway routes, and the government itself sent exploring expeditions there, which reported evidences of goldfields. This created on the part of the whites a strong desire to occupy the region, and the disaffection of the Indians soon developed into open hostilities.

Spotted Tail was a wise and really great chief. Red Cloud had been a noted warrior, but at that time was conservative and diplomatic. Both these hereditary chiefs had counseled peace, but the war spirit prevailed. Crazy Horse was the incarnation of ferocity, a fierce, restless warrior who, at the age of twenty-six, had become the leader of the Oglalas, the most warlike tribe of the Sioux nation. Sitting Bull of the Hunkpapas was an older man; he had made his reputation as a leader of the hostile element and by his intense hatred of the white race. He was a perfect type of the savage Indian—a born leader of men. Though not a hereditary chief, when any great war council was held, he was the central figure and the head of the war element. He became leader of the strongest and best-armed confederation of Indians ever created on this continent. Their warriors numbered several thousand, and had congregated in eastern Wyoming and Montana.

Against this body of hostile Indians, three columns of troops were moved in the spring of 1876—the troops from the south under General Crook, those from the east under General Terry, and those from the west, also in General Terry's department, under Bvt. Maj. Gen. John Gibbon. The defeat of General Crook's command, June 17, and the massacre of five troops of cavalry under

Nelson A. Miles as a major general.
NELSON A. MILES. *PERSONAL RECOLLECTIONS AND OBSERVATIONS.*

Colonel Custer, June 25, were most disheartening to the troops in the field and occasioned the sending of reinforcements.

After weeks of tedious steamboating up the Missouri to Fort Buford and then up the Yellowstone, we finally reached the mouth of the Rosebud, and I reported my command to General Terry. A series of long marches was at once made. This, however, failed to bring the troops into action with the Indians, but occupied nearly two months of time, and then the forces under Terry, Crook, and Gibbon were withdrawn to winter quarters.

With the withdrawal of the other troops, my command was directed to remain and shelter itself by building a cantonment. I intended, however, to do more than hibernate that winter. I believed that a winter campaign could be successfully made, even in that extremely cold climate. I told General Terry that if he would give me supplies and a reasonable command, I would clear a zone of hostile Indians before spring. He said that it would be impossible for troops to endure the severity of those northern winters and that I could not contend against the elements. I was, however, confident of success and equipped my troops as if they had been going to the arctic regions. They had campaigned in the Southwest in the winter, with the thermometer at twenty-eight degrees below zero. To attempt it in a country where the temperature was known to fall to sixty degrees below was a different proposition; but they were supplied with an abundance of woolen and fur clothing, even to masks for covering their faces.

The command consisted of my regiment, the 5th Infantry, two companies of the 22nd Infantry, a few pieces of artillery, and a small company of scouts, interpreters, and friendly Indians. At times I had with me the most noted scouts and guides in the western country. A prince among these was William F. Cody, better known as Buffalo Bill, who was then one of the handsomest men I have ever seen; very tall and straight, an abundance of golden hair falling to his shoulders, like the cavaliers of old, large brilliant brown eyes, auburn mustache and goatee, and features as perfect as if they had been chiseled out of marble. L. S. Kelly,[2] known as "Yellowstone" Kelly, was a remarkable man, of the type of Kit Carson or Daniel Boone—well educated, very intelligent, and a native of New York, but he lived on the remote frontier because he loved nature.

In order to know the position and disposition of the Indians, I adopted the same system of espionage that I had found successful in the Southwest. I soon learned by this means that the Indians had separated, and I determined, if possible, to prevent their reassembling. In this I was successful. I learned that Sitting Bull, with three tribes, the Hunkpapas, Minneconjous, and Sans Arcs, was moving north of the Yellowstone to the valley of the Big Dry, a tributary of the Missouri, and that Crazy Horse, with the Oglalas and Cheyennes, was moving to the headwaters of the Tongue and Rosebud Rivers. In addition to these powerful tribes, there were warriors from the disaffected elements of other tribes. The Indians intended to hunt buffaloes and gather their yearly supply of robes, and at the same time send out raiding parties for plunder. These great camps would, when located, be about a hundred miles apart. I determined to use my available force against them in detail.

Their young warriors lost no time in opening hostilities. They commenced by attacking isolated commands, stealing stock, and harassing the troops in many ways. One night my camp was attacked by the Indians charging close to our tents in their efforts to stampede our saddle horses and train animals. They fired two shots through my tent just over my cot. Our animals were, however, securely placed, and the troops soon repulsed the assault. Sitting Bull, with a large number of warriors, attacked one of our supply trains and held it in check until its escort was strongly reinforced.

My first move was against Sitting Bull's camp. I took the available part of my regiment, 394 riflemen and one piece of artillery, and leaving a small guard at the cantonment, our temporary base, moved northeast. On the fourth day, October 21, we suddenly discovered a strong force of a thousand or more warriors, each armed with a rifle and plenty of ammunition. They were gorgeously decorated with feathers, beadwork, and war paint, well supplied with fur robes, and splendidly mounted on fleet, hardy war ponies. As we approached their position, deployed in order of battle, they sent out a flag of truce, saying that Sitting Bull desired to meet the commanding officer. Their object appeared to be to delay us and ascertain our strength. I afterward learned that they had a well-laid plot to surprise us and attempt a massacre. As I desired to learn more of the location of their camp, I consented to meet Sitting Bull with six men under a flag of truce, halfway between the two forces.

With Lieutenant Bailey[3] and five privates I went out to meet him, the regiment taking up a commanding position in the rear. Sitting Bull spread a large robe on the ground and prepared to talk with much formality. I explained to him that it was useless for them to contend against the white race; that if they would discontinue their warlike attitude and depredations and go upon a reservation, I could assure them of the goodwill of the government and my earnest efforts in their behalf; but all this was fruitless. They scorned the friendly proposition and scoffed at the idea of any power being able to subdue the Sioux warriors. Sitting Bull said that Almighty God had made him an Indian and not an agency Indian, and he did not intend to be one. He said there never was a white man who did not hate the Indians, and there never was an Indian who did not hate the white race. They were at that time flushed with victory. They believed the Sioux warriors superior to any body of white troops. During the conversation, through the interpreter, named Bruguier, a half-breed, I told Sitting Bull that I knew when he would be on the Yellowstone and where he was going. This so surprised him that he instantly changed from an adroit, mild-mannered man to an enraged savage. His appearance was more like that of a wild beast than a human being. Every feature showed his intense emotions and fierce nature. His strong jaws were firmly set, and his eyes were like liquid fire. While we were thus talking, the officers and soldiers, with their rifles ready for action, had been anxiously watching the scene and had observed a few warriors move down from the hills, one at a time, and take position near Sitting Bull. One was observed to place a short rifle under his buffalo robe. This was also observed by the men with me, and by myself. Their object, I learned, was to encircle and destroy us, the same as had been done with General Canby a few years before in the Lava Beds of Oregon. I informed Sitting Bull that unless those warriors returned to the main body of the Indians, our conversation would at once terminate. Seeing our determination and also our readiness for action, he assented. Looking abashed, he told the young warriors to return, which they did very reluctantly; to discontinue the council without violence, and without divulging our purpose, I told Sitting Bull he could, during the night, consider what I had said to him, and I immediately withdrew to my command and then marched back about three miles to the nearest timber and water to camp for the night.

The next morning, the command moved very early in the direction of what we believed to be the main camp of the Indians and, marching about ten miles, came in sight of it.[4] Sitting Bull again sent out a flag of truce, asking for a talk,

Colonel Miles meets Sitting Bull between the lines. W. F. BEYER. DEEDS OF VALOR.

which was granted. I told him my command had come out to bring him and his followers in peaceably, if possible; forcibly, if we must. This was answered with scorn, and I finally told him that I would give him fifteen minutes and no longer to accept the terms of the government. With a huge grunt, he turned on his heel and rushed back, shouting to his chiefs and warriors to prepare for battle. The prairie was immediately alive with Indians dashing in every direction. They assembled [and] took position en masse on the prairie behind mounds and hills, wild with excitement and anxious for combat. My command was deployed into a large, open square, and we moved forward. The Indians surrounded us, assumed a menacing attitude, and set fire to the dry prairie grass. At the end of fifteen minutes hostilities commenced. At the first shot, a soldier remarked, "That shot ends the talk now for some fighting."

The infantry soldiers, presenting but a small target, with their skilled, long-range marksmanship, kept the Indians at a good distance. That, with the artillery fire, was evidently a surprise to the Indians. The troops maintained excellent order and moved steadily on, driving the Indians through their camp, where they abandoned much property and a few horses. Thus they were pursued for two days, a distance of forty-two miles. Wherever they made a stand, the troops would deploy and drive them out. They would never remain for a close decisive battle, although they outnumbered us at least three to one.

They were driven south across the Yellowstone and finally, October 25, sent in a flag of truce, asking for terms. They agreed to go to their agencies and surrender, and placed in our hands five of their principal chiefs as hostages for the surrender of some two thousand of their people. We learned at the same time that Sitting Bull, Gall, Pretty Bear, and quite a large camp had broken away and gone north. Returning to the cantonment, I soon equipped another command, of 434 riflemen and a detachment of artillery, to move north in pursuit of Sitting Bull. That country at that time was entirely unknown. Steamers had passed up and down the Yellowstone and Missouri Rivers, but the Indians had held the country so tenaciously that it had never been surveyed, and it was a blank on the official maps. At times we would find indications of Indians and strike their trail, but the blinding snowstorms of November and December obliterated all traces, and often we were obliged to march solely by the compass. We crossed and recrossed the Missouri River with artillery and loaded trains on the solid ice, the cold being intense. Some days the soldiers were obliged to march single file, taking turns in advance to break down the snow. Usually at night we would camp in the valleys where dry wood could be obtained, but at other times, in crossing the high divides, we could not obtain fuel, and the soldiers were obliged to lie down at night on the snow without fires. Still, they were so well equipped that although they suffered much from the cold, it caused no permanent injury. By dividing my command into three columns, I was enabled to reconnoiter a wider zone of territory; one column, under the command of Captain F. D. Baldwin,[5] struck Sitting Bull's camp on the Big Dry, drove him out, and captured a large quantity of camp equipage and a few horses.[6] Sitting Bull had now been driven far enough north to be practically out of the field of operation, and the command returned to the cantonment.

Within six days, I had organized another command for a campaign against the large camp of Oglalas and Northern Cheyennes under Crazy Horse, Big Crow, Little Big Man, Hump, Two Moons, and White Bull, which was located about eighty miles to the southwest, near the head of the Rosebud and Tongue Rivers. On the last of December [December 29, 1876], I moved up the valley of the Tongue River with 436 riflemen of the 5th and the 22nd Infantry and two pieces of artillery, which I concealed in my wagon train by covering the guns and carriages with wagon bows and canvas, intending to surprise the Indians. The snow was a foot deep on the level, and the streams were frozen solid. During the march, we were somewhat harassed by the Indians, and once they surprised and killed two of our soldiers. As we approached their camp, extending for three miles along the Tongue River, they retreated. Their evident object was to secure a stronger position in the more mountainous country. Skirmishing frequently occurred, and one day [January 7, 1877] our advance guard captured a warrior,[7] three women, and three children as they were returning to their camp. As these belonged to prominent families in the hostile camp, their capture had quite important results. The command advanced into what was known as the Wolf Mountains; well named, as they are rugged, rough, and most unattractive. We were then three hundred miles from the nearest settlement on the west and four hundred miles from the terminus of the Northern Pacific Railroad on the east. In the impending engagement with this powerful body of Indians, defeat would mean annihilation, and it would have been weeks before our fate would have been known. Every officer and soldier realized his responsibility.

On the evening of January 7, the command took up a strong position and camped for the night. The following morning, the Indians were reported in great numbers coming down the valley. They found us ready for action. From a high bluff, with a field glass, I watched them come out of the canyon and move down the valley—at least a thousand or twelve hundred well-armed and well-mounted warriors. They shouted their determination to make it another massacre. In fact, they yelled to the soldiers, "You have had your last breakfast!"[8] The response was equally defiant. When within range, the infantry opened fire, and the coverings were quickly removed from what had appeared to be harmless wagons but now became effective artillery.

The battle of Wolf Mountain. ARMY AND NAVY JOURNAL, 1877.

The Indians completely surrounded the command, but the key to their position was a high bluff in front of the left of our line. To charge and capture this point was a difficult undertaking for our troops. They were, however, gallantly led by Captains Casey and Butler and Lieutenants MacDonald and Baldwin. The last was very conspicuous as he rode at the front of his line, waving his hat. As they advanced, a prominent chief, Big Crow,[9] who had made his followers believe that his "medicine" was so strong that no white man's bullet could harm him, proved the strength of his superstition by his dauntless courage. As the troops, encumbered by their heavy clothing and impeded by the deep snow, ascended the hill, firing as they advanced, this most noted leader dashed out in full view of the soldiers, whooping and yelling defiance with savage bravado. He was gorgeously bedecked in war costume, with eagle feathers reaching nearly to the ground. His strong voice could be heard up and down the valley whenever there was a lull in the firing. He was unharmed for a time, as it is not easy to hit a man when he is in quick action; but some coolheaded soldier fired more deliberately and dropped him dead, just as the troops charged up and took possession of the bluff. This caused a retreat, which soon became a panic and rout of all the Indians in the valley. We followed them a short distance up the valley to make sure of their precipitous retreat and then moved back to camp, masters of the situation and with the great satisfaction that our laborious efforts had been crowned with success. The command then returned to the cantonment. The captives were kindly treated, well fed and clothed, and after keeping them a month, I sent three of them with an interpreter to the hostile camp with a message demanding their surrender. The Indians were surprised to see their relatives alive and to learn that they had been well treated.

After the engagement of January 8, the Indians had retreated west to the base of the Bighorn Mountains and camped in the deep snow, where they suffered from the intense cold and many of their horses died from exposure. Thus the demand for their surrender came at an opportune time. The result was that a delegation of nineteen chiefs and warriors[10] came down to the cantonment to learn what terms would be granted them. They were told that they must surrender their arms and war ponies; the latter would be sold and the proceeds returned to them in domestic stock; that so long as they remained at peace and complied with the directions of the government, they would be justly treated.

The meeting of the captives and their relatives, who came in with this delegation, was one that fully illustrated the Indian character. The women were hysterical with emotion; they bewailed the misfortunes and woes of their race, and at the same time they shed tears of joy at seeing again those nearest and dearest to them. The Indian warriors scorned to show any emotion of grief, joy, or fear. One was observed to take up a little child in his arms with the utmost tenderness, yet his face was as motionless as a bronze statue. One beautiful Indian girl looked in vain among the warriors for the face of her lover, and although she inquired anxiously for him, she was turned away by them with some thoughtless remark or jest, little realizing the depth of the heart wound they were inflicting. We were unaware of this romance until it resulted in a sad tragedy. One morning, a sharp report was heard coming from one of the tents occupied by the Indians, and it was found that the young Indian maiden had committed suicide with a small pistol that she had concealed all the time since their capture. Her companions then reported that she was overcome with grief because her lover had not come in to see her, but it was afterward learned that he knew nothing of the warriors leaving camp; that he was away hunting at the time and did not return until several days after their departure—too late to join them.

The delegation, upon returning to camp with the conditions before mentioned, found their people willing to accept our terms; and the whole camp, over three thousand, moved over the divide and down the valley of the Tongue River en route to the cantonment. At the mouth of Otter Creek, they were met by a runner from the Spotted Tail agency, who urged them to come in there and

The surrender of Little Chief. NELSON A. MILES. *PERSONAL RECOLLECTIONS AND OBSERVATIONS.*

surrender, saying they would be granted better terms and be with their friends, etc. The camp halted, and a delegation of over one hundred principal chiefs and warriors came down to see if more liberal terms would be granted. They were told that they must surrender at the agencies or to the military in the field; that the country must be cleared of hostile Indians. With all the power I possessed, I urged them to discontinue their hostilities and accept the best terms they could get from the government, assuring them that if they did, I would cease to be their enemy and become their friend. At the close of my remarks, absolute silence prevailed for at least five minutes. Those were most anxious moments. They were to determine peace or war. Finally Little Chief, a noted warrior and their principal orator, came forward with great dignity and deliberation and threw back the rich buffalo robe from his shoulders, like the toga of a Roman senator, finally letting it drop until it remained suspended from his belt. In making their oratorical efforts, some of our politicians remove their collars and even their coats, but this Indian orator threw off everything above his waist, displaying the scars of the Sun Dance on his upper arms and breast. His manner, movements, and gestures were the perfection of dignity and grace. With eloquence and deep feeling, he recited the misfortunes of his race, their devotion to their country, and their effort to defend and retain it. Finally he said, "Your terms are cruel and harsh, but we are going to accept them." I have never heard more welcome words. They meant peace instead of war, friendship instead of hostility, prosperity instead of desolation, and safety and security in place of terror. To make their assurance doubly sure, White Bull, the head warrior of the Cheyennes, said that he would remain as hostage for the good faith of the Cheyennes; Hump, the leading warrior and most popular man of his tribe, said he would remain for the good faith of the Oglalas; and others did the same until I checked them, saying it was enough. They had manifested their willingness to pledge their lives for their tribes and race. Little Hawk, the uncle of Crazy Horse and a prominent chief, promised that within a certain number of days he would bring in Crazy Horse or have him surrender at the lower agencies, and this promise he kept. Within a short time, more than three hundred came in and surrendered; the remainder continued their journey south and surrendered to the agencies, except Lame Deer's band of about three hundred. These declared they would never surrender. Those that came in surrendered their arms and ponies and afterward remained at peace. Sitting Bull, who had been concealing his small following, retreated to Canada.

When the Indians had become settled and confidence restored, I organized a command to go after Lame Deer's camp, then on the upper Rosebud. We moved up the Tongue River, passing over the trail of the Indians when they moved from that valley to the Rosebud, and making a day's march beyond, went into camp for the night [May 5, 1877], believing that the Indians would be watching us from the hills. After dark, I took a battalion of mounted troops and made a forced march directly across the country for about thirty miles, and before daylight concealed the command, sending out three Indian scouts in different directions to look for signs of Indians. They soon discovered smoke rising above Lame Deer's camp, about fifteen miles distant. I crawled up behind a bluff, and looking through my field glass, could discern what appeared to be a mist or light cloud against the foothill. So keen eyed were the Indians that they said it was the smoke of a village and that they could see ponies grazing.

To approach it without being discovered was an art. Our Indian guides took us up one ravine and down another in a winding course, always keeping some object between the command and the hostile camp. We finally rested and waited for the night. After midnight, we started again, and just at the dawn of a beautiful spring morning, we passed up a tributary of the Rosebud on which the camp was located. I detached one company of mounted men under Lieutenants Casey and Jerome,[11] with orders to charge up the valley and stampede the horses, while, with a battalion of the 2nd Cavalry, I attacked the camp. This was successful, and four hundred fifty horses, mules, and ponies were captured.

As we dashed up to the village, I told our friendly Indians to call out to the hostiles that we would spare their lives if they surrendered. The retreat of several of the Indian warriors was cut off, and they laid down their arms. I rode up to the principal chief, Lame Deer, extending my hand, and said, "How, how, cola," meaning friend. He took my hand, and as I was trying to assure him of safety, in the intense excitement a white scout rode up behind me; before I could check him, [he] covered the Indian with his rifle. Evidently suspecting treachery, Lame Deer jerked his hand from mine, grasped his rifle, stepped

The Lame Deer fight. NELSON A. MILES. *PERSONAL RECOLLECTIONS AND OBSERVATIONS.*

back a few paces, and fired. As he did this, I whirled my horse to the right, and the bullet passed by my breast, killing a brave soldier nearby. The chief was instantly killed by Captain Whelan,[12] and the fight continued until fourteen warriors were killed and many more wounded. The Indians who escaped were driven into the rough, mountainous country and followed until they finally surrendered to the south agencies.

Thus ended Indian hostilities in that vast country. When peace and security had been fully established, one of the first steamboats to come up the river in June 1877 brought my wife and little daughter, from whom I had been separated for nearly a year. With them came a sister of Mrs. Miles, Miss Elizabeth Sherman. These were the first white women to visit that remote region and call a soldier's camp and bivouac their "army home," but they were soon followed by the families and relatives of other officers and some of the soldiers.

Winter Campaigning Against Indians in Montana in 1876

FRANK D. BALDWIN[1]

Winners of the West 9, no. 10 (September 1932): 2–3, 8

In summer, the Indian was prepared for war; in winter, wholly unprepared. In summer, they had their thousands of ponies, which they could depend upon for remounts and means for transporting their supplies. Their food supply consisted of buffalo and other game, which in abundance was always in close proximity. The troops were necessarily encumbered with heavy wagon and pack trains which must, under strong guard, follow from camp to camp, and never did the troops have more than one mount, which in a few weeks became exhausted from excessive marching and lack of forage. Under these conditions, it is readily seen what great advantage the Indian had over the troops in the way of mobility. It was only after strenuous efforts that the troops would come in conflict, except at the discretion of the Indian, who was ever watchful and took advantage of every opportunity to attack and harass the troops and emigrants either on march or in camp.

When the first snows came and winter set in, the Indians always gathered in large camps near their agencies, in protected localities in the vicinity of abundance of wood and excellent grass. During the summer, they had gathered plenty of meat and robes for the winter, but their ponies were poor and must be recuperated and in condition for the summer's raids, either against the white man or the buffalo.

They would enter into treaties with the government, promising to remain in perpetual peace, the government promising them everything that the fancy of the Indian might suggest, which was seldom if ever fulfilled by either party. During the winter, the Indian would secure a plentiful supply of the best arms and ammunition from the traders, giving in exchange buffalo robes and other valuable products. In fact, it was during the winter that the Indian prepared for war, and in the summer waged a most relentless war upon our frontiers. After years of experience, this was realized. One of the best and oldest maxims of war is "Strike your enemy in its most vital point and time." First its bases of supplies, then at a period of least preparedness. This maxim was finally observed, and with most gratifying results, but it entailed the condition of the greatest exposure and hardship that ever civilized troops underwent and overcame with success crowning their efforts.

We will now attempt in a way to give you a word illustration of a winter campaign in Montana.

Following the unsuccessful and in one sense disastrous campaign of Generals Terry, Crook, and Custer against the Sioux and confederated bands of Indians in Montana during the summer of 1876, their troops were withdrawn from the field, leaving Lt. Gen. Nelson Miles, then colonel of the 5th U.S. Infantry, with his regiment and six companies of the 22nd Infantry on the Yellowstone, with headquarters at the mouth of Tongue River.

The withdrawal of the troops had hardly been completed when Sitting Bull, Gall, and other leading chiefs with their following returned to the field of their summer operations. Emboldened by their success during the summer months, they were now in prime condition for war, which they urged without hesitation, attacking our troops who were escorting wagon trains, and even the troops en route on the road.

On October 21, Colonel Miles, with the greater strength of his regiment and one field gun, met Sitting Bull and his following on Cedar Creek, a small tributary of the Yellowstone, flowing from the north. A conference was held between the heads of the opposing factions. After an hour's effort to reach some terms as to cessation of hostilities, without result, the battle opened and continued until dark. It was resumed the following morning, when the superior marksmanship, coupled with the nerve and the discipline of the troops, had its effect. The Indians were driven from the field, abandoning much of their plunder.

On returning to the cantonment at the mouth of Tongue River, it was learned that Sitting Bull, Gall, and other leading chiefs, with a large following, had gone north after the Cedar Creek fight, while a considerable number had recrossed the Yellowstone, going south to join Crazy Horse, who had located his following on the Tongue River in the Wolf Mountains.

The colonel determined to go for the Indians who had gone north without delay. To do this, a command was organized composed of four hundred fifty infantry, two field guns, scouts, and a train of twenty-five six-mule teams [and] wagons, loaded with necessary supplies to their full capacity.

This command crossed the north of the Yellowstone the early part of November 1876. The snow was from one to two feet deep on the level, and a blizzard raging. Had the men not been clad with an abundance of extra wool and fur garments, mostly improvised by themselves, their suffering would have been to the limit, but so well clad were they that their exposure to the extreme cold resulted in no permanent disability. On two occasions before we reached the Missouri River, we were obliged to bivouac in the snow without fuel of any kind.

After a most fatiguing march of seven days, we reached the Missouri River opposite Fort Peck, an old trading station. At that time, the country we had traversed was virtually unknown. To determine our course, we were obliged to rely on the compass almost entirely.

Reports were received that Sitting Bull had moved up the river. Fortunately the river was frozen over. The colonel having decided to follow the Indians, we crossed to the north bank with six companies of infantry and one field gun and train, proceeding up the left bank of the river as far as the mouth of the Musselshell, about the same climatic conditions obtaining, but we did have an abundance of good, dry cottonwood for fires.

Finding no traces of the Indians, it was decided to endeavor to recross the river and thoroughly examine the southern tributaries of the Missouri. At this point, the current was very rapid, the ice was broken up, and the river covered with floating ice. Several miles up and down, it was found that it was not strong enough to effect a crossing, and the only way to get over it at all was by rafts, two of which were constructed of dry cottonwood logs lashed together with lariats and chains. The first one was launched all right and boarded by a dozen men, who attempted to make the crossing, but after pushing out through the ice floes a distance of forty or fifty feet, we were struck by a great sheet of ice that skidded well up on the raft and came very near wrecking us, but the men on shore had hold of the tiller rope, which we had attached to the craft, and soon pulled us to the shore, but wet through and a wrecked raft as a result.

We were no more successful with the second raft, except one man did cross on it but was wrecked in returning.

During the construction, launching, and efforts to float these crafts, many men had been thoroughly drenched and were suffering from the cold. We all felt that the commanding officer should help us out. The medical officer [Maj. Henry R. Tilton] was consulted. The fires were all right so far as they would reach, but while one side of the person next to the fire was being roasted, the opposite side was freezing. Hot coffee was suggested, but it would take an hour to prepare it; besides, we only had the limited ration and could not afford to use it all at once. The medical officer was a firm man, a religious man, and a great temperance man. He was asked if he had any liquor among his supplies. His answer was affirmative, he had fifty-two quarters. The remedy was at hand, and instructions were given that each man who had gotten wet during the day should be given a good, stiff dram of whiskey.

There was no hesitancy in coming forward, not only those who had been drenched, but those who had not. Each man was inspected as to his eligibility, [and] it was soon found that no one but the bona fide wet man would be served. Whereupon an officer whose name it is not necessary to mention, but who is now a resident of this beautiful city [Denver], went to the river and deliberately waded out to his waist in the water, and with chattering teeth presented himself and got his dram. No one discovered the ruse until he told it himself. I was not the culprit. Here the old adage was demonstrated again, "A soldier will go to any extreme to get a dram."

The evening of the second day [November 29], scouts came into camp reporting that they had learned that Sitting Bull, with 199 lodges, had moved

Crossing the ice-bound Missouri River. W. F. BEYER. *DEEDS OF VALOR.*

east of Fort Peck and was located somewhere on Milk River, a northern tributary of the Missouri.

Reports as to the movements and whereabouts of the Indians were so conflicting that about the only thing we could do was to investigate as many of these rumors as was possible. As we were not satisfied as yet that the Indians were not somewhere in the upper Missouri region, Colonel Miles decided to divide his command again, each division consisting of three companies of infantry and one field gun. I was assigned to the command of one of these battalions, which was to retrace our steps down the river, taking the wagon train, which by this time was empty, to Fort Peck, under instructions, if possible, to find Sitting Bull's camp, attack it, and follow him as I deemed advisable.

We must keep in mind the fact that there had been no letup in the severity of the weather, entailing, more than ordinarily, obstacles which must be surmounted to ensure any kind of success. The companies were small; I had only 121 men in the ranks, with a large, cumbersome train to protect. No long forage and only four pounds of grain to the animal per day, which was soon exhausted, and two days' ration on the person.

The following morning, December 2, as I was about to move out, the colonel said to me, "Baldwin, you know my plans and what is desired to be accomplished. I know you will do the best you can. I shall be anxious until I hear from you. If you meet with ill success, I can take responsibility for the movement; if you are successful, it will be very creditable to you. I hope you will be successful. If you do no more than keep them moving, you will do well."

Arriving at Fort Peck early on the morning of December 7, I learned that the hostiles, numbering two hundred lodges, were camped at the Fort Buford road crossing of Milk River, twelve miles from Fort Peck. I determines to lose no time and at once set to work organizing for the enterprise: three officers mounted, one hundred men, one hundred rounds of ammunition, and two days' rations on the person; ten packs and two riding mules, twenty thousand rounds ammunition on packs; extra man with pack to lead and prevent escape of animals; mounted men and four packs in advance to break the trail through the snow; two companies, remainder of pack train, one company bringing up the rear.

In this order the command silently left camp at 9:00 P.M., moving well outside of the stockade which surrounded the fort, so as not to arouse Indians who were held inside under guard and prevent the possibility of these notifying the hostile camps of our movements. We soon swung back to the road and, as rapidly as practicable, floundering through the snow, reached a spot about a mile from Milk River without anything unusual occurring, but here a lone Indian put in an appearance. [He] only remained a few seconds, when he wheeled about and disappeared out of sight as suddenly as he had appeared.

He was the outpost of the hostile camp. Quickening our pace, we soon struck the camp, or where it had been a short time before. They had evidently left in great haste, as their campfires were still burning and much plunder lay scattered about. We soon found their trail, which was at least thirty yards wide;

the snow was firmly tramped down by them, which made our progress easier, and we followed with much less fatigue.

Just before daybreak, several Indians rode up to my pack train and attempted to stampede it, but they were very promptly driven out, losing one of their number at least. His body was left on the trail. We at once moved into a bunch of timber and prepared for action, either offensive or defensive. It was bitter cold; still, it was not safe to build fires. As soon as day broke, the command moved in line toward the river, which was only a short distance away. We struck the point where the Indians had just crossed on the ice. Their rear guard was still on the ice, and their long caravans of women, children, and ponies with packs, rushing with frightened haste, could be seen wending their way through the timbered foothills to the south. Fire was opened on the retreating Indians, but soon the opposite bank of the river was lined with their warriors to the number of several hundred.

A brisk exchange of shots was continued for two hours. In the meantime, a large number of Yanktonais had gathered in my rear. These Indians were reputed to be friendly, but we had grave doubts to this, and I felt obliged to take steps to meet any acts of hostility on their part. This necessitated the withdrawing of one company from the front and placing it in my rear, with orders to open fire on the Yanktonais if they did not leave at once, which they had been warned to do, and did so on the deployment of the company. My line was advanced across the frozen river, driving the Indians well back, but as soon as their families had gotten well out of range, the warriors commenced to congregate in large numbers.

Taking into consideration that my rear was menaced by the Yanktonais, who no doubt would have in some degree participated in the attack had I engaged the opposing hostiles in my front, which would certainly have required every man I had to hold them in check, I decided to retire across the river, as a defeat, with the great river, covered with thin ice which was liable to break up at any moment and become impassable, between my command and my base, would have proven most disastrous in case of defeat.

Reaching the north bank of the river without loss, we went into a grove of cottonwood timber and quickly surrounded ourselves with a substantial breastwork composed of logs, where I felt secure, for a time at least, against all the Indians in the country. My men were greatly exhausted with the excessive cold and lack of sleep or rest. Fires were built, food prepared, one half of the command under arms at all times, while the other half were sleeping. All day long the hostiles were in sight, often venturing so close that they were in fairly good range when shots were exchanged. As the day advanced, the thermometer went lower, and by the middle of the afternoon, a furious blizzard was oncoming from the west.

About 5:00 P.M., the Indians had entirely disappeared; our worst enemy, the cold blizzard, was increasing its fury. My men were not prepared to withstand it very long without ample food and protection. I had learned from past experience that these severe storms last from three to five days without cessation. I decided to return to Fort Peck. After preparing and consuming all the food that remained, the packs were adjusted, and we started on the return tramp,[2] satisfied with the results of our efforts, as we had driven the Indians out of their winter camp at the most inclement season of the year. The suffering of the troops, although great, could in no way be compared with that of the Indians, including that of their women and children.

With the pack train in the lead to break the trail [and] the raging storm in our faces, the march was necessarily slow. The men began to get numb, and some of them more or less listless, which caused drowsiness. It was not long before they would throw themselves in the snow, sound asleep. Any of you who have ever been at the point of freezing will realize that these were your sensations and feelings.

This was a condition that must be met and overcome. We were on the great plains, no shelter or fuel available. A man once down could not be aroused by a simple shaking or dragging him. Hence, six or eight of the strongest men of the command were selected and, with fixed bayonets, placed in the rear, [and] an officer in rear of each company with orders that if a man laid down, he was to be probed with the bayonet if he did not move instantly when spoken to. These orders were effectually carried out. A long rope was attached to a mule and strung out to the rear. The men took hold of this and would hang on like grim death. Occasionally the mule would put to a slow trot the men holding onto the rope, which caused a quicker pulsation of the blood. This, of course, was beneficial.

Overcoming these trying conditions, the command reached Fort Peck at 7:00 A.M. on the ninth, with no other damage than frozen ears, fingers, and feet. Fifty-seven men of the command were treated for these causes at the hospital. As an example of the character of the well-disciplined and thoroughly seasoned soldiers, we will give an instance following this most trying, hazardous, and exacting experience of my life. I had sent a mounted man on with directions that breakfast should be prepared for my men. It was in readiness as soon as the men could lay off their equipment and thaw out a little. After consuming this bountiful and well-prepared meal, the men were turned loose on the carcass of a large buffalo, which had been killed near the camp the day before. This was entirely consumed by noon, when they contentedly took their blankets and slept until supper time.

The mercurial thermometer had frozen up during the night, but the spirit thermometer registered forty-two or better below zero; a little chilly for an eighteen-mile night march through the snow. To allow my men to recover somewhat from their extraordinary exposure of the past two days, I was obliged to remain at Fort Peck a few days. I could learn nothing definite as to the point to which the hostiles had retreated; still, I felt sure they had gone south and would probably establish themselves on some one of the tributaries of the Missouri River, and as the Redwater presented the most favorable conditions on account of timber, etc., I decided to make the head of this tributary my next objective field of operations.[3] Repairing the transportation, gathering a supply of buffalo meat, we remained in camp three days. On the fourth day, we started the entire outfit down the left bank of the Missouri, following the main road toward Fort Buford, hoping to mislead the Indians as to my intentions. We marched to Wolf Point several miles further east than was necessary. Having secured the services of two excellent scouts, [Joseph] Culbertson and [Edward] Lambert, I left Wolf Point at nightfall with three sacks of grain for one hundred fifty animals and three days' rations for the men.

We were entering a country wholly unknown, in the midst of winter, and without any delay it was at least five days' marching to our cantonment (Tongue River). Before leaving Fort Peck, I had sent by couriers a request to the cantonment that supplies be sent down the Yellowstone to meet me. I remained at Wolf Point one day[4] and then crossed the river. I had to unhitch the teams and drag the wagons across on the ice by long ropes on account of the thin ice. Accomplishing the crossing successfully, we moved up Wolf Creek for a few miles, then crossed a small divide into the valley of Redwater. Here we halted a few hours for rest. The snow was so deep that often we were obliged to dig our way through heavy drifts, which delayed our progress and added an unusual amount of fatigue to both men and animals. After a few hours of rest in this, our first camp on Redwater Creek, we again started moving up the valley until dark, when we camped for the night, only allowing small fires to be built at daybreak. The following morning, December 18, 1876, found us again on the move, floundering through snow, carefully holding to the valley so as not to expose our whereabouts.[5]

About 1:00 P.M., as we were nearing the head of Redwater Creek and the bluffs, which was the divide between the Yellowstone and the Missouri Rivers, an Indian mounted was discovered in our front, and shortly thereafter, smoke was plainly seen rising from the Indian camp, not more than two miles away. Had we been mounted, a few moments would have found the command in the Indian camp. Scarcely slackening our pace, the train was closed up, forming in four columns, the infantry in line, one company in front and one on each flank, with a small guard in the rear. We moved forward as rapidly as possible direct for the camp, which was soon attacked; the Indians were driven out, thoroughly stampeded, leaving quantities of plunder.

The camp consisted of 122 lodges, many of which were left standing. Sixty head of stock, buffalo robes, meat in large quantities, and nearly every kind of supplies such as are usually issued at their agencies—such as sugar, tea, flour, calico, red cloth, blankets, etc.—were found in this camp and fell into our hands, and such as could be made useful was loaded into the wagons; the balance was destroyed. I will here mention an instance that demonstrated the minds of my men. From causes incident to the campaign, there were nearly forty of the men riding in wagons, not being able to endure the fatigue of keeping in the ranks. When the order for formation for attack was given, there was not one of these men that did not join his company and, struggling along as best they could, remain there until the affair was settled.

My camp for the night was made near that just vacated by the hostiles. We had secured an abundance of food and hundreds of robes and blankets, each man utilizing what he wanted for his comfort, enough being left so that even the animals had a covering, and for once every man and beast was comfortable, despite the fact that the thermometer registered forty and more degrees below zero. Subsequently these robes and blankets were distributed among the men and were made up into garments and sleeping bags of some sort and added greatly to the comfort of all. The next morning, camp was broken and the march was continued over the divide and down into the valley of the Yellowstone, where we halted for the night. The Indians had hovered about our camp all last night and on our flanks all day, and just before the sun set, the camp was attacked quite vigorously, but the Indians [were] quickly driven away.

From this camp, I sent a courier to the cantonment reporting my whereabouts and saying that we had an abundance of rations, in fact everything but forage, and it would not be necessary to send supplies. But the train had already started, which we met about noon the next day, loaded with good eatables and sundries for both men and beasts; also a note from Colonel Miles, in part as follows: "I am delighted to learn that you have been successful in your engagement and without loss. I sent Captain Ewers[6] out with supplies for you. I want to see you as soon as you can get near enough. Take what mounted men you want and come in in the night."

As soon as we had gotten comfortably supplied, after dark I mounted my famous horse, "Redwater," which had carried me night and day more than three hundred miles during this, the most severe and exhausting, as well as exacting, campaign, considering its short duration, that I have ever experienced. Accompanied by one mounted man, I started for the cantonment about thirty miles distant, arriving at 2:00 A.M., December 21, 1876, when I was greeted by a most hearty and gratifying reception.

We had not only kept the Indians moving, but had two spirited encounters and destroyed and captured large quantities of their supplies, and some of them were killed.

Terror of the Badlands: The Sioux Expedition, Montana Territory, 1876 and 1877

EDWIN M. BROWN

Edwin M. Brown Papers, Montana Historical Society, Helena

>Written for John L. Penwell by Ed. M. Brown,
>Trumpeter, B Company
>CANTONMENT ON TONGUE RIVER

The 5th U.S. Infantry, under command of Col. N. A. Miles, left Fort Leavenworth, Kansas, July 12, 1876; the command comprising six companies of said regiment, viz., Companies B, E, F, G, H, and K. After a long and tedious ride, after leaving the cars at Yankton, Dakota, on board the steamer *E. H. Durfee*, we at last reached the mouth of the Rosebud, on the Yellowstone, where we left the boat and joined General Terry's command, which was then stationed at that point.

With this command, we proceeded up the Rosebud in search of the trail of Sitting Bull, who was supposed to be camped somewhere on the river. The third day out, about noon [August 9, 1876], one of our Ree Indian scouts came galloping back and reported a large body of Sioux coming in the distance; we could see a heavy cloud of dust rising up above the treetops, and we knew only a large body could be able to raise such a dust. Our Indians put on their war bonnets, painted themselves, and rode in the advance, prepared for battle. There was a great commotion on both sides, for they could be seen also preparing for action. As our wagon train came to the top of the hill, they (the supposed enemy) saw it, and in a moment a mounted man was seen coming towards us from them. After he came in view, he was recognized as an officer of the 7th U.S. Cavalry, and it was General Crook's command that was before us. They were about to open fire on us when they seen [*sic*] our wagons and recognized us instantly. Soon amicable feelings were restored, which a moment since was all hostility.

One of our Indians ventured a little too close before they recognized us, and the consequence was that he met his death from the unerring aim of William Cody, "alias" Buffalo Bill, who was performing his duty as scout for General Crook. We laid over a couple of hours, during which time the officers had formed some conclusion in regard to the route which was to be taken.

Our regiment started back the same night for the Yellowstone, a distance of about sixty-five miles. We marched all that night and stopped at daylight, made coffee, and again started on the road; we made the Yellowstone about 4:00 P.M. That was one of the most difficult marches the 5th Infantry ever made, for it was through dust and burning sand, which nearly suffocated us; when we stopped at the Yellowstone, I assure you that there was more than one sore and blistered foot, both among the boys and officers, for they marched as well as we did, for they had no horses on this trip. But I take notice they provided themselves with horses as soon as they got in the post, so as not to be caught afoot again.

We got aboard the steamer *Far West* that night; started down the Yellowstone, for Colonel Miles had received orders to patrol the river and to station troops at various points to prevent Indians from crossing. Company H, 5th Infantry, was stationed at Stanley's old ford, near a stockade which was built by Colonel Custer in the expedition of 1873.[1] They had been there but a few days when the Indians paid them a visit; the Indians fired a few ineffective shots and left.

Company B, 5th Infantry, was stationed six miles below Tongue River, the present cantonment. There were only forty-two men in the company, and it seemed but folly to place so small a number on the vast prairie alone, with orders to prevent Indians from crossing; we would have been but a mouthful had Mr. Sitting Bull visited us with a thousand warriors. Meanwhile, Colonel Miles, with the remainder of the command, moved up and down the river on the *Far West,* occasionally visiting the companies stationed at the fords.

We were then taken from this point and stationed at Buffalo Rapids, about twelve miles below on the Yellowstone. We had left our former station scarcely an hour, so the scouts say, when a party of about three hundred Indians crossed the river with their lodges and families. They must have been concealed in the brush on the opposite side, and on account of their papooses and squaws being with them, they remained quiet until we left.

While we were camped at the rapids, the cantonment was being built by the remainder of the 5th Infantry, who had previously arrived from Kansas under command of our lieutenant colonel, J. N. G. Whistler.[2] Our company was then detailed on escort duty, escorting the Diamond R wagon train from a post below us to Tongue River.[3] We remained on duty for about six weeks escorting, when we were relieved by a part of the 22nd Infantry. We reported for duty at Tongue River with the remainder of the regiment. We commenced to erect winter quarters. Every man had to work with his musket by his side, for any moment we were liable to be attacked, for the Sioux kept watch continually on our movements. They often came right in our camp and ran off our stock. There have been about four hundred head of cattle run off since we commenced building the post.

Our quarters were not completed when a scout arrived at camp and reported that the Diamond R was corralled by the Indians about forty miles from the post.[4] We were ordered to pack up with one day's ration in our haversacks. We started at about 4:00 A.M. next morning [October 17, 1876] for the rescue. [We] marched all day through clouds of dust and burning sand, which nearly choked and blinded us; we stopped at sundown, made a cup of coffee, and again took up the line of march. [We] marched till daylight, when we were allowed two hours to rest and get breakfast. After breakfasting, we proceeded up [Custer] Creek. When within about an hour's march of where the train was corralled, our scouts, who were in advance, could be seen coming in the distance, followed by a party whom we supposed were Indians in chase of them, but they proved to be a party of scouts and some of the officers in charge of the wagon train. Presently the train came in sight. The Indians were aware of our proximity and had abandoned the train. The train camped with us overnight.

Next morning, the train started for Tongue River and we after Sitting Bull, for Colonel Miles was determined on giving him a chase, after our coming this far. We marched all that day [October 19]. Parties were sent out to kill buffalo for the command. We camped on [Cherry] Creek; next morning, started very early and marched till about 11:00 A.M., when a scout came in and reported a large body of horsemen coming toward the command. We had come to a valley[5] and halted to rest when the Indians, as they proved to be, appeared on the bluff to our left with a white flag. They sent a chief in with a request to Colonel Miles to come out halfway and hold a council. The colonel granted them this request, [and] with a small escort went out to meet the famous Sitting Bull. They held a long powwow, but no satisfaction could they gain from the colonel, who wanted them to surrender on the spot or fight; they wanted to think the matter over before giving an answer. Colonel Miles said that he would give them ample time to form a conclusion; then, if they did not give satisfactory answer, he would open fire on them. They withdrew a few rods and held a powwow among themselves. Finally a chief rode up to Colonel Miles,

Sitting Bull attacking Miles's supply train. W. F. BEYER. *DEEDS OF VALOR.*

asking him to withdraw his troops and give them till the morning to decide the matter, and they would come and camp with us and give us a satisfactory answer in regard to their surrendering.

In the meantime, the Indians had worked their way all around the command to find out our actual number. They did not like our mode of deploying, for we had a hollow square of skirmishers around the wagons, with skirmish lines on front, rear, and both flanks, and a Rodman gun which was posted on a high bluff to our left frowned down upon them. They left in disgust from their examination, for they had expected to find the troops all huddled in a mass.

The request was granted by Colonel Miles, who marched us back eight miles and went in camp. I suppose the colonel began to think they were shamming and were only asking this request in order to give their camp time to move. Early next morning, we pulled out and started in pursuit of them. Before we got to them, we could see them watching us from the bluffs. Colonel Miles had surmised correct; they were indeed moving their village. We could see them in the distance. They looked like a vast herd of buffalo. The warriors had all stopped back to give us a reception.

When we came up to them, a chief rode out and said Sitting Bull wished to know why we had broken faith and were following them. Colonel Miles replied that they had lied, but as they would not come to camp with him, he would come and camp with them. The chief rode off to the Indians who were occupying the bluffs on the left and front. An Indian was seen setting the prairie on fire about one hundred yards from the command. The colonel ordered a scout to go out and put a stop to his work. The scout rode and shouted at him, but fired at the same time. The Indian rolled over on the burning grass. We did not stop to ascertain if he were dead, but marched straight ahead towards the Indians which occupied the bluffs ahead of us. The bluffs were literally swarming with the "red varmints."

By this time, the prairie was a solid wall of fire all around us. After the scout had shot this Indian which set the prairie on fire, the "opera" commenced. Bullets whistled lively over our heads and around us for a short time. Many a strong heart grew weak, as our thoughts flew back to the Custer massacre. We began to think our case was hopeless, for indeed the odds were against us. No doubt had we been cavalry, they would have killed every one of us, but as we were enabled to fight them on their own principles, it was much to our advantage.

As we were down in the ravine, the big gun, which was planted on the summit of a high bluff, broke loose, which scattered them in all directions. They kept so far away after the cannon opened on them that it was only our best marksmen [who] were able to cause them to bite the dust.

We fought them all that day through fire and smoke, which nearly suffocated us. That night we camped on five hills, companies occupying the hills, with the wagon train in the valley in the center. As we did not camp with Sitting Bull that night, we did camp where he camped the night before. Shots were fired from the picket posts nearly all night, for some of the most venturesome of the Indians would creep up with the intention of picking them off their posts. But many of them were mistaken, for the sentries were not asleep, as dead bodies of Indians could be seen outside of the picket lines, which was evidence of a vigilant guard.

All night the redskins could be seen dancing through the flames and yelling like fiends. It reminded one of a representation I once saw of hell in the panorama of Milton's *Paradise Lost*. Many was the poor wretch that never shut an eye that awful night. Fires shone all around us. It made me think of torch-light processions. A fellow was almost afraid to go to sleep for fear he might never waken. I was one of them; all my sins rose up before me like huge mountains. I began to think of the good advice which I had scorned. I began to think of home and friends and almost wished I was back in the Buckeye State once more, far from the scenes of carnage and warfare, where one could lie down peaceably to rest without the fear of his scalp being torn from his cranium by these red and bloodthirsty fiends. I assure you I was not the only one, for I heard more than one remark that they wished we were back in camp at Tongue River. If there ever in this world [was] a case of homesickness, I was the worst case at that time that ever was known.

The morning dawned at last. The Indians were still ahead of us, ready to renew the contest, but not willing to come to close quarters. We had scarcely moved out of camp when we received a volley from the rear, wounding two men. It seems the Indians had laid in the bluffs behind us for this purpose; all the injury we received on this trip was two wounded and several horses killed. After this volley from the bluffs to the rear, the Indians were only seen occasionally in the distance. They kept continued watch of our progress. They were surprised at the tenacity with which the "walk-a-heaps," as they call us, followed their trail.

We kept direct on their trail. We could track them much faster and easier than before, for the trail was clear and distinct. Then, their ponies were more liable to give out with no grass. We had a little forage on hand and managed to get along without grazing our stock. They would occasionally fire a shot at us to gain our attention, that their families might gain on us and make the Yellowstone before we reached them; no use, for we were on their trail, and Colonel Miles said he would not give up till he caught them, if he followed them to the Bighorn Mountains. We knew that the colonel was a man of his word; therefore, we dared not grumble, but went cheerfully on.

We followed them about seventeen days, till we came to the Yellowstone, where they had crossed. The Indians could not have been far ahead, for lodge poles, ponies, both dead and crippled, were scattered all along their trail, for they abandoned them in order to make faster progress.

Before we reached the Yellowstone, a party of Indians rode out to meet us with a flag of truce. While the colonel was holding a conversation with the Indians in front, some redskins were seen to the left and rear of the column. They were endeavoring to cut off our wagonmaster from the command. He had gone out to bring in some ponies that were straggling on the prairie. The men on the artillery wheeled the gun around and fired a shell among the Indians with such precision that it burst immediately beneath the horses of the Indians; blankets, saddles, horses, riders, and everything were seen flying in all directions. Had it not been for the promptness of the artillerymen, the wagonmaster would have been a gone "gosling," but the novelty of the affair was to see a conversation of peace in the front of the command and war in the rear. The Indians in front rode off after holding a short council; they said they would go to their people and if possible get them to come back and make peace.[6]

We stopped at the river and began to prepare to cross, when a few Indians were seen on the opposite bank. They wanted to see the "paleface chief." Colonel Miles sent Yellowstone Kelly, the scout, and a few more scouts over the river to bring them across. They came over and held a long powwow and smoked the pipe of peace with the colonel. The result was that about eleven hundred of the band surrendered to us. The Indians said Sitting Bull would not surrender, for he, with a few chosen warriors, had left this band before they came to the river and had started back towards Fort Peck to join a larger band of hostiles.

Colonel Miles took five of their principal chiefs as hostage that they would report to their agencies.[7] He sent the chiefs under guard to Standing Rock, Dakota. He gave the remainder of the band thirty days' permission to hunt buffalo for winter supply.

We again took up the line of march for Tongue River. [We] took on supplies for a forty-day scout, for Colonel Miles was determined that Sitting Bull, Crazy Horse, and the rest of the hostile bands should not have a moment's peace in which to hunt their winter's meat. This trip was about three hundred miles. We arrived at Tongue River November 3, 1876, laid over one day, and started the morning of the fifth. As I kept no accurate account of this trip, I must give the camps and distances as near as possible from memory.

We first crossed the Yellowstone, marched fifteen miles, and went into camp; plenty of wood and water. Our pack mules, on starting out that morning, did not fancy the idea of being decorated with camp kettles, bundles of blankets, frying pans, and cooking utensils of various description, and forthwith raised a row; the kettles, pans, and everything flew in all directions.

[We] started early next morning; marched only nine miles in order to have wood and water, [and] went into camp. Next day we marched all day till dark, making about thirty-two miles; no wood, burned sagebrush to cook with. Next day we marched twenty-nine miles and struck the Dry Fork of the Missouri; went in camp, wood and water. Next day we took up line of march, following in the dry bed of the river; about 2:00 P.M., it commenced to snow. [We] marched till dark, went in camp; still snowing, continued till midnight.

Next day [we] marched twenty-five miles to big sand hills [and] went in camp; plenty of moccasin tracks crossing river. Next day [November 15] started early and marched about ten miles, when we left the riverbed and struck across the prairie in direction of Fort Peck. About 2:00 P.M., the mounted party came back and reported Indians on the bluffs in the front. Skirmish lines were deployed and the scouts sent out. Presently they came back and reported that it was only two miles to Fort Peck.[8] The Indians were friendly (for a wonder) and were only watching us through curiosity. We went in camp, making a march of twenty-two miles. The thermometer stood at five degrees below zero; grew very cold after dark.

[The] distance from Tongue River to Fort Peck in a direct line is considered 108 miles, but the route we came was over one hundred thirty. We laid over two days on the opposite side of the Missouri from Peck. The command divided here. Six companies went across the river with Colonel Miles and went in camp, the four companies under Captain Snyder[9] remaining. Companies with the colonel were A, B, E, G, H, and J; companies with Captain Snyder were C, D, F, and K.

Colonel Miles, after taking on more supplies, started up the Missouri on the north side. We marched about two hundred miles when Company B, under Captain A. S. Bennett,[10] left the command and struck off in a northwesterly direction; our object was to make for a trader's post on the Missouri.[11] Everything went smooth the first day; plenty of buffalo, antelope, deer, elk, etc., so there was no necessity for our starving. Next day we started early. In the distance, to the left, could be seen the Crazy Woman's Mountains. About 9:00 A.M., our guide left us and told the captain to be sure and keep to the right, on the tableland. He was going over the bluffs to see if he could see the river. But instead of going as the guide directed, the captain took us to the left and marched us about eight miles, till we found ourselves hemmed in on both sides and front by huge and almost perpendicular bluffs. There was no alternative but to turn back, which was done, and as we gained the top of the tableland, the guide could be seen in the distance coming toward us. He knew that we did not take the route he pointed out and had come back to find us. As it was getting late, we went in camp on the open prairie. Some of the boys found a buffalo wallow with stagnant and slimy water in it. We filled our kettles and gathered some sagebrush to cook coffee. It was relished as well as if it had been made of pure spring water.

Next morning we struck out towards the Crazy Woman's Mountains till about noon, when we went in a southerly direction towards the pine bluffs. We were then about eight miles from the trading post, and as it was late, we went in camp in the bluffs; plenty of pine wood but no water. We melted snow and cooked our supper. After supper we melted snow for breakfast so as not to be delayed in the morning.

Early next morning we struck out, thinking that we could make the post about noon, but with the rough traveling through the pine bluffs, it was late when we arrived at the Missouri River. The post was on the opposite side, and as it was unsafe to undertake to cross with our teams on the ice at night, we went in camp. Next day we crossed, first taking over the mules, then the empty wagons, afterwards carrying over the baggage. We camped at the trading post all next day, during which time the captain performed what duty he had to do, which, I think, was to make investigations in regard to the amount of ammunition and arms the trader had on hand and to issue an order prohibiting him to trade the same to Indians.

Next morning we started, on the south side of the river, to join the command of Colonel Miles. After three days steady marching, we saw the campfires of the command among the bluffs. After reaching them and reporting, we took up the line of march for Tongue River. They had a much worse time in crossing the [Missouri] river than we had, for the ice was floating all along the river. It seems the place where we crossed was very tough, as it was in a bend, but a mile on either side of this, the ice was much broken. They made rafts and crossed the mules, wagons, and baggage, afterwards crossing the command. The best joke is on the colonel; for while he was on the raft, it broke from its mooring and carried him downstream till it struck a snag. There he was, our shipwrecked colonel, as the boys called it. He was on the raft from 8:00 A.M. till 4:00 P.M. [November 25]. Every effort to throw ropes to him proved fruitless, when a lad of Company E, 5th Infantry, volunteered to take a rope out to him. He took the rope and shouted, "God save our gallant General," leaped into the cold water, and swam through the floating ice and rescued the colonel from his unpleasant situation. The colonel was so well pleased that he gave the lad thirty days' furlough.

While the colonel was on the raft, a herd of elk ran into camp and the picket commenced firing into them. The colonel yelled out, "What is the meaning of that firing?" Some rogue responded, "Indians coming." As the colonel was down below the bank out of sight and could not see what was going on, [he] began to cry "Fall in! Fall in!", giving orders in a true military style deserving of credit. After the true state of affairs were communicated to him, his appearance became more calm, but I would not have been in the fellow's boots that shouted "Indians" for a mint of money, if the colonel had found him out, for I almost know a volcano of wrath was burning in his bosom, which was ready to burst with a vengeance on the guilty wretch who raised a false alarm.

After a few hours' labor, everything was safely landed on the opposite bank, with exception of Lieutenant Baldwin, who with three companies started towards Fort Peck on the north side of the river. The companies under Baldwin were G, H, and I of the 5th Infantry.

Our command took up line of march [on December 2] through the pine bluffs till we came to Crooked Creek; camped on this creek, and the next day left creek and struck the Musselshell, crossed over and struck Squaw Creek [December 5]; we followed Squaw Creek for about seventy-five miles through some of the most winding canyons and over rocky bluffs, which greatly impeded our progress. Often we had to cut down the hills in order to pass our wagon train. For nearly two weeks, it was just such traveling, after which the prairie became more level.

We struck the trail of Captain Snyder, which was going in the direction of the post. Followed trail all that day [December 12] till dark, stopped to make coffee and cook some buffalo meat, and again took up the march. As it was a very dark night, we could scarcely keep the trail; such feeling with hands and striking matches I never heard of. The scouts went ahead and fired their guns in the air. All we could see was a flash, then all was darkness. We would go in the direction of the flash till we came to the scouts, and they would then go ahead again. About 11:00 P.M., we struck [Sunday] creek and went into camp. The weather began to turn severely cold. Next day we again took the trail and followed it till within three days' march of Tongue River, when our mules began to die from starvation. We found dead mules along the trail which died from Captain Snyder's command; we also seen [sic] wagons which they had abandoned in order to not impede them. We sent a scout in to have them send us out forage enough to bring us in. Our mules grew so thin that you could almost read a newspaper through them. After the forage arrived, we stopped over a day that the mules might fill up and recruit their strength.

We arrived in Tongue River in good condition, with the exception of a few frozen feet and hands. The thermometer stood at about thirty-five degrees below zero most all the way back from the Missouri. Just imagine taking a cup of coffee from the fire boiling. Before getting it to your mouth you could cut it out in slices; how's that for sliced coffee for dessert?

Let us follow Lieutenant Baldwin. After leaving the command, he marched the three companies direct to Fort Peck. On his arrival there, he was informed that Sitting Bull and his band were camped on the river about eight miles below the post. They left their wagons here, and with pack mules, they started that night [December 2] for the hostile camp. They marched within a few miles of them and laid over to make an early attack on the Indians.

At daylight [December 7], they came in sight of the camp, which to the surprise of the troops outnumbered them by five to one; the Indians numbered about six hundred. They knew the troops were coming and were all prepared to meet them. They did not seem desirous of fighting, but motioned the troops to leave them, saying there would be another massacre similar to Custer's. Lieutenant Baldwin is a man of prudence and, knowing that his number was too small, withdrew while he had a chance, for no telling what moment the Indians would turn on them and corral them, and then there would be no hopes of success.

They went back to Peck and took their wagons and started for Tongue River to inform Colonel Miles of the whereabouts of the hostiles. He marched his men day and night till they almost dropped in the ranks (the boys tell me this is a fact). They say they imagined all sorts of things; some thought they were riding in steam cars, others that they were about to get in an ambulance when some unseen hand would pull them back again, others thought they saw parks, lakes, and cities, when it was nothing but the vast snow-covered prairie before them. I hope I may never have the pleasure of taking a trip under Lieutenant Baldwin. Colonel Miles marches us hard enough, but then he is reasonable and permits us to rest a moment when he sees we are tired. Before they reached the cantonment, their rations ran short and they were compelled to send after; almost read a New York *Herald* through their carcasses.

As I am not of a romantic turn of mind, I will not try to describe the grand scenery of Montana more than just given, but shall leave it to those of a more romantic nature. But if it be romantic to tramp over a wild, barbarous country, with the expectation of losing one's "top knot" in the bargain, I will take none for mine, but shall close this little sketch of the Sioux campaign and bid you adieu, hoping I have given satisfaction, I am,

Most respectfully yours,
Edwin M. Brown, Company B,
5th U.S. Infantry,
Camp on Tongue River,
Montana Territory.

Campaigning against Crazy Horse

DAVID T. MEARS[1]

Proceedings and Collections of the Nebraska State Historical Society
15 (1907): 6877[2]

In 1875–76, I was in Washington, D.C. In January, I received a letter from General Crook, who was then in command of the Department of the Platte, to report to him at Cheyenne, Wyoming, as soon as possible to organize his transportation for a summer campaign against the Sioux and other Indians who were then on the warpath, killing settlers and committing all kinds of depredations. I landed in Cheyenne in due time and went to work at once. My particular business was to organize pack trains.

Right here is a good place to describe a pack train. It consists of a lot of medium-sized mules, on which to carry supplies for the army when we cut loose from wagon trains. We could then keep up with the command, let the soldiers go when and where they would or travel as fast as they wished. The pack train was right at their heels, with their provisions, blankets, ammunition, tents, or feed for the horses. A pack train generally consists of about sixty pack and ten riding mules, led by one bell horse. An army horse will do, just so he is gentle and is a good kicker. Mules are very playful, and the horse that kicks, bites, and fights them most is the horse that suits them best. Keep the bell horse in hand, and Indians will get very few mules in case of a stampede.

We had eight such trains as above described when we left Cheyenne for the Bighorn country in Wyoming. besides about one hundred wagons divided into four trains, each train under the supervision of a wagonmaster and one assistant.

About March 1, 1876, we left Cheyenne on our Indian hunt. The weather was very cold nearly all the time we were gone on that trip. We went via Ft. Laramie and Ft. Fetterman. The latter fort was close to where the village of Douglas, Wyoming, now stands. From there we went over to the Dry Fork of Powder River, where we had our first alarm from Indians. We had some beef cattle with the command and every few days had one killed. There were about a dozen left, and as Indians are very fond of beef, they will run some chances to get the cattle. One night they shot the herder, ran off all our beef cattle, and we never saw any of them since. Our scouts from here were sent out in advance to locate the Indian village. They were to meet the command at the crossing of the

Crazy Woman's Fork of the Powder River. The scouts returned and reported that they had seen signs of Indians, and after a needed short rest were again sent ahead to locate, if possible, their village.

After a few days, the scouts returned with what they called good news. They had located a village of about sixty tepees. For two days, we had orders not to shoot under any circumstances, nor to make any undue noise, as we had to make a sneak to surprise the Indians. The night before we jumped the Indians was one of the coldest nights I had ever experienced. We left camp about 2:00 A.M. of March 17 and opened the campaign on St. Patrick's Day. Several companies rode through the village, shooting right and left, and stampeded the Indians, who soon rallied, returned, and bravely defended their families. A great many people have an idea that Indians are not brave, that they will only sneak on the enemy; but let such be undeceived. Indians will average with white men in bravery. I noticed on this trip that when the troops were surprised in camp, as occurred several times during the summer, they would try to dodge every bullet that came. After the fight in the early morning, several soldiers were found killed. How the Indians suffered in killed and wounded we never knew, as the troops never went back to the battlefield, but left their dead in the hands of the Indians.

General Crook decided to return to Cheyenne to reorganize for a summer campaign against the same Indians. We were in rendezvous camp near Cheyenne several weeks. We had about six hundred men, having left about three hundred to guard the wagon train. We also had eighty Shoshones, eighty Crows, and fifty Pawnees as allies. They made good scouts and did good work. They all acted very brave, each tribe vying with the others to outdo in acts of bravery.

I had a very close call myself at this Rosebud fight. We were half a mile from the creek and needed water badly, especially in the hospital. I started with several canteens, went on foot, and kept well out of sight, going down a ravine. There was a Shoshone Indian who had left his saddle at the creek when the fight started and was going after it. We kept together for several hundred yards. He then left me and went alone for his saddle, as I could strike the creek in a nearer way. The first thing we knew, the Sioux had us cut off from the command. There were eight or ten of them who opened fire on us. I got behind a bank and stood them off until some of the troops came toward me and drove the Indians away, but they got my Indian friend. When I saw that the Sioux had him going ahead of them, I knew he would not last long. He turned around and fired at the Sioux, and when they found his gun empty, a couple of Sioux ran up so close on him that he had no time to load his gun. The Shoshone jumped off his pony and sprang over a bank of the creek. A Sioux who was at his heels lit upon him and stabbed him in the back with a butcher knife, leaving the knife in the Shoshone's back. After the day's battle, I went directly to find my Indian and found him lying on his face, dead, with the knife through his heart. I pulled it out and returned it to its scabbard, which was lying on the ground where the Sioux Indian had left it in his hurry to save his own scalp. He did not even scalp the Shoshone, which proves what a great hurry he was in.

The Rosebud battle lasted from about 9:00 A.M. until near sundown, when the Indians withdrew and were soon out of sight. The battle was fought on June 17, 1876. The Indians had gained their point, which was to hold us there until they could get their camp moved about forty miles from the Rosebud and go into camp again on the Little Bighorn, where eight days after, Colonel Custer met them and was utterly defeated by them. We had ten men killed and several badly wounded in this fight. The Indians suffered a good deal, as we afterwards learned. General Crook returned with his command to the wagon train and went into camp on Goose Creek to await orders from General Sheridan. We were in camp a long time without hearing from the outside world. The Indians were very brave, thinking they had got the best of it at the Rosebud, and I guess they had as much to crow over as anybody. They would often fire into our camp.

At last, about the Fourth of July, a courier came from Ft. Fetterman with the news of the Custer massacre, which had been known all over Europe eight or nine days before we heard of it, although we were within sixty miles of where it occurred. General Crook had tried to get in communication with General Terry, who was in command of the Department of Dakota, but the scouts always returned with the cry of "too many Indians" between the commands. We were in camp until troops arrived from all points that could spare a corporal's guard, when we broke camp and relieved the monotony by marching through the Indian country with two thousand men and ten days' rations. We went where we wished with a command so large, though the Indians still had the best of it numerically, and their knowledge of the country gave them a chance to run or fight. We soon made a junction with General Terry on the Yellowstone River, but the Indians had scattered, and we were not molested much by them.

We left General Terry and started for the Black Hills, thinking to come across some Indians. They had divided up into small bands, which would give them a better chance to depredate against the settlers in the vicinity of Deadwood. General Crook scoured the country all he could, but as the rainy season had set in it, was very difficult to do much scouting. The next twelve days was one of the hardest marches United States troops ever made. We came down to horse meat for rations, and that so poor there was not fat enough on a dozen horses to season the gruel for a sick grasshopper. The horses were not killed until they gave out and could go no farther. With the last meal of beans we had in the pack train, I concluded to have quite a blowout and invite the general to breakfast. Next morning our cook got all the beans he could get together for one grand mess. He cooked them in the evening, and some soldiers came around camp and offered him $20 for the beans. The cook told me of the offer. I told him not to sell for any money, as I had invited General Crook and staff to breakfast. Well, the next morning, the beans were all gone—stolen. The cook swore he did not sell them, neither did he eat them, but I will always think that the cook got what he could eat and sold the balance.

It rained every day. The horses were giving out, soldiers walking through mud. In the evening when we went into camp, there was not a thing to eat but meat from poor horses, ten or fifteen of which were killed each evening and eaten with no seasoning whatever. Seventy-five miles from Deadwood, we surprised a large band of Indians, about forty tepees, American Horse's band. We kept out of sight until daybreak, when we made the attack. Several were killed on both sides, and a great many soldiers wounded. American Horse soon had runners out to other Indian camps. Crazy Horse was soon on hand with all his force and made it very interesting for us for six hours.

After this battle, called Slim Buttes, we fared a little better for something to eat. We had buffalo meat, and besides the Indian ponies were fat and we had plenty of them. I really thought that horse meat was good and wondered why we did not eat more horse at home. We could not follow the Indians on account of lack of rations, and the only thing that I could hope for was that the man who stole the beans was killed.

We arrived at Deadwood and were met by the citizens of that place with open arms and a generous hospitality that only those bighearted miners know how to give. From there the command came to Ft. Robinson, Nebraska, where a great many Indians had come in to give themselves up. We found them to be generally women and children and old and decrepit men with no guns. This was just what the fighting Indians wanted—to get rid of those noncombatants who were only an encumbrance to them. Let the government feed the squaws while the bucks fought the troops.

General Crook was not satisfied with the surrender and decided to make a winter campaign against Mr. Crazy Horse. We started again from Ft. Robinson and Ft. Laramie in November 1876 with a large command, which required an extra amount of transportation to carry supplies. We arrived at Crazy Woman's [Fork and] went into camp, having seen no Indians, but the scouts had been busy and had located a large village in the Bighorn Mountains, on the headwaters of the creek we were then camped on.

Here again is where the pack trains came into play. We cut loose from the wagon train and proceeded up the creek, where it would be impossible for wagons to go. It began to get cold. After a march of twenty miles, we laid in camp all day expecting to make a night march. We dared not build a fire, as the Indians would see our smoke. Cold? Well I should say, "Yes." Our spread for dinner was frozen beans, frozen bread, with snowballs and pepper on the side; supper the same, less the beans. We began to think that the government was treating us rather cool. Horse meat would have been a Delmonico dinner.

The scouts came into camp in the evening and reported the Indian camp, supposed to be that of Crazy Horse, Standing Elk, and Young American Horse.[3] We made the attack at daybreak [November 25, 1876] and completely surprised the Indians, who soon rallied and came very near turning the tables on us, when eighty packers left their mules in the rear of the command and joined in the fight, and soon had the Indians on the retreat, We looted the village and burned everything we could not take away. This was the most telling battle against the

Sioux that was fought during that 1876 campaign. It had more to do to make them surrender than all the other fights. We found that Crazy Horse was not in that fight, but was camped on Powder River. Had he been there with all his determined braves, the battle might have had a different termination. He was so disgusted with that camp for retreating and giving up everything that he would hardly let the starving, freezing Indians come into his camp. His action in this case had its effect on him at his final surrender. General Crook made up his mind to try to strike Crazy Horse if possible before he left the country, but the cavalry horses and wagon mules were getting poor, the snow so deep, and the weather so terribly cold that it was beginning to tell on the men, and he concluded to give up the chase. We made a detour of a few days' march on the Powder River and headwater of the Belle Fourche and Cheyenne Rivers, which brought us to Pumpkin Butte, where we camped on Christmas Eve, just twenty-six years ago this day, and a colder day and night I never slept out of doors. Several mules froze stiff and fell over during the night. So on December 25, we left Pumpkin Buttes and Crazy Horse behind and started for Cheyenne, which caused a general rejoicing among men and mules. The backbone of the Indian war was broken, but the main vertebra was still defiant, viz., Crazy Horse.

The next summer, General Crook started again. He sent troops in all directions to bring in all Indians that had not previously surrendered. They had been coming in during the winter to Chief Red Cloud's camp, which was then situated near Ft. Robinson, Nebraska. General Crook went personally to Fort Robinson to superintend the surrender as they arrived. They were coming and going all the time, and he intended to put a stop to that. So he issued an order that no Indian should leave the agency without his permission. That made the Indians "heap mad," and they concocted a scheme to kill him. They were to call a council to talk with him about the surrender, when someone was to shoot him and have a general fight. An Indian, whom General Crook had befriended at some time, told Crook all about the plan. When the time came for the talk, the general had the whole place surrounded with troops. When the Indians saw such an array of soldiers, they thought better of the plan, and the assassination did not take place. The Indians appeared to be undecided what to do, whether to go out again on the warpath or to surrender.

Crazy Horse was still out and had runners going back and forth all the time. They kept him posted about affairs at the agency. General Crook concluded to disarm the Indians and set a time for them to appear and give up their arms. When the time arrived, three-fourths of the Indians started out again on the warpath. They went about twenty-five miles and entrenched themselves on Chadron Creek, just four miles from where I am now writing. The general had "Boots and Saddles" sounded, and a large body of troops took along with them a couple of mountain howitzers and a Gatling gun. When they arrived within gunshot, no shot having been fired as yet, the commanding officer called to the Indians under a flag of truce and told them he would just give them five minutes to surrender. When the five minutes were up, he let go his cannon, and the flag went up instantly. They were taken back to the agency, where they were all disarmed.

Crazy Horse was on his way to the agency, the general having sent friendly Indians out to meet him. His marches were very slow, as his ponies were very poor, the squaws and children worn out, cold, and hungry. When within twenty miles of the agency, he stubbornly refused to go further, but the general sent him word by other Indians that he would bring him in if he had to call all the troops in the United States. He sent some of his aides-de-camp with plenty of provisions, and wagons to haul the women and children. After a long talk, and being assured he would not be hurt, he reluctantly agreed to come in. There was a general rejoicing among the Indians when he agreed to come in, and he was met by nearly all the Indians at the agency. It was an imposing sight to see all those Indians, several thousand in all, headed by Crazy Horse himself, who was riding beside Lieutenant Clark of Crook's staff. He was escorted directly to General Crook, who shook hands with the chief and directed that he should be made comfortable as well as all his people. The next day was set to disarm Crazy Horse's band. They had come into the fort, and the agency was located a short distance away. In the morning, Crazy Horse personally was not at the fort but was said to be at the agency, where he was found by the Indian police that had been sent after him. But he refused to return to the fort with them; the police so reported on their return to the fort. General Crook sent the police back—those police were all Indians—to take an ambulance with them and bring Crazy Horse to the fort. We all expected it would bring on a big fight, as the Indian police were very determined, but they brought him in without much of a demonstration from the other Indians. He was put in the guardhouse, where there was the usual guard, and as a precaution, several Indians were detailed as extra guards. Crazy Horse was very sullen and morose. All of a sudden, he jumped up, brandishing a large knife, and made for the door. An Indian jumped on his back and pinioned his arms. The soldier guard sprang forward with his gun at a charge. Crazy Horse was seen to fall. When the excitement was over, Crazy Horse was dead, having been pierced through the body with either a knife or the bayonet of the soldier. Thus died one of the greatest Indian war chiefs that ever fought a battle with the white men.

# PART SEVEN

The Odyssey of the Northern Cheyennes, 1871–90

Some Experiences with the Cheyennes

GEORGE A. WOODWARD

United Service 1, no. 4 (April 1879): 184–95

The latest blossoming of our Indian policy, as exemplified in the case of Dull Knife's band of the Northern Cheyennes, has attracted widespread attention, and not a little adverse comment. It exhibits, in epitome, the baneful consequences that must ever attend the working of a system of divided responsibility in the conduct of Indian affairs. Not being in possession of sufficiently authentic and detailed information on which to base an intelligent judgment, I shall not attempt to impute blame to either the civil or military officials connected with this affair; had I such information, I should have neither the disposition nor the right to criticize or find fault, my purpose and only legitimate province in this paper being to jot down for the entertainment of the readers of *The United Service* some experiences of my own with the Northern Cheyennes in times gone by, when Dame Fortune was more benign to them than she has proven of late. I cannot, in passing, however, restrain expression to the thought, that has doubtless occurred to many of us, of how great the pity is that gallant soldiers, the peers of the best humanitarians in all the refinement and susceptibilities that belong to gentlemen, should be compelled by the stern requirements of duty to turn their arms, under such circumstances as attend this occurrence, against a people whose wild love of liberty and home could make them do, and dare, and die so bravely as have the Cheyennes.

In the spring of 1871, the 14th Infantry, of which I was then the lieutenant colonel, was ordered to Forts Laramie and Fetterman, in the Territory of Wyoming; the regimental headquarters, with six companies, going to the former post, and I, with the remaining four companies, to the latter. Fort Fetterman, named for the gallant but unfortunate officer who, with his entire command, was slaughtered by the Sioux Indians near Fort Phil Kearney in 1866, [was] situated at the junction of La Prele Creek and the North Platte River, and was, at the time of which I speak, the extreme outpost of the Platte River region. Fort Laramie was eighty miles distant in a southeasterly direction, but for all that, was our nearest neighbor. Medicine Bow Station, on the Union Pacific Railroad, ninety miles to the southwest, was the nearest point to us touched by that great artery of travel and commerce. We had a mail once a week, which we got by sending a party to Horseshoe Creek, halfway between us and Fort Laramie, where it was met by a similar party from the latter post, between whom our outgoing and incoming mails were exchanged. We had, besides, telegraphic connection with Fort Laramie and with department headquarters at Omaha.

At this time we were nominally at peace with all of the northwestern tribes. This peace was not exactly the kind that politicians habitually denominate "profound," but was rather a one-sided affair, in which we were to presume all Indians to be peacefully inclined until the contrary were shown, a principle that did not operate beneficently as to parties that might meet the copper-colored gentry at the moment their savagery—emotional, like the insanity of the modern murderer—got the better of their plighted faith.

The situation of Fort Fetterman made it a convenient house of call for roving bands of the Oglala Sioux, the Northern Arapahos, and the Northern Cheyennes, the two latter of which tribes, although claimed by Red Cloud to belong to his jurisdiction, and therefore appurtenant to his agency, repudiating such claim, had been allowed by the government to receive their supplies at Fetterman, and the post had therefore become practically their agency, and its commanding office *ex officio* their agent.

I had been in command at Fetterman but a short time, when one day runners came in bringing intelligence that Little Wolf,[2] one of the three headmen of the Cheyennes—the other two being Turkey Legs and Dull Knife—would arrive the next day with the larger part of the tribe, who were returning from the great autumn hunt in the Powder River country. And the next day, about 10:00 A.M., the sentinel whose beat commanded a view up the valley of the Platte reported the approach of Indians. Although still some miles away, we could easily, by aid of field glasses, separate what to the unaided eye seemed only a dark, moving mass into its constituents of warriors, squaws, children, ponies, and dogs.

The column came on, moving slowly, but with such order and precision as gave token of skilled leadership and soldierly discipline. Arriving near the post, a halt was called and immediate disposition made for camping, the labor involved falling, as all labor does among savages, upon the women. The unloading of the ponies and their picketing out, the erection of the tepees, the carrying in and stowing away of the bundles of robes, bags of pemmican, strings of dried meat, and the few utensils employed in culinary operations, that constitute the impedimenta of Indian marching, all devolve upon the squaw.

Leaving the women to their labors, Little Wolf, accompanied by a select few of his warriors, came up to the post for a talk with the commanding officer, stopping on his way at the log cabin just outside the fort, where lived our guide and interpreter, Joe Merival, "Old Joe," as he was popularly called, whose services were indispensable on all occasions of councilor talk. Joe was a grizzled Mexican whose whole life had been spent among the Indians, formerly as a trapper, but for many years in the capacity he held at Fetterman, of guide and interpreter. Joe was a character, and his dialect was something all his own. Indeed, until use made it familiar and to some degree intelligible, his speech needed interpreting nearly as much as that of the Indians themselves. One of Joe's dialectic peculiarities was the excision or clipping off of the last syllables of words, as though he disapproved of redundancy and boldly rejected what he regarded as surplus in language. For example, "Bible" with Joe became "Bibe," and "you ain't the Bibe" was Joe's mode of telling one with whom he differed in opinion that he was not infallible. Joe was also indifferent to gender and habitually spoke of woman—"gooman" he called her—as "he." On one occasion he was telling a party of officers about a game of monte he once saw in Mexico, and was illustrating how deftly the dealer cheated the players. "But Joe," said one of the officers, "I should have thought they would have knifed him." "Oh, no, no," said Joe; "*he* was a gooman."

Well, Little Wolf, having secured Joe's services, came to my office, and filing in with his dusky aides, each as they entered shaking my hand and ejaculating, "How," he took a proffered chair, while the others ranged themselves around the walls of the room, squatting or sitting on the floor. The Indian in council is the most deliberate of mortals, and beyond uttering his "how" on entering—and that is not invariable—not a word will he speak until the pipe has been produced, slowly filled with kinnikinnick, passed to the end man at the right, by him lighted, devotionally tendered first, by a downward gesture, to Mother Earth, and then, by an upward one, to the Great Spirit above, then a whiff or two taken, and the pipe handed to the next man towards the left, who, repeating the proceedings of the first, hands it to his left-side neighbor, and so on till its circuit of the assemblage is completed. At least once, often twice or three times, the pipe makes its rounds before the talking begins. Then the chief or headman of the party rises, offers his hand to the person he is about to address, says, "How," and begins his speech. On this occasion, Little Wolf, after telling me that he was glad to see me and that his heart was good towards me, went on to say that they had had a prosperous hunt in the fall and had procured a large supply of skins, which they had dressed and were now anxious to trade for the various articles of use and ornament that suit the Indian taste. Besides our regular post trader, there had gathered near the post a number of others provided with Indian goods, in anticipation of this coming in of the Cheyennes, and Little Wolf wanted me to say what rules should be observed in dealing with them. He inform me that he had "made soldiers"—equivalent to posting sentinels—and that none but those I saw with him would be permitted to leave their village, or camp, till he had my permission to open trade. Having listened to what I had to say in reply, and receiving permission to make the best bargains he could, and with whom he chose, he and his companions took their departure and spent the rest of the day in stalking solemnly about from one trader's camp to another, getting from each of the competing dealers a "feast," consisting mainly of coffee and crackers, and receiving at the same time proposals for their robes and other peltry. The next day, Little Wolf gave his people loose rein, and they were soon discovered everywhere about the post. Many of the women and children, more curious than avaricious, dropping out of the crowds that pressed around the counters of the post trader, would come up to the officers' quarter and hang for hours about the windows, peering in and frequently flattening their noses against the panes to get a more satisfactory view of our interior life, which seemed to possess for them irresistible attraction. Most of our ladies were sufficiently familiar with Indians not to be seriously alarmed by their presence, but to the more timid and nervous among them, the sudden apparition of an aged crone, whose hand, no doubt, had often brained or scalped the white victim of Indian savagery, would be far from exhilarating. Others of the Indian women, however, were not a whit behind their sisters of the pale face in their propensity for shopping, and would stand hour after hour, ranged two and three deep, along the counters in the post trader's storehouse, feasting their eyes on the bright beads and particolored calicoes and flannels with which his shelves were loaded, producing from time to time, for the purposes of barter, a buffalo tongue, dried and cured, or a dressed skin of some of the smaller objects of the chase, which up to that moment had been carefully hidden somewhere about their persons. Some of them on this occasion perpetrated a fraud on the post trader that for a time gave promise of largely increasing their personal estate at his expense. In the rush of business, which he was taking at its flood, he and his assistants had no time to make any orderly disposition of the wares he was receiving, and as fast as gathered in, the buffalo tongues and peltry were tossed under the counters, discovering which, some of the Indian women managed quietly to detach one of the boards forming the front of the counter and, reaching in, would abstract the wares already once paid for and unblushingly swap them again.

From this time forth, during nearly my whole stay at Fetterman, I had a good deal of experience with the Cheyennes. Every five days, when they were in the neighborhood, they came in to receive their rations, the issuing of which nearly always had to be prefaced by a councilor talk, the object of which, however it might at first be masked by a pretence of other business, generally proved to be a demand for an increased supply of subsistence stores. For a long time, they insisted that I was not giving them credit for the number of people they had, and to prove it, they would bring to the councils a bundle of small sticks of uniform size and length, which constituted their census, each stick counting for a person, and they thought it very hard that I would not accept this return as final and conclusive. I invariably told them that whenever they would submit to be counted, I would increase the number of their rations if my enumeration proved their claim to be well founded, but until such time, I would adhere to the existing practice of estimating their number from the number of tepees or lodges constituting their village. In common, I believe, with Indians generally, they were averse to being counted, whether because of some superstition or because their actual number being once ascertained, it would not be so easy to magnify it on occasion, I do not know. However, they finally yielded, and at an appointed time, they formed a great circle in a grassy spot just across the Platte, and accompanied by my adjutant and quartermaster and the interpreter, I rode over and, passing slowly around inside the circle, made my count, while each of my companions made his, and when we were through, we compared and verified our several enumerations. The result was that they were found to have a considerably greater number than I had been issuing to. On this occasion, the whole Northern Cheyenne tribe were present, with the exception of one small band whose numbers were pretty accurately known, and as this was the first time that an acual enumeration of them had been successfully attempted, the information obtained was not without value.

Of the three headmen of the Cheyenne, Dull Knife[3] was, I think, greatly the superior. Tall and lithe in form, he had the face of a statesman or church dignitary of the grave and ascetic type. His manner of speech was earnest and dignified, and his whole bearing was that of a leader weighted with the cares of state. Little Wolf had a less imposing presence, but looked more the soldier

Little Wolf. BUREAU OF AMERICAN ETHNOLOGY, SMITHSONIAN INSTITUTION.

than the statesman. Turkey Legs looked his character, which was a very bad one. His appearance was mean and forbidding, and bespoke the very incarnation of treachery and cruelty. The ascetic-looking Dull Knife was, however, not superior to a fondness for sweets. Somebody about the post had given him once [a] can of preserved pineapple, and this he had found so toothsome that he resolved if possible to have it included in the issue of rations made to him. Accordingly, the next issue day, he told Joe that he wanted him to ask the colonel for some pineapple. Joe told him that it was useless to ask for it, as he would only be refused. "You do as I tell you," said Dull Knife. "You ask the colonel for it, and accident (Joe, for accidentally) he may be in humor, and may give it to us."

Turkey Legs distinguished himself on one occasion at Fetterman by a wonderfully successful fishing exploit that he and his people accomplished with a seine belonging to one of the companies at the post, which had been loaned him on condition that all the pickerel he should take with it should go to the company, he retaining such other of the finny denizens of the Platte as might be captured. Taking the seine, the whole band—men, women, and children—proceeded to the river, and selecting a spot where the channel was much narrowed by a projection of the opposite shore, the men, wading in, stretched the seine across the upper end of the narrowest part; while the women and children, mounted on their ponies, formed a line across its lower end, and cling in upon the party with the seine with a great noise of shouts and splashing of water, they drove the fish into the seine as it was slowly swept shoreward, the *net* result being a take of nine hundred fish, of which the pickerel, the part going to the company, filled a handcart to overflowing. Much elated at their success, they were out to repeat the experiment, when Joe, fearful that they would depopulate the stream, forbade further attempt in that direction.

The only hostile act of which any portion of the Cheyennes was guilty during the time the tribe was under my supervision—at least the only one committed anywhere in the region over which the protection afforded by Fort Fetterman could be regarded as extending—was an attack made by a small party of them on a quartermaster's wagon train at La Bontee Creek, twenty-two miles from the post on the Laramie road, in the month of May 1872, and the subsequent killing of Sergeant Mularkey of my command, who, being in charge of the mail party en route for Horseshoe Creek the same day that the wagon train was attacked, had incautiously ridden ahead of his party, and coming upon the Indians just after they had been repulsed in their attack upon the train, fell a victim to their rage and disappointment. In this affair, the Indians succeeded in killing the sergeant, taking the mule he rode, and escaping into the hills before his party could come up, the first intimation the latter had of the presence of the hostiles being their coming upon the dead body of the sergeant lying in the road, watched over by a faithful dog that had accompanied him.

This was the work of Cheyennes; not, however, of those of them that had been receiving the bounty of the government at Fort Fetterman, but of a small

The murder of Sergeant Mularkey. HARPER'S WEEKLY, 1889.

band of irreconcilables under a leader appropriately named Old Bear, who persisted in maintaining an attitude of hostility towards the whites despite the influence and example of their more tractable brethren. Indeed, the great body of the Cheyennes were on the very day of this occurrence encamped near the post, preparing to start for their hunting grounds on the Powder River, and their presence there materially complicated the solution of the problem as to who were the perpetrators of the Mularkey murder, for Indians never, when it can be avoided, expose themselves with their women and children to the danger of reprisal and retaliation. Their own maxim of conduct being "a life for a life," their presence with their families near a military post is pretty good prima facie evidence of their innocence of any act of killing committed in that immediate neighborhood. The Cheyenne village on this occasion was perfectly commanded by a gun that could at any moment have been trained upon it, hurling destruction and death upon all it contained, and I found it very difficult, therefore, to believe that with such means of retribution menacing them, the Cheyennes were the perpetrators of this outrage. Besides the Cheyennes, the Arapahos were also encamped near the post, so that the same presumption of innocence as to this particular act existed in their case also, thus leaving the Sioux, roving bands of whom were frequently in the neighborhood, obnoxious to the strong suspicion of being the slayers of Mularkey. Having no mounted force, any attempt to find and take up the trail of the hostiles in time to effect a successful pursuit would be futile. I, however, sent for the headmen of the Cheyennes and Arapahos, and giving them to understand that I was very angry with Indians generally, asked them if they had anything to say respecting this outrage. They, of course, denied all participation in or knowledge concerning it. Then, addressing myself to the Cheyennes, I told them that I had reason to think that the party who killed the sergeant had gone up the Powder River road, the same that they were about to move on, and that I should expect them to find out the guilty ones and arrest and bring them back to me, and that they should recover and return to me the mule and equipments. This they finally promised to do if they could. I did not rely very confidently, however, on anything coming of it all, and therefore my surprise was almost as great as was my gratification when, a few days after the Cheyennes had departed, runners from them returned to the post bringing me word from Little Wolf and Dull Knife that they had ascertained that Old Bear's band were the perpetrators of the Mularkey murder, and that they intended to catch and punish them, and this was supplemented a few days later by the arrival of Little Wolf himself, bringing back the mule the sergeant had ridden. Little Wolf informed me that they had come up with Old Bear's party at night, and that his young men had charged their camp and had captured it and the mule, but that Old Bear and his followers had escaped. Some of this I took *cum grano salis,* but the substantial fact of the rendition of the mule there was no disputing. Having properly acknowledged this evidence of good faith on their part, I made Little Wolf and his companions a present of some rations, and they set out to rejoin their people.

    The most powerful influence operating within our Indian system is that of the trader. From top to bottom of the Indian service, its personnel from time to time changes—all except the trader; he is perennial. Theoretically, he too has his time to fall, but practically he stays. His counting room is the point of radiation of lines of influence as minute as the capillary ducts of the human body, and as powerful. If *his* Indians go to Washington to visit their Great Father, he goes with them; the interpreter, who is probably deep in his debt, varies the utterances of the chiefs to suit his purposes, and by his wily machinations, he manages to defeat all efforts in behalf of Indians that do not coincide with his interests. My relation to the Cheyennes at Fort Fetterman was detrimental, of course, to the trading interest at the Red Cloud agency, where it was claimed these Indians properly belonged, and unceasing were the efforts made to effect a rupture of that relation. The Cheyennes themselves, although connected with the Sioux by marriage and generally allied with them in war, were extremely averse to being associated with them in their village life, for the reason that, being weaker in numbers, they were robbed and lorded over by the Sioux, and for the further reason that the principles and the practice of the Sioux in regard to female chastity differed widely, for the worse, from that of the Cheyennes.

What the Cheyennes most earnestly desired was the establishment of an agency for themselves, somewhere in the northern country, or if that could not be compassed, their continuance under military management at Fort Fetterman. The scheme of the government respecting them was to effect their transfer, peacefully if possible, to a southern reservation, and it was the partial consummation of this scheme that led to the recent tragic event in their history. In all of my councils with them, I persistently endeavored to bring their minds to an acceptance of the government scheme of removal to the south, but without much success. Meanwhile, I regarded it as of prime importance that, pending their final disposition, they be kept away from the Red Cloud agency, because I knew that the influences to which they would be subjected there would be opposed to the realization of the government scheme; moreover, anticipating the hostilities with the Sioux that have since occurred, I deemed it better military policy, while the Cheyennes should remain in the northern country, to have them so in hand that we might utilize them as our allies against the Sioux, rather than add them as a reinforcement to the latter.

Finding my effort to induce them to acquiesce in the policy of a removal to the south ineffectual, I tried to persuade them to ask for permission to visit Washington, hoping that by an interchange of views with the authorities there, either the government might succeed in winning them over to acceptance of its scheme, or if that failed, they might be permitted to have an agency of their own. After repeated refusals to accept this advice, they finally adopted it and, coming to me, asked that I would communicate to the Great Father their request to be allowed to visit Washington. This I immediately did, but the moment was inopportune, for as it happened, Red Cloud was just then on one of his periodical visits to the capital, accompanied by his retinue of traders and interpreters, and the request of the Cheyennes being communicated to him, he was made to say that a delegation from them was unnecessary, that they belonged to him, and that he would represent them. In consequence of this opposition of Red Cloud to their suit, the Cheyennes failed to obtain the personal hearing at Washington which they so ardently desired, and which, had it been accorded them, I cannot but think would have resulted happily both for the government and for them.

Even after my *quasi* agentship had been terminated, and both the Cheyennes and Arapahos had been remitted to the Red Cloud agency for their subsistence and government oversight, they were constantly touching at Fetterman in their journeys to and from the Powder River country and their forays against the Shoshones, and it was seldom that the tepees of members of one or the other of these tribes were not visible near the post. The Cheyennes and Arapahos got along very peaceably together. The latter were only about half as strong in numbers as the former, and although originally among the most fierce and warlike of the Indians of the plains, they were, much more rapidly than the former, taking on a milder type of manners and character. Their declining numbers had doubtless much to do with this decadence from their pristine eminence in savage traits, and they had among them, moreover, a man whose influence probably operated as an auxiliary towards the same result. The man to whom I allude was "Friday," whose singular history, albeit not falling strictly within the purview of my subject, merits a passing notice. The tribe, many years ago, breaking up their village on the Cimarron branch of the Arkansas River, divided into two bands, each taking its own direction. Friday was at that time a boy of about seven years of age. By some misadventure, he found himself accompanying one band while his parents and family had gone with the other. Upon making this discovery, he left the party he was with and started to find the one his parents had accompanied. He lost his way and wandered about for days in a vain search for the right trail, till at last, overcome by hunger, fatigue, and cold, he lay down, as he supposed, to die. A passing trader found him, however, before life was extinct, and carrying him to Missouri, turned him over to the Jesuit fathers at St. Louis. By them he was cared for and instructed, with a view to making him, in after years, a missionary to his people. He proved intelligent and apt, and became a respectable scholar in Hebrew, Greek, and Latin. When he had attained the age of sixteen, his parents then, for the first [time] having learned his whereabouts, made requisition on the government for him, and with much reluctance, both on his part and on that of the worthy fathers who had so long nurtured him, he was delivered to his parents at a spot near one of the military posts, in what is now the state of Colorado. So little, however, did he joy the prospect of a return to the savage life that as soon as the shades of night had fallen upon the Indian village, he stole forth and made a break for the camp of the party that had brought him out from the states. His attempt at escape was speedily discovered and promptly frustrated by pursuit and recapture, and he was compelled to take up again the nomadic life of the plains. Had he been of mature age at the time of this rendition or, perhaps, had his character been of tougher fiber, the store of language, dead and living, and, let us hope, the precepts of religion and morality with which the good fathers had furnished him, might have proved a valuable equipment for effort on his part toward civilizing and Christianizing his people; but being what he was, only a boy, and sharing with us all that human tendency towards bondage that makes descent into savagery much easier than rising out of it, he became what he was when I knew him—as thoroughly an Indian, to all outward seeming, as any of his companions. Almost his only distinguishing characteristic, beyond his knowledge of English, was a fondness for "firewater" that could only be regarded as distinctive by reason of the proportions it had attained. And yet, despite all this, I believe, as I intimated before, that unconsciously to himself, and imperceptibly by his people, Friday has been an auxiliary of no mean effect in toning down the savagery of the tribe, and so rendering them somewhat more amenable to civilizing influences.

The Arapahos, at the time of which I speak, were without a recognized chief, their headship being divided between Friday and a splendid specimen, the young Indian brave named Black Coal. The two called one day at my quarters on some business just as I had finished dinner, and as I was alone at the time, my family having gone to the states, I invited them to eat; an invitation which an Indian as invariably accepts as does that approximate congener of his—civilization's latest human product—the tramp. My man of all work reset the table with the same attention to detail that he would have given it had my guests been in velvet and ermine instead of blankets and paint. Whether influenced thereto by a sentiment of respect for the aborigines, a hope that he might be gratefully remembered should the vicissitudes of war cast him upon their tender mercies, or simply by the fact of their being his master's guests, I could not say.

Black Coal watched his proceedings with an expression of countenance that seemed to indicate uneasy feeling in his mind, which, had it found vent in words, would probably have formulated itself into "heap dishes, mighty little grub," the to him unfamiliar display of china, glass, and cutlery giving forth a somewhat chilly aspect that was but faintly relieved by the piece of butter, midway of the table, which constituted all the food in sight, pending the warming up of the joint and vegetables. Friday's reminiscences of civilized ways enabled him to possess his soul in patience until the board, duly set, was ready to receive him and his companion, when he still further indicated the training of his youth by displaying a perfect familiarity with the several table articles and their uses, while Black Coal was much hampered in the appeasing of his appetite by the necessity he was under of learning by observation of his more accomplished friend the mode of using the knives and forks and spoons with which civilization has supplemented aboriginal fingers.

My last council with the Cheyennes was a stormy one. It was after Fort Fetterman had ceased to be their appointed base of supplies that one day about five hundred of them came in, hungry and cross, asking for food. At the beginning of the council, they were glum and moody, but not insolent. I received them kindly, but told them that I could not issue rations to so large a number of them without first obtaining permission of the Great Father at Washington, as it was no longer intended that they should be subsisted at Fetterman, but at the Red Cloud agency, all of which they perfectly well understood. I further said to them that as they seemed to be really suffering for food, I would ask the Great Father, by telegraph, for permission to issue them bread and beef sufficient to subsist them en route to the agency; that I might receive a reply that afternoon, but that possibly it would be delayed till next morning; that I would them again in the afternoon and tell them whether I had received an answer to my dispatch or not. At the time for the reassembling of the council in the afternoon, no reply had been received, and upon my informing them of this fact, they began to manifest a very ugly spirit. Two of their young men had been killed by whites just previous to this, between Fort Laramie and the railroad, and one of their speakers commenced arraigning me and the whites generally for this offense, his harangue finding great acceptance with his companions, who, by their grunts of applause and angry looks, were evidently being worked up to a high pitch of excitement. When he had finished, I replied to him that the young men who were killed were stealing cattle, and had no business to be where they were under any circumstances; furthermore, that I had an unsettled account with them in the matter of my sergeant, whom their people had killed. To this they vouchsafed no immediate reply, but one of them, rising with great excitement of manner, ejaculated somewhat after this fashion, "What are you doing in this country, anyhow? You come here and kill our game; you cut our grass and chop down our trees; you break our rocks (prospecting for mines), and you kill our people. This country belongs to us, and we want you to get out of it." Joe having got thus far in his interpreting, I stopped him and directed him to tell the Indians that I had heard all that I proposed to listen to of that kind of talk, and that if they were not more civil I would turn them off the reservation, and if they ever set foot on it again I should treat them as enemies.

The aspect of affairs at this juncture was threatening: The Indians were all armed, while the few of us who were present were unarmed; they were angry and excited, and except for a diversion which most opportunely occurred, serious results might have ensued. But fortunately, just at this moment, the telegraph operator came in and handed me a reply to my dispatch, authorizing me to issue the bread and beef. Transferring it to Joe, I told him to interpret it to the Indians. The effect was magical and strongly controverted the traditional stoicism that they are credited with, for no sooner did they learn the contents of the dispatch than all their sullenness disappeared, smiles took the place of scowls, they crowded around me and the other officers present with a general shaking of hands and ejaculations of "How," and one enthusiastic brave, seizing my hand, intimated to me his opinion that the killing of my sergeant and of their two young men about balanced matters in that line, and that we ought now to drop the subject.

This, as I have said, was my last council with the Cheyennes. The Sioux were becoming restive, and the greed of traders, made potential by the unfortunate system, at the core of which it nestles like the "worm in the bud," had forced the Cheyennes to amalgamate with them and undergo conversion from peaceful wards and possible allies of the government to active and relentless foes. Now, nearly eight years since the incidents I have narrated, old Dull Knife lies stark and stiff among the Nebraska bluffs,[4] his warriors are either dead or in irons, the widows of his braves find refuge with their sisters of the Sioux, and Little Wolf plays the avenger among the ranchmen of the Niobrara.

A Finish Fight for a Birthright

EDGAR B. BRONSON[1]

Pearson's Magazine 11, no. 1 (January 1909): 103–9

Dull Knife's Provocation

To behold the inroads of autumn upon the foliage of a noble forest; to watch a rose fade and see its withered petals fall to earth; to see a beast in its death throes; to witness the last agony of a fellow mortal, even though he be a stranger and nothing to you in the world—any of these is a sufficiently saddening incident to a man of average susceptibility.

Happily enough, therefore, it has come to few men to witness the final dissolution of a people, even though that people be a savage tribe, every page of whose history is dark with deeds of barbarism. Such, however, has been my lot, and the scenes, incidents, and characters of the dread spectacle are as fresh on my mind today as if they were of yesterday.

In the autumn of 1877, I bought my first herd of cattle at Cooper Lake on Laramie Plains, west of the main range of the Rockies. The country lying between the Union Pacific Railway and the Platte was then fairly well stocked and the best ranges occupied. But up to that time, the North Platte River had stood the dead line between the Sioux and the ranchmen, a dead line never crossed by ranchmen, except in occasional trailing parties in pursuit (and usually a hopeless pursuit) of stolen horses taken by the raiding Sioux.

All of the two-thirds of Wyoming lying to the north of the North Platte River, all of the two-thirds of Montana lying to the east of a line drawn through Bozeman and Fort Benton, all of the two Dakotas west of Fort Pierre and Yankton, and all of the northwest quarter of the state of Nebraska—a vast area of roughly three hundred thousand square miles, greater in extent than all of New England with the states of New Jersey, New York, Ohio, Pennsylvania, Virginia, West Virginia, and half of Kentucky thrown in—held no white man's habitation, save the little camp of miners in the Black Hills, and had for its only tenants nomad bands of Cheyennes and of Oglala, Brule, and Unkpapa Sioux, the ancient lords of this most noble manor.

To be sure, a treaty had been had, and the Sioux title proper was recognized by the government over none of this territory excepting a part of the two

Dakotas lying west of the Missouri and north of the White River. Thus, technically, the rest of this great area was open to occupation and settlement, but it was still ranged from end to end by war parties resentful of the treaty terms, which had taken from them the best-beloved part of their domain, the Black Hills, and limited them to the wastes of the Dakota Badlands.

With the country to the south of the Platte more or less crowded with ranches, it was plain the time had come when seekers for attractive free ranges must venture north of the Platte into the Sioux domain; and bar one ranch located by Pratt and Ferris immediately on the Platte River to the east of Fort Laramie, I was the first man to carry a herd of cattle into the heart of the Sioux country, and there locate and permanently maintain a ranch.

Starting from Cooper Lake on Laramie Plains rather late in the autumn of 1877, trailing through the Rockies, by Collin's Cut Off, to the Sabille, thence down to the Laramie River, and down the Laramie to Butch Phillips's ranch, I there crossed to the Platte River, and we were fortunate enough to arrive in time to swim it the very night before it froze over. With the cold weather come on, it became imperative to go into winter quarters, and we wintered on the Cottonwood, twelve miles northwest of Fort Laramie.

In October 1877, over twelve thousand Oglala Sioux were removed from their old agency on White River, a mile east of Fort Robinson, to Bijou Hill, on the Missouri, only to be moved back a year later to what still remains their present agency, between Wounded Knee and White Clay Creeks.

In the months of January and February, accompanied by two men, I made a scouting trip to the north and east down the Niobrara to Pine Creek, crossing north to White River and thence back by the head of White River to my winter camp on the Cottonwood, a journey of sixty days without meeting a single white man.

With my future location decided by this trip, so soon as the cattle could be gathered in the spring, I moved one hundred miles north of the Platte River and took up and occupied White River from its head down to Fort Robinson, twenty miles, and also twenty miles of the Niobrara, averaging fourteen miles to the south of the White River range.

This territory embraced the very heart of what had been the favorite home camping ground of the main band of Oglala Sioux for generations. Indeed, the head of White River was, bar none, the most beautiful country I have ever seen in the West, a rolling hill country, open timbered with pines like a park; with springs of clear, cold water breaking out in almost every gulch; with tall, white limestone cliffs to north and south that gave the valley perfect shelter against winter storms; and all the land matted thick with juicy buffalo grass.

The home ranch I located on Dead Man's Creek, a small tributary of the White River, five miles south of Fort Robinson. While chosen only for its value as a ranch site, this location proved the most fortunate choice I could have made. The Sioux name of the Creek was Wi-nogi-waka-pala, meaning "Ghost Creek," or "Dead Man's Creek" and we later learned that the Sioux had such a superstitious dread of it that no Indian ever ventured near Dead Man's Creek at night. This superstition came from the tradition of a camp of Indians on the Dead Man many years before, which was attacked by a contagion so deadly that not enough living were left to bury the dead. Thus it happened that, while we could never abate our watchfulness, no night raid upon this ranch or the horse herd ranging near was ever made by the Sioux, while ranches far to the south of mine suffered often and severely. Fort Robinson was then a little two-company garrison, which had been built at the close of the Sitting Bull campaign of 1876, at the junction of Soldier Creek and White River, built really to help to awe and hold in check the restless Oglala Sioux, whose agency then lay a mile down the river from the Fort.

But this story deals with the Sioux only incidentally. The people whose virtual extermination I came to witness were the Northern Cheyennes, belonging to Dull Knife's band, captured on Chadron Creek by Capt. J. B. Johnson, of the 3rd Cavalry, in October 1878 and held as prisoners in barracks at Fort Robinson until January 1879. The band numbered 149 people, of whom forty were warriors. Their capture by Johnson was the closing scene of the most remarkable campaign in the history of Indian warfare.

The Cheyennes were natives of these same plains and mountains, highlanders whose hereditary domain embraced the magnificent ranges of the Bighorn and the Black Hills; here through generations were they born, here their dead were buried. Allied more or less with the Sioux, intermarried with them to some extent, here they dwelt and maintained themselves against all comers in a veritable aborigine's paradise, the plains alive with buffalo and antelope, the mountains full of deer, elk, mountain sheep and bear, the streams swarming with fish, and everywhere a thick carpet of juicy buffalo grass that kept their ponies fat as seals. Numerically weaker than the Sioux, they were an infinitely bolder and more warlike race.

But at last, in 1876, came the fatal day that sooner or later arrived for all Indian titles—that which the Pale Face most covets was discovered in the very heart of their domain; gold was found in the Black Hills, and miners began to stream in. This part of the story was well told by General Brisbin[2] (then commanding Fort Ellis) in an interview with a newspaper correspondent:

> That the Indians do not make war unless pressed, you, as a resident here since 1870, must admit. You remember my first operation here after my arrival in 1876. I allude to the rescue of the garrison at Fort Pease, at the mouth of the Bighorn. Some forty whites had left Bozeman and located in the heart of Sitting Bull's country, and without any authority in the world had built a fort there. The Sioux and Cheyennes attacked, and were on the point of capturing it, when the besieged men appealed to me for aid. Sitting Bull had one thousand five hundred warriors, and we had only four hundred men, but we hastened to relieve the settlement. He could have beaten us, but doubtless thinking

it best to permit the removal of the cause of the trouble, he drew off, only too glad to see the departure of the intruders. I had hardly again reached Fort Ellis, when I was notified of the approach of Colonel Gibbon with seven companies of infantry from one direction, and General Terry and Custer with his regiment from another. We all returned to Sitting Bull's country—then the Bighorn and Rosebud fights occurred.

At the first encroachment on their reservation, the Indians had petitioned the government for protection. As usual, the petition was "read and referred." Meantime, their country was being invaded. Small parties of venturesome miners were coming into the Black Hills from Fort Pierre on the east, Cheyenne and Sidney on the south, and Bozeman on the west.

For a time, the Indians waited patiently for the government to interfere in their behalf. Had they considered the long, shameful story of the treatment of the red race by the white, they probably would not have waited so long. Instead of help, more miners came. At last, losing hope of any aid, they went the way all people go in one manner or another directly they find themselves being despoiled—they went to war. War parties attacked the trespassing whites. Quickly the wires brought to the East stories of Indian atrocities, and soon two military columns were set in motion to crush those whom they should rather have been sent to protect.

This was the origin of the 1876 campaign, in which the gallant Custer and his brave 7th were wiped out, and which ended in the defeat of Sitting Bull and the capture of Crazy Horse's Sioux and Dull Knife's Cheyennes. Then we had a treaty, and the Sioux and Cheyennes "ceded" the Black Hills to the government. With proper prompt action in the beginning, this "cession" might have been negotiated with honor to the government and satisfaction to the Indians, and the 7th spared their terrible sacrifice.

In rude old feudal days, when they took a man's land, they usually hacked off his head. But the rude old feudal customs, convenient though they may be, quite shock modern sensibilities. Thus the then-ruling humanitarians of the Indian Bureau decided that Dull Knife's Cheyennes, who were the boldest and most independent of the lot, should be removed six hundred miles south to the Indian Territory, a country and climate with no pleasing prospect for them unless of an early and certain translation—by disease and death—to the Happy Hunting Grounds, which represent the future paradise of the red man.

So away they were marched in 1877 to Fort Reno, a grim band of warriors, squaws, and papooses, their robes, *parfleches,* and other rude equipment trailing on travois. Their war chief was Dull Knife; two senior chiefs, Old Crow and Wild Hog; the junior war chief, Little Wolf. Dull Knife had a history worth telling, but suffice it here to say that all army officers who encountered him held high esteem for his generalship and indomitable courage.

"The head men of the tribe appealed to the government."
EDGAR B. BRONSON. *REMINISCENCES OF A RANCHMAN.*

Unaccustomed to the enervating climate of the South, they rapidly fell its victims. Easy prey to the fevers there prevalent, it was not long before there was scarcely a lodge free from the shrill death chant of mourners and the dull roar of the medicine tom-tom. Out of two hundred and thirty-five bucks who arrived at Fort Reno in August 1877, twenty-eight died within a twelve-month, while the mortality among the women and children was greater still.

The head men of the tribe appealed to the government. They pleaded as men can only plead for life. They showed that they were dying like sheep on their new reservation. They begged to be permitted to return to their old home in the highlands of the North. They promised to be obedient and peaceful if allowed to return. To be sure, it was an Indian promise, and the government had gotten in the bad habit of discrediting Indian promises, notwithstanding the indisputable fact of history that once frankly pledged, the Indian faith has rarely been broken. Therefore, their prayer was denied, and they were told to content themselves where they were.

As a piece of humanity, this decision was like telling a well man to sleep with a leper; as public policy, like courting war; as justice, like robbing a man of his home, and then compelling him to dwell roofless in an atmosphere of contagion. However, it was the decision, a decision from which the Cheyennes possessed only one right of appeal—the appeal to arms—and they took it. This was the *raison d'etre* of the Cheyenne outbreak of 1878.

It was a campaign begun early in September 1878, far south on the banks of the Canadian River, in the (then) Indian Territory, now Oklahoma, and only finished when, late in October, Little Wolf, with the younger and stronger members of Dull Knife's band, although constantly pursued and intercepted by troops, had successfully fought his way through four great military lines of interception—which included all the troops the War Department was able to put in the field against him—to the complete escape and safety of a junction with Sitting Bull's Hunkpapa Sioux in the British Northwest Territory, one thousand miles to the north; and when Dull Knife and the elders of the tribe, entirely spent of strength and ammunition, were captured in the Niobrara sand hills of northern Nebraska, six hundred miles from their starting point; a campaign that for generalship and strategy, for boldness of conception and sheer, desperate, reckless courage of execution, surpasses in every detail even the famous outbreak of the Nez Perces under Chief Joseph, or of the Apaches under Victoria; a campaign inspired by a holy purpose no man who knows the love of fatherland can gainsay, if ever warfare had a holy purpose in this world. To be sure they left a trail red with the blood of many an innocent victim, gray with the ashes of many a plundered ranch and farmhouse. Still they were only savages, fighting according to the traditions of their race.

It was September 9, 1878. Night had fallen over the valley of the Canadian, one of those clear, bright nights of early autumn on the plains when the stars seem hovering about the tops of the cottonwoods. The moon was nearly full, for the savage, much of whose strategy is learned from the wild beast, chooses the night—and always a moonlit night—for his forays. No Indian ever sought the warpath in the dark of the moon.

The Cheyenne camp was pitched in the valley, at some distance from the fort.[3] The tall tepees, gleaming gray in the moonlight, stood in clusters in a narrow belt of cottonwoods that lined the stream. Usually at this hour, an Indian village was bright with the flames of campfires and noisy with romping children, above whose piping voices from time to time rose the weird, monotonous chant of some old folklore song of the race, recounting the world-old story of dangers doughtily withstood by heroes gone long before; groups of warriors lounged about the campfires, the elders spinning yarns of the chase and the raid, stories of hunting, of war, and of love that stirred the young bucks mightily. But this night, while there was an unwonted activity in the camp, there was no noise. The great herd of ponies, usually grazing out on the divide where the juicy buffalo grass grows thick, had been quietly brought into the camp. Men, women, and youths were rapidly but silently lariating their mounts and adjusting their rude bridles and saddles. This finished, they attacked the tepees. Tall, grim, blanketed figures bent quickly to the work. The buffalo robe or canvas covering of the tepees was soon stripped off the poles, rolled, and packed on the ponies. The tepee poles were left standing, for the preparations making were as well for a flight as a fight. The column must travel light; no needless impedimenta could be taken, and there would be no time to set up tepees on this march.

The few poor stores at their disposal were soon stowed in *parfleches* and tied on the pack animals. Then the column was ready to move. Papooses were quickly slung in the slack of the blanket on the mothers' backs and the mothers mounted; the children were tossed up astride behind their mothers; the bucks tightened their belts, slung their arms, and swung swiftly into the saddle; the column, in loose, irregular order, with seldom more than two or three riding abreast, moved softly out of camp, headed northward on as desperate a sortie as forlorn hope ever drove men to.[4]

Dawn came at last. A sleepy sentinel on post yawned, rubbed his eyes, and walked to the edge of the bluff, where he could look down on the Cheyenne camp. But presto, the camp had disappeared. Only the ghost of a camp remained, for where had stood the gleaming canvas of the tepees, naught appeared but the gaunt pole skeletons of these primitive habitations. The sentry quickly called the sergeant of the guard; he, the officer of the day; he, the commanding officer.[5] The "assembly" was promptly sounded. A patrol was ordered out, a patrol which soon reported a deserted village and a trail leading straight-away across the divide toward the north. The story was told in the trooper's brusque phrase, "Dull Knife's jumped the reservation."

No time was lost. Within half an hour, two troops of cavalry rode out of Fort Reno on the trail.[6] The chase was on. And what a hopeless chase none but an old trooper or frontiersman familiar with Indian methods and troopers' limitations can realize. The trooper was always at a disadvantage. He had only his single mount, accustomed to high grain feeding and stable care, that quickly went footsore and lost condition in such a pursuit. Once afoot, the trooper could not forage on the country for a fresh mount.

A band of Indians, on the other hand, always carried with them a herd of loose ponies. They rode at great speed, they rode on and yet on till their mounts fell from fatigue. The throats of the fagged beasts were then quickly cut to prevent their falling into the hands of pursuers, fresh mounts caught, and the flight resumed. Their own supply of fresh horses exhausted, the band then raided ranches and farms for others. By these means, extraordinary marches were made. At the time of the last outbreak of Geronimo from the San Carlos reservation, his first march covered one hundred and forty miles without a halt.

This small initial pursuing column was the least difficulty Dull Knife had to contend with. The outbreak had instantly been telegraphed by Major Mizner, commanding at Fort Reno, through the usual official channels, to the War Department. Dull Knife's skill and daring as a leader were only too well known to the department. Instantly the whole available force of the United States Army was set in motion to effect his capture. Within a few days, no less than two thousand troops, seasoned veterans trained in the great Sioux-Cheyenne War of 1876, had taken the field against Dull Knife. To accomplish this, three departments of the army were drawn upon; and from Cantonment in the Bighorn Mountains of Montana to Camp Supply in the Indian Territory, from Omaha to Salt Lake, grim columns were moving to crush or subdue this handful of hostiles. General Pope,[7] commanding the Department of the Missouri, directed the immediate pursuit. [On] September 12, 1878, he reported to General Sheridan:

> The following dispositions have been made to intercept the Northern Cheyennes: One hundred mounted infantrymen leave by special train tomorrow for Fort Wallace to head off the Indians if they cross the railroad east or west of that post. Two companies of infantry leave Hays this evening to take post at two noted crossings of Indians on the Kansas Pacific between Hays and Wallace. One infantry company from Dodge is posted on the railroad west of that point. Two cavalry companies from Reno are close on the Indians and will be joined by the cavalry company from Supply. Colonel Lewis[8] will assume command of them as soon as they reach the vicinity of Dodge. The troops at Fort Lyon are ordered to watch the country east and west of that post. All are ordered to attack the Indians wherever found unless they surrender at once, in which case they are to be dismounted and disarmed. Whatever precautions are possible should be taken on the line of the Platte.

The same day witnessed similar activity in the Department of the Platte. Four companies, under Captains Burrowes, Bowman, Brisbin, and Trotter of the 4th, 9th, and 14th Infantry, were ordered to rendezvous at Sidney, Nebraska, on the Union Pacific Railroad, whence scouts were to be kept out on watch for the hostiles, and a special train was kept in constant readiness to carry the troops east or west.

[On] September 14, General Crook hurried westward over the Union Pacific to direct operations, and Major T. T. Thornburgh[9] took command of the troops at Sidney. Meantime, the Cheyennes were pushing forward night and day, stealing horses, ravaging the country, and killing all who came in their path. Notwithstanding the presence of their women and children, they were making fifty to seventy miles a day, and the pursuers, struggle as they might, seemed to be on a hopeless stern chase.

It was believed at the time in the Department of the Platte that Dull Knife had been in communication with Sitting Bull, and that a consolidation of forces had been planned. This sufficiently points [out] the high estimate placed by experienced army officers of the day upon the daring and generalship of Dull Knife; for at the time, Sitting Bull and his band of hostiles were in the mountains between Calgary and McLeod, in the British Northwest Territory, one thousand miles from Fort Reno.

The hostiles were reported checked by the troops at a point twenty miles from Fort Wallace, Kansas, on September 16. This, however, proved a mistake, for on the eighteenth a detachment of Dull Knife's band fought a desperate engagement with two companies of the 4th Cavalry and fifteen cowboys near Dodge City. In this fight, several Indians were captured, and many were wounded on both sides. But the Cheyennes succeeded in beating off the troops and resumed their flight to the northwest.[10] Of their mastery in this engagement, they left behind them terrible evidence in the smoking ruins of several houses no more than three miles from Dodge City.

Notwithstanding the cordon of troops stretched along the Kansas Pacific Railway from Fort Wallace eastward, on the twentieth it was reported that the main band of the Cheyennes had skillfully eluded the troops, had crossed the railway, and were rapidly advancing against the second line of military interception on the Union Pacific Railway, north of the South Platte River.

On the second line of interception, General Crook had concentrated every available man of his department. Here the Cheyennes were certainly to be stopped, but knowing well and highly valuing Dull Knife's generalship and resolution, the veteran Crook took no chances and ordered Colonel Bradley, at Fort Robinson, one hundred and twenty-five miles north of the Union Pacific Railway, to hold his command in readiness for an emergency order, and directed Colonel Wesley P. Merritt of the 5th Cavalry to move his command down the flanks of the Bighorn Mountains to the vicinity of Fort McKinney, Wyoming, one hundred miles to the northwest of Robinson. A correspondent on the ground at the time wrote to the [New York] *Herald:*

> These Cheyennes are considered the finest horsemen in America; they ride their animals as if glued to them, and load and fire with the precision of foot soldiers. Besides this they have the bravery which comes

from desperation and continued ill treatment. It is more than suspected things were rotten at their agency, and they preferred to fight rather than starve.

A band of two hundred Northern Cheyennes under Little Chief was brought into Sidney September 16 by the 7th Cavalry. They were being escorted, virtually as prisoners, from their homes in the north to the Cheyenne Reservation at Fort Reno. [On] September 22, General Crook held a council with them. Little Chief said, "We are sorry to hear of the outbreak of our people. Many of our relatives must be killed. We do not propose to join them, but we hear we are going to a poor country where the Indian dies. We are leaving our own hunting grounds in the Black Hills where we were born, where our fathers are buried, and we are sad." From this speech, it would seem that Little Chief's character justified his name; he had none of Dull Knife's greatness of soul and iron courage.

[On] September 27, Dull Knife fought his fifth engagement with the troops since leaving Reno—five fights in a fortnight. The battle occurred in the canyon of Famished Woman's Fork,[11] near Fort Wallace. Lt. Col. W. H. Lewis, 19th Infantry, commanded the troops. The battle lasted two hours. The fighting was desperate. When leading a line of skirmishers within one hundred and fifty yards of the enemy, Colonel Lewis's horse was shot under him. Disengaging himself from his fallen mount, he seized a carbine and advanced with his line. Fifty yards farther on, a ball cut the femoral artery in his left leg, and he quickly bled to death. Lewis was an experienced Indian fighter of a noble record in the desperate plains service of those days, and greatly mourned by all who knew him. At nightfall the Indians withdrew, leaving one dead warrior and seventeen dead ponies on the field. Besides the loss of Colonel Lewis, three troopers were wounded.[12]

Still the indomitable band held their northward course, fighting for freedom and fatherland. On October 2, two separate engagements were fought by detached bands of the Cheyennes. In one engagement, Lieutenant Broderick, of the 23rd Infantry, was wounded, and Corporal Stewart, of Company I, and five soldiers were killed; in the other, a hand-to-hand fight between Indians and ranchmen, eighteen ranchmen were killed and five wounded. The bodies of the dead were brought into Buffalo Station. As usual, the Indians carried off their dead and wounded, and their losses were unknown. Most of the dead ranchmen were settlers on the Beaver, Sappa, and Frenchman Creeks.

Scouts from Thornburgh's command on October 3 sighted a band of Cheyennes on the Frenchman and estimated their number at two hundred fifty. In the three days previous, the Cheyennes had stolen two hundred and fifty horses and left sixty dead or worn out behind them on the trail.

At high noon of October 4, the splendid old general Dull Knife, having assembled his scattered columns into one body, boldly forded the South Platte River and led his main command north across the Union Pacific Railway, a half mile east of the town of Oglala, Nebraska. As quickly as the Indians were sighted, the news was wired to Sidney, and by 4:00 P.M. Thornburgh had arrived with his command at Oglala, and immediately struck out on Dull Knife's trail. Shortly thereafter, he was followed by the command of Captain Mauck, who had been pursuing the Indians constantly since Lewis's death in Famished Woman's Canyon.

Astounded and dismayed by Dull Knife's marching and desperate fighting, General Crook began to feel uncertain whenever and wherever the old chief could be brought to a final stand. This same day, therefore, he ordered Major Carlton's[13] five troops of the 3rd Cavalry to leave Fort Robinson, scout the Niobrara Sand Hills, and try to intercept and hold the Cheyennes until Thornburgh's column could overtake and strike their rear, and also ordered into the field ten troops of the 7th Cavalry, then in cantonment at Bear Butte (now Fort Mead), Dakota, on the northeast edge of the Black Hills, nearly two hundred miles to the north of Carlton, to form the fourth line of military barrier against Dull Knife's advance. Two days later (October 6), dispatches came in from Thornburgh reporting his column sixty miles north of Oglala in the midst of terrible sand hills, wherein, after leaving the North Platte, they had traveled thirty miles without water. No Indians had been seen, and the trails indicated that they were scattered in all directions, singly and in pairs, scattered like a flock of quail, for concealment and rest.

Thus further immediate pursuit became hopeless. The Nebraska sand hills were then and are still a great, trackless waste, in extent ninety miles north and south by two hundred miles east and west, bounded on the south by the Platte River and on the north by the Niobrara—a veritable Sahara of loose, drifting sands in which horse or man sinks ankle-deep at every step; an arid desert region affording no water except in a few isolated lakes; a region impossible to know because the landmark of one day is removed by the winds of the next; a weird, mysterious, awful country in which, looking south, one sees naught but an endless sea of yellow, rolling sand waves, while turning and looking to the north, the eye takes in a limitless expanse of waving red-top grass, higher than one's stirrups. How to pursue hostiles in such a country? It was clearly impossible.

In this dilemma, Major Carlton of the 3rd Cavalry, who had reached Dog Lake, south of Niobrara, was directed to march his column back north and patrol the divide between the Niobrara and White River, in an attempt to prevent a junction of the Cheyennes with Red Cloud's Oglala Sioux, then on their agency on White Clay Creek.

Pearson's Magazine 11, no. 2 (February 1909): 205–13

Little Wolf's Escape and Dull Knife's Capture

Late in September, I had ridden into Cheyenne from the ranch to buy and bring out the winter supplies for my outfit and there first learned of the

Cheyenne outbreak. Naturally, more or less anxiety was felt by men having ranches north of the Platte, but with the great number of troops in the field, news was expected from day to day that the Cheyennes had been rounded up and captured. When, however, on the afternoon of October 5, news arrived that Dull Knife's main war party had crossed the Union Pacific at Oglala, it became plain that temporizing must cease and the time for action had come; so, leaving instructions that no supplies should be forwarded until after peace was restored and the safety of the trails assured, I struck out northward on the morning of the fifth alone.

My mount for the journey, fortunately, was the best cow pony I ever owned or ever saw: a square-built, short-backed, deep-barreled, dark red bay, with great, blazing eyes, alert and watchful as any of his long line of wild mustang ancestors; a horse whose favorite gait was a low, swift, daisy-clipping lope, easy as a rocking chair to the rider, and no more tiring to the beast than a trot to an average pony—good old "ND."

Early in the afternoon, ND and I made the Dater ranch on Bear Creek, fifty miles north from Cheyenne, the last cattle ranch between Cheyenne and my place. Next morning, starting at dawn, before sunrise, having no trails and striking straight across country through Goshen's Hole, we swam the Platte and by noon had reached the ranch of Nick Janisse, lying on the north bank of the Platte, twenty-eight miles east of Fort Laramie.

Janisse was an old French voyageur squaw man, who had lived and traded thirty years among the Sioux, and who had then been for some years settled in this isolated valley, within a stout-walled sod stockade.

I had expected to spend the night with Janisse, but shortly after my arrival, his son-in-law, a half-breed named Louis Changro, rode in from the east with the news that he had seen a party of eighteen Cheyenne bucks about fifteen miles east of the ranch, heading northwest directly into the hill country between Sheep Creek and the head of Snake Creek, which I had to cross to get home—this evidently a small scouting party sent out ahead by Dull Knife. Of course, it was madness to expect to cross in daylight the seventy-six intervening miles between Janisse's ranch and mine with Cheyenne scouts out, although it was probable that they were prowling ahead more in the hope of rounding up fresh ranch horses than anything else. So I decided the ride home must be made that night. Although the task was a heavy one for a horse that had already done his forty-five miles in the forenoon, I felt old ND could make it.

Just at twilight, a tremendous thunderstorm broke, very conveniently, for the moon was not due to rise until after 10:00 P.M. As soon as it was dark, we struck out on an old United States government wagon trail long disused, which I would never have been able to follow but for the constant flashes of lightning. Luckily the storm held until time for the moon to rise, and by that time we were getting up out of the valley of Sheep Creek upon the drier uplands, where I could let out ND into the free, easy stride he loved. We had only one alarm throughout the night. Toward midnight, relying more on ND's alert watchfulness than my own, tired and dozing comfortably in the saddle (a knack all cowboys know and practice when traveling a trail), suddenly old ND made a bound to one side that nearly unseated me. Of course, I could fancy nothing but Cheyennes, but, jerking my pistol and looking quickly round about in the dim moonlight, could see nothing. Still old ND shied away as if in deadly fear of something behind him on the ground and, looking closely back, I was surprised to see a skunk following us, literally charging after us as if mad—and mad I have no doubt he was, as often have I heard of men being bitten, while sleeping on the plains at night, by these little animals, and later dying with all symptoms of hydrophobia. Hesitating to take the chance of stirring up some marauding neighbor by shooting my little pursuer, I gave ND his head and we soon left him behind. Few greater performances by horseflesh than old ND achieved that night are recorded, for when, a little after dawn the next morning, we reached the Dead Man home ranch, old ND had completed 121 miles between sun and sun, and had done it without quirt or spur.

With the garrison only five miles away and a military wire to the railroad, I found the boys already had news of the approaching enemy and learned that Johnson's and Thompson's troops of the 3rd Cavalry were patrolling the heart of my range from Robinson to the head of White River, and were scouting daily for the approaching Cheyennes.

Two days after my arrival, October 8, two of my cowboys reported to the garrison having seen Indians on Crow Butte, two miles east of our ranch, signaling to the southeast with looking glasses, and dense clouds of smoke were seen to the north in the direction of Hat Creek, the smoke signaling probably the work of the little scouting party Changro had seen crossing the Platte on the fifth.

Late in the night of the thirteenth, a little band of hostiles raided Clay Deer's store at the old Red Cloud agency, a mile east of Fort Robinson, and successfully got away with all of his horses, escaping safely south to Crow Butte; and the Sioux scouts told us all that saved our horses on Dead Man was the Indians' superstitious dread of venturing into the valley of Wi-nogi-waka-pala at night.

The next day, patrols of troopers reported to Robinson that the main band of hostiles was encamped on the summit of Crow Butte, the most natural point of defense for a desperate final stand in all the country for one hundred miles round about—a high, isolated butte, in ancient times an outer buttress of the tall range of hills rising above the White River Valley to the south, worn by erosion until it stood a detached peak, precipitous on all sides and accessible even to footmen only at one point. Four troops of cavalry were promptly sent to surround Crow Butte, arriving near nightfall at its lower slopes.

The position was one impossible of direct assault, and therefore pickets were set at short intervals surrounding the butte. Then the commanding officer laid himself comfortably down to rest, with the happy certainty it had fallen to his lot to be the lucky one to succeed in entrapping Dull Knife and his redoubtable band. But the Indian hosts were by no means yet ready to become

Fort Robinson and vicinity.
JOURNAL OF THE MILITARY SERVICE INSTITUTION OF THE UNITED STATES, 1914.

hostages, and thus it fell out that when morning came it was found the band had flown-had slipped quietly through the picket lines at night and were far away to the north. Later it was learned that this band was led by the junior war chief, Little Wolf, and comprised something over two hundred of the younger and stronger members of the band who were still able to travel and to fight.

Before scattering in the sand hills, a council had been held, for the situation of the Cheyennes had become utterly desperate. Here they were beyond the settlements, with no more ranches to raid for horses, food, or ammunition. All were worn and exhausted by the march, until it was apparent that the elders of the band would be powerless to fight their way through to Canada, unless through some diversion. It was therefore decided that Little Wolf should lead the stronger on a last desperate dash for the liberty they hoped to find somewhere in the north, while the elders should rest themselves in the hope the main pursuit might be led off by Little Wolf, leaving the elders able to slip through later unobserved.

Successfully eluding the Bear Butte column and still another barrier of troops situated along the Yellowstone, Little Wolf led his band safely through, without the loss of another man, to a junction with Sitting Bull, across the Canadian border.

This march is not excelled in the annals of warfare. It covered a distance of more than one thousand miles in less than fifty days, with a column encumbered with women and children, every step of the trail contested by all the troops of the United States Army that could be concentrated to oppose them; a march that struck and parted like ropes of sand the five great military barriers interposed across their path: the first across the Kansas-Pacific Railway, commanded by General Pope; the second along the Union Pacific Railroad in Nebraska, commanded by General Crook; the third along the Niobrara, commanded by Colonel Bradley; the fourth the Bear Butte (7th Cavalry) column, stretched east from the Black Hills; the fifth along the Yellowstone, commanded by Colonel Gibbon.

In the early evening of October 14, we of the Dead Man Ranch were anything but easy in our minds or certain how long we might continue to wear our hair. Early in the afternoon, Tobacco Jake, one of my cowboys, had brought the news that the main band of the Cheyennes lay on Crow Butte, two miles to the east of us. Immediately we circled and rounded up all our horses and put them under guard within our strongest stockaded corral. The Indians were so desperate for fresh mounts we felt certain of an attack—certain that even their dread of the haunting spirits with which their savage superstition had peopled the valley of Wi-nogi-waka-pala would not prevent them from making a fight to take our fat ponies.

It was therefore a relief when one of the guards entered my room about 10:00 P.M. and reported a body of men coming up the valley, who, in the moonlight, appeared to him to be marching in such regular order he felt sure they were soldiers. This proved to be true, and presently arrived before the ranch a sergeant and ten men of Troop B, with two Sioux scouts, Woman's Dress and Red Shirt, the sergeant bringing me a note from dear old Jack Johnson, saying that while he felt we were quite able to take care of ourselves, it seemed to him expedient to give us reinforcements to help defend our horses, the lifting of which by the Cheyennes would add enormously to the difficulty of subduing the band.

From this most welcome increase to our little force, I doubled the guards around ranch and corrals, and we retired in perfect ease of mind, for the ranch was so placed as to command an open plain on all sides for three or four hundred yards, without cover for an attacking party, and so we were warned against a hostile approach; we felt entirely secure behind our loopholed log walls. This night and the next day passed without incident, and we later learned that Little Wolf had been so closely invested by troops he could not venture upon a foray.

The next week was indeed an anxious one, for it was known that approximately a third of the Cheyennes still remained grouped or scattered in the sand hills a few miles to the southeast of us. White River was lined with patrols of troopers, from the head down to Chadron Creek, watching for Dull Knife's advance. He could not go south, for Thornburgh lay behind him; he could not go east or west, for lack of water—he must come north.

During this week, Dull Knife succeeded in getting runners through with messages to Red Cloud, of whom, in Dull Knife's name, they besought aid. They pleaded the blood ties which existed between many of their families. They pleaded the ancient alliance of the two tribes in many a bloody fray with their common enemies, the Crows, the Pawnees, and the whites. But wise old Red Cloud was even a greater statesman than warrior and had realized long years before the utter hopelessness of resisting the whites. Indeed, had his counsels prevailed against those of Sitting Bull, the campaign of 1876 would have never happened. Thus, Dull Knife's messengers returned with nothing better than words of sympathy and advice to Dull Knife to surrender and submit himself to the Great Father's will.

After waiting a week without any sign of movement on the part of the hostiles, Major Carlton sent out from Fort Robinson, on October 21, troops commanded by Capt. Jack Johnson, and consisting of Johnson's Troop B and Lt. J. C. Thompson's Troop D, 3rd Cavalry, accompanied by twenty-two Sioux scouts under Chiefs American Horse (Red Cloud's son-in-law and now head chief of the Oglala Sioux) and Rocking Bear. Their orders were to scout the sand hills for the Cheyennes and harry or capture them.

Two days later, when well into the sand hills and near the sink of Snake Creek, Johnson located a band of sixty hostiles, including the Chiefs Dull Knife, Old Crow, and Wild Hog. In rags, nearly out of ammunition, famished and worn, with scarcely a horse left that could raise a trot, no longer able to fight or fly, suffering from cold, and disheartened by Red Cloud's refusal to receive and shelter them, the splendid old war chief and his men were forced to bow to the inevitable and surrender. Later in the day, Johnson succeeded in rounding up the last of Dull Knife's scattered command and headed north for White River with his prisoners, 149 Cheyennes and 131 captured ponies.

The evening of the twenty-third, Johnson camped at Louis Jenks's ranch on Chadron Creek, near the present town of Chadron, Nebraska. A heavy snowstorm had set in early in the afternoon, and the night was so bitter and the Indians so weakened by their campaign that Johnson felt safe to leave them free to take the best shelter they could find in the brush along the deep valley of Chadron Creek.

This leniency he was not long in regretting. Dull Knife and his band had been feeding liberally for two days on troopers' rations and had so far recovered strength of body and heart that when morning came on the twenty-fifth, the sentries were greeted with a feeble volley from rifle pits in the brush, dug by Dull Knife in the frozen ground during the night. And here in these pits, indomitable old Dull Knife fought stubbornly for two days more—fought and held the troops at bay until Lieutenant Chase[14] brought up a field gun from Fort Robinson and shelled them to a final surrender.

Cavalry in a blizzard. HARPER'S WEEKLY, 1888.

Thus ended the first episode of Dull Knife's magnificent fight for liberty and fatherland, and yet had he had food, ammunition, and mounts, the chances are a hundred to one that his heroic purpose would have been accomplished, and the entire band that left Reno, barring those killed along the trail, would have escaped in safety to freedom in the then wilds of the Northwest Territory. And that even in this apparently final surrender to hopeless odds, Dull Knife was still not without hope of further resistance was proved by the fact that when he came out of his trenches, only a few comparatively old and worthless arms were surrendered, while it later became known that twenty-two good rifles had been taken apart and were swung, concealed, beneath the clothing of the squaws.

After taking a day's rest, Johnson marched his command into Fort Robinson, arriving in the evening in a heavy snowstorm, where the Cheyennes were imprisoned in one of the barracks and their meager equipment dumped in with them, without further search for arms or ammunition. Later it was learned that that night, the Indians quietly loosened some of the flooring of the bar rack and hid their arms and ammunition beneath it, so that when a more careful search of their belongings and persons was made two days later, they were found to be absolutely without weapons of any description.

Fort Robinson was a good type of the smaller frontier posts of the 1870s. It stood on a narrow bench to the north of and slightly elevated above the valley of Soldier Creek. Facing the parade ground, on the north were eight sets of officers' quarters; on the east, a long company barrack; at the southeast angle, another barrack; beyond this, to the west, the guardhouse, then the adjutant's office, then the quartermaster's and the commissary warehouses; back and to the south of these, the company stables and corrals; on the west, the hospital; at the northwest angle, Major Paddock's sutler's store. A half mile down the valley of White River stood the old ruined cantonment of Camp Canby. Dull Knife and his people were confined in the log barrack at the southeast angle of the parade ground. No doors were locked or windows barred. A small guard patrolled the barrack prison night and day.

What to do with these indomitable people puzzled the Indian Bureau and the army. The states of Kansas and Nebraska were clamoring for their temporary custody for the purpose of the identification, prosecution, and punishment of individual members for killings committed during their march north in October. The Sioux, with whom they were closely federated and allied, wanted them released and settled in the Sioux reservation; and Sioux wishes could not be idly disregarded, for the best military authorities then agreed it would need discreet handling to prevent the Sioux from taking the warpath again so soon as green grass rose in the spring.

The question of any particular justice in the claim of the Cheyennes that the agreements of the government (made upon their surrender in 1876) had not been kept, and that their return to the Indian Territory meant speedy death from fevers, received no serious consideration. In his reports to the general of the army for 1878, General Sheridan made the following noble plea:

> There has been an insufficiency of food at the agencies, and as the game is gone, hunger has made the Indians in some cases desperate, and almost any race of men will fight rather than starve. The question of justice and right to the Indian is past and cannot be recalled. We have occupied his country, taken away his lordly domain, destroyed his herds of game, penned him up on reservations, and reduced him to poverty. For humanity's sake, let us give him enough to eat and integrity in the agent over him.

In December, a great council was held in the barrack prison. The Sioux chiefs, Red Cloud, American Horse, Red Dog, and No Flesh, came over from their agency to attend it. The government was represented by Captains Wessells[15] and Vroom and their juniors. The Cheyennes were gathered in a close circle, the officers and visiting chiefs near its center, the bucks back of them, and farther back still the squaws and children.

Red Cloud was the principal Sioux speaker. He said in substance:

> Our hearts are sore for you. Many of our own blood are among your dead. This has made our hearts bad. But what can we do? The Great Father is all powerful. His people fill the whole earth. We must do what he says. We have begged him to allow you to come to live among us. We hope he may let you come. What we have we will share with you. But remember, what he directs, that you must do. We cannot help you. The snows are thick on the hills. Our ponies are thin. The

game is scarce. You cannot resist, nor can we. So listen to your old friend and do without complaint what the Great Father tells you.

The old Cheyenne war chief, Dull Knife, then stepped slowly to the center of the circle, a grim, lean figure. Erect despite his sixty-odd years, with a face of a classical Roman profile, with the steady, penetrating glance and noble, commanding bearing of a great leader of men, Dull Knife stood in his worn canvas moccasins and ragged, threadbare blanket, the very personification of the greatness of heart and soul that cannot be subdued by poverty and defeat. Never when riding at the head of hundreds of his wild warriors, clad in the purple of his race—leggings of golden yellow buckskin, heavily beaded, blanket of dark blue broadcloth, war bonnet of eagles' feathers that trailed behind him on the ground, necklace of bears' claws, the spoils of many a deadly tussle—never in his life did Dull Knife look more a chieftain than there in his captivity and rags.

He first addressed the Sioux:

We know you for our friends, whose words we may believe. We thank you for asking us to share your lands. We hope the Great Father will let us come to you. All we ask is to be allowed to live, and to live in peace. I seek no war with anyone. An old man, my fighting days are done. We bowed to the will of the Great Father and went far into the south where he told us to go. There we found a Cheyenne cannot live. Sickness came among us that made mourning in every lodge. Then the treaty promises were broken, and our rations were short. Those not worn by disease were wasted by hunger. To stay there meant that all of us would die. Our petitions to the Great Father were unheeded. We thought it better to die fighting to regain our old homes than to perish of sickness. Then our march was begun. The rest you know.

Then, turning to Captain Wessells and his officers:

Tell the Great Father Dull Knife and his people ask only to end their days here in the north where they were born. Tell him we want no more war. We cannot live in the south; there is no game. Here, when rations are short, we can hunt. Tell him if he lets us stay here, Dull Knife's people will hurt no one. Tell him if he tries to send us back, we will butcher each other with our own knives. I have spoken.

Captain Wessells' reply was brief—an assurance that Dull Knife's words should go to the Great Father.

The Cheyennes sat silent throughout the council, all save one, a powerful young buck named Buffalo Hump—old Dull Knife's son.[16] With the thin strip of old canvas that served as his only covering drawn tightly about his tall figure, his bronze face aflame with sentiments of wrong, of anger, and of hatred, Buffalo Hump strode rapidly from one end to the other of the long barrack room, casting fierce glances at the white men, the very incarnation of savage wrath. From beginning to end of the council, I momentarily expected to see him leap on some member of the party and try to rend him with his hands.

Of course, nothing came of the council. The War and Interior Departments agreed that it would be imprudent to permit these unsubduable people to be merged into the already restless ranks of the Sioux. It was therefore decided to march them back south to Fort Reno, whence they had come. Fearing disturbance and perhaps outbreak among the Sioux when this order became known, Capt. P. D. Vroom, with four troops of the 3rd Cavalry, was ordered to reinforce the two companies of the garrison commanded by Captain Wessells. Captain Vroom's column reached Robinson early in January 1879 and went into quarters at Camp Canby, one mile east of the post, and Vroom reported to Wessells, the ranking captain, for orders.

January opened with very bitter weather. Six or eight inches of snow covered the ground. The mercury daily made long excursions below zero. Even the troops in cantonment at Canby were suffering severely from the cold—some with frozen feet and hands. It was all but impossible weather for marching. Nevertheless, on January 5, Captain Wessells received orders from the War Department to immediately start Dull Knife's band, as quietly and peaceably as possible, and under proper escort, on the march to Fort Reno, six hundred miles away in the South. This was the decision of the Indian Bureau, and the secretary of war was requested to have the decision immediately enforced. Hence the order which reached Captain Wessells.

Captain Wessells sent a guard to the barrack and had Dull Knife, Old Crow, and Wild Hog brought into his presence at headquarters. On the arrival of the Indians, a council was held. Captain Wessells advised them of the order of the department that they were to return to the Indian Territory. Dull Knife rose to reply. His whole figure trembled with rage; his bronze cheeks assumed a deeper red; the fires of suppressed passion blazed through his eyes until they glittered with the ferocity of an enraged beast at bay. Nevertheless, he spoke slowly and almost calmly. He did not have much to say. He made no threats or gestures. He said he had listened to what the Great Father had ordered. It was the dearest wish of him and his people to try to do what the Great Father desired, for they knew they were helpless in his hands. But now the Great Father was telling them to do what they could not do—to try to march to the Indian Territory in such weather. Many would be sure to perish on the way, and those who reached the reservation would soon fall victims to the fevers that had already brought mourning into nearly all their lodges. If, then, the Great Father wished them to die—very well, only they would die where they then were, if necessary by their own hands. They would not return to the South, and they would not leave their barrack prison.

Captain Wessells knew that Dull Knife's complaint was well founded. Still, bound by the rigid rules of the service, he had absolutely no latitude whatever. He therefore directed the interpreter to explain to Dull Knife that the orders were imperative and must be obeyed, and to assure him that the cavalry escort would do all in their power to save the Indians from any unnecessary hardship on the journey. Dull Knife, however, remained firm, and his companions, when appealed to, only growled a brief assent to Dull Knife's views. "Then, interpreter," said Wessells, "tell them their food and fuel will be stopped entirely until they conclude to come peaceably out of their barrack, ready to march south as ordered."

The three chiefs silently heard their sentence and were then quickly marched back to their barrack prison by a file of soldiers. All this occurred shortly after guard mount in the morning.

Apart from its inhumanity, Wessells's order was bad policy. Hunger drives the most cowardly to violence. Then, to add to the wretched plight of the Indians, they were all but naked. No clothing had been issued to them since their capture, and they were clad only in tattered blankets and fragments of tent cloth. Requisitions for clothing had been sent to the Indian Bureau, but none had come. Thus, half naked, without food or fires, these miserable people starved and shivered for five days and nights, but with no thought of surrender. Captain Wessells sent the interpreter to propose that the children be removed and fed, but this they refused; they said they preferred to die together.

For five days and nights, the barrack rang with the shrill, terrible death chants. It was clear that they had resolved to die, and weakening fast indeed they were under the rigors of cold and hunger, weakening in all but spirit. The morning of January 9, the fifth day of their compulsory fast, Captain Wessells again summoned Dull Knife, Old Crow, and Wild Hog to a council. Only the two latter came. Suspecting violence, the Indians refused to let their old chief leave the barrack. Asked if they were ready to surrender, Wild Hog replied that they would die first. The two chiefs were then ordered seized and ironed. In the struggle, Wild Hog succeeded in seriously stabbing Private [Thomas] Ferguson of Troop E, and sounded his war cry as an alarm to his people.[17]

Instantly, pandemonium broke loose in the Indian barrack. They realized the end was at hand. The war songs of the warriors rang loudly above the shrill death chants of the squaws. Windows and doors were quickly barricaded. The floor of the barrack was torn up, and rifle pits were dug beneath it. Stoves and flooring were broken into convenient shapes for use as war clubs. The twenty-odd rifles and pistols which had been smuggled into the barrack, by slinging them about the waists of the squaws beneath their blankets at the time of the capture, were soon brought from their hiding place and loaded.

They expected an immediate attack, but none came. And all day long, the garrison was kept under arms, ready for any sortie by the Indians. Night at last came, and notwithstanding the terrible warnings of the day, no extraordinary precautions were taken. A guard of only seventeen men were under arms, and of these only a few were on post about this barrack full of maddened savages. All but Captain Wessells were so certain of a desperate outbreak that night that

The defiance of Dull Knife. EDGAR B. BRONSON. *REMINISCENCES OF A RANCHMAN.*

Lieutenant Baxter[18] and several other officers sat fully dressed and armed in their quarters, awaiting the first alarm.

Taps sounded at 9:00 P.M., the barracks were soon darkened, and the troopers retired. Only a few lights burned in the officers' quarters and at the trader's store. The night was still and fearfully cold, the earth hid by the snow. 10:00 P.M. came, and just as the "all's well" was passing from one sentry to another, a buck fired through a window and killed a sentry,[19] jumped through the window and got the sentry's carbine and belt, and sprang back into the barrack. Then two or three bucks ran out of the west door, where they quickly shot down Corporal [Edward F.] Pulver [of Troop L] and Private [Peter] Hulse of Troop A, and Private [James] Emory of Troop C.

At doors and windows, the barrack now emptied its horde of desperate captives, maddened by injustice and wild from hunger. Nevertheless, they acted with method and generalship, and with a heroism worthy of the noblest men of any race.

The bucks armed with firearms were the first to leave the barrack. These formed in line in front of the barrack and opened fire on the guardhouse and upon the troopers as they came pouring out of neighboring barracks. Thus they held the garrison in check until the women and children and the old and infirm were in full flight. Taken completely by surprise, the troops nevertheless did fearfully effective work. Captain Wessells soon had them out, and not a few entered into the fight and pursuit clad in nothing but their underclothing, hatless and shoeless.

The fugitives took the road to the sawmill crossing of White River, only a few hundred yards distant from their barrack, crossed the White River, and started southwest toward my ranch, where they evidently expected to mount themselves out of my herd of cow ponies, for they carried with them all their lariats, saddles, and bridles to this point. Here, pressed hopelessly close by the troops, their gallant rear guard of bucks melting fast before the volleys of the pursuers, the Indians dropped their horse equipments, turned and recrossed White River, and headed for the high, precipitous divide between Soldier Creek and White River, two miles nearer [to] their position than the cliffs about my ranch. They knew their only chance lay in quickly reaching hills inaccessible to cavalry.

All history affords no record of a more heroic, forlorn hope than this Cheyenne sortie. Had the bucks gone alone, many would surely have escaped, but they resolved to die together and to protect their women and children to the last. Thus more than half their fighting men fell in the first half mile of this flying fight. And as the warriors fell, their arms were seized by squaws and boys, who wielded them as best they could.

In the gloom of night, the soldiers could not distinguish a squaw from a buck. Lieutenant Cummings[20] fell into a washout near the sawmill nearly atop of two Indians. They attacked him with knives, but he succeeded in killing both with his pistol—only to find that they were squaws.

Dull Knife's Cheyennes struggling toward the divide between Soldier Creek and White River. HARPER'S NEW MONTHLY MAGAZINE, 1897.

The struggle was often hand-to-hand, and many of the dead were powder-burned. For a long distance, the trail was strewn thick with bodies. A sergeant and several men were pursuing two isolated fugitives, who proved to be a buck and squaw. Suddenly the two fugitives turned and charged their pursuers, the buck armed with a pistol, the squaw with a piece of an iron stove. They were shot down.

This running fight afoot continued for nearly a mile, when the troops, many of them already badly frozen, were hurried back to the garrison to get needed clothing and their mounts.

Pearson's Magazine 11, no. 3 (March 1904): 257–62

Soldier Creek Ambuscades

That night at ten o'clock, I sat in my room at the Dead Man Ranch, five miles south of Fort Robinson, writing a letter descriptive of the day's incidents, and of the peril threatening us, to my then partner, Clarence King.

I had ridden into the garrison that morning for my mail, and was passing the headquarters building at the very moment the fight occurred, in which Dull Knife and Old Crow were seized and bound—in fact, dismounted and got into the building in time to see the finish of the fight. I had remained in the garrison until midafternoon, a witness of the desperate temper of the captives. Indeed, I do not think there was an officer in the garrison, outside of the commanding officer, who did not feel perfectly certain in his mind that the Cheyennes would, in a few hours at the most, make a finish fight for liberty, for from the hour of the seizing of the two chiefs, all day long death chants and war songs were ringing in the barracks.

In the event of such an outbreak, our position at the ranch was serious, for mine was the only large band of horses then in the immediate neighborhood, and any who might succeed in cutting their way through the troops and temporarily eluding pursuit were certain to seek mounts from my *caballadas*. I therefore returned to the ranch in time to have the horses rounded up and thrown in stockade, about which a guard was set at dark. At precisely 10:00 P.M., one of my cowboy guards sprang into my room and cried, "The ball's opened down thar at the fort, an' she's a hell of a big one!"

Hurrying outside into the clear, still, bitterly cold night, I could plainly hear heavy rifle fire at the post that proved a desperate engagement was on.

The north end room of the ranch house itself was a stable, in which, on emergency nights like this, each of us had his best horse ready saddled. Leaving eight men to guard the ranch and corrals, I immediately mounted and took with me a boy named Matthews on a run for the fort, with the purpose to learn if there was any likelihood of any of the Cheyennes escaping in our direction.

Halfway into the garrison, we could hear heavy firing on our left, which told us the chase led west up the White River Valley. Then suddenly all firing ceased. Spurring rapidly ahead at full speed, we soon reached a high, conical hill about two hundred yards south of the sawmill, a hill which commanded a full view of the garrison, and we rode to its summit.

There beneath us, across the valley, lay Fort Robinson in the moonlight, calm and still. In the entire garrison, only one lamp was alight, and that at Major Paddock's trader's store. No one could fancy that Death had been at work there in one of his most terrible forms.

"Old man," said Matt, "I reckon we better pull our freight for the ranch. From all that shootin', 'pears to me like there cain't be many left alive, and that damned still valley don't look to me no good country to go into."

However, I decided to ride on into the garrison, and we descended the hill toward the river. Presently, nearing the narrow fringe of timber that lined the stream, we could see ahead of us a broad, dark line dividing the snow: It was the trail of pursued and pursuers—the line of flight. Come to it, we halted. There at our feet, grim and stark and terrible in the moonlight, lay the dead and wounded, so thick for a long way that one could leap from one body to another; there they lay, grim and stark, soldiers and Indians, the latter lean and gaunt as wolves from starvation, awful with their wounds, infinitely pathetic on this bitter night in their ragged, half-clothed nakedness.

We started to ride across the trail, when in a fallen buck I happened to notice I recognized Buffalo Hump, Dull Knife's son. He lay on his back, with arms extended and face upturned. In his right hand, he held a small knife, a knife worn by years and years of use from the useful proportions of a butcher knife until the blade was no more than one quarter of an inch wide at the hilt, a knife descended to domestic use by the squaws as an awl in sewing moccasins, and yet the only weapon this magnificent warrior could command, in this his last fight for freedom. As I sat on my horse looking down at Buffalo Hump, believing him dead, the picture rose in my mind of the council in which he had stalked from end to end of the barrack, burning with an anger and hatred which threatened even then and there to break out into violence, when suddenly he rose to a sitting position and aimed a fierce blow at my leg with his knife. Instinctively, as he rose, I spurred my horse out of his reach and jerked my pistol, but before I could use it, he fell back and lay still—dead. So died Buffalo Hump, a warrior capable, with half a chance, of making martial history worthy even of his doughty old father.

I dismounted, took the little knife from his hand, cut its tiny leather sheath from his belt, and had just remounted when we got the sharp challenge, "Who goes there?" from the dense plum thicket to the west of the trail, to which we were not slow in answering, "Friends," when out of the brush marched Lt. George Baxter at the head of his half-dressed, dismounted troopers, hastening back to the garrison for their horses.

"Where are your Indians, George?" I called.

"Every mother's son gone but those laid out along the trail, old man," he answered.

Then Matt and I rode on into the post, meeting Lt. Jim Simpson[21] and Dr. Pettys, out with a wagon and detail of men, gathering up the dead and wounded.

Immediately on hearing the fire, Vroom, at Camp Canby, had thrown two troops in skirmish order across the valley to prevent escape to the east, and hurried into Robinson himself at the head of a third troop. Already mounted, Vroom was the first to overtake and reengage the flying Cheyennes, whose knowledge of the geography of the country proved remarkable. They had selected a high bluff two miles west of the post as their means of escape, its summit inaccessible to horsemen for more than six miles from the point of their ascent.[22]

Almost daily for months had I ridden beneath this bluff, and would readily have sworn not even a mountain goat could ascend to its summit; but hidden away in an angle of the cliff lay a slope accessible to footmen, and this the Indians knew and sought. Just below this slope, Vroom brought the rear guard to bay, and a brief, desperate engagement was fought. The Indians succeeded in holding the troops in check until all but those fallen under the fire of Vroom's command were able to reach the summit. Here on this slope, fighting in the front ranks of the rear guard, the "Princess," Dull Knife's youngest daughter, was killed.

Further pursuit until daylight being impossible, the troopers were marched back into the garrison.

By daylight, the hospital was filled with wounded Indians, and thirty-odd dead—bucks, squaws, and children—lay in a row by the roadside near the sawmill, and there later they were buried in a common trench. At dawn of January 10, Captain Wessells led out four troops of cavalry, and after a couple of hours' scouting, found that the Indians had followed for ten miles the summit

Captain Wessells sets out after Dull Knife's band.
HARPER'S NEW MONTHLY MAGAZINE, 1897.

of the high divide between White River and Soldier Creek, traveling straightaway westward, and then had descended to the narrow valley of Soldier Creek, up which the trail lay, plain to follow through the snow as a beaten road. Along this trail, Captain Vroom led the column at the head of his troop. Next behind him rode Lt. George A. Dodd,[23] then a youngster not long out of West Point, and later for many years recognized as the crack cavalry captain of the army. Next, behind Dodd, I rode. Ahead of the column a hundred yards rode Woman's Dress, a Sioux scout.

For seventeen miles from the post, the trail showed that the fugitives had made no halt. A marvelous march on such a bitter night for a lot of men, women, and children, many of them wounded, all half clad and practically starved for five days.

Presently the trail wound round the foot of a high, steep hill, the crest of which was covered with fallen timber, a hill so steep the column was broken into single file to pass it. Here the trail could be seen winding on through the snow over another hill a half mile ahead. Thus an ambush was the last thing expected, but after passing the crest of the second hill, the Indians had made a wide detour to the north, gained the fallen timber on the crest of this first hill, and had there entrenched themselves.

So it happened that at the moment the head of Vroom's column came immediately beneath their entrenchment, the Cheyennes opened fire at short range, emptied two or three saddles, and naturally and rightly enough stampeded the leading troop into the brush ahead of and back of the hill, for it was no place to stand and make a fight. And here a funny thing happened. Dodd was a youngster then, fuller of fight than experience, and at the first fire, realizing the hopelessness of work in the saddle on such ground, he sprang off his horse and had no more than hit the ground before his horse jerked loose from him, and looking about, he found himself alone on the hillside, the only target, and a conspicuous one, for the Cheyennes' fire. Nothing remained but to make a run for the brush, and a good run he made of it, but encumbered with a buffalo overcoat and laboring through the heavy snow, he soon got winded and dropped a moment for rest behind the futile shelter of a sagebrush.

Meantime, the troopers had reached the timber, dismounted, taken positions behind trees, and were pouring into the Indian stronghold a fire so heavy that Dodd was soon able to make another run and escape to the timber unscathed. Arrived there, Vroom noticed Dodd rubbing the back of his neck and asked him what was the matter, when Dodd answered, "Mighty heavy timber I was lying under out there, wasn't it? You know, the limbs cut off by the Indians' fire and falling on the back of my neck felt like strokes from a baseball bat!" A humorous sarcasm on the scanty shelter of a sagebrush and the slender sage twigs Tommy was picking out of the back of his collar.

The Indian stronghold on the hilltop was soon surrounded and held under a desultory long-range fire all day, as the position was one impregnable to a charge. No packs or rations having been brought, at nightfall Captain Wessells built decoy campfires about the Indians' position and marched the command back into the garrison.

Early in the afternoon of the tenth, shortly after the troops had surrounded the hill held by the hostiles, I rode alone back into the garrison and started for my Dead Man Ranch. About a mile south of the sawmill, I met a trooper riding at high speed for the garrison, and turned and rode with him. He told me Lieutenant Baxter, with a detachment of ten men, had located, on the slope of a bluff a mile east of the Dead Man Ranch, a camp of Indians which he believed represented a large band of the hostiles still loose. Pointing to a spur of the bluffs three or four hundred feet high, standing well out into the valley a scant mile east of my ranch, the trooper hurried on into the garrison for reinforcements, and I spurred away for the bluff, and soon could see a line of dismounted troopers strung along the crest of the ridge.

As I rode up to the foot of the bluff, skirmish firing began on top of the ridge. After running my horse as far up the hill as its precipitous nature would permit, I started afoot climbing for the crest, but finding it inaccessible at that point, started around the face of the bluff to the east to find a practicable line of ascent, when suddenly I was startled to hear the ominous, shrill buzz of rifle balls just above my head, from the skirmish line on the crest of the ridge—startled, indeed, for I had supposed the Indians to be on the crest of the bluff, farther to the south.

Dropping behind a tree and looking downhill, I saw a faint curl of smoke rising from a little washout one hundred yards below me, and crouched beside the smoldering fire in the washout, a lone Indian. This warrior's fight and death was characteristic of the magnificent spirit which had inspired the band from the beginning of the campaign at Fort Reno. In midafternoon, scouting to the south of the garrison for trails, Lieutenant Baxter had discovered this campfire, and quite naturally assuming that none but a considerable band of the Indians would venture upon building a campfire so near to the garrison, had immediately sent a trooper courier into the garrison with advice of his discovery. Then he dismounted his command and approached the campfire in open skirmish order, until it was plain to be seen that the fire was deserted. The trail of a single Indian led into the washout, and imprints in the snow showed where he had sat, evidently for some hours, beside the fire. But of the washout's fugitive tenant no trace could be found, no trail showing his route of departure. In one direction, along a sharp ridge leading toward the hogback's crest, the snow was blown away, the ground bare, and this seemed to be his natural line of flight from Baxter's detachment.

After what all believed a thorough search of the vicinity of the fire, Lieutenant Baxter left Corporal [W. W.] Everett and a trooper near the fire and, remounting, led the balance of his men up the slope with the view to cut the Cheyenne's trail wherever it might again enter the snow.

Baxter was gone barely ten minutes when he was startled by two rifle shots in his rear, from the vicinity of the fire! Looking back, he saw his two troopers prostrate in the snow, and later learned that Everett and his mate, while stamping about to keep warm, had approached a little shallow washout within thirty yards of the fire that all vowed they had looked into, and suddenly had discovered the Indian lying at its bottom, wrapped in a length of dirty old canvas the precise color of the gray clay soil, which doubtless had served to conceal him through the earlier search. The moment the Indian made sure he was discovered, he cast open his canvas wrap and fired twice with a carbine, shooting Corporal Everett through the stomach and killing him almost instantly, and seriously wounding his mate.

Thus rudely taught that humanity was useless, and that it must be a fight to the death, observing "Papa" Lawson[24] approaching from the fort at the head of his troop, Baxter swung his own men up and along the top of the ridge, where they could better command the old Cheyenne's position, and opened on him a heavy fire—and it was just at this juncture I arrived. Immediately after I first sighted the Indian, Papa Lawson swung around the foot of the hill with his troop, dismounted, and charged up on foot—thus making sixty men concentrated upon one. The old Cheyenne kept up his rapid fire as long as he could. Toward the last, I plainly saw him fire his carbine three times with his left hand, resting the barrel along the edge of the washout, while his right hand hung helpless beside him. Suddenly I saw him drop down in the bottom of the washout, limp as an empty sack.

When we came up to him, it appeared that while the shot that killed him had entered the top of his head, he nevertheless earlier in the engagement had been hit four times—once through the right shoulder, once through the left cheek, once in the right side, and a fourth ball toward the last had completely shattered his right wrist. It was apparent that he had been making a desperate break to reach my horses, which usually ran in the very next canyon to the west, for he still carried with him a lariat and bridle; but his unprotected feet had been so badly frozen during the night that he had become entirely unable to travel farther, and realizing himself to be utterly helpless, in sheer desperation had built a fire to get what poor, miserable comfort he could for the few minutes or hours remaining to him.

A curious incident here followed. An ambulance had come with Lawson's troop to the field, in which the body of Everett and his wounded mate were placed, while the body of the dead Cheyenne was thrown into the boot at the back of the conveyance. Upon arrival in the garrison, Lieutenant Baxter discovered that the body of the Indian had been lost out of the boot on the short four-mile journey into Robinson, and sent back a sergeant and detail of men to recover it. But the most careful search along the trail failed to reveal any trace of the body, and whatever became of it to this day remains a mystery.

On the night of the tenth, fifty-two Indians had been recaptured, approximately half of them more or less badly wounded, and thirty-seven were known to have been killed, leaving a total of sixty unaccounted for. Still without food, on the morning of the eleventh, the seventh day of their fast, and unable to march farther, Captain Wessells's column found the fugitives occupying a strong position in the thick timber along Soldier Creek, at the foot of the hill upon which they had been entrenched the day before, better sheltered from the severity of the weather. Again, long-range firing was the order of the day, for a charge would have incurred needless hazard.

During this day, the Indians succeeded in killing a troop horse on an exposed hillside within three or four hundred yards of their position. The rider

Fighting the entrenched Cheyennes on Hat Creek Bluffs.
HARPER'S NEW MONTHLY MAGAZINE, 1897.

narrowly escaped with his life. The ground where the horse fell was so openly exposed the carcass had to be left where it had fallen, and that night, after Captain Wessells had again marched his command back into the garrison, the carcass furnished the first food these poor wretches had eaten for seven days. That their hearts were firm as ever, and that all they needed was a little physical strength, the next few days effectually proved.

The eleventh they lay eating and resting, and when on the thirteenth Wessells's column returned to the attack, the Indians were found six miles farther to the west, well entrenched on the Hat Creek Bluffs, and there again an ambush was encountered in which two troopers were wounded. On this day, a twelve-pound Napoleon gun was brought into action, and forty rounds of shell were thrown into the Indians' position, without dislodging them. This same day, Captain Wessells and Lieutenants Crawford and Hardie crept near the rifle pits with an interpreter and called to the Cheyennes to bring out their women and children, promising them shelter and protection. A feeble volley was the only reply. Realizing the Indians had now reached a cattle country in which they could kill meat and subsist themselves, Captain Wessells had brought out a pack train, with blankets and rations, to enable him to surround the Indians' position at night and, should they slip away, to camp on their trail.

This night they were surrounded, but at dawn of the fourteenth, Lieutenant Crawford discovered the wily enemy had again slipped through the picket lines, headed southwestward along the high bluffs which lined the southern edge of Hat Creek Basin. For six days more, the same tactics on both sides prevailed;

the Indians were daily followed in running fight or brought to bay in strong positions practically impregnable of direct attack, surrounded at nightfall, only to glide away like veritable shadows during the night, and, of course, more or less were killed in these daily engagements.

On January 20, Captain Wessells's command was joined by Lieutenant Dodd and a large band of Sioux scouts. Tuesday, the twenty-first, saw the finish. At a point on the Hat Creek Bluffs near the head of War Bonnet Creek, forty-four miles a little to the south of west of Fort Robinson, the Cheyennes lay at bay in their last entrenchment, worn out with travel and fighting, and with scarcely any ammunition left. They were in a washout about fifty feet long, twelve feet wide, and five feet deep, near the edge of the bluffs. Skirmishers were thrown out beneath them on the slope of the bluff to prevent their escape in that direction, and then Captain Wessells advanced on the washout, with his men formed in open skirmish order.

A summons through the interpreter to surrender was answered by a few scattering shots from the washout. Converging on the washout in this charge, the troopers soon were advancing in such a dense body that nothing saved them from terrible slaughter but the exhaustion of the Cheyennes' ammunition. Charging to the edge of the pit, the troopers emptied their carbines into it, sprang back to reload, and then came on again, while above the crash of the rifles rose the hoarse death chants of the expiring band.

The last three warriors alive—and God knows they deserve the name of warriors if ever men deserved it—sprang out of their defenses, one armed with an empty pistol and two with knives, and madly charged the troops. Three men charged three hundred. They fell, shot to pieces like men fallen under platoon

"*The little washout was a shambles.*" HARPER'S NEW MONTHLY MAGAZINE, 1887.

fire. And then the fight was over. The little washout was a shambles, whence the troops removed twenty-two dead and nine living, and of the living all but two (women) were badly wounded.

These were all that remained out of the sixty unaccounted for after the fighting near Fort Robinson, excepting five or six bucks, among them Chief Dull Knife, who had been cut off from the main band in the first night's fight and had escaped to the Sioux. And among the Oglala Sioux thereafter, till he died, dwelt Dull Knife, grim and silent as Sphinx or dumb man; brooding his wrongs; cursing the fate that had denied him the privilege to die fighting with his people.

Across the Country with the Cheyennes

ALBERT G. FORSE

Order of the Indian Wars Collection, U.S. Army Military History Institute, Carlisle Barracks, Pennsylvania

In the month of September 1887, two troops of the 1st U.S. Cavalry were ordered from Fort Custer, Montana, to the Tongue River agency on Lame Deer Creek. The reservation for said agency is situated on the Tongue River, Rosebud, Muddy and Lame Deer Creeks, Montana.

The distance from Custer to the agency is about sixty-five miles, half of it over the Badlands, on the divide between the Little Bighorn River and Rosebud Creek. In many places the roads were sidling and steep, and as the wagons were heavily loaded with rations and grain for a long journey, the march was necessarily a slow one.

Twelve miles from Custer, we passed the monument erected on the memorable battlefield of the Little Bighorn where Custer and his five troops of cavalry were exterminated by the Sioux, led by Chief Gall, on the fated June 25, 1876. A young officer who was sent ahead to select a suitable place for our first camp, on East Tullocks, came suddenly upon a fine, large deer, drinking at the stream. Both saw each other at the same moment and both were equally surprised, but the deer, not having the "buck fever;" was the first to recover himself and to remember that he had urgent business elsewhere, and good lungs and sinewy legs to carry him there. When the lieutenant bethought himself of his weapon, the deer was over the divide, and the command had bacon for supper.

While descending the divide, the second day, a wheel of one of our overloaded wagons broke, causing a long delay on account of having to transfer the load to other wagons. The day's march was a short one, and we went into camp on the Rosebud, whose name, no doubt, would suggest many pleasant possibilities to one not acquainted with the peculiarities of the country, but which was only another alkaline stream. Prairie chickens, pintails, were abundant and in good condition. The men had fine sport hunting them.

The object of the expedition was to take back to the Pine Ridge agency, in South Dakota, the renegade Cheyennes who had left their reservation and had come to the Tongue River agency to be with their friends and relatives.

After the Northern Cheyennes had been whipped into submission in 1877, they were put down in the Indian Territory with the Southern Cheyennes, on the Cheyenne and Arapaho reservation. In 1881, four hundred Northern Cheyennes were transferred from the above mentioned agency to the Pine Ridge. In 1882, two hundred Northern Cheyennes left the Pine Ridge reservation and went to Fort Keogh, Montana, where they remained until 1884, when the reservation on the Tongue, Rosebud, and other streams was set apart for them.

So many changes had separated many families and relatives, and the Cheyennes at Pine Ridge, who had relatives and friends at the Tongue River agency, quietly took their departure, and after a three-hundred-mile journey arrived at the latter agency with the firm determination to remain with their friends, and to escape the taunts of the Sioux at the Pine Ridge, who twitted them for eating the food that belonged to them and to which they said they had no right.

Knowing that the Cheyennes would object to another reservation and treat with scorn an order without a substantial backing, in addition to the two troops of cavalry, five companies of the 5th Infantry, under Major Snyder, had been ordered from Fort Keogh, Montana. At the end of our third day's march down the Rosebud, past the mouth of the Muddy and up the Lame Deer to the agency, we went into camp near the infantry command.

Nothing of interest transpired the first day. The Indians were in an unfriendly and sullen mood, and would have been in a worse one had they known that some inquisitive soldiers, without superstition and with a rudimentary development of the olfactory nerve, had crawled into the cave where Lame Deer, the old chief of the Cheyennes, was buried, hauled out his remains, and unrobed them. We were camped on the battlefield where the chief had been killed in his fight with General Miles some years before. Fortunately, the knowledge of the desecration was conveyed to the commanding officer, who soon had the culprits on their hands and knees dragging back the disturbed remains to the place where they belonged.

The following day, a council was held at the agency. A few of the officers attended, but most of them were in camp where the command was held in readiness to act upon a moment's notice.

The council was a stormy one. American Horse, one of the chiefs, was very bitter; [he] declared that the Cheyennes would not be separated from their friends and relatives; that if it came to that they might as well die, and counseled resistance to any attempt made to move them. Red Cherries spoke to the same effect, acted like an enraged lion, hurled threats and defiance without stint, and in speaking of the agent, whom he wished to designate as an "old fossil," said "he was not born, he was dug out of the bank." Red Cherries had cause to be angry: His daughter, who had married an Indian at the Tongue River agency, was to be taken with her child back to the Pine Ridge agency.

Among the speakers was one, not a chief, whose motions and gestures were so graceful, whose manner was so impressive, that we named him "the senator." There was one new feature of the council that surprised even the old campaigners: A squaw spoke, and her speech was as bitter and hostile as the others to which we had been treated. Her right to speak was given her for some act of bravery that had benefited the tribe in one of their hostile expeditions. Two Moon, a subchief, standing six feet two inches in his moccasins, was also among the number who spoke violently and counseled resistance to the last.

The general drift of the savage oratory seemed to be carrying us to unpleasant and depressing probabilities. We knew that the chief and subchiefs were angry, but we had hoped that some of them, especially the older ones who had suffered so much in their last campaigns, would have learned wisdom from experience and counseled obedience. The unfriendly sentiments of Two Moons were a great disappointment, as we had counted upon him to give good advice. When he went against us, it certainly looked as though we would have to use force, which meant a long and bloody war and many lives lost, as the Cheyennes, next to the Nez Perces, are the bravest and hardest fighting-warriors on the continent.

In all the speeches, there was not one advising separation, although the Indians knew that the Tongue River reservation was not large enough to furnish farming and grazing lands for so many. Many whites had taken up claims and were living on them when the government selected the reservation, and their titles being good, they could not be removed. All these convincing facts seemed to have no effect, and the result of the council was extremely unsatisfactory.

Our first ray of hope came from the belligerent and disappointing Two Moon, who stealthily came to our camp in the evening and, through an interpreter, gave us to understand that he did not mean what he had said in the council; that his warlike speech was simply a political dodge to gain favor with the tribe; that he and American Horse were both striving to be head chief, and as opposition to separation was decidedly popular, he could not ruin his chances by publicly favoring it. "But," said he, after smilingly telling us that his deceptive speech was meant only for the unsuspecting ears of his fellow Indians, "I will do all I can to make them go, and they will go."

After four days of many talks and much patient persuasion, in which, no doubt, the two troops of cavalry and five companies of infantry acted as a powerful incentive to the persuasiveness of the red man, they all decided to go back to Pine Ridge.

How to take so many was the next question to be considered, and how to feed them caused still greater anxiety. We could not give them transportation and had only enough rations for our own command. The agent was finally induced to let us have some light wagons belonging to the Interior Department, to use as trains behind the army wagons, but he seriously objected to taking the responsibility of giving the rations belonging to his Indians. But as the visitors could not, and would not, go without rations, and would be driven to killing cattle to keep from starvation if they remained, he at last consented.

Many preparations were necessary before starting, and for several days there was great activity and pleasant excitement. Beeves were killed and the meat cut in thin slices and jerked (dried) to keep it from spoiling. The Indians, having accepted the situation, were doing the sensible act of making the best of it, and all was going well until the interpreter, Seminole, while assisting in shooting the beeves, fired an unlucky bullet that struck the horn of a beef, glanced off, and killed one of the many Indians festooning the corral fence. The Cheyennes had no great love for Seminole, and the dead man's friends declared that the killing had been intentional. The excitement was of such a threatening character that the agent sent to the commanding officer for assistance, and a troop of cavalry was ordered to the agency.

The Indians, wild with rage, were searching for Seminole, who had been secreted in the cellar of the agent's house, from which he was safely escorted to the Indian guardhouse, and a guard put around the building to keep the dead Indian's friends from shooting him through the windows.

In order to prove, if possible, that the shooting was accidental, the acting assistant surgeon was ordered to make a post mortem examination. The head men were requested to be present, and fortunately for Seminole, the course of the bullet was followed through the body and found lodged in the muscles of the back, not having struck a bone. Examination of the ball plainly showed the marks made by the wrinkles at the base of the horn from which it had glanced, and continuing the investigation at the corral, it was proved from the position of the beef and the Indian killed that it could not have been a direct, but a glancing, shot. All were satisfied except the immediate friends of the dead man, who probably held out for pecuniary solace to heal their woes.

During the post mortem, the squaws and relatives of the deceased gathered near the building and gave voice to their lamentations in dismal cries and ear-splitting howls. They were in deep mourning. The hair cut short, a little dark paint on the face, the legs scarified, swollen, and covered with blood from the knees down to the ankles are to these savage people the same as the conventional black robe and long crape veil are to the civilized world; much less expensive emblems of grief, but decidedly more painful. Why blood poisoning does not set in is surprising, as all the laws of surgery and hygiene are disregarded. Neither before nor after the operation are the legs washed; neither are the knives, and the blood flowing from the wounds is allowed to coagulate and remain until it wears off.

The Indians object to any mutilation of their dead, and although their consent had been gained, after much and long persuasion, the fury of the relatives when they crowded into the building after the post mortem was simply devilish when they discovered what had been done. The doctor, unfortunately for his general peace of mind, was the only white man left in the room, and the very man wanted by the enraged crowd of relatives. Drawing their knives, they made a rush at him, but with the instantaneous conviction that "absence might make their hearts grow fonder," the doctor ingloriously fled, and made double quick time to a place of safety.

Finally the day of our departure arrived. The two troops of cavalry were to escort the Cheyennes to Pine Ridge, and the infantry to remain in camp near the agency. It was nearly 9:00 A.M. before we got under way; there were so many last words to be spoken, so many sorrowful partings to be made.

Crossing the divide, between Rosebud and Tongue Rivers, we followed down Stebben's Creek from the summit, and camped at its mouth where it empties into the Tongue. Our march was slow and tedious, having a great deal of road making and grading to do to get our heavy wagons over and to prevent them upsetting. After leaving the camp at the mouth of Stebben's Creek, there was no road to follow, and our map of the country was not correct; it was one gotten up by the cattlemen, and our Indian guides had crude ideas of where wagons should go.

The general direction was southeast. Our guides led us up the Tongue River to the mouth of Otter Creek, up Otter to Three Mile Creek, which was only a two-mile creek to us, for finding it impossible to go farther with our heavy wagons, we went into camp. The Indians kept well to themselves and showed no disposition to be friendly.

That night a most terrific thunderstorm was let loose upon us. For hours there were continuous flashes of vivid lightning, followed by deafening peals of thunder. The lightning seemed to be striking all around us, and we feared that some of the Indians might be struck. They are in abject terror of the lightning, believing it to be a great bird that lives in the Bighorn Mountains, and to be struck by it means the anger of the Great Spirit and a bad omen for any expedition or war they may be engaged in. Fortunately, no damage was done beyond a thorough soaking to all who had not the best of tepees. The morning came clear and beautiful, and we made a backward march to Otter Creek, and up that creek through a valley that would have been pleasant to look at if the grasshoppers had not paid it a visit and eaten every green thing in it. We had another big storm during the night, and although we were camped on a level bench several feet above the creek, to which the surface water had free access, the rain fell in such torrents that in the morning, which again came clear and bright, we had the unexpected surprise of seeing our boots and shoes floating in the water that formed miniature lakes in our tents.

Marching up Otter to Indian Creek, and nearly to the head of the latter, we camped near a hay and cattle ranch kept by two brothers. After breaking camp the following day, we left Indian Creek and reached the summit of the divide between Tongue and Powder Rivers. After following the ridge for some time, the guides made a sudden descent down a steep grade which they said was a road to Powder River, and as they had done well since our trouble at Three Mile Creek, we got well down the grade before the unwelcome possibility dawned upon us that we might be getting into a place that would be hard to get out of. The little valley narrowed into a deep canyon, and the quartermaster, sent ahead to find out what kind of a road was before us, returned with the information that it would be impossible to get our wagons through. Unfortunately, some of the wagons had gotten too far down to be turned back.

The evening was spent in trying to find an egress better than the steep grade down which we had come into the pocket, but we were not successful, and reluctantly we went into camp. The next morning, the drivers, by doubling the teams, got the wagons on the ridge again, along which we marched until we struck Corral Creek, down which we found a road that brought us to the Powder River. The river being high and muddy, and the water bad, we ascended the left bank to Bitter Creek. We crossed and went up the creek to a ranch that had an excellent spring of water, the first good water we had had since leaving the agency.

As we were approaching the game country, the Indians were given ammunition for hunting. The hunters were placed so that they could be counted, and the cartridges equally divided. Noticing that the Indian distributor kept none for himself, an explanation was asked, and the astonishing answer came that the distributor, who was never the same Indian twice in succession, would not take the cartridges for fear he might be suspected of taking more than his share. It was a nice little point of pride, and had its reward by the distributor receiving his share after the others had left.

Before leaving the agency, we naturally wanted to know how many Indians were to go with us, but the nervous agent said they considered it "bad medicine" to be counted and refused to assist us. Owing to our difficulties and delays on account of storms and bad roads, we were unable to count them until one lucky day when they had to pass through a narrow defile; the counting was so quietly done that the confiding savages had not the faintest suspicion that they were taking bad medicine. There were 203. We had started with 205, but some friends of Red Cherries' daughter had carried her child back to the agency. She was allowed to go back to get it, but did not return. Her intentions were good, as she left all her property with us.

Up Bitter to Rabbit Creek, up Rabbit to the divide, which was soon crossed to the head of White Tail Creek, where an unexpected spring of fine water gave relief and comfort to men and horses after the hot and dusty ride. A long distance down the valley, two men were in a field plowing, and so engaged in their agricultural occupation that they did not see the soldiers but saw our Indian hunters coming from different directions into the valley. Fearing they might be hostiles, the men unhitched their horses, mounted, and started on a mad gallop for their ranch, hoping to get there in time to protect their women and children. It would have been hard lines for the latter if the Indians had been hostiles, for when the men reached the house it was surrounded by the hunters, looking with quiet curiosity at the badly scared inmates.

We continued down White Tail to Little Powder, where we expected to have a refreshing bath in the "flowing waters of the river." The poetical part of it was about all we had. The waters were flowing all right enough, but the heavy rains had washed down so much white clay from the highlands that the flowing water looked more like a stream of whitewash than anything else. By digging holes in the sand a little distance from the river, we managed to get water clear enough to cook with, but the sylvan dream of a bath in the river failed to materialize.

Discovering that the Indians were amusing themselves shooting at prairie dogs, birds, rabbits, and everything they came across, a council was held and they were asked why they had not kept the promise they had made to use the ammunition given them only for large game. "We're are not using the cartridges you gave us," a young warrior answered, "we are shooting these at the small game," showing us one that had been reloaded. Making inquiries, we found they had bullet moulds and made cartridges for their guns when they could not buy them. The Indians can buy lead, powder, and primers, but it is contrary to the law to sell them fixed ammunition, but they get it if they have the money to pay for it. The average frontier storekeeper does not harass his mind with the mandates of the law, and a red man's dollar for cartridges is just as acceptable as a white man's dollar for canned tomatoes.

Just before breaking camp on the Little Powder, Seminole, the interpreter, came with the information that one of the Indians was not getting ready to move, but was planning to remain quietly in the timber on the river bottom until the soldiers were at a safe distance, and then put back for the agency. Seminole's watchfulness put a quietus on this sharp little game, and the would-be deserter made a hurried packing and fell into line with the others. That evening the chiefs were told that one of their men had attempted to go back, and that unless they would promise that there would be no more such attempts, the whole outfit would be under guard day and night; none would be allowed to leave the camp, and there would be no more hunting.

After a long parley (an Indian is never in a hurry when there is talking to be done), the chiefs promised that there would be no more attempted escapes, but said, "It is pretty hard to punish all if one or two does wrong." It was hard, but as we did not know the contented from the discontented and were responsible for their safe delivery at Pine Ridge, our only recourse was to make the chiefs responsible for their followers. Knowing their great affection for their families, there was nothing risked in giving them hunting passes so long as we had the squaws and children.

[Frederick] Remington should have been with us to sketch the column of eighteen trail wagons filled with squaws and children (dilapidated old buggies owned by the Indians), with a hundred ponies following, some carrying squaws, some children, some packs, and some drawing travois made of lodge poles, the large or butt ends fastened to both sides of the pony and the smaller ends dragging on the ground. Traveling a la travois is really quite luxurious: The poles being long and springy, the motion is quite easy. Countless dogs followed their dusky friends; an eagle, a ground owl, and other pets of various kinds, with a contingent of unwalkable puppies, were tied in the wagons and on the travois, out of which the puppies would fall and hang strangling in midair till some sympathetic squaw would utter a bloodcurdling shriek and rush to the rescue.

The heaviest bundles were carried in the wagons. These bundles were wrapped in watertight matting, or skins, so that neither rain nor dampness could harm their contents, and they were looked after with the greatest care, especially the bag containing the good medicine and the charms of the medicine man.

Continuing our march up the Little Powder to Horse Creek and along the right bank, we reached the Cottonwood, where we halted, unloaded our wagons, pitched our tents, and gazed with hungry admiration at the game that our successful hunters had brought into camp: Deer, elk, antelope, bear, rabbits, ducks, and prairie chickens made a mighty feast and brought sweet forgetfulness of the army bacon. The Indians are too crafty to risk long shots while hunting; they take advantage of the ridges to crawl up on the game and seldom risk a shot over a hundred yards.

Up the Cottonwood, over the divide, down Dry Creek to the North Fork of the Cheyenne, we reached Kaufman's ranch on the west side of the Black Hills. We had passed over a rolling country with abundant grass, but without trees except a few pines on the highest points and the cottonwoods along the streams. A fine cattle country if the cattlemen could afford to feed their stock when an unusually severe winter comes, but as a herd of thousands of cattle is a different affair from the eastern farmer's gentle bovines coming home to the evening meal, feeding them would soon cause disaster to the cattleman's exchequer. If the winter is not too severe, the cattle paw through the snow and manage to get enough grass to keep them alive till spring, but if the winter comes with heavy snows whose surface melts and then freezes to a hard crust, the cattle die by thousands.

Our Indians, who at first kept to themselves in sullen seclusion, became, as time passed, quite friendly, and evinced a desire to be sociable that was quite embarrassing. The red man *is* interesting, but there are various and uncomfortable reasons why he should be kept at a distance. Our friend, the "senator," was an anomaly among his kind and deserves public mention. As soon as we got into camp, he helped his squaws put up the tepees, brought wood and water, did all the hard work (he seemed to think it no disgrace) and was always cheerful, beaming with smiles when spoken to. The other noble red men would hunt or ride all day while the squaws looked after the children, rescued the dangling puppies, and kept an eye on the pack ponies. Arriving in camp, the copper-hued maidens would unpack their belongings, put up the tepees, bring wood and water, do the cooking, and rest themselves afterwards by jerking venison or curing the skins, while their lords and masters smoked and slept.

Leaving the North Fork of the Cheyenne, we made camp on Buffalo Creek, near some agents of the Interior Department who were looking for testimony to prosecute dishonest men for taking up land fraudulently. In taking up tillable soil, the government requires so many acres to be enclosed, plowed, and fenced, but the would-be owners of the soil in question had such vague conceptions of what a fence should be that in the judgment of the investigating agents, it was not a fence but a pretense, and the turning up of the soil to the depth of one or two inches on the outer edges of the piece, and diagonally from corner to corner, was not considered, in the stern opinion of the law, a strict fulfillment of the "I hereby swear that the land has been cultivated" clause.

Marching up the Buffalo was not pleasant. The weather was dark and rainy, and the roads were bad and became so much worse when we crossed over to the head of the Beaver that we went into camp on the high bluff above the creek, which had cut quite a respectable canyon at that point. One of the officers, hearing that a sick child was in one of the tepees, and having a tender place in his heart for suffering humanity when it comes with tender years, took an evening stroll to the tepee to inquire how the child was getting on and if it needed anything. The mother of the child was old, ugly, and dirty, but the father, being in a state of happy oblivion to these few drawbacks, accused the philanthropic son of Mars of coming under the guise of friendship to make love to his wife. Alas! for our best and purest motives when they bump their innocent heads against the adamantine convictions of a jealous husband.

Cold, wet, and disagreeable as our camp was, we left it with regret, knowing the discomforts that lay before us. The rain came down with pitiless persistence, and the roads were so bad that men had to walk on each side of the wagons, knocking the mud, or gumbo, as it is called, from the wheels to enable us to make even one poor mile an hour. The only amusing thing in the whole day's proceedings was the story of Tobacco Eating Jake's pet beaver. Jake was a halfbreed Canadian, a simple-minded fellow, knowing one or two Indian dialects and the sign language, and was one of our interpreters. Jacob Sasey was the man's real name, but Jacob's intimate friends, becoming convinced that the name was too barren of meaning to bring to public attention the principal peculiarity of the man owning it, had given him the all comprehensive sobriquet of Tobacco Eating Jake. Jake had captured the beaver when it was in the impressionable period of youth and had tamed and petted it into living in happy contentment in his shack, or hut. One day Jake, who was evidently a free and easy housekeeper, left an open sack of flour on the floor with a bucket of water in close proximity. The beaver, feeling lonely, amused himself by jumping into the flour sack, then into the bucket of water, and back into the flour sack, varying the monotony of flour and water by rolling on the floor and in Jake's bed, then back into the flour and water until the latter was exhausted. When Jake returned, he was fully impressed with the sorrowful conviction that there was "no place like home." Dough, flour, and water were over everything. The joyous beaver had become sad and dejected. His many coats of flour and water had dried into such a tough crust that he could scarcely move. Let us hope that he had enough suppleness of muscle to make a safe retreat from that blighted abode.

Our second camp on Beaver Creek was, if possible, more disagreeable than the first. Everything was covered with the thick, black mud which clung to our boots in such generous quantities that walking was a feat of strength too great for careless indulgence, and the campfire, the one spot that always has some suggestion of cheerfulness, became the principal point of attraction. Each day's march along Beaver Creek was a repetition of discomforts and hard work that taxed the most Christian spirit, if anything coming under that head could be found in the wet and muddy outfit laboriously making its way through the driving rains and clinging mud, building great fires in the wet camps to dry the soaked clothing and blankets, and wondering if the rain would never cease and the sun ever shine again. The country was rolling, and in the distance to the left could be seen the Black Hills, and black enough they appeared to us till our last day on the Beaver, when the clouds disappeared and the sun shone once more. But we left it without regret, and when we reached the South Fork of the Cheyenne and came to a large ranch with a store and post office, we felt that we had reached the very center of civilization. After crossing the South Fork, the weather was fine, the country more level and easier to march over.

When within three days' march of the Pine Ridge, an unusual activity was suddenly developed among the Indians. As soon as we got into camp, they were washing themselves, their clothes, and everything they could get hold of. So little washing had been indulged in, notwithstanding the dust and mud that we had come through, that this sudden outburst of cleanliness took the camp by surprise.

Reaching the town of Oelrich, named after the superintendent of a big cattle company, we halted a couple of hours, then continued the march and camped on Black Tail Creek, a branch of the White River. All through the country, the caravan excited the greatest interest. Accustomed as the ranchers were to seeing Indians, they had never before seen such an accumulation of old wagons, buggies, carts, travois, and ponies. Most of the vehicles, not belonging to the government, were held together by rawhide, and how they made the long journey without falling to pieces still remains a mystery. The wheels were at all angles to the axles and made serpentine trails in the dust and mud.

Marching east, we camped on the eastern bank of White River, just below White Clay Creek, both well named, as the aqueous part of them had more the appearance of liquid clay than water. The mysterious washing, scrubbing, and cleaning still continued, and the carefully packed bundles opened and examined. Morning on White River came dark and cloudy, but the appearance of the Indians had changed as if by magic. Old shirts, leggings, dresses, and moccasins had given way to gorgeous clothing, bright, clean, covered with beads and hundreds of elk teeth, the latter worth from twenty-five to fifty cents apiece, making the jackets ornamented with them worth a small fortune to the lucky owners. Faces shone with red paint, varied by streaks of other colors, and all were ready to meet their friends at Pine Ridge, and as desirous of making a good impression as Lieutenant Forse was when he asked his striker for his white shirt and undress suit. Gunny sacks are useful and excellent for carrying grain and flour, but when one takes the place of a valise and is packed with a promiscuous assortment of boots, shoes, brushes, blacking, candles, and clothing, with the general appearance of having been arranged by a private cyclone, it is not surprising that the lieutenant was somewhat astonished when the white shirt and undress suit were brought into view.

Fine raiment, personal beautifying, and vanity having no weight with the elements, the rain poured down in torrents the morning of our last day's march to Pine Ridge, but the welcome sunshine came in the afternoon, and by the time we filed into the agency, our soaked clothes had dried to a comfortable degree of dampness. The Indians were met by their friends, and there was such general rejoicing that when they were turned over to the agent, the bad medicine of being counted was submitted to quite cheerfully. The following day, the cavalry troops started on the homeward journey by the way of Fort Robinson, Nebraska, old Fort Fetterman, Wyoming, and Fort McKinney, and rode into Custer after an absence of two months and a march of nearly nine hundred miles.

PART EIGHT

The Death of Crazy Horse, 1877

The Capture and Death of an Indian Chieftain

JESSE M. LEE

Journal of the Military Service Institution of the United States 54, no. 189 (May–June 1914): 323–40

In my rustic childhood days, I was often thrilled with wonder as I listened with eager ears and bulging eyes to the recital from my venerated elders of the cruelties, dangers, and hardships incident to life on the frontier among Indians, until by treaty or compulsion they were driven toward the setting sun— never to return to the homes of their fathers.

When I heard those hair-raising tales, I little thought that much of my after life would be spent in the remoter West among Indians of similar type, who were then vainly struggling to stay the wave of the white man's civilization that has now engulfed them and probably doomed to ultimate extinction the vanishing Indian race.

About eighteen years ago, I read a lyceum essay to my brother officers, relating the events leading up to the killing of one of the most fanatical and bravest war chiefs of the Sioux nation. This occurred at Camp Robinson, near Red Cloud Indian Agency in Northwestern Nebraska in the fall of 1877. This and Spotted Tail agency, forty miles distant, were two of the largest Indian agencies in our country.

I may remark in passing that in December 1890, over thirteen years afterward, in this same vicinity the widespread "Messiah" or "Ghost Dance" craze among the Plains Indians culminated in the slaughter of Big Foot's band of about two hundred Sioux at Wounded Knee Creek.

In March 1877, it fell to my lot to enter on duty as military Indian agent, in charge of the Brule Sioux, at what was then known as the Spotted Tail agency in Northwestern Nebraska. The great Sioux war was in its closing stage—a war in which the Indian displayed the highest qualities of generalship and, considering his limited resources, prolonged the conflict to a surprising degree and achieved victories which will long endure in the annals of warlike history. This war brought into marked prominence Indian chieftains, warlike leaders whose skill and prowess gave renown to the names of Crazy Horse and Sitting Bull.

At this time, the spring of 1877, the result with respect to losses was decidedly favorable to the Indians; but having no base of supplies other than rude nature afforded; being dependent upon their enemies, the whites, for such arms and ammunition as they might capture in conflict or obtain through clandestine traffic; being necessarily encumbered with their wives and children, and kept constantly on the move by recurring military expeditions against them, the thoughtful Indian warriors gradually realized that prolonged resistance would be suicidal.

Under these conditions, two prominent causes contributed to the general cessation of hostilities: first, the splendid success of Colonel Miles in the North, which resulted in his securing prominent hostages for the surrender of the hostiles in the spring of 1877; second, in the latter part of January 1877, General Crook induced Spotted Tail, one of the noblest Indian chiefs of modern times, to go out in the midst of Dakota blizzards with about two hundred of his Brule headmen and persuade the hostiles to come in and surrender at the Spotted Tail and Red Cloud agencies. As a direct result of Spotted Tail's mission, two hostile Sioux bands, numbering about one thousand, under Touch-the-Clouds, Roman Nose, and Red Bear, surrendered at Spotted Tail agency in April 1877.

The Cheyennes, of about nine hundred souls, who had met with defeat by Colonel Mackenzie in November 1876, were the next to surrender at Red Cloud; but all the authorities were anxiously awaiting the coming of the invincible chieftain, Crazy Horse. His gradual approach from day to day was heralded by swift couriers, and his numbers much exaggerated. He arrived at Red Cloud about May 15, 1877, where he was met by General Crook's representatives, Colonel (now Major General) Randall[2] and Lt. Philo Clark. He had 140 lodges, numbering by actual count less than a thousand men, women, and children, mostly Oglala Sioux.

Crazy Horse did not surrender with the humility of a defeated, broken-spirited chief. He was an unsubdued warrior, a great soldier chief, and had come in to make such terms as would bring peace and rest to his people, who had scarcely known defeat under his valiant leadership. To his mind there was no "unconditional surrender" about it. He was willing, at least for a time, to give up the uncertain buffalo for the certain agency beef; to exchange the old, worn-out skin lodges for new and handsome tepees of army duck. Crazy Horse consented to peace, but demanded plenty. He was the ideal captain, who was not only in touch with his soldier braves, but who fired their souls with his own martial ardor. It was Crazy Horse's voice that rang out when some of the advance warriors recoiled from Custer's fire, "Come on! Die with me! It's a good day to die! Cowards to the rear!" and by deeds that surpassed his words, it was he who first broke Custer's line. At Red Cloud, Crazy Horse made a dignified semblance of surrendering, giving as a token of peace a small percentage of arms.

About a month prior to Crazy Horse's surrender, General Crook, at Spotted Tail, in council with the friendlies and the former hostiles, promised them, and especially the latter, that when matters got settled down, they should all go out on a big buffalo hunt in the early fall. This announcement was loudly greeted with a chorus of enthusiastic "Hows!" This promise, which was also explicitly made to Crazy Horse, was deemed wise at that time, but its attempted fulfillment became fraught with danger, as the sequel will show.

Shortly prior to this, considerable numbers of Indian scouts had been enlisted at both agencies, and after the usual feastings and promises, a very good representation, numerically, was obtained from those who had recently surrendered. The chiefs were rated as noncommissioned officers and their trusted braves selected as privates, all receiving good pay and having but little to do. The promise was made and reiterated by Colonel Randall and Lieutenant Clark, who had a right to speak on the subject to the scouts, and especially to the late hostiles, that they were enlisted to preserve peace and good order at the agencies and vicinity and protect themselves and their ponies against white horse thieves.

Colonel Mackenzie had been in command of the District of the Black Hills during troublous times, and upon his departure to another field of duty of equal importance, Colonel Bradley,[3] of the 9th Infantry, was selected to command the important district. This able officer had won marked distinction in the Civil War; since then, by his splendid capacity, cool judgment, and untiring energy, [he] had successfully met the grave responsibility affecting both Indians and whites, and contributed in an eminent degree to the prosperous development of the frontiers of that region.

Lieutenant Clark was stationed at Camp Robinson, near Red Cloud agency, having a general oversight over the recent hostiles, especially Crazy Horse and his Oglalas, and it was his duty to keep General Crook fully and directly informed as to anything of interest. Lieutenant Clark possessed in a high degree a personal magnetism and pleasing manner that charmed everyone. His selection by General Crook for this most difficult of duties was a high compliment to his marked ability and splendid accomplishments. He was, without doubt, one of the most talented and promising officers in the army, and his untimely death deprived the country of one who would probably have adorned a high niche in the temple of military fame, had the opportunity offered. He was successful in almost every move and was only overreached by the wily Crazy Horse, whose unfettered will would consciously brook no mastery.

At the other agency, Spotted Tail was king in fact as well as in name, and every Indian, half-breed, and squaw man yielded obedience to him. He spoke for his tribe, and when he had done, nothing more need be said. He was a keen diplomat, a logical reasoner, and an orator of the highest rank, and was consulted by generals, philanthropists, and peace commissioners.

As the summer wore along, the Northern Indians at both agencies were looking forward to the buffalo hunt with more or less anxiety. Everything was peaceful, but these Indians had gotten well enough attached to agency ways for this departure on a long and questionable hunting expedition. Crazy Horse was eager to go, and it seemed that the promise of months before, whether wisely or unwisely made, would have to be fulfilled. There was also some talk about getting a large delegation of the principal chiefs to go to Washington for a powwow with the Great Father. On August 5, we received word from Clark that all Indians who desired could go on the hunt, and the trip to Washington would occur later. At Spotted Tail agency, we felt that probably a crisis had come. If all the Indians, wild and tame, or all of the former and some of the latter, went out on a general buffalo hunt with all the wild Indians from Red Cloud, trouble might ensue, and many would slip away and join Sitting Bull, who had gone north of the line. Spotted Tail held this view and vehemently supported it, and his right-hand subchief, Swift Bear, said, "The man who planned this hunt needs a heart and a brain."

Major (later General) Burke, the efficient commanding officer of Camp Sheridan, at Spotted Tail agency, and I, as agent, had a long and trying council with the chiefs. We agreed with Spotted Tail that it might be a question of peace or war; a holding fast to what had been gained or the undoing of all that had been accomplished. After twenty-four hours of almost incessant work, the eloquence and unanswerable arguments of Spotted Tail carried the day. We felt that we had broken the backbone of the buffalo hunt at our agency. Crazy Horse at Red Cloud was probably disappointed, and even his reluctant acquiescence would enable him at any time to accuse the authorities with breach of faith. Detectives were watching his movements and listening to all that he said, and reporting anything that boded of ill. He was now approached on the subject of going with the delegation to Washington, to which he replied he "was not hunting for any Great Father. His father was with him, and there was no Great Father between him and the Great Spirit."

About this time, Colonel Randall informed Major Burke and myself that "Crazy Horse was all right, was doing just what they wanted him to do, that he was talked to too much, but if they would let him alone and not 'buzz' him so much he would come out all right." Soon after this, Clark wrote, "Crazy Horse told me he wanted to do right, but wanted plenty of time to consider, and so matters rest and nothing has been determined in regard to the hunt," showing that Crazy Horse had not forgotten this promise.

Two weeks later, Clark again wrote that "rumors between the two agencies have grown into such proportions; their influence is so bad and pernicious, keeping the Indians in an unsettled, restless state, I hope we can stop them. The Northern Indians at both agencies have done well, and as long as they are trying to do what is right, it is not fair or just that they should be kept constantly on nettles by stories of damage that is going to be done to them." We at Spotted Tail agency had tried hard to prevent this very thing, by keeping our business affairs and councils separate from such matters at Red Cloud.

Clark further added, "In the event of any trouble, which I am quite confident we need not fear, I will send a courier to you at once with written information; so do not place any reliance on any other kind."

A few days later (near the last of August), Touch-the-Clouds,[4] whose honesty Major Burke and I could not doubt, informed us that he and one or two other northern chiefs had been sent for by Clark to go to Red Cloud, for some purpose we knew not what, but on the next day we received instructions from Red Cloud agency that sixty Indian scouts were wanted to go out northwest and fight the Nez Perces. As a result, all was hubbub and excitement among the Indians. The Northern Indian scouts did not take to this measure with much zest, but finally we succeeded in getting them ready to go, and then came an order to suspend action.

On August 31, just four days before the trouble culminated, Clark wrote Major Burke as follows: "General Crook left Omaha this morning. Crazy Horse and Touch-the-Clouds with High Bear came up and told me that they were going north on the warpath. I hope you and Lee can at least postpone any starting of the Northern Indians. Crazy Horse has worked Touch-the-Clouds exactly round to his way of thinking. Perhaps after he gets cooled off, and Spotted Tail and the rest can get at him, he will change, but it certainly shows that his reformation is not very deep."

The above clearly showed that a breach had suddenly occurred, and the resulting events show how even the most careful man may be misled as to the real intent of Indians, and that, too, through a mistake of an interpreter, however honest. Next day, official word came from Red Cloud agency that the Northern Indians there were to be surrounded, and asking that the same thing be done at our agency.

That Touch-the-Clouds had agreed to go north with Crazy Horse and fight the whites surprised us very much, for he had ever acted honorably and as far right as we could expect. Major Burke directed that as soon as Touch-the-Clouds and High Bear returned from Red Cloud, they be sent to the post. They at once came up, without excitement or concern, and many, in fact all, circumstances showed nothing wrong. We went to Major Burke's house. There were present Major Burke and several other officers. Of the interpreters, Louis Bordeaux[5] and Charlie Taggett (two of the most competent interpreters in the Sioux nation), besides Frank Grouard, General Crook's famous guide, and the well-known old Mexican scout and interpreter, Joe Merival. Of Brule loyal Indian chiefs, Spotted Tail, Swift Bear, Two Strike, and White Thunder; of northern chiefs, Touch-the-Clouds, Red Bear, and High Bear. We asked Touch-the-Clouds to repeat what he said and explain what he meant at Red Cloud the day before. Louis Bordeaux interpreted, and the other interpreters were cautioned to follow every word. It soon became evident that Frank Grouard had, through honest mistake, no doubt, misinterpreted Touch-the-Clouds (perhaps Crazy Horse too). Bordeaux and Grouard were soon engaged in a wordy dispute, and Touch-the-Clouds, apparently for the first time comprehending how Grouard had misinterpreted him at Red Cloud, told Grouard, with earnest indignation, that he lied; that he never said that he was going to fight the whites, but that he had told "White Hat" (Clark) that when he came here, he was promised absolute peace, but that the Great Father, General Crook, and others had deceived him and now wanted him and his people to go on the warpath, a thing which he violently condemned as a breach of faith; that first, it was give up his gun and he did it; then it was to enlist as a scout to keep peace and order at the agency, and he did that; then he was asked to throw away the buffalo hunt, and he did that; then, like a horse with a bit in its mouth, his head was turned toward Washington, and he looked that way; now the Great Father, the "Gray Fox" (General Crook), and White Hat put blood on their faces and turned then to war; that he and Crazy Horse had been deceived and lied to, but now they would do as White Hat said, and war it would be! They would all go north and fight; the troops would have to go north and fight, too, and when they met the Nez Perces (meaning they would conquer them), "all would soon be peace."

In this way, Touch-the-Clouds repeated and explained all that he and Crazy Horse had said, and added that Grouard had given it a meaning they had not intended. Naturally, Grouard disliked to admit the correctness of Touch-the-Cloud's statement, as interpreted by Bordeaux, but in answer to a question as to whether he now believed Touch-the-Clouds meant to go north to renew hostilities against the whites, he responded in the negative, saying, "I don't believe he intends doing so now." It is believed that this whole trouble originated in asking these Northern Indians to go out and fight the Nez Perces, something they could not understand. Clark, however, acted on Grouard's interpretation, and additional troops were sent for to come to Red Cloud, augmenting the force to probably over seven hundred cavalry and infantry, with the addition of about three hundred Indian allies, making a total of not less than one thousand well-armed men. We had at Spotted Tail a garrison of about 90 men, which of itself would have been powerless to protect the agency and post in the event of an Indian outbreak, where there were six thousand Indians—but Spotted Tail, with his faithful Brules, was a tower of strength on our side.

To avoid a crisis or an outbreak at Spotted Tail agency, on September 2, I proceeded to the post at Red Cloud agency and found that General Crook had arrived and events of great importance were near at hand. Clark had suddenly lost all confidence in Crazy Horse, including Touch-the-Clouds and all our Indians belonging to northern bands. I at once saw General Crook and Colonel Bradley and told them there was some mistake; that all the Indians at Spotted Tail agency were quiet and had no intention of going north on the warpath. I was directed to see Clark and tell him all about it, which I did, but he seemed positive that there was no mistake. I tried to explain the dispute at Spotted Tail as to the meaning of what was said about going to war. I repeated all that had occurred at the interview with Touch-the-Clouds; all that Touch-the-Clouds said; Frank Grouard's apparent discomfiture as to the mistake which the interpreters said he made, and his partial admission to that effect, as above stated.

In the course of the discussion, which was by no means tame, I said I would guarantee that no Indian from Spotted Tail agency would go north, at which Clark smiled incredulously. I reiterated that there was certainly a mistake as to Touch-the-Clouds. I finally succeeded in getting myself listened to, and was greatly relieved when General Crook and Colonel Bradley said they were glad I had come. General Crook said, "Mr. Lee, I don't want to make any mistake, for it would, to the Indians, be the basest treachery to make a mistake in this matter."

Having accomplished enough to secure peace at Spotted Tail, I felt easy. One strong and conclusive fact was that the remnant of what was once Lame Deer's hostile band was coming in to our agency and giving up some horses and a considerable number of arms, which would not be the case had our Indians any intention of going out; but it still seemed to be the intention of Clark to have something done to Crazy Horse and his band—just what, I did not then know.

On September 3, four troops of cavalry came in from Laramie. I heard other troops were approaching from different points, and it was evident something startling was likely to happen before long. In the afternoon of that day, I was told, confidentially, that Crazy Horse's camp would be surrounded next morning. I asked if word had been sent to Major Burke at Spotted Tail agency of the intended surround, and was told, "No, that had not been done." I urged that it was vital that he should know it beforehand, so as to prevent a stampede from there; that an Indian courier from the Indians would probably get there first, with exaggerated news of fighting; that wild excitement would follow, and all the work of the year might be undone. Without my knowledge, Chief Spotted Tail had been sent for by the authorities at Camp Robinson and was then at Red Cloud, and it was urged by me that he be at once sent back to aid in controlling matters at his agency through the trouble. Feeling it my duty to get him back as soon as possible, I obtained Colonel Bradley's permission to start after midnight. On the morning of the fourth, we started at three o'clock, well armed for what some thought might be a perilous journey, but which proved to be perfectly safe, as I had believed.

I must not forget to say that the last words I said to Clark before leaving were, "Don't let Crazy Horse get away; he might come to Spotted Tail agency." Clark replied, with a trace of sarcasm, "Lee, don't you worry about that! Crazy Horse can't make a move without my knowing it, and I can have him whenever I want him. I'll send you the news of our success in writing, by a good courier." This was not idle talk, for Clark had detectives with ears quick to catch each word that might fall from Crazy Horse's lips, and eyes keen to note his every movement.

Spotted Tail and I reached his agency about 10:00 A.M. and found everything quiet and Major Burke busily engaged in counting the remnants of the hostiles who had just arrived from the north for surrender.

We soon called the chiefs together and told them that probably some trouble might occur at Red Cloud, but it must not affect them, and for all to remain perfectly quiet and have no fear. We then had only to wait. Imagine, if you please, being compelled to sit down over a powder magazine, with sparks flying around, and wondering how long it would be until the blowup comes. We felt certain an explosion would occur, but uncertain as to the hurt it might do. Well, we had not long to wait. About 4:00 P.M., an Indian courier arrived in the northern camp—not to us—his quivering horse all white with foam, and with the startling news that "their friends were fighting at Red Cloud, and that the troops were coming to Spotted Tail agency."

The old scout Joe Merivale, well known and respected by the Northern Indians, had been sent to their camp with some reliable agency chiefs to meet just this contingency and allay excitement. By dint of hard effort, they were succeeding fairly well, when Black Crow came to us and said, "Crazy Horse is in the northern camp." This came like a clap of thunder from a clear sky. Could it be possible that the one Indian of all others to be secured had made good his escape and come to our agency?

The arrival of the Indian courier from the Red Cloud Indians had produced intense excitement, but when he was soon followed by Crazy Horse, there was a wild scene, beggaring description. The bold warrior, the venerated hero of his braves, who had often led them to victory, was in the midst of devoted friends, and to them a hunted victim of rank injustice and cruel persecution. All the three hundred or more tepees in that camp came down with magic swiftness, and had it not been for White Thunder and other loyal Brules, a stampede would have resulted at once; merciless slaughter of unsuspecting whites on the line of flight would probably have followed, and another Indian war inaugurated.

The "reliables" surrounded and harangued the camp and restored some degree of quiet. Word was sent to the Indians under Touch-the-Clouds to bring Crazy Horse to the post. Major Burke, Dr. [Elgon] Koerper, and myself, with interpreter Louis Bordeaux, started for the northern camp, about three miles from the post. When over halfway out, we met over three hundred mounted armed Indians in good line of battle, not so much guarding as escorting Crazy Horse in the direction of the post. There were war bonnets and war shirts in profusion, and had it not been for a score or more of reliables intermingled with the three hundred, we might have had serious trouble. Touch-the-Clouds was on one side of the great warrior and the brave, handsome White Thunder on the other, with the desperate Black Crow just in the rear. Just here I would add that White Thunder and Black Crow had determined to shoot Crazy Horse should he make a break.

We took Crazy Horse to the post, or perhaps I would better say he and his 300 friends were taking us there. Just as we reached the little parade ground of Camp Sheridan, Spotted Tail, the able planner that he was, arrived from another direction with not less than three hundred of his trusty Brule soldiers, all armed with good breechloaders, principally Winchesters. This number, with more who joined soon after, gave good solid backing, and with our ninety soldiers at quarters, ready to aid at a moment's notice, turned the scale and kept it safely in our favor. As if by intuition, these forces of Indians formed on either side of a walk, leaving a small space about six by eight feet in the center. It was a wild, weird scene; and had the spectacle been for display, it would have been grand beyond compare but, as it meant most serious business and was fraught with danger, every nerve was under the severest strain. For once Crazy Horse realized that his prestige had forsaken him; for once he was in the presence of one whose mastery he dare not, then and there, dispute. Spotted Tail, the coolest man of all the assembled hundreds, in the plain Indian blanket garb, without any insignia of chieftainship, stepped into the arena and, in a few words, delivered in a clear, ringing voice, with dignity and eloquence addressed Crazy Horse, who was almost within touch: "We never have trouble here; the sky is clear, the air is still and free from dust. You have come here and you must listen to me and my people. I am chief here. We keep the peace. We, the Brules, do this. They obey me, and every Indian who comes here must listen to me. You say you want to come to this agency and live peaceably. If you stay here you must listen to me. That is all."

It is hard to justly render an Indian speech, especially on such an occasion; but had you heard its telling points and pauses, emphasized and punctuated by the click of loaded rifles, you would have thought it one of the most effective speeches ever delivered. Its conclusion was greeted with four hundred vociferous "hows." One frenzied Northern Indian, believing his friend Crazy Horse was to be harmed, wanted to sacrifice himself in his place. He caught hold of Major Burke's arm and excitedly exclaimed, "Crazy Horse is brave, but he feels too weak to die today. Kill me! Kill me!" The Brule guns were already loaded, and had a shot been fired, serious trouble would have begun.

After a few more words, and as night was coming on, the crowds dispersed, and we got Crazy Horse into Major Burke's quarters to have a talk. He seemed like a frightened, trembling, wild animal brought to bay, hoping for confidence one moment and fearing treachery the next. He had been under a severe nervous strain all day, and it plainly showed.

Before proceeding with what was the last talk or council, let me go back a little. Soon after we heard Crazy Horse had reached our agency, a courier arrived from Red Cloud with the following message from Clark: "There has been no fight. Crazy Horse's band is just going into camp and will give up their guns without trouble in all probability. Crazy Horse has skipped out for your place. Have sent after him. Should he reach your agency, have Spotted Tail arrest him, and I will give any Indian who does this $200." Soon thereafter, a squad of fifteen or twenty Indian scouts arrived from Red Cloud, having been sent after Crazy Horse to arrest and take him back. It was understood then, and afterward known to be a fact, that they overtook Crazy Horse as he was riding along quite leisurely with his sick wife, and when they asked him to go back with them, the prestige of his name and warlike deeds overawed them when he said, "I am Crazy Horse! Don't touch me! I'm not running away!"

At our talk in Major Burke's quarters, Crazy Horse seemed to realize his helplessness. We assured him we had no reason to do him any hurt, and he promised, almost at the outset, to go with me next day to Camp Robinson. The best solution of the matter was to get Crazy Horse back to Red Cloud safely and quietly; let him make his talk there with the authorities who could decide what should be done as to granting or refusing his desire for transfer to our agency. He said he wanted to get away from trouble; that he had brought his sick wife to be treated and came for that purpose only. I told him I would remember what he said and repeat his words to the authorities at Camp Robinson. Several of the chiefs were held responsible, under a binding Indian pledge, for Crazy Horse's safekeeping during the night and his reporting to Major Burke next morning at nine o'clock.

Crazy Horse reported at the appointed time next morning and said he had changed his mind about going back to Red Cloud because he "was afraid something would happen." He asked us to go down without him and fix up the matter for him and his people. We assured him we had no thought of harming him in any way; that he owed it to his people at Red Cloud to return, and we insisted upon his return peaceably and quietly, to which he agreed, upon the following conditions, which, under the circumstances, Major Burke and I felt we could make: first, that neither Crazy Horse nor myself should take arms; second, that I would state to the soldier chief at Red Cloud all that had occurred at Spotted Tail agency, and that if Crazy Horse made a statement of the facts, I would say to the soldier chief that Major Burke, Spotted Tail, and I were willing to receive him by transfer from Red Cloud, if the district commander so authorized; that Crazy Horse might state what occurred; how he had been misunderstood and misinterpreted; that he wanted peace and quiet, and did not want any trouble whatever. We made Crazy Horse no promise that he would be transferred to Spotted Tail agency, because we knew and he knew that could be settled only by higher authority. Crazy Horse asked to ride horseback, which request was granted.

We started from the northern camp on the morning of September 5. In the ambulance with me were Louis Bordeaux; Black Crow and Swift Bear, two reliable agency chiefs; and High Bear and Touch-the-Clouds, Crazy Horse's friends. By consent, seven Northern Indians, friends of Crazy Horse, went along to see fair play, but Good Voice, Horned Antelope, and a few other reliables rode with Crazy Horse to take care of him and prevent his escape.

When about fifteen miles out, small parties of Spotted Tail's Indian soldiers began to arrive, and when halfway, about twenty miles, I had over forty reliable Indian soldiers. Crazy Horse then realized that he was practically a prisoner.

At one time, Crazy Horse dashed ahead and disappeared for a moment over the brow of a hill, one hundred yards away. It was here he probably obtained a knife of an Indian family stampeding to Spotted Tail. He was soon overhauled and said he went ahead only to water his horse. He was then directed to ride immediately in the rear of my ambulance, and he saw at once he was closely guarded. He seemed nervous and bewildered, and his serious expression seemed to show that he was doubtful of the outcome. I tried to reassure his friends by telling them that I would do exactly as had been promised in presenting his case.

When within fifteen miles of Red Cloud, I sent a note to Clark, by a swift Indian courier, asking whether I should take Crazy Horse to the post or the agency. I also stated briefly and explicitly that we had to use tact and discretion in securing Crazy Horse without precipitating serious trouble, and that we had promised him that he might state his case, and wished when we reached Red Cloud that arrangements be made accordingly. When within four miles of Red Cloud, I received this answer, in writing: "Colonel Bradley wishes you to drive direct to his office with Crazy Horse." I had built the post and knew that the commandant's office was next to the guardhouse. This brief note, being silent as to the important part of my request, signified to my mind that Crazy Horse was to be put in the guardhouse, but I still hoped that he would be allowed to say a few words in his own behalf.

We proceeded to the post, my Indians on either side of the ambulance, with pieces ready for instant use, and Crazy Horse in the center. Upon arriving at the commandant's office, I was met by the adjutant, who informed me that the general directed that Crazy Horse be turned over to the officer of the day. I said, "No, not yet," and asked if Crazy Horse could say a few words to the commanding officer before this was done. I was referred to the colonel. I had Crazy Horse dismount, go into the office, and sit down, and Swift Bear, Touch-the-Clouds, High Bear, Black Crow, and Good Voice went in with him. I stationed an Indian soldier at the door with orders to admit no one while I was away. I then went to the colonel's quarters, some two hundred yards distant, and in earnest and respectful language preferred my request, and he informed me, in no doubtful terms, that it was no use. The orders were peremptory; he could not change them; General Crook himself could not change them, and nothing further need be said, and the sooner I turned over Crazy Horse the better. I tried to explain what had been done; just what had been said in securing Crazy Horse, to all of which Colonel Bradley said, "It's too late to have any talk." I replied, "Can he be heard in the morning?" The colonel looked at me steadily for an instant but did not answer. I was again ordered to deliver Crazy Horse to the officer of the day, and tell him to go with the officer of the day and not a hair of his head should be harmed.

Colonel Bradley was every inch a soldier. An order to him was law and gospel and met with prompt, undeviating obedience, and woe betide the one who dared question, evade, or fail in obeying his orders. I knew the colonel too well to attempt to prolong the interview, yet as I retraced my steps to the office, I had a glimmering hope that on the morrow Crazy Horse might be heard. I told Crazy Horse the night was coming on and the soldier chief said it was too late for a talk; that he said for him to go with the officer of the day and he would be taken care of and not harmed.

At the conclusion of my message, the chiefs uttered a joyous "How!" Crazy Horse's face lighted up hopefully, and he stepped across the room to the door and took the officer of the day, Captain Kennington,[6] warmly by the hand. My duty, my military duty, was done, but I took Touch-the-Clouds and High Bear, Crazy Horse's friends, to one side to explain to them, as best I could, the situation of affairs, and how it was that I was entirely subject to higher authorities there.

Crazy Horse willingly went along with Captain Kennington, closely followed by two soldiers of the guard with sidearms, straight to the guardhouse and into the main door. When he reached the prison room, he saw the dungeon cells, the small grated window, and some prisoners in irons, it was said. Across the puzzled brain of this Indian leader, whose life had been as free as the wind, there no doubt flitted the terrible thought of prison chains and ignominious death. To his mind he was, then and there, at last brought face to face with what the white man had in store for him. No doubt feeling that he was abandoned by his friends, alone in his extremity and surrounded by a score or more of his armed enemies, he sprang, with the desperation of an infuriated tiger, into the main guardroom, and drawing from his clothing a long, glittering knife, attempted to plunge it into Captain Kennington, but the captain's drawn sword diverted this purpose; he then sprang outside, striking right and left among the guard and struggling to make his way to where his seven friends were.

At this juncture, Little Big Man,[7] an erstwhile friend and warrior comrade of Crazy Horse, appeared on the scene. He seized Crazy Horse by the arm and attempted to force him to the ground. The great chief, even in his frenzy, was too magnanimous to try to seriously wound Little Big Man, but merely cut his arm to free himself from his unwelcome, if not treacherous, grasp. He then tried hard to kill a soldier of the guard who blocked his way. Swift Bear, Black Crow, and Fast Thunder (loyal Brules) caught him, and in the struggle, Captain Kennington called out, "Kill him! kill him!"[8] and just then an infantry soldier of the guard made a successful lunge and Crazy Horse fell, mortally wounded, with a deep bayonet thrust in his right side.

The friendly Indians prevented Crazy Horse's friends from firing on the guard. All the Indians were taken by surprise, and upon the pressing appeal and earnest demand of his friends, Crazy Horse was carried into the office whence he had come. Confusion followed, troops turned out, and pandemonium seemed to have broken loose in the populous Indian camps. Even the friendlies, though they disliked Crazy Horse, were not pleased with the result, and there was not much that could then be explained to their satisfaction.

Crazy Horse's uncle at once sought to take revenge, but two friendlies caught and led him away. Touch-the-Clouds asked permission to take Crazy Horse to an Indian lodge and let him die there, but it was refused. He then asked to remain in the office with him, and that was granted on condition that he give up his gun. I recall his remarkable reply, "You are many, I am only one. You may not trust me, but I will trust you. You can take my gun." I think Crazy Horse's old father and mother were also finally allowed to remain with him. About 10:00 P.M., Touch-the-Clouds sent word that Crazy Horse wished to see me before he died. I went to the office. Crazy Horse was lying on the floor, as he desired. He took my proffered hand and said, between his dying moans, "My friend, I don't blame you for this; had I listened to you, this trouble would not have happened to me." He died about midnight, and thus passed away the restless, untamed spirit of as brave an Indian chief as ever drew a bow or wore a moccasin.

After his death, I was informed, and the statement is, I believe, in the official reports, that he had threatened to kill General Crook should the general scold or speak roughly to him at a proposed council to be held at Crazy Horse's camp some days prior to this trouble. General Crook was on his way in an ambulance to the camp without escort for the talk, when one of the scouts, or someone who was watching Crazy Horse, met him with news of this impending danger, and the general returned to the post without meeting Crazy Horse. This may have all been true, but whether it was merely an idle threat announced in a spirit of bravado or, if made and meant, he would have sought an excuse to carry it into execution can never be known.

A field officer of cavalry, then a captain, 3rd Cavalry,[9] has since informed me that his troop was detailed to take Crazy Horse from the guardhouse that night at midnight and push on rapidly to the railroad, and from there he was to be sent as a prisoner to the Dry Tortugas.[10] Manifestly this was the mandatory order which Colonel Bradley had received from higher authority, and of course he could neither suspend nor modify it in any way. When Crazy Horse died, Touch-the-Clouds shook hands with all present, thus showing he had no bad heart toward anyone.

Crazy Horse's father[11] made some pathetic remarks as to the life and character of his son. He asked that he might take the body away and give it an Indian burial, and consent was given. The offer of an ambulance was declined, and at daylight, September 6, the gray, bare-headed, wailing, wretched old father and mother[12] followed on foot, out of the post, the travois on which was lashed the body of their only son and protector. Their pitiable condition appealed to the sympathy of everyone, and as they passed Major Burrowes's[13] quarters, they were kindly offered something to eat, which they accepted with apparent gratitude, and then resumed their mournful journey.

With respect to Crazy Horse, I neither eulogize nor condemn. It may be said that he was an intractable Indian chieftain, a bitter hater of the pale faces, insensible to fear in battle, and intensely fanatical in his religious devotions from the Indian's standpoint. I have merely stated the facts as they occurred, mainly under my own observation, or as told to me by reliable eyewitnesses. There is no Indian journalist, author, or reporter to present the warlike chief's side of the story of his tragic fate. With the lapse of time, his name and fame may linger for a while in the traditions of his tribe, and then fade away forever. History will make but little record of him save to note a point, perhaps, in the onward western march of our Christian civilization.

While I would gladly banish the remembrance of some things affecting me in this tragedy of long ago, yet, not for one instant would I utter aught of censure or reproach for mistakes which may have been made in the trying ordeal. Some of the prominent actors now sleep in honored graves. Let their errors, if they made them, be forgotten, and recall only the great work which they accomplished in solving the crucial problems of somewhat perilous times.

Crazy Horse is forever at peace; he sleeps in an obscure and lonely Indian grave on the cliffs of Wounded Knee Creek, where it may be that his hovering spirit, in the closing days of 1890 (the practical extermination of Big Foot's following), caught once more the sound of the white man's guns that sent to bloody graves in indiscriminate slaughter men, women, and children of a kindred band, imbued with the same fanaticism and contempt of death which had characterized his stormy life and his untimely end.

The Murder of Chief Crazy Horse

HENRY R. LEMLY

EDITED BY E. A. BRININSTOOL

Hunter–Trader–Trapper (May 1933): 7–10

The greatest fighting chief of the Sioux nation, after the practical retirement of Red Cloud following the Wagon Box fight [of] 1867, was unquestionably Crazy Horse. Although a young man, even at the time of his treacherous murder, he had won his spurs in the defeat of Reynolds on March 17, 1876, on Powder River and [in] the practical defeat of Crook in the Rosebud fight of June 17, to say nothing of the leading part he played in the annihilation of Custer's command two weeks later on the Little Bighorn. After that, his reputation among his own people was secure.

Crazy Horse had come in and surrendered about the middle of May [1877], at Red Cloud agency, with about one hundred forty lodges of his people, numbering by actual count around one thousand men, women, and children, most of them being Oglala Sioux.

But Crazy Horse did not surrender because he wanted to. Far from it. He was by no means a subdued warrior. He was actually starved out and really came in to make such terms with the military authorities as would bring rest and peace to his people, who were always his first consideration, and who had scarcely known defeat under his able and valiant leadership.

The author [Brininstool] engaged in correspondence with Capt. H. R. Lemly, U.S.A. retired, in 1925. He has since passed away. This correspondence, together with Captain Lemly's signed account of the murder of Chief Crazy Horse, follows.

———◆———

ARMY AND NAVY CLUB,
Washington, D.C., June 17, 1925

E. A. Brininstool, Esq.,
Los Angeles, California
Dear Sir:

I take pleasure in trying to answer your letter of the sixth. Crazy Horse was approximately forty years old when killed. Lt. Philo

Clark, whom I knew well, had nothing to do with Crazy Horse's incarceration and his intended transfer to Fort Marion, Florida, unless through his influence with General Crook or with General Sheridan, who said, "The only good Indian is a dead one."[2]

The three-fourths-breed daughter of Louis Richard, a half-breed interpreter at Red Cloud agency, and married to a squaw, had eloped to Crazy Horse.[3] The agent asked the Indian Bureau in Washington to forcibly restore her to her father. Telegraphic orders were sent by the War Department to General Sheridan in Chicago; by him to General Crook at Fort Laramie; and by him to Colonel Bradley at Camp Robinson. Both girl and Crazy Horse refused such restoration, and when General Crook wired he would take her, Crazy Horse grimly replied, "Tell the Gray Fox to try it."

General Crook ordered Maj. J. W. Mason[4] from Fort Laramie to Red Cloud agency by night marches. At daybreak, we arrived at Crazy Horse's village, seven troops of cavalry, but Crazy Horse had fled with his people during the night to Spotted Tail agency, where Lt. J. M. Lee was acting Indian agent. Lee persuaded Crazy Horse to return to Red Cloud agency with him for a talk with Colonel Bradley, and gave Crazy Horse verbal safe conduct.

Meanwhile, Colonel Bradley had received orders from General Sheridan, through General Crook, to confine Crazy Horse and send him to Fort Marion, where Geronimo was confined.[5]

I was to take him at midnight, with my troop of cavalry, rapidly to Fort Laramie, thence by coach to Cheyenne and by train to Florida. When Crazy Horse saw the cell, he attempted to escape, but was bayoneted in the bowels by a member of the guard at the door. He fell to the ground in convulsions. The wound bled internally. Some thirty to fifty mounted and dismounted Indians had formed a semicircle in front of the guardhouse. When Crazy Horse fell, they produced hidden carbines from under their blankets, cocked them, and cornered all of us. Firing was averted by the quick action of Baptiste Pouriere, the interpreter, and Crazy Horse was carried to the adjutant's office, where he died about 12:15 A.M., after singing the Indian death song. Lieutenant Lee saw him during the evening, but only the contract surgeon, Dr. McGillycuddy, Touch-the-Clouds, Baptiste, and myself were present when he died. Next day his body was taken by Indians to Red Cloud agency. Tom-toms were kept beating night and day for a week, and we even feared an attack on Camp Robinson. Crazy Horse's body was kept several days before it was removed to Spotted Tail agency. I do not know where it was buried. At that time the Indians put their dead on scaffolds, not in the ground.

Crazy Horse was a lithe, slender Indian of medium or more height, weighing perhaps 155 to 165 pounds. I never saw him except before his death, clad in a red blanket, and later, lying upon it on the floor in the adjutant's office before his death.

Louis Richard's daughter, who fled to Crazy Horse, was said to be very pretty. Crazy Horse must have been good-looking to have attracted her. Because of the Custer battle, he had great prestige with his own followers, with Red Cloud's Oglalas, and Spotted Tail's Brules.

In a letter I wrote to the New York Sun, and which Mr. E. P. Mitchell, editor, wrote me was the best piece of border correspondence he had read in a long time, I sent a somewhat different account, September 6, the day following Crazy Horse's death. I was only a second lieutenant, and I was afraid of getting into trouble if I betrayed my identity.[6]

Crazy Horse was seized by Little Big Man, agency Indian police, whom he badly cut with a keen sharp knife drawn from the folds of his blanket, and the attempt was made to make the Indians believe that Crazy Horse accidentally stabbed himself in the scuffle. I think a soldier of the guard inflicted the wound. General Crook had left only two days before on the fourth. I think he did not like to be around when he did not exercise direct and immediate command, but he must have been at Fort Laramie, not at Omaha.

Colonel Bradley did all he could to have the order of incarceration revoked, wiring General Crook at Laramie about the safe conduct given by Lieutenant Lee, but I think General Sheridan in Chicago was at fault, or the matter may not have been properly understood by him. Sitting Bull was similarly killed by treacherous Indians. In this letter [to the New York *Sun*] I find that I said Crazy Horse was to be taken to Spotted Tail agency, fifty miles north, where his people were, and this was no doubt done. In my letter, he died about 12:15 A.M., September 6, 1877.

Crazy Horse, it seems, had been enlisted by the United States as a Sioux scout. There were both friendly (enlisted) and hostile Sioux present, and many dismounted Indians as well at the killing.

Hoping this may serve your purpose, I am
                Very truly yours,
                H. R. Lemly, Major U.S.A.
                (retired)

Captain Lemly's story follows:[7]

After the massacre on the Little Bighorn, many of the Indians returned to Spotted Tail and Red Cloud agencies, but Crazy Horse and Sitting Bull, accompanied by their most devoted followers, evaded the troops, crossed the Yellowstone River, and escaped into Canada, where they remained several years.[8] Finally, after considerable negotiation, and when assured of immunity by the United States government, they rejoined their tribes, Crazy Horse going to Red Cloud agency in Nebraska.

At this time the resident interpreter at this agency was a half-breed descendant of a French voyageur named Louis Richard, who had a beautiful daughter, and of her Crazy Horse became enamored.[9] He was a tall, lithe Indian, still young, with the prestige of his military attainments surrounding him, and apparently the love was returned. At any rate, after sending several ponies to her father—after the Indian fashion of buy-and-sell marriage—Crazy Horse carried off the young woman to his tepee. But the interpreter entertained other view for his daughter and caused the agent to demand her return. Crazy Horse, it was said, referred the matter to the girl herself, who in turn defied her father's messengers and announced her desire and intention to remain with her Indian husband. At this juncture, General Crook, who commanded the Department of the Platte, was appealed to, and an officer of the army, stationed at Camp Robinson, near Red Cloud agency, was sent to Crazy Horse with the threat that he would have to suffer the consequences if he did not return the girl to her father. To this menace, Crazy Horse made the laconic reply, "Tell Gray Fox (General Crook) to come and take her."

Immediately telegraphic instruments began to click, and a battalion of the 3rd Cavalry under Maj. Julius W. Mason was ordered to proceed from the nearest contiguous post (Fort Laramie) to Red Cloud agency, which was protected by a half regiment of infantry stationed at Camp Robinson. The column of cavalry was directed to so time its arrival, after a night march, that it could surround the village of Crazy Horse at daybreak.

All went well. The Gray Fox had seemed to plan admirably in sending for the remoter troops and providing for a night approach, but when they arrived upon the bluffs supposed to overlook the village, there were no tepees in sight. The bird had flown! After a short halt and an examination of the trail, the troops returned to Camp Robinson.

At that time, Lt. Jesse M. Lee of the 9th Infantry, stationed at the adjacent post of Camp Robinson, was acting Indian agent, and [he] finally persuaded Crazy Horse to accompany him to Camp Robinson and talk over the matter with Col. Luther P. Bradley, a distinguished old officer of the Civil War, in command of the post, and of what was then known as the District of the Black Hills. No more honorable officers ever lived than Colonel Bradley and Lieutenant Lee, and the part they played, inadvertently or by compulsion, that day was no doubt revolting in the extreme. Somebody high up had blundered, but orders had to be obeyed.

I happened to be crossing the parade ground when Colonel Bradley, walking upon the veranda of his quarters, observing that the approaching ambulance containing Lieutenant Lee and Crazy Horse was followed by mounted Indians, hurriedly called and directed me to post Troop E, 3rd Cavalry, in the vicinity of and surrounding the guardhouse. At the same time, he gave instructions to Captain Kennington, 14th Infantry, the officer of the day.

When the ambulance halted in front of Colonel Bradley's office, Lieutenant Lee, accompanied by Crazy Horse and Touch-the-Clouds, an extremely tall Indian, as his name implies, dismounted and entered the building; but shortly after, Lieutenant Lee appeared and crossed the parade ground to Colonel Bradley's quarters, from which he presently emerged and returned to the commandant's office. After a few minutes, I saw Captain Kennington and the Indian (Crazy Horse) proceed to and enter the guardhouse. As they did so, the guard, which had formed at sight of the officer of the day, by the latter's orders, faced the door of the building.

When Crazy Horse entered, I observed for the first time that he was accompanied by Little Big Man. This Indian, so named because of his small stature, double joints, and great strength, was known to the officers as a paid spy in the employ of the agency.

Thus far, Crazy Horse had proceeded apparently unconscious of danger. Against his protest, Lieutenant Lee had been directed to inform him that it was too late for a council, and that he must spend the night in charge of the guard, and that no hair of his head would be harmed. But when Crazy Horse saw a narrow and barred cell in front, fearing that it was for himself, he immediately made a rush for the door.

Instantly he was grappled by Little Big Man, who attempted to force him to the floor; but whipping out a long and slender knife from the folds of his red blanket, Crazy Horse drew its keen edge across the wrist of his assailant and cut it to the bone. Captain Kennington drew his sword, but with one bound Crazy Horse gained the door of the building, and with another leap fell upon the ground outside, pierced through the groin and abdomen by the bayonet of the guard. Here he lay and writhed in convulsions, but uttered no sound.

"Pick up that Indian and carry him to the guardroom," shouted Captain Kennington. Four members of the guard dropped their rifles and started to obey, when, as if with a single click, thirty carbines were cocked and aimed at us by as many mounted Indians, who had formed a semicircle about the entrance to the guardhouse.

"For God's sake, Captain, stop," exclaimed Big Bat, the post interpreter, "or we are all dead men."

I was within the semicircle, and my own men mounted outside, posted according to my instructions, but literally unavailable at the moment, as were the members of the guard, and we were taken unawares. For a few seconds, our lives hung in the balance, when Big Bat, taking advantage of the ominous silence, assured the Indians that Crazy Horse was ill and proposed taking him to the council chamber at the other end of the building, where he could be attended by the surgeon. To this they assented, for the bayonet thrust had been unseen, and presently the carbines were lowered and the dangerous hammers released.

At the same time, Crazy Horse was gently conveyed to the adjutant's office and placed upon his extended blanket on the floor. Touch-the-Clouds and Big Bat accompanied him, and shortly after, Dr. McGillycuddy, the post surgeon, appeared. Later I was given special charge of the wounded chief, but not until I had seen his followers dash wildly from the garrison, firing their carbines in the air and yelling like fiends as they galloped off to their camps, from which the sound of tom-toms and of war dancing soon warned us of a possible night attack.

Had the Sioux present been fully cognizant of the cause and nature of Crazy Horse's malady, trouble could scarcely have been averted, but when they learned of his death, it was too late.

For several hours, Crazy Horse remained unconscious. The hemorrhage was internal and gradually sapped away his strength. When the impression was sought (unofficially) to be conveyed that the wound was self-inflicted by Crazy Horse himself in his struggle with Little Big Man, the conversation by members of the guard, which I overheard, convinced me that, although I did not actually see the stroke, Crazy Horse was killed by a thrust from a bayonet. When he recovered consciousness, he sent for Lieutenant Lee, whom he acquitted of all blame, saying, "This would not have happened if I had listened to you."

Already it had been planned to imprison the chief in Fort Marion, at St. Augustine, Florida. He was to have been taken in an ambulance at midnight, with a troop of cavalry for an escort, to Fort Laramie, thence by the Deadwood coach to Cheyenne, and by trains east and south. Death kindly intervened. As the fatal moment approached, consciousness returned, and the dying chief, supporting himself upon his elbow, for the first time gave vent to his feelings. Touch-the-Clouds was visibly affected. Big Bat interpreted.

"I was not hostile to the white men," said Crazy Horse. "Occasionally my young men would attack a party of Crows or Arikaras and take their ponies, but just as often they were the assailants. We had buffaloes for food and their hides for clothing, and we preferred the chase to a life of idleness and the bickering and jealousy, as well as the frequent periods of starvation at the agencies.

"But Gray Fox came out in the snow and bitter cold and destroyed my village. All of us would have perished of exposure and hunger had we not recaptured our ponies. Then Long Hair came in the same way. They say we massacred him, but he would have massacred us if we had not defended ourselves and fought to the death. Our first impulse was to escape with our squaws and papooses, but we were so hemmed in that we had to fight. The government would not let me alone. Finally I came here to Red Cloud agency. Yet I was not permitted to remain quiet. I took a half-breed Indian wife after the Indian fashion. She came to me willingly, and I sent her father ponies in exchange. I told her to go if she wished, but she refused. She said she loved me and would remain with me.

"Again Gray Fox sent soldiers to surround me and my village, but I was tired of fighting. All I wanted was to be let alone, so I anticipated their coming and marched all night to Spotted Tail agency while the troops were approaching the site of my camp. Touch-the-Clouds knows how I settled at Spotted Tail agency and asked that chief and his agent to let me live there in peace. The agent told me I must first talk with the big white chief of the Black Hills. Under his care, I came here unarmed, but instead of talking they tried to confine me, and when I made an effort to escape, a soldier ran his bayonet into me. I have spoken."

And then, in a weak and tremulous voice, he broke into the weird and now-famous death song of the Sioux. Instantly there were two answering calls from beyond the lines of pickets, and Big Bat told me they were from Crazy Horse's old father and mother, who begged to see their dying son. I had no authority to admit them and resisted their appeal, piteous as it was, until Crazy Horse fell back with the death gurgle in his throat. The end had come.

When the little old couple, gray and wrinkled as only old Indians can become, were finally allowed to enter, they bent over and crooned to the prostrate form of their dead son, and fondled it as if he had been a broken doll and they strangely withered children or pygmies.

The next day, Crazy Horse's body was given to his people for burial. The beating of tom-toms and the war dancing continued for several nights, but it was finally discontinued.

Some years later, Sitting Bull met a similar fate at the hands of the Indian constabulary.

(Signed)   H. R. LEMLY

The Death of Crazy Horse

VALENTINE T. MCGILLYCUDDY

Valentine T. McGillycuddy to Elmo S. Watson, April 13, 1922, Elmo S. Watson Papers, Ayers Collection, Newberry Library, Chicago[2]

In September 1877, [Brig.] Gen. George Crook, commanding the Department of the Platte, held an important council at Fort Robinson, Nebraska, with the famous Chief Crazy Horse and his people, he having surrendered with 1,500 of the northern hostiles the previous April. The object of the council was to secure the assistance of Crazy Horse and his band in arresting Chief Joseph and his Nez Perces, then in hostility in Montana.

I was in the Crazy Horse camp that day, and the council was a heated one and finally broke up with no results, except to create the belief in Crook's mind that Crazy Horse was meditating desertion and an attempt to rejoin Sitting Bull, still in British America, where he [Sitting Bull] had found refuge under the British flag after the Custer massacre in June 1876. This impression regarding the desertion of Crazy Horse was the result of a purposeful misinterpretation by the government interpreter [Frank Grouard], who was an enemy of and feared Crazy Horse, and of this I was informed by Louis Bordeaux, a reliable man who checked the interpreting. The feeling was added to by Red Cloud's jealousy of Crazy Horse's increasing power and importance.

Three days later, a courier arrived from General Crook, who had gone sixty miles west to Fort Laramie, Wyoming, with orders to Colonel Bradley, commandant at Fort Robinson, to arrest Crazy Horse, and next morning a force of three troops of cavalry and a field piece, and myself as medical officer, left the post an hour before daylight for a march of five miles to the camp to make the arrest. We arrived at daylight and found but a deserted campground. Crazy Horse and his people, lodges, and everything had scattered and gone. That evening a courier arrived from Major Burke, commanding at the Spotted Tail agency, forty-three miles east, that Crazy Horse had arrived alone and was in Spotted Tail's camp.

Orders were sent to Major Burke to arrest Crazy Horse and return him to Fort Robinson. Burke informed Chief Spotted Tail of his orders, [and] Spotted Tail's reply was, "Crazy Horse is a chief. He is my guest. He cannot be arrested, but if the soldier chief will set the time, we will council with him."

549

At 9:00 A.M. the next day [September 5, 1877], Spotted Tail and Crazy Horse appeared at Burke's office. Crazy Horse was not informed that he was a prisoner, but that Colonel Bradley, commanding at Fort Robinson, wanted him there for a council. His reply was, "It is well, I will go," and entering the waiting ambulance surrounded by Indian scouts and cavalry escort, they started to Fort Robinson.[3]

At 5:00 P.M., they arrived at the adjutant's office. In the meantime, Bradley had issued orders to Captain Kennington, officer of the day, that immediately upon his arrival, Crazy Horse was to be confined to the guardhouse. Anticipating the arrival, I was standing in front of the adjutant's office and shook hands with Crazy Horse on his arrival. He entered and said he was there for council, but instead of meeting Bradley, he was taken charge of by Kennington and was led to the guardhouse, which they entered quietly. However, when he observed the steel bars between the guard room and the cells, he gave an outcry, "This is a prison," and seizing a knife in each hand from his belt, fought his way to the parade ground where I was standing, Kennington hanging on to one wrist, Little Big Man, a northern scout, the other. Then, as the cowboy would say, hell broke loose. The guard to the number of twenty closed in on and surrounded Crazy Horse; Indians hostile and friendly closed in on us by the hundreds; the soldiers formed in their quarters; and a general fight was imminent. In the meantime, Crazy Horse, surrounded by the guard, suddenly fell to the ground, writhing and groaning. I worked my way in between the guard and examined him. He was frothing at the mouth, pulse weak and intermittent, blood trickling from the upper edge of his hip.

A private of the 9th Infantry had transfixed him with his bayonet, and his case was hopeless. I then worked my way to American Horse,[4] the friendly chief who was sitting on his horse, and informed him that Crazy Horse was badly hurt and that we would place him in the guardhouse, and I would care for him. "No, Wasichu Wakan, he is a chief and cannot be put in prison."

The officers were at their quarters, orderlies had vanished, and [there was] no one to carry orders, so I tried to arrange matters and advised Kennington to hold the ground, while I crossed the parade ground to the colonel's quarters to explain matters, which resulted as follows: "Please give my compliments to the officer of the day; he is to carry out his original orders and put the Indian in the guardhouse."

I returned to Kennington, and we proceeded to put the Indian in the guardhouse. We started to lift him, when a tall Northern Sioux grasped my hand, and in the sign language [said] that they did not want to see me hurt, and to desist; the Indians had begun cocking their rifles, so another trip to the colonel to explain matters [was necessary]. I remarked to him as follows: "Colonel, I know the temper and feelings of these Indians. You may be able to imprison Crazy Horse, but it will mean the death of a good many soldiers and Indians, and if you will pardon me for suggesting it, we may be able to compromise on the adjutant's office, where I can care for him, for he will die before morning."

After much reluctance he acquiesced, and I returned to the scene. On being informed, American Horse dismounted, spread his blanket on the ground, on which the Indians placed the chief and carried him into the adjutant's office.

By administration of hypodermics of morphia, I eased his suffering. I remained with him until his death at 11:00 P.M., and there was present Kennington, Lemly, old man Crazy Horse, and the northern chief Mahpia Yutan (Touch-the-Clouds), six feet four in height. When Crazy Horse died, this chief drew the blanket over the face and, standing up, remarked, pointing to the body, "There lies his lodge," then, pointing up, "The chief has gone above." I then returned to my quarters across the parade ground, accompanied by Touch-the-Clouds, who slept on his blanket outside my door through the night, as there was still danger of trouble.

After I retired, word of the death of the chief got out, and we could hear the wails and death songs from all quarters, as we were surrounded for miles by the camps. The whole garrison was kept on guard for the night, but matters finally adjusted themselves.

Next day the body was removed to the Spotted Tail agency and placed on the usual platform. Later in the fall, when we moved the Indians three hundred sixty miles to the Missouri River, it accompanied us, and in the fall of 1878, when the Indians were moved back to the present Pine Ridge agency, the body was brought back and is concealed there.

When the son died that night, the old father lamented and talked, remarking, "We are Northern Sioux. We do not belong here, but the Gray Fox (Crook) kept sending word to us [to] come in. We came in, and hard times have come on me. My son is dead now. We may not have remained long. Red Cloud was jealous of my boy. We did not want the white man's beef; we preferred the buffalo on our hunting grounds. We did not want to be agency Indians."

PART NINE

The Ghost Dance and Wounded Knee, 1890–91

The Story of the Ghost Dance

GEORGE SWORD

The Folklorist, Journal of the Chicago Folklore Society 1, no. 1 (July 1892): 28–31

In the story of the ghost dancing, the Oglalas heard that the Son of God was truly on earth in the west from their country. This was in the year 1889. The first people who knew about the Messiah to be on the earth were the Shoshones and the Arapahos. So in 1889, Good Thunder, with four or five others, visited the placed where the Son of God was said to be. These people went there without permission.[2] They said the Messiah was there at the place, but he was there to keep the Indians, and not the whites, so this made the Indians happy to find out this.

Good Thunder, Cloud Horse, Yellow Knife, and Short Bull visited the place again in 1890 and saw the Messiah. Their story of the visit to the Messiah[3] is as follows:

From the country where the Arapahos and Shoshones dwell, we start in the direction of northwest, in the train for five nights, and arrived at the foot of the Rocky Mountains. Here we saw him, and also several tribes of Indians. The people said that the Messiah will come at a place in the woods, where the place was prepared for him. When we went to the place, a smoke descended from heaven to the place where he was to come; when the smoke disappeared, there was a man of about forty, which was the Son of God. The man said, "My grandchildren, I am glad you have come, far away, to see your relatives. These are your people who have come back from your country."

When he said he wanted us to go with him, we looked and we saw a land created across the ocean, on which all the nations of Indians were coming home, but as the Messiah looked, the land which was created and reached across the ocean again disappeared, he saying that it was not time for that to take place.

The Messiah then gave to Good Thunder some paints, Indian paint, a white paint, a green grass, and said, "My grandchildren, when you get home, go to farming and send all your children to school, and on the way home, if you kill any buffalo, cut off the head, the tail, and the four

Wovoka. W. FLETCHER JOHNSON. *LIFE OF SITTING BULL.*

feet, and leave them, and that buffalo will come to live again. When the soldiers of the white people's chief want to arrest me, I shall stretch my arms, which will knock them to nothingness; or, if not that, the earth will open and swallow them in. My father commanded me to visit the Indians on a purpose. I have come to the white people first, but they are not good; they killed me, and you can see the marks of my wounds on my feet, my hand, and on my back. My father has given you life, your old life, and you have come to see your friends, but you will not take me home with you at this time. I want you to tell, when you get home, your people to follow my examples. Any one Indian who does not obey me and tries to be on the white's side will be covered over by a new land that is to come over the old one. You will, all the people, use the paints and grass I give you. In the spring, when the green grass comes, your people who have gone before you will come back, and you shall see your friends then, for you have come to my call."

The people from every tepee sent for us to visit them; they are people who died many years ago. Chasing Hawk, who died not long ago, was there, and we went to his tepee. He was living with his wife, who

The Ghost Dance. FOURTEENTH ANNUAL REPORT, BUREAU OF ETHNOLOGY, 1892–93.

was killed in war long ago. They live in a buffalo-skin tepee—a very large one, and he wanted all his friends to go there to live. A son of Good Thunder, who died in war long ago, was one who also took us to his tepee, so his father saw him.

When coming home, we came to a herd of buffalos; we killed one and took everything except the four feet, head, and tail, and when we came a little ways from it, there was the buffalo come to live again and went off. This was one of the Messiah's words that came to truth.

The Messiah said, "I will shorten your journey when you feel tired of the long way, if you call upon me." This we did when we were tired. The night came upon us; we stopped at a place, and we called upon the Messiah to help us because we were tired of our long journey. We went to sleep, and in the morning, we found ourselves at a great distance from where we stopped.

The people came back here and they got their people, both those loyal to the government and those not in favor of the whites, and held a council. The agent's soldiers were sent after them and brought Good Thunder and two others to the agency, and they were confined to the prison.[4] They were asked by the agent and Captain Seward[5] whether they saw the Son of God, and whether they held councils over their return from their visit, but Good Thunder refused to say yes.

They were confined to the prison for two days, and upon their promising not to hold councils about their visit, they were released. They went back to the people and told them about their trouble with the agent, and thus they dispersed without a council.

The Ghost Dance and Wounded Knee, 1890–91

An unconscious ghost dancer. FOURTEENTH ANNUAL REPORT, BUREAU OF ETHNOLOGY, 1892–93.

In the following spring, the people at Pine Ridge agency began to gather at the White Clay Creek for councils. Just at that time, Kicking Bear,[6] from Cheyenne River agency, Dakota, went on a visit to the Arapahos and said that the Arapahos there have ghost dancing. He said that people partaking in the dance would get crazy and die. Then the Messiah is seen, and all the ghosts dance. When they die, they see strange things. They see their relatives who died long before. They saw these things when they died in the Ghost Dance, and came to life again. The person dancing becomes dizzy and finally drops dead, and the first thing they see is an eagle coming to them, and it carries them to where the Messiah is with his ghosts. The man [Kicking Bear] said this:

> The persons in the ghost dancing are all joined hands. A man stands, and then a woman, so in that way forming a very large circle. They dance around in the circle in a continuous time, until some of them become so tired, and overtired, that they become crazy, and finally drop as though dead, with foam in the mouth, all wet by perspiration. All the men and women made holy shirts and dresses, which they wore in the dances. The persons that dropped in the dance would all lie in a great dust the dancing made.
>
> They painted the white muslins; they made holy shirts and dresses out of it, with blue across the back, and alongside of this is a line of yellow paint. They also paint in the front part of the shirts and dresses. On the shoulders and on the sleeves, they tie eagles' feathers. They said that the bullets will not go through these shirts and dresses, so they all have these dresses for war. Their enemies' weapons will not go through these dresses. The ghost dancers all have to wear eagle

Another view of a Ghost Dance. FRANK LESLIE'S ILLUSTRATED NEWSPAPER, 1891.

feathers on their heads; any man would be made crazy if fanned with this feather. In the Ghost Dance, no person is allowed to wear anything made of any metal, except the guns made of metal are carried by some of the dancers. When they come from ghosts, or after recovery from craziness, they brought meat from the ghosts or from the supposed Messiah. They also brought water, fire, and wind, with which to kill all the whites or Indians who will help the chief of the whites. They made a sweathouse, and made holes in the middle of the sweathouse, where they say the water will come out of these holes. Before they begin to dance, they all raise their hands toward the northwest and cry in supplication to the Messiah, and then begin the dance with the song "Ate Nusun-Kala."

The Wounded Knee and Drexel Mission Fights

LLOYD S. MCCORMICK

Edward S. Luce 7th Cavalry Collection, Little Bighorn National Monument, Crow Agency, Montana[2]

An account of the conditions and events which precede the collecting of United States forces at several places in South Dakota during the fall and winter of 1890–91 will be necessary in order that the reader may understand the peculiarities of the problem which was presented for solution, and the difficulties to be encountered in a real effort to meet the emergency.

During the late summer and fall of 1890, the Indians throughout the country, but particularly those at the agencies in North and South Dakota, had shown signs of unrest. In many cases, they had refused to obey their agents, and generally had adopted a very arrogant bearing. The cause of this change was not at first apparent, and the authorities, as a rule, were puzzled to account for it. Although it was known in a general way that the Indians were engaging in some unusual ceremonies, it was well into the fall before the more serious aspects of the matter appeared to the military authorities. By this time, fanatic zeal had so possessed a large number of Indians that there was a general belief that a Messiah was soon to appear, and that with him would be a return of the buffalo, a resurrection of the dead Indians, and the annihilation of the white man. A feverish excitement pervaded most of the agencies, and different medicine men took advantage of this condition to so play on the feelings of the savages as to convince a large percentage that the rule of the white man could easily be terminated. Such a desirable change appealed strongly to their superstitious natures, and when the Indians had been worked up to the top notch of ardor, the announcement was made that the bullets of the white men could not harm them if they would wear the "ghost shirt." The material from which these were made was the unbleached muslin issued to the Indians at the agencies; but the shirt must be made up by certain squaws designated by the medicine men of each band. The shirts sold for five dollars each, and it was thought by not a few that the trade in shirts was sufficient stimulus to unusual efforts in convincing the deluded savages that by means of the shirt alone could they hope to reap the benefits to accrue as soon as the Messiah should appear.

560   EYEWITNESSES TO THE INDIAN WARS

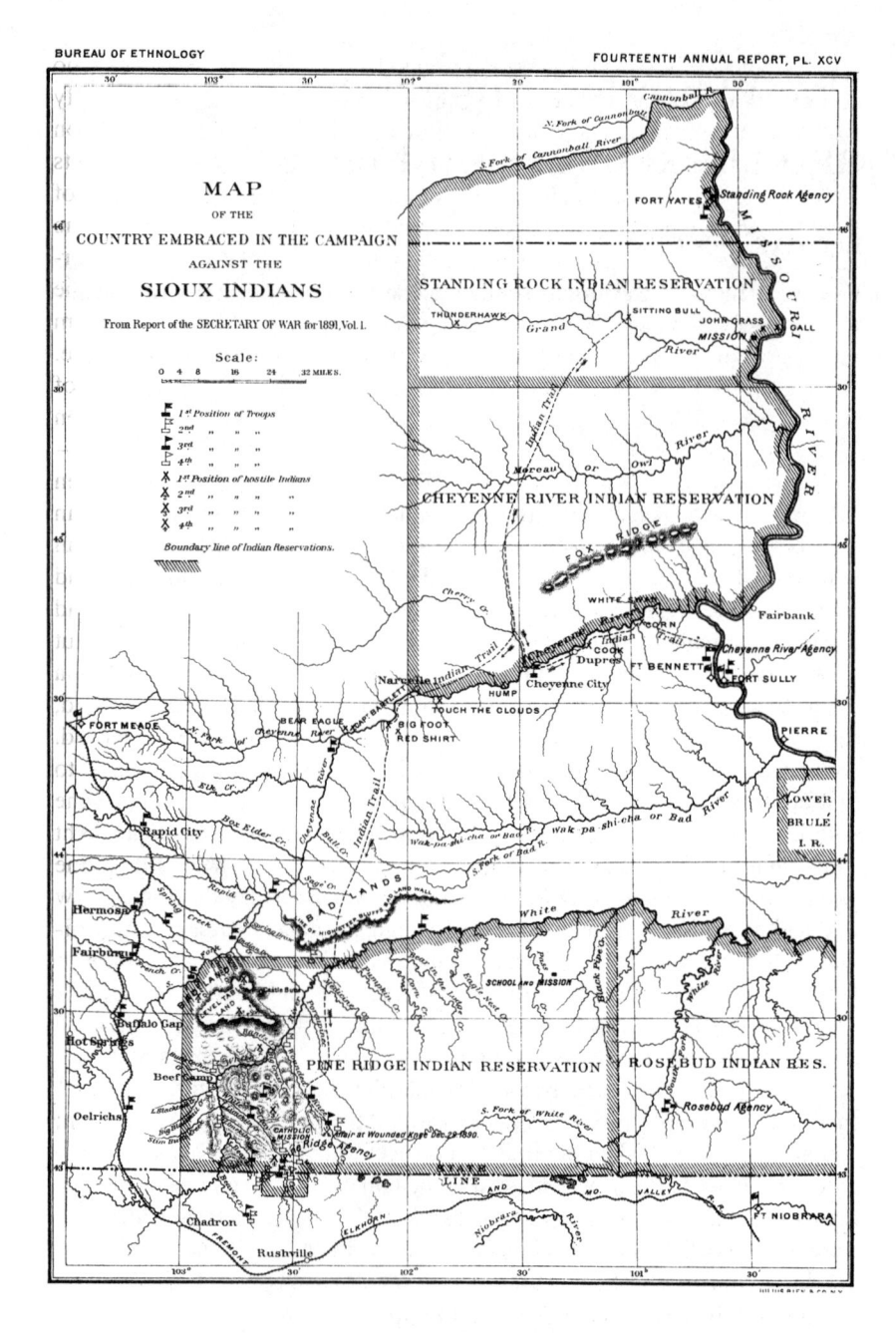

The 1890–91 Sioux campaign. FOURTEENTH ANNUAL REPORT, BUREAU OF ETHNOLOGY, 1892–93.

With such sentiment prevailing, it is not to be wondered at that agents, who had little or no experience in handling Indians, should be amazed at their surly and impudent demeanor, and that some of them should jump to the conclusion that a general war was to be proclaimed by the red man. A few of the agents had the nerve to meet the emergency in a partly effective manner, but many of them seemed helpless and at a loss to institute any measures to counteract the tendencies. And it is a question whether these could have been wholly overcome, and a more or less serious conflict averted. The religious element was the most potent factor in this fanatic zeal and ardor, and it is well known that from the earliest times, such a disturbance has been the most difficult to overcome.

Although this feverish unrest had, to a certain extent, taken possession of the Indians at all the agencies of the country, those in the Northwest had been much more generally affected than those south of the Union Pacific Railroad—due possibly to the less interrupted communication. There is kept up between all of the northern agencies an almost continual connection by means of Indian runners and so-called hunting parties. This disaffection was rapidly reaching an acute stage, when the agent at Pine Ridge, South Dakota, deserted his post and asked for military protection, asserting that the Indians at his agency had become intractable.[3] This was one of the largest agencies and was located about thirty miles north of Rushville, Nebraska. The Indians here were Sioux, and a more unfavorable place for the agent to fall down could not have been selected, as the Sioux is a warlike and turbulent tribe, more easily aroused than quieted.

The forces at several military posts had, in the meantime, been directed to hold themselves in readiness for field duty, so we were not surprised when the telegraphic order arrived at Fort Riley, Kansas, for the headquarters and eight troops of the regiment, stationed at that post, to proceed at once by rail to Pine Ridge and report for duty to Brig. Gen. John R. Brooke,[4] who had arrived a few days before and was personally in charge of the military preparations. The officers who accompanied the command were:

Col. James W. Forsyth, 7th Cavalry, commanding;
Maj. Samuel M. Whitside, commanding 1st Squadron;
Capt. Charles S. Ilsley, commanding Troop E and 2nd Squadron;
1st Lt. L. S. McCormick, regimental adjutant;
Capt. and Asst. Surgeon J. Van R. Hoff, Medical Department, surgeon;
1st Lt. and Asst. Surgeon James D. Glennan, Medical Department;
Capt. Myles Moylan, commanding Troop A;
1st Lt. Ernest A. Garlington, with Troop A;
Capt. Charles A. Varnum, commanding Troop B;
1st Lt. John C. Gresham, with Troop B, acting quartermaster;
2nd Lt. Edwin C. Bullock, with Troop B;
Capt. Henry Jackson, commanding Troop C;
1st Lt. Luther R. Hare, with Troop C;
2nd Lt. T. Q. Donaldson, Jr., with Troop C;
1st Lt. W. H. Robinson, Jr., commanding Troop D;

2nd Lt. S. R. H. Tompkins, with Troop D;
1st Lt. Horatio G. Sickel, with Troop E;
2nd Lt. Sedgwick Rice, with Troop E;
Capt. Winfield S. Edgerly, commanding Troop G;
1st Lt. Edwin P. Brewer, with Troop G;
Capt. Henry J. Nowlan, commanding Troop I;
1st Lt. William J. Nicholson, with Troop I;
2nd Lt. John C. Waterman, with Troop I;
Capt. George D. Wallace, commanding Troop K;
1st Lt. James D. Mann, with Troop K.

Veterinary Surgeon Daniel LeMay, 7th Cavalry, accompanied the command. 1st Lt. Ezra B. Fuller, regimental quartermaster, was left back a few days to turn over the public property at the post, but joined and relieved Lieutenant Bullock of his duties as quartermaster before the first fight. Capt. Edward S. Godfrey joined from detached service soon after we arrived at Pine Ridge and was present in command of his troop (D) in both fights. 2nd Lt. Herbert G. Squiers joined from detached service, but was ordered to appear for examination for promotion before a board sitting at Fort Leavenworth, Kansas. 2nd Lt. J. F. Bell joined from detached service. Lieutenants Hare and Bullock were sent back to Fort Riley on account of sickness. The four last named officers were unfortunate in not being able to take part in the fight. From Fort Riley also went as part of the command Light Battery E, 1st Artillery, with the following officers: Capt. Allyn Capron, 1st Lt. Albert Todd, and 2nd Lt. Harry L. Hawthorne.

The railroad trip from Fort Riley to Rushville, Nebraska, was noteworthy only in the poor service rendered by the company, both as to speed and accommodations for men and animals. After many and unaccountable delays, we reached Rushville about daybreak on November 24, detrained, and marched about eight miles and went into camp. While on the way to the agency next day, almost continual firing was suddenly heard to the right front. This firing was at a distance, and the only explanation seemed to be that a fight was in progress between the Indians and the few troops already at the agency, although the absence of any word from General Brooke, who had been apprised by telegraph of our approach, left this in doubt. Two troops were sent at a gallop in the direction of the firing, and the remainder of the command took the trot. After marching nearly two miles at these gaits, word was received from the two troops in advance that the firing was caused by the Indians killing the cattle as they were issued to them. This information was a great relief, as everyone knew that the small force at the agency could not hold out very long if hostilities had begun.

We arrived at the agency about noon, November 25, without further incident, and by General Brooke's direction went into camp in the bottom south of the agency. There remained in and around the agency a large number of Indians, but a great many bucks had left and were camped in the Badlands, about thirty miles north, and with these General Brooke had been negotiating. Their

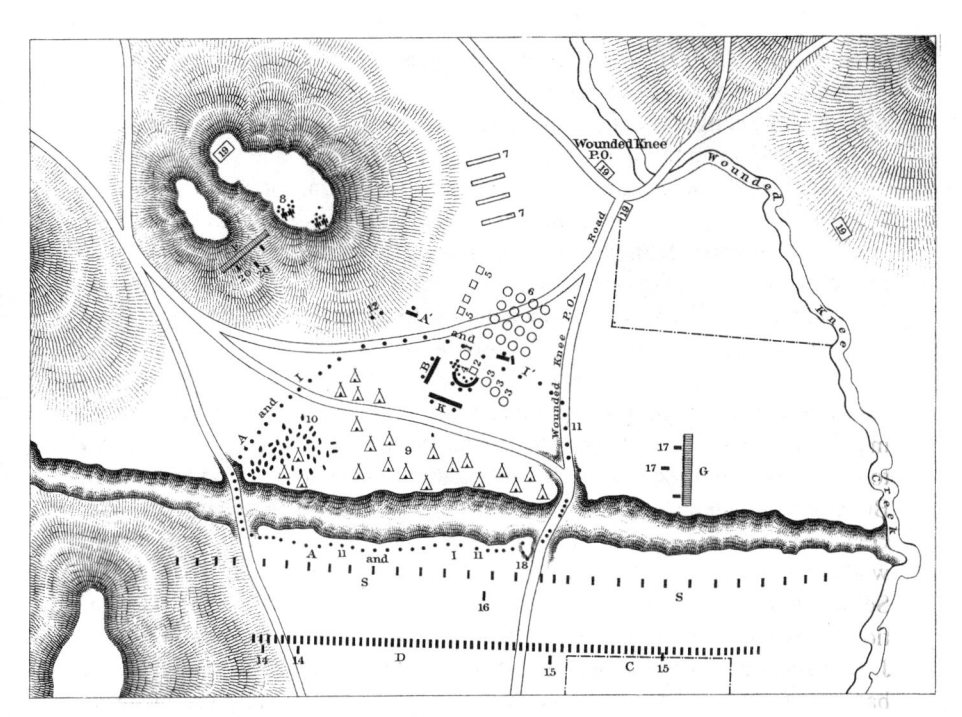

The Wounded Knee battlefield. (A, I) Troops A and I in dismounted line of sentinels. (B) Troop B dismounted in line. (C) Troop C mounted in line. (D) Troop D mountd in line. (E) Troop E mounted in line. (G) Troop G mounted in line. (K) Troop K dismounted in line. (S) Indian scouts. (1) Tent where a warrior shot two soldiers. (2) Tent where Big Foot was killed. (3) Tents put up for Big Foot's band. (4) Council ring. (5) Officers' tents, First Battalion. (6) Enlisted men's tents, First Battalion. (7) Bivouac of Second Battalion. (8) Four Hotchkiss guns and detachment of First Artillery. (9) Indian village. (10) Indian ponies. (11) Dismounted line of sentinels. (12) Ilsley and Moylan. (13) Garlington and Waterman. (14) Godfrey and Tompkins. (15) Jackson and Donaldson. (16) Taylor in command of Indian scouts. (17) Edgerly and Brewer. (18) Nowlan and Gresham. (19) Indian houses. (20) Sickel and Rice. CYRUS T. BRADY. *INDIAN FIGHTS AND FIGHTERS.*

camp was known as the "hostile camp," and in it were also several disaffected bands from other points. The Indians who had remained at the agency were not considered, by officers who had much experience in such matters, any more inclined to peace than those in the hostile camp; this belief was confirmed when the first actual conflict occurred later at Wounded Knee by nearly every Indian hastily leaving for the hostile camp and firing into the agency as he went. However, these negotiations were continued by General Brooke with a view to getting all the Indians to come from the hostile camp to the agency—the idea apparently being that this would settle the question. Almost daily communication was kept up, but with true Indian cunning, very little was accomplished toward committing the Indians to a peaceful acquiescence. One day the report would be very favorable, the next, matters would be at a standstill.

This backing and filling continued until the killing of Sitting Bull near Standing Rock agency, December 15, 1890. Sitting Bull was a chief and the head medicine man of the Sioux, who had for years devoted himself in every possible way to stirring up discontent. To curb this dangerous influence, his arrest was ordered and accomplished; but within a few moments thereafter, he uttered a signal shout, to which his band at once responded, and in the fight which followed, he, with several others on each side, was killed. This event, however beneficial it ultimately proved to be, caused a suspension of Brooke's negotiations, and for a few days it looked as if nothing short of force would accomplish any desired results. The negotiations were, however, soon resumed.

There were several bands of Indians out from the Missouri River agencies, and troops from different posts were in the field watching them. One of these bands was under Big Foot,[5] a very surly and treacherous Indian. His camp was on the Cheyenne River, and after Sitting Bull's death, his following was very much increased by small parties of bucks from different points. During the night of December 22, Big Foot and his band escaped from the force whose duty it was to control him. To prevent his joining the hostile camp north of Pine Ridge was of the utmost importance, and for this purpose Colonel Forsyth, under orders from General Brooke, sent Whitside on December 26 with his squadron (Troops A, B, I, and K) and two Hotchkiss guns under Lieutenant Hawthorne to the Wounded Knee Post Office to intercept Big Foot if possible. Assistant Surgeon Glennan accompanied this command.

Maj. Gen. Nelson A. Miles, commanding the division [of the Missouri], was at Rapid City, South Dakota, exercising command of all the forces in the field. He had more than once, since Big Foot's escape, forcibly reminded Brooke of the danger attending his freedom, and of the absolute necessity of again having him under control. This was the tenor of all the orders and instructions given regarding Big Foot.

Whitside captured Big Foot [on] December 28 about six miles from Wounded Knee and brought the entire party into his camp. He sent a request to Brooke at Pine Ridge for the remainder of the 7th Cavalry and the battery. This request was complied with, and at 8:45 P.M. that night, the entire Fort Riley contingent (excepting a small camp guard) and a company of Indian scouts under 1st Lt. Charles W. Taylor[6] and 2nd Lt. Guy H. Preston,[7] 9th Cavalry, were at Wounded Knee Post Office, eighteen miles from the agency. Whitside had already located the Indian village on the flat about 150 yards southwest of his camp. He had counted the band and had issued rations to 120 bucks and 230 women and children. He had detailed Troops A and I as guard for the night, dividing them into two reliefs, with an officer in charge of each relief. The two captains divided the night in the duties of officer of the day. Forsyth's force

A parley with Big Foot. COSMOPOLITAN, 1911.

joined Whitside's with as little commotion as possible, and as it had no baggage of any kind, it bivouacked for the night, and no change was made in Whitside's dispositions.

Brooke's order to Whitside was to "find Big Foot, move on him at once and with rapidity, and if he fought, to destroy him." Those elements of the order, without condition, had been completely executed. Capture by United States forces has never inspired Indians with very much terror. It is always followed by an issue of rations, which is repeated at regular intervals, and finally terminated, as a rule, with liberty and forgiveness for all crimes and disorders, no matter how serious have been the consequences. On Forsyth, as will be seen, was imposed the ticklish business of disarming this band of fanatics; this has always been the critical stage in dealing with Indians—even when not inflamed to the point of insanity by religious zeal. In fact, complete disarmament has been so rare that the rules of chance have not yet presented any variety of results. A fight will always take place, and it is absurd to even hope for the contrary. To the Indian, a gun is the most cherished of all earthly possessions. The cost almost precludes the possibility of any one Indian buying more than one gun during a lifetime. How persistently would the civilized white man cling to any of his treasures if he saw no prospect of replacing them! The Indian recognizes the superiority of the white man's gun over his bow and arrow for hunting purposes, and as his hunting is for subsistence alone, and is not for the mere fun of seeing animals die, it is not hard to understand this intensity of feeling. It would be instructive to see the workings of a law (assuming that it would be constitutional) requiring the citizens of this country to surrender their sporting guns, and to note the protestations, concealment, lies, and even forcible resistance which those executing such a law would encounter. The noble red man himself could pick up points; yet we like to consider him as the culmination of all that is troublesome, unreliable, and treacherous. And this band did possess all of these attributes to a marked degree.

Whitside hoped to so overawe its members by numbers as to convince them that resistance to the demand that was to follow would be useless, and thus accomplish the purpose without loss of life. Believing as they did that their ghost shirts would protect them from the bullets of the soldiers, he might as well have tried to overawe so many lions. Forsyth's orders from Brooke were "to disarm the Indians where they were camped, to under no circumstances allow any of them to escape, and to destroy them if they resisted." The difficulties coincident with the execution of this duty have been partially explained, and no subordinate ever had a more delicate service to perform. In this connection, it must be remembered that Forsyth could not take the initiative in actual conflict with the Indians. Had such a course been in accord with the policy of the government, he could have announced his ultimatum of immediate surrender of arms or destruction, and governed himself accordingly. Instead, by the limitations of this policy, he was chiefly occupied in an endeavor to obey his order "to disarm" without resorting to the alternative "to destroy"—though at the same time taking the necessary precautions to meet what all feared would follow.

Early in the morning of December 29, Forsyth made his disposition for the coming contest in diplomacy, it was hoped; but in force, it was feared. Whitside's sentinels from Troops A and I and the remainder of the guard were left as morning found them—one-third on post around the village, and the other two-thirds stationed at suitable points from which to support the sentinels in case of necessity. Troops B and K were held in reserve, to be used as the occasion demanded. These four troops remained dismounted, their horses being left at the picket lines in camp. Troops C, D, E, and G were mounted and stationed at such sheltered positions as were available around and at some distance from the flat on which the village was located. The artillery was placed on a rise of ground north of and overlooking and controlling the flat, with Troop E near at hand. All were cautioned to avoid doing anything to excite suspicion on the part of the Indians.

When these arrangements were completed, Forsyth called a council and took his place on the flat between Whitside's camp and the village. Only a part of the bucks responded, and after showing themselves, they returned to the village. This constant moving back and forth continued for half an hour or more, the bucks paying no attention to Forsyth's instructions to listen to what he had to say. Finally, Big Foot, who was ill with pneumonia, was brought from the tent which had been pitched for his comfort and treatment, and in front of which Forsyth stood, and was persuaded to cause his bucks to assemble. Even then they paid little or no attention to the purpose of the council, and many of them returned to the village in defiance of every effort to restrain them.

It then became necessary to adopt some method by which they could be held until Forsyth could explain what he had been ordered to demand of them. For this purpose, Troops B and K were moved to the flat between the village and the place of council and placed in effective position. Several bucks, at different times, tried to push themselves through these lines toward the village, and it required the greatest forbearance on the part of the officers and men to prevent an outbreak.

After the placing of these two troops to hold the bucks, Forsyth plainly told them that he was ordered by higher authority to secure their arms and tried to impress them with the fact that the government would deal fairly and kindly with them. Just here is where the real trouble began. His announcement was received with the sullen defiance so often displayed by strikers during labor troubles—with this effective difference, that the Indians believed themselves to be absolutely safe from all attacks by white men. It was surprising to see the perfect confidence they had in their ghost shirts. Big Foot gave some instructions, and as a result, a few broken and worthless guns were brought over from the village. He was then informed that those few guns could not be taken as a compliance with the orders of the government. He replied that his people had no more guns, that they had been burned by the troops on the Cheyenne River. His statement was not believed, and it was apparent that to get any serviceable arms, we would have to find and take them.

Forsyth then ordered Whitside to have the village searched. The captains of Troops B and K (Varnum and Wallace), with small details, were designated for this duty—Wallace starting on the flank of the village farthest from our camp, and Varnum on the other flank, each working toward the center. The Indians had evidently expected this search and had taken every possible precaution. Several tepees on each flank had been searched without result, when someone noticed a squaw sitting on the ground with her clothes spread out more than usual. She would not get up when told to do so, and it was necessary for two soldiers to take her by the hands and raise her to her feet, disclosing two guns which had been very cleverly concealed.

The search was resumed, and under nearly every squaw and child was found some sort of a weapon. Wallace and Varnum were cautioned against allowing their details to use any more force than necessity demanded in making these searches. A number of knives, war clubs, and about forty guns, many of which were unserviceable, were taken out of the village. Forsyth, satisfied that full results had not yet been obtained, again demanded from Big Foot a compliance with the orders, calling his attention to the fact that every buck had a gun at the surrender the day before. Big Foot simply repeated his former assertion about having been deprived of his guns on the Cheyenne River. Every place had been searched except the persons of the bucks, and Forsyth could not feel that he had fully executed his orders to disarm this band if any place was left unsearched, so instructions were given for each buck to be examined. To properly accomplish this, the Indians were told to return to their village by passing through the intervals between Troops B and K, and to allow the details at that point to search them for arms and ammunition.

It was then about 9:30 A.M., and the medicine man of the band had been indulging in an almost continuous harangue. Little attention had been given to this by Forsyth until Interpreter P. F. Wells[8] of Lieutenant Taylor's company of scouts, who had been acting as interpreter in the council, informed him that the Indian had suddenly changed the tenor of his address and was then trying to induce his comrades to resist the personal search, claiming that they could not be harmed by the bullets of the soldiers. Forsyth had a great deal of trouble in causing his men to cease his efforts in this direction, but finally he sat down, although his manner plainly indicated that he was still determined to carry his point if possible. Father F. M. J. Craft, a Catholic priest from the agency,[9] had been present at the council, doing all he could to persuade the Indians to submit. The personal search began, and about half a dozen of the older Indians had passed through the interval designated and allowed the details to search under their blankets, when the medicine man reached down, gathered a handful of dust, and threw it into the air. Captain Varnum, although some little distance away assisting in the search, saw this sign, recognized it, and called, "Look out, they've broken!"

Although the blankets fell from the Indians as suddenly as a fireman is deprived of his bedding when an alarm is turned in, and every buck began to use his gun as rapidly as possible, Captain Varnum's warning no doubt brought to many a young soldier a realization of the fact that he was in his first fight and gave him a bracer in the knowledge that all of his comrades had heard the warning and were with him to the end. The Indians broke in the general direction of their village and endeavored to penetrate the line of Troops B and K, but the soldiers stood their ground and returned the fire to the best of their ability. It should be remembered that every shot fired by the Indians at this stage was toward their own village, in which were their women and children, and that not a single soldier was so placed as to fire in that direction, but exactly the opposite.

About the time the order was given to prepare for the personal search, it was noticed that the squaws and children were saddling ponies, hitching their teams, and loading considerable plunder in their wagons. When asked for an explanation of this, the bucks said they were simply getting ready so that they would not delay the command. At the first shot, the squaws leaped in the wagons and drove out of their village, and took an old road leading along the base of the hill on which the artillery had been located. The bucks soon scattered around the flanks of Troops B and K and endeavored to follow their families, some of which had been unable to reach the old road and had then crossed a deep ravine, which was the southern limit of the flat. No wagons escaped in this direction, and the number of bucks was not large, although several followed up the ravine and in that way tried to reach the foothills.

Yellow Bird throws dust in the air.
HARPER'S WEEKLY, 1891.

Those Indians who were not killed in the first clash, and who succeeded in getting in rear of their women and children, necessarily now drew our fire in their direction. Troops B and K, in order to allow the other troops to open fire, gradually changed their position to the hill where the artillery was. Troops A and I (those were the troops that furnished the sentinels and supports) held the positions they occupied, and on them the sentinels assembled. The artillery had not yet had a chance to take part without endangering our own men, but was ready and watching for the first opportunity. The Indian scouts disappeared early in the action. The mounted troops (C, D, E, and G) dismounted at the first shot, and after placing their horses as safely as possible, waited for orders. The troops' commanders allowed a few of their sharpshooters to fire at certain Indians, but the rest of the men were kept ready for any call.

This fight on the flat was very hot, and by the time Troops B and K had changed their positions to the hill, not many bucks were possessed of motive power, and a number of those who had escaped around the flanks of the line had been killed by the sharpshooters of Troops C, D, E, and G. Several had, however, succeeded in reaching the foothills and the dense brush growing in the ravines. Whitside's squadron had borne the brunt of the fight and had, in less than an hour, permanently disposed of most of the bucks. Forsyth sent orders to Troops C, D, and G of the other squadron to pursue those Indians who had escaped and to capture or kill the men, and to capture the women and children. The three troops mounted and set out at a gallop, and a running fight took place with these Indian bucks for two or three miles, when all who had not been killed were captured. During this time, the killed and wounded were being collected, and the latter attended to in the best possible manner by Captain Hoff and Lieutenant Glennan. The results of Captain Hoff's continued and efficient instructions of the company bearers of the regiment were so remarked as to produce general praise. He received several bullets through his clothing while dressing wounds on the field.

Instead of fleeing to the hills, two or three bucks had secreted themselves in the brush near the head of the deep ravine south of the flat, and by moving about had escaped destruction, although a Hotchkiss gun under Lieutenant Hawthorne and detachments of Troop E had been trying to dislodge them. It was while on this duty, with his gun advanced to short range in order to get better control of the brush, that Lieutenant Hawthorne received a severe wound in the groin. Earlier in the action, Captain Wallace had been killed, and Lieutenant Garlington severely and Lieutenant Gresham slightly wounded. 1st Lt. John Kinzie,, 2nd Infantry,[10] present but not on duty of any kind, was shot through the heel. Father Craft had been stabbed through the body from behind, and Interpreter Wells's nose had been almost severed from his face. Captain and Assistant Surgeon C. B. Ewing was present but not on duty with any organization.

In the meantime, Captain Jackson's troop had captured a number of Indians, principally women and children, in the foothills, when he was confronted by about a hundred bucks who had come out from the agency (whom the authorities had supposed to be peaceful Indians), and had sent back for rein-

The opening of the fight at Wounded Knee. HARPER'S WEEKLY, 1891.

forcements. Troops D and G were ordered to move from their work in the adjacent hills to Jackson's assistance, and Troop E was assembled and was about to go to the same point when Jackson sent word that the agency Indians had retired. A counting of dead bucks had been going on for some little time, and as all but two or three of Big Foot's band were accounted for, every effort was directed towards the care of our dead and the wounded of both sides. About this time, a train of ten or fifteen wagons appeared on the scene, loaded with rations and forage from the agency, and intended for Whitside's squadron in escorting Big Foot's disarmed band to a station on the railroad, whence they were to be taken to some reservation at a distance.

Up to this time, the transportation present was so limited that moving the dead and wounded was an impossibility; a beginning had been made to construct temporary entrenchments on the hill north of the flat, as it seemed a foregone conclusion that we would have to remain there until such time as means for moving the wounded were sent to us. The hostile camp was not a great distance west of us, and an attack from that quarter was not at all unlikely as soon as news of the fight could reach it, and the temper of the agency Indians was very apparent from Jackson's encounter in the hills. The arrival of this train offered a solution. The wagons were unloaded and a layer of sacked oats placed in the bottom, over which was spread a thick layer of hay, and in these wagons the dead and wounded were taken to Pine Ridge that night, in order to get them where they could be properly cared for. After all our wagons were loaded, there were four or five wounded Indians not provided for. One of the Indian wagons was secured for these, and by gathering pieces of harness from different parts of the field, we finally had all ready for the terrible ride of eighteen miles. There were two ambulances, and in one of them Lieutenants Garlington and Hawthorne were placed, and in the other Father Craft and a noncommissioned officer. The transportation of these four was bad enough, but it was heavenly when compared with the springless jolts of the freight wagons. It took us from 5:00 P.M. until about 11:30 P.M. to march in—the rate being regulated by that of the wagons.

To recapitulate, we started with the bodies of one officer and twenty-four enlisted men of the 7th Cavalry, and one hospital steward; of wounded, one officer and thirty-three enlisted men of the 7th Cavalry, one officer of the 1st Artillery, and one of the 2nd Infantry, one interpreter, and one civilian. Three of the wounded enlisted men died of wounds in the wagons, and five afterwards as a result of their wounds. As it was impossible to bury the dead Indians, they were left on the field, but all the wounded Indians were given the best attention possible and taken with us to the agency. A party was sent out in a few days and buried 146 on the field. With very few exceptions, all the bucks were still there.

When we arrived at the agency, Forsyth stopped and made a verbal report to General Brooke. The regiment and battery went to their camps, cared for their horses, and speedily sought their blankets. A great many of the Indians who had been living at the agency, and who had by some been considered as friendly, had disappeared in the direction of the hostile camp. Just when they would appear again, and whether as an attacking force or as rations receivers, was a question. There was considerable excitement among the troops, which prevented much sleep.

Immediately after reveille next morning, December 30, we were summoned to go to the help of the train of a squadron of the 9th Cavalry, which was following that squadron to its camp at the agency. Maj. Guy V. Henry, commanding, had come in ahead with three of the troops, leaving one troop as a guard to the train. It had been attacked by Indians, and one corporal killed. This squadron had made quite a long march, and the 7th Cavalry was considered in better condition for the work. After a gallop of about three miles, we found the train and escorted it to the agency.

Within an hour, the 7th Cavalry and Light Battery E, 1st Artillery, were again called for to go to the Drexel Mission,[11] about four miles away, on the report that Indians were burning the mission. An interview with those in charge convinced Forsyth that the mission was in no danger, and he had given orders to return to the agency, when a report came in from the advance guard that one of the scouts claimed that he heard the firing of heavy guns from the direction of the hostile camp. Forsyth had already executed the orders under which he had been sent to the mission, but could not well turn back in the face of this report, particularly as it was quite possible that a fight was in progress in his front between the forces known to be in that direction and the unknown number of Indians. Deciding to investigate matters a little more, he sent a report to Gen-

Henry's squadron rescues the 7th Cavalry near Pine Ridge.
COSMOPOLITAN, 1911.

eral Brooke with [a] request for the 9th Cavalry squadron to join him, and continued his march down the valley. The advance guard developed and drove back a small party, but soon afterwards a much larger force was opposed to us. Proper dispositions were made on commanding ground about two miles below the mission. There was nothing to indicate that there was any fight in our front, and as Forsyth was not expected to bring on an unnecessary engagement, and as our men had practically been without food for forty-eight hours, he gave orders for the return to camp, withdrawing Whitside's squadron and the artillery first, and leaving Ilsley's squadron in position until Whitside could occupy one in rear, when Ilsley was to withdraw to the rear of Whitside.

Whitside's squadron was approaching its position when a sharp fire was directed against it from the hills on its right flank. Part of the squadron was formed toward the right and occupied a crest, which controlled the situation. As Ilsley's squadron retired, it was so utilized as to aid in the withdrawal. About this time, Henry's squadron of the 9th Cavalry arrived from the agency and, under Forsyth's direction, was used for the same purpose. One enlisted man was killed in this affair, and 1st Lt. James D. Mann[12] and six enlisted men were wounded. Lieutenant Mann afterwards died as a result of this wound. The loss to the Indians was never known. The command arrived at the agency about 4:00 P.M.

As a sequel to these two fights, Colonel Forsyth was relieved from command of his regiment by General Miles and subjected to an investigation of his conduct of the two engagements. The following endorsements show the action taken by the major general commanding the army, and the secretary of war, on the reports of the investigation.

February 4, 1891

Respectfully submitted to the Secretary of War:

The interests of the military service do not, in my judgment, demand any further proceedings in this case, nor any longer continuance of Colonel Forsyth's suspension from the command of his regiment.

The evidence in these papers shows that great care was taken by the officers and generally by the enlisted men to avoid unnecessarily killing women and children in the affair at Wounded Knee, and shows that the conduct of the 7th Cavalry, under very trying circumstances, was characterized by excellent discipline and, in many cases, by great forbearance. In my judgment, the conduct of the regiment was well worthy of the commendation bestowed upon it by me in my first telegram after the engagement.

(Signed) J. M. Schofield,
Major General, Commanding

War Department,
Office of the Secretary,
Washington, February 12, 1891

Respectfully returned to the major general commanding

From the testimony taken by Major Kent[13] and Captain Baldwin, two officers of General Miles's staff, ordered by him to investigate the fight at Wounded Knee, it appears that before the action, Big Foot's band had been joined by Sitting Bull's following, and these bands embraced the most fanatical and desperate element among the Sioux. They surrendered because of the necessities of their situation rather than from a submissive spirit. It was the sullen and unwilling yielding of a band of savage fanatics, who were overmatched and out of food, to superior force. It was not in good faith on the part of the younger braves, at least, but yet not with any definite prearranged plan of treachery.

The surrender was made to Major Whitside, commanding the 1st Battalion of the 7th Cavalry, on the afternoon of December 28. Colonel Forsyth was ordered up to his support and arrived at 8:45 P.M.

It was manifestly an imperative necessity to prevent the escape of any of these desperados during the process of disarming or as a consequence of the attempt to disarm them, for such escape would probably have resulted in a destructive raid upon the settlements. The troops appear to have been well disposed to prevent an outbreak, which was not and could hardly have been anticipated by anyone, under the circumstances, even in dealing with Indians, and the dispositions made appear to have had the desired effect of convincing at least a majority of the Indians of the futility of any escape. If treachery was premeditated by any of the Indians, which seems extremely improbable, the majority of them were deterred from attempting to execute it until incited by the speech of the ghost dancer.[14]

The disarmament was commenced, and it was evident that the Indians were sullenly trying to evade the order. To carry out this order, the men had been ordered from their camp, to separate them from their women and children, and were formed about a hundred yards away, and Troops K and B were posted midway between them and their tepees. When ordered to surrender their arms, they produced two broken carbines and stated that was all they had, but when the partial search of the tepees was made before the firing commenced, about forty arms were found, the squaws making every effort to conceal same by hiding and sitting on them, and in various other ways evincing a most sullen mien. The disarmament was much more thorough than they expected, and when they found that the arms were to be taken from their tepees, and those they had concealed under their blankets were to be taken away also, they were carried away by the harangue of the ghost dancer and, wheeling about, opened fire. Nothing illustrates the madness of their outbreak more forcibly than the fact that their first fire was so directed that every shot that did not hit a soldier must have gone through their own village. There is little doubt that the first killing of women and children was made by this first fire of the Indians themselves.

They then made a rush to break through and around the flanks of Troop K, commanded by the gallant Captain Wallace, and reached their tepees, where many of them had left their arms with the squaws, and they continued the firing from among their own women and children, and when they started from their camp, their women and children were mingled with them. The women and children were never away from the immediate company of the men after the latter broke from the circle. Many of them, men and women, got on their ponies, and it is impossible to distinguish buck from squaw at a little distance when mounted. The men fired from among the children and women in their retreat. Cautions were repeatedly given both by officers and noncommissioned officers not to shoot squaws and children, and the men were cautioned individually that such and such Indians were squaws. The firing by the troops was entirely directed on the men in the circle and in a direction opposite from the tepees until the Indians after their break mingled with their women and children, thus exposing them to the fire of the troops, and as a consequence, some were unavoidably killed and wounded, a fact which was universally regretted by the officers and men of the 7th Cavalry. This unfortunate phase of the affair grew out of circumstances for which the Indians themselves were entirely responsible. Major Whitside emphatically declares that at least fifty shots were fired by the Indians before the troops returned the fire. Several special instances of humanity in the saving of women and children were noted. That it resulted in the loss of the lives of many good soldiers and the wounding of many others, as well as the almost total destruction of the Indian warriors, was one of the inevitable consequences of such acts of insane desperation.

The bodies of an Indian woman and three children who had been shot down three miles from Wounded Knee were found some days after the battle and buried by Captain Baldwin of the 5th Infantry on January 21, but it does not appear that this killing had any connection with the fight at Wounded Knee, nor that Colonel Forsyth is in any way responsible for it. Necessary orders will be given to ensure a thorough investigation of the transaction and the prompt punishment of the criminals.

No doubt the position of the troops made it necessary for some of them to withhold their fire for a time in order that they might not endanger the lives of their comrades, but both Major Kent and Cap-

Sioux dead at Wounded Knee. FOURTEENTH ANNUAL REPORT, BUREAU OF ETHNOLOGY, 1892–93.

tain Baldwin concur in finding that the evidence "fails to establish that a single man of Colonel Forsyth's command was killed or wounded by his fellows." This fact, and indeed, the conduct of both officers and men through the whole affair, demonstrates an exceedingly satisfactory state of discipline in the 7th Cavalry. Their behavior was characterized by skill, coolness, discretion, and forbearance, and reflects the highest possible credit upon the regiment, which sustained a loss of one officer and twenty-four enlisted men killed, and two officers and thirty-one enlisted men wounded.

    The situation at Wounded Knee was a very unusual and a very difficult one, far more difficult than that involved in an ordinary battle, where the only question is of gaining a victory without an effort to save the lives of the enemy. It is easy to make plans when we look backward, but in the light of actual conditions, as they appeared to the commanding officer, there does not seem to be anything in the arrangement of the troops requiring adverse criticism on the part of the department. I therefore approve of the endorsement of the major general commanding, that the interests of the military service do not demand any further proceedings in this case. By the direction of the president, Colonel Forsyth will resume the command of his regiment.

                                      (Signed) Redfield, Secretary of War

The Indian Troubles and the Battle of Wounded Knee

WILLIAM F. KELLEY[1]

Transactions and Reports of the Nebraska State Historical Society 4 (Lincoln: State Journal Company, Printers, 1892): 30–50

It may be said that conflicts with Indian tribes have been features of American civilization from the beginning of the seventeenth century. The natural progressiveness and constant extensions of the white race have made Indian wars unavoidable. Enterprise has gradually deprived the red man of his former domains. Many times he has not relinquished his possessions without a bitter strife. Although vanquished habitually, the struggle has left enmity deep and enduring within his breast. From the Indian's own peculiar nature, in his opposition to the modes of civilization, and in the ever trespassing tendencies of the whites, were found the sources of these constant conflicts. In brief, it has been the old tale of energy and thriftiness, in combat with ignorance and idleness. In not a few of these many struggles has the Indian proven a foe formidable to his more civilized pursuer. Though conquered for the moment, the struggle was not in vain in the lesson left behind. Unable to be the victor, the Indian, to men at least, has proven the prowess of his kind; at the mention of his name and cruelties, women speak with trepidation.

Tardy legislation has often urged the Indian to perpetrate unmentionable cruelties and crimes, in hope of redress. Indian officials have been men without character, who have pilfered and abused him, or have not been solicitous as to his needs. The Indian's fiery nature has again broken from all restraint, upon trivial pretext, inaugurated a strife that has cost many lives and the destruction of much property. In quarrels begun without adequate cause, in effect the Indian was, of course, the loser. Military regulations were more strictly enforced; his confines became more and more limited; but the instincts of his nature were not subdued. The prospect of an Indian war is an object to be dreaded by those most directly concerned. It is productive of great damage, not only during the period of the conflict, but for an indefinite time succeeding. Visions of the Indian's anger and ferocity haunt the people in the surrounding country. This is sufficient to put a check upon progress and development, and is detrimental to commerce and trade. No safety for man or property is felt in his vicinity. The Indian's enmity, when aroused, is not soon suppressed; time is needed for it to slumber into extinction. Therefore, an anxiety, warranted by past experiences, was felt throughout some of the western states during the summer, fall, and winter of 1890, on account of the threatening cloud of trouble with several of the Indian tribes.

During the summer months, rumors, both many and varied in character and sometimes thrilling in detail, were sent over the country, indicating an uprising of various Indian tribes within the states of Dakota, Wyoming, Montana, and Utah Territory. So incessant were these reports of that which the Indian was doing, or about to do, that gradually a feeling of alarm and fear became definable and took possession of settlers in these various states nearest to the different Indian reservations situated therein. That these apprehensions were needless and almost causeless appears now to be true except in regard to the several Sioux tribes in South Dakota. These latter had some real and some fancied grievances that, sooner or later, diplomacy or force of arms would have been compelled to meet and adjust. The Ghost Dance was the immediate cause of these disturbances.

A few words as to this almost universal infection, for so it may be termed, are necessary to an understanding of the subject. An increasing excitement for months had been visible among the tribes over the supposed coming of the Indian Messiah. It was suspected, and became well known subsequently, that the best informed and most intelligent among the Indian chiefs placed no faith in this novel doctrine; still, they awaited in silence, or from ambitious motives;

Ghost dancers in prayer. FOURTEENTH ANNUAL REPORT, BUREAU OF ETHNOLOGY, 1892–93.

while many, aspiring to as yet a secret result, encouraged their more credulous brethren in this belief. The Christ was reputed to be coming in the form of a buffalo; it was said that he would cause the vast herds of buffalo and deer again to inhabit the plain and mountains; that he would renew the youth of the aged; that the Indian dead would be resurrected; and that the white man would disappear. Again would the Indian's home be the whole of the North and West, whose eastern boundary would be the great river, the Mississippi. These promises were all very alluring to the Indian's heart and well calculated to arouse Indian sentiment to an extraordinary degree. It is difficult to comprehend that the Indian could sincerely believe in such promises, and that such events as these predicted would take place; but it is nevertheless a fact that in them, many Indians had implicit faith. So old and experienced a chieftain as Red Cloud himself sent two couriers to the Far West to ascertain any news of the Messiah, as well as to investigate the authenticity and sources of information concerning the Messiah, of which he had heard so much.

The report soon became general that the Messiah had been seen in Washington, then in Oregon, and finally in Utah; that he was moving eastward, visiting the several Indian tribes. Representatives were sent from the Sioux at Pine Ridge and Rosebud, the Cheyennes at Tongue River agency, the Arapahos, Shoshones, and other tribes, to behold and to converse with the Messiah, at a designated point in Utah, among the mountains, where he was reputed to be at that time.

A few of these messengers returned and reported that they had seen the Messiah at a distance, and generally at night; but they became frightened and dared not approach him. Others, through various adverse circumstances, were unable to reach him, but were more firmly convinced than ever of the reliability of his near approach. As a consequence, the excitement increased rapidly; agency business of all kinds was at a standstill; progress was retarded or forgotten; schools were abandoned wholly or partially; and other undertakings beneficial to the Indians' daily welfare were sacrificed to this popular idea and idol of the moment.

Among the different tribes, and about their reservation, the agitation had thus far been harmless, as far as any actual danger to white men and their families was concerned. Some of the less courageous settlers had been seized with fright and fled, but it must be said such hasty actions were without sufficient cause. Ghost dancing was being freely indulged in and becoming more attractive to all the Indians. It was said the Messiah had commanded them to dance six days and nights at the beginning of every new moon. The dances at these times were always largely attended, so many enthusiasts were created. These prolonged dances were usually followed by feasts, while at other times the dancing went on when desired. The dancing Indian would continue the monotonous tread, until in exhaustion he fell to the ground in a fainting condition. While in this state, he was to hold communion and receive revelations from the

Christ. No weapons, other than a knife, perhaps, were allowed by the Indians to be on their person during the progress of the dance.

As nothing of a serious nature developed from the dancing of the various tribes, except the Sioux, we shall confine our attention wholly to them. The agent and his Indian police soon had under control the Cheyennes and other tribes, but the Sioux were by far too numerous and excited to be thus restrained. The demoralizing influence of the craze increased among the Sioux with great rapidity when once it had obtained a start. The first indication of what the craze was leading to was exhibited on August 22, 1890, by their demeanor and defiance of authority. A large number of Indians[2] met on White Clay Creek to hold a religious festival. Agent Gallagher, of the Pine Ridge agency,[3] with a few of his Indian police, went to the appointed place to reason with the Indians and disperse the dancers to their homes. Upon the agent's appearance, many fled, others ran to their tepees for their arms and stripped themselves for a fight, ordering the police and agent not to approach. The agent, being greatly outnumbered and seeing a fight likely to ensue, thought discretion better than valor, and with his force withdrew to the agency. The incident is trivial, otherwise than as it illustrates the dangerous spirit prevailing in thus bidding defiance to the government's agent, Sometime afterwards, Dr. Royer, who had succeeded Gallagher as agent, was openly assaulted, without provocation, by a few Indians at the agency proper. A mob gathered which threatened to burn the government storehouses. This feeling was with much difficulty quieted and peace restored.[4]

At Pine Ridge, the situation was becoming perilous to life and property. The agent, with a small force of Indian police at his command, was unable to maintain order. At this time the Standing Rock agency Indians and those at the agency on the Cheyenne River (Big Foot's band) were beyond police control, as were also the Brules at the Rosebud agency. They refused to discontinue dancing, and the agent's orders were treated with contempt in all other matters. Royer at once took prompt measures. He called for troops to protect the government property, and stated to the department that they were needed at once. The leaders of the young men were sublimely passive when appealed to by the agent for assistance in quelling these disorders. These young chiefs were at that time using this dance as cover under which to plan an outbreak, and also encouraging the dance as a means of uniting the turbulent into a common cause. As the young men advocated these popular measures, and were determined to be the leaders, the older men among the chiefs were more or less compelled to give a tacit assent, or see themselves and their power set aside. It should be remembered that from first to last, these disturbances were instigated and animated by the young chiefs.

The Indians were assuming an impudent attitude at all the Sioux agencies toward the government and its representatives, committing some petty depredations; but the spirit of the hour was not on the wane. The dancing was causing them to become wilder as each day passed. The Indian police were frightened and afraid to cope with them.

In accordance with instructions from the War Department, General Brooke, with five companies of the 2nd Infantry and three troops of the 9th Cavalry, arrived at Pine Ridge on November 20. Several companies were at and near Rosebud. Reinforcements were sent to Standing Rock and vicinity, the home of Sitting Bull's band. That wily chieftain had not as yet committed himself to any act of hostility. While he was too intelligent to be a ghost dancer himself, yet he openly encouraged it among his band and friends, though often requested by his agent to do the contrary.

Upon the arrival of General Brooke and his troops, an order was sent to all the Indians scattered over Pine Ridge reservation to come and camp at that agency. Those who complied would be considered as friendly; the others would be treated as hostile. Whether friendly or hostile, soon an immense camp was established about the agency consisting of several thousand Indians and their families.

More troops were constantly arriving at Pine Ridge. The government, through the War Department, evidently intended to assume no half-hearted attitude. Five more companies of the 2nd Infantry and eight troops of the 7th Cavalry were soon in the field; also some batteries of artillery arrived, with Hotchkiss and Gatling field pieces and a few rifled cannon. With these additional troops, affairs began to look reasonably secure about the agency for the first time, notwithstanding the immense numbers of Indians around Pine Ridge. These Indians were much divided in regard to their position and intentions toward the government. The principal source of trouble it was supposed would be at Pine Ridge, on account perhaps of the number of Indians at that place. But no sooner had the greater number of troops begun to concentrate at that point than news reached them that more than two thousand Brules had worked away from the Rosebud agency under the leadership of Two Strike, Short Bull, and Kicking Bear; the latter was a prominent and noted young warrior and the high chief of the ghost dancers among all the Sioux. These Brules made direct for the Badlands, situated north of the White River, and destroyed everything in their path to that place. The greater part of the damage to property during the entire trouble was done by these Brule Indians on their flight to the Badlands. They had too great a start to be overtaken, and any attempt made to check them would have been futile. Small bands circled out from the main body and pillaged the country on every side, wantonly destroying all that could not be carried away with them. No white settlers were in this region; the country through which they passed was the reservation of the Oglalas. The property, consisting of domestic effects and Indian annuities, was unprotected or in the charge of squaws whose husbands were at Pine Ridge and friendly, obeying the order of the authorities to camp there for the present. The stock of ponies and cattle was largely the property of squaw men and half-breeds.

In all the United States, there could not have been found a better spot for these hostiles to select than these Badlands. They were wholly inaccessible except in one or two narrow places. There was a scarcity of water; it was found in one place only, in a group of springs about which the Indians were camped. If the troops should be successful in entering, horses and army conveyances would be unable to traverse the country, owing to the steep declivities, the narrow gullies, and the rocky nature of the ground. At this place these Brules spent a month, holding a high carnival, having a merry Ghost Dance each day, and constantly receiving small accessions from their Oglala sympathizers. They maintained a semimilitary discipline about their camp, no Indians being permitted to leave the same.[5] One or two peace embassies only, of the many sent to them, were allowed to enter the limits of the camp and depart; usually they were forced to remain on the outside, and were but the bearers of insolent messages to the commander of the troops in his endeavors to have them come to Pine Ridge or to return to their own reservation.

As a diversion soon after their arrival, these Brules confiscated a herd of nearly two thousand government cattle grazing in the vicinity and killed a faithful herder, named [Henry] Miller. After this these Brules lived in the midst of such luxury and abundance as they had perhaps never before experienced, and such as it is probable they will never experience in the future. It may well be supposed something more than vague and uncertain promises as to the future, and in regard to what would be their punishment, was necessary to tempt the Indians to abandon this easy and comfortable life. Some more definite conditions than the commander of the troops was authorized to make them was needed. The one condition that the Brules on their part always did insist upon was that the troops be taken away from Pine Ridge before they would consent to leave the Badlands. Evasive answers were, of course, the reply of the military authorities. Peace parties of friendly Indians were continually sent to the Badlands. Those that succeeded in entering the limits of the hostile camp passed through an experience they did not wish to have repeated. Fanaticism was king of the hour.

The most successful of these peace commissions was that headed by Father Jutz, a most estimable Catholic priest, who has devoted his life to mission work among the Indians. He prevailed upon Turning Bear, High Hawk, and some other leaders of the young men to come in and hold a council with General Brooke and officers. When all had spoken, the council adjourned with many promises on the Indians' part, which in the end availed nothing, if we except, on the Indians' behalf, immense quantities of crackers and tobacco, which they induced the military commander to give them to vary their daily diet, after their return to the Badlands, during their deliberations over his propositions.

While matters were thus progressing at and near the Pine Ridge agency, an episode of a startling nature occurred near the Standing Rock agency which culminated in the death of the famous Sitting Bull and some others. Sitting Bull with his small band was on the point of setting out to join the Brule hostiles in the Badlands; his arrest was attempted by the Indian police, and in the melee, his death took place. It was thought this death would prove an unfortunate vent, but in the Indian world, he was a man of less power and influence than was generally supposed. Clothed as he had been by numerous writers with all those virtues and characteristics that approach the idyllic in manly character, his friends among the white people in the country—and he had many—had become fascinated by this so-called patriot of his race. His supposed leadership at the Custer massacre gave the fame and luster to his name, as did also to some extent the subsequent retreat of the Sioux over the border into Canada, pursued by a large military force. That his influence among his people was much overestimated by the American public is best shown, perhaps, by the fact that at his death, no more emotion or sensation was aroused among the Sioux than would have been by the death of a chief of humbler pretensions. The sudden death in this manner of any one of a dozen chiefs would have caused extreme commotion or violence, but of these Sitting Bull was not one. He was not a warrior, neither was he a leader at the Custer fight, as is popularly supposed. He was present with his tribe but not in any sense a participant on that day. Sitting Bull was a crafty and shrewd politician. He used every device at all times to fix public attention upon himself. He was successful to a degree that speaks well for his ability as a politician. Those who knew him best say that he was a genial, manly companion. His death marked no change, as was apprehended by the country at large; it was a benefit to the Indian and white man alike; his bitter hatred of the whole white race was well known; he was an uncompromising opponent of every measure advocated towards civilization for his people; he was a born agitator whose mind was never at peace; his nature demanded it, and because of it, he came to an unexpected death.

Life at Pine Ridge was varied by the arrival of a man, [A. C.] Hopkins by name, who appeared among the Indians, claiming to be the long awaited Messiah. His advent in the friendly Indian camp was not known for some days, during which time he lived quietly, praying among the Indians constantly. His presence becoming known, his arrest by the Indian police followed; he was finally conducted to Chadron and dismissed. The Indians treated him with consideration and respect, as is their custom to the demented. That he was not the Christ was best proven to them in that he was wholly ignorant of their language. The man was modest, genteel in bearing, an attractive man in person. In conversation, he was singularly well versed in natural theology, philosophy, and the sciences. He modestly but firmly maintained that he was the Messiah. The unfortunate man soon disappeared.[6]

The troops heretofore mentioned extended across the country from Pine Ridge to Rosebud agencies, and to the northeast, as a protection and to prohibit any raids being made toward the south; while on the north and northwest were stationed infantry companies at various points, but the 6th and 8th Cavalry in detachments of troops or battalions were the effective forces of guards in these directions. Some citizen soldiery of South Dakota, under the command of Colonel [H. R.] Day, on the staff of Governor [Arthur C.] Mellette, did some service in patrolling the country across the South Fork of the Cheyenne River, which is on the northern and north western side of the Badlands.

It will thus be seen from the positions of all these troops that each detachment of troops formed a segment of a huge military circle, or nearly so, extending on every side of the hostile Brules in the Badlands.

General Miles established his headquarters at or near Rapid City, South Dakota, and the operation and movements on the north were under his direction, while those on the south were under the immediate supervision of Brigadier General Brooke. It was Miles's intention not to permit them to break through or be upon the outside of this military cordon. If there was to be war, to keep them in one large body was his purpose. The advantage of the idea consisted in the practical prohibition of small raiding bodies of Indians, whose excursions have always been so destructive to life and property in Indian wars. To the successful completion of this project, General Miles threw all the energy of his character, and all the ingenuity derived from a successful military education in wars with many Indian tribes. To hold the Indians on the reservation at all hazards was his aim, for then no settlers' lives could be endangered. To prevent them from crossing the South Fork of the Cheyenne River, into a region where there are so many ranches and thousands of cattle, as there are also to the west of the Badlands in Wyoming, was another important part of his plan. Should the hostile Brules have escaped from the Badlands, they would unquestionably have gone in one or both of these directions, for then they would have found all the conditions favorable to Indian warfare: cattle for food in abundance, and a mountainous country in which it would have been difficult for soldiers to pursue them. This was surely General Miles's conception of the situation when he came to the seat of hostilities and located at Rapid City, where he remained until after the fight on Wounded Knee Creek.

At no time was there any danger of raids to the south, along the Elkhorn railway in Nebraska, except in the minds of a thoroughly frightened people. Surely there was no plausible reason to tempt the Indians southward. The country is fairly well populated, at least much more so than the country to the north and west of the Badlands. Towns of considerable size are found, and but few miles apart; the country is open and presents no places for concealment; and finally, the Indian would place himself between the troops extending east and west between the Pine Ridge agency and the various towns in Nebraska. Some time previously, Big Foot's band, which was reputed to be a desperate body of Indians, all implicit believers in the Messiah craze and the infallibility of the ghost shirt, had left the Cheyenne River agency. It was supposed that it was their intention to join the hostile Brules in the Badlands. Soon after, they were captured by Colonel Sumner[7]—from whom they subsequently effected their escape—near a small town called Smithville; now they were supposed to be heading again for the Badlands.

On the afternoon of December 24, an order was received from General Miles ordering a cavalry force to be at once dispatched to intercept Big Foot. Within an hour, Col. Guy Henry, with four troops of the 9th Cavalry and three Hotchkiss guns strapped to the backs of mules, was on the march. Their haste was such that they marched forty miles over the desolate prairie before day dawned. The command scouted over the country near the Badlands without success. They were unable to find the Indians. This force returned to Pine Ridge agency on the morning of December 30, the morning after the battle at Wounded Knee, arriving in haste, to protect the agency from a threatened and anticipated attack. It is worthy of mention that these troops marched over eighty miles in the twenty-four hours preceding their arrival. These Negro cavalrymen constituted one of the very best regiments in the United States Army. Its degree of excellence in soldierly qualities and duties was high. Several of the colored privates of this battalion of the 9th Cavalry were the fortunate possessors of gold medals voted to them by Congress for bravery in action and distinguished merit, which they proudly bore at all times pinned to the breasts of their uniforms. This mark of distinction is a rare one among the privates of the army.

Exciting events were now to be the destiny of each day. Thrilling rumors concerning the surrounding Indians were so plentiful as to seem to be floating on the air, inhaled by the inhabitants of the agency. The Indians about the agency were becoming decidedly hostile in spirit and in demonstrations. The war cloud which had hung apparently suspended for some weeks seemed now about to break. Notwithstanding the increasing hostility of the Indians about the agency, on December 26, four troops of the 7th Cavalry, commanded by Major Whitside, left Pine Ridge in a terrific sandstorm, in an endeavor to intercept the band of Big Foot. Success was destined to be the fate of the brave soldiers of this veteran regiment.

For some reason, the military authorities were fearful of the presence and influence of Big Foot's tribe, and for a week had been making every possible effort to learn his location and destination. During the afternoon, the 7th Cavalry removed to the northeast twenty miles; at evening, as dusk approached, some scattering Indians were encountered, but they could not be overtaken by the troops, who rushed hotly in pursuit. A camp on Wounded Knee Creek was established for the night. Attempts were made all the following day, by means of numerous scouting parties, to learn some tidings of the much-wanted Indians, but without avail.

On Sunday the task was renewed, and about midday they were discovered about ten miles distant by Little Bat [Pouriere], a noted half-breed scout. The Indians were marching over the prairie, carelessly enough, in the direction of Pine Ridge agency, and evidently wholly unaware of the near presence of the troops. The troops, upon this report, in haste set out from the camp on a gallop. As they neared the vicinity of the Indians, they moved stealthily and with caution. The troops were formed into line, and with a Hotchkiss gun in the center, they dismounted and lay quietly upon the ground, concealed near the top of a high ridge running across the plain, waiting for the Indians to approach, which they soon did, men, women, and children straggling along in an indifferent manner. An order was sent forward demanding an immediate surrender.

Astonishment and consternation took possession of the Indians at the appearance of these unexpected cavalrymen. Joy and exultation seemed to fill the breasts of these veteran troopers at the prospect of combat. The Indians soon recovered from their surprise but were at a serious disadvantage to make any resistance, encumbered as they were with women and children. After some delay spent in parleying, during which a considerable number of Indians sought to congregate about the Hotchkiss piece, also, in a casual manner, to flank both ends of the line of troops, which maneuvers were promptly and sternly checked by the commander, Big Foot and band were prisoners of war. For once the Indians had been taken and overcome by surprise. The command was at once put in motion toward the camp on Wounded Knee, the Indians closely watched by the cavalrymen. Stringent measures were taken to guard them through the night. They still were in possession of their arms. Sullen anger was depicted upon each countenance. Their tepees for the night were pitched within the camp line of the troops. A chain guard encircled them. Loaded Hotchkiss guns were trained upon their camp from a slight elevation nearby.

In the band were one hundred and forty bucks and some two hundred and fifty women and children. Many of this band were outlaw Indians, and with their reputation for desperateness, it was thought inadvisable to attempt to disarm them with the present number of troops, a number but few more than the number of male Indians. The mere presence of a larger body of troops was deemed to be a better insurance against any disturbance in disarming them. An Indian values his gun almost as life itself, and parts with it only from urgent necessity. A courier brought Colonel Forsyth with the remaining battalion of the 7th Cavalry from Pine Ridge.

Soon after reveille in the morning [December 29], most of the troops were mounted and massed about the Indian camp at varying distances. The Indian men were ordered to come from their tepees and stand in a line a few paces forward from their tepees, which, after considerable hesitation and demur, they were persuaded to do, 131 in number. Every man of them was decorated in full war paint and clad in their hideous ghost shirts. About their shoulders was folded a blanket, under which was concealed a rifle or carbine, unknown to the soldiers about them. That they were on the eve of a bloody conflict entered the mind of neither officer nor private. Absolute safety was felt from attack or opposition by the superiority in numbers of the troops; and yet every precautionary measure was observed to produce an effect upon the Indians. Eight troops of cavalry and a few artillerymen were there present—nearly four hundred men. Two dismounted troops, one hundred in number, were placed within ten yards of the Indian line.

For one hour and more did these troops there stand, and yet not a suspicion was aroused as to these hidden guns. Twenty Indians were counted off and the

The battle of Wounded Knee. W. F. BEYER. *DEEDS OF VALOR.*

order given to them to go to their tepees and turn over their arms. The designated Indians withdrew to the rear and returned with two or three worthless guns. A search of the tents, women, and camp outfit was at once begun by a detachment of troops, ending by some forty pieces being found, nearly all of which were valueless as weapons. Surprised at this scarcity, when but the day previous all the Indians were seen to be well armed, the command was given to search the Indian men in the line. A detachment moved forward for the purpose, the order was about to be executed, when at this critical moment, without a word, a cry, or symptom of warning, a shot was fired and a soldier fell. The medicine man had reached forward to the ground for a handful of earth; he tossed it high above his head, threw back his blanket, and fired.[8] Almost instantly, with hardly a perceptible pause, was he followed by his comrades. So rapidly was this done that the whole line of Indians had fired ere the soldiers realized and comprehended the situation.

But these veterans of our army, Custer's old command, were not for a moment thrown into confusion, unexpected as the assault was; it was an unexcelled instance of discipline. They stood their ground bravely, and soon a bloody carnage was ensuing. Single-handed combats were many. Knife and Indian club wounds were numerous; but the fire was too close, too severe, to endure long at this short distance. The Indians stood heroically for a time, until fifty-two of their comrades were dead upon the spot, and then retreated back among their tepees, firing as rapidly as possible the meanwhile.[9]

The Ghost Dance and Wounded Knee, 1890–91 589

When the Indians had moved away from the troops, the Hotchkiss guns, not fifty yards distant, began sending their destructive little shells among them; this quickened their pace, causing them to run to the adjoining hills or to take refuge in a neighboring ravine. The Indians were soon followed by the mounted troops, and as they refused to surrender in almost every instance when overtaken, very few Indian men lived to tell the story of that bloody day's treachery. As the Indians stood forward from their tents only a few yards, about which were the women and children, a large number of these latter were accidentally struck by the fire of the soldiery, before they could seek shelter in the ravine or flee to the bluffs from the open prairie where the conflict was taking place. The results of the fight were disastrous to both sides. In reality, the brunt of the battle was borne by the two dismounted troops. Of the troops, twenty-five were killed on the field and thirty-five wounded; many of the latter died soon after from the severe character of their wounds.

Captain Wallace was among the dead, a man beloved alike by his brother officers and by the men of his troop. Wallace had acquired a reputation in the army, in a previous Indian war, equaled by few young officers, for bravery and skill in his profession. His death was deeply lamented by the whole command. Lieutenants Hawthorne and Garlington were among the severely wounded, the latter of arctic fame, who made an unsuccessful attempt to rescue Greeley in the frozen north.

The Indian loss was 116 dead, including Big Foot; and among the women and children, sixty or seventy killed and about the same number wounded;

The wounding of Lieutenant Hawthorne. HARPER'S WEEKLY, 1891.

among the latter, a sister of Sitting Bull. The death and injuries of the women and children were much deplored, but, from their position, it was certainly unavoidable. No one could have shown them greater kindness than did these soldiers afterward when the opportunity was presented them in the hospital at Pine Ridge agency.

The casualties were appalling, considering the numbers engaged, the most disastrous that had occurred in any Indian battle for thirty years, if we except the last fight of Colonel Custer. It was indeed a severe lesson to the Indians. While nearly all the Indians had guns under their blankets, it is difficult to believe any large number contemplated engaging the troops. Subsequent consideration of many trifling incidents, not attracting attention at the time, seemed to confirm the supposition of some that a considerable number did have that intention rather than give up their guns. But when the first gun was fired, owing to the close proximity of the contestants, there could be no opportunity to distinguish friend from foe. If there were those whose intentions were pacific at the onset, they seemed instantly to comprehend that their only chance for life was to fight—and to fight desperately. In their position, that chance was indeed a poor one. Their misfortune, however, was brought on by the foolhardiness of some of their own people. Before night, the Indians had set the prairie on fire in every direction toward Pine Ridge agency; miles of prairie were a slumbering mass of fire, and it was with much difficulty that the column hastened to the agency at night to the protection of that place with their dead and wounded. The Indians were left where they had fallen.

Upon the 7th Cavalry's arrival at Pine Ridge after midnight, they found the people gathered at that place, panic-stricken and convulsed with fear. But few infantrymen were guarding the agency, and the Indians had occupied the afternoon shooting into the agency from the surrounding hills. The return of this force restored peace and order for a time. The following day, a wagon train but two miles from the agency was attacked by a body of Indians. Two colored troopers were slain before assistance arrived.[10]

The 7th Cavalry, pursuing the Indians for some miles, brought on an engagement which lasted for several hours. The troops were unable to get near the Indians, who were scattered about and estimated to be from six to eight hundred in number. As evening approached, the 9th Cavalry came to the relief of the 7th, who were in a difficult position and surrounded by Indians. As the bugles sounded over the hills, denoting the coming of the 9th, the Indians hurriedly fled.[11] Less than a dozen were killed and wounded upon each side, the Indians keeping well protected during the combat. Among the wounded was Lieutenant Mann, the remaining officer of ill-fated Troop K; he died soon afterward.

After these two days of fighting, affairs began to assume a serious aspect. General Miles and the 1st Infantry at once came to Pine Ridge agency from the north. A decided change was at once manifest as to what would be the policy of the future. No more time would be spent in the endless coaxing; the hostile Brules were to be answered with decision. General Miles, with his accustomed

Digging trenches at Pine Ridge.
HARPER'S WEEKLY, 1891.

energy, began making preparations and taking vigorous measures for a winter's campaign. Fortifications of earth and logs, behind which were mounted cannon and Gatling pieces, were placed upon the highest hills around the agency proper, while rifle pits were scooped out across the top of nearly every small knoll, within these outer breastworks. These signs did not pass unnoticed and unheeded by the Indians. It was the remedy needed. The 7th Cavalry was camped to the south of the agency, and hardly enough troops were left in the agency to form a sufficient guard, most of the soldiers being sent to strengthen the huge military circle.

A period of indescribable panic and confusion now commenced, never to be forgotten by those who passed through it. The Indians, to the number of five or six thousand, had at last come out of the Badlands and were encamped ten miles away. General Miles had succeeded so far, yet the Indians refused to come to the agency and surrender. Almost hourly for several days were reports brought to the agency, by friendly Indians, that this large body of Indians were determined to come in at night and burn the agency and government storehouses. Each night was their firing kept up on the outposts and picket lines, which gave color to the reports. As each night passed, the attack was thought more certain to take place on the next. As day faded and darkness gathered, every living thing was infected with the terror and excitement of the hour. Numbers of half-breed women passed the night through cringing with fear at the distant report of the guns. Their condition was pitiable to behold. Men with demeanor hardly more manly moved about with loaded weapons in their hands, not daring to sleep, such were their apprehensions of danger and attack.

As the first streaks of day dawned, unuttered prayers of gratitude were in the hearts of these creatures that another day of life was before them. Time went by and the danger passed. From an Indian standpoint, it would have been the severest blow they could have inflicted upon the government, within their power, and it might have been accomplished with comparative ease by this large body of Indians.

Grave apprehensions of danger were felt to be imminent beyond the borders of Pine Ridge agency. Two regiments of the Nebraska militia, under Brigadier General [L. W.] Colby, were soon stationed at or near the towns along the Elkhorn railway, southward from the Indians. These militia did good service in quieting the fears of the people and in being ready to afford protection in case of necessity.

While the situation was becoming hopeful, the unfortunate death of an accomplished young officer, by the Indians, ensued. Lieutenant Casey, in command of the Cheyenne scouts, ventured too near the hostile camp and was shot as a spy. The grief over the loss of this young officer was sincere and heartfelt, but it must be said his own rashness was responsible for his death. He was a man who sincerely had the welfare of the Indian race at heart; in his death they lost a sympathetic friend.

General Miles had accomplished, so far, his object in preventing the Indians from scattering in small bands. Some attempts to disperse had been made by them, but they invariably had been driven back. Miles was putting his troops daily through a series of skillful maneuvers, to and fro; however, not to such an extent as to seriously frighten the Indians. He was slowly but surely drawing this military circle of three thousand United States troops closer about the hostile camp. Vigilance was the watchword of troops and commander. The Indians were beginning to comprehend the danger of their position. Troops were between them and the Badlands, their stronghold, and it was hardly possible for any considerable number of them to escape through the ever tightening human band around them. Still defiant, many were beginning to see their helplessness and the folly of further resistance.

The collapse and end was not far away. The Brules indeed were still fierce and ready for war, while the Oglalas under Red Cloud and Little Wound, who had fled to the Brules after the Wounded Knee fight, wished to leave the Brules and surrender. Bitter dissensions were known to exist in the hostile camp. The rival factions clashed daily and often came to blows. The Oglalas several times attempted to desert the Brules but were prevented by force. A few chiefs of the former tribes finally succeeded in getting to General Miles, and held a council upon the terms to be granted them; unconditional surrender was the demand. The 6th Cavalry and Carr were only twenty miles to the north; the Indians must decide quickly, and yet they hesitated from day to day.

The man for the emergency was at hand. Young-Man-Afraid-of-His-Horses, who had been absent in Wyoming for some months, suddenly returned to the agency. He was one of the four most powerful of the Sioux chiefs, and what was more, he was a friend of the white man. Through his ability and by his directions, the Oglalas did desert their comrades and joined the large friendly camp of the same tribe on the south side of the agency. The Brules would not yet abandon the struggle, hopeless as it was becoming. Under the pressure of troops, however, they again moved up, this time to within three miles of the agency. The troops were moved sufficiently to keep the Indians uneasy without making a positive hostile demonstration. The Brules' young men were wild and fierce at their position. Pandemonium reigned in their camp. They fought one another. It seemed that they were drawn as by a magnet nearer and nearer the goal, against their individual will and inclination. Should no unfortunate accident occur, it was deemed now that the end was near at hand. Time, and time alone, would cool their warlike ardor. That element was best needed to do the remainder after this prolonged period of excitement. Councils were held in vain. No definite promises could be obtained from General Miles. Kindness was awarded the Brules on every hand. Gifts of provisions and tobacco were plenty. Their hearts must soften. Again they moved nearer. Troops were in sight all about them, and the great Indian scare was terminated by the Brules, signifying their intention to move into the agency.

The ending was picturesque; the Indians' vanity for theatrical parade was strikingly exhibited. Kicking Bear, a Brule leader and the host dancing chief, strode forward with haughty step and form erect, with folded arms; he sternly eyed the military commander; defiance faced defiance for a moment; but in recognition of submission, this proud savage humbly laid his carbine at the feet of General Miles. What three months before had threatened to develop into an extensive and bloody war had been averted, but not before a large part of three states had been effectually frightened. The result had been accomplished by tedious persuasion and gentleness rather than by force, yet the lesson administered at Wounded Knee had not been without its effect. The punishment of treachery was swift; the voice of governmental authority must be obeyed.

Fully ten thousand Indians were camped about Pine Ridge. Quiet for a time ensued; then a demand was made for the Brules to surrender their arms. Less than a hundred were voluntarily obtained. It was thought best not to enforce this order by seizure. The Indians were too many in number; the outcome of such a course would be doubtful if the Indians should resist. The Brules were soon sent to their own reservation at Rosebud; and some time afterward, without pretext and without ostentation, thirty of the leaders of the trouble, including the famous Kicking Bear and Short Bull, were obtained and transported to Fort Sheridan, near Chicago. Later it was thought that European travel might be beneficial to them; that it might awaken inclinations by which they might profit by beholding civilization abroad—if not in their own country—by viewing the sights and the musty monuments of the Old World; accordingly, under the chaperonage of Colonel Cody, many of these Brule captives accompanied that gentleman to foreign shores. The grand finale was a review of all the troops engaged in the campaign by General Miles, and soon most of them were homeward bound to their several posts.

It is worthwhile to notice that the progressive and Christian Indians, those who had been influenced by Indian schools, were almost universally loyal. They participated in none of the disturbances and were unaffected by the Messiah craze.[12] Some, indeed, were forced by circumstances or by their chiefs to go to the Badlands, but they contributed no small part to the final termination by their desertion of the hostiles at the critical moment. These friendlies suffered greatly by their loyalty, in having their property ruined or stolen. The government was prompt in its legislative action and made an appropriation immediately to reimburse them for their loss. This justice of the government at once allayed antagonistic feelings, which it was thought might terminate in future trouble. Had not this appropriation been made at once and when needed, resentment would have displaced friendship among many of these loyal Indians, which would have been the principal source of apprehension as to any renewal of the trouble in the spring of 1891.

As has been stated before, the disturbances were instigated and fostered by the young men. The Ghost Dance had its purpose in the minds of aspiring leaders. But the Sioux had grievances; at least a portion of them had; no prospect of redress being visible, ambitious chiefs were ready to seize the opportunity. The very large reduction of the great Sioux reservation, brought about by the Sioux commission, composed of Major Warner, General Crook, and the present secretary of the treasury, Foster, some time previous, had been a constant source of dissatisfaction, especially among the young men. While the reduction was made with the consent of a large majority, it was bitterly opposed by an influential minority, who afterward allowed no opportunity to pass to stir up dissension among those who had favored the agreement in consideration of certain allowances. A change was made by the committee in the boundary line between the Rosebud and the Pine Ridge reservations. The line had been replaced farther eastward, and consequently had given more land to the Oglalas, who report to the agency at Pine Ridge. The Brules thus affected were given other quarters equally as good. No trouble or hardship was made them, but owing to their irritable mood, dissatisfaction prevailed. The boundary line was thus changed to make the amount of land proportionate to the number of Indians at each agency, the Oglalas exceeding the Brules in number.

Two censuses taken, each by special agents [A. T.] Lea and [James G.] Wright of the Indians at Rosebud, showed that the Rosebud Indians had been drawing rations largely in excess of what was due the actual number of Indians at that place. A decrease of rations at once took place, based upon the census. Again, one condition promised by the Sioux committee, in lieu of the lands ceded away, was the unchanged amount of provisions per capita. Not long afterward, by the reduced and delayed appropriations of Congress, the amount of rations and supplies were for a time reduced. No suffering or want was necessitated, but those who opposed the cession of lands did not forget or allow others to forget their position on that question at that time. The next year, the winter of 1891, after the disturbance, Congress put the rations back to the former amount by appropriating sufficient funds. The question of rations is of supreme importance to the Indian; nothing, in fact, lies so close to his heart. The amount of his happiness is measured by the amount of rations obtainable.

These are, in brief, the principal causes of dissatisfaction that led to the hostile position assumed by the Sioux; and they apply more particularly to the Brule Sioux than to the other branches of that tribe. Other reasons were now and then heard of, but they were on the whole unworthy of notice.

Belief in the Ghost Dance among the Sioux has long since passed away. The Indian victims at Wounded Knee and other places, wherever reliance was placed in the ghost shirt to prove the ineffectiveness of bullets, have all tended to enlighten the less intelligent among them regarding this unique theory. Many Indians bitterly resented the consequences of this delusion, into which they and their friends had been led by their leaders and others. Since 1876–77, no trouble of note had been experienced with the Sioux Indians. In that time, many thousands of male children had risen to the estate of young manhood. The traditions of their race are all of war. A large number of these young men were ardent sympathizers of the young chiefs in their efforts to inaugurate a war, as decidedly in its favor as the older Indians were opposed to it. It offered a means for them to elevate themselves to distinction among their fellows, and as young blood is full of ambition and spirit, they naturally at once favored any avenue leading to that end.

    Schools and education among these Indians are fast accomplishing their task. Most of the schools are largely attended voluntarily by the children, and with the consent of their parents. Thus progress and contentment are rapidly on the increase. Every year marks a greater proportionate change in this direction. Many of the older and most powerful war chiefs in their prime are enthusiastic reformers and personally take an interest in these changes for the welfare of their people, and freely discuss with the authorities plans and ideas leading to that result. Many of the real, influential men among these (the Sioux) Indians today are those who endorse and assist in these progressive tendencies. It will not be many years ere the sullen, idle brave of the past, disdainful of labor, will have no important place among them. Theirs is a peculiar nature. Patience and kindness to guide them while they learn the habits and benefits of civilized life is the rule needed. Sensitive to rebuff and pained by sternness, it is only necessary now carefully to nurture these ideas awakened at last among a considerable number of these Indians. Education will swiftly do its work when actual interest is manifested. The intelligent Indian among the Sioux knows as well as his white brother that the race is doomed to extinction if it continues in the paths of ignorance and idleness. Those who are the real lovers of the welfare and happiness of their people, and there are many such Indians, are the sincerest supporters and patrons of the changed conditions. May the time be not far distant when this hitherto unfortunate race of people shall be welcomed into the ranks of the prosperous and happy among the heterogeneous people of this continent.

The True Story of the Death of Sitting Bull

EDMOND G. FECHET[1]

Cosmopolitan 20 (March 1896): 494–500

More than five years have passed since the most famous Indian warrior of his time lost his life while resisting arrest by lawful authority, and as yet the general public has never been given the true story of the events which led up to and culminated in the death of Sitting Bull and some of his most devoted adherents. Many accounts have been written, few of which had more than a faint color of truth. The different versions were many, and nearly all simply absurdities.

During the Sioux outbreak of 1890–91, the writer, then a captain of the 8th Cavalry, was stationed at Fort Yates, North Dakota. The post was commanded by Lt. Col. William F. Drum,[2] 12th Infantry. The garrison consisted of two companies of the 12th Infantry and two troops of the 8th Cavalry. The Standing Rock agency is on the north side of the post and only a few hundred yards away. Maj. James McLaughlin was the agent and had held the position during the eight or nine previous years.

During the summer of 1890, it became apparent that the Indians of the agency were becoming imbued with the Messiah craze. Major McLaughlin, aided by his wife and seconded by the well-known warrior Gall and other loyally disposed chiefs, used his utmost efforts to stem the tide of fanaticism. Sitting Bull, who had proclaimed himself high priest, was thus in direct opposition to his agent. The exertions of the latter confined the "disease" to the settlements on the Upper Grand River, which were largely composed of Sitting Bull's old followers.

In a letter to Mr. Herbert Welsh[3] of Philadelphia, Major McLaughlin says,

> Sitting Bull always exerted a baneful influence over his followers, and in this craze they fell easy victims to his subtlety, believing blindly in the absurdities he preached of the Indian millennium. He promised them the return of their dead ancestors and restoration of their old Indian life, together with the removal of the white race; that the white man's gunpowder should not throw a bullet with sufficient

597

Sioux of the Standing Rock Agency.
HARPER'S WEEKLY, 1888.

force in the future to injure true believers; and even if Indians should be killed while obeying this call of the Messiah, they would only be the sooner united with their dead relatives, who were now all upon earth (having returned from the clouds), as the living and the dead would be united in the flesh next spring.

Those whom Sitting Bull had converted to his views gave up all industrial pursuits, abandoned their homes, gathered around him, and raised their tepees near his house, which was on the Upper Grand River and about forty-two miles from Fort Yates. Here they passed the time in dancing the Ghost Dance and in purification baths.

Rations were issued at the agency every second Saturday. Previous to October, Sitting Bull seldom failed to come in person and draw his share. From that time on, he sent some member of his family to procure his rations, and no inducement of the agent could tempt him to appear at the agency. This determination of Sitting Bull frustrated one of the schemes to get him into safekeeping. In the event of his coming in, Colonel Drum had intended quietly to surround the agency with troops. Each company and troop had its position designated, and on signal were to move up quickly. Sitting Bull, by remaining at home, declined to walk into the trap laid for him.

On November 14, 1890, Major McLaughlin was advised by telegram "that the president had directed the secretary of war to assume a military responsibility for the suppression of any threatened outbreak among the Sioux Indians," and on December 1, 1890, he was instructed "that as to all operations intended to suppress any outbreak by force, the agent should cooperate with and obey the orders of the military officers commanding on the reservation." These orders practically placed the whole conduct of affairs in the hands of Colonel Drum, and he and Major McLaughlin were at all times in perfect accord. Throughout the entire civil and military services, two men better fitted for the trying and delicate duty to come could not have been found.

As each day passed, it became more and more apparent that the sooner Sitting Bull could be removed from among the Indians of the Standing Rock agency, the fewer hostiles there would be to encounter when the "outbreak by force" came. In the meantime, everything had been put in shape for a sharp and quick movement of the cavalry squadron, the troopers and horses designated for duty (fifty from each troop), gun detachments for the Gatling and Hotchkiss guns told off and drilled, one day's supply of rations and grain, buffalo overcoats and horse covers, extra ammunition—all packed, ready to be loaded. The transportation was one spring escort wagon, drawn by four horses, and one Red Cross ambulance.

Meanwhile, Major McLaughlin had quietly sent his company of Indian police by small parties to points on the Grand River, above and below Sitting Bull's house. They were scattered for some miles, ostensibly cutting timber, but as a matter of fact keeping close watch on the actions of Sitting Bull and his partisans.

With the coming of December, McLaughlin was all anxiety to have the arrest made without delay, and arranged with Colonel Drum that the event should take place on the sixth. McLaughlin selected that date as it was the next issue day, and as the greater number of his Indians would be in at the agency, he believed that the arrest could be effected with the least trouble and alarm. As the sixth drew near, McLaughlin became doubtful of his authority to make the arrest, inasmuch as it might be in conflict with the instructions from Washington, referred to before as received on November 14 and December 1, 1890. To settle his doubts, he referred the matter by telegraph to the commissioner of Indian affairs, receiving a reply on the evening of the fifth to the effect that no arrest whatever should be made, except on orders from the military or order of the secretary of the interior. Colonel Drum, not having orders from higher authority, felt that he could not take the responsibility of ordering the arrest; consequently, no movement was made.

Both Drum and McLaughlin chafed under the delay, as they felt that each day of waiting only added to the difficulties of the situation. Their anxiety was quieted by the receipt of the following telegram on the afternoon of the twelfth:

> HEADQUARTERS DEPARTMENT OF DAKOTA
> ST. PAUL, MINN., December 12, 1890
> *To Commanding Officer, Fort Yates, North Dakota:*
> The division commander has directed that you make it your especial duty to secure the person of Sitting Bull. Call on the Indian agent to cooperate and render such assistance as will best promote the purpose in view. Acknowledge receipt, and if not perfectly clear, report back.
> By command of General Ruger.
> (signed) M. BARBER,
> Assistant Adjutant General

After consulting with Major McLaughlin, who ahered to his idea that it was best to make the arrest on an issue day, Colonel Drum consented to wait until the twentieth, which was the next ration drawing. Early on the morning of the thirteenth, Colonel Drum imparted to me his orders and plans for their execution. As I was to command the force intended to cooperate with the Indian police, he directed me to make the necessary preparations quietly in order not to attract attention, as he felt confident that Sitting Bull had his spies watching both post and agency. There was but little to do, everything having been previously attended to.

But an event came which caused us to act before December 20, as the sequel will show. On the fourteenth, about 6:00 P.M., as we were enjoying the usual after-dinner cigars beside our comfortable firesides, "officers' call" rang out loud and shrill on the clear, frosty air. In a few minutes, all of the officers of the post were assembled in Colonel Drum's office. He informed us briefly that the attempt to arrest Sitting Bull would be made that night; then, turning, he said that charge of the troops going out would be given to me, that my orders would be made out in a short time, and that my command would move at midnight.

Orders were at once given to load the wagon. A hot supper was served to the men at 11:00 P.M. Then, after seeing that my orders were in process of execution, I went over to Colonel Drum's house for final instructions and to ascertain the cause of the change of program. With Colonel Drum I found Major McLaughlin, and learned that Henry Bull Head, the lieutenant of police, in charge of a company on Grand River, had written to the agent that Sitting Bull was evidently making preparations to leave the reservation, as "he had fitted his horses for a long and hard ride." Couriers had started at 6:00 P.M. with orders to Lt. Bull Head to concentrate his men near Sitting Bull's house, to arrest him at daybreak, place him in a light wagon, move with all speed to Oak Creek, where my force would be found, and transfer the prisoner to my custody. The lieutenant of police had been instructed to send a courier to await my arrival at Oak Creek, to let me know that the police had received their orders, and to give me any other information that might be for my interest to know.

By this time, my written orders had been handed to me. I found it directed me to proceed to Oak Creek, and there await the arrival of the Indian police with Sitting Bull. This seemed faulty to me, as Oak Creek was eighteen miles from Grand River, and my force would not be within supporting distance of the police if there should be a fight. Moreover, if he should succeed in escaping from the police, it was the intention to pursue him to the utmost, and in the race for the Badlands which would ensue, he would have a start of at least thirty miles.

After some discussion with Colonel Drum and Major McLaughlin, it was agreed that I should go some ten or twelve miles beyond Oak Creek, toward Grand River.

The squadron consisted of Troop F, 8th Cavalry, Lieutenants S. L. H. Slocum, M. F. Steele, and forty-eight enlisted men; Troop G, 8th Cavalry, Capt. E. G. Fechet, Lieutenants E. H. Crowder, E. C. Brooks, and fifty-one enlisted men; Capt. A. R. Chapin, medical officer, and hospital steward August Nickel; two Indians scouts, Smell-the-Bear and Iron Dog; and Louis Primeau, guide and interpreter. The artillery, consisting of one Gatling gun with Troop G and one Hotchkiss breech-loading steel rifle with Troop F, was under the immediate command of Lieutenant Brooke. Transportation, one four-horse spring wagon and one Red Cross ambulance.

For the first four miles, the squadron moved at a quick walk; a halt was then made, and the men were told to fix their saddles and arms securely, as I intended to make a rapid ride to Oak Creek.

The ride to Oak Creek was taken at a brisk trot; two or three short halts were made in order to tighten the girths and to change the troop leading the column. On reaching the creek at about 4:30 A.M., I was greatly surprised and concerned to find that the scout whom Bull Head had been directed to send to meet me at that point had not arrived. Although bewildered by this event, I realized that there was but one thing to be done, to push my command to Grand River as rapidly as possible and act according to the situation found. The gallop was the gait from this time on. I was pushing the animals, but still not too fast to impair pursuit beyond Grand River, should I find that Sitting Bull had escaped.

Just in the gray of the dawn, a mounted man was discovered approaching rapidly. He proved to be one of the police, who reported that all the other police had been killed. I forwarded to Colonel Drum the substance of his report, with the additional statement that I would move in rapidly and endeavor to relieve any of the police who might be alive. This courier (Hawk Man), by the way, was mounted on the famous white horse given to Sitting Bull by Buffalo Bill.

The men at once prepared for action by removing and stowing away their overcoats and fur gloves. While they were doing this, I rode along the line, taking a good look at each man. Their bearing was such as to inspire me with the fullest confidence that they would do their duty.

The squadron was now advanced in two columns, the artillery between the heads, ready for deployment. The line had just commenced the forward movement when another of the police came in and reported that Sitting Bull's people had a number of the police penned up in his house; that they were nearly out of ammunition and could not hold out much longer. At this time, we could hear some firing. In a few minutes, we were in position on the highlands overlooking the valley of Grand River, with Sitting Bull's house surrounded by the camp of the ghost dancers, immediately in front and some twelve hundred yards distant. The firing continued and seemed to be from three different and widely separated points: from the house, from a clump of timber beyond the house, and from a party, apparently forty or fifty, on our right front and some eight or nine hundred yards away. At first there was nothing to indicate the position of the police. Our approach had apparently not been noticed by either party, so intent were they upon the business on hand. The prearranged signal (a white flag) was displayed, but was not answered. I then ordered Brooks to drop a shell between the house and the clump of timber just beyond. It may be as well to state here that the Hotchkiss gun would not have been up on the line at this time but for the courage and presence of mind of Hospital Steward Nickel. In going into position over some very rough ground, the gun was overturned and the harness broken, so that the animals drawing it became detached. Steward Nickel, a man of exceptional physical strength, coming up with his Red Cross ambulance, seeing the plight the gun was in, seated himself on the bottom of the ambulance, bracing his feet against the tailgate, took a good grip with his hands on the shafts, told his driver to go ahead, and in this way dragged the gun up to the line.

The shell from the gun had the desired effect, and a white flag was seen displayed from the house. Slocum[4] and Steele,[5] with their men dismounted;

Crowder[6] with Troop G was ordered to move along the crest and protect the right flank of the dismounted line. Brooks threw a few shells into the timber, also against the party which had been on our right front, but was now moving rapidly into the valley. As Slocum's line approached the house, the police came out and joined it. The line was pushed into the timber, dislodging the few hostiles who remained.

I now caused the dismounted line to fall back to the vicinity of the house, pickets being left at the farthest point gained by the advance. All the hostiles having disappeared, Crowder was recalled. I had moved with the dismounted line and in passing the house had noticed Sitting Bull's body on the ground.

On returning, when the advance fell back, I saw the evidence of a most desperate encounter. In front of the house, and within a radius of fifty yards, were the bodies of eight dead Indians, including that of Sitting Bull, and two dead horses. In the house were four dead policemen and three wounded, two mortally. To add to the horror of the scene, the squaws of Sitting Bull, who were in a small house nearby, kept up a great wailing.

I at once proceeded to investigate the causes which brought about the tragedy. The inquiry showed that the police entered the house about 5:50 A.M. and arrested Sitting Bull. He occupied considerable time in dressing, and at first accepted his arrest quietly; but while dressing, his son, Crow Foot, commenced upbraiding him for agreeing to go with the police. On this, Sitting Bull became obstinate and refused to go. After some parleying, the police removed him from the house, and found themselves and prisoner in the midst of the whole crowd of ghost dancers frenzied with rage. As to the occurrences outside the house, I will again quote from Major McLaughlin's letter, the details of which are more complete than my notes, and were distinctly corroborated by investigations on the spot, made within three hours after the fight:

> The policemen reasoned with the crowd, gradually forcing them back, thus increasing the open circle considerably; but Sitting Bull kept calling upon his followers to rescue him from the police; that if the two principal men, Bull Head and Shave Head, were killed, the others would run away; and he finally called out for them to commence the attack, whereupon Catch-the-Bear and Strike-the-Kettle, two of Sitting Bull's men, dashed through the crowd and fired. Lt. Bull Head was standing on one side of Sitting Bull, and Sgt. Shave Head on the other, with Sgt. Red Tomahawk behind, to prevent his escaping. Catch-the-Bear's shot struck Bull Head on the right side, and he instantly wheeled and shot Sitting Bull, hitting him in the left side, between the tenth and eleventh ribs, and Strike-the-Kettle's shot having passed through Shave Head's abdomen, all three fell together. Catch-the-Bear, who fired the first shot, was immediately shot down by Pvt. Lone Man.

The death of Sitting Bull.
W. FLETCHER JOHNSON. *LIFE OF SITTING BULL.*

The fight now became general. The police, gaining possession of the house and stables, drove the ghost dancers to cover in the timber nearby. From these positions, the fight was kept up until the arrival of my command.

While engaged in the investigation, breakfast had been prepared for the men and grain given to the horses. Going to the cook fire for a cup of coffee, which I had just raised to my lips, I was startled by the exclamation of the police, and on looking up the road to where they pointed, saw one of the ghost dancers in full war array, including the ghost shirt, on his horse, not to exceed eighty yards away. In a flash, the police opened fire on him; at this he turned his horse and in an instant was out of sight in the willows. Coming in view again some four hundred yards farther on, another volley was sent after him. Still further on, he passed between two of my picket posts, both of which fired on him. From all this fire he escaped unharmed, only to fall at Wounded Knee two weeks afterward.

It was ascertained that this Indian[7] had deliberately ridden up to our line to draw the fire, to test the invulnerability of the ghost shirt, as he had been told by Sitting Bull that the ghost shirt worn in battle would be a perfect shield against the bullets of the white man. He, with some others of the most fanatical of the party, fled south, joining Big Foot's band. He was one of the most impetuous of those urging that chief not to surrender to Colonel Sumner, but to go south and unite with the Indians in the Badlands, backing up his arguments by the story of the trial of his shirt. Who can tell but that the sanguinary conflict at Wounded Knee, December 28, would have been averted if the Indian police had been better marksmen and had brought down that daring Indian, and that Captain Wallace and his gallant comrades of the 7th Cavalry, who gave up their lives that day, would still be among us?

The excitement over the bold act of the ghost dancer had hardly died away when another commotion was raised by the discovery of two young boys concealed in the house where the squaws were. They were found under a pile of buffalo robes and blankets, on which several squaws were seated. These boys were taken to the agency and turned over to Major McLaughlin, not murdered before the eyes of the women, as one newspaper account stated.

About 1:00 P.M., the squadron commenced the return march. Before leaving, the bodies of the hostiles were laid away in one of the houses and the squaws of Sitting Bull released, they having been under guard during our stay. Well knowing that they would communicate with their friends on the withdrawal of the troops, I sent a message to the hostiles to the effect that if they would return and stay peaceably in their homes, they would not be molested.

The dead and wounded Indian police and the remains of Sitting Bull were taken with the command to the post. On arriving at Oak Creek about 5:00 P.M., a courier was met with a message from Colonel Drum to the effect that he would join me some time in the night with the infantry. About midnight, Colonel Drum, with the companies of Captains [David J.] Craigie and

[Harry L.] Haskell, marched in, bringing with them food, forage, and tents, all of which we needed sadly. The cold was intense and fuel so scarce that only very small fires could be made. Our stomachs were in a state of collapse, as we had had but one light meal since leaving the post twenty-four hours before, during the first seventeen of which the entire command had ridden over sixty miles, and part of it nearly seventy miles. Supper was cooked in short order, and the infantry generously sharing their blankets with us, the balance of the night was passed comfortably.

After a long and anxious conference with Colonel Drum as to further operations, it was decided that pursuit might possibly do much harm by causing many Indians to flee into the Badlands. Accordingly, Colonel Drum ordered the command to Fort Yates, the movement to commence at daylight. Subsequent events proved the wisdom of Colonel Drum's decision, as, in response to messages sent by Major McLaughlin by runners who had left the reservation, 160 returned in a few days and, two weeks later, eighty-eight more were added to the 160. Of those that held their way to the south, 168 men, women, and children surrendered to Lt. Harry C. Hale, 12th Infantry, on the twenty-first near the mouth of Cherry Creek, a tributary of the Cheyenne River. Only about thirty-eight men, women, and children went to Big Foot's camp. Had pursuit been made, all the Indians of Sitting Bull's faction would undoubtedly have been forced into the band of Big Foot, thus swelling the force which met Colonel Forsyth at Wounded Knee.

The Sioux Outbreak in South Dakota

FREDERIC REMINGTON

Harper's Weekly, January 24, 1891

We discussed the vague reports of the Wounded Knee fight in the upper camps of the cordon, and old hands said it could be no ordinary affair because of the large casualties.

Two days after, I rode into the Pine Ridge agency, very hungry and nearly frozen to death, having ridden with Captain Baldwin, of the staff, and a Mr. Miller all night long. I had to look after a poor horse and see that he was groomed and fed, which require considerable tact and "hustling" in a busy camp. Then came my breakfast. That struck me as a serious matter at the time. There were wagons and soldiers—the burial party going to the Wounded Knee to do its solemn duty. I wanted to go very much. I stopped to think; in short, I hesitated, and of course was "lost," for after breakfast they had gone. Why did I not follow them? Well, my natural prudence had been considerably strengthened a few days previously by a half hour's interview with six painted Brule Sioux, who seemed to be in command of the situation. To briefly end the matter, the burial party was fired on, and my confidence in my own good judgment was vindicated to my own satisfaction.

I rode over to the camp of the 7th United States Cavalry and met all the officers, both wounded and well, and a great many of the men. They told me their stories in that inimitable way which is studied art with warriors. To appreciate brevity, you must go to a soldier. He shrugs his shoulders and points to the bridge of his nose, which has had a piece cut out by a bullet, and says, "Rather close, but don't amount to much." An inch more, and some youngster would have had his promotion.

I shall not here tell the story of the 7th Cavalry fight with Big Foot's band of Sioux on the Wounded Knee; that has been done in the daily papers; but I will recount some small talk current in the Sibley tepees, or the "white man's war tents," as the Indians call them.

Lying on his back, with a bullet through his body, Lieutenant Mann grew stern when he got to the critical point in his story. "I saw three or four young bucks drop their blankets, and I saw that they were armed. 'Be ready to fire, men; there is trouble.' There was an instant, and then we heard sounds of firing in the center of the Indians. 'Fire,' I shouted, and we poured it into them."

"Oh yes, Mann, but the trouble began when the old medicine man threw the dust in the air. That is the old Indian signal of defiance, and no sooner had he done that act than those bucks stripped and went into action. Just before that, someone told me that if we didn't stop that old man's talk, he would make trouble. He said that the white man's bullets would not go through the ghost shirts."

Said another officer, "The way those Sioux worked those Winchesters was beautiful." Which criticism you can see was professional.

Added another, "One man was hit early in the firing, but he continued to pump his Winchester; but growing weaker and weaker, and sinking down gradually, his shots went higher and higher, until his last went straight up in the air."

"Those Indians were plumb crazy. Now, for instance, did you notice that before they fired, they raised their arms to heaven? That was devotional."

"Yes, captain, but they got over their devotional mood after the shooting was over," remonstrated a cynic. "When I passed over the field after the fight, one young warrior who was near to his death asked me to take him over to the medicine man's side, that he might die with his knife in the old conjurer's heart. He had seen that the medicine was bad, and his faith in the ghost shirt had vanished. There was no doubt but that every buck there thought that no bullet could touch him."

"Well," said an officer, whose pipe was working into a reflective mood, "there is one thing which I learned, and that is that you can bet that the private

A cavalryman in winter uniform.
HARPER'S WEEKLY, 1891.

soldier in the United States Army will fight. He'll fight from the drop of the hat anywhere and in any place, and he'll fight till you call *time*. I never in my life saw Springfield carbines worked so industriously as at that place. I noticed one young fellow, and his gun seemed to just blaze all the while. Poor chap! He's mustered out for good."

I saw the scout who had his nose cut off.[2] He came in to get shaved. His face was covered with strips of court plaster, and when informed that it would be better for him to forego the pleasure of a shave, he reluctantly consented. He had ridden all day and been in the second day's fight with his nose held on by a few strips of plaster, and he did not see just why he could not be shaved; but after being talked to earnestly by a half dozen friends, he succumbed.

"What became of the man who did that?" I asked of him.

He tapped his Winchester and said, "Oh, I got him all right!"

I went into the hospital tents and saw the poor fellows lying on the cots, a little pale in the face, and with a drawn look about the mouth and eyes. That is the serious part of soldiering. No excitement, no crowd of cheering comrades, no shots and yells and din of battle. A few watchful doctors and Red Cross stewards with bottles and bandages, and the grim specter of the universal enemy hovering over all and ready to dart down on any man on the cots who lay quieter and whose face was more pale than his fellows.

I saw the Red Cross ambulances draw up in line and watched the wounded being loaded into them. I saw poor Garlington. His blond mustache twitched under the process of moving, and he looked like a man whose mustache wouldn't twitch unnecessarily. Lieutenant Hawthorne, who was desperately shot in the groin while working the little Hotchkiss cannon, turned his eyes as they moved Garlington from the next cot, and then waited patiently for his own turn.

I was talking with old Captain Capron, who commanded the battery at the fight—a grim old fellow, with a red-lined cape overcoat and nerve enough for a hundred-ton gun. He said, "When Hawthorne was shot, the gun was worked by Corporal Weimert, while Private Hertzog carried Hawthorne from the field and then returned to his gun. The Indians redoubled their fire on the men at the gun, but it seemed only to inspire the corporal to renewed efforts. Oh, my battery was well served," continued the captain, as he put his hands behind his back and looked far away.

This professional interest in the military process of killing men sometimes rasps a citizen's nerves. To the captain, everything else was a side note of little consequence, so long as his guns had been worked to his entire satisfaction. That was the point.

At the mention of the name of Captain Wallace, the Sibley became so quiet that you could hear the stove draw and the wind wail about the little canvas town. It was always "Poor Wallace" and "He died like a soldier, with his empty six-shooter in his right hand, shot through the body, and with two jagged wounds in his head."

Watching the Brule stronghold. Lieutenant Casey is in the center with binoculars; Frederick Remington stands to his left with his hands in his pockets. HARPER'S WEEKLY, 1891.

I accosted a soldier who was leaning on a crutch while he carried a little bundle in his right hand. "You bet I'm glad to get out in the sunlight; that old hospital tent was getting mighty tiresome."

"Where was I shot?" He pointed to his hip. "Only a flesh wound; this is my third wound. My time is out in a few days; but I'm going to reenlist, and I hope I'll get back here before this trouble is over. I want to get square with these Injuns." You see, there was considerable human nature in this man's composition.

The ambulance went off down the road, and the burial party came back. The dead were for the time forgotten, and the wounded were left to fight their own little battles with stitches and fevers and suppuration. The living toiled in the trenches or stood out their long term on the pickets, where the moon looked down on the frosty landscape, and the cold wind from the north search for the crevices in their blankets.

The Surrender of Red Cloud

CHARLES W. TAYLOR[1]

Order of the Indian Wars Collection, U.S. Army Military History Institute, Carlisle Barracks, Pennsylvania[2]

During 1889–1890, there was a widespread spirit of unrest among the Indians located on reservations in our western and northern states. This condition was due to a semi-religious-spiritual craze caused by a medicine man (a Paiute Indian named Jack Wilson, or Wovoka), promulgating what was claimed to be the coming of a Messiah who would return to the Indians all their lost territory together with complete subjugation of the white race. This idea, it is understood, started in Nevada with a medicine man who claimed to have had a vision in which was revealed the complete return of the Indian to his pristine state.

Spreading rapidly among the different tribes, the announcement of this vision took form in what was known as the Ghost Dance, in which the dancers wore shirts made of buckskin or cloth, painted in bright colors; these shirts were [said] to be bulletproof against the fire of the white man, who would be stricken helpless at [the] sight of them.

These dances went on for months, having a varying effect among the different tribes, depending largely upon the counsel of the chiefs, medicine men, and white men associated with them. The craze took firmer root, apparently, among the Northern Sioux tribes than elsewhere, and had its culmination at Pine Ridge, December 1890. The agents at Pine Ridge, Rosebud, and Standing Rock were rapidly losing control, and turmoil began.

In November, the agent at Pine Ridge came to Fort Robinson, Nebraska, where I was then stationed, giving alarming accounts of affairs at his agency and asking that troops be sent at once. Report was sent to headquarters, and those of us who saw the handwriting on the wall prepared for field service. In a few days, orders came which dispatched six troops of [the] 9th Cavalry from Fort Robinson and the 2nd Infantry from Fort Omaha to Pine Ridge. Later the command was augmented by other troops.

Red Cloud's immediate following was in camp at the agency and apparently quiet. It must be understood that many Indians were loyally inclined to the government and took no part in hostilities.

Soon after arrival at Pine Ridge, I was ordered to organize a troop of Indian scouts; this was promptly done. These scouts, 110 in number, were composed of men from Standing Elk's band of Cheyennes and friendly Oglala Sioux, among them such tried and true old-timers as No Neck, Woman's Dress, Yankton Charley, Red Shirt, Standing Soldier, and others. I am glad to avail myself of this opportunity to testify to the faithful services of these men in many campaigns, should this ever reach their friends and relations. Most of the actors themselves are dead. The Brule Sioux at Rosebud agency left their reservations and went into the Badlands, where it was planned to have a general gathering of all those hostilely inclined. Sitting Bull, the most vicious and influential of all medicine men, was creating much trouble at Standing Rock, and his arrest was ordered. Defying authority and resisting arrest, this old scoundrel was killed by the agency police. Big Foot, with his notoriously bad band, broke away and headed for the Badlands. A squadron of cavalry and Indian scouts were sent to intercept him and in due time located him at Wounded Knee Creek, about sixteen miles east of Pine Ridge. Col. J. W. Forsyth, 7th Cavalry, with Capron's Battery, 5th Artillery, with Hotchkiss guns, and the troop of scouts, were at once ordered to the scene. On the morning of December 29, a fight occurred resulting in the practical extermination of Big Foot's band. Some persons, for reasons best known to themselves, have sought to make it appear that the soldiers started the fight and were responsible for it. I am a living witness to the contrary.

Colonel Forsyth had called the leading men of the band before him to demand their surrender and receive instructions. These men were ugly from the start. They wore ghost shirts enveloped in longer white cloth sheets, under which, as it later transpired, arms were concealed. They soon began to sing their war and death chants, finally throwing dirt in the air. My interpreter, Philip Wells, went to inform Colonel Forsyth that this meant defiance and trouble was imminent. Wells had hardly reached the colonel when the warriors threw off their shirts, threw out their guns, and fired into the soldiers nearby.

In an instant, all was ablaze; most of the killing was over in a few minutes. A running fight followed, lasting probably an hour before the band was either killed, wounded, or prisoners; the prisoners were women and children almost entirely. News of the fight reached the agency by Indian means in an incredibly short time, and Red Cloud's camp instantly went into the air, all starting for the Badlands. General Brooke, in command, would not allow these people to be fired upon, so all made good their escape. Early the next morning, the wagon train of the 9th Cavalry was attacked as it was nearing the agency. Later the mission four miles north of the agency was attacked. Fighting was carried on for several hours, finally terminating in a charge of the 9th Cavalry.

Matters were now concentrated in the Badlands. Additional troops had been hurried from a distance, and a cordon practically established around the Badlands. It was here that Red Cloud came to the front and played his last part in Indian warfare. While the old chief was no longer young, his dominating influence was nevertheless felt. Through the scouts daily touch was kept with the hostile camp and all that transpired there. Messages began to come, but all were ignored except those directly or indirectly from Red Cloud. This wily, experienced old warrior recognized the uselessness of further resistance and acted accordingly, but his opponents, largely among the young men, held out for some time. Finally there was evidence of this turbulent element cooling down. This was aided by the cooling process of Dakota winter weather. Red Cloud sent word that he was ready to come as soon as he could escape from camp unnoticed. He made two or three ineffectual attempts. After some two or three weeks, a message was received saying another attempt would be made that night which promised to be successful. Accordingly, scouts were on the alert to render any assistance that might be required. It was a miserable night following a wet snowstorm—cold, raw, with a heavy damp mist prevailing. About dawn, a scout reported that Red Cloud was coming, and soon a stealthily moving figure could be distinguished against the skyline. In [the] course of time, the old chief, assisted by scouts, staggered into camp. He was placed on a box in my tent close to a Sibley stove in which a fire burned.

A squaw and a young girl had accompanied him, as his eyesight was failing him and he experienced difficulty in walking alone. Certainly he was a wreck. All in a tremble, cold, wet, exhausted, hardly able to articulate. It struck me at the time "how art the mighty fallen"—a rap under the chin, the toe of a boot at the base of the spine, would have launched one more brave in the "Happy Hunting Ground." But the army has always been known as the Indian's best friend; has always stood up for him, so far as possible, against all the abuse, dishonorable treatment, broken pledges heaped upon him, officially and otherwise. Acting along those lines in this case, it was up to me to care for this poor down-and-out old man. Accordingly, I gave him a drink of good whiskey. Miracles may have been performed—and works of magic—but one thing is certain, that drink of whiskey was magical in its effects, for in a few minutes a wonderful change took place: The old man put his hands toward the fire, rubbed them feebly, loosened the woolen scarf around his head, opened his coat, and began to straighten up. Light came into his eyes, and quickly he began to talk, his voice increasing in strength. He took from his clothing a pistol and handed it to me, saying it had belonged to Lieutenant Casey, who had been murdered near the Badlands by an Oglala buck [Plenty Horses], a graduate of the Carlisle Indian School who, after his education, had been sent back to the life of a blanket Indian with no chance to work in the white man's way or profit at all by an education. Red Cloud then proceeded to describe the situation among the hostiles in full, giving as his opinion that they would soon give up and come into the agency. This proved to be correct.

After a thorough warming and some breakfast, the revived old-time warrior was taken to General Miles, who was pleased to see him.

After some further delay and exchange of messages, those from this side calling for complete surrender only, the hostile camp broke up and moved in near the agency. It was up to me to go to a big powwow at this camp arranged by the friendly chiefs. Hot dog boiled in the kettle with the bark on was indulged in, and oratory, some of it forceful and excellent, prevailed for hours. Short Bull and Kicking Bear held out sullenly, but finally were prevailed upon to quit, return to their reservations, and be good forever more. Following the usual custom, a delegation of the principal performers was sent east for a parley with the high authorities. All members, however, were in camp at Fort Sheridan a few weeks later. The arms turned in were in the nature of a joke, as almost always has happened in such cases. Somewhere I have the gun turned in by Kicking Bear, an old battered and broken muzzle-loading squirrel rifle, such as was used about the time of the Revolution.

Old man Red Cloud died some years later, his life seemingly prolonged by a drink of good whiskey. Had anything happened to the great chief at this critical moment, just after his coming in, the result might have been disastrous, not only in the hostile camp, but among the Indians at large.

The Battle of Wounded Knee Creek

EDWARD S. GODFREY

Winners of the West 12, no. 2 (January 1935): 1

Cookstown, New Jersey
May 29, 1931

Chief of the Historical Section,
Army War College,
Washington, D.C.
Dear Sir:

Pursuant to your letter of March 25, 1931, requesting information as to the engagement at Wounded Knee, South Dakota, December 29, 1890, I submit the following.

At the time of the so-called "Ghost Shirt" or "Ghost Dance" unrest at the Sioux Indian agencies in 1890, I was stationed at Fort Leavenworth, Kansas, as a member of the U.S. Tactical Board. Our work was nearing completion, and when my regiment, the 7th U.S. Cavalry, was ordered to the field, I made application to be relieved and to join my troop. The application was granted.

Upon my arrival at Chadron Creek, I found a detachment of recruits from Jefferson Barracks for the 7th Cavalry and a wagon train of supplies for the troops, awaiting escort. I assumed command of the detachment and supply train, and about the middle of December arrived at the Pine Ridge agency, where I joined my troop.

It is my recollection that on December 27, Major Whitside's squadron, 7th Cavalry, and Lieutenant Taylor's Indian scouts were ordered to intercept Big Foot's band and at all hazards to prevent it from joining the Indians at Pine Ridge agency. It was generally understood that the orders of the division commander were to capture and disarm or destroy Big Foot's band.

Major Whitside met Big Foot's band on the twenty-eighth, and after some maneuvering, Big Foot surrendered, and he and his followers were conducted to Wounded Knee under guard. Major Whitside did not feel that his force was strong enough to attempt the disarmament, and he called for reinforcements.

Late in the evening of December 28, "To Horse" was sounded at the headquarters of the 7th Cavalry. The 2nd Squadron (troops C, D, E, and G) and Hawthorne's section of Hotchkiss guns of Captain Capron's Battery, 1st Artillery, under Col. J. W. Forsyth, arrived at Whitside's camp at Wounded Knee about midnight. Captain Wallace claimed me as his guest, and from him I learned the events of the day and the dispositions of the troops on guard for the night.

About 8:00 A.M. December 29, I received orders to take my troop (D) to position. En route, I passed where there were a number of Indian warriors squatting between two troops (B and K dismounted) and facing inward about a V-shaped formation, the apex next to the Indian village, near which was a small pile of what looked to me like old guns. My routing took me by two sides of the village, which lay to my left. On my right was a high ridge overlooking the village, and on this ridge were posted two troops of cavalry and Hawthorne's section. I passed down a ravine on a road that led across another and deeper ravine, which I crossed, then turned to the left and reported to Captain Jackson.[1] I then formed on his left, facing the village and opposite the ridge on which were posted the two troops, mounted, and the artillery as above mentioned. The deep ravine lay between our line and the village. Between the ravine and us were Taylor's Indian scouts and also some dismounted soldiers, who I understood were the night guards not yet relieved.

After we had been there some time, the quiet was suddenly broken by a shot, and after a very short interval there came two or three more shots, followed by a continuous fusillade. At the first shot, I remarked to Lt. S. R. Tompkins, "I'm afraid there has been a mistake. Too bad. Too bad." The whole village was in commotion, and in a short time the mass of Indians started in our direction. The troops on the ridge opposite us opened fire on them with small arms and Hotchkiss guns. As the mass neared the deep ravine, some bullets ricocheted to our position. I went to Captain Jackson (behind whose troop was a small field, enclosed by a barbed wire fence) and said we ought to change our position and get out of range of our own troops. Jackson said he thought of taking his troops back of the field. I told him I would like to take my troop to a hill on my left and rear. He said, "All right, go ahead."

I rallied my troop on the hill, dismounted to fight on foot, and posted my men in position. Large groups were approaching and opened fire on us. I cautioned the men not to shoot at women and children and gave the order to commence firing. As soon as firing from the groups ended, I gave the order that firing should cease. The time

Sioux dead at Wounded Knee. The body in the foreground with upraised arms is that of Yellow Bird. HARPER'S WEEKLY, 1891.

between the commands seemed incredibly short—probably not more than five minutes, though some firing continued by Jackson's men.

During the firing, I had observed some Indians escaping up the deep ravine. I sent Lieutenant Tompkins[2] with half my men to take and hold the ravine at all hazards. There were no more escapes up that ravine after Lieutenant Tompkins got there. A large dismounted group, however, had assembled in the ravine bordering the upper flank of the village and made their escape over a ridge.

Some time after all firing had ceased, Major Whitside came to my position and said a group of Indians had escaped over the ridge, and that Colonel Forsyth sent his compliments and wished me to take my troop and go in pursuit. I explained that I had sent Lieutenant Tompkins with half of my men, and as there were occasional shots, it seemed to me the ravine should be guarded. I then asked if I should leave that detachment or take it with me. Whitside hesitated a moment and then said, "Do as you please." I said I would leave it. I mounted my men (fourteen) and went in pursuit. I followed the trail for some time beyond the ridge to a wide, open country, but the group had dispersed, leaving no trace.

I marched several miles in the general direction indicated by the trend of the trail toward a partly wooded valley, climbed prominent points for observation, but saw nothing to indicate the Indians who had escaped.

My return march was down a partly wooded valley containing clumps of bushes with dead leaves on them. In the blizzard two days after the engagement, the dead leaves were blown off. I put flankers on each side on the ground. As we entered one of these clumps. the advance discovered some Indians running to a hiding place. I at once dismounted to fight on foot and called out, "How, cola! Squaw, papoose, cola!" Hearing no response, and finding that the men were becoming anxious, lest we get into a trap, I instructed each man to advance until he could spot an Indian, but not to fire till I gave the command. I kept repeating my phrase, "How, cola! Squaw, papoose, cola!" Getting no response, I commanded, "Ready," and then "Commence firing."

The firing was a volley and was followed by screams and the order to cease firing. No man fired more than one shot. I gave the commands, "Forward, march!" and ran to where I heard the screams. There I found one squaw and two children in the agonies of death and what appeared to be a man, sprawled face down, clothed with civilian clothes and with coat turned over his head, perfectly quiet, and I supposed dead.

Just as I was about to leave, Blacksmith Carey, who was one of the flankers, joined me. As I turned to join my skirmishers, I heard him exclaim, "This man ain't dead," and "Bang!" went his gun. He had turned back the coat tail, discovered a movement, and shot. I saw that the body was that of a boy whom I judged to be fourteen or fifteen years old, and that he had been shot in the head. I told Carey to come along and join the skirmish line. I was shocked by the tragedy, but thought Carey had acted from fright, and the well-known sentiment in the army at that time was to take no chance with a wounded Indian. Carey was one of the detachment of recruits that I found at Chadron and which joined the regiment with me. (After stables the next morning, December 30, I had Carey in my tent to question him as to his motive in shooting the boy. He was very penitent and began to cry, saying he was scared and only thought of self-defense; that he had been warned not to trust a wounded Indian or taken any chances, and that he shot on the impulse of the moment. Just then "To Horse!" was sounded, and the troop joined the regiment to go to the Drexel Mission affair. I was perfectly satisfied that Carey was actuated by sudden fear and the instinct of self-defense.)

Further search revealed no sight of Indians, and I resumed my return march. Seeing a group of men and horses on a high point, I directed my march to that place. I found that it was at the head of the ravine at which I had left Lieutenant Tompkins, about one and a half to two miles from the village, and that the group was Troop C.

As I was leaving Captain Jackson, I noticed a mounted Indian riding rapidly from the direction of Pine Ridge to a high hill a couple of miles away. He circled his horse, and a large number of Indians were galloping to join him. Then he started in our direction on the run. Satisfied that Jackson did not sense the danger, I called to him to get his horses under cover and prepare for defense, since I was certain that the Indians were going to attack. I dismounted and deployed my men. As the leading warriors neared, Jackson's men, getting into position, opened fire, and then my men, at command, also began firing. There were probably one hundred fifty or more warriors in this attack. Captain Jackson sent a courier to the regiment for help. Captain Edgerly, with his troop, came up and joined in the firing, and soon afterward the Indians withdrew. We had no casualties in this encounter. I understood later that this attack was made by Little Wound.[3]

On my return to camp, I reported my movements and results to headquarters. Late in the afternoon, the command and captives started on the return march to Pine Ridge agency. The captives were hauled in their wagons, and we detailed as rear guard. Sometime after midnight, we arrived at Pine Ridge, where I turned over my prisoners.

In the foregoing, I have endeavored to state circumstances relating to acts and facts connected with my troop, D, 7th Cavalry.

The story of the opening of the firing was to this effect: The medicine man [Yellow Bird] was exhorting the warriors that the ghost shirt would protect them from the bullets of the soldiers. The interpreter warned Colonel Forsyth that trouble was brewing. The medicine man was tossing dust from his hands. Colonel Forsyth forbade him exhorting, and the medicine man threw the handful of dust in the air. A warrior fired a pistol shot,[4] which was followed by other shots, and then the firing became general from both soldiers and warriors.

I do not believe that there was any wanton killing of women and children. I did not see or hear of any drunkenness at any time at Wounded Knee.

Respectfully submitted,
E. S. GODFREY,
Brigadier General, U.S.A., Retired

Personal Recollections of the Messiah Craze Campaign

AUGUST HETTINGER

Winners of the West 11, no. 1 (December 1934): 1, 3

Only a soldier can realize what we suffered—or thought we did—during the four years in the sand hills in Nebraska, for with the exception of a short summer maneuver, there was absolutely no excitement whatever. But the storm finally burst on November 25, 1890, and the Sioux Indian "Messiah Craze" campaign, as it is officially known, was on.

As the order came at 9:00 A.M. to march at 2:00 P.M., there was sure some excitement in the fort, and to make matters worse—or better—most of the soldiers started a jollification at the canteen; the officers also laid in a supply for strictly private use, but I regret to say a good deal of this private stock disappeared in a mysterious way before the wagon train left the fort. To my own knowledge, the quartermaster came to me and stated that two of his gallon jugs had been found empty, and he asked me to take care of one. I managed to get the one he turned over to me to the Rosebud agency by putting it in a nosebag and filling it to the top with oats.

Promptly at 2:00 P.M., the general call sounded, and we were off: A, B, F, and H Companies of the 8th Infantry, and two troops of the 9th Cavalry. We crossed the Niobrara River and then left the main road to Valentine, turned sharply to the right, crossed the Minieatosa, and climbed the steep bluffs along the north side of the river and followed a dim trail leading straight across the prairie to the Rosebud agency, forty miles away. Unluckily, on crossing the Minieatosa, the H Company wagon upset, and the boys had the pleasure of seeing their bedding, extra supply of tobacco, stationery, etc., going down the river; everything was fished out again, but the supplies were ruined; writing paper and postage stamps were at a premium during the coming winter. But the funny part of it was that the teamster of this wagon, a noted character of our company known by the nickname of "Limber," always bragged that all he needed was a piece of buckskin to drive a six-mule team around a ten-cent piece, and then he upset our bed wagon with all our precious possessions in the river before we were two miles from the fort.

Before we got away from the fort, a little incident happened that nearly landed me in the guardhouse. It seems that at the last moment, the department commander decided to organize a battery of one-pound Hotchkiss [guns] as a part of each expedition, the members of which were to be drawn from the different companies. I was detailed to drive the four-mule ammunition wagon. That sure got my goat; here was a likely campaign in sight, for which we had waited for years, and after one Charles Baker and myself had agreed to be bunkies, I was told to drive mules in a different organization. Only a soldier can realize my predicament. The company means everything to a soldier, but as the first sergeant threatened to put me in the guardhouse unless I reported to the quartermaster immediately, I had to go or miss the expedition altogether. The whole incident proved to be a piece of luck afterwards, for the reason that my own company was left at the Rosebud agency during the campaign, while the two troops of cavalry, the battery of light artillery, and Company A of the 8th Infantry were detailed to go to the assistance of the 7th Cavalry just before the battle of Wounded Knee, and by being a member of the battery I got to see the whole show.

The forced march of forty miles from Fort Niobrara to the agency was a heartbreaker to most of the infantrymen, but nevertheless we arrived there at daylight [November 30]. It was just bright enough to see Short Bull pull out with almost fifteen hundred warriors in the direction of Eagle Pass.[2]

A forty-mile march is no particular feat for an infantry command to make after they are two or three days on the road, but to make forty miles under heavy pack the first day out can only be accomplished by the American doughboy. In this connection, it may be mentioned that at that time, in 1890, Company K held the world record: They marched fifty-eight miles in twenty-four hours during the Geronimo campaign in Mexico. But this feat was tied by A Company, 8th Infantry, during the march from the Rosebud to the assistance of the 7th Cavalry, when they made fifty-eight miles in twenty-four hours in from twelve to fifteen inches of snow; and in three days and three nights they marched 128 miles.

But I am digressing from the story. After breakfast, we pitched camp in the agency, and for nearly a month, the command was busy getting in shape for a winter campaign. The weather was unusually cold, but everybody was busy drilling, target practice for the recruits, breaking in a string of sixty pack mules, drilling a detachment of Indian scouts, organizing the remaining five hundred or six hundred Indians, and issuing rations. The Hotchkiss field guns amused the Indians a great deal; we used a big lime rock and, for a while, an old cabin a mile away as a target, but as the cabin lasted only one hour for a target, we had to fall back again on a large limestone cliff across the valley. They could understand the workings of the gun, but the explosion of the shell remained a mystery to the old Indians, and they actually were afraid of the shell; you could not get one to as much as touch the cartridge.

An infantryman in winter uniform.
HARPER'S WEEKLY, 1891.

About a week after the outbreak, General Miles took command of all the forces in the field, and as he had no superior as an Indian fighter and organizer, everything went off according to schedule. The weather was fierce at times, but right at the start, General Miles equipped all the troops with suitable clothing. His strategy consisted in making a big drive from all directions to one common center; this center was the Pine Ridge agency. And he succeeded admirably; when the roundup was complete, there was something like eighteen thousand hostile Indians in one camp on White Clay Creek, guarded by something like 3,500 soldiers in four different camps.

But I am getting ahead of the story. Nothing very exciting occurred at the Rosebud except that we received a big batch of recruits, which nearly doubled the strength of the companies. It was, of course, quite a change for these boys from some quiet farm in Indiana, where most of them came from, to an Indian agency in the middle of winter, where to go beyond the protection of the camp meant certain death. The issuing of beef on the hoof to the Indians was a revelation to most of them, for it was nothing to see an Indian riding through the camp at top speed with one hundred feet of gut tied to the horn of his saddle, rope fashion; the gut represented his share of the beef; or to see a number of otherwise attractive young squaws sitting around the agency building chawing raw beef gut, the same as a white girl would gum, while the blood was running down both sides of their jaws. However, they soon got bravely over being surprised at anything, and by the time they got into Fort McKinney the following spring, they were veterans in every sense of the word. They also had no more illusions about the Indian.

Christmas Day came and went, a little more dreary than it would have been at a fort, but not much more so. This holiday is always a heart-wringer to young soldiers, no matter where stationed. A soldier in the Regular army in those days had to depend on his own resources for recreation; [of] companionship outside of the fort, we had none. A great many civilians, badly informed about the history of our own country, had the very annoying habit of looking down on the regular soldier, but in every crisis, recent history has shown that he has not his peer in any country.

But to resume. Like a flash out of the sky came the order to march at 9:30 P.M. on December 27, 1890. This made a stir, as it was thirty minutes after taps had sounded. The camp was full of wild rumors, but nobody outside of the commanding officer knew where we were going; all we knew even was that we had to march at midnight.

The command consisted of two troops of the 9th Cavalry, the mountain guns, and Company A, 8th Infantry, to guard the wagon train. Captain Whitney[3] was in command and Charles Taggett was chief of scouts, of which we had six. Young Spotted Tail was a member of the scouts. This Charles Taggett was a half-breed, his father having been a missionary for forty years among the Brule Sioux. He was highly educated, and all the tribes had the greatest confidence in him. He became chief interpreter during the big powwows the Indians and General Miles had in February 1891, as the Indians refused pointblank to have Frank Grouard act in that capacity. I nearly forgot to mention Foolish Elk, the best Indian scout at that time in Dakota, outside of Charles Taggett.

I was sorry that my own company was not selected as an escort, because A Company had the worst reputation in the Regular army as a feeder, and I was assigned to this outfit for rations. No matter what the ration consisted of, in this company you received only hardtack, bacon, and coffee. Even beans were considered a luxury. On the other hand, my own company furnished the most substantial meals I ever saw anywhere. Here, as nowhere else, one can see the value of management and honesty; the members of one company perpetually went hungry, while the next company lived on the fat of the land on the identical rations.

Winners of the West 11, no. 2 (January 1935): 3

Promptly at midnight, we pulled out. The new moon went down before we were a mile on the road. The cavalry disappeared in the darkness, and we just plodded along the best we could; sometimes we noticed that we were on a trail; sometimes for miles we followed old buffalo trails. If we were going into action, we knew it could not be a surprise, for we could see the Indian signal fires sixty miles to the northwest as soon as we left the agency, and so the chances were the Indians in the Badlands knew more about our movements than we knew ourselves. But we never worried over the future; we were happy to be on the road again, no matter where it would take us. It was bitterly cold, but we were equipped for a winter campaign; [we] were young and optimistic.

It sounds funny, but the only thing that we ever worried about was to keep our stomachs full of chow, and to tell the truth, we had good reason to worry about that if we had to live with A Company. We did suffer terribly at times for the want of water. This was on account of the sow-belly diet, improperly cooked, and sometimes, in these Badlands, where there was no wood, not cooked at all. But on the whole, we could eat snow, but we could not help but be sorry for the mules. We fed corn, all they could eat, but no hay sometimes weeks for a time. All the springs were frozen tight, unless we came to a good-sized spring, and [as] this happened but twice in 128 miles, the work and pack animals received no water. We could, of course, not turn them loose for a minute, for the Indians would stampede them in spite of all we could do.

But you must remember that the field army is always made up of young men who can stand anything; the same rule applies to the mules. We received most of the pack and team mules fresh and unbroken from Kentucky, and they were a congregation of devils. There were only a few that would not bite, strike, and kick at the same time, and what that means with sharp-shod animals after being tied all night, in a blizzard, to a wagon wheel, without hay, must be lived through. You cannot imagine it. The wagon boss nearly had his ear bitten off one day by what was supposed to be a mule, but really was a bulldog.

Well, just at break of day we came to White River; quite a large stream at this place, something like one hundred fifty feet wide and from three to four feet deep. The ice was thick enough to hold up the cavalry horses, but not the heavy loaded six-mule wagons, so a passage had to be cleared out. After much difficulty getting the wagons down the steep banks without upsetting them, we got the wagon trains across and camped on the other side to cook coffee.

One six-mule team would not tighten a tug for some reason after they got in the stream, and so another six-mule teamster had to get in that ice water up to his hips and hitch on another team. While this was going on, the atmosphere turned blue, and not from the cold, either. After we filled up on sow belly and alkali water, we pulled out again about 8:00 A.M. [December 29]. The cavalry left us here again, and we did not catch up with them until next day about noon, when we found them standing by their horses near a dry lake, during a blizzard. We ourselves camped at 9:00 P.M. on a bare hillside without wood or water that night, and raw bacon and snow was our supper. We had marched twenty-one hours and were fifty-eight miles from the Rosebud agency.

At 4:00 A.M. [December 30], a sharp reveille sounded, and as there was nothing to cook and the mules would not eat their corn unless they were watered, and there was no water, it did not take us long to get ready. At 5:00 A.M., we pulled out in a blizzard. We pounded along [with] the cavalry, and then pulled out about four miles further to where the scouts thought we could get some water. We camped here about one hour and watered the poor mules and filled them up on corn, for we were told that there was nearly a twenty-mile hike ahead of us before camp would be made for the night. We made camp this night something like three hours after dark at an old deserted ranch. In spite of hunger and cold, we slept like dead men, and it seemed only an hour when reveille called us again to put icy harness on the mules and frozen shoes and overcoats on ourselves. At 5:00 A.M., we were on our way.

By daylight, when we were something like six or more miles out, Foolish Elk, who was always the furthest out, came loping back to the command with another scout, a white man. After they had a short talk with the major, we left our line of march and struck out northward through those desolate hills of Dakota. We knew that this scout had brought important news. The command was kept in close order; only the Indian scouts were from one to three miles out. We were told that no stop would be made for coffee that day and not to spare the buckskin. As we had been running a race with the Devil for the last three days and nights, we were as anxious as the commanding officer to get someplace, no matter where, and we all pushed to the limit. We naturally thought that the race since 5:00 A.M. was made for the purpose of heading off a band of Indians, and the day's march would wind up with a fight. We knew that Short Bull had left the Badlands with nearly one thousand warriors, and several other subchiefs had done likewise, but we were disappointed in our hopes before the sun went down on this day.

Between 2:00 P.M. and 3:00 P.M., we saw several Indian scouts galloping back to the command, and a few minutes later, we were halted and the command given to corral the train. In the meantime, Captain Whitney advanced over the hill with the cavalry, but before we got the train in shape for defense, an orderly came back and ordered us to advance again. About half a mile further on, we crossed the brow of a small hill and beheld a small valley about one-half mile wide, spread out in front of us. A small creek fringed with brush and cottonwoods meandered down through the center and finally disappeared to the northwest in some pine-covered rough hills.

This was our first sight of Wounded Knee Creek. Between us and the creek, there was a small, egg-shaped hill, approximately fifty feet higher than the surrounding bottomland. The hill was occupied by the cavalry, whom we soon joined. We were told that a battle had taken place the day before, on December 29, just across a creek from us, but with whom we had no way of knowing. We could see on the other side of the creek the ground strewn with the bodies of horses and even wagons, and the remnants of a burned camp and what looked like the bodies of human beings could be seen over an area of two hundred or three hundred acres.

The first thing the troops did was to start a trench large enough to hold all of the 120 men in the command. The job actually took several days, for the ground was frozen as hard as flint. Before we got something to eat, Captain Whitney took the scouts, the doctor, the stretcher bearers, and my ammunition wagon with hospital supplies and went over to the battlefield to take care of the wounded, if there were any. I got just as far as the first dead pony and Indian when the mules gave the place just one whiff and look and stampeded, as luck would have it, toward the creek, where they finally tangled themselves up in the woods. Here I tied them, took my gun, and went back to the battlefield. The dead Indians were laying around, single and in bunches, over about two hundred acres, and the first sight of the mutilated bodies and the expressions of the faces had the effect of turning one sick. But of course, you get used to it.

Our first effort was to look for wounded in order to find out what regiment had been in the fight; we found after a careful search five live wounded Indians. We packed them to an old cabin and made them as comfortable as possible. They didn't, however, answer a single question of the scouts. The only word they ever uttered was "water." We never found out until the next evening that the fight had been between the 7th Cavalry and Big Foot's tribe. These wounded had been lying on the battlefield a little over twenty-four hours, and we knew they could not live.

One squaw was shot five times through the body. But to the last they were defiant, and our reward for making them comfortable were looks of the blackest hatred. You could not help but admire such courage in the face of death. As I stated, we made them as comfortable as possible for the night, but we found them all dead next morning.

The battlefield was divided by a deep washout thirty to forty feet wide and all of fifteen feet deep; several cow trails crossed this dry gulch, and near the lower end, toward the creek, a wagon road crossed also. In searching for the wounded, I ran down this road, and on coming out on the other bank, I was confronted by a pile of dead Indians. On top of all, and in a sitting position, with his arm extended full length and the forefinger pointed straight up in the sky, was an Indian, painted green as grass from head to toe, and looking wide open, clear-eyed, straight at me. It startled me, and the next second I had a bead on his forehead, but second thought made me hesitate about pulling the trigger, for while a soldier will kill in the line of duty, unnecessary shooting is murder nevertheless, and so, after looking at him for a minute over the sights of the gun, I noticed that he never batted his eyes, and so I came to the conclusion that he was dead, and so he was. Lucky for me I did not shoot—the boys would have guyed me to death.

The next day, we were busy getting the camp in shape for defense; we even dug a round trench deep enough at each end of the hill to hold the Hotchkiss, for after all, we were only a small command of ninety-six officers and men, and there were [several] thousand Indians roaming around, and about the poorest policy a commander of troops could follow was to get careless or underestimate the fighting qualifications and determination of the Sioux Indians.

Along in the afternoon, a scouting party with dispatches from General Miles came into camp, and as the escort of the dispatch rider consisted of troopers from the 7th Cavalry who had been in the fight, we got the first account of the battle. We tried to get one of these troopers to go over the battlefield with us to show us on the ground just how it happened, but he stated that his bunkie got killed and he never wanted to see the place again. It seems that the 7th Cavalry had been on the road for several days, from the Badlands to the Pine Ridge agency, with the tribe of Indians as prisoners, but they were not disarmed. The government throughout this campaign insisted on the Indians giving up their arms, but the Indians refused to the last to comply with this condition. They told General Miles again and again they would [not] surrender their arms, and the battle of Wounded Knee was proof of their contention.[4]

Winners of the West 11, no. 3 (February 1935): 3–4

The night before the battle, they [the 7th Cavalry and Big Foot's band] camped on what turned out to be the last camping ground for all of the Indians but one tiny papoose and a great many of the soldiers.[5] The guy ropes of the soldiers' tents and the tepees joined. Forsyth had orders, it seems, to disarm the tribe before bring them to the agency, and as this was the last day's march, he called the chiefs for a powwow early in the morning of December 29. While this powwow was going on, a row started among the soldiers and the Indians, and at the first shot, the chiefs pulled their war clubs, which they had concealed under their blankets, and fell on the officers, knocking the brains out of Captain Wallace and wounding several others.[6]

In two minutes, it was a free-for-all fight, and the foul-up was so great that the soldiers were killing one another,[7] so the colonel sounded "Boots and Saddles." The soldiers extricated themselves as best they could, made for their horses, mounted, and rode over a low hill, halted here, formed into their proper organization again, and prepared to charge the Indians and their own camp.

At this stage of the game, the Indians made a fatal mistake. When they saw the soldiers ride over the nearest hill four hundred yards away, they thought they were running away, so they crossed the dry gulch on foot and horseback, and some even in wagons, and started across the short flat and up the hill. The leaders, who were on fast horses, nearly got to the top of the hill when the soldiers came back as fast as their horses could charge. The Indian farthest up the hill was a young squaw on a pinto pony, and it looked as if she received the first fire from all the troopers in the regiment, for she was literally riddled with bullets. I counted over forty bullet holes in the upper part of her body.

The troopers shot and ran the Indians across the flat and into the dry gulch; they got no chance to make a stand here, for the soldiers were right on top of them. The gulch was literally piled full in places with horses, wagons, and dead Indians. Some tried to climb up the cow trails on the other side, but few managed to do it and get to the tepees which were just beyond. At the bottom of every trail, there was a pile of dead, and you could see by their positions that they tumbled back down in the gulch after being shot on the trail above. The whole thing happened so quickly that all of the Indians did not get a chance to pursue the soldiers; about seventy-five bucks, most of the squaws, and all of the papooses were in and around the tepees yet, and these now cut slits in the tepees and opened a murderous fire on the soldiers on the other side of the

Corporal Weinert working his Hotchkiss gun.
W. F. BEYER, *DEEDS OF VALOR.*

gulch, only seventy-five to one hundred yards away, with telling effect. But the Hotchkiss opened up on these with case shot and soon silenced them. During this last phase of the fight, all the papooses but one were killed; of course, this was very sad, but it could not be avoided. This one papoose was found alive and uninjured by an officer, who raised and educated it as his own daughter.[8]

As soon as the firing ceased, the soldiers gathered around their tents; one lifted up the flap of the tent to step inside, when he was shot down by a wounded Indian who was concealed behind the stove inside. All the soldiers were, of course, very much excited from the battle, and when they saw their comrade shot down, three others pulled their revolvers and started for the tent, only to be shot down dead one after the other.

At this stage of the game, a corporal in charge of the Hotchkiss [Paul H. Weinert] told them all to stand away; he trained his gun at the center of the tent and let it fly. The shell made a clean hole through the stove and caught the Indian, who was lying on his stomach behind the stove, on the chin, and ripped him wide open. The fire from the stove was scattered over the bedding, and everything went up in flames, roasting the Indian like a barbecue beef.

This battle was not a massacre, but a fight to the finish. The evidence on the ground showed that the squaws fought as desperately as the bucks. I counted as many as twenty-three empty shells by the side of the dead squaws.

As the 7th Cavalry had been the heaviest sufferer at the hands of the Sioux during nearly thirty years of warfare, it was fitting they should administer a severe and last lesson with a heavy hand.

Short Bull's Story of the Battle of Wounded Knee

COURTNEY R. COOPER[1]

The Red Man (February 1915): 205–212[2]

It was in a South Dakota blizzard that I found him huddled in his flapping tent, far out upon the Sioux reservation of Pine Ridge. The marks of the warrior were absent, a frayed fur overcoat covered the somewhat undersized form that once had known the dancing bustle and the ghost shirt, and cotton gloves shielded the wrinkled hands which held once the war club and the rifle.

Under the banking of the tent, the wind sifted its snow; the old stovepipe rattled; in a corner, huddled and shivering, sat a wrinkled squaw, awaiting in stubborn silence the return of the sun. From a rope at the top of the tent—the tepee of earlier days had vanished—hung a few shreds of jerked beef left from the rations of the agency. It was a home of poverty and of hopelessness, the home of Ta Ta La Slotsla, Short Bull, blamed for a quarter of a century for an Indian war which called forth half the troops of the United States and cost lives by hundreds—the war of the Messiah.

So to explanation. Consult history and there comes the story of a strange, an unknown being who, in 1890, incited the Indians to rebellion; who, in personification of Jesus Christ, gave the promise that once again the prairies should be the Happy Hunting Grounds of the red man, where again would roam the elk, the antelope, and the buffalo, and that the white man would vanish into the eastern seas. Consult history and it tells the story of how the representatives of the Indian tribes from Canada to Oklahoma journeyed to Pyramid Lake, Nevada, that they might hear a message of war and hatred; of how the ghost shirt, supposedly impervious to bullets, was fashioned; and particularly of how it was Short Bull of the Sioux who spread the news and brought about the war which followed.

Therefore, it was because of this history that they had told me upon the reservation not to talk to Short Bull. He would say nothing. He would be taciturn. He would be evasive, for what could he say, now that his fabled ghost shirt had been riddled with many an army bullet, now that the white man had built cities where the buffalo were to have grazed, and the Indian braves who were to have driven their enemies into the eastern ocean had lain these twenty-three years in their trenches atop the battlefield of Wounded Knee? No, Short Bull would be hardly the man to care to talk. And yet. . . .

We entered—Horn Cloud, the interpreter, and myself. There went forth my message, the question of the cause of the war of the Messiah. A smile of greeting from the little man beside the rickety, rattling stove, an outstretching of arms; a cry from the squaw in the corner. The little man in the frayed overcoat had risen, his eyes glistening, his face alight.

"How kola!" he called. "How kola! Was' te—was' te!"

And there can be no Indian greeting of more friendliness. I tried to answer in what little Sioux I had learned. It was impossible. Short Bull—he who is blamed for a war—was talking excitedly, gesticulating. Horn Cloud turned.

"He says you're the first man who ever asked that," came from the interpreter. "He say to thank you—maybe now he get to tell the truth."

And so there was something wrong with history? I smiled at that, but when I spoke of it to Horn Cloud, he smiled also and shook his head. Evidently there was a great deal wrong with history, at least from the standpoint of the man blamed for a war. Evidently—but Short Bull had doffed his coat now and was standing with outstretched arms. His face had grown suddenly serious.

"Ask the white man," came through the interpreter, "whether he comes through friendship or through curiosity. Ask the white man whether he will hear the story of Ta Ta La Slotsla and remember it as he tells it. Ask the white man whether he wants to hear the truth and nothing but the truth from Short Bull—Short Bull who saw the Messiah."

A silence except for the flapping of the tent, the shrill of the wind. I nodded. Short Bull raised his arms.

"Tell white man to forget what he has read in history, for my story is different. Tell him that I deny that I caused the war of the Messiah. Tell him that I preached peace, not war."

And so a new phase of history came forth. There was a conference. Horn Cloud was telling the little man to begin at the beginning. Once again, Short Bull raised his arms.

"There was starvation in 1888 and 1889," he said slowly. "The tepees were cold for want of fires. Up on the Rosebud agency, where I lived, we cried for food, as they did down here at Pine Ridge. The white man had forgotten us. We were going toward the sunset. Then, one day—it seemed we all heard it at once—there came a message that the Messiah was soon to come to us. The white man had turned him out, long ago. Now he was coming to the Indian. We danced for joy. The Messiah perhaps would bring us food and warmth and clothing. There was a letter, too, from Red Cloud on Pine Ridge. Red Cloud said, too, that the Messiah was coming and to choose the hard-hearted man of the tribe to meet him. I was that man."

The little Indian swallowed hard and looked at the ground. The interpreter turned. "He means brave-hearted," came the explanation. "How!"

Short Bull heard the command to continue. He folded his hands. "There were twelve of us, each from a different tribe. One by one we traveled to the head of Wind River and met. The Messiah was in Nevada at Pyramid Lake. Some of us had horses. Others walked. We did not care for fatigue or for hunger. One must suffer to see God. We traveled on. We reached Pyramid Lake. And then—"

"How!"

It was the command of Horn Cloud again. Short Bull smiled the least bit.

"Some way we all knew where he would come and when he would come, at sunset by the great rocks. So we waited. I had not believed. They had taught me in the parish churches not to believe too much. So I stood there and watched and looked here and there to see where he would come from. I looked hard and rubbed my eyes. He had not come at all. He was there. Just as if he had floated through the air."

Short Bull was biting his lips the least bit. Horn Cloud turned from him and faced me.

"I know how that happen," he explained in his Indian English. "Big rocks—see? The Messiah, he get on a wagon and have it pulled up so it'll be hidden by them rocks. Then he jumps out from behind the rocks like he floats through air—see? Wait!" A moment of Indian gutturals, then a smile from Horn Cloud. "Short Bull, he say he go behind rocks next day and see a wagon there."

And so, in this little explanation of an Indian interpreter came the first glimpse of the truth about the so-called Messiah—some street-corner orator with a great scheme and with the spirit of the faker to carry it through. The questions went on. Short Bull, looking into the past with all the superstition of the Indian, hesitated and moistened his lips.

"He was the Holy Man. His gown was like fire. It caught the sun rays and sent them back to the west. It glowed like the fire of a feast. It changed colors. All over the robe there were crosses, from his head to his feet. Some of them were in white—some were in red. We could not see much, for he looked at us and we were afraid of him. He raised his arms, and there seemed to be fire all about him. We fell down and worshipped. And when we raised our heads, he was gone."

They had fallen and worshipped, worshipped with all the superstition and all the faith of the Indian race, worshipped a man in a changeable silk robe who had come mysteriously from behind a pair of great rocks by aid of an unseen wagon. But Short Bull was continuing.

"There was a little house by the side of the lake, and we went back there. We did not talk much. We were afraid to. The next morning, a little white boy came to us and told us his father was ready to see us and talk to us down in the willow grove by the lake. We . . ."

But I had interrupted. "His father?"

"The Messiah had a little boy," came from Short Bull. "The little boy said the Messiah was his father."

And so this fanatic of Pyramid Lake had given God a grandson in his masquerade. But the Indians had not doubted it. How could they? It had been many years since the Messiah had been on earth. The Messiah was the son of God; therefore, why not a grandson? And so they went to the willow patch, still trusting.

"So we went to the willow patch"—Short Bull was in the past now, his face brightened by a wonderful memory—"and he was here, just as we had seen him the night before. He talked to all of us, but he talked to me the most. He came close to me. He laid his hand on my forehead, and I thought that fire had gone through me. He held my hands, and they turned numb. His hands were hot when they touched me. When they left me, they were cold—cold like the wind outside. Then he talked. 'A long time ago,' he said, and he talked slowly, as if it hurt to remember, 'I came among the white people. But they did not like me. They sent me away. They crucified me.'"

Short Bull raised his hands and pointed to his palms. He raised his beaded, moccasined feet and pointed there. He bared his breast and patted it above his heart.

"He was the Holy Man," he almost shouted, and there was a strange, an awed something in his voice. "I saw. He showed me. Here, and here, and here—where they had nailed him to the crucifix! He was the Holy Man!"

Horn Cloud, educated and somewhat worldly, turned, wondering. "What make that?" he asked.

And there was only one answer—reality, self-imposed torture, such as few men can stand, or the acid burns that are known to every professional faker the world over. But it would have done no good to tell that to Short Bull. Nothing could take away the glamour of the vision. He had seen God. Besides, Short Bull was talking again.

"But after the Holy Man said that, he smiled and shook his head. That was a long time ago that the white people did that, and now he didn't care. Now he had come back to bring peace. He said, 'I have come back to bring you news. You have fought with the white man. That is wrong. I want you to go back to your tribe and tell them what I have said. You must say that the white man and the Indian shall live in peace. You shall say that the Indian must learn the white man's way and the white man's religion. There may be trouble. Stamp it out like a prairie fire. They may try to kill you, Short Bull, and even if they should, do not fight back. You must live in peace. Your children must go to the white man's school, and your children's children must grow to become the husbands and the wives of the white man and the white woman. And some day there will be no Indian. There will be no white man. You will all be one, and then will be peace. Listen to me and listen to each other. I am the Holy Man. I am the Messiah. Listen to the white man and the white man shall listen to you. Do as I say, and on earth you will be together—and in heaven you will be together. And then there shall be no nights, no sleeps, no hunger, no cold. You shall be with me!'"

And even as he spoke, the words interpreted by jerks and fragments, there was an oratory in the recital of the little man, a resemblance as he quoted to the forms of the Scriptures. He continued, "'You have come unto me,' the Holy Man said, "to learn the news. I have told it to you, and now you must journey forth to tell it to the others who wait by the tepees. Tell them to be merciful unto each other. Tell them the Father says to do no harm, but to live in peace.' And he told this to each one of us. To me he told it in Sioux. He told it to the others in their own language. Could any man but God have done it? There is no man who can talk all the languages. He taught us to dance, and he says this is the dance we must perform. He showed us his robe and told us that we should worship him by wearing robes like this. He told us that we must throw away the rifle and the war club. 'Live in peace,' he said, 'and let the white man live in peace with you.' And that was all he said. Pretty soon he was gone, and we turned and came home. Yes, that was all."

But history had interfered. History tells a different story of the Messiah—of someone who desired war between the white man and the Indian; of someone who told of the coming back of the Happy Hunting Grounds; of the return of the buffalo and the antelope and the elk, and the fading of the white man from the land. The questions came. But Short Bull only smiled.

"Yes, history say that," he answered, "but history lies. It was not the Messiah." His face suddenly hardened. His hands clenched. "It was the men who have made us suffer, who have brought the wrinkles to these cheeks and the trembling here!"

He held out his hands. His voice rose high. "I went home—and all before me there was singing and happiness. They had heard of the Messiah. All down through Pine Ridge, they sang and danced, and pretty soon Red Cloud and American Horse and Fast Thunder sent for me to come home. I knew what they wanted. They wanted war. They did not want to do as the Holy Man said. And so I went. I talked to them, and they laughed at me. Then they brought me the ghost shirts to bless. I blessed them—and then—then," the muscles of Short Bull's face were drawn tense, "then they went back to their people and told them I had said that bullets would not pierce the ghost shirts. They went back and told their people I had brought a new message from the Messiah, but that I could not give it directly. They told their people I had said the white man was to be driven out and that there must be war. But I did not know then. When I heard it was too late. All through the reservations, they were dancing now—and dancing for war—because American Horse and Fast Thunder and Red Cloud wanted war. They had blamed it all on me—and yet I only told what the Messiah had ordered me to tell. I begged them to listen to the Holy Man—to hear the news he had sent and live in peace with the white man. I did not want war; I did not want it! The Messiah had told me what to do, and I was trying to do it. I had told my people we should dance for the Messiah when the grass turned brown, but the police from the agency came out and told me to stop. Then they told me the soldiers were coming. And then Fast Thunder and American Horse

"The last scene of the last act of the Sioux War" —a Sioux woman mourns her slain husband. HARPER'S WEEKLY, 1891.

and Red Cloud called for me to come to Pine Ridge and fight the white man. But I said, 'No! No! The Messiah had said there must be no war.' Old Two Strikes moved his camp from the Little White River toward Pine Ridge, but I stayed. The Brules moved from the Rosebud toward Pine Ridge, but still I stayed. I had seen the Holy Man, and he had told me to live in peace. Then the young men of the Rosebud came to me and ordered me to follow Two Strikes. I followed. They talked to me about cartridges, but I would not help them get them. I did not want war; I wanted to do what the Messiah had told me. We went to the Badlands. They told me that now I must fight against the whites. I cried out to them, 'No! No!'"

The little man was striding up and down the narrow space of his tent now. The squaw was wailing in a corner.

"'No! I keep calling to you; you do not hear me. I try to tell you that there shall be no war; you will not listen. You say the white soldiers will kill me? Then they can kill; I will not fight back. Once I was a warrior, once I wore the shield and the war club and the war bonnet; but I have seen the Holy Man. Now is peace; now there shall stay peace. You chose me as the hard-hearted one to journey to the sunset to see the Messiah. I saw him, and I brought you his message. You would not hear it. You changed it. Now, I am silent.'"

There was a long pause. The death song from the old squaw in the corner rose high and shrilling, as shrilling as the wind of the blizzard without. Short Bull folded his hands.

"The next day I saddled my horse. I rode away. I came to the pine hills and looked out in the distance. They were fighting the battle of Wounded Knee. I kept on. They fought the battle of the missions, and they blame me for it—me, who saw the Holy Man. They were jealous; I was a hard-hearted man, and I was a chief. They did not like me, so they blame me for a war—my own people, my people who had sent me to the sunset that I might talk to Him, the Holy Man!"

So there is the story of Short Bull, whatever history may say. This is the story told me by that wrinkled, little heartbroken old Indian who lives in the past, standing there in the willow patch, listening to the message of the Messiah.

NOTES

Introduction
1. For various population estimates, see Frederick W. Hodge, ed., *Handbook of American Indians North of Mexico (Smithsonian Institution Bureau of American Ethnology, Bulletin 30)*, 2 vols. (Washington, G.P.O., 1912): 2, 989, 991.
2. The description of the Lakota people and their culture that follows is drawn largely from Hodge, *Handbook of American Indians,* and Robert M. Utley, *The Lance and the Shield: The Life and Times of Sitting Bull* (New York: Henry Holt and Company, 1993).
3. Quoted in Utley, *Lance and Shield,* 1.
4. Utley, *Lance and Shield,* 32.
5. Utley, *Lance and Shield,* 12.
6. Robert M. Utley, *Frontiersmen in Blue: The United States Army and the Indian, 1848–1865* (New York: Macmillan Publishing Company, 1967), 115.
7. Peter Cozzens, *General John Pope: A Life for the Nation* (Urbana: University of Illinois Press, 2000), 240–41.
8. Cozzens, *General John Pope,* 256.
9. Leroy R. Hafen and Ann W. Hafen, eds., *Powder River Campaigns and Sawyers Expedition of 1865* (Glendale, CA: Arthur H. Clarke Company, 1961): 48–49.
10. Utley, *Lance and Shield,* 73.
11. Robert M. Utley, *Frontier Regulars: The United States Army and the Indian, 1866–1890* (New York: McMillan Publishing Company, 1973), 99.
12. Cozzens, *General John Pope,* 276.
13. Jacob P. Dunn, Jr., *Massacres of the Mountains: A History of the Indian Wars of the Far West* (New York: Harper, 1886), 585.
14. Utley, *Lance and Shield,* 115.
15. Dunn, *Massacres,* 590.
16. Utley, *Frontier Regulars,* 247.
17. John S. Gray, *Centennial Campaign: The Sioux War of 1876* (Norman: University of Oklahoma Press, 1976), 324–57.
18. Utley, *Frontier Regulars,* 257.
19. Gray, *Centennial Campaign,* 145.
20. Hamlin Garland, "General Custer's Fight as Seen by Two Moon," *McClure's Magazine* 9 (September 1898): 445.
21. Utley, *Lance and Shield,* 158.
22. *Ibid.,* 160–61.
23. Jerome A. Greene, *Slim Buttes, 1876: An Episode of the Great Sioux War* (Norman: University of Oklahoma Press, 1982), 37.
24. Utley, *Frontier Regulars,* 271, 291–92.
25. Jerome A. Greene, *Yellowstone Command: Colonel Nelson A. Miles and the Great Sioux War, 1876–1877* (Norman: University of Oklahoma Press, 1991), 120.
26. Utley, *Lance and Shield,* 182.
27. Utley, *Frontier Regulars,* 282.
28. Utley, *Frontier Regulars,* 410.
29. Utley, *Frontier Regulars,* 401.

PART ONE: PLATTE RIVER BRIDGE AND THE POWER RIVER EXPEDITION, 1865

S. H. Fairfield: The 11th Kansas Regiment at Platte Bridge
1. S. H. Fairfield (1833–post-1908) moved to Kansas from Massachusetts in 1856. He served with the 11th Kansas Volunteer Cavalry from September 1861 to September 1865. Later in life, he was elected the treasurer of Wabaunee County, Kansas, and also was a trustee of Washburn College.
2. Henry Grimm died on January 3, 1904, in Wabaunee County, Kansas, a wealthy farmer. Despite suffering all his life from arrow wounds received at the battle of Platte River Bridge, he fathered fourteen children.
3. Fort Laramie was located on the Laramie River about one-half mile from its confluence with the North Platte River.
4. A reference to the Sand Creek massacre of November 29, 1864.
5. Brig. Gen. Robert B. Mitchell (1823–1992), commander of the Military District of Nebraska.
6. Traders from British Canada, and not Mormons, were then a principal source of firearms to the disaffected tribes.
7. Grenville M. Dodge (1831–1916) was a civilian engineer who rose to the volunteer rank of major general during the Civil War. He was appointed chief engineer of the Union Pacific Railroad in 1866 and became one of the principal railroad men of his day.
8. Preston B. Plumb had been elected major of the 11th Kansas Volunteer Cavalry at its muster in in September 1861. He served as a U.S. senator from Kansas from 1877 until his death in 1891.
9. Confederate major general Sterling Price raided Missouri with a small army in the fall of 1864 before being turned back at the battle of Westport, Missouri, on October 23, 1864.
10. The 11th Kansas arrived at Fort Kearny, Nebraska, on March 4, 1865.
11. Thomas Moonlight (1833–99) was a Scottish immigrant who served as an enlisted man in the Regular army prior to the Civil War. After mustering out of the 11th Kansas Volunteer Cavalry, he held a variety of federal and state offices, becoming governor of Wyoming in 1884.
12. On August 7, 1864, a Cheyenne war party killed Joseph Eubanks, a stage driver and station keeper, and all the family except his wife and eighteen-month-old daughter.
13. Patrick E. Connor (1820–91) was an Irish immigrant who enlisted in the Regular army in 1839. He served as a Texas volunteer during the Mexican War. As colonel of the 3rd California Infantry and commander of the District of Utah during the Civil War, Connor earned the hatred of the Mormons. Nonetheless, after mustering out in 1866, he settled in Salt Lake City, where he founded the first daily newspaper in the state and industriously promoted the mining industry.
14. Martin Anderson (1817–97) was a founding member of the Republican Party in Kansas and an influential state legislator before the Civil War. After the war, he returned to farming.
15. Amos J. Custard (1827–65) came to Kansas from Pennsylvania in 1853 to farm.
16. Collins did not volunteer for the mission, which he believed to be suicidal, but rather was ordered to go out by Major Anderson. J. W. Vaughn, *The Battle of Platte Bridge* (Norman: University of Oklahoma Press, 1963), 56–57.
17. The war party consisted principally of Sioux warriors and members of the Cheyenne Dog Soldier warrior society.

18. Camp's horse was killed and he himself wounded. Three other soldiers dragged Camp to safety.
19. Vaughn, *Platte Bridge,* 78–81, says Shrader took four men with him.
20. Accounts vary as to the location of Collins's body, with some placing it as far as three miles from the battlefield. Vaughn, *Platte Bridge,* 94–95.

Henry E. Palmer: The Power River Indian Campaign of 1865

1. Henry E. Palmer (1841–post-1910) left his Wisconsin home to join the Pikes Peak gold rush in 1860. Palmer rose to the rank of captain of the 11th Kansas Volunteer Cavalry during the Civil War. After the Powder River expedition, Palmer went first to the Montana mines, then to eastern Nebraska to engage in business. In the 1880s, he moved to Wyoming and worked in livestock management and land promotion. He was an active member of the Kansas State Historical Society.
2. Palmer presented his paper on the Powder River expedition to the Nebraska chapter of the Military Order of the Loyal Legion of the United States in February 1887. He revised it in February 1900, correcting a number of significant errors. The earlier version was published in the *Transactions and Reports of the Nebraska State Historical Society* for 1887, and a portion reprinted in Leroy R. Hafen and Ann W. Hafen, *Powder River Campaigns.* It is the revised text that is presented here.
3. Samuel R. Curtis (1805–66), a member of the West Point Class of 1831 and a major general of volunteers during the Civil War.
4. The attack occurred on August 8, 1864. The Cheyenne and Sioux war party killed eleven white men and carried off a woman and a boy. George B. Grinnell, *The Fighting Cheyennes* (Norman: University of Oklahoma Press, 1956), 155.
5. John M. Chivington (1821–94) was one of the West's most controversial figures, venerated by many fellow Coloradoans and despised by eastern humanitarians for his conduct at Sand Creek. For a study of the affair, see Stan Hoig, *The Sand Creek Massacre* (Norman: University of Oklahoma Press, 1974).
6. On September 3, 1855, Brig. Gen. William S. Harney, with six hundred Dragoons, attacked the Brule Sioux camp of Little Thunder at Ash Hollow on Blue Water Creek, Nebraska, killing eighty-five.
7. Palmer's estimates of Indian losses are probably exaggerated. See Grinnell, *Fighting Cheyennes,* 183–86, for the Native American version of the Julesburg fight.
8. Palmer apparently is mistaken as to the identity and number of Indians, as Grinnell, *Fighting Cheyennes,* 189, 449, says that Two Face and Big Crow were both names for the same individual.
9. Jacob L. Humphreyville (1841–1916) enlisted in the 11th Ohio Infantry in April 1861 and rose through the ranks to a captaincy in the 11th Ohio Cavalry. He earned a Regular army commission as a lieutenant in the 9th U.S. Cavalry in 1866. Humphreyville resigned his commission after eight years' service on the Southern Plains and later authored *Twenty Years among Our Hostile Indians.*
10. Samuel Walker (1822–93) was promoted to lieutenant colonel in the 16th Kansas Volunteer Cavalry in 1864. After muster out, he held public office in Kansas.
11. Nelson Cole (1832–99) ended the Civil War as colonel of the 2nd Missouri Artillery. After the Powder River campaign, he was mustered out and went into business in St. Louis. Cole was reappointed a brigadier general of volunteers during the Spanish-American War.
12. Walker also had with him a detachment of the 15th Kansas Volunteer Cavalry and two mountain howitzers.
13. The La Bonta (or La Bonte) stage station was located near the mouth of La Bonte Creek and some seven miles south of present Douglas, Wyoming.

14. Minton "Mitch" Boyer (c. 1846–76), a half-breed Crow, was a protégé of Jim Bridger, after whom he was considered the best scout between the Bozeman Trail and the Platte road.
15. Pumpkin Buttes is located twenty miles east of present Sussex, Wyoming.
16. Christened Fort Connor, the post was renamed Fort Reno on November 11, 1865, in honor of Maj. Gen. Jesse Reno, a Union general killed at the battle of South Mountain during the Civil War.
17. Luther H. North (1846–1935) and his brother Frank J. North settled near the Pawnee reservation in Nebraska in 1861, where Frank found work. Luther began scouting for the army during the 1864 Sioux campaign. In 1867, Col. C. C. Augur authorized Frank to enlist a battalion of Pawnees; Luther became captain of one of its companies. The scouts were mustered out ten years later, after which the North brothers became ranchers.
18. For an account of the fight, see George B. Grinnell, *Two Great Scouts and Their Pawnee Battalions* (Cleveland: Arthur H. Clark Co., 1928), 89–94.
19. A wickiup was a temporary shelter, usually with an oval base and rough frame, and covered with mats, grass, or brushwood.
20. Pierre-Jean De Smet (1801–73) was a Jesuit missionary who began his frontier work with the Flatheads in 1840. Said one authority on his life, "No white man has ever come close to equaling his universal appeal to the Indian." Dan L. Thrapp, *Encyclopedia of Frontier Biography* (Spokane: Arthur H. Clark Company, 1988, 1994), 1:366–68.
21. There also were some Cheyennes camped beside the Arapaho village.
22. Estimates of the number of Arapaho ponies seized range from six hundred to Palmer's eleven hundred. Grinnell, *Fighting Cheyennes*, 210.
23. James A. Sawyers (1824–1903) was an Iowa merchant who became commanding officer of the Iowa Northern Border Brigade following the Sioux uprising of 1862. He supervised the building of a chain of forts and stockades across northeastern Iowa, then turned to cattle, freighting, and river transportation businesses in Sioux City. On March 14, 1865, the secretary of the interior appointed him superintendent and disbursing officer for the survey of a wagon road from the mouth of the Niobrara River, in Nebraska Territory, to Virginia City, in Montana Territory. In later years, Sawyers engaged in mining in California.
24. In his official report, Cole repeats these wildly high estimates of Indian losses during his early September fights with the Sioux and Cheyennes. Indian sources have one warrior killed in the largest of the running engagements with Cole. Grinnell, *Fighting Cheyennes*, 214.
25. The reception for Connor was held on the evening of October 14, 1865.
26. I have omitted the last seven pages of Palmer's paper, as they deal with matters subsequent to the Powder River campaign.

Charles W. Adams: Raiding a Hostile Village
1. I was unable to determine the identity of "Popcorn."
2. The Connor expedition left Fort Laramie on July 30, 1865.

Ovando J. Hollister: An Interview with General Connor
1. Ovando J. Hollister was the editor of the *Daily Mining Journal* and the author of *The Mines of Colorado* (Springfield, MA: Samuel Bowles and Company, 1867). Hollister rode with the 1st Colorado Volunteer Cavalry during the 1862 New Mexico campaign and chronicled the regiment's experiences in the *History of the First Regiment of Colorado Volunteers* (Denver: Thomas Gibson and Company, 1863).

Albert M. Holman: A Fifteen Day Fight on Tongue River
1. Albert M. Holman worked for the Sioux City *Journal* before joining the Sawyers's expedition as a teamster.
2. The men were killed on August 15, 1865, when they became separated from the expedition. Sawyers placed the number of attacking Indians as from five hundred to six hundred. Hafen, *Powder River Campaigns,* 255.
3. The expedition reached the fort on August 19.
4. Holman's written reminiscences of the expedition appeared in Albert M. Holman and Constant R. Marks, *Pioneering in the Northwest, Niobrara-Virginia City Wagon Road* (Sioux City: Deitch and Lamar Company, 1924). They agree in most respects with his oral recollections published in *Winners of the West.*
5. In his official report, Sawyers said the expedition consisted of fifty-three men, plus another ninety belonging to a private freight train that accompanied them. Hafen, *Powder River Campaigns,* 228–29.
6. August 31, 1865.
7. Sawyers gives the name as Dillelend.
8. Here Holman's memory fails him. The chief guide for the expedition was Benjamin F. Estes (b. 1835). Baptiste Defond, a half-breed Yankton Sioux, signed on in June 1865 as an additional guide.

PART TWO: RED CLOUD'S WAR, 1866–68

"W": A Bloody Prospecting Trip in the Bighorn Mountains
1. The mail escort, which had left Fort C. F. Smith for Fort Phil Kearny on September 11, 1866, was under the command of Sgt. John Murphy. Barry J. Hagan, *"Exactly in the Right Place": A History of Fort C. F. Smith, Montana Territory, 1866–1868* (El Segundo, CA: Upton and Sons, 1999), 60.
2. The wounded man was Pvt. Charles Hackett of Company D, 27th U.S. Infantry.
3. September 22.
4. Nathaniel C. Kinney (d. 1881) had been brevetted major in the Regular army for gallantry at the battle of Stones River, and lieutenant colonel for meritorious service during the Civil War. He was transferred from the 18th to the 27th U.S. Infantry in September 1866 and resigned his commission in January 1867.
5. James Marr had been mustered out of the volunteer army a short time before and had come to Montana in search of gold. A. C. Leighton was the post sutler at Fort C. F. Smith.
6. Other contemporaneous accounts substantiate W's allegations of misconduct on the part of Kinney but do not mention drunkenness. Hagan, *Exactly in the Right Place,* 66–67.
7. Kinney was accused of cowardice for failing to retrieve the bodies of Cpl. Alvah Staples and Pvt. Thomas Fitzpatrick, both of Company D, 27th U.S. Infantry, who had been killed while hunting buffalo for a hay-cutting detail on September 20.

William Murphy: The Forgotten Battalion
1. Red Cloud (1822–1909) of the Oglala Sioux was known to the whites as chief of the hostile element of the Sioux tribes until he signed a peace treaty in November 1868. He visited Washington, D.C., on several occasions thereafter and became something of an elder statesman of the Sioux.
2. Crazy Woman's Fork was a tributary of Powder River.
3. Located twelve miles north of where the Bozeman Trail crossed Crazy Woman's Fork.

4. Capt. Nathaniel C. Kinney was detached on August 3, 1866, to construct Fort C. F. Smith.
5. Henry B. Carrington (1824–1912) was a graduate of Yale University. Although he rose to the rank of brigadier general of volunteers during the Civil War, Carrington saw no combat duty. He retired from the army in December 1870.
6. Horatio S. Bingham (d. 1866) was a Canadian who had been commissioned a lieutenant in the 2nd Minnesota Volunteer Cavalry in 1863. He received a regular commission in the 2nd U.S. Cavalry in February 1866.
7. Two enlisted men were also wounded in the encounter. *Chronological List of Actions, etc., with Indians, from January 15, 1837, to January 1891* (Washington, D.C.: G.P.O., 1891), 25.
8. William J. Fetterman (c. 1833–66) was commissioned a first lieutenant in the 18th U.S. Infantry and transferred to the 27th U.S. Infantry as a captain in 1866, having earned two brevets for gallantry in the Civil War.
9. Tenodor Ten Eyck enlisted in the 12th Wisconsin Infantry in 1861 and rose to brevet major during the Civil War. He retired from the army a captain in 1891.
10. John E. Smith (1816–97) was treasurer of Jo Davies County, Illinois, before the Civil War and a friend of Ulysses S. Grant. A capable volunteer officer, he rose to the brevet rank of major general of volunteers during the Civil War. He was appointed colonel of the 27th U.S. Infantry in July 1866.
11. Philip St. George Cooke (1809–95), of the West Point Class of 1827, compiled a distinguished record on the antebellum frontier, but saw principally staff duty during the Civil War. He retired from the army in 1873, after more than fifty years of service.
12. The train belonged to the firm of Proctor and Gilmore and was under the charge of civilian contractor J. R. Porter.
13. Brown was a civilian cook for the wood party.
14. The war party that attacked the wagon-box corral consisted principally of Oglala Sioux under Crazy Horse and Minneconjou Sioux under High Backbone. There were a handful of San Arcs Sioux and some sixty Cheyennes under Little Wolf. Whether Red Cloud was on hand remains uncertain. Jerry Keenan, *The Wagon Box Fight: An Episode of Red Cloud's War* (Conshohocken, PA: Savas Publishing Company, 2000), 23.
15. Verling K. Hart (d. 1883) began his military career as a captain in the 19th U.S. Infantry in October 1861. He received brevets through the rank of lieutenant colonel in the Regular army during the Civil War.
16. For a biographical sketch of James Bridger, see his "Indian Affairs in the Powder River Country," elsewhere in this volume.

George Weber: Cold Cheer at Fort Kearny

1. George Weber was a member of Company C, 27th U.S. Infantry.
2. Winfield S. Matson served as a private in the 6th Indiana Cavalry during the Civil War. He was commissioned a second lieutenant in the 18th U.S. Infantry in April 1866 and resigned in January 1870.
3. The Holliday coach road, as that portion of the Bozeman Trail leading from Fort Phil Kearny to Fort Reno was known.
4. Capt. Fredrick H. Brown (d. 1866) enlisted in the 18th U.S. Infantry in July 1861. He was commissioned a second lieutenant in October 1861 and served as regimental quartermaster until May 1866.
5. On September 23, 1886, Brown chased a band of Indians who had run off a herd of civilian cattle. After a ten-mile chase, he overtook the raiders, killing six.

John Guthrie: A Detail of the Fetterman Massacre
1. John Guthrie (d. 1923) enlisted in September 1865 at Philadelphia and was honorably mustered out of Company C, 2nd U.S. Cavalry, as a private three years later. Guthrie successfully promoted a congressional bill to erect a monument to the dead of the Fetterman battle.
2. George W. Grummond (d. 1866) enlisted as first sergeant of Company A, 1st Michigan Infantry, in May 1861 and ended the Civil War the lieutenant colonel of the 14th Michigan Infantry. He was commissioned a second lieutenant of the 18th U.S. Infantry in May 1866.

Anonymous: Letters from Fort Phil Kearny
1. Fetterman took with him forty-nine infantrymen.
2. The Indian war party numbered between fifteen hundred and two thousand warriors.

Thomas W. Cover: The Murder of John Bozeman
1. Thomas W. Cover (1831–84) was a prospector and frontiersman who, after attending a business academy in Mount Vernon, Ohio, went west around 1850. In 1864, he and a partner established the first sawmill near Virginia City, Montana; a few months later, they built a gristmill at the present site of Bozeman, Montana, from which they supplied all the grain they could grind at Virginia City and to military posts along the Bozeman road. Cover and his friend John M. Bozeman were traveling to Fort C. F. Smith to arrange a flour contract when Blackfeet warriors accosted them. Thrapp, *Encyclopedia*, 1:330.
2. Thomas F. Meagher (1823–67) was the rabble-rousing son of a wealthy Irish merchant. In 1861, he organized a New York Zouave company, rising to the rank of brigadier general of volunteers during the Civil War. In late 1865, he was appointed territorial secretary of Montana. Meagher fell from the deck of a steamboat into the Missouri River while on a drunken spree on July 1, 1867; his body was never recovered.
3. John M. Bozeman (1835–67) of Georgia arrived at Virginia City with his wife in June 1862. Seeking a more direct route into the Montana Territory, he led numerous parties along a trail east of the Bighorn Mountains that came to be known as the Bozeman Road.

James Bridger: Indian Affairs in the Powder River Country
1. James Bridger (1804–81) was one of the preeminent mountain men, an invaluable guide to the army and an expert fur trapper and organizer of fur-trapping companies. In the words of one authority, Bridger was "one of the very greatest frontiersmen of the American saga, a man of outstanding character and worth." Thrapp, *Encyclopedia*, 1:167–68.
2. One enlisted member of the 2nd Battalion, 18th U.S. Infantry, was killed and four wounded in the July 17 skirmish along Reno Creek. *Chronological List*, 23.
3. Napoleon H. Daniels (d. 1866) was commissioned a first lieutenant in the 18th U.S. Infantry in February 1866. Daniels was killed while riding alone ahead of a wagon train for which he was part of the escort. An enlisted man was also killed.

E. A. Brininstool and Samuel S. Gibson: The Wagon Box Fight
1. Earl A. Brininstool (1870–1957) was a Los Angeles newspaperman and student of frontier history. He wrote or edited numerous books on the subject.
2. Samuel S. Gibson (1849–post-1920) was a private in the 27th U.S. Infantry at the time of the Wagon Box Fight. An ex-shoemaker from Nottingham, England, known to his comrades as "Whitey," Gibson had immigrated to the United States in 1865, enlisting in the army the following year. Keenan, *Wagon Box Fight*, 27.
3. James Powell (d. 1893) enlisted in the 11th U.S. Infantry in 1848. He was promoted to captain of the 18th Infantry in September 1864 and was brevetted major for gallantry during the Atlanta campaign. Transferred to the 27th U.S. Infantry in September 1866, Powell earned a brevet to lieutenant colonel for gallant conduct in the Wagon Box Fight. He retired in January 1868.
4. Brininstool's estimate is preposterous. In his report of the fight, Captain Powell estimated that "there were not less than sixty Indians killed on the spot and 120 severely wounded." Even Powell's seemingly conservative guess may have been too high. Keenan, *Wagon Box Fight*, 45–46.
5. Max Littman, formerly a cigar maker in Germany, was a twenty-year-old immigrant who spoke no English.
6. John C. Jenness (d. 1867) served in the New Hampshire volunteers during the Civil War. He was commissioned a second lieutenant in the 27th U.S. Infantry in July 1866 and promoted to first lieutenant the following March.
7. Whether the leader of this charge was the nephew of Red Cloud is uncertain.
8. Benjamin F. Smith (d. 1868) of the West Point Class of 1853 served as colonel of the 126th Ohio Volunteer Infantry during the Civil War. He was brevetted a brigadier general of volunteers for gallant and meritorious service at Petersburg. Smith was appointed a major in the 27th U.S. Infantry in July 1866.

George B. Grinnell: An Indian Perspective on the Wagon Box Fight
1. George B. Grinnell (1849–1938) graduated from Yale in 1870 and joined the Black Hills expedition as naturalist and paleontologist. He became editor and later owner of *Forest and Stream* magazine. Grinnell developed a profound interest in the Plains Indians and became one of the finest chroniclers of the Pawnee, Cheyenne, and Blackfoot ways of life. An ardent conservationist, Grinnell founded the Audubon Society in 1886.
2. Much of Grinnell's article consists of a review of the literature on the Wagon Box Fight, as well as a general discussion of Plains Indian methods of warfare. I have reproduced here only that portion of the article drawn from information that Grinnell obtained on the Wagon Box Fight from his Native American informants.
3. Col. Richard I. Dodge, author of several late-nineteenth-century works on the western frontier.

PART THREE: THE YELLOWSTONE EXPEDITION, 1873

George A. Custer: Battling with the Sioux on the Yellowstone
1. George A. Custer (1839–76), of the West Point Class of 1861, earned brevets of major general in both the Regular army and volunteers during the Civil War. He was assigned to the 7th Cavalry as lieutenant colonel upon its organization in July 1866.
2. David S. Stanley (1828–1902), of the West Point Class of 1848, served with distinction during the Civil War, ending the conflict a major general of volunteers. He retired a brigadier general in the Regular army.

3. Thomas L. Rosser (1836–1910) resigned from West Point in April 1861, two weeks before he would have graduated. Rosser rose to the rank of major general in the Confederate army. After working as chief engineer of the Northern Pacific and later the Canadian Pacific railroad, Rosser settled near Charlottesville, Virginia, as a gentleman farmer. He served as a brigadier general of U.S. Volunteers during the Spanish-American War.
4. Fort Rice, North Dakota Territory, was established in 1864 as a supply base for operations against the Sioux. It was located on the right bank of the Missouri River, ten miles north of the mouth of the Cannonball River.
5. Myles Moylan (1838–1909) enlisted in the 2nd Dragoons in 1857. He fought in the eastern theater during the Civil War, and in December 1866 he was commissioned a first lieutenant in the 7th Cavalry, becoming a captain in March 1872. He retired a major in the 10th Cavalry in 1893.
5. Thomas W. Custer (1845–76) was a younger brother of George A. Custer. Tom Custer earned two Medals of Honor during the Civil War.
7. James Calhoun (1845–76) enlisted in the 23rd U.S. Infantry in January 1864. He was assigned to the 7th Cavalry as a second lieutenant in January 1871.
8. Charles A. Varnum (1849–1936), of the West Point Class of 1872, served until 1907, when he was retired for disability after service in the Philippines. He was recalled to active duty as a colonel during the First World War.
9. Bloody Knife (c. 1837–76) was the son of a Hunkpapa father and Arikara mother. Growing up with the Sioux, he was discriminated against because of his Arikara blood, which bred in him a hatred for the Sioux. Bloody Knife enlisted as a corporal in the U.S. Army Indian scouts in May 1868 and served faithfully until his death at the Little Bighorn.
10. Custer refers to his brother by his Civil War brevet rank.
11. The main body was under the command of Captain Moylan.
12. Here Custer seemingly embellishes greatly, as the *Chronological List*, 55, gives hostile losses as just one warrior wounded. The 7th Cavalry lost the regimental surgeon and a civilian sutler killed, and reported one trooper missing in action.

Louis E. Hills: With General George A. Custer on the Northern Pacific Surveying Expedition in 1873

1. Thomas M. McDougall (1845–1909) served as a second lieutenant at age seventeen during the Civil War and saw wide service in the postwar frontier army.
2. Thomas H. French (1843–82) began his military career as a private in the 10th U.S. Infantry in 1864.
3. Augustus Baliran (c. 1843–73) was a French immigrant who served in the Confederate army during the Civil War. If Capt. Frederick Benteen is to be believed, Baliran dealt principally in liquor and high-stakes card games. Thom Hatch, *The Custer Companion: A Comprehensive Guide to the Life of George Armstrong Custer and the Plains Indian Wars* (Mechanicsburg, PA: Stackpole, 2002), 112.
4. John Honsinger (c. 1824–73) served as an army veterinary surgeon with the rank of sergeant major. He served in the Union army during the Civil War and may have accompanied John C. Frémont on several of his western expeditions. Hatch, *Custer Companion*, 128.
5. The priest that Hills encountered could not have been the famous Jesuit Pierre-Jean De Smet (1801–73), as he had died on May 23, 1873. De Smet did not, as some believed, baptize Sitting Bull, although the Sioux chief did accept religious articles from him. Thrapp, *Encyclopedia*, 1:396–97.
6. Charles A. Reynolds (1842–76), better known as "Lonesome Charley," was a well-educated frontier army scout who had moved to Kansas with his parents from Illi-

nois in 1859. He served on the Missouri frontier during the Civil War. Unlike many of his fellow scouts, Reynolds was abstemious, using neither tobacco nor liquor.
7. Sitting Bull (1834–90), the great Hunkpapa Sioux medicine man and chief, was by the mid-1870s generally regarded as the most able chief of all the Dakota bands.

Charles Braden: The Yellowstone Expedition of 1873

1. Charles Braden (1847–1919) was a member of the West Point Class of 1869. The wound he sustained during the Yellowstone campaign compelled his retirement in 1878. Braden settled near West Point and taught at a preparatory academy that graduated hundreds of successful candidates for cadetship at the Military Academy. He served for thirty-one years as secretary of the Association of Graduates of West Point.
2. John F. Weston was a volunteer officer during the Civil War and in August 1867 was commissioned a second lieutenant in the 7th Cavalry. He retired a brigadier general in the Regular army after the turn of the century.
3. The blizzard began on Sunday night, April 13, 1873. Residents of Yankton later referred to it as "the Custer storm of 1873." Jeffry D. Wert, *Custer: The Controversial Life of George Armstrong Custer* (New York: Simon and Schuster), 297.
4. Alexander M. McCook (1831–1903) was an instructor in tactics at West Point at the outbreak of the Civil War. He rose to corps command before being shelved after the Union defeat at Chickamauga. McCook advanced to the rank of major general in the Regular army in 1894, retiring a year later.
5. Lt. Col. James W. Forsyth (1834–1906), a graduate of the West Point Class of 1856, served as Philip H. Sheridan's military secretary from 1873 to 1878. In 1886, he became colonel of the 7th Cavalry.
6. Elizabeth Bacon Custer, *Boots and Saddles; or, Life in Dakota with General Custer* (New York: Harper and Brothers, 1885).
8. The infantry component of the expedition consisted of the Headquarters Company and Companies D, F, and G, 22nd U.S. Infantry; Companies A, B, C, F, H, and K, 8th U.S. Infantry; Companies A and F, 17th U.S. Infantry; Companies A, D, E, F, H, and I, 9th U.S. Infantry; and a small detachment from the 6th U.S. Infantry.
8. The Rees, or Arikaras, were blood enemies of the Sioux. They were often called the Corn Indians from their habit of living in relatively permanent villages and raising crops.
9. Daniel H. Brush, of the West Point Class of 1867.
10. The expedition departed Fort Rice on June 24, 1873.
11. The expedition numbered approximately fifteen hundred troops and four hundred civilians, along with a train of 275 wagons.
12. George W. Yates (1843–76) enlisted in the 4th Michigan Volunteer Infantry in 1861 and rose to the rank of brevet lieutenant colonel of volunteers during the Civil War. Commissioned a second lieutenant in the 2nd Cavalry in March 1866, Yates became a captain of the 7th Cavalry in June 1867, remaining with the regiment until his death at the Little Bighorn.
13. Edward P. Pearson began his military career as a private in the 25th Pennsylvania Volunteer Infantry in 1861. He rose to become colonel of the 10th U.S. Infantry and was a major general of volunteers in the Spanish-American War.
14. The veterinary surgeon was Dr. John Honsinger; the sutler was named Baliran.
15. Rain-in-the-Face (c. 1835–1905) was a great Hunkpapa Sioux warrior, but he was never, as Braden implies he was, a chief of the tribe.
16. Hiram H. Ketchum (d. 1898) earned a brevet for gallantry during the August 11, 1873, action near the mouth of the Bighorn River.

17. This article originally appeared as "An Incident of the Yellowstone Expedition of 1873." Although published anonymously, the distinguished Custer scholar Fred Dustin, in his landmark bibliography of sources on the general and his campaigns, credits the article to Braden. Dustin cites an undated reprint, with addenda, entitled "Experiences of Lt. Charles Braden on the Yellowstone Expedition of 1873," as evidence of authorship. Dustin's conclusion seems inescapable, as no one but Braden could have provided the details offered in this article. W. A. Graham, *The Custer Myth: A Source Book of Custeriana* (Harrisburg, PA: Stackpole, 1953), 383.
18. James P. Kimball was a Regular army surgeon. His widow wrote a reminiscent biography of him, entitled *A Soldier-Doctor of Our Army* (Boston: n.p., 1917).
19. For a biographical sketch of Edward S. Godfrey, see his "Captain Benteen's Command," elsewhere in this volume.
20. Jenifer Smallwood, of the West Point Class of 1869. He resigned his commission in December 1873.
21. For a biographical sketch of Andrew S. Burt, see his "Dispatches from Crook's Column," elsewhere in this volume.
22. For a biographical sketch of Samuel J. Barrows, see his "Crossing the Big Muddy [Creek]," elsewhere in this volume.

Samuel J. Barrows: Crossing the Big Muddy [Creek]
1. Samuel J. Barrows (b. 1844), a divinity student at Harvard University, accompanied the Yellowstone expedition as a correspondent for the New York *Tribune*. In later years, he became a Unitarian minister, editor of the *Christian Register*, and a Republican member of Congress from Massachusetts.
2. Patrick H. Ray began his military career as a private in the 2nd Wisconsin Volunteer Infantry in 1861. He rose to the rank of colonel of volunteers during the war with Spain.
3. Eugene M. Baker (d. 1884), of the West Point Class of 1859, was commissioned a second lieutenant in the 2nd Dragoons after graduation and served with that regiment (later the 2nd U.S. Cavalry) for most of his career.
4. John J. Dougherty, of the West Point Class of 1872.
5. Edwin F. Townsend, of the West Point Class of 1854. He retired a colonel in 1895.

PART FOUR: THE BLACK HILLS AND BEYOND, 1874–76

George A. Custer: The Black Hills Expedition: Dispatches and Letters
1. For a biographical sketch of William Ludlow, see his "The Black Hills Expedition," elsewhere in this volume.
2. Newton H. Winchell (1839–1914) graduated from the University of Michigan in 1866 and was appointed state geologist of Minnesota in 1872, a position he held until 1900. He was a founder of the American Geological Society.
3. Aris B. Donaldson (d. 1883) was a member of the faculty of the University of Minnesota and a correspondent for the St. Paul *Daily Pioneer*.
4. George D. Wallace (1849–90) joined the 7th Cavalry after graduation from West Point in 1872. He was with Maj. Marcus Reno's wing at the Little Bighorn and served on the plains until his death at the Wounded Knee affair.
5. Other eyewitness accounts suggest that the shooting of the fleeing Indian was intentional. An enlisted soldier of the 7th Cavalry recalled that the Arikara had painted and stripped for war when the Oglala camp was found, and it was only with the greatest difficulty that they were prevented from massacring the Sioux. Donald

Jackson, *Custer's Gold: The United States Cavalry Expedition of 1874* (New Haven, CT: Yale University Press, 1966): 79.
6. Present-day Vanderlehr Creek.
7. That cheery estimate did not include Pvt. James King of Company H, 7th Cavalry, who fell ill on August 12 and died the next afternoon of heatstroke and dysentery. His battalion commander, Maj. Joseph G. Tilford, disobeyed Custer's order that King be buried that evening, saying that no man of his battalion would be buried so soon after dying if he could prevent it. Tilford buried him on the morning of August 14, after Custer departed with the left wing and the wagon train. Captain Benteen read the service. Jackson, *Custer's Gold*, 96–97; Ernest Grafe and Paul Horsted, *Exploring with Custer: The 1874 Black Hills Expedition* (Custer, SD: Golden Valley Press, 2002), 147.
8. The Santee were an eastern division of the Dakota Sioux and had settled on a reservation in Nebraska in 1862.
9. Winchell repeated his belief that there was no gold in the Black Hills during a lecture before the Academy of Natural Sciences in Minneapolis in September 1874, saying he had seen none, nor had anyone shown him any gold. Jackson, *Custer's Gold*, 108.
10. A reference to the Hunkpapa Sioux warrior Rain-in-the-Face, whom Custer arrested but for want of evidence was unable to bring to trial for the killings. Rain-in-the-Face later boasted of his guilt.

William Ludlow: The Black Hills Exposition

1. William Ludlow (1843–1901), of the West Point Class of 1864, entered the Civil War in time to receive brevets up to lieutenant colonel. As a brigadier general of volunteers in the Spanish-American War, he commanded a brigade in the attack on El Caney. Promoted to major general of volunteers, he served briefly as governor of Havana, dying in New Jersey while under orders to go to the Philippines. Ludlow's preliminary report first appeared in the September 14, 1874, number of the *New York Times*.
2. Othniel C. Marsh (1831–99) was a famous Yale paleontologist and personal friend of Lt. Gen. Philip H. Sheridan.
3. Capt. J. W. Williams (d. 1889), a graduate of the National Medical College in Washington, D.C., had been surgeon-in-chief with the 1st Cavalry Division of the Army of the Shenandoah in the latter months of the Civil War. Williams apparently was drunk during much of the expedition, and he died a narcotics addict. Jackson, *Custer's Gold*, 69–70.
4. William H. Illingworth (1842–c. 1893) studied photography in Chicago. In 1866, he accompanied the Fisk emigrant expedition to Montana, and the stereoscopic pictures he made formed the basis for a studio-gallery that he opened at St. Paul, Minnesota, in 1867. Illingworth committed suicide shortly after divorcing his third wife. His photographs of the Black Hills expedition are beautifully reproduced in Grafe and Horsted, *Exploring with Custer*.
5. Sgt. Charles Becker was in charge of the two-wheeled odometer cart. In July 1876, he would ride the same cart about the battlefield of the Little Bighorn, charting the final positions of Custer's command during an army investigation of the defeat. Jackson, *Custer's Gold*, 63.
6. For a biographical sketch of William H. Wood, see his "Reminiscences of the Black Hills Expedition," elsewhere in this volume.
7. The expedition emerged from the Black Hills on August 14, 1874.
8. William Ludlow, *Report of a Reconnaissance of the Black Hills of Dakota, Made in the Summer of 1874* (Washington, D.C.: U.S. Army, Engineer Department, 1875).

William H. Wood: Reminiscences of the Black Hills Expedition
1. William H. Wood (1844–post-1928) was born in Ontario but moved to Michigan with his family as a small boy. Wood's father was a surveyor and ran the surveyor's office in St. Paul, Minnesota, after 1857. Wood learned surveying from his father. He worked for the railroads and also helped lay out Fort Abraham Lincoln.
2. Custer had a command of 951 soldiers and teamsters, plus a large number of military and civilian aides.
3. Gouverneur K. Warren, then a lieutenant and later a major general during the Civil War, was the topographical engineer on Brig. Gen. William S. Harney's 1855 punitive expedition against the Sioux, which skirted the Black Hills. Warren returned to the area two years later on a mapping expedition.
4. Custer's expedition left Fort Lincoln on July 2, 1874, and returned on August 30.

Alfred Bear: Story Told by Strikes Two and Bear's Belly of an Expedition under Custer in 1874
1. The title of the article, as it originally appeared, incorrectly gave the date of Custer's Black Hills expedition as 1875.
2. Alfred Bear was the interpreter who translated the stories of the Arikara scouts Strikes Two and Bear's Belly.
3. This is the cave that Custer christened Ludlow's Cave.
4. The quarrel involved two soldiers from Company M, George Roller and George Turner. Roller killed Turner, apparently in self-defense, after the latter cross-hobbled Roller's horse and then tried to draw on him. Both were regarded as "desperate characters." Grafe, *Exploring with Custer,* 21–23.

Guy V. Henry: A Winter March to the Black Hills
1. Guy V. Henry (1839–99), of the West Point Class of 1861, became colonel of the 40th Massachusetts Volunteer Infantry in 1863 and earned three brevets and a Medal of Honor during the Civil War. He was commissioned a captain in the 3rd U.S. Cavalry in 1870. Henry was severely wounded in the battle of the Rosebud, losing an eye. He rose to the rank of brigadier general in the Regular army and served as a major general of volunteers in the Spanish-American War.
2. William L. Carpenter (d. 1898) served as an enlisted man during the Civil War and was commissioned a second lieutenant in the 9th U.S. Infantry in April 1867.

Philip H. Sheridan: The Black Hills
1. Philip H. Sheridan (1831–88) was commander of the Military Division of the Missouri.
2. Sheridan served in the Pacific Northwest during the 1850s, participating in the October 1855 campaign against the Yakima Indians of Oregon. Sheridan lived for some time on the Grande Ronde Indian Reservation of northeast Oregon with a Rogue River Indian girl.
3. The area Sheridan describes was more commonly known as the Bighorn Mountains.
4. George A. Forsyth (1837–1915) earned lasting fame when his company of frontier scouts fought off a large band of Cheyennes, Arapahos, and Brule Sioux at Beecher Island in September 1868. He retired a colonel in 1890.

5. Sheridan ended up sending Lt. Col. James W. Forsyth of his staff, rather than George A. Forsyth, up the Yellowstone River with Grant. Frederick Dent Grant was the son of President Grant.
6. Fort Brown, Wyoming, was located on the south bank of the Little Wind River, at its junction with the North Fork. It was renamed Fort Washakie in December 1878.
7. Anson Mills (1834–1924) helped lay out the city of El Paso, Texas, while a surveyor in 1857. He left Texas at the outbreak of the Civil War and was commissioned a first lieutenant in the 18th U.S. Infantry, emerging from the conflict with brevets to lieutenant colonel. He retired a brigadier general in 1897. Mills invented an improved cartridge belt and other equipment for soldiers and sportsmen, making a fortune in the process.

Frederick Schwatka: The Sun Dance of the Sioux

1. Frederick Schwatka (1849–92), of the West Point Class of 1871, attained fame when he led an arctic expedition from March 1878 to October 1880 searching for the remains of the doomed Sir John Franklin polar expedition of 1847–48. During the journey, his party completed the longest sledge journey on record, of 3,251 miles. Schwatka returned to the artic on a *New York Times* financed expedition in 1886. He authored several books, including *Along Alaska's Great River* and *Nimrod of the North*. He died of an overdose of laudanum, which he was taking for a chronic stomach ailment.

Robert E. Strahorn: "Alter Ego" on the Power River Expedition

1. Robert E. Strahorn (1852–1944), known to his readers as "Alter Ego," was a correspondent for the *Rocky Mountain News*, Chicago *Tribune*, Cheyenne *Sun*, and other newspapers from 1866 to 1877. Strahorn owed his place on the expedition to his friendship with Maj. Thaddeus H. Stanton of Crook's staff. He remained with Crook's command until the surrender of Crazy Horse in 1877. Fellow correspondent John F. Finerty described Strahorn as a "distinguished Western newspaper correspondent who in every situation proved himself as fearless as he was talented." Strahorn maintained a lasting friendship with Crook, who once said of him, "It mattered not what the cost was; Bob was every inch a soldier . . . and he never failed to work his rifle as well as his pen." Strahorn worked in the publicity department of the Union Pacific Railroad from 1877 until 1883, then went on to a variety of promotional, industrial, and railroad enterprises. He eventually settled in Spokane, Washington. Thrapp, *Encyclopedia*, 3:1376; Oliver Knight, *Following the Indian Wars: The Story of the Newspaper Correspondents among the Indian Campaigners* (Norman: University of Oklahoma Press, 1960), 170–71.
2. George Crook (1829–90), of the West Point Class of 1852, saw extensive frontier service in the Pacific Northwest prior to the Civil War. During that conflict, he rose to the brevet rank of major general of volunteers. Prior to assuming command of the Department of the Platte in May 1875, he had campaigned extensively against the Apaches in Arizona and northern Mexico.
3. Commissioner of Indian Affairs E. P. Smith issued the order in question to his agents at the Red Cloud, Spotted Tail, Standing Rock, Cheyenne River, Fort Peck, Lower Brule, Crow Creek, and Devil's Lake agencies on December 6.
4. A reference to the Fetterman fight.
5. Strahorn's criticism is disingenuous, as heavy snows had prevented most runners sent from the agencies with the order from reaching the roving bands until after the January deadline had expired.

6. The expedition was divided into six battalions, composed and commanded as follows:
   1st Battalion: Companies E and M, 3rd Cavalry, Capt. Anson Mills, commanding.
   2nd Battalion: Companies A and D, 3rd Cavalry, Capt. William Hawley, commanding.
   3rd Battalion: Companies I and K, 2nd Cavalry, Capt. Henry E. Noyes, commanding.
   4th Battalion: Companies A and B, 2nd Cavalry, Capt. T. B. Dewees, commanding.
   5th Battalion: Company E of 2nd Cavalry, and Company F of 3rd Cavalry, Capt. Alexander Moore, commanding.
   6th Battalion: Companies C and I, 4th Infantry, Capt. E. M. Coates, commanding.
   In his official report, Reynolds said the expedition consisted of 30 commissioned officers, 35 scouts and guides, 662 enlisted men, 62 pack train employees, 89 wagon train employees, and 5 ambulance drivers, for a total of 883 men. J. W. Vaughn, *The Reynolds Campaign on Powder River* (Norman: University of Oklahoma Press, 1961), 26–27.
7. Strahorn's estimate—which the military shared—reflects the entire Teton Sioux population, not simply those away from their agencies or who had never set fought on an agency. The Bureau of Indian Affairs in late 1875 calculated the number of potential hostile Sioux at 3,000, to which historian John S. Gray, in his meticulously documented *Centennial Campaign: The Sioux War of 1876* (Norman: University of Oklahoma Press, 1988), 320, adds some four hundred Cheyenne, for a total of 3,400, of whom 850 might be counted fighting men.
8. For a biographical sketch of Thaddeus H. Stanton, see his "A Review of the Reynolds Campaign," elsewhere in this volume.
9. The mortally wounded herder was named Jim Wright.
10. Edwin M. Coates earned a Regular army commission during the Civil War. He retired a colonel in 1900.
11. Samuel P. Ferris (d. 1881), of the West Point Class of 1861.
12. Frank Grouard (1850–1905) was one of the best of the frontier army scouts. Born in the South Pacific, the son of a Mormon missionary and a native woman, he came to Utah with his father in 1852. He ran away at age fifteen, settling in Helena, Montana. Four years later, while a mail carrier, he was captured by the Sioux and for six years lived among them.
13. Little is known of the Indian village and its occupants, except that they were principally Northern Cheyenne, with perhaps sixteen Sioux lodges under He Dog thrown in. Vaughn, *Reynolds Campaign,* 122–30, deemed it unlikely that Crazy Horse was present, as his village rested three days distant, and suggests that the principal Cheyenne chiefs present were Two Moon, Old Bear, and Little Wolf.
14. For a biographical sketch of John G. Bourke, see his "The Battle of Slim Buttes," elsewhere in this volume.
15. James Egan (d. 1883) was an Irish immigrant who enlisted in the 2nd Cavalry in 1856 and rose from the ranks.
16. The approximate time was 8:30 A.M.
17. Looking at his watch as he gave the order to charge, Egan noted the time as 9:05 A.M.
18. Strahorn neglected to mention that his own horse became frightened and ran away during the charge, breaking its neck after falling over a precipice. Strahorn continued into the village on foot. Vaughn, *Reynolds Campaign,* 84.
19. Alexander Moore (c. 1835–1910) was an Irish immigrant who served as a volunteer officer through the brevet rank of lieutenant colonel during the Civil War. He was commissioned a captain in the 38th U.S. Infantry in 1867 and transferred to the 3rd Cavalry in 1870.

20. John B. Johnson (d. 1896) was commissioned a second lieutenant in the 6th U.S. Colored Infantry in 1863. He was assigned to the 3rd Cavalry in 1870.
21. Henry E. Noyes (1839–1919), of the West Point Class of 1861, served through the Civil War in the 2nd U.S. Cavalry, earning two brevets for gallantry in action.
22. Lt. William C. Rawolle of the 2nd Cavalry was slightly wounded, having received a contusion on the left leg from a rifle ball
23. To reiterate, it was a Northern Cheyenne village, with some lodges of visiting Sioux.

Thaddeus H. Stanton: A Review of the Reynolds Campaign

1. Thaddeus H. Stanton (1835–1900) was commissioned a captain in the 18th Iowa Infantry in 1862. In October of that year, he transferred to Paymaster Corps. In 1895, Stanton became paymaster of the army, with the rank of brigadier general. He was paying troops at Fort Fetterman when Crook assembled the Powder River expedition. Crook wanted a correspondent from the friendly New York *Tribune* to go along to "present all the facts to the country." Editor Whitlaw Reid had none available and suggested instead that Stanton go as special correspondent. Crook agreed and made Stanton chief of scouts—a role for which he was unqualified.
2. The headquarters of the Department of the Platte were located at Omaha, Nebraska.
3. A reference to Col. John Gibbon's Montana column, which had left Fort Ellis on April 1, 1876.
4. The Red Cloud agency was located in Nebraska, on the left bank of the White River, near its source. The Spotted Tail agency was located on the right bank of the West Fork of Beaver Creek, twelve miles above its confluence with the White River, and some forty miles downriver from the Red Cloud Agency.
5. Little is known of the Indian village and its occupants, except that they were principally Northern Cheyenne, with perhaps sixteen Sioux lodges under He Dog thrown in. Vaughn, *Reynolds Campaign,* 122–30, deemed it unlikely that Crazy Horse was present, as his village rested three days distant, and suggests the principal Cheyenne chiefs present were Two Moon, Old Bear, and Little Wolf.
6. Crook initially was pleased that Reynolds had found and destroyed a large hostile village. It was only after he heard from Stanton, Strahorn, Bourke, and others present at the attack that Crook grew angry that more had not been accomplished and preferred court-martial charges against Reynolds, Noyes, and Moore. Gray, *Centennial Campaign,* 57. Reynolds was tried in January 1877 at Cheyenne, Wyoming, and found guilty of the charges and specifications. He was sentenced to be suspended from rank and command for a year. President Grant remitted the sentence, but Reynolds never recovered from the stigma, and he retired on account of disability in June 1877. Historian J. W. Vaughn, who carefully examined both the campaign and the court proceedings, concluded that the findings were "cruelly unjust to Colonel Reynolds." Thrapp, *Encyclopedia,* 3:1211. An excellent officer withal, Captain Noyes was found guilty of having permitted his men to unsaddle and make coffee at a critical juncture in the fight for the village. He was reprimanded for his action. Captain Moore was found guilty of the rather nebulous charge of conduct to the prejudice of good order and military discipline and was sentenced to six months' suspension from command, which President Grant remitted in view of his good Civil War record.
7. Lt. George A. Drew, the quartermaster of the expedition, and Captain Noyes and Lieutenant Rawolle all agreed that they could not have loaded the meat on the Indian ponies, as there were no packers with the command. Vaughn, *Reynolds Campaign,* 112.

8. Crook was uncertain of the location of Sitting Bull's camp, which was located east of Chalk Buttes on Beaver Creek, near the present Ekalaka, Montana. Ibid., 134, 156.
9. Stanton exaggerates Crook's predicament. The Indians had failed to recapture 180 ponies, and Crook's scouts drove in another 40 or 50.
10. Although unsigned, this harsh denunciation of Colonel Reynolds and Captain Moore clearly was penned by Stanton. He, Lieutenant Bourke, and Robert E. Strahorn were all harshly critical of the behavior of Colonel Reynolds and Captain Moore at the March 17 battle for the Indian village. Stanton, who shared a tent with Crook, was the most vocal of the three, and helped Capt. Anson Mills pen charges against Reynolds while the command was still in the field. During his subsequent court-martial, Colonel Reynolds had occasion to condemn Stanton's letter to the Washington *Chronicle,* as well as his earlier articles to the New York *Tribune.* Said Reynolds:

> The United States Army is entitled to know whether a noncombatant paymaster can be taken from his legitimate duties, to act as a newspaper correspondent on an Indian campaign, and giving strength to his statements by his official position, can, under the smiles and encouragement of the department commander, denounce in public print as cowards and imbeciles his fellow officers, both his superiors and inferiors in rank, and not even have his conduct inquired into.

The court agreed with Reynolds. It reprimanded General Crook for allowing Stanton to accompany the expedition as a newspaper correspondent in violation of regulations, saying, "This court cannot but regard such a practice as pernicious in the extreme and condemns it as unsoldierly and detrimental to the efficiency and best interests of the service." Among the members of the court were a number of distinguished senior officers, including Brig. Gen. John Pope, Col. John Gibbon, Col. Jefferson C. Davis, and Col. George Sykes. Vaughn, *Reynolds Campaign,* 172–78.
11. Stanton testified at Reynolds's court-martial that he had told Moore: "We might as well be in Cheyenne as here. The Indians will all escape." Vaughn, *Reynolds Campaign,* 75.

PART FIVE: THE SUMMER CAMPAIGN OF 1876

Daniel C. Pearson: Military Notes, 1876
1. Daniel C. Pearson (1845–1920), of the West Point Class of 1870, was commissioned a second lieutenant in the 2nd Cavalry. He served on the frontier continuously from 1874 to 1891. Pearson retired a lieutenant colonel in 1904.
2. The crossing took place on May 25 and 26, 1876.
3. Frederick W. Sibley (1852–1918), of the West Point Class of 1874, rose to the rank of brigadier general before his retirement in 1916. He served with Pershing's Mexican punitive expedition as colonel of the 14th Cavalry.
4. The combined commands of Crook and Terry remained at the Powder River supply camp from August 17 to 25, 1876.
5. Robert H. Montgomery began his military career in 1860 as a private in the 5th U.S. Cavalry. He retired a major in 1892.
6. Capt. Anson Mills' column discovered the village on the afternoon of September 8 but waited until the following morning to attack it.

7. Lt. Henry D. Huntington (d. 1886), of the West Point Class of 1875.
8. A reference to the wound that Lt. Adolphus H. von Leuttwitz sustained during the battle of Slim Buttes.

Henry W. Daly: The War Path

1. Henry W. Daly (1850–1931) was an Irish immigrant who roamed Canada and northern Mexico before taking up employment as a civilian packer for the army. He became a skilled pack specialist and a particular favorite of General Crook. Daly became the first chief packer for the Quartermaster Department and wrote manuals on pack operations while an instructor at West Point in the early 1900s. He served in the Quartermaster Corps during the First World War as a major.
2. Valentine P. McGillycuddy, who served as a surgeon on the Rosebud campaign, penned this wonderful character sketch of Calamity Jane:

> As to Calamity Jane. She was born at Fort Laramie, Wyoming, in 1860, the daughter of a private soldier [named] James Dalton. He was discharged from the army in the fall of 1861 and made a little home for the family on the La Bonte, 120 miles northwest of Fort Laramie, and shortly thereafter he was killed by a war party of Sioux. His wife made her way back to Fort Laramie with the child on foot, subsisting on roots and herbs for eight days. Shortly after reaching the post, she died from exhaustion, and the child was adopted by Sergeant Basset of the 14th U.S. Infantry, and became known as Calamity Jane Dalton by reason of her misfortune. There she remained a protege until the fitting out of the Black Hills expedition in the spring of 1875, when she had reached the mature age of fifteen.
>
> When riding past the wagon train guard of the expedition when about three days out from post one morning, I heard a beautiful array of expletives delivered in a gentle feminine voice, with no skirt in view, but finally located Calamity, in full soldier attire, riding on a horse with the guard, having volunteered as the sole member of her sex as an assistant of the expedition, under the special "protection" of First Sergeant Shaw, Troop A, 3rd Cavalry, much to the worry and disapproval of his company commander, [1st Lt. Joseph] Lawson.
>
> Necessarily she was soon excluded from the soldiers' camp, and she attached herself to the teamsters' camp for the season, and thence forward for many years she became a camp follower with several expeditions, or made her home in the frontier towns. Being gregarious in her tastes, she practiced "serial polygamy" and had many husbands. As necessity required, she became an expert rifle shot, an experienced scout, could hold her own with any man at his own game, drinking, swearing, or holding forth all night in a frontier dance hall. As a girl she was comely, well built, and attractive, but years of dissipation and exposure roughened her, and she died in the early nineties, a wreck, and was buried by her old friends of the frontier in Mt. Moriah Cemetery near Deadwood, in the Black Hills, in the shadow of the monument erected to Wild Bill [Hickok], the famous scout.
>
> Was she immoral? That depends on one's point of view. I knew her well, and I might term her *unmoral,* the victim or product of

unfortunate heredity, environment, conditions, and opportunity. She was not a hypocrite. She was withal a woman. I have seen her carousing one night in a frontier den, the next morning nursing and sharing her last cent with some sick man needing care.

3. Thomas Moore (1832–96) began his packing career in the Salmon River, Idaho, mines in the 1850s. Beside the Rosebud campaign, he also service with Brig. Gen. O. O. Howard against the Nez Perces, again with Crook in Arizona from 1883 to 1886, and at Wounded Knee.
4. For a biographical sketch of David T. Mears, see his "Campaigning against Crazy Horse," elsewhere in this volume.
5. Daly errs in his depiction of Terry's role and responsibilities. Both Crook and Terry were department commanders. Sheridan did not plan for them to work in concert and permitted them wide discretion in the conduct of their campaigns. "I have given no instruction to Generals Crook or Terry," he explained to the commanding general of the army, William T. Sherman, "as I think it would be unwise to make any combination in such a country as they will have to operate in." Paul A. Hutton, *Phil Sheridan and His Army* (Lincoln: University of Nebraska Press, 1985), 303–3.
6. Crook's command reached old Fort Reno, ninety miles out of Fort Fetterman, on June 2, 1876.
7. On the evening of June 9, a war party of Cheyennes under Little Hawk raided Crook's bivouac in an unsuccessful effort to steal horses.
8. From Indian sign he had picked up along the way, Grouard supposed the Sioux were camped on the Rosebud, but was less certain than Daly represents.
9. The battle of the Rosebud began earlier than Daly recalls—at approximately 8:30 A.M. on June 17. J. W. Vaughn, *With Crook at the Rosebud* (Harrisburg, PA: The Stackpole Company, 1956), 50.
10. What Daly describes as the battlefield, and disposition of forces, reflects the situation at 8:30 A.M., when the first shots of the Sioux attack were heard over the low ridges north of Crook's command. The 150–yard-wide space he refers to was a valley bounded by the left (north) bank of the Rosebud and the first line of low ridges north of the river. Through this valley, Crook's left column, consisting of five companies of the 2nd Cavalry, two infantry companies, and the scouts and packers, was marching; the ten companies of the 3rd Cavalry were moving in column along the right (south) bank of the Rosebud. Neil C. Mangum, *Battle of the Rosebud: Prelude to the Little Big Horn* (El Segundo, CA: Upton and Sons, 1987), 52–53.
11. In his recollections, Daly has jumped ahead three hours, from the opening shots of the battle to 11:30 A.M., when Lt. Col. William B. Royall's cavalry was driven from its third position on the field, and the Indians launched a general attack all along the line.
12. William B. Royall (1825–95) served with distinction with the Missouri volunteers during the War with Mexico. Promoted to first lieutenant in the 2nd U.S. Cavalry, he saw action against the Comanches in the late 1850s. Royall ended the Civil War a brevet lieutenant colonel. He served competently on the postwar frontier and retired a colonel in 1887.
13. Although his son, Goose Feather, participated in the fight, it is not certain that Chief Dull Knife was at the battle of the Rosebud. Grinnell, *Fighting Cheyennes,* 341; Vaughn, *With Crook,* 45.
14. Snow was shot through both forearms.
15. The battle lasted nearly six hours.
16. In the *Chronological List of Actions,* 61, army losses are given as nine men killed and one officer and twenty-men wounded. Only the eleven hostiles whose bodies remained on the field were listed as Indian casualties.

17. A reference to Lt. Frederick W. Sibley's scout in the Bighorn Mountains and running engagement with Sioux and Cheyenne war parties, from June 6 to 9, 1876.
18. Daly is being charitable. Crook was not conducting a reconnaissance, but rather leading a party on a hunting trip to the summits of the Bighorn Mountains.
19. Here Daly refers to four Crow scouts whom Colonel Gibbon had sent to Crook with a duplicate of Terry's dispatch. They arrived in Crook's camp on July 19.
20. Daly's comments regarding Custer's body may have been made to spare the feelings of his widow, Elizabeth Bacon Custer. Although Custer's remains were less mutilated than those of many others (he was not scalped, for instance), there is evidence that one thigh had been slashed, an arrow shot into his genitals, and a finger cut off. Larry Sklenar, *To Hell with Honor: Custer and the Little Big Horn* (Norman: University of Oklahoma Press, 2000), 327–29.

Anonymous: Brave Boys Are They: The Newspaper Correspondents with Crook's Army

1. A reference to Capt. Anson Mills's movement against the rear of the Sioux at 1:30 P.M. on June 17, 1876, near a spot on the Rosebud battlefield called Conical Hill, as they were massing for an attack on Lt. Col. William B. Royall's command.
2. On July 6, 1876, Lt. Frederick W. Sibley of the 2nd Cavalry set off with twenty-five hand-picked troopers on a scout of the Bighorn Mountains, a three-day ordeal in which his command was attacked by several strong war parties and nearly annihilated.
3. Frederick S. Schwatka took up writing for the Chicago *Inter-Ocean* upon MacMillan's departure.

James E. H. Foster: From Fort Fetterman to the Rosebud

1. James E. H. Foster (d. 1883) enlisted in Battery A, Independent Pennsylvania Light Artillery, in May 1864. He was commissioned a second lieutenant in the 3rd U.S. Cavalry in October 1873.
2. A reference to Reynolds's Powder River campaign.
3. John W. Bubb enlisted as a private in the 12th U.S. Infantry in September 1861. He was commissioned a second lieutenant in the regiment in February 1866. In 1872 he transferred to the Quartermaster Corps.
4. Frederick Van Vliet (d. 1891) was commissioned a second lieutenant in the 3rd Cavalry in 1861 and promoted to captain in 1866.
5. Crook's command camped on Prairie Dog Creek on the night of June 6.
6. A reference to Ben Arnold, whose life on the frontier is retold in Lewis F. Crawford, *Rekindling Camp Fires: The Exploits of Ben Arnold, an Authentic Narrative of Sixty Years in the Old West* (Bismarck, ND: Capital Book Co., 1926).
7. Thomas B. Dewees (d. 1886) was commissioned a second lieutenant in the 2nd Cavalry in 1861.
8. Peter D. Vroom (1842–1926) was commissioned a second lieutenant in the 1st New Jersey Infantry in August 1862. He remained in the army after the war, serving with the 3rd Cavalry until 1889. He retired a brigadier general in the Regular army in 1903.
9. Gray, *Centennial Campaign*, 118, calculated the village then to have consisted of some 450 lodges, for a total of just under one thousand fighting men.
10. Avery B. Cain (d. 1879) was commissioned a second lieutenant in the 4th Infantry in 1861.

11. William H. Andrews (d. 1880) was commissioned a captain in the 108th New York Volunteer Infantry in 1862. After the Civil War, he was commissioned a second lieutenant in the 12th U.S. Infantry and transferred to the 3rd Cavalry in 1870.
12. Crook ordered Royall to halt his advance and return from his exposed position at 10:00 A.M.
13. Azor H. Nickerson (1837–1910) emerged from the Civil War a brevet major for gallantry at Antietam and Gettysburg. He served on Crook's staff for ten years, until his promotion to major in June 1878.
14. The time was approximately 12:30 P.M.
15. Mangum, *Battle of the Rosebud,* 78, estimates the number of men in Royall's defensive line—exclusive of horse holders—as closer to one hundred.
16. For a biographical sketch of Henry R. Lemly, see his "The Murder of Chief Crazy Horse," elsewhere in this volume.
17. It was now shortly after 1:00 P.M.
18. Foster exaggerated the losses. General Crook reported nine men killed and one officer and twenty enlisted men wounded in the battle of the Rosebud. Mangum, *Battle of the Rosebud,* 129.
19. Gerald Russell was an Irish immigrant who earned a commission as a second lieutenant in the 3rd Cavalry in 1862. He retired a major in 1890.

Charles King: Custer's Last Battle

1. Charles King (1844–1933) graduated from West Point with the Class of 1866. During the Civil War, the sixteen-year-old King enlisted as a volunteer mounted orderly to his father, Brig. Gen. Rufus King. Badly wounded at Sunset Pass in Arizona in 1874, King recovered enough to participate with Crook's command in the Sioux War of 1876. Retired for disability in 1879, King returned to his native Milwaukee and began writing of his Indian War experiences for the Milwaukee *Sentinel*. His articles on the Sioux War formed the basis of his highly regarded book *Campaigning with Crook* (New York: Harper and Brothers, 1890). King became a prolific writer of war novels and pursued a second military career as adjutant general of the Wisconsin National Guard and a brigadier general of volunteers during the war with Spain.
2. Alfred Sully (1821–79), son of the famous painter Thomas Sully, led a 3,400–man command into the Sioux country on a four-month expedition during the summer of 1864. At the climactic battle of Killdeer Mountain, he inflicted 150 killed on the Sioux, at a loss of only 2 killed and a handful wounded.
3. King exaggerates the hostile population of the Northern Plains. For a more accurate estimate of the Native American population of the Northern Plains at the time of the Sioux War of 1876, see Charles A. Eastman's "The Indian Version of Custer's Last Battle," elsewhere in this volume.
4. Gray, *Centennial Campaign,* 320, calculates the number of hostile warriors involved in the 1876 summer campaign at 2,150.
5. Major Reno conducted his scout of the Powder and Rosebud Rivers from June 10 to 19.
6. William H. Low (d. 1886), of the West Point Class of 1872.
7. Thomas M. McDougall (1845–1909) was commissioned a second lieutenant of the 48th U.S. Colored Infantry in February 1864. After the Civil War, he earned a commission as a second lieutenant in the 14th U.S. Infantry. McDougall joined the 7th Cavalry in December 1870. He was retired for disability in 1890.
8. Donald McIntosh (1838–76) was a younger brother of the noted scout Archie McIntosh. He entered the army as a second lieutenant in August 1867.
9. Benjamin H. Hodgson (1848–76) of the West Point Class of 1870.

10. The story of Reno firing his pistol blindly at the distant foe may have been apocryphal; it was told by Lieutenant Edgerly at the Reno Court of Inquiry.
11. Also dead near the river was Dr. James DeWolf.
12. The nature of Curley's escape has been the source of much debate. Only in recent years have scholars come to credit his assertion of having been at Custer's side all the way to Calhoun Hill. See in particular Sklenar, *To Hell with Honor,* 281–86, and John S. Gray, *Custer's Last Campaign, Mitch Boyer and the Little Bighorn Reconstructed* (Lincoln: University of Nebraska Press, 1991), x–xi, 372–82.
13. King is mistaken; DeWolf was with Reno's column and fell in the retreat across the Little Bighorn.
14. Mark H. Kellogg (1833–76) became assistant editor of the Bismarck *Tribune* in 1873. He worked as the foreman of a hay camp near Bismarck the following year.
15. Comanche died on November 6, 1891, at the age of twenty-eight. He presently stands on display at Dyche Hall on the campus of the University of Kansas at Lawrence.
16. As an elder chief and spiritual leader, it was the place of Sitting Bull to remain in the village and protect the women and children from harm while the younger war chiefs directed the fight against the 7th Cavalry; there was nothing shameful in that.

Charles A. Eastman: The Indian Version of Custer's Last Battle

1. Charles A. Eastman (1858–1939) was the son of Many Lightnings, a full-blooded Santee Sioux. His mother, the half-blood daughter of an army officer, died soon after childbirth, and Eastman was raised by an uncle, who, after the 1862 Sioux uprising, left Minnesota. When they returned to the states eleven years later, Eastman went to school at his uncle's insistence, graduating from Dartmouth College and the Boston University School of Medicine. As the government physician at the Pine Ridge agency he treated victims of the Wounded Knee massacre of 1890. Dr. Eastman later entered practice at St. Paul, Minnesota, and for a time was traveling secretary of the Young Men's Christian Association among the Indians. He devoted much of his life to bettering the conditions of Native Americans and researching and writing about their history. He was active in the Boy Scouts and Campfire Girls of America and was appointed U.S. Indian inspector in 1920.

    Eastman's remarkable account of the Little Bighorn was drawn from interviews with Sioux and Cheyenne participants. It is of the first importance; as the historian John M. Carroll observed, the "versions as told to him, another Indian, are far more reliable than those told to non-Indian historians." The early Custer scholar, Fred Dustin, failed to recognize the worth of Eastman's narrative, saying merely that it was "of some value as checking white men's stories of the battle." John M. Carroll, *Custer in Periodicals* (Fort Collins, CO: Old Army Press, 1975), 14.
2. Edward S. Godfrey, "Custer's Last Battle," *Century Magazine* 43, no. 3 (January 1892). This article was reprinted many times. Brig. Gen. James B. Fry's comments on the article appeared in the same issue.
3. In the summer of 1850, a regular expedition under Capt. Nathaniel Lyon attacked four hundred Clear Lake Indians on an island on the northern California lake of the same name, killing nearly 150.
4. Historian John Gray, who made a careful study of available sources concerning the hostile population, reached a conclusion similar to that of Eastman. Gray placed the number of lodges at 1,000, and the number of adult males at 1,780. Gray, *Centennial Campaign,* 356.
5. Hamlin Garland, "Custer's Last Fight as Seen by Two Moon," *McClure's Magazine* 11, no. 5 (September 1898), reprinted in Graham, *Custer Myth,* 101–103.

6. A probable reference to Major Reno's departure from the skirmish line with G Troop, which he took into the timber, ostensibly to attack the hostile village. Sklenar, *To Hell with Honor*, 177–78.
7. Probably a reference to A Troop, which Captain Moylan tried to shift to the right to fill in the gap on the skirmish line that G Troop's departure had opened. Instead, Moylan's troop gradually melted into the timber in disorder. The remainder of the skirmish line unraveled in short order. Ibid., 180–86.
8. Here Eastman relates the confused retreat of Reno's battalion across the Little Bighorn. Reno led A Troop and part of G Troop out of the timber first; the remainder of G Troop and M Troop came out on their own and lost heavily. Ibid., 242–52.
9. E and F Troops under Capt. George W. Yates.
10. E and F Troops on Last Stand Hill; I Troop and one platoon of C Troop along what is known as the Keogh Sector of Custer Ridge; L Troop on Calhoun Hill and one platoon of C Troop on nearby Finley Ridge.
11. L Troop and Harrington's platoon of C Troop.

Theodore W. Goldin: On The Little Bighorn with General Custer

1. Theodore W. Goldin (1858–1935) was born in Wisconsin and adopted by Reuben W. and Elizabeth Goldin. His birth name is unknown. On April 8, 1876, seventeen-year-old Goldin enlisted in the army, claiming his age as twenty-one. He was assigned as a clerk to Company G, 7th Cavalry. His parents appealed Goldin's fraudulent enlistment, and he was discharged from the army on November 13, 1877. Returning to Wisconsin, Goldin resumed his schooling, and in 1882, he was admitted to the state bar and also elected clerk of the circuit court of Green County. From 1882–85 he also served as assistant chief clerk of the Wisconsin Assembly. He moved to Janesville in 1885 and became a partner in a highly successful law firm. Before the age of thirty-one, he was appointed a colonel in the Wisconsin National Guard. In 1896, Goldin was awarded the Medal of Honor for having been part of at least one detail that brought water from the Little Bighorn River to the wounded on Reno Hill during the battle of June 25–26. After the death of his wife in 1911, Goldin is said to have gone "all to pieces." He moved about the Southwest, working for a short time for the Mexican Northwestern Railroad. In 1924, Goldin suffered a stroke. He returned to Wisconsin and retired to the Masonic Home in Dousman. By 1929, he was afflicted with poor eyesight, impaired circulation, and neuritis. Nonetheless, he maintained a vigorous correspondence with several Custer historians, among them W. J. Ghent and E. A. Brininstool. The foregoing sketch of Goldin's life is drawn from Larry Sklenar, "Theodore W. Goldin: Little Big Horn Survivor and Winner of the Medal of Honor," *Wisconsin Magazine of History* 6 (1996–97): 106–23.
2. The original issues of *Army Magazine* being unobtainable, I have relied for the text of Goldin's article on John M. Carroll, *Custer in Periodicals* (N.p., 1975), 98–114.
3. John Martin (1853–1922), born Giovanni Martini in Italy, emigrated to the United States in 1873 and enlisted in the army the following year. On June 25, 1876, he was detailed as an orderly to Colonel Custer. Martin remained in the service until 1904, when he retired a sergeant.
4. Custer fell out of favor with President Grant for his hostile testimony before a congressional impeachment hearing against Secretary of War William W. Belknap. Grant first deprived Custer of his command, then forbade him even to accompany the upcoming summer 1876 expedition against the Sioux and Cheyennes. Grant relented in the face of bad press and protests, and Custer resumed command of the 7th Cavalry.

5. Opinions of Custer among the rank and file of the 7th were decidedly mixed. While most admired his courage, many also considered him to be a martinet.
6. The 7th Cavalry went into camp on the east bank of the Little Missouri River at 9 A.M. on May 30, 1876.
7. Upwards of 120 men were left at the Yellowstone depot for lack of mounts.
8. These were warriors killed in the battle of the Rosebud on June 17.
9. The conference apparently began at 2 P.M. and concluded before 4 P.M. Gray, *Custer's Last Campaign*, 202.
10. Gray, *Custer's Last Campaign*, 205, calculates that the 7th Cavalry marched twelve miles on June 22.
11. Gray, *Custer's Last Campaign*, 205, calculates that the 7th Cavalry marched thirty-three miles on June 23.
12. After what Gray, *Centennial Campaign*, 228, calculates to have been a seven-mile march, the 7th Cavalry halted at 3:30 A.M.—dawn broke early in the Northern Plains summer—on June 25 at the point where Davis Creek connects with the Rosebud.
13. The 7th Cavalry halted on Davis Creek after a march of just under four miles. After an officers' call, at which Custer determined to attack the hostile village on the Little Bighorn, the regiment resumed the march at 11:45 A. M. Gray, *Centennial Campaign*, 228.
14. Goldin presumably obtained this interpretation of Custer's instructions to Benteen from Benteen himself in the course of their extensive correspondence, which has been published as John M. Carroll, *The Benteen-Goldin Letters on Custer and His Last Battle* (New York: Liveright, 1974).
15. Custer swung clear of Reno and out of sight near a point known as the Flat, two and three-quarter miles west of the Lone Tepee.
16. Did Goldin take a message to Reno? Judging Goldin largely by his confused and semifictitious accounts of the battle offered in correspondence in his declining years, and from a blatantly manufactured account he wrote in a letter to Cyrus T. Brady in 1904, Custer historians Walter A. Graham and W. J. Ghent say no—emphatically. Graham (*Custer Myth*, 267–78) buttressed his opinion with statements from Colonel Varnum and Trumpeter Martin, declaring that they were unaware of Goldin having borne any message from Custer.

   I disagree. Whether Goldin delivered the message to Reno at the moment he said he did, it seems entirely plausible that he would have been entrusted with such a duty. And whatever lies and half-truths Goldin later told about himself and the Little Bighorn, his account in *Army Magazine* is well written, modest in tone, and otherwise in accord with known facts of the battle. Benteen read Goldin's draft of the articles, and while he was unquestionably anxious to portray Custer in as unfavorable a light as possible, it is unlikely he would have condoned Goldin's fabricating a story about a final message to Reno.

   Little Bighorn historian Larry Sklenar undertook an exhaustive look at the known evidence on Goldin's life and carefully reviewed his accounts of the battle, particularly the 1894 *Army Magazine* articles. Finding myself in accord with most of his conclusions about Goldin's "last message" from Custer (Sklenar, "Theodore W. Goldin," 113–14), I repeat them here verbatim. However, Sklenar believes that Goldin did not deliver his message until after the retreat to Reno Hill; I am less in accord with that conclusion.

   > It may be tempting to dismiss the story as just more of the same from a long line of "last survivors," those imposters and pretenders who usually surface well after the fact, when there is no one left to challenge their claims; but in Goldin's case, he made the statement

while Reno, Moylan, and other officers and men who might contest his account were still living. Additionally, and more importantly, it made sense—indeed it was mandatory—for Custer to send a message to Reno in response to the two he had received from his subordinate. That Goldin was chosen to carry such a message is also plausible, it being his contention that as a clerk with the headquarters command, he had been detailed to serve as orderly with the general's adjutant, Lieutenant Cooke, who was the conduit between Custer and the components of the regiment. Goldin was at least a competent horseman. [And, I would add, a bright and energetic young man, as his rapid rise in the civilian world after his army discharge demonstrated; precisely the type of soldier to deliver an important dispatch.] Lastly, when all of Goldin's accounts are analyzed, he cannot be positively located with any other element, including his own G Troop, which was riding with Reno. After a thorough examination of all available source material I [Sklenar] have concluded that Goldin did carry such a message from Custer, he failed to deliver it as described in any of his accounts because, by the time he would have reached Reno's command, it was virtually surrounded by very angry Indians.

17. Several survivors of Reno's command recalled having seen Custer silhouetted briefly on the high ground across the river.
18. John Aspinwall (d. 1881) of the West Point Class of 1869; he was dropped from army rolls in July 1874.
19. The identity of the trooper who tried to help Hodgson was never determined. Two eyewitnesses said that Hodgson was standing in the river when Trumpeter Charles Fischer of M Troop drew rein and offered him a stirrup; another said that Hodgson and Pvt. John Meier of M Troop had both lunged after a loose horse, Meier mounting it, and Hodgson grabbing a stirrup for the crossing. Sklenar, *To Hell with Honor,* 255.
20. Scout George B. Herendeen (1846–1919) was detached from Gibbon's column to Custer's command on June 22.
21. However, several packs came loose and were cut free to save time.
22. A probable reference to Captain Moylan, whom numerous eyewitnesses accused of having hid among the pack animals during the fighting on Reno Hill. Goldin himself said in a July 8, 1886, letter to the Janesville (Wisconsin) *Daily Gazette* that the men called Moylan "hardtack Mick" because he cowered behind the bacon and hardtack boxes until the night of June 26. Sklenar, *To Hell with Honor,* 318.
23. Benteen may have concocted the story that Reno intended to abandon the wounded. Sklenar, *To Hell with Honor,* 314–15.

John Silversten: Reminiscences of the Reno Fight
1. John Silversten was a member of Troop M, 7th Cavalry at the Little Bighorn. Col. Henry Hall visited him at the National Soldier's Home in Washington, D. C. in 1916 and recorded his experiences, as presented here.
2. Charles White of M Troop was wounded in the early stages of the fight, while coming off the skirmish line.
3. Here Silversten's narrative is somewhat misleading. DeRudio did not cross the Little Big Horn and ascend the bluffs with Silversten and his comrades. DeRudio and Pvt. Thomas O'Neil became separated from the others and remained in hiding on a small island in the river until the afternoon of June 26.

Edward S. Godfrey: Captain Benteen's Command
1. Edward S. Godfrey (1843–1932) enlisted in the 21st Ohio Volunteer Infantry in 1861. He received an appointment to the Military Academy in 1863 and graduated with the West Point Class of 1867. He was commissioned a second lieutenant in the newly formed 7th Cavalry and participated in all the regiment's campaigns through Wounded Knee. Godfrey retired a brigadier general in 1907. His writings on the Little Bighorn—particularly his "Custer's Last Battle," which first appeared in the January 1892 issue of *Century Magazine* and has been reprinted many times—are among the most consulted primary accounts on the subject. His letter from the field reproduced here represents his first written comments on the fight and has not been reprinted previously.
2. It is odd that Godfrey would say Weir had been sent to look for Custer. Historians agree that Weir had a bitter quarrel with Reno while trying to persuade the major to go to Custer's relief. Having failed at that, Weir rode off without—and perhaps in defiance to—orders to an elevation a mile from Reno Hill. Godfrey related the episode in "Custer's Last Battle" as follows: "Captain Weir and Lieutenant Edgarly, after driving the Indians away from Reno's command on their side, heard the firing, became impatient at the delay, and thought they would move down that way, if they should be permitted. Weir started to get this permission, but changed his mind and concluded to take a survey from the high bluffs first." Graham, *Custer Myth*, 142.

Frederick Schwatka: With Crook's Expedition
1. Wesley Merritt (1834–1910), of the West Point Class of 1860, rose to the rank of major general of volunteers during the Civil War. He became lieutenant colonel of the 9th Cavalry in 1866 and rose to the rank of major general in the Regular army. In 1898, he commanded the expedition to the Philippines and captured Manila.
2. Louis Richard (c. 1846–97) worked on his father's tollbridge over the Platte River before hiring on as an army scout.
3. William F. "Buffalo Bill" Cody (1846–1917), Pony Express rider, plainsman, and famed showman, began his army scouting career in 1862 for Kansas volunteers operating on the Santa Fe Trail.
4. Not found.
5. For a biographical sketch of Nelson A. Miles, see his "Rounding Up the Red Men," elsewhere in this volume.
6. The main hostile village had encamped on July 27 at the spot where Crook's and Terry's commands turned east.
7. Schwatka neglected to mention that the temperature hovered near the 105-degree mark throughout the day. Jerome A. Greene, *Slim Buttes, 1876: An Episode of the Great Sioux War* (Norman: University of Oklahoma Press, 1982), 26.
8. I have omitted Schwatka's lengthy description of the Sun Dance ritual.
9. The smoke seen in the valleys of the Tongue and Powder Rivers could only have been that of small hunting or war parties, as the main Indian village had moved eastward, beyond the northern reaches of the Powder River, on August 5, splitting into smaller bands as it went.
10. Emmet Crawford (1844–86) enlisted in the 71st Pennsylvania Infantry Volunteers in 1861 and was commissioned a first lieutenant in a black regiment three years later. One of Crook's favorite—and most capable—subordinates, he was killed by Mexican irregulars during the 1885 Geronimo campaign.
11. John W. "Captain Jack" Crawford (1847–1917) was an Irish immigrant and Civil War veteran who drifted into the Black Hills after the Custer expedition of 1874.

He became a rancher and popular writer, authoring three plays and more than a hundred short stories.
12. John J. Upham (d. 1898), of the West Point Class of 1859. He retired a colonel in 1892.

Andrew S. Burt: Dispatches from Crook's Column

1. Andrew S. Burt began his military career at the outbreak of the Civil War as a private in the 6th Ohio Volunteer Infantry. He ended the conflict a captain in the 18th U.S. Infantry with two brevets. Burt retired a brigadier general in April 1902.
2. For a biographical sketch of Nelson A. Miles, see his "Rounding Up the Red Men," elsewhere in this volume.
3. Another instance of the army badly exaggerating the strength of the Indian attackers at the Rosebud, who numbered between 850 and 1,500.
4. Not found.
5. More importantly for the Shoshones, it was annuity time at their agency.
6. A reference to a pamphlet entitled *Our Barren Lands; the Interior of the United States West of the One Hundredth Meridian and East of the Sierra Nevadas* (Cincinnati: R. Clarke Printers, 1875) which William B. Hazen authored to spread his view that the Great Plains were uniformly arid and uninhabitable.
7. Two officers—Captain Munson and Lieutenant Bourke—dragged the woman and the children to safety.

John G. Bourke: The Battle of Slim Buttes

1. John G. Bourke (1846–96) enlisted in the Union army at age sixteen, winning a Medal of Honor at the battle of Stones River. After the Civil War, he attended West Point and was commissioned in the 3rd U.S. Cavalry. Bourke joined General Crook's staff when the latter took command of the Department of Arizona in 1871 and served with him for the better part of the next fifteen years. A dedicated ethnologist and meticulous observer, Bourke published widely on the Indians with whom he came into contact. He also authored several invaluable historical works, the most noteworthy of which is the classic *On the Border with Crook*.
2. William Philo Clark (1845–84), of the West Point Class of 1868, was called by General Terry "one of the best officers of his grade in the army." He died suddenly while in Washington, D.C. on special duty with General Sheridan, a loss lamented within the army. Thrapp, *Encyclopedia*, 1:278–79.
3. Jonathan White (c. 1841–76) had fought with the Confederate cavalry leader "Jeb" Stuart during the Civil War. Charles King wrote of him that "a simpler-minded, gentler frontiersman never lived. He was modesty and courtesy itself." And King disputed Bourke's labeling of him as a liar, saying he "never heard him swear, and no man ever heard him lie." Ibid., 4:1552.
4. Pvt. John M. Stevenson, Company I, 2nd Cavalry.
5. Samuel Munson (d. 1887) rose from the ranks during the Civil War and was commissioned a captain in the 9th Infantry in September 1865.
6. American Horse had been shot in the abdomen, and his bowels spilled into his clutched hands as he walked toward General Crook.
7. Daniel W. Burke (1841–1911) enlisted in the 2nd U.S. Infantry in 1858, rising to the rank of brigadier general in 1899.
8. Alfred B. Bache (d. 1876) was appointed a second lieutenant in the 5th Cavalry from civilian life in 1867. He died in November 1876 of chronic rheumatism.

John F. Finerty: The Fellows in Feathers:
An Interview with General Crook

1. John F. Finerty (1846–1908) came to the United States from Ireland in 1864 and enlisted in the 94th New York Infantry. After the war, he became a Chicago newspaperman. His dispatches to the Chicago *Times* on the Sioux War formed the basis of his well-regarded book, *War-Path and Bivouac*. Finerty traveled to Mexico in 1878, becoming the first American newspaperman to interview President Porfirio Diaz. He served as a member of Congress from 1883 to 1885.
2. Crook badly exaggerated the number of warriors he had confronted at the Rosebud. In his well-documented study, *Centennial Campaign,* 318–20, historian John Gray calculated the number of hostile warriors to have been 2,150, of whom he estimated 850 participated in the battle of the Rosebud. Other historians have placed the number closer to 1,500.
3. Crook was among the few who believed he had thrashed the Indians.
4. James S. Hastings had assumed the duties of agent at the Red Cloud agency in late 1875. He first encountered Crook's displeasure during the Powder River expedition of March 1876, when he denied the general's charges that arms, ammunition, or supplies had found their way to the hostile camps, or that few if any of his Indians had been with the roaming northern Sioux during the winter. Despite convincing evidence to the contrary, Hastings similarly denied that his charges had participated in the summer campaign against the army. Responding to army pressure, on July 18, 1876, the commissioner of Indian Affairs dismissed Hastings. James S. Olson, *Red Cloud and the Sioux Problem* (Lincoln: University of Nebraska Press, 1965), 216–23.
5. The Sitting Bull here referred to is not the famous Hunkpapa medicine man, but rather an Oglala leader who spoke and wrote fluent English. He took part in the Fetterman fight but later settled with Red Cloud on the agency. He traveled twice to Washington, D.C. On his second visit, in the spring of 1875, he was presented with a Winchester carbine, engraved as a gift from the president in remembrance of previous aid he had given the army. He was ambushed by a war party of Crows and killed while returning from a peace mission to Crazy Horse in December 1876.
6. Perhaps not overt opposition, but there was considerable worry about the advisability of the move. Captain Munson of the 9th Infantry complained to Lieutenant Bourke at the outset of the march that "there was much solicitude among officers and men to know what General Crook's purposes were." And the loyal aide Bourke himself confessed to his diary that he "shared to a considerable extent Captain Munson's apprehensions, as it was certainly a gloomy prospect to have an expedition of two thousand men left without rations in the midst of the desert." Gray, *Centennial Campaign,* 244.
7. A reference to Reuben H. Davenport, whose reporting throughout the summer campaign had been critical of Crook.
8. That Crook fared little or no better than his men is borne out by Bourke's diary entry for September 8 (Bourke Diary 8:864, 890):

> Horse meat has now become our staple food; as one of our mess pithily remarked, "The steaks we munch have a horse or a mule shoe at one end of them." . . . General Crook celebrated his birthday this evening. He drew out from the breast pocket of his coat a pint flask of whiskey, which he had concealed there the day before we left the Yellowstone, and passing it around to the members of his mess and the other officers present, called upon them to drink to his health. There were thirteen or fourteen in the group, and the flask

held a little shot of sixteen ounces, making just a taste for each one. Then those of us who had pieces of cracker in their pockets ate them; those who had none went without. Take it for all in all, it was decidedly the thinnest birthday celebration I have ever attended.

9. Finerty's question to Crook about Davenport had been a journalistic lob. Both Finerty and Joe Wasson, who were close to Crook, ridiculed Davenport in their own dispatches. Said Finerty of Davenport's uncomplimentary version of the battle of the Rosebud: "A flashy New York sheet calls for his [Crook's] removal because he did not please that paper's reporter on the day of the Rosebud. The *Herald*'s warrior must have been awfully excited if he calls the Rosebud a defeat." Knight, *Following the Indian Wars*, 243–44. In his own report, Finerty characterized the battle as a draw.
10. Convinced that Red Cloud was sympathetic to the hostiles, on the night of October 22 Crook sent Col. Ranald Mackenzie with eight companies of cavalry from Camp Robinson to Red Cloud's camp on Chadron Creek, about thirty miles from the agency, and disarmed them at dawn of the twenty-third without incident.
11. Red Cloud was incredulous that Crook had replaced him as chief of the agency Oglala with his rival Spotted Tail, who was a Brule. "What have I done," he purportedly asked, "that I should receive such treatment from him whom I thought my friend?" Olson, *Red Cloud,* 233.
12. Little Wound had been considered a protégé of Red Cloud after the latter elevated him to a subchieftaincy upon signing the Treaty of 1868—to the extent that any chief could "appoint" a leader in a warrior society in which leadership was based upon merit and consent of the tribe. Little Wound, however, sometimes acted contrary to Red Cloud's desires, as his support for Spotted Tail demonstrated. Olson, *Red Cloud,* 21.

Charles S. Diehl: Terry's Tribulations

1. Charles S. Diehl (1854–1946) began his newspaper career as a newsboy in Ottawa, Illinois, at the age of nine. After five years apprenticing in print shops, Diehl joined the reportorial staff of the Chicago *Times*. He was chosen to replace Mark Kellogg, killed with Custer at the Little Bighorn, as the *Times* correspondent on the Sioux campaign. Diehl subsequently enjoyed a distinguished career as a journalist, becoming assistant general manager of Associated Press in 1887. From 1911 until 1924, he published the San Antonio (Texas) *Light*. Diehl's *The Staff Correspondent: How the News of the World Is Collected and Dispatched by a Body of Trained Press Writers* (San Antonio: Clegg Company, 1931) tells of his varied newspaper experiences, from the western frontier to Revolutionary Mexico.
2. William B. Hazen (1830–87), of the West Point Class of 1855, saw antebellum service in the Pacific Northwest and Texas. He was severely wounded in a fight with the Comanches in 1859. Hazen emerged from the Civil War a major general of volunteers. In 1880, he was appointed chief signal officer of the army, with the staff rank of brigadier general, a post he held until his death.
3. William W. Belknap (1829–90), a brigadier general of volunteers during the Civil War, was impeached by the House of Representatives in March 1876 for having extorted $24,000 from the post trader at Fort Sill in exchange for immunity from removal. Belknap resigned before the Senate could take action on the impeachment.
4. Elwell S. Otis (1838–1909), a Maryland lawyer, rose to the volunteer rank of lieutenant colonel during the Civil War. He became lieutenant colonel of the 22nd U.S.

Infantry in 1866 and served on the frontier until 1881. He established the United States Infantry and Cavalry School at Fort Leavenworth and commanded all American forces in the Philippines from 1899 to 1902, when he retired a major general in the Regular army.
5. The skirmish occurred on July 29, 1876. The *Chronological List,* 62, lists one enlisted man as having been wounded in the encounter, and none killed.
6. Gray, *Centennial Campaign,* 224–28, concluded that the trail, which was that of the main hostile camp, was nearly two weeks old.
7. Joseph N. A. Whistler (d. 1899), of the West Point Class of 1846, fought in the Mexican War and the Civil War, emerging from the latter conflict a colonel of volunteers and a major in the Regular army. He retired a colonel in 1886.
8. During the fight, Diehl grabbed a rifle and joined in the fray until Captain Weston reprimanded him, saying, "Come out of that. You're not paid to get killed. We are." Clifford Hicks, "Charles Sanford Diehl's Coverage of the Indian Wars," 1, 3, unpublished manuscript in the Elmo S. Watson Papers, Ayers Collection, Newberry Library, Chicago.
9. Edmund Rice served as lieutenant colonel of the 19th Massachusetts Volunteer Infantry during the Civil War. He was commissioned a first lieutenant in the 40th U.S. Infantry in 1866 and was promoted to the rank of colonel of the 19th Infantry in 1902.
10. Edward Ball (d. 1884) began his military career under an assumed name as a private in the 4th U.S. Infantry in 1844. He retired a major in the 7th Cavalry in 1884.
11. Gray, *Centennial Campaign,* 356, concludes that there were no more than twenty-five Yanktonai warriors among the hostiles during or after the Little Bighorn campaign.
12. Diehl's estimate of Reno's scout, certainly obtained from conversations with Terry's staff, does the hapless major a disservice. Terry had ordered Reno to scout the Powder and Tongue Rivers, to be followed by a two-pronged offensive aimed at trapping the main hostile village on the lower Rosebud between Gibbon's command and that of Custer. The trouble was, the Indians were farther to the west, along the Little Bighorn River. In violating his orders and following the hitherto undiscovered trail in that direction, Reno took a reasonable course of action. And as John Gray observed, "Terry's claim that Reno's defiance had sabotaged his plan was a gross misrepresentation. The fact is, Terry's plan was doomed from the start. Reno's violation of orders led to securing the proof of the plan's futility. Reno thereby saved Terry from an ignominious wild goose chase, and at the same time handed him some intelligence upon which to build a better plan." Gray, *Centennial Campaign,* 126–37.
13. I have omitted Diehl's concluding dispatch, which appeared in the September 20, 1876, Chicago *Times.* It was largely a summation of all that he had written in preceding articles.

PART SIX: THE WINTER CAMPAIGN OF 1876–77

Jerry Roche: The Dull Knife Fight
1. John G. Bourke remembered Jerry Roche as "a companionable, scholarly gentleman, who has since abandoned journalism and become possessed of considerable means in Texas." Knight, *Following the Indian Wars,* 290.
2. It had been snowing for a week or more, and the temperature was far below freezing. Jerome A. Greene, ed., *Battles and Skirmishes of the Great Sioux War, 1876–1877: The Military View* (Norman: University of Oklahoma Press, 1993), 174.

3. George A. Gordon (d. 1886), of the West Point Class of 1854.
4. Clarence Mauck (d. 1881) began his army career as a second lieutenant in the 1st U.S. Cavalry in March 1861.
5. Joseph H. Dorst, of the West Point Class of 1873. He was still on active duty as colonel of the 3rd Cavalry in 1903.
6. Hayden DeLany (d. 1890) began his army career as a private in the 30th Ohio Volunteer Infantry in December 1861. He was commissioned a second lieutenant in the 9th Infantry in 1867 after two years at West Point.
7. Walter S. Schuyler, of the West Point Class of 1870, saw wide service in Arizona and on the Northern Plains. He also served in the Philippine Insurrection as colonel of the 45th U.S. Volunteer Infantry.
8. The headwaters of the North Fork of the Powder River.
9. John A. McKinney, of the West Point Class of 1871.
10. John M. Hamilton (d. 1898) entered the army as a private in the 33rd New York Volunteer Infantry in 1861. He was killed at the battle of San Juan, Santiago, Cuba, during the Spanish-American War.
11. Harrison G. Otis, of the West Point Class of 1870. He resigned his commission in 1881.
12. Alfred B. Taylor entered the army as a private in the 22nd New York State Militia in 1862. He was commissioned a second lieutenant in the 5th U.S. Cavalry in October 1863.
13. Wirt Davis (1839–1914) enlisted in the Union army as a private in the 1st Cavalry in May 1860. He rose steadily through the ranks, retiring as a brigadier general in 1904.
14. This figure is also given in the *Chronological List,* 63.
15. James N. Allison, of the West Point Class of 1871.

Nelson A. Miles: Rounding up the Red Men

1. Nelson A. Miles (1839–1925) was a volunteer officer who was four times wounded during the Civil War and emerged from the conflict a major general of volunteers. Appointed colonel of the 5th U.S. Infantry in 1869, he saw service in the Red River War of 1874 and the Great Sioux War. He captured Chief Joseph of the Nez Perce in 1877. An unpleasant self-promoter of inordinate ambition, Miles become commander-in-chief of the army in 1895.
2. Luther S. Kelly (1849–1928) enlisted in the 10th New York Volunteer Infantry in the waning days of the Civil War and served out his enlistment in the Dakota Territory. He remained in the region, trapping, hunting, and serving occasionally as a dispatch courier. He began his army scouting career in 1873 and was chief scout for Miles from 1876 to 1878. Afterward, he was a War Department clerk. In 1898 and 1899, he guided exploring expeditions in Alaska. As a captain of volunteers, he saw action in the Philippines, then served as agent of the San Carlos Apache Reservation before retiring to a fruit ranch in Pasadena, California, where he died.
3. Hobart K. Bailey was commissioned a second lieutenant in the 5th Infantry in 1872. He served again on General Miles's staff as aide-de-camp with the rank of lieutenant colonel from 1900 to 1901.
4. The Sioux camp was located on the East Fork of Cedar Creek.
5. For a biographical sketch of Frank D. Baldwin, see his "Winter Campaigning against Indians in Montana in 1876," elsewhere in this volume.
6. Baldwin attacked Sitting Bull's camp on Ash Creek, a tributary of the Big Dry River, on December 18, 1876, with three companies of the 5th Infantry
7. What Miles terms a warrior was a fourteen-year-old boy.

8. The hostiles yelled to the soldiers that they "would eat no more fat meats," which Miles interpreted as meaning the men had eaten their last breakfast. Jerome A. Greene, *Yellowstone Command: Colonel Nelson A. Miles and the Great Sioux War, 1876–1877* (Lincoln: University of Nebraska Press, 1991), 166.
9. Big Crow was a Cheyenne medicine man, not a chief.
10. The mixed delegation of Sioux and Northern Cheyenne chiefs that arrived at the Tongue River cantonment on February 19, 1877, included such notables as Hump, White Bull, Little Chief, and Two Moon.
11. Edward W. Casey (1850–91), of the West Point Class of 1891, and Lovell H. Jerome (d. 1935), of the West Point Class of 1866.
12. Miles's recollection is faulty. Lame Deer escaped in the confusion, only to be gunned down after running two hundred yards by a volley of gunfire from soldiers of Company L. Greene, *Yellowstone Command*, 210.

Frank D. Baldwin: Winter Campaigning against Indians in Montana in 1876

1. Frank D. Baldwin (1842–1923) was one of Miles's most trusted and able subordinates. He won the Medal of Honor during the Civil War and on the frontier during the Red River War. He served with distinction during the Philippine insurrections and retired a brigadier general.
2. Baldwin began the return march at 9 P.M. on December 7.
3. Baldwin was influenced in this decision by word he received from Indian agent Thomas J. Mitchell, who arrived at Fort Peck from the Wolf Point Indian Agency with Assiniboines, that Sitting Bull had gone to Redwater Creek after fleeing from Baldwin's troops four days earlier. Greene, *Yellowstone Command*, 139.
4. While at the Wolf Point agency, Baldwin replenished his supplies with flour, oats, and hams.
5. Baldwin's command was now moving along the valley of Ash Creek, a southeastwardly flowing tributary of the Redwater. Ibid., 141.
6. Ezra P. Ewers entered the army as a private in the 19th Infantry in January 1862. He saw service as a brigadier general of volunteers during the Spanish-American War and retired a lieutenant colonel in the Regular army in 1901.

Edwin Brown: Terror of the Badlands: The Sioux Expedition, Montana Territory, 1876 and 1877

1. This was a short distance below the mouth of the Powder River.
2. Joseph N. G. Whistler (1822–99), of the West Point Class of 1846, served in the Mexican War and the Civil War, earning a brevet to brigadier general of volunteers. He retired a colonel in 1886.
3. The Diamond R train was a civilian wagon train bearing supplies from Glendive, Montana, to the Tongue River cantonment.
4. On October 15, 1876, Lt. Col. Elwell S. Otis led an eighty-six-wagon train out of Glendive for the Tongue River cantonment with 185 men as escort. Near Spring Creek, he was attacked by a large Sioux war party under Sitting Bull. Otis continued his march, and a two-day skirmish ensued before the Sioux broke contact.
5. Seven miles east of Cedar Creek.
6. Brown may have been mistaken as to the sequence of events, as other sources identify the man as a herder, rather than the wagonmaster, and place the incident on October 24, one day before Miles met with the party of Indians that included the great Hunkpapa war chief Gall. That council lasted two days and, as Brown relates,

concluded with the promise of several Minneconjou and Sans Arc chiefs to surrender their people. Greene, *Yellowstone Command,* 106–8, 268n.
7. The hostages were the Minneconjous Red Skirt and White Bull the elder, and Sans Arc headmen Black Eagle, Sun Rose, and Foolish Thunder.
8. Fort Peck, Montana, was an agency for the Yanktonais, Assiniboines, and Gros Ventres.
9. Simon Snyder began his army career in 1861 as a lieutenant in the 5th U.S. Infantry. He retired a brigadier general in 1902.
10. Andrew S. Bennett (d. 1878) served as a lieutenant in the 5th Wisconsin Volunteer Infantry during the Civil War. He was commissioned a first lieutenant in the 15th U.S. Infantry in 1867 and transferred to the 5th Infantry in 1871. He was killed in action during the Bannock War.
11. On November 25, Miles ordered Captain Bennett to march his company to Carroll City, on the Missouri River, about twenty miles above the mouth of the Musselshell River, to seize ammunition that the trader there reportedly was selling to the hostiles. Ibid., 124–25.

David T. Mears: Campaigning against Crazy Horse

1. David T. Mears (1833–post-1903) was born in Pennsylvania. At age fifteen, he took up work on Ohio and Mississippi River steamboats. In 1856, he went to the Pacific coast, where he engaged in mining and freighting. He settled near Fort Niobrara, Nebraska, in 1880 and was one of the commissioners appointed to organize Cherry County. Mears served in various public offices, among them mayor of Chadron, police, judge, water commissioner, and justice of the peace.
2. Mears read his paper before the annual meeting of the Nebraska State Historical Society on January 14, 1903.
3. The village was Cheyenne, belonging to Chiefs Dull Knife and Little Wolf.

PART SEVEN: THE ODYSSEY OF THE NORTHERN CHEYENNES, 1871–90

George A. Woodward: Some Experiences with the Cheyennes

1. George A. Woodward began his military career in May 1861 as a captain in the 2nd Pennsylvania Reserves. He ended the Civil War a colonel of volunteers and was commissioned a lieutenant colonel in the 45th U.S. Infantry in July 1866. Woodward was transferred to the 14th Infantry in March 1869, becoming its colonel in January 1876. He retired in March 1879.
2. Little Wolf, or Ohkom Kakit (c. 1820–1904), was chief of the Bowstring Soldiers, a Northern Cheyenne tribal military society. He remained a "respected figure with an alert mind" until his death. Thrapp, *Encyclopedia,* 862–63.
3. Dull Knife, or Tash-me-la-pash-me (c. 1810–83), was a Northern Cheyenne chief who took part in the hostilities following the Sand Creek massacre of 1864 and subsequently signed the Fort Laramie Treaty. Dull Knife's warriors may have fought with the Sioux against Crook and Custer in 1876, but Dull Knife himself apparently was not involved.
4. Early reports that Dull Knife had been killed during the January 1879 Cheyenne breakout from Fort Roinson were incorrect.

Edgar B. Bronson: A Finish Fight for a Birthright

1. Edgar B. Bronson was a nephew of the famed abolitionist Henry Ward Beecher and cousin of Lt. Fred Beecher, who had been killed at the battle of Beecher Island in September 1868.
2. James S. Brisbin (d. 1892) began his army career as a second lieutenant in the 1st Dragoons in 1861. He earned brevets through major general of volunteers during the Civil War and died while on active duty as colonel of the 8th U.S. Cavalry.
3. Fort Reno, which stood on the North Fork of the Canadian River, about two miles from the Cheyenne and Arapaho Indian Agency, also known as the Darlington agency.
4. The followers of Dull Knife and Little Wolf who left the agency numbered 353, of whom only 60 or 70 were seasoned warriors. John A. Monnett, *Tell Them We Are Going Home: The Odyssey of the Northern Cheyennes* (Norman: University of Oklahoma Press, 2001), 43.
5. The commanding officer at Fort Reno was Maj. A. K. Mizner, who himself had been appalled at the scanty rations accorded the Cheyennes at the Darlington agency. Ibid., 32–33.
6. Capt. Joseph Rendlebrock led Troops G and K of the 4th Cavalry out of Fort Reno at 8:00 A.M. on September 9.
7. Brig. Gen. John Pope (1822–92) was commander of the Department of the Missouri.
8. William H. Lewis, of the West Point Class of 1849.
9. Thomas T. Thornburgh (d. 1879), of the West Point Class of 1867, was killed in action against the Utes in September 1879.
10. The fight in question, known as the Sand Creek skirmish, took place on September 22, not the eighteenth as Bronson records. Four troops of the 4th Cavalry under Captain Rendlebrock, two companies of the 16th U.S. Infantry from Fort Dodge, and some twenty cowboys from nearby ranches took part in the engagement. No casualties were reported in official channels. *Chronological List,* 68.
11. Better known as Punished Woman's Fork.
12. The *Chronological List,* 69, gives army losses as one enlisted man killed, one officer mortally wounded, and five enlisted men wounded.
13. Caleb H. Carlton (occasionally misspelled as Carleton), of the West Point Class of 1859. He retired a brigadier general in 1897.
14. George F. Chase, of the West Point Class of 1871.
15. Henry W. Wessells, Jr., attended the U.S. Naval Academy for two years before enlisting in the 7th U.S. Infantry in 1864. He retired a colonel in 1901.
16. Buffalo Hump was also known as Bull Hump.
17. Wild Hog was wrestled to the ground after stabbing Private Ferguson—who recovered from his wound—and placed in irons.
18. John Baxter, of the West Point Class of 1877.
19. Pvt. Frank Schmidt of A Troop, 3rd Cavalry.
20. Joseph F. Cummings, of the West Point Class of 1876. He was dismissed from the army in 1884.
21. James F. Simpson (d. 1899) began his army career as a second lieutenant in the 14th Connecticut Volunteer Infantry in 1862. He retired a captain in 1887.
22. The high ground was known as the Hat Creek Bluffs.
23. George A. Dodd, of the West Point Class of 1876.
24. Joseph Lawson (d. 1881) entered the service as a second lieutenant in the 11th Kentucky Volunteer Cavalry (U.S.) in 1862. He was commissioned a second lieutenant in the 3rd U.S. Cavalry in 1866.

Albert G. Forse: Across the Country with the Cheyennes

1. Albert G. Forse (1841–98) graduated with the West Point Class of 1865 and was commissioned a second lieutenant in Company E, 1st U.S. Cavalry. Except for two years of recruiting duty, Forse served in the West until the Spanish-American War. As a major of the 1st Cavalry, he was killed leading his squadron in the assault on San Juan Hill, Cuba.

PART EIGHT: THE DEATH OF CRAZY HORSE

Jesse M. Lee: The Capture and Death of an Indian Chieftain

1. Jesse M. Lee (1843–1926) began his distinguished military career in 1861 as a private in the 59th Indiana Volunteer Infantry. Commissioned a second lieutenant in the 39th U.S. Infantry in July 1866, Lee served as an Indian agent in Nevada from 1869 to 1870. Lee was an agent at Spotted Tail agency from 1877 to 1879; he and Chief Spotted Tail became good friends. Lee retired from the Regular army a major general in 1902. Interpreter Louis Bordeaux said Lee "was a sincere and warm friend of the Indians; had their highest good at heart; treated them upon the principle that they were men; trusted them; considered their claims and wishes, and yielded to them no doubt far beyond his instructions because he understood them and it was the better way." Richard G. Hardoff, *The Surrender and Death of Crazy Horse: A Source Book about a Tragic Episode in Lakota History* (Spokane: Arthur H. Clark Company, 1998), 103.
2. George M. Randall (1841–1918) was a superb officer and, like Jesse M. Lee, a friend of the Native American. He did good service as an Indian agent with both the Apaches and the Sioux. Randall commanded the scouts during the latter weeks of Crook's Bighorn and Yellowstone expedition in 1876 and was at Wounded Knee. He retired a major general in the Regular army in 1905.
3. Luther P. Bradley (1822–1910) began the Civil War as a lieutenant colonel in the 51st Illinois Volunteer Infantry and emerged from the struggle a brigadier general of volunteers. He was commissioned a lieutenant colonel of the 27th U.S. Infantry in 1866. Bradley served widely on the frontier and retired a colonel in 1886.
4. Touch-the-Clouds (c. 1837–1905), the son of Lone Horn, became a Minneconjou subchief upon his father's death in 1875. He may also have been related to the mother of Crazy Horse. Touch-the-Clouds was so named because of his remarkable height; he was said to have been seven feet tall.
5. Louis Bordeaux (1849–1917) was born near Fort Laramie, the son of William J. Bordeaux and a Brule woman. He was well educated and as an interpreter accompanied the first Sioux delegation to Washington in 1869. Later in life, he established a successful ranch in Todd County, South Dakota.
6. James Kennington (d. 1897) was an Irish immigrant who rose from the ranks. Known for blind devotion to duty, he retired a captain in 1887.
7. Little Big Man was an Oglala warrior and may also have been Crazy Horse's cousin.
8. Lee may have softened Kennington's actual language. According to Louis Bordeaux, Kennington screamed, "Stab the son of a bitch! Stab the son of a bitch!" Hardoff, *Crazy Horse,* 110.
9. A reference to Capt. Henry R. Lemly, whose "The Murder of Chief Crazy Horse" appears as the next article in this volume.

10. Apparently at the suggestion of Lieutenant Clark, on September 5 General Crook ordered Colonel Bradley to arrest Crazy Horse and send him under a strong escort to department headquarters at Omaha. Hardoff, *Crazy Horse,* 179–80.
11. Crazy Horse's father, the Oglala warrior Worm (c. 1811–81), was also known by the family name of Crazy Horse, which had been passed down from one generation to the next. After his son's death, Worm and his second wife settled among the Brules on the Rosebud reservation. Ibid., 56.
12. The woman with Worm was not Crazy's Horse's mother, Rattle Blanket Woman, who had committed suicide in 1844, but rather the old man's second wife, a sister of Spotted Tail.
13. Thomas B. Burrowes (d. 1885) of the 9th Infantry.

Henry R. Lemly and E. A. Brininstool: The Murder of Chief Crazy Horse

1. Henry R. Lemly, of the West Point Class of 1872, served with the 3rd Cavalry until 1898, when he was promoted to captain of the 7th Artillery. He retired in 1899.
2. Lieutenant Clark had reported to Crook repeatedly of Crazy Horse's intransigence. On August 18, he wrote Crook that he had "cultivated the friendship and confidence of all the northern Indians and Crazy Horse in particular and succeeded in getting on excellent 'dog-eating' terms with them and him, but it is impossible to work him through reasoning or kindness. Force," continued Clark, "is the only thing that will work out a good condition in this man's mind." Hardoff, *Crazy Horse,* 171–72.
3. Lemly apparently is mistaken as to the parentage of Helen Laravie, Crazy Horse's last wife. He Dog, a noted Oglala warrior and later a judge to the Pine Ridge Court of Indian Offenses, told Crazy Horse biographer Mari Sandoz that Helen Laravie was the son of a mixed-blood French trader named Joseph Laravie and a Southern Cheyenne woman. He Dog also said Helen Laravie was no relation to Louis Richard. Hardoff, *Crazy Horse,* 118.
4. Julius W. Mason (1837–82), a graduate of the Kentucky Military Institute, was commissioned a second lieutenant in the future 5th Cavalry at the outbreak of the Civil War. He served with that regiment until the end of the Sioux campaign of 1876, when he was transferred to the 3rd Cavalry.
5. Geronimo was not imprisoned at Fort Marion until 1886.
6. Lemly's letter was printed in the September 14, 1877, number of the New York *Sun* and is reproduced without attribution in Hardoff, *Crazy Horse,* 238–44.
7. I have omitted the opening paragraphs of Lemly's account, which consist merely of a summary of the Powder River and Little Bighorn campaigns. The signed account that Lemly sent Brininstool had been published previously as "The Passing of Crazy Horse," *Journal of the Military Service Institution of the United States* 54 (1914): 317–22.
8. Lemly is mistaken here. Crazy Horse did not accompany Sitting Bull into Canada.
9. Lemly's claim that Crazy Horse's incarceration was related to his marriage to Helen Laravie seems suspect—particularly as he misidentifies her father as Louis Richard—and is not borne out by other sources. On the other hand, Mari Sandoz speculated that Lt. Philo Clark was romantically involved with Helen Laravie, both before and after Crazy Horse's death. If this were true, and if Crazy Horse's dying words, as purportedly given to Lemly and Pourier, were true, then he might have believed his elopement with Laravie had so angered Clark, or Helen's father, as to be the proximate cause of his arrest. This is an intriguing possibility. I think that Hardoff, *Crazy Horse,* 30, is too dismissive of Sandoz's claim.

Valentine T. McGillycuddy: The Death of Crazy Horse

1. Valentine T. McGillycuddy (1849–1939) was a multitalented man who served as a topographer on the U.S. Boundary Survey in 1874 and later as an army surgeon. He was the first mayor of Rapid City, South Dakota, and a pioneer president of the South Dakota School of Mines. McGillycuddy was named agent for the Oglala Sioux in 1879, a post he held until 1886.
2. During the 1920s, Dr. McGillycuddy also corresponded with the western historian E. A Brininstool and with fellow participant William Garnett about the death of Crazy Horse. McGillycuddy's correspondence with Garnett can be found in Robert A. Clark, ed., *The Killing of Chief Crazy Horse* (Lincoln: University of Nebraska Press, 1988), 107–36.
3. Other accounts say Crazy Horse rode his horse.
4. American Horse (c.1840–1908) was an Oglala chief who had participated in the Fetterman fight in 1866 and later accompanied Red Cloud to Washington, D.C., on several occasions. He also toured with Buffalo Bill's Wild West Show. American Horse died of natural causes at the Pine Ridge agency.

PART NINE: THE GHOST DANCE AND WOUNDED KNEE, 1890–91

George Sword: The Story of the Ghost Dance

1. Capt. George Sword was the highly capable head of the Pine Ridge Indian police force. He wrote his account of the Ghost Dance in his native Oglala. Emma Sickels, a schoolmaster at Pine Ridge, translated the account. Sword was a convert to Christianity who became a deacon in the church. As he later said of himself, "When I believed the Oglala Wakan Tanka was right I served him with all my powers. In war with the white people I found their Wakan Tanka the superior. I then took the name of Sword and have served Wakan Tanka according to the white people's manner with all my power." Robert M. Utley, *The Last Days of the Sioux Nation* (New Haven, CT: Yale University Press, 1963), 34.
2. In the fall of 1889, the Oglalas of the Pine Ridge Indian Agency held a council to discuss the rumors of the Messiah. Similar councils were held at the Rosebud and Cheyenne River agencies. As emissaries to the purported Messiah, the Pine Ridge council selected Good Thunder, Yellow Breast, Flat Iron, Broken Arm, Cloud Horse, Yellow Knife, Elk Horn, and Kicks Back. Short Bull and Mash-the-Kettle represented the Rosebud council, and Kicking Bear went on behalf of the Cheyenne River council. Utley, *Last Days,* 60–61.
3. The Messiah was a Paiute named Wovoka (c. 1856–1932), who had been raised with the family of a white rancher named David Wilson, who named him Jack Wilson. Wovoka was friendly to the whites and preached a nonviolent creed of Native American revival. In 1887, he claimed to have had a vision of passing "up to the other world." There he met God, who told him to return to earth and teach his people to love one another, live in peace with the whites, and work hard to better themselves. The belligerent turn given his teachings as they traveled east to the Sioux, culminating in the Wounded Knee tragedy, was said to have depressed Wovoka greatly.
4. In the spring of 1890, the agent at Pine Ridge, Hugh D. Gallagher, summoned Good Thunder and two others and interrogated them about the Ghost Dance. When they refused to answer, he locked them in jail.
5. An apparent reference to William T. Selwyn, the postmaster at Pine Ridge.
6. Kicking Bear was a forty-one-year-old Oglala mystic and medicine man who had ridden with Crazy Horse during the Great Sioux War. He was uncompromising in his hatred of the whites. Utley, *Last Days,* 62.

Lloyd S. McCormick: The Wounded Knee and Drexel Mission Fights

1. Lloyd S. McCormick, of the West Point Class of 1876, was commissioned a second lieutenant in the 10th Cavalry upon graduation but transferred to the 7th Cavalry eleven days later, on June 26, 1876, the day after the battle of the Little Bighorn.
2. McCormick wrote this account in December 1904, while stationed at Fort Leavenworth, Kansas.
3. The agent at Pine Ridge, Daniel F. Royer, was placed in charge of Pine Ridge on October 9, 1890, as a consequence of political patronage, replacing the experienced and competent Hugh Gallagher. Royer knew nothing about Indians and was so visibly fearful of them that the Oglalas dubbed him "Young-Man-Afraid-of-Indians."
4. John R. Brooke entered the army as a captain of the 4th Pennsylvania Volunteer Infantry in 1861. He earned brevets through major general of volunteers during the Civil War and in July 1866 was appointed lieutenant colonel of the 37th U.S. Infantry. He was promoted to brigadier general in the Regular army in 1888. Brooke retired a major general in 1902.
5. Big Foot, or Si-tanka (c. 1825–90), was a Minneconjou chief, outstanding as a strategist and politician rather than as a warrior. Although briefly an advocate of the Ghost Dance, Big Foot desired peace and tried to quell turbulence among the restless young warriors of his band.
6. For a biographic sketch of Charles W. Taylor, see his "The Surrender of Red Cloud," elsewhere in this volume.
7. Guy H. Preston, of the West Point Class of 1888.
8. Philip F. Wells was a mixed-blood Sioux and white.
9. Francis M. J. Craft was an extroverted, hard-drinking Catholic missionary who was popular with both the Sioux and the army. He survived a knife wound in the lung at Wounded Knee.
10. John Kinzie was commissioned a second lieutenant in the 2nd U.S. Infantry in 1872. He retired a captain in 1897.
11. The Drexel Mission was the popular name for the Holy Rosary Mission and School, which seventy-seven-year-old Father John Jutz had founded at Pine Ridge in 1888.
12. James D. Mann, of the West Point Class of 1877.
13. Jacob F. Kent, of the West Point Class of 1861. He was appointed a major general of volunteers during the Spanish-American War and retired a brigadier general in the Regular army in October 1898.
14. A reference to Yellow Bird, a medicine man virulent in his hatred of the whites.

William F. Kelley: The Indian Troubles and the Battle of Wounded Knee

1. William F. Kelley was an employee in the business office of the *Nebraska State Journal,* with no reporting experience prior to the Wounded Knee tragedy.
2. These were members of Chief Torn Belly's Oglala band.
3. Hugh D. Gallagher was a Democrat who had obtained his position at Pine Ridge during the Cleveland administration. He was, by all accounts, a good agent.
4. The incident in question occurred on November 11, 1890, ration day at the Pine Ridge agency, when a Sioux warrior wanted for killing agency cattle defied the police. Agent Royer ordered his arrest, but two hundred ghost dancers mobbed the agency police. Only the intervention of the respected Chief American Horse averted bloodshed. The ghost dancers, however, prevented the arrest of the warrior. Utley, *Last Days,* 107–109.

5. The area of the Brule ghost dancers' camp was a triangular piece of tableland some two miles wide by three miles long, projecting northward from the higher Cuny Table and known as the Stronghold. A narrow land bridge, barely wide enough for a wagon, connected the Stronghold with the Cuny Table. The Cuny Table, in turn, separated the White and Cheyenne Rivers.
6. Hopkins continued on to Sioux City. There he called at the office of the Sioux City *Journal* on Christmas Eve. After chatting with a reporter, he departed, leaving a note that read, "To America and the world. Greeting: God's peace be with you. The Messiah. Christmas Eve, 1890."
7. Edwin V. Sumner (1835–1912) was the son of a Civil War major general of the same name. The younger Sumner was commissioned a second lieutenant in the 1st U.S. Cavalry in August 1861. He served on the Pacific Coast from 1866 to 1880 and saw action in the Modoc, Nez Perce, and Bannock Wars. Sumner retired a brigadier general in March 1899.
8. Eyewitness sources differ as to whether Yellow Bird himself fired a weapon. Most agree that five or six young warriors near him drew rifles from beneath their blankets and opened fire on the men of K Troop. Utley, *Last Days*, 212.
9. Reporter Kelley was not idle during the fight. He emptied his revolver into one warrior who charged him, then picked up a carbine and shot at least three more.
10. Only one trooper was killed during the attack on the 9th Cavalry wagon train, two miles east of the Pine Ridge agency. The attack occurred on the evening of December 29, not the following day as Kelley records.
11. A squadron under Maj. Guy V. Henry, composed of four troops of the 9th Cavalry, drove off the attacking Sioux from the vicinity of the Drexel Mission.
12. The notable exception was Plenty Horses, who killed Lieutenant Casey while the lieutenant was conferring amicably with several hostile Sioux, trying to coax them into the agency. Plenty Horses had been educated at the Carlisle Indian School. At his murder trial, he explained his reason for killing Casey. "I am an Indian. Five years I attended Carlisle and was educated in the ways of the white man. I was lonely. I shot the lieutenant so I might make a place for myself among my people. Now I am one of them. I am satisfied." Plenty Horses was acquitted of murder, the judge ruling that he had acted as a combatant during a state of war. Utley, *Last Days*, 257–58, 266–67.

Edmond G. Fechet: The True Story of the Death of Sitting Bull

1. Edmond G. Fechet (1844–1910) entered the army in 1861 as a sergeant in the 7th Michigan Volunteer Infantry. In July 1866, he was commissioned a second lieutenant in the 8th Cavalry. Fechet retired a major in 1898. From then until his death, he taught military science at the University of Illinois, Champaign.
2. William F. Drum (d. 1892) spent two years as a cadet at West Point in the early 1850s. He enlisted as a private in the 3rd Ohio Volunteer Infantry in 1861 and ended the Civil War as colonel of the 5th New York. He was commissioned a major in the 14th U.S. Infantry in 1882.
3. Herbert Welsh was the corresponding secretary of the influential Indian Rights Association.
4. Herbert J. Slocum, of the West Point Class of 1876.
5. Mathew F. Steele, of the West Point Class of 1883.
6. Enoch Crowder, of the West Point Class of 1881.
7. The warrior in question was Crow Woman, one of the most devoted adherents to the new faith. Utley, *Last Days*, 163.

Frederic Remington: The Sioux Outbreak in South Dakota
1. Frederic Remington (1861–1909) attended the Yale School of the Fine Arts. After graduation in 1880, he traveled to the Pacific Northwest, and there he found his life's work, to record "the living, breathing end of three American centuries." His western art is known for its authenticity and meticulous attention to deal. Thrapp, *Encyclopedia,* 3:1205.
2. The interpreter Philip Wells had had his nose sliced nearly off by a Sioux warrior during the Wounded Knee melee.

Charles W. Taylor: The Surrender of Red Cloud
1. Charles W. Taylor was a member of the West Point Class of 1879. He was commissioned a second lieutenant in the 9th Cavalry in June of that year.
2. A somewhat condensed version of Taylor's narrative appeared in the *Frontier Times* 13, no. 2 (November 1935): 133–36.

Edward S. Godfrey: The Battle of Wounded Knee Creek
1. Henry Jackson was an English immigrant who enlisted in the 14th Illinois Volunteer Cavalry in 1863. He ended the Civil War as sergeant major of the 5th U.S. Cavalry and was commissioned a second lieutenant in the regiment in May 1865. He retired a colonel in 1901.
2. Selah R. H. Tompkins was commissioned a second lieutenant in the 7th Infantry in 1884; he was transferred to the 7th Cavalry two years later.
3. Godfrey is mistaken; the warriors who attacked Jackson and Godfrey belonged to Two Strikes's band of Brules.
4. Most other eyewitness accounts said the first shot was fired from a rifle. Utley, *Last Days,* 212.

August Hettinger: Personal Recollections of the Messiah Craze Campaign
1. August Hettinger was an enlisted member of Company H, 8th U.S. Infantry during the Wounded Knee campaign.
2. On November 30, the largely Brule camps of Short Bull and Two Strike broke camp and marched in the direction of Cuny Table. The Pine Ridge agent, Daniel F. Royer, estimated that the combined camps consisted of five hundred lodges, with perhaps six hundred warriors. Utley, *Last Days,* 121.
3. Folliot A. Whitney (d. 1900) was commissioned a second lieutenant in the 1st Maryland Cavalry (U.S.) in 1862. In May 1866, he received a Regular army commission as a second lieutenant in the 8th U.S. Infantry.
4. Hettinger confuses the sequence of events, as General Miles did not assume direct command of the campaign until after the battle of Wounded Knee.
5. Few of Big Foot's followers escaped death or injury, but there were other survivors beside the papoose whose fate Hettinger relates. Fifty-one wounded were admitted to the hospital at Pine Ridge, forty-four of whom survived. Another twenty to thirty wounded may have escaped under their own power or been borne from the field by fellow Sioux. Utley, *Last Days,* 227–28.
6. Other accounts say that the top of Captain Wallace's head was carried away by a bullet. Wallace was carrying a stone war club that he had picked up in the Sioux camp when he was shot; perhaps some surviving members of the 7th Cavalry assumed it had been the instrument of his death.

7. This is a most revealing remark. Colonel Forsyth and the officers of the 7th Cavalry insisted that no soldier was struck by friendly fire; they hardly could be expected to have said otherwise, as to confess to any such chaos as Hettinger describes might have cost them their commissions. Hettinger's informants undoubtedly were enlisted men of the 7th, with no shoulder straps to protect. I find their characterization of the fight, as related to Hettinger, far more plausible than the self-serving testimony of the officers given during the postbattle inquiry by Kent and Baldwin and in later reminiscences.
8. The baby girl of three or four months was said to have been found under the snow, carefully wrapped in a shawl beside her dead mother. On her head was a little cap of buckskin, upon which was embroidered the American flag. She was adopted by Brig. Gen. L. W. Colby, commander of the Nebraska state troops, which participated peripherally in the campaign. James Mooney, *The Ghost Dance Religion and the Sioux Outbreak of 1890* (Lincoln: University of Nebraska Press, 1991), 879.

Courtney R. Cooper: Short Bull's Story of the Battle of Wounded Knee
1. Courtney R. Cooper was a reporter with the New York *Sun*.
2. *The Red Man* was published at the United States Indian School in Carlisle, Pennsylvania, from 1910 to 1917 by Indian School students as part of their printing training.

INDEX

Adams, Charles W., 43–44
Agard, Louis, 161
Allison, James N., 428
American Horse (d. 1875), 382, 466
American Horse (Sioux chief), xlii, 284, 303, 364, 466, 497, 634
Anderson, Martin, xxiii, 6, 9
Andrews, W. H., 277
Arapahos, xvii, 224, 282, 479, 480
 Platte Bridge, battle of, xxi, xxiii, 2–12
 Powder River campaign, xxiv–xxv, 30–31, 33–34
Arikaras (Rees), 108, 115, 125, 130, 141–142, 179–182, 239
Augur, Christopher C., xxviii, 105
Ayers, Lorenzo E., 223

Bache, Alfred B., 384
Baeber, 71–72
Bailey, Hobart K., 434
Baker, Eugene M., xxx, 151
Baldwin, Frank D., xliv, 436, 442–450, 460, 461, 575–577
Baliran, A., 124, 147, 170
Ball, Edward, 405
Barrows, Samuel J., 149, 150–153
Baxter, John, 504, 507, 509–511
Bear, Alfred, 179–182
Bear Butte, 164–166
Bear's Belly, 179–182
Belknap, William W., xxxi, xxxiv, 393
Bell, J. F., 562
Belle Fourche, 159, 173–174
Bennett, A. S., 458
Bent, George, xviii, 14, 15

Benteen, Frederick W., xxxviii, xl, 257, 288, 293, 320, 321, 326, 327, 329, 330, 341–342
Big Crow, 436, 437–438
Big Foot, xlviii–xlix, 564, 567, 586, 589, 612, 615
Bighorn Mountains,
 prospecting trip in the, 58–63
Big Road, 301
Bingham, Horatio S., xxvii, 69, 91
Black Bear, 30
Black Coal, 480
Black Crow, 16, 206, 535, 537
Blackfeet (Siouan), xv, xvi, xix, xxxiv, 285, 291, 297
 murder of John Bozeman, 88–89
Black Foot (warrior), 4, 16
Black Hills
 Bear's description of, 179–182
 Crook's march to, xli–xlii, 200–226
 Custer's description of, 156–171
 gold, xxxi–xxxii, 169, 175, 188–190, 484
 Henry's description of, 183–187
 Ludow's description of, 172–175
 Sheridan's description of, 188–191
 Wood's description of, 176–178
Black Kettle, xxi, 14, 15
Black Moon, 301, 305
Bloody Knife, 108–109, 115–117, 125, 133, 160, 179
Bordeaux, Louis, 532, 537, 549

Bourke, John G., xxxiii, xlii, 218, 220, 224, 255, 278, 378–384, 419
Bowers, Sergeant, 69
Bozeman, John, 88–89
Bozeman Trail, xii, xxiv, xxvi, xxviii, xxix
Braden, Charles, 128–149
Bradley, Luther P., 530, 538, 545–546
Braided Locks, 101
Brewer, John S., 19
Bridger, James, 78, 90–92
Bridger, Major, 27–28
Brinnstool, E. A., 93–100, 542–548
Brisbin, James, xxxvi, 484
Bronson, Edgar B., 482–514
Brooke, John R., xlviii, 561, 563, 582, 585
Brown, Albert, xxiv, 20, 25–26, 35
Brown, Edwin M., 451–462
Brown, Frederick H., 71, 79, 81, 82, 84, 86
Brown, J. Willard, 20
Brules, xv, xvi, xxxiv, xlviii
 Ghost Dances, 582–583
 Little Bighorn, 284, 285, 294, 296–298, 301, 303, 306
 Platte Bridge, 3
 surrender of, 593–594
Brush, Daniel, 130
Bryan, W. C., 224
Bubb, John W., 265
Buffalo Hump (Bull Hump), 500–501, 507
Buffalo Wallow, 66
Bull Head, Henry, xlviii, 601
Bullock, Edwin C., 562
Burke, Daniel W., 383, 531, 532
Burke, J., 300–301
Burt, Andrew S., 149, 262–263, 367–377, 383

679

Cain, Avery B., 276
Calamity Jane, 250
Calhoun, James, 108, 110, 111, 321
Camp, George, 8, 9
Campbell, Sergeant, 331
Carlton (Carleton), C. H., 492, 497
Carpenter, William L., 183
Carrington, Henry B., xxvi, xxvii–xxviii, 69, 71–72
Casey, Lieutenant, 592, 613
Cedar Creek battle, xliv, 433–436, 443, 451–462
Chambers, Alexander, 205
Chandler, Zachariah, xxxi
Charging Bear, 382
Chase, G. F., 497
Cheyennes, xv, xviii, xix, 282
  Bronson's description of, 482–514
  1865–1891, battles of, xxi, xxxiv
  Forse's description of, 515–525
  Little Bighorn, xl, 296–298, 301, 303, 306
  Little Blue Valley, 4, 13, 14
  Miles talks with, 436–441
  Platte Bridge, battle of, xxiii, 2–12
  Red Fork, battle of, xliii–xliv
  Rosebud, battle of, 251–260
  resettlement of, xlvi–xlvii
  Wagon Box Fight, 75–78, 92–102
  Woodward's description of, 470–481
Chicago *Inter-Ocean*, 263
Chicago *Times*, 262
Chicago *Tribune*, 262–263
Chippewas, xv, 282
Chivington, John M., xxi, 3, 15, 105
Clark, Philo, 529, 530–532, 533, 534, 542–543
Clark, W. P., 381, 418, 419
Coates, Edwin M., 210

Cody, William F., 349, 354, 433, 452
Cole, Nelson, xxiv–xxv, 19, 35, 37–38, 40–41
Cole, Osmer F., 51, 54
Collins, Caspar W., xxiii, 8, 9
Comanche, Keogh's horse, 296
Connor, Patrick E., xxii, 16
  interview with, 45–48
  Platte Bridge, battle of, 5–6
  Powder River campaign, xxiv–xxv, 17–21, 22, 30, 31, 40–41
Conquering Bear, xix
Conrad, George, 20
Cook, Lieutenant, 288, 295
Cooke, Philip St. George, xxvii, xxviii, 73
Cooke, William W., xxxix–xl, 321
Cooper, Courtney R., 630–636
Cover, Thomas W., 88–89
Craft, Francis M. J., 568, 570, 572
Crawford, Emmet, 362, 363
Crawford, John W., 364
Crazy Horse, 431
  campaign against, 463–468
  Crow's description of Crazy Horse's battle with Custer, 256–258
  death of, xlv–xlvi, 468, 528–551
  destruction of village, Strahorn's description, xxxiii, 200–226
  1865–1891, battles of, xxvii–xxviii, xxx, xxxiv, xxxv, xlv
  Little Bighorn, xxxix, xl, 296–298, 303, 305–306
  Rosebud, battle of, 251–260
Crazy Woman's Fork, 66, 91, 209–212, 414–430
Cree, 239, 282
Crittenden, Lieutenant, 321

Crook, George, xxxi, xxxii, xxxiii–xxxiv, xliii, 42, 200, 217
  campaign against Crazy Horse, 463–468
  dispatches from, 367–377
  Finerty's interview with, 385–390
  Little Bighorn, xxxv, xli
  Little Bighorn, Goldin's description of, 311–312
  march to Black Hills, xli–xlii, 200–226
  Rosebud, battle of, 251–260, 285
  Schwatka's description of Bighorn and Yellowstone expedition, 350–366
Crow, xv, xviii, xxx, 76–77, 239, 252, 254, 256, 274–275, 282, 300, 368–369
Crowder, Enoch, 601, 603
Crow King, 301, 305
Curley, 294, 333–334
Curtis, Samuel R., xxiii
Custard, Amos J., 8–9
Custer, Elizabeth B., 130, 148, 392
Custer, George A., xxx
  Barrows description of Yellowstone expedition, 150–153
  battle with Sioux on the Yellowstone, 104–119
  Black Hills expedition, xxxi, 156–171
  Braden's description of Yellowstone expedition, 128–149
  Crow's description of Crazy Horse's battle with, 256–258
  disfavor with Grant, xxxiv, 312
  Little Bighorn, xxxvi–xli
  Little Bighorn, Goldin's description of, 310–337
  Little Bighorn, Indian version of, 299–309

Index

Little Bighorn, King's
   description of, 282–298
   Northern Pacific Railroad
     surveying expedition,
     xxx, xxxi, 104, 105,
     106, 120–127
   Rosebud, battle of, 251
Custer, Thomas W., 108,
   110, 111, 112, 139,
   288, 295, 425
Custer Avengers, xli

Dakotas, xv, xx, 179–182,
   282, 300
Daly, Henry W., 250–260
Daniels, N. H., 91
Davenport, Reuben B.,
   261–262
Davis, Wirt, 423
Dawes Act (1887), xlvii
Defond, Baptiste (Desfond,
   Estes), 55
DeLany, Hayden, 419
Denver *Rocky Mountain
   News*, 263
DeRudio, Lieutenant, 320,
   322, 338
De Smet, Pierre-Jean, 124,
   188, 189, 268
Dewees, T. B., 216, 270
DeWolf, Doctor, 320, 324
Diehl, Charles S., 391–412
Dilliner (Dillelend), James,
   52, 54
Dodd, George A., 508, 509,
   513
Dodge, Grenville M., xxii,
   xxiv, 3, 11
Dodge, Richard I., 101
Donaldson, A. B., 160
Donovan, John, 69
Dorst, Joseph H., 419
Dougherty, John J., 151
Dowdy, Peter, 223
Doyle, Tommy, 98
Drew, W. Y., 6
Drexel Mission, 572–577
Drum, William F., xlviii,
   597, 599–602, 605–606
Dull Knife, xxiii, xliii, xlvi,
   xlvii, 471
   Bronson's description of,
     482–514

   capture of, 492–505
   fight with, 414–430
   Hat Creek Bluffs and Sol-
     dier Creek fights,
     506–514
   provocation of, 482–492
   Rosebud, battle of,
     251–260
   Woodward's description
     of, 474, 475, 481

Eastman, Charles A.,
   299–309
Edgerly, Lieutenant, 320,
   327, 619
Edmunds, Newton,
   xxii–xxiii
Egan, James, xxxiii, 219,
   220–222, 225
Elk Head, 301
Eubanks, Mrs. 4, 13, 14,
   16–17
Eubanks family, 13
Ewers, E. P., 450

Fairfield, S. H., 2–12
Fast Thunder, 634
Fearless Bear, 303
Fechet, Edmond G., xlviii,
   597–606
Fetterman, William J.,
   xxvii–xxviii, 71, 79,
   81, 82, 84, 86, 94,
   267–268
Fetterman Massacre of
   1866, 69–72, 79–87,
   91–92
Finerty, John F., 262,
   385–390
Fisher, Isaac, 71, 79, 87
Flanagan, James, 326
Foolish Elk, 623
Forse, Albert G., 515–525
Forsyth, George A., 190,
   191
Forsythe, James W.,
   xlviii–xlix, 129, 160,
   396, 564, 566, 567,
   568, 570, 572, 577, 612
Fort Fetterman, 200, 202,
   205, 227, 239, 470
Fort Kearny (Fort Childs),
   60, 284

   abandonment of, 77–78
   building of, xxvi, xxvii,
     64–69, 93
   Fetterman Massacre of
     1866, 69–72, 79–87,
     91–92
   Foster's description of,
     267–268
   life at, 73–75
   Wagon Box Fight, xxviii,
     75–78, 92–102
Fort Laramie, 470
   Treaty, xviii–xix, 90
Forts
   Brown, 191
   Buford, xxviii, xxix,
     394–399
   Custer, xlv
   Ellis, xxx
   Keogh, xlv
   Lincoln, xxx, xxxii, 156,
     168, 173, 176, 179, 391
   Peck, 300, 301, 443, 446,
     448, 458
   Reno (Connor), xxvi, 24,
     50, 77–78, 211, 251,
     266, 284
   Rice, xxiii, xxix, xxx,
     105, 106, 107
   Robinson, 484, 498
   Russell, 78
   Smith, xxvi, xxvii, xxviii,
     60, 62, 69, 73, 77–78,
     284
Foster, James E. H.,
   265–281
Fouts, W. D., 4, 5
French, T. H., 123, 139, 320,
   322, 327, 329, 338, 339
Friday, 479–480
Fry, J. B., 300
Furay, John B., 20

Gall, xxix–xxx, xxxiv, xl,
   xliv, 260, 303, 304,
   305, 436
Gallagher, Hugh D., 581
Garlington, Ernest A., 570,
   572, 589, 609
Geier, George, 93
Ghost Dance, xlvii–xlix,
   554–558, 579–581, 611

Gibbon, John, xxxiv, 407
　Little Bighorn, xxxvi,
　　311, 317–318
　Rosebud, battle of, 251,
　　285–286
Gibson, Samuel S., 93–100,
　320
Gilmore and Porter bull
　train, 75
Glennan, James D., 570
Godfrey, Edward S., 300,
　320, 329, 341–342,
　562, 615–619
gold, xix
　in the Black Hills,
　　xxxi–xxxii, 169, 175,
　　188–190, 484
　prospecting trip in the
　　Bighorn Mountains,
　　58–63
Goldin, Theodore W.,
　310–337, 345–349
Good Thunder, 554–556
Gordon, George A., 418,
　419, 421
Grant, Frederick D., 178,
　190
Grant, Ulyssess S., xxiii,
　xxxi–xxxii, xxxiv, 11,
　312
Grattan, John L., xix
Gray Head, 429
Greer, James E., 6, 8
Gresham, John C., 570
Grimm, Henry, 2, 7, 8, 9
Grimm, Phil, 9
Grinnell, George B.,
　101–102, 158, 172, 174
Grouard, Frank, xxxii, 217,
　218, 219, 224,
　251–252, 266, 278,
　352, 362, 363, 364,
　380, 423–425, 428,
　532, 533, 549, 623
Grummond, G. W., 81, 82,
　84, 86
Guthrie, John, 81–83

Haggerty, Henry, 98
Half Yellow Face, 326
Hamilton, John M., 421

Hankammer, Sergeant, 8
Hare, Luther R., 320, 326,
　562
Harney, William S., xix, 105
Harney's Peak, 162–164,
　174, 177–178, 189
Harney Springs, 185
Harrington, Lieutenant, 320
Hart, V. K., 78
Hastings, James, 300, 386
Hat Creek Bluffs, 506–514
Hawley, William, 216
Hawthorne, Harry L., 562,
　570, 572, 589, 609
Hazen, William B., 393
Henry, Guy V., xlix,
　183–187, 279, 572, 586
Henry, John, 279
Herendeen, G. B., 326
Hettinger, August, 620–629
High Back-Bone, xxviii
High Bear, 537
Hills, Louis E., 120–127
Hodgson, Benjamin H., 144,
　291, 293, 320, 324
Hoff, J. Van R., 570
Hollister, Ovando J., 45–48
Holman, Albert M., 49–55
Honsinger, John, 124, 147,
　170
Hopkins, A. C., 584
Horn Cloud, 631
Hubbard, Josiah M., 9
Hump, xlviii, 301, 436, 440
Humphreyville, J. L., 17, 20,
　36
Hunkpapas, xv, xvi, xix, 285
　Cedar Creek battle, xliv
　1865–1891, battles of,
　　xxi–xlix
　Little Bighorn, xxxix,
　　291, 297, 301, 303

Ilsley, Charles S., 574
Indian Appropriations Act,
　xxii
Inkpadutas, 301
Iron Bull, 77
Iron Dog, xliv
Iron Star, 301, 303, 306

Jackson, Henry, 570–571,
　616, 619
Jenness, John C., xxviii, 81,
　97, 98
Jewett, Oscar, 18, 20, 24, 25,
　34
Johnson, J. B., 220, 222,
　484, 497, 498
Jumping Bull, xxxiv

Kansas Regiment, 11th,
　2–12
Kelley, William F., 578–596
Kellogg, Mark, xxxvii, 295
Kelly, Luther S., 433
Kennington, James,
　538–539, 546, 550
Kent, Jacob F., 575–577
Keogh, Myles, 288, 295,
　296, 321, 379
Ketchum, H. H., 139
Kicking Bear, xlvii, xlviii,
　xlix, 557–559, 582,
　594, 614
Kidd, J. H., 20, 25
Kimball, James P., 143, 144,
　148
King, Charles, 282–298
Kinney, N. C., 62
Kinzie, John, 570

Lakotas
　culture of, xvi–xvii
　1865–1891, battles of,
　　xxi–xlix
　Ghost Dance, xlvii–xlix
　Little Bighorn, xxxix, xl
　meaning of name, xvii
　Platte Bridge, battle of,
　　xxiii, 2–12
　subtribes, xv–xvi
　Wounded Knee,
　　xlviii–xlix
Lame Deer, xlv, 301,
　440–441
Lame White Man, xl
Latham, Charles M., 31
Laurant, C. J., 19, 20
Lee, Jesse M., 528–541,
　543, 545–546
Left Heron, xvi
Leighton, A. C., 62

Index

Lemly, Henry R., 280, 542–548
Lewis, W. H., 489, 491
Little Bighorn, xxxv–xli
  Crow's description of Crazy Horse's battle with Custer, 256–258
  Goldin's description of, 310–337
  Indian version of, 299–309
  King's description of, 282–298
  Nugent's description of, 343–344
  Silversten's description of Reno fight, 338–340
Little Big Man, 284, 539, 544, 546, 550
Little Blue Valley, 4, 13, 14
Little Chief, 439, 491
Little Crow, xx
Little Hawk, 301, 440
Little Horse, 301, 303, 306
Little Priest, 54, 55
Little Thunder, xix
Little Wolf, xliii, xlvi, 429
  escape of, 492–505
  Woodward's description of, 471–475, 477, 481
Little Wound, 619
Littman, Max, 93, 96
Lone Bull, 303, 304
Lord, Doctor, 335
Louissant, chief, 254
Low, W. H., 287
Low Dog, 301, 306
Ludlow, William, 157, 172–175, 177
Ludlow's Cave, 157, 179

Mackenzie, Ranald S., xliii, 415, 416, 418, 419, 422
MacMillan, T. C., 263
Mann, James D., 574, 590, 607–608
Marr, James, 62
Marsh, O. C., 172
Marshall, Levi G., 20, 25, 38
Martin, John (Giovanni Martini), xl, 310, 333
Mason, J. W., 543, 545
Matson, W. S., 79

Mauck, Clarence, 418, 419, 422, 492
McCannon, Michael, 223
McCook, Alexander M., 129
McCormick, Lloyd S., 559–577
McDougall, Thomas M., 121, 124, 157, 288, 320, 326, 329, 330
McGillycuddy, Valentine T., 543, 549–551
McIntosh, Donald, 291, 293, 320, 321, 322–323, 425
McKinney, John A., 421, 428, 430
McLaughlin, James, xlviii, 597, 599–600
Meagher, T. F., 88
Mears, David T., 250, 463–468
Merival, Joe, 471–472, 532, 535
Merrill, E. G., 52, 54
Merritt, Wesley, xli, 350, 402
Messiah (Wovoka), xlvii, 554–558, 579–581, 611, 620–629, 631–636
Metzgar, trumpeter, 269
Miles, Nelson A., xli, xlv, 367, 397, 401, 402, 431–441
  Cedar Creek battle, xliv, 433–436, 443, 451–462
  Wounded Knee, 564, 585, 590, 592–593, 622
Mills, Anson, xxxiii, xxxv, xlii, 191, 216, 220, 222, 277, 278, 361–365, 378, 379, 380
Miniconjous, xv, xvi, 183, 206
  Cedar Creek battle, xliv
  1865–1891, battles of, xxviii–xxix
  Ghost Dance, xlviii
  Little Bighorn, 285, 297, 301, 303, 306
Mitchell, Robert B., 3
Mizner, A. K., 489
Montgomery, R. H., 247
Moonlight, Thomas, 3, 4, 5, 16, 17

Moore, Alexander, xxxiii, 216, 219–220, 221, 222, 229, 233
Moore, Thomas, 250
Moylan, Myles, 108, 110, 111, 112, 113, 114, 136, 158, 320, 323, 329
Mularkey, Sergeant, 475–477
Munson, Samuel, 381
Murphy, E. B., 14
Murphy, William, 64–78

Nash, E. W., 20
Nation, Carrie, 250–251
Nehring, Sebastian, 8, 9
New York *Herald*, 261–262
New York *Tribune*, 263–264
Nickerson, A. H., 278
North, Frank, xxiv, 20, 24, 25, 33, 36, 38
Northern Pacific Railroad, xxx, xxxi, 104, 105, 106, 120–127, 128
No Water, 301
Noyes, Henry E., xxxiii, 216, 220, 223
Nugent, William D., 343–344

O'Brien, Nicholas J., 15, 17, 19, 25
Oglalas, xv, xvi, xlviii, 593
  See also Red Cloud
  1865–1891, battles of, xxi–xlix
  Little Bighorn, xxxix, 285, 294, 296–298, 301
  Miles talks with, 436–441
  Platte Bridge, battle of, 3
  surrender of, xlv
Old Bear, 429, 476, 477
Old Crow, 501, 502
Old David, 30
Old-Man-Afraid-of-His-Horses, xxi, xxiii, xxvi, xxix, 284
One Stab, 161, 162
Otis, Elwell S., xli, 397
Otis, Harrison G., 421
Otter Creek, Strahorn's description of camp on, 215–217
Ould, Dr., 79

Palmer, Henry E., 13–42
Pawnees, 24–25, 282, 419–420, 424, 428
Pearson, Daniel C., 236–249
Pearson, Edward P., 133
Pine Ridge agency, 581–596
  See also Wounded Knee
Platte Bridge Station, battle of, xxiii, 2–12
Plenty-of-Bears, 206
Plumb, P. B., 3, 4, 6
Pope, John, xx, xxi–xxv, 11–12, 489
Porter, Doctor, 320
Porter, Lieutenant, 321
Pouriere, Baptiste, 251–252, 256, 380, 382, 543, 586
Powder River campaign
  description of, xxiv–xxvii, xxix, 13–44, 90–92
  interview with Connor, 45–48
  review of, 227–234
  Sawyers expedition, xxiii, 49–55
  Strahorn's description, xxxiii, 200–226
Powell, James, xxvii, xxviii, 93, 94
Preston, Guy H., 564
Pretty Bear, 436

Rain-in-the-Face, 100, 124, 134, 170, 298, 303, 304, 305
Randall, George M., 529
Rawolle, W. C., 219–220
Ray, Patrick H., 141, 151–153
Red Bear, 529
Red Cloud, 227, 284, 299, 300, 431, 499–500, 634, 635
  battles of, xxi, xxiii, xxv, xxvi, xxviii, xxix, xxx, xliii, 65
  massacre of 1866, xxvii, 69–73, 267
  surrender of, 611–614
  Wagon Box Fight, 75–78, 92–102
Red Dog, 267, 284
Red Leaf, 267

Ree Indians. *See* Arikaras (Rees)
Reilly, Lieutenant, 321
Remington, Frederic, 607–610
Reno, Marcus A.,
  Eastman's description, 304–305
  Goldin's description, 312, 314, 320, 321–322, 323, 327, 329, 330, 337
  King's description, 286, 288, 290–291, 293, 294, 297
  Little Bighorn, xxxv–xxxvi, xxxviii–xli, 257, 258, 260
  Silversten's description, 338–340
Reynolds, Charles A., 125
Reynolds, Joseph J., xxxiii, 201, 222, 227–234
Rice, Edmund, 404
Rice, J. N., 59–60
Richard, Louis, 351–352, 543, 545
Richards, A. V., 20
Robbins, Sam, 20
Roche, Jerry, 414–430
Rocking Bear, 497
Roman Nose, xxiii, 364, 382, 429, 529
Roper, Laura, 14, 17
Rosebud Creek, xxiv
  battle of, xxxiv–xxxvi, 250–260, 464–465
  Foster's account of, 265–281
  King's description of, 282–286
Rosser, Thomas L., 106–107
Royall, William B., xxxv, 254, 280–281
Royer, agent, 581
Russell, Gerald, 281

San Arcs, xv, xvi, xxxiv
  Cedar Creek battle, xliv
  Little Bighorn, 285, 297, 301, 303
Sand Creek massacre, xxi, xxii, 15

Santees (Nakotas), xv, xx, xxxiv, 167, 300
Sawyers, James A., xxiii, 49–55
Scalp dances, 141–142, 352–353
Schneider, George, 223
Schulyler, W. S., 419, 421
Schwatka, Frederick, 192–199, 350–366
Sheridan, Philip H., xxxi, xxxii, xxxv, xliii, xlv, 169, 188–191, 251
Sherman, William T., xxv–xxvi, xxviii, xlvii, 105
Short Bull, xlvii, xlviii, 582, 594, 614, 621, 630–636
Shoshones (Snakes), 9, 239, 252, 254, 274–275, 282, 352–353, 368, 419, 421
Shoup, George L., 15
Sibley, Frederick W., 243
Sibley, Henry H., xx
Silversten, John, 338–340
Simpson, J. F., 507
Sioux
  See also under name of lodge/tribe
  Custer's battle with, on the Yellowstone, 104–119
  Little Bighorn, Indian version of, 299–309
  Missouri River, 3
  origin of name, 282
  population statistics, 299–302
  Rosebud, battle of, 251–260
  Sun Dance, xvi, xxxiv–xxxv, 192–199
  Tetons, xv, 300
  Wagon Box Fight, 75–78, 92–102
Sitting Bear, 415
Sitting Bull, 126, 229, 285, 431
  Black Hills and, xxxi, xxxii
  Brown's description of fight with, 451–462

in Canada, xliv
Cedar Creek battle, xliv,
  433–436, 443, 451–462
death of, 564, 583–584,
  597–606
1865–1891, battles of,
  xvii, xxi, xxiii, xxv,
  xxix–xxxi, xxxiv
Ghost Dance, xlviii,
  554–558, 579–581, 582
Little Bighorn, xxxix, xl,
  xli, 260, 297–298
Miles' fight with,
  433–436, 443
Sun Dance ceremony,
  xxxiv–xxxv, 297
Yellowstone, battle of,
  xxix–xxxi
Sitting Bull, Oglala leader,
  387
Slim Buttes, battle of,
  378–384, 466
Slocum, Herbert J., 601, 602
Smith, Benjamin F., 100
Smith, E. P., xxxii
Smith, E. W., xxxvii
Smith, John E., 73, 76, 77,
  78
Smith, J. W., 59–60
Snake Indians. *See*
  Shoshones
Snow, Elmer A., 255
Snyder, Simon, 458
Soldier Creek, 506–514
Spotted Bear, xxxi
Spotted Eagle, 301, 303, 304
Spotted Horn Bull, 297
Spotted Tail, xxvi, xliii, xlv,
  192, 193, 227, 284,
  299, 300, 431, 530,
  531, 532, 533, 534
Squiers, Herbert G., 562
Standing Elk, xxvi, xxxi,
  192, 193, 466
Standing Rock, 300, 301
Stanford, Jeff, 58
Stanley, David S., xxx, 105,
  130, 132, 133, 140,
  144, 150, 151
Stanton, Thaddeus H., 202,
  218, 220, 222, 227–234
Steele, Mathew F., 601, 602

Strahorn, Robert E., xxxiii,
  200–226, 263
Strikes Two, 179–182
Sturgis, Lieutenant, 320, 392
Sully, Alfred, xx–xxi, xxii,
  282
Summer campaign of 1876
Benteen's command,
  341–342
dispatches from Crook's
  column, 367–377
Foster's account of Rose-
  bud, 265–281
Little Bighorn, Goldin's
  description of, 310–337
Little Bighorn, Indian
  version of, 299–309
Little Bighorn, King's
  description of, 282–298
Little Bighorn, Nugent's
  description of, 343–344
Little Bighorn, Silver-
  sten's description of
  Reno fight, 338–340
military notes of Pearson,
  236–249
newspaper correspondents
  reports, 261–264
Rosebud, battle of,
  250–260
Schwatka's description of
  Bighorn and Yellow-
  stone expedition,
  350–366
Slim Buttes, battle of,
  378–384
Sumner, Edwin V., xix,
  xlviii, 585
Sun Dance, xvi, xxxiv–xxxv,
  192–199
Sutaios, xv
Swift Bear, 537
Sword, George, 554–558

Tackett, Charlie, 532
Taggett, Charles, 623
Taylor, Alfred B., 421, 422
Taylor, Charles W., 564,
  611–614
Taylor, Edward B., xxv, xxvi
Ten Eyck, T., 71, 72, 79, 84

Terry, Alfred H., xxxii,
  xxxiv, xliii, 105, 131,
  244
Diehl's description of,
  391–412
Goldin's description of,
  345–349
Little Bighorn,
  xxxv–xxxvi, xli, 312,
  314, 339–340
Rosebud, battle of, 251,
  285–288
Thompson, J. C., 497
Thornburgh, T. T., 490, 492
Three Bears, 428
Tiernay, Francis, 269
Tompkins, S.R.H., 616, 617
Tongue River
Sawyers expedition, xxiii,
  49–55
Strahorn's description of
  camp on, 212–215
Touch-the-Clouds, 529,
  531–533, 535, 537,
  539, 540
Townsend, Edwin F., 151
Tubbs, W. H., 20
Turkey Legs, 471, 475
Two Face, 4, 14, 16
Two Kettles, xv, xvi, xxxiv
Two Moon, xxxix, xl,
  xlvi–xlvii, 301,
  302–303, 306, 517
Two Strike, 582

Vandever, William, 386
Van Vliet, Frederick, 266,
  278
Varnum, Charles A., 108,
  110, 117, 118, 320,
  568–569
von Leuttwitz, A. H., 362,
  363, 383, 384
Vroom, P. D., 274, 501,
  507–508

Wagon Box Fight, 75–78,
  92–102
Wakan Tanka, xvi
Walker, Samuel, xxiv–xxv,
  19
Wallace, George D., 160,
  320, 322, 326–327,

329, 568, 570, 589,
609, 616, 627
War Dance, Pawnee, 25
Ware, Eugene F., 19
Wasson, Joseph, 263–264
Watkins, E. C., xxxii
Weber, George, 79–80
Weinert, Paul H., 629
Weir, Thomas B., xl, 293,
320, 327, 329, 342
Wells, Philip F., 568, 570,
612
Welsh, Herbert, 597
Wessels, Henry W., xxviii,
499, 500, 501–502,
508, 511, 512, 513
Weston, John F., 128, 134,
136, 137, 143, 393
Wheatley, James S., 71, 79,
87
Wheeling, Robert, 20, 26
Whistler, Joseph N. A., 401,
403, 452
White, Charles, 338
White, Jonathan, 381
White Antelope, 15, 255
White Buffalo Woman, xvi
White Bull, xxiii, xl, 301,
306, 436, 440
Whitney, F. A., 623, 625
Whitside, Samuel M., xlviii,
564, 566, 570, 574,
586, 615–616

White Thunder, 535
Wild Hog, 501, 502
Williams, J. W., 172
Winchell, N. H., 158, 169,
172, 174
Winnebago Indians, 54, 55
Winter campaign of
1876–77
Bronson's description of,
482–514
Brown's description of,
451–462
campaign against Crazy
Horse, 463–468
Dull Knife fight, 414–430
Miles' description of,
431–441
in Montana, 442–450
Wolf Chief, 101
Wolf Mountain, battle of,
436–438
Wood, William H., 172,
176–178
Woodward, George A.,
470–481
Wounded Knee, xlviii–xlix
Godfrey's description of,
615–619
Hettinger's description of,
620–629
Kelley's description of,
578–596

McCormick's description
of, 559–577
Remington's description
of events after,
607–610
Short Bull's description
of, 630–636
Wounded Knee Creek, 184
Wovoka (Messiah), xlvii,
554–558, 579–581,
611, 620–629, 631–636

Yanktonais, 447
Yanktons, xv, 300
Yantonais, xv, xxxiv
Yates, George W., xl, 132,
139, 288, 295, 321
Yellow Bird, xlix, 575, 588,
619
Yellowstone expedition,
xxix–xxxi
Barrows' description of,
150–153
Braden's description of,
128–149
Custer's battle with Sioux
on the, 104–119
Diehl's description of,
391–412
Schwatka's description of,
350–366
Young-Man-Afraid-of-His-
Horses, 593

CANADA

Milk River

Missouri River

Fort Shaw

MONTANA

Rocky Mountains

Fort Logan

Little Bighorn River

Redw
18

Fort Ellis

Little Bighorn 1876

Tongue R.

Fort Custer

Roseb 1876

Bozeman Trail

W
Mou
18

Virginia City

Fort C. F. Smith

Wagon Box Fight 1867

Fette Mas 18

Fort Phil Kearny

Fort Reno

Bighorn River

IDAHO

WYOMING

Fort Caspar

Platte River Bridge 1865

Union Pacific Railroad

UTAH TERRITORY

Scale in miles

0   10